Fodor's 2016

NEW YORK CITY

WELCOME TO NEW YORK CITY

From Wall Street's skyscrapers to the neon of Times Square to Central Park's leafy paths, New York City pulses with an irrepressible energy. History meets hipness in this global center of entertainment, fashion, media, and finance. World-class museums like MoMA and unforgettable icons like the Statue of Liberty beckon, but discovering the subtler strains of New York's vast ambition is equally rewarding: ethnic enclaves and shops, historic streets of dignified brownstones, and trendy bars and eateries all add to the urban buzz.

TOP REASONS TO GO

★ **Landmarks:** With towering edifices and awe-inspiring bridges, the skyline says it all.

★ **Shopping:** Whether you're in the market for top designers or inexpensive souvenirs.

★ **Food:** Dim sum to pizza and everything in between, NYC has what you're craving.

★ **Museums:** Art is it, with museums like the Guggenheim and galleries all over town.

★ **The Dazzle:** From the lights of Broadway to celebrity sightings, NYC is full of stars.

★ **Brooklyn and Elsewhere:** Cool neighborhoods and restaurants are a subway ride away.

Fodor's NEW YORK CITY 2016

Publisher: Amanda D'Acierno, *Senior Vice President*

Editorial: Arabella Bowen, *Editor in Chief*; Linda Cabasin, *Editorial Director*

Design: Tina Malaney, *Associate Art Director*; Chie Ushio, *Senior Designer*

Photography: Jennifer Arnow, *Senior Photo Editor*; Mary Robnett, *Photo Researcher*

Production: Linda Schmidt, *Managing Editor*; Evangelos Vasilakis, *Associate Managing Editor*; Angela L. McLean, *Senior Production Manager*

Maps: Rebecca Baer, *Senior Map Editor*; Mark Stroud (Moon Street Cartography), *Cartographers*

Sales: Jacqueline Lebow, *Sales Director*

Marketing & Publicity: Heather Dalton, *Marketing Director*; Katherine Punia, *Publicity Director*

Business & Operations: Susan Livingston, *Vice President, Strategic Business Planning*; Sue Daulton, *Vice President, Operations*

Fodors.com: Megan Bell, *Executive Director, Revenue & Business Development*; Yasmin Marinaro, *Senior Director, Marketing & Partnerships*

Copyright © 2016 by Fodor's Travel, a division of Penguin Random House LLC

Writers: Jessica Colley, David Farley, Laura Itzkowitz, Kristin Iversen, Christina Knight, Jacinta O'Halloran, Anuja Madar, Megan Eileen McDonough, Marisa Meltzer, Chris Molanphy, John Rambow, Matt Rodbard, Josh Rogol, Emily Saladino, Sarah Spagnolo, Christina Valhouli

Editors: Caroline Trefler (lead editor) and Mike Dunphy

Production Editor: Jennifer DePrima

ISBN 978-1-101-87827-9

ISSN 0736–9395

SPECIAL SALES

This book is available at special discounts for bulk purchases for sales promotions or premiums. For more information, e-mail specialmarkets@penguinrandomhouse.com

PRINTED IN THE UNITED STATES OF AMERICA

10 9 8 7 6 5 4 3 2 1

CONTENTS

MAPS

ABOUT THIS GUIDE

Fodor's Recommendations

Everything in this guide is worth doing—we don't cover what isn't—but exceptional sights, hotels, and restaurants are recognized with additional accolades. **Fodor's Choice★** indicates our top recommendations; and **Best Bets** call attention to notable hotels and restaurants in various categories. Care to nominate a new place? Visit Fodors.com/contact-us.

Trip Costs

We list prices wherever possible to help you budget well. Hotel and restaurant price categories from **$** to **$$$$** are noted alongside each recommendation. For hotels, we include the lowest cost of a standard double room in high season. For restaurants, we cite the average price of a main course at dinner or, if dinner isn't served, at lunch. For attractions, we always list adult admission fees; discounts are usually available for children, students, and senior citizens.

Hotels

Our local writers vet every hotel to recommend the best overnights in each price category, from budget to expensive. Unless otherwise specified, you can expect private bath, phone, and TV in your room. For expanded hotel reviews, facilities, and deals visit Fodors.com.

Top Picks	Hotels &
★ **Fodor's**Choice	**Restaurants**
	⊡ Hotel
Listings	⤴ Number of
✉ Address	rooms
✉ Branch address	⌾⃝ Meal plans
☎ Telephone	✕ Restaurant
🖷 Fax	⌸ Reservations
⊕ Website	⌂ Dress code
✎ E-mail	⊟ No credit cards
⬚ Admission fee	$ Price
⊙ Open/closed times	**Other**
Ⓜ Subway	⇨ See also
⊹ Directions or Map coordinates	☞ Take note
	🏌 Golf facilities

Restaurants

Unless we state otherwise, restaurants are open for lunch and dinner daily. We mention dress code only when there's a specific requirement and reservations only when they're essential or not accepted. To make restaurant reservations, visit Fodors.com.

Credit Cards

The hotels and restaurants in this guide typically accept credit cards. If not, we'll say so.

EUGENE FODOR

Hungarian-born Eugene Fodor (1905–91) began his travel career as an interpreter on a French cruise ship. The experience inspired him to write *On the Continent* (1936), the first guidebook to receive annual updates and discuss a country's way of life as well as its sights. Fodor later joined the U.S. Army and worked for the OSS in World War II. After the war, he kept up his intelligence work while expanding his guidebook series. During the Cold War, many guides were written by fellow agents who understood the value of insider information. Today's guides continue Fodor's legacy by providing travelers with timely coverage, insider tips, and cultural context.

EXPERIENCE
NEW YORK CITY

NEW YORK CITY TODAY

The phrase "in a New York minute" is clichéd for a reason: in this frenetic city, things really do change in a flash. With the constant ebb and flow, it can be hard to keep up. Here is just some of what New Yorkers are talking about.

Economy

A few quick positive economic indicators: New York is experiencing its biggest hotel expansion in a generation, attracting a host of new brands—from high-end boutiques to budget chains—all across the city. The city has 122 hotels in the pipeline to open by 2017, with half of these properties slated for the outer boroughs—a key indicator of the recent visitor trend to visit, and stay in, boroughs beyond Manhattan. And tourists keep on coming: 2014 had a record number of visitors—over 56 million, up from the previous year's 54 million, and the city is expecting to exceed that number by the end of 2015.

Battle of the Boroughs

While visitors are discovering all things Brooklyn right now, New Yorkers are looking at—and raving about—Queens. With its longstanding residential communities, cheap ethnic eats, established attractions like MoMA PS1, the second-biggest Chinatown in the country, and Long Island City's skyline views and hop-skip-jump subway ride to Midtown, it's no wonder. Add less-expensive-than-Manhattan (and Brooklyn) hotel rooms and rents, the current and projected development boom, and proposed projects like the QueensWay (aka "the Queens High Line"), and it seems Queens is where it's at for 2015 and 2016. That said, it's Brooklyn Pope Francis will visit in late 2015, not Queens.

The Arts

Some of the biggest movers and shakers in the New York art scene will be moving and/or shaking off dust after renovations in 2015 and 2016, perhaps suggesting that the art world will be more focused on exhibition spaces than the exhibitions themselves. In early 2015, the Whitney Museum of American Art debuted its state-of-the-art new space in the Meatpacking District, complete with terraces opening onto the High Line and stunning views of the Hudson. Meanwhile, the Metropolitan Museum of Art is leasing the Whitney's old digs to display its growing collection of contemporary art while it refines plans to gut-renovate its Modern Wing. The Tenement Museum

WHAT'S NEW?

"SuperPier," the Pier 57 development at West 15th Street in Hudson River Park, originally earned its "super" status in 1952 when it opened as a shipping terminal. But the name applies just as easily to the pier under construction today, which will reopen (hopefully in 2016 or 2017) with a riverfront spa, a beach club, restaurants, and retail stores housed in repurposed shipping containers.

Lincoln Center's Avery Fisher Hall, home to the New York Philharmonic, will receive a $500 million gut renovation to create an exciting new concert venue to address evolving performances and audiences. Thanks to a new donor, the hall will also receive a new name: David Geffen Hall. Lincoln Center is reviewing design proposals and plans to begin construction in 2017.

is expanding to recreate the life of immigrants in New York post–World War II. The American Museum of Natural History is planning a six-story addition to improve navigation and add facilities for research and education, while the Frick is battling public disapproval of its plan to build a tower in its gated garden.

Sports

If there's something the quintessential New Yorker can't get enough of, it's sports, so if you're looking to make small talk with a local, just pick a team. Basketball fans can support the trendy Brooklyn Nets in their digs at the Barclays Center in Brooklyn or the New York Knicks at Madison Square Garden (Spike Lee is practically the team mascot). In late 2015, the New York Islanders hockey team moves from their suburban Long Island stadium to their new home at Barclays Center. The Islanders haven't won a Stanley Cup since the early 1980s; maybe Brooklyn will help them get their mojo back. The Islanders compete with the New York Rangers for the hearts—and ticket sales—of New York hockey fans. Baseball lovers can choose between the New York Yankees (Yankee Stadium in the Bronx) or the New York Mets (Citi Field in Queens). New York football fans declare their loyalty to either the New York Giants or the New York Jets—both teams play at MetLife Stadium in New Jersey. Soccer fans can choose between the city's two Major League Soccer teams, the New York Red Bulls and the newly formed New York City Football Club, who might sway fairweather fans with their field in the hallowed baseball grounds of Yankee Stadium in the Bronx. If you can't pick a team, pick a less contentious sport, like tennis; the U.S. Open brings the best in tennis to the USTA Billie Jean King National Tennis Center in Queens in late summer.

Plans—and shovels—are finally underway to overhaul the South Street Seaport, replacing the existing complex at Pier 17 with a new $200 million glass retail complex. Reopening is scheduled for late 2016.

Coney Island's New York Aquarium is open but undergoing a $150 million renovation. New features will include a roof deck and a walk-through coral tunnel with sharks swimming overhead. It's set to open in 2016.

Staten Island is hoping to become a destination as it redevelops the waterfront to include a mall, a giant observation wheel, an open-air pedestrian mall, restaurants, and a hotel. The first spin on the Wheel is scheduled for early 2017.

PLANNER

When to Go

New York City weather is a study in extremes. Much of winter brings bone-chilling winds and an occasional traffic-snarling snowfall, but you're just as likely to experience mild afternoons sandwiched by cool temperatures.

In late spring and early summer, streets fill with parades and street fairs, and Central Park has free performances. Late August temperatures sometimes claw skyward, bringing subway station temperatures over 100°F (no wonder the Hamptons are so crowded). This is why September brings palpable excitement, with stunning yellow-and-bronze foliage complementing the dawn of a new cultural season. Between October and May, museums mount major exhibitions, most Broadway shows open, and formal opera, ballet, and concert seasons begin.

Getting Around

On Foot. The best way to explore New York is on foot. No matter what neighborhood you're headed to, you'll get a better sense of it by wandering around; you can check out the architecture, pop into cool-looking shops and cafés, and observe the walk-and-talk of the locals. And if you get lost, New Yorkers are actually very helpful with directions.

By Bike. Since Citi Bike's bike sharing program rolled out in 2013, there have been glitches but ridership continues to increase and New York City's program now boasts the largest fleet of bikes in the nation, and there are plans for the system to double in size by 2017. The city is slowly acclimating (its bike lanes and attitudes) to the popular new mode of transportation but it's no Copenhagen . . . yet. Ride off-peak if possible, keep out of Midtown, and stay alert!

By Public Transportation. New York's subway system is probably the most efficient and cost-effective way to get around, and it runs 24 hours a day. The subway is safe, but be smart: try to avoid riding alone (especially late at night) and avoid riding in empty cars.

If you prefer to stay above ground, and you're not in a rush, consider taking a bus. They're especially good if you need to travel crosstown, between the East and West sides of the city. What a city bus lacks in efficiency (especially at rush hour), it makes up for in people-watching and city views.

By Taxi. If you'd rather be comfy than thrifty, hail a yellow cab (the new apple-green "Boro Taxis" serve the outer boroughs and won't make pickups south of East 96th Street or West 110th). A taxi is available if the center panel of the roof light is lit and the side panels are dark. It's best to give your destination address using cross streets: ask to be taken to "55th and Madison" rather than "545 Madison." Avoid trying to hail a cab between 4 and 4:30 pm, when drivers change shifts. And remember that the subway is often faster than a cab, especially during rush hour.

E-hail Car Services. Uber, Lyft, Gett, and SheRides are some of the app-based car services available in Manhattan. ⇨ *For more information about getting around, check out the Travel Smart chapter.*

A Guide to the Grid

The map of Manhattan is, for the most part, easy to follow: north of 14th Street, streets are laid out in a numbered grid pattern. Numbered streets run east and west (crosstown), and broad avenues, most of them also numbered, run north (uptown) and south (downtown). The main exception is Broadway, which runs the entire length of Manhattan on a diagonal. Below 14th Street, street patterns get chaotic. In the West Village, West 4th Street intersects West 11th Street, Greenwich Street runs roughly parallel to Greenwich Avenue, and Leroy Street turns into St. Luke's Place for one block and then becomes Leroy again. There's an East Broadway and a West Broadway, both of which run north–south, and neither of which is an extension of Broadway, leaving even locals scratching their heads.

Street Smarts

You'll look—and feel—less conspicuous if you replace maps with apps. If you have a smartphone or tablet, download a subway map app from the MTA's website to help you plan your trip (by fastest route or fewest train changes), find nearby stations, and stay up-to-date on any service disruptions. Most major NYC attractions—from Central Park to the Met Museum—have their own apps to help you make the most of your time so download accordingly before you visit. Even better, download just one app—the Fodor's NYC app—for attraction overviews and handy suggestions of what's nearby.

New York City is a safe city, but it's still a city, so keep jewelry out of sight on the street; better yet, leave valuables in your hotel safe.

When in bars or restaurants, don't hang your purse or bag on the back of a chair.

Expect to have yourself and your possessions inspected thoroughly in such places as airports, sports stadiums, museums, and top attractions. Police officers reserve the right to check your bags before you pass through the turnstile to enter the platform.

We suggest politely ignoring panhandlers on streets and subways, people who offer to hail you a cab, and limousine and gypsy-cab drivers who (illegally) offer rides.

Opening Hours

Subways and buses run around the clock, as do plenty of restaurants. Some shops and services have longer hours than you'll find elsewhere in the United States, so you can get groceries, or get your nails done, at 11 pm. In general, though, you can safely assume that most shops are open seven days a week, from about 10 to 7 Monday through Saturday, and from noon to 6 on Sunday. Bars generally close at 4 am, though some after-hours clubs are open later.

Money-Saving Tips

Consider buying a CityPass, a group of tickets to six top-notch attractions in New York: the Empire State Building, the Guggenheim Museum or Top of the Rock, the American Museum of Natural History, the Museum of Modern Art (MoMA), the Metropolitan Museum of Art (including the Cloisters), and Circle Line Cruises or admission to Liberty and Ellis islands. The $109 pass, which saves you almost half the cost of each individual ticket (and all that time on ticket lines), is good for nine days from first use.

Sign up for social discount shopping sites like Groupon, Gilt City, Amazon Local, and LivingSocial a month before your visit to New York to score discounts on everything from trendy restaurants and clubs to beauty treatments and attractions.

WHAT'S WHERE

Numbers refer to chapters.

2 Lower Manhattan. The Financial District, NY Harbor, and TriBeCa. Heavy-duty landmarks anchor the southern tip of Manhattan, including Wall Street and the waterfront parks of Battery Park City. Ferry terminals dispatch boats to Ellis Island and the Statue of Liberty. The 9/11 Memorial, the 9/11 Memorial Museum, and North America's tallest building—One World Trade Center—are also down here.

3 SoHo, NoLIta, Little Italy, and Chinatown. Luxe shops dominate in SoHo these days, while NoLIta, to the east, has lots of boutiques and restaurants. Little Italy is a shrinking zone of touristy red-sauce eateries. Farther south, Chinatown teems with street vendors selling knockoff handbags and side streets with Chinese herb shops and noodle joints.

4 The East Village and the Lower East Side. Once a gritty neighborhood of artists and punks, the East Village is now a gentrified melting pot of NYU students, young professionals, and old-timers, but it still feels like a neighborhood. You'll get some of the best people-and-pooch-watching in the city from a bench in Tompkins Square Park. The once seedy, now trendy Lower East Side has live-music clubs, independent clothing shops, and wine bars.

5 Greenwich Village and the West Village. Artists with rent-controlled apartments, out-and-proud gays, and university students still live in the Village, but because those townhouses have become so expensive, residents also include wealthy media moguls, celebrities, and socialites. From 14th Street south to Houston and from the Hudson River east to 5th Avenue, the blocks are a jumble of jazz clubs, restaurants, former speakeasies, and rainbow flags.

6 Chelsea and the Meatpacking District. With hundreds of galleries in a seven-block radius, Chelsea is still the center of the city's contemporary art scene, even if real estate development has pushed some galleries elsewhere in the city or to Brooklyn. To the south, the Meatpacking District has evolved into a swanky clubbing and restaurant scene by night and—with the High Line, the new Whitney Museum of American Art, and high-end boutiques—a shopping and strolling destination by day.

7 Union Square, the Flatiron District, and Gramercy Park. Bustling Union Square Park hosts the city's best greenmarket. On the 14th Street edge are broad steps where break dancers and other performers busk for onlookers. Nearby, private, elegant Gramercy Park is surrounded by storied mansions and townhouses.

WHAT'S WHERE

8 Midtown East and Murray Hill. Midtown from 5th Avenue to the East River is the refined big sister of flashy Midtown West, with grand hotels, grand shopping, the Chrysler Building, and Grand Central Terminal. Murray Hill is a mix of quiet tree-and townhouse-lined streets and attractions like the Empire State Building and the Morgan Library.

9 Midtown West. Head to 42nd Street to see Times Square in all its neon and massive-TV-screen glory. Towering office buildings line Broadway up to Columbus Circle at the edge of Central Park. At Rockefeller Center are the famous ice rink and Christmas tree (in season), and nearby are swank shops like Saks and Bergdorf Goodman.

10 The Upper East Side. The Upper East Side is home to more millionaires than any other part of the city. Tucked into this stretch of 5th Avenue are the Museum Mile and Madison Avenue's haute boutiques.

11 Central Park. Frederick Law Olmsted's ode to the pastoral in the heart of New York, Central Park is the place to escape the bustle of the city. There's a small zoo, a boathouse, and activities as diverse as rock climbing, softball, and Frisbee.

12 The Upper West Side with the Cloisters. Wide sidewalks and ornate prewar buildings set the tone, and the American Museum of Natural History and Lincoln Center are big draws. Farther north is the Cloisters, a branch of the Metropolitan Museum of Art housing medieval works in a reconstructed monastery.

13 Harlem. A hotbed of African American and Hispanic American culture for almost a century, Harlem still sizzles. The brownstone-lined blocks are being refurbished, boutiques and restaurants are popping up, and music venues from the 1920s and '30s are still in full swing.

14 Brooklyn. New York's largest borough counts among its stars Prospect Park and the Brooklyn Botanic Gardens. Its distinctive neighborhoods include Williamsburg, DUMBO, Fort Greene, Coney Island, and Brighton Beach.

15 Queens, the Bronx, and Staten Island. Queens is known for its ethnic communities and Citi Field. The Bronx may be best known for Yankee Stadium, but the New York Botanical Garden and the Bronx Zoo also score home runs. Staten Island's best-known feature might be the ferry, but there are reasons to stick around, including a children's museum and New York City's only historic town and farm: Historic Richmond Town.

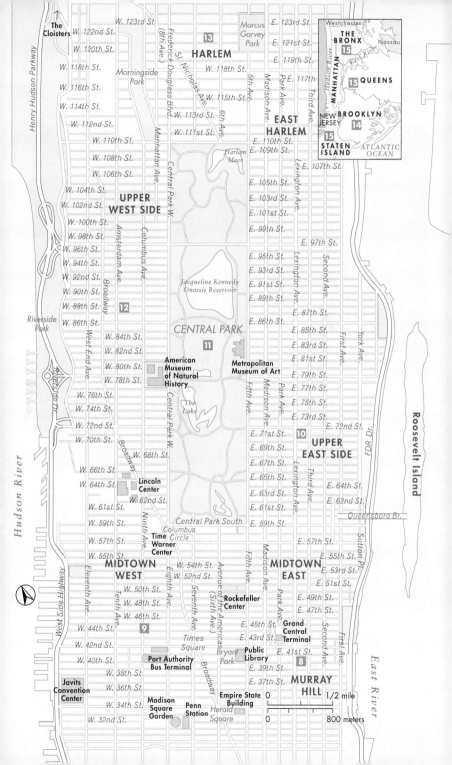

NEW YORK CITY
TOP ATTRACTIONS

Metropolitan Museum of Art

(A) The largest art museum in the Western Hemisphere, the Met is a mecca for art lovers. Treasures from all over the world and every era of human creativity make up its collection. If you need a breather, you can always retire to the Temple of Dendur or the rooftop café.

Times Square

(B) Times Square is the most frenetic part of New York City: a cacophony of languages and flashing lights, outré street performers, shoulder-to-shoulder crowds, and back-to-back billboards. These days it's also a pedestrian-friendly zone, so you won't have to take your eyes off the excitement to watch for traffic.

Empire State Building

(C) It may not be the tallest building in New York anymore (Freedom Tower reclaimed that title for the World Trade Center in May 2012), but its status as most iconic will never change. Take in the panoramic views of the city from its observatories, or just enjoy it from afar—after dark it's illuminated by colored lights that correspond to different holidays and events.

Museum of Modern Art

(D) Airy and spacious, with soaring, high-ceiling galleries suffused with natural light and masterpieces that include Warhol's *Campbell's Soup Cans* and Van Gogh's *Starry Night,* this one-of-a-kind museum designed by Japanese architect Yoshio Taniguchi is as famous for its architecture as for its collections.

Brooklyn Bridge

(E) New York City's most famous bridge connects the island of Manhattan to the borough of Brooklyn, and serves thousands of pedestrians, vehicles, skaters, and bicyclists a day. Walking across is an essential New York experience.

Statue of Liberty

(F) Presented to the United States in 1886 as a gift from France, Lady Liberty is a near-universal symbol of freedom and democracy, standing 152 feet tall atop an 89-foot pedestal on Liberty Island.

American Museum of Natural History

(G) The towering reassembled dinosaur skeletons that greet you when you enter this museum might stop you in your tracks, but there's much more to see here, including exhibits of ancient civilizations, the live Butterfly Conservatory (October–May), a hall of oceanic creatures overseen by a 94-foot model of a blue whale, and space shows at the Rose Center for Earth and Space.

Central Park

The literal and spiritual center of Manhattan, Central Park has 843 acres of meandering paths, tranquil lakes, ponds, and open meadows. For equestrians, softball and soccer players, strollers, skaters, bird-watchers, boaters, picnickers, and outdoor performers, it's an oasis of fresh air and greenery amid the hustle of the city.

9/11 Memorial and Museum

The National September 11 Memorial and Museum at the World Trade Center site is a moving tribute to the lives lost on 9/11. The free memorial features two large waterfalls and recessed pools, set within the footprints of the Twin Towers. The below-ground museum memorializes the lives of those lost through personal artifacts, multimedia displays, and first-person accounts.

The High Line

A botanical garden, a bridge to nowhere, a local hangout, and a work of art using the city's architecture, greenery, and people as part of its composition, this once-abandoned railroad track rises above the west side of Chelsea neighborhood.

LIKE A LOCAL

New Yorkers love this city, and with good reason: there's no other place like it on earth. Living here can be challenging, from the high rents to battling crowds at Sunday brunch, but locals have plenty of tricks up their collective sleeve. Follow our tips and before you know it, you'll be stopped by visitors seeking directions and ignored by tourist-seeking vendors.

Getting Around

Hit the ground walking

Spend a day in a New Yorker's shoes and you'll quickly realize that New Yorkers walk, and they walk fast. Pounding the pavement is often the fastest way to get around, but remember: move quickly. If you can't keep up the pace or you need to check your smartphone or take a photo, step to the side of the sidewalk and get out of the way. Hurry!

Take the subway

If weather, distance, or time rules out walking, locals head underground; it's cheaper than a cab and usually faster. If you truly want to look like a local you'll skip the double-decker bus tours and get yourself a MetroCard. The subway runs 24 hours a day, 7 days a week. There are maps posted in all stations, but locals are more than happy to show off their knowledge of the subway lines if you need directions. Even seasoned New Yorkers ask for or confirm directions, so don't be shy. If you're traveling with a smartphone, apps like HopStop and NYC Subway Map will help you figure out the best route. As for safety, the same advice applies here as to traveling in any major city: be alert, watch your bag, and don't travel on your own late at night.

E-hail a taxi cab

Many visitors to the city expect to find locals summoning taxis with a loud whistle or a brash "Hey, Taxi!", but in reality, locals are much quieter about it, preferring to hail cabs with a raised arm or via a smartphone app. Several e-hail services are available in the city, but Uber and Lyft are the most popular with locals. Once you've signed up, a simple tap will search for a car and track it in real time as it comes to you; you pay with a prestored credit card. Uber is the most established and best-known on-demand car service, but their "surge pricing" for high-traffic times like holidays and inclement weather have not endeared the service to locals (the practice may be banned if a new law goes into effect). If you're a woman traveling solo, or you prefer a female driver, you can hail a car from the city's newest e-hailing app—and the only car service app tailored to the needs of women—SheRides.

Food and Drink

Drink decent coffee

There might be a chain coffee shop on every corner in New York City, but you won't find many locals there. The so-called "city that never sleeps" is fueled with coffee, but not just any coffee. Locals are particular (some might say snobby) about coffee, so wait those few extra minutes for the best freshly roasted beans and pour-over brews. Join discerning locals at gourmet hot spots like Blue Bottle Coffee, Everyman Espresso, Joe the Art of Coffee, La Colombe, Ninth Street Espresso (which has locations other than 9th Street), Stumptown, and Third Rail Coffee. Most offer the added bonus of homemade pastries and treats.

Follow that truck

New Yorkers haven't lost their appetite for the various food trucks parked around the city, offering everything from Korean tacos and vegan sandwiches to gourmet doughnuts and Belgian waffles. Twitter feeds and blogs track their whereabouts (try ⊕ *NYCTruckFood.com*).

Support local farmers

New Yorkers do eat in on occasion (crazy rents to pay, after all), and when they do, they shop local. Local greenmarkets like the Union Square farmers' market offer a range of fresh fruit and vegetables, as well as locally sourced meats, fish, and specialty foods. If you don't have a kitchen to prepare a meal, shop for the makings of a great picnic. Join hungry locals to shop the stands on Monday, Wednesday, Friday, and Saturday from 8 am to 6 pm.

Skip the food fair

Beloved food festivals like Smorgasburg and Hester Street Fair are a huge local draw, especially on warm summer weekends, but now that the word is out and the lines are long, locals are heading back indoors to the city's new crop of highly curated food courts. Indoor markets like Gotham West Market, Gansevoort Market, Chelsea Market, and Hudson Eats feature artisan vendors and affordable eats, and sometimes live music and extended hours.

Do brunch

Your mother might have told you that breakfast is the most important meal of the day but on the weekends, this means brunch: eggs Benedict, bagels with cream cheese and smoked salmon, fruit-filled pancakes, decadent French toast, or fried chicken and waffles, accompanied by mimosas or bloody marys or specialty brunch cocktails. Most places start serving at 11am; the more popular spots will have a line so either plan to wait or get there early. These days, just about every restaurant worth its menu serves brunch on the weekends, even if they don't serve lunch during the week.

Entertainment

Take in a show

You won't cross paths with many locals in the heart of packed Times Square, but New Yorkers are not so jaded as to ignore the wealth of Broadway and Off-Broadway theatrical and musical offerings—they just don't like to pay full price for the experience. Do as locals do and find discounted tickets at social buying sites like Groupon, Gilt City, and Living Social, or score deals at discount ticket booth TKTS (though you'll make better use of your time if you line up at the less-trafficked booth in Brooklyn or South Street Seaport than the one in Times Square). ■ TIP➡ Use the free TKTS App for up-to-date ticket availability at each of the city's three booths. Otherwise we favor the Off-Off-Broadway experience, staying in-the-know with sites like ⊕ *OffOffOnline.com*.

Support the arts

Take advantage of the city's amazing museums, but make like a local and going during off hours, like early mornings on weekdays, to avoid the crowds. If you visit regularly, become a member of your favorite museums (as much to skip lines as to support the arts). Many museums have free or pay-as-you-wish nights (or days), but these can get very crowded. Another popular (and free) local art activity is skipping the major museums altogether and hopping from gallery to gallery in Chelsea.

SITTING IN A TV AUDIENCE

Tickets to tapings of TV shows are free, but can be hard to get on short notice. Most shows accept advance requests by email, phone, or online—but for the most popular shows, you might have to wait a few months. Same-day standby tickets are often available, but be prepared to wait in line for several hours, sometimes starting at 5 or 6 am, depending on how hot the show is, or the wattage of that day's celebrity guests. Remember that standby tickets do not guarantee a seat in the audience.

The Shows

The Dr. Oz Show. With tapings twice a day, three days a week, fans of "America's Favorite Doctor" have a good chance— or rather, six good chances a week—to bask in the polished bedside manner of Oprah's former health expert. No topic is off-limits so audience members must be over 18. Request tickets in advance online; your reservation will be confirmed by email two weeks in advance if there are seats available. Advance ticket holders receive updates about show segments with opportunities for audience involvement. Standby tickets are available at the studio Tuesday, Wednesday, and Friday at 8:50 am and 1:50 pm. ⊠ *320 W. 66th St., Upper West Side, New York* ⊕ *www. doctoroz.com/tickets* Ⓜ *1 to 66th St.–Lincoln Center.*

Good Morning America. Robin Roberts and George Stephanopoulos host this early-morning news and entertainment show. It airs live, weekdays from 7 to 9 am, and ticket requests (required only if you want a studio tour after the show) should be made online four to six months in advance. Gather before 7 am on the corner of West 44th Street and Broadway to participate in outdoor segments. ⊠ *7*

Times Sq., 44th St. and Broadway, Midtown West, New York ⊕ *abcnews.go.com/ GMA/mailform?id=12943471* Ⓜ *1, 2, 3, 7, N, Q, R, S to Times Sq.–42nd St.*

The Late Show with Stephen Colbert. After hosting the *Late Show* for 22 years, David Letterman passed the torch to former *Colbert Report* host, Stephen Colbert, in May 2015. While Colbert's fictional conservative persona did not follow him to his new gig in the Ed Sullivan Theater, his loyal audience did, so expect competition for tickets. The show is taped Monday to Wednesday at 4:30 and Thursday at 3:30 and 6 pm; check the website for updated ticket details. You must be 18 or older to sit in the audience. ⊠ *Ed Sullivan Theater, 1697 Broadway, between 53rd and 54th sts., Midtown West, New York* ☎ *212/975–5853* ⊕ *www. lateshowaudience.com* Ⓜ *1 to 50th St.; C, E to 50th St.; B, D, E to 7th Ave.*

Late Night with Seth Meyers. *Saturday Night Live* alum Seth Meyers took the reins as host of *Late Night* on NBC in 2014, when former host Jimmy Fallon departed for the *Tonight Show.* Tickets are available online up to two months in advance. Same-day standby tickets are handed out at 9 am at the NBC Experience Store (49th Street entrance). If all else fails, monologue rehearsal tickets are available at the NBC Experience Store at 12:30. Guests must be 16 or older to be in the audience. ✉ *30 Rockefeller Plaza, Midtown West, New York* ☎⊕ *www. showclix.com/event/latenightseth* Ⓜ *B, D, F, M to 47th–50th Sts./Rockefeller Center.*

Live! with Kelly and Michael Sparks fly on this morning program, which books an eclectic roster of co-hosts and guests. Tickets are available online about six weeks in advance. Standby tickets become available weekdays at 7 am at **ABC Studios** (*7 Lincoln Sq., 67th St. and Columbus Ave., Upper West Side*). Children under 10 are not permitted in the audience. ✉ *Midtown West, New York* ☎ *212/456–3054* ⊕ *live-kellyandmichael.dadt.com* Ⓜ *1 to 66th St.–Lincoln Center.*

Saturday Night Live. After four decades of laughs, *SNL* continues to push buttons, nurture comedic talents, and captivate audiences—all "live from New York." Standby tickets (only one per person) are distributed at 7 am on the day of the show at the West 49th Street entrance to 30 Rockefeller Plaza. You may ask for a ticket for either the dress rehearsal (8 pm) or the live show (11:30 pm). Requests for advance tickets (two per applicant) must be submitted by email only in August to *snltickets@nbcuni.com*; recipients are determined by lottery. You must be 16 or older to sit in the audience. ✉ *NBC Studios, 30 Rockefeller Plaza, between W. 49th and W. 50th Sts., Midtown West, New York* ☎ *212/664–3056* ⊕ *www.nbc. com/tickets* Ⓜ *B, D, F, M to 47th–50th Sts./Rockefeller Center.*

Today. The *Today Show* doesn't have a studio audience, but if you get yourself to the the corner of Rockefeller Center and West 49th Street before dawn, with posterboard and markers (fun signs always get camera time), comfortable shoes (you'll be on your feet for hours), and a smiley, fun attitude, you might get on camera. America's first morning talk-news show airs weekdays from 7 to 10 am in the glass-enclosed, ground-level NBC studio. ✉ *Rockefeller Plaza, W. 49th St., Midtown West, New York* ⊕ *www.today. com* Ⓜ *B, D, F, M to 47th–50th Sts./Rockefeller Center.*

The Tonight Show Starring Jimmy Fallon. In early 2014, musician, singer, actor, and comedian Jimmy Fallon packed up his impressions and sketches, his roster of star friends, and his house band (the Roots) and moved from *Late Night* to the *Tonight Show*, into the big comedic shoes of Jay Leno and Johnny Carson before him. He also moved the show back to New York, where it had resided until 1972. Visit the website to reserve free tickets: each month they're released during the first week of the prior month. ■TIP→ Each month's ticket release date and time is announced exclusively on the show's Twitter feed (@FallonTonight). ✉ *30 Rockefeller Plaza, Studio 6B, Midtown West, New York* ☎ *212/664–3506* ⊕ *www.showclix.com/event/thetonightshowstarringjimmyfallon* Ⓜ *B, D, F, M to 47th–50th Sts./Rockefeller Center.*

FREE AND CHEAP

Sometimes it seems like everything in New York costs too much, but in fact the city has tons of free (or cheap) attractions and activities; you just need to know where to look for them. Note that NYC is at its most free (mentally and financially) in summer when there are all sorts of outdoor events, but you can find a "wealth" of freebies year-round.

Free Art

The $25 admission fee to the **Metropolitan Museum of Art**, the $22 fee to the **American Museum of Natural History,** and the $16 admission to the **Brooklyn Museum** are actually *suggested* donations. Smaller donations may get some eye-rolling from the cashier, but it's a small price to pay for access to world-famous works of art. The **Museum at FIT**, "the most fashionable museum in the city" at the Fashion Institute of Technology, is home to a collection of some 50,000 garments and accessories from the 18th century to the present. It's free, off-the-beaten-museum-path, and fabulous. Another less trafficked—and free—gem, the **American Folk Art Museum**, features traditional folk art as well as contemporary works by self-taught artists. The museum's diverse collection includes everything from drawings, paintings, and ceramics to mummylike sculptures, decorative furniture, and a beautifully stitched quilt made by female slaves on a Southern plantation. **The National Museum of the American Indian (Smithsonian Institution),** in a beautiful Beaux Arts building on the south side of Bowling Green in Lower Manhattan, is a small museum (by New York standards) but it offers free admission as well as free music and dance performances and an extensive permanent collection of textiles, ceremonial objects, and decorative arts. Decidedly on the beaten path, and for good reason, **MoMA** is free

on Friday between 4 and 8 pm, when the $25 entry fee is waived. Arrive as close to 4 as you can, and once you get your ticket (the line is long but fast), avoid the crowds by working your way down from the fifth floor. If you want to avoid the crowds altogether—and get ahead of the art game—take a gallery-crawl in and out of the hundreds of **galleries in Chelsea** for free access to up-and-coming and superstar artists alike. Unlike major museums, galleries are rarely crowded (except for Thursday, when they often host openings with free wine and cheese). You'll also find a trendy art scene in Williamsburg, Brooklyn.

Free Entertainment

If you don't see enough movie stars wandering around New York City, you can catch stars on a big screen—under the stars—with a free summer flick. There are free screenings all across the five boroughs in summer, from Brooklyn Bridge Park to Bronx Terminal Market (⊕ *www. nycgovparks.org/events/free_summer_ movies*). In Manhattan take your blanket and picnic basket to **Bryant Park**: a tradition since 1992, watching films alfresco surrounded by tall Midtown buildings is a summertime rite of passage for New Yorkers. Be prepared to stake out a good spot on the lawn early in the day. Movie schedules are posted at ⊕ *www. bryantpark.org*.

If you prefer live entertainment, catch tango dancers and jazz musicians outside Lincoln Center at the annual, free, monthlong **Out of Doors** festival, held in August. It includes more than 100 performances. You can also experience free music performances, film screenings, and artist conversations at Lincoln Center's **David Rubenstein Atrium**; check the online

calendar before you visit. **Central Park SummerStage** is your free ticket to big-name performers like Afrobeat bandleader Seun Kuti and Columbia University's own Vampire Weekend. There's also a series of concerts in Brooklyn.

Catch rising stars in music, drama, and dance at the **Juilliard School**'s free student concerts (check ⊕ *www.juilliard.edu* for a calendar of events). Free tickets are available at the Juilliard box office for theater performances; standby tickets are available an hour before the show.

One of the city's most beloved events (and the hottest free ticket in town) is **Shakespeare in the Park,** which usually features celebrities earning their olde English acting chops in outdoor performances in Central Park. Get in line early at the Public Theater for a shot at tickets, or head to the Delacorte Theater in Central Park. ⊕ *www.shakespeareinthepark.org.*

Like your theater a little less scripted? Get gratis giggles at the **Upright Citizens Brigade Theatre**'s improv comedy shows, where professional comedians, including UCB cofounder and *Saturday Night Live* alumna Amy Poehler, are sprinkled in with amateurs during the performances. Many of the shows are just $5; some are free. ⊕ *www.ucbtheatre.com.*

Another way to save your pennies for dinner is to catch a free reading at one of the city's bookstores—big (Barnes & Noble) and small (Housing Works Bookstore Café). Or you can get your fix of free words at KGB in the East Village, where authors have been reading since 1993. In Brooklyn, Pete's Candy Store and Franklin Park (both bars) have reading series.

Free Rides

One of the best free rides in the city is on the **Staten Island Ferry.** A one-way trip takes 30 minutes and offers magnificent views of the Statue of Liberty, Ellis Island, and the southern tip of Manhattan—plus there's inexpensive beer and snacks. Note that you have to disembark at St. George Terminal in Staten Island before your return trip. Another cheap/sometimes-free ferry sure to (ahem) float your boat is the seven-minute ferry ride from Lower Manhattan to **Governors Island,** a 172-acre island oasis in the heart of New York Harbor. You can visit the former military base turned sculpture park and public playground daily from late May to late September to bike, picnic, wander forts, take in views of Lower Manhattan, and enjoy a variety of cultural offerings and festivals. Ferries are free on weekend mornings and $2 round-trip (for adults) on all weekday and weekend-afternoon ferries. Give your sea legs a rest and take to the sky for an almost-free aerial ride on the **Roosevelt Island Tramway.** For the price of a subway ride ($2.75), you can glide over the East River on the only commuter cable in North America and score stunning city views while you're at it. The trip takes only a few minutes (board at the East 59th Street and 2nd Avenue station) so you have plenty of time to explore Roosevelt Island and FDR Four Freedoms Park before you make the return trip.

MIDTOWN ARCHITECTURE: LOOK UP!

Midtown is the heart of New York City during the workday, with people rushing to and from work in the morning and to lunch or coffee in the afternoon, all with that vibrant energy that is synonymous with Manhattan. What those rushing by might miss, though, are the many beautiful architectural sights. We say, don't be embarrassed to look up at them—just get out of the way of other people speed-walking down the sidewalk.

The East Side: From the United Nations to Grand Central

Start near the East River, at New York City's first glass-curtain skyscraper, the **UN Building** (*760 United Nations Plaza*), completed in 1949 and designed by Le Corbusier. (Technically, it's not on New York land, but we still count it.) The iconic structure is a monument to diplomacy, but being the city's first skyscraper isn't all glory: the air-conditioning is famously persnickety in summer. Continuing west, you'll pass the murals of the **Daily News Building** (*220 E. 42nd St.*) on the south side of the street. The lobby is home to a giant globe (from the era when the *News* had international correspondents) and murals are in the WPA style, since the Art Deco building was finished in 1929. Also a can't-miss: the **Chrysler Building** (*405 Lexington Ave.*), which out–Art Decos any other structure in New York. (Dig the wheels with wings in place of gargoyles on the exterior.) Continue walking and you'll get to **Grand Central Terminal** (*1 E. 42nd St.*), the largest train station in the world. This Beaux Arts structure was saved from the wrecking ball by concerned citizens in the '70s, a fate that the similarly styled old Penn Station didn't escape. Step inside for a look at the constellations painted on the soaring ceiling, for a nibble at the Grand Central Oyster Bar, or for a cocktail at the swanky Campbell Apartment.

Midtown: Bryant Park and the New York Public Library

By the time you hit 5th Avenue, you'll be staring at the lions that guard the **New York Public Library** (*455 5th Ave.*). Built in 1911, the structure is a hub of learning and hosts many lecture series throughout the year. It's abutted by **Bryant Park,** which offers free Wi-Fi, ice skating in the winter, and films in the summer.

The West Side: The Heart of Times Square

Keep walking west and you'll hit the razzle and dazzle of **Times Square.** It's better than it's ever been. No, not from Giuliani's cleanup—those seedy days are long since passed, and Disney predominates—but thanks to a series of pedestrian-friendly improvements, including the closure of some lanes to traffic and the addition of lawn chairs, making it easier to navigate. Be sure to note the futuristic-looking **4 Times Square,** where Vogue magazine dictates the world of style from on high, and the kid-friendly confines of **Madame Tussauds** (*234 W. 42nd St.*). Finish off by seeing the lights of Broadway from the many theaters on this stretch between 8th and 9th avenues. If you keep walking, you'll get to the pedestrian path along the Hudson River.

1

Where to Start:	United Nations, especially for those who are architecturally inclined
Length:	1½ miles (two hours)
Where to Stop:	Grand Central, Bryant Park
Best Time to Go:	Early afternoons; weekends
Worst Time to Go:	Weekday evenings, when the after-work crush is at its peak
Highlights:	Grand Central, Chrysler Building, New York Public Library

NYC'S WATERFRONT PARKS

If Central Park makes you think, "Been there, done that," head to one of the city's several waterfront parks. Many New Yorkers are just now discovering some of these green getaways, too.

Battery Park City

Built on landfill jutting out into the Hudson River, Battery Park City is a high-rise residential neighborhood split in two by the World Financial Center and its marina. The Hudson River Park promenade borders Battery Park City along the West Side Highway. There are several reasonably priced outdoor restaurants with stunning views of the Statue of Liberty. If you have kids, don't miss the excellent Teardop Park, with its huge slide, and the park's newest attraction, SeaGlass, an aquatic-themed carousel ride that simulates a descent to the ocean's floor.

Getting Here

By subway: South Battery Park: 1, R to Rector Place; 4, 5 to Wall Street. North Battery Park: 1, 2, 3, A, C to Chambers Street; E to World Trade Center. By bus: M9, M20, M22.

Brooklyn Bridge Park

Over in Brooklyn, a former industrial site running along a narrow stretch of Brooklyn waterfront from Vinegar Hill to Brooklyn Heights has been turned into a 1.3-mile-long park featuring grassy lawns, rocky outcrops, bike paths, playgrounds, a pop-up pool in summer, soccer fields, basketball courts, volleyball courts, and a carousel. There are picnic areas, seasonal food stands by high-profile restaurants, food and film festivals in summer, water-taxi service to Governors Island, and thousands of visitors and locals taking advantage of it all. Perhaps the best feature of this new hipster destination is one that's been here all along: the picture-postcard views of the Brooklyn Bridge and the city skyline, now framed by a thriving greenway and best appreciated from the rough-hewn granite-block seating under the Manhattan Bridge.

Getting Here

By subway: A, C to High Street; F to York Street. Instead of taking the subway, you could take a water taxi (⊕ www.nywatertaxi.com) to Fulton Ferry Landing, the East River Ferry (⊕ www.nywaterway.com) to Fulton Ferry Landing, or by walking across the Brooklyn Bridge.

The East River Park

This recently landscaped waterfront park, stretching from Montgomery Street to 12th Street along the Manhattan side of the East River, is one of the Lower East Side's best-kept secrets, with ball fields, bike paths, tennis courts, playgrounds, gardens, and picnic areas—along with impressive views of the Brooklyn skyline and the Williamsburg Bridge. You have to cross a footbridge over the FDR Drive to get to the park.

Getting Here

By subway: J, M, Z to Essex Street; F to 2nd Avenue.

Governors Island

A recent addition to the city's parks scene, this little island feels like a small town just 800 yards from the tip of Manhattan. Tourists love the unparalleled views of the New York Harbor and Lower Manhattan, and locals love the out-of-city experience. The 172-acre park, built in part from landfill from subway excavations, was a base for the U.S. Army and Coast Guard for almost two centuries. Until 2003, it was off-limits to the public, which could be why the 19th-century homes here are

so well preserved. The island is open to the public daily from May to October, with programs including art showings, concerts, and family events. You can take a bike over on the ferry or rent one on the island. For more information, including updated ferry schedules and a calendar of activities, go to ⊕ *www.govisland.org.*

Getting Here

A $2 seven-minute ferry ride (free on weekend mornings) takes passengers to Governors Island from a dock at 10 South Street, next to the Staten Island Ferry. Get to the ferry by subway: 1 to South Ferry; 4, 5 to Bowling Green; or R, W to Whitehall Street. By bus: M1 (weekdays only), M6, M9, and M15.

The High Line

Once an elevated railroad track that serviced the long-ago factories along the lower west side, the High Line was converted into a park (really more of a promenade) that integrates landscaping with rail-inspired design and provides a fresh perspective on the city. Vegetation here includes 210 species of plants, trees, and shrubs intended to reflect the wild plants that flourished for decades after the tracks were abandoned in 1980. The park—30 feet above street level—is open between Gansevoort Street in the Meatpacking District and 34th Street in Midtown. Sweeping views of the Hudson River, an extended sight line of the Meatpacking District, and the new Whitney Museum of American Art are the highlights. For information on tours, public programs, and a calendar of events, go to ⊕ *www. thehighline.org* or call *212/500–6035.*

Getting Here

The High Line is accessible at Gansevoort and every two blocks between 14th and 30th streets with elevator access at 14th,

16th, 23rd, 30th and 34th streets (no bikes allowed). It's two blocks west of the subway station at 14th Street and 8th Avenue, served by the A, C, E, and L. You can also take the C, E to 23rd Street and walk two blocks west. The 1, 2, 3 stops at 14th Street and 7th Avenue, three blocks away. By bus: M11 to Washington Street, M11 to 9th Avenue, M14 to 9th Avenue, M23 to 10th Avenue, M34 to 10th Avenue.

The Hudson River Park

This 5-mile greenway park hugs the Hudson River from 59th Street to Battery Park. Although the park has a unified design, it's divided into seven distinct sections that reflect the different Manhattan neighborhoods just across the West Side Highway. Along with refurbished piers with grass and trees, there are also attractions like the *Intrepid* Sea, Air, and Space Museum at Pier 86 across from 46th Street. A few blocks south, the Circle Line and World Yacht offer boat tours of the Hudson. At piers 96 and 40, the Downtown Boat House (⊕ *www.downtownboathouse.org*) offers free kayaking. There's a mammoth sports center, **Chelsea Piers,** between piers 59 and 61, and a playground, mini-golf course, and beach volleyball court at Pier 25. The park also sponsors free tours and classes, including free fishing. For a calendar of events and activities, go to ⊕ *www. hudsonriverpark.org.* North of Hudson River Park is one of Manhattan's better-known parks, **Riverside Park.**

Getting Here

Hudson River Park is on the far west side of the city, adjacent to the West Side Highway. Crosstown buses at 14th, 23rd, and 42nd streets will get you close, but you'll still have to walk a bit. It's worth it.

NEW YORK CITY WITH KIDS

From space shuttles to vintage trains, climbing walls to climbing coasters, not to mention zoos, parks, playgrounds, kid-centric shows, and more—the city that never sleeps has plenty of ways to tire out your kids.

Museums

There's a museum for every age, interest, and attention span in New York City. Some are aimed squarely at the younger set, but you shouldn't limit yourself or your kids to "children's" museums; most—especially the big players like MoMA, the Guggenheim, the Met, and the Whitney—offer programs to engage younger visitors (just ask at the admission desk). That said, sometimes toddlers want play places designed specifically for them, like the play center and interactive exhibits created for the under-five set at the **Children's Museum of Manhattan** and the arts and crafts rooms and ball pit at the **Children's Museum of the Arts**. The **American Museum of Natural History** is a top choice for kids of all ages and interests, visitors and locals alike: the giant dinosaurs and the huge blue whale alone are worth the trip, as is the live Butterfly Conservatory (October through May). You'll also find an IMAX theater, ancient-culture displays, and fabulous wildlife dioramas. The space shows at the Hayden Planetarium (tickets sold separately) are a big bang with kids. Nearby, the often overlooked **DiMenna Children's History Museum**—in the New-York Historical Society—invites kids (8 and up) to connect to the lives of real New York children from the past through hands-on activities that include video games, cross-stitching, and interactive maps. The **Lower East Side Tenement Museum** also offers a glimpse into the lives of early New Yorkers, in this case immigrant families. Guided tours (for ages 6 and up) visit restored tenement apartments where costumed "residents" bring history to life. You can also explore the history of public transit in NYC—from horse-power to the subway—at the **New York Transit Museum**. Housed in an old subway station in Brooklyn Heights, this museum has an old bus to pretend-drive, vintage subway cars, and retro ads and maps. Also in Brooklyn is the **Brooklyn Children's Museum**, which, although a trek from the subway, has great hands-on exhibits (best suited for under-8s) like an interactive greenhouse. The **Intrepid Sea, Air and Space Museum**, an aircraft carrier turned museum, houses the world's fastest jets, a Cold War–era submarine, the first space shuttle, the interactive Exploreum Hall, flight simulators, and more. When museums try to make learning fun, they often fall flat, but the new kid museum on the block, the **Museum of Mathematics**, makes learning kaleidoscopic, and yes—fun—through interactive puzzles, games, displays, and hands-on tools like square-wheel tricycles.

Parks and Playgrounds

If you're looking for space to let off steam in Manhattan, the 843-acre **Central Park** is a good start. You can row boats on the lake, ride a carousel, explore the zoo, rent bikes, picnic, or just wander and enjoy the park's musicians, performers, and 21 playgrounds.

Head to **DUMBO** (short for Down Under the Manhattan Bridge Overpass) for family-friendly **Brooklyn Bridge Park**, a picnic-perfect waterfront park with several inventive playgrounds, Jane's Carousel, the Brooklyn Ice Cream Factory, a public swimming pool, and a variety of kid-centric music, arts, and kite-flying festivals.

If it's too hot, too cold, or the kids just want too much of a good thing in one easy location, head to **Chelsea Piers**, between 18th and 23rd streets along Manhattan's Hudson River. With a climbing wall, batting cages, ice-skating rinks, basketball and volleyball courts, indoor soccer fields, bowling, sailing, golf, gymnastics, and an Explorer Center with a ball pit and slides, it's a five-block energy outlet for local and visiting kids of all ages.

Attractions

With all the screeching and honking, wild colors, and crazy behavior, New York City can feel like one big zoo, but if the kids want the real deal, there's a zoo in every borough of Manhattan. The **Bronx Zoo** is the city's—and country's—largest metropolitan wildlife park, and home to more than 4,000 animals, including endangered and threatened species. Plan to spend a whole day here so your kids don't have to choose between Congo Gorilla Forest and the Siberian cats at Tiger Mountain. Manhattan's **Central Park Zoo** is small but popular, and known to little kids as the setting for the animated *Madagascar* films. You'll find red pandas, snow leopards, a penguin house, performing sea lions, grizzly bears, and a petting zoo. You can get face-to-face with even more interesting creatures in **Coney Island,** where the whole family can enjoy a walk along Coney Island's famous boardwalk to take in the beach, Luna Park's amusement rides, the landmark Cyclone wooden roller coaster (54-inch height requirement), minor league baseball games at the Cyclones' stadium (MCU Park), and Nathan's hotdogs. While the **New York Aquarium** is still only partially open due to continuing renovations (after 2012's Hurricane Sandy), the adorable sea lion shows at its newly renovated Aquatheater are always a hit

with kids. If adorable creatures of the robotic variety are called for, hit the **Sony Wonder Technology Lab.** The line to get into this futuristic fantasy world might be long (entry is free) but a talking robot keeps everyone entertained while you wait. Inside, kids can program their own robots; record their own digital music, movies, and games; and perform open-heart surgery using Haptic technology.

Shows

Once upon a time, it seemed like the only truly kid-friendly show on Broadway was *The Lion King*. These days, adults could complain that Broadway is selling itself to the youngest bidder, but who's complaining when the shows are so adult-friendly, too. *The Lion King* is still a firm favorite with kids, but it has solid competition with the likes of *Aladdin, Matilda, Wicked,* and Off-Broadway shows like *Stomp,* the *Gazillion Bubble Show,* and *Blue Man Group*. Kids shows are popular, so it's rare to find tickets at TKTS booths; book ahead if possible. Preteens and teens who are too cool for the Disney musical experience might appreciate Sam Eaton's mind-boggling display of magic and mentalism in **The Quantum Eye,** Off-Broadway at Theatre 80 in St. Mark's Place. The **New Victory Theater** is New York City's only theater dedicated to presenting family-friendly works; tickets are affordable, and shows are entertaining, never condescending, and, yes, cool. Kids ages 3–9 can partake of music, dance, comedy, storytelling, and dancing at Just Kidding at **Symphony Space,** a performing arts center on Broadway and West 95th Street that inspires and entertains with established and emerging family-friendly artists. Interacting is encouraged.

NEW YORK CITY MUSEUMS, AN OVERVIEW

From the grand institutions along 5th Avenue's museum mile to an underground museum in a converted subway station in Brooklyn, to the dramatic new Whitney Museum in the Meatpacking District, New York City is home to an almost overwhelming collection of artistic riches, so it's a good idea to plan ahead. This overview includes museums listed elsewhere in the book; check the index for full listings.

Major Museums

It's hard to create a short list of top museums in New York City, because, well, there are just so many top museums. That said, ambitious art lovers will likely focus on the Big Five. One of the most-visited museums in the world, the **Metropolitan Museum of Art** (known locally as "the Met," not to be confused with the Metropolitan Opera, also known as "the Met") is a must. It's collection consists of more than 2 million works of art representing 5,000 years of history. From its world-famous dinosaur halls, its halls of fossils, gems, and human evolution, and its planetarium, the **American Museum of Natural History** is one of the most celebrated museums in the world. Both the **Museum of Modern Art (MoMA)** and the **Solomon R. Guggenheim Museum** are known for their incredible spaces—MoMA, a maze of glass walkways, was designed by Yoshio Taniguchi, and the nautilus-like Guggenheim was designed by Frank Lloyd Wright—as well as for their superlative collections of contemporary art and curated shows. The **Whitney Museum of American Art**, which moved from its Upper East Side home to the Meatpacking District in spring 2015, is the city's hottest museum ticket, as much for its High Line and Hudson views as for its expansive indoor and outdoor exhibition spaces.

Other Top Museums

There are many other important museums in the city. The **Frick Collection,** an elegant museum in the neoclassical mansion of industrialist Henry Clay Frick, is especially worthy of a visit. The **Morgan Library and Museum** is another mansion-museum founded on the vast and varied collections of a magnate—in this case J. P. Morgan. The **American Folk Art Museum** is dedicated to American folk art and the work of contemporary self-taught artists. The **New Museum** is the only museum dedicated solely to contemporary art in Manhattan. There are several museums to satisfy design lovers including the **Museum of American Illustration and Museum of Comic and Cartoon Art at the Society of Illustrators,** the **Museum of Arts and Design**, the **Museum at FIT**, the **Skyscraper Museum**, and the newly redesigned **Cooper Hewitt, Smithsonian Design Museum,** packed with hands-on activities for grown-ups. Speaking of lovers, the provocative, adults-only **Museum of Sex** explores the history, evolution, and cultural significance of sex while the **Museum of American Finance** satisfies our obsession with all things money.

New York–Specific Museums

It's appropriate that the city's oldest museum, the **New-York Historical Society,** is dedicated to the city itself. Founded in 1805, this neighbor of the American Museum of Natural History offers a unique and comprehensive overview of New York's history, as well as quirky and compelling exhibits. Other NY-centric museums include the **Museum of the City of New York,** the **Lower East Side Tenement Museum,** the **Merchant's House Museum,** the **Fraunces Tavern Museum,** the **Ellis Island Immigration Museum,** the **New York City Police Museum,** the **New York City Fire Museum,** the

9/11 Memorial Museum (at Ground Zero), and the New York Transit Museum.

Culturally Specific Museums

New York City is often referred to as a melting pot, which explains the profusion of culture-specific museums dedicated to sharing the broad and specific stories, struggles, and experiences of certain cultural and ethnic groups—often overlooked in mainstream museums. El Museo del Barrio focuses on Latin American and Caribbean art and features a popular collection of hand-carved wooden folk-art figures from Puerto Rico. The Hispanic Society of America Museum and Library houses paintings by Goya, Velázquez, and El Greco, as well as an unsurpassed collection of Spanish, Portuguese, and Latin American artifacts. The National Museum of the American Indian (Smithsonian Institution) explores the diversity of the Native American peoples through cultural artifacts, and regular music and dance performances. The Jewish Museum, the Museum of Jewish Heritage, and the Museum at Eldridge Street explore Jewish culture and art, and the Jewish experience in New York. The Asia Society and Museum, the Museum of Chinese in America (MOCA), the Japan Society, and the Rubin Museum of Art are dedicated to the art and experiences of Asian communities. Other notable ethnic- or culture-specific museums include the Leslie + Lohman Museum of Gay and Lesbian Art, the Ukranian Museum, and the Studio Museum in Harlem (for artists of African descent locally, nationally, and internationally).

Museums Farther Afield

The Brooklyn Museum is the second-biggest museum in New York City and home to an impressive collection of European and American paintings and sculptures, an outstanding Egyptian collection, and a sculpture "memorial garden" of salvaged architectural elements from throughout New York City. A visit to Queens means innovative and experimental art at MoMA PS1 and the small museum and garden of the Noguchi Museum, dedicated to the art of Isamu Noguchi, a prominent Japanese-American sculptor. Other top museums in Queens include the Museum of the Moving Image and the Queens Museum of Art. The Cloisters Museum and Gardens (an outpost of the Met museum) in Fort Tryon Park in Upper Manhattan is a bit of a trek relative to other city museums but we can pretty much guarantee you'll think it worth the trip.

Children's Museums

Some kids museums are fun just for the kids, like the Children's Museum of the Arts, the Children's Museum of Manhattan, and the Brooklyn Children's Museum, but many are fun for the entire family. Kids of all ages will appreciate the fleet of jets, the flight simulator, and other hands-on activities, the space shuttle *Enterprise*, and the *Growler* submarine at the Intrepid Sea, Air and Space Museum. Other crowd-pleasers include Madame Tussauds New York, the Museum of Mathematics, and the New York Transit Museum. The DiMenna Children's History Museum (at the New-York Historical Society) has interactive exhibits geared to help kids connect with children throughout New York's history.

Galleries

There are many art galleries in Manhattan and Brooklyn worth visiting; check neighborhood chapters for specific listings. It can also depend on what shows are on at what times, so we also recommend checking the listings in *New York Magazine* and the *New York Times*.

NEW YORK CITY FESTIVALS

There's always *something* going on New York City, but if you want to put a finger on the real pulse of New York, you should participate in a *big something* while you're here. Summer is an especially good time for festivals. Here are a few of our favorites:

Spring

Spring means the start of baseball season with home openers, usually in the first week of April, for both of New York's Major League teams: the Yankees and the Mets.

Sakura Matsuri Cherry Blossom Festival. New Yorkers come out of hibernation en masse every spring to witness the extremely popular annual Sakura Matsuri Cherry Blossom Festival at the Brooklyn Botanic Garden. In addition to the blooming cherry trees, there are Taiko drumming performances, Japanese pop bands, samurai swords, martial arts, tea ceremonies, and more. ⊠ *New York* ⊕ *www.bbg.org* ⊙ *Apr.* Ⓜ *2, 3 ro Eastern Parkway-Brooklyn Museum; 2, 3, 4, 5 to Franklin Ave.*

Tribeca Film Festival. Founded by Jane Rosenthal and Robert De Niro to contribute to the long-term recovery of Lower Manhattan after 9/11, the Tribeca Film Festival has become one of the most prominent film festivals in the world. There are upward of 250 films, more than 1,000 screenings, and even more buzz. ⊠ *New York* ⊕ *www.tribecafilm. com* ⊙ *Mid- to late Apr.*

Summer

With festivals and events on city streets, at the beaches, and in almost every city park, New Yorkers take full advantage of the long summer days and nights. Free outdoor movie festivals are a huge draw in summer: choices include sci-fi movies with a view of Brooklyn Bridge Park (⊕ *www.*

brooklynbridgepark.org); indie movies on city rooftops (⊕ *www.rooftopfilms. com*); and classics screened every Monday night in Midtown's Bryant Park (⊕ *www. bryantpark.org*).

Celebrate Brooklyn! Launched in 1979 to bring people back into Prospect Park after years of neglect, Celebrate Brooklyn! is one of the city's most popular, free, outdoor performing arts festivals, and *the* place to catch excellent live music in the great Brooklyn outdoors. The artists and ensembles reflect the borough's diversity, ranging from internationally acclaimed performers to up-and-coming musicians. The lineup also includes kids shows, movies with live music, ballet, and more. Performances are rain-or-shine and free (there is a suggested donation of $3), with the exception of ticketed benefit concerts, which directly support the festival. Seats for free shows are first-come, first-served. Local restaurants provide the food. Get there early and bring a blanket and an umbrella for shade. ⊠ *Prospect Park Bandshell, 9th St. and Prospect Park W. entrance, Park Slope, Brooklyn* ⊕ *www.bricartsmedia. org/performing-arts/celebrate-brooklyn* ⊠ *Free* ⊙ *Jun.–Aug.* Ⓜ *F, G to 7th Ave.; 2, 3 to Grand Army Plaza.*

Midsummer Night Swing. If dancing in the street is your thing, join the Midsummer Night Swing festival, an outdoor music and dance party in Lincoln Center Plaza. Take lessons with pros or just take your chances on the floor! ⊠ *New York* ⊕ *www.midsummernightswing.org* ⊙ *Late June–early July* Ⓜ *1 to 66th St.*

Museum Mile Festival. For one day every June, thousands of locals and visitors celebrate the Museum Mile Festival when 10 museums along 5th Avenue open their doors for free. ⊠ *New York* ⊕ *www.museummilefestival.org* ⊗ *Early June.*

Summer Streets. On three consecutive Saturdays every August, you can join hundreds of thousands of locals to let loose on nearly 7 miles of pedestrianized city streets for Summer Streets. From the Brooklyn Bridge to Central Park, along Park Avenue and connecting streets, New Yorkers hit the car-free streets to rock climb, zip line, dance, work out, experience art, or just ramble along the city's streets in a new way—all for free. ⊠ *New York* ⊕ *www.nyc.gov/summerstreets* ⊗ *Aug.*

Other popular summer festivals and events include Coney Island's **Mermaid Parade,** the **New York International Fringe Festival, SummerStage,** and **Shakespeare in the Park.**

Fall

Brooklyn Book Festival. The Brooklyn Book Festival is a huge, (mostly) free public event with an array of established and emerging authors, readings, panels, discussions, parties, games, and signings—all held in clubs, parks, theaters, and libraries across Brooklyn. ⊠ *New York* ⊕ *www.brooklynbookfestival.org* ⊗ *Sept.*

Feast of San Gennaro. Every year, thousands of locals and visitors flock to Little Italy for the 11-day Feast of San Gennaro. This festival is a mix of religion, delicious food, colorful parades, and live entertainment. Don't miss the cannoli-eating competition at the end of the week. ⊠ *New York* ⊕ *www.sangennaro.org* ⊗ *Mid- to late Sept.*

New York City Marathon. Even if you're not joining the almost 50,000 runners taking a 26.2-mile run through New York's five boroughs on the first Sunday in November, you'll want to experience the electric atmosphere and the very best of New York with the 2 million spectators. ⊠ *New York* ⊕ *www.tcsnycmarathon.org* ⊗ *1st Sun. in Nov.*

Other top fall events include the **Village Halloween Parade, Macy's Thanksgiving Day Parade,** and the **Rockefeller Center Tree Lighting Ceremony.**

Winter

Sure, it can be icy-cold in New York in winter, but locals know that the best way to stay warm is by running/skating from one event to another.

Holiday Train Show. The New York Botanical Garden's Holiday Train Show is one of the city's top seasonal attractions, especially for families. You'll find electric trains, more than 150 miniature replicas of city landmarks (made out of twigs and bark), and magical landscapes—all housed in a conservatory, so winter weather can't dampen your spirits. ⊠ *New York* ⊕ *www.nybg.org* ⊗ *Mid-Nov.–mid-Jan.*

To ring in the **Lunar New Year,** the streets of Chinatown give way to food vendors hawking traditional eats, colorful costumes and decorations, and a major parade of elaborate floats, marching bands, and dragon troupes running from Little Italy through Chinatown and Lower Manhattan. Festivities also take place in Sunset Park in Brooklyn and in the Flushing neighborhood of Queens (⊕ *www.betterchinatown.com*).

If you want to join in on a little local tomfoolery, join tens of thousands of "Santafied" locals who tear up the town for **SantaCon** (⊕ *nycsantacon.com*), or sign up for a **No Pants Subway ride** in January (⊕ *www.improveverywhere.com*).

BEST TOURS IN NEW YORK CITY

Sometimes a guided tour is the way to go, even if you usually prefer to fly solo. It can be a great way to investigate out-of-the-way areas, to get an insider's perspective on where locals eat and play in the city, and to learn about interesting aspects of the city's history, inhabitants, or architecture. Whether you want the classic hop-on, hop-off bus tour to get oriented in the city or a more personal, interest-specific walk, you'll find it here. ■TIP➔ Some of the bigger tour companies offer discounts if you book in advance online.

Boat Tours

Circle Line Sightseeing Cruise. In good weather, a Circle Line Sightseeing Cruise around Manhattan Island is one of the best ways to get oriented in the city. A "Best of NYC" 2½-hour, $40 cruise runs at least once daily. Shorter options are available, too, including the 30-minute thrill-ride, the Beast. ⊠ *Pier 83, W. 42nd St., Midtown West, New York* ☎ *212/563–3200* ⊕ *www.circleline42. com* ⌫ *From $29.*

Manhattan By Sail. Looking for a more historical experience? Manhattan By Sail has an 82-foot yacht dating from the 1920s that makes daily 90-minute public sails and Sunday brunch sails from mid-April through mid-October. Themed sailings include a wine-tasting sail, lobster and beer lovers sail, and a jazz sail against stunning moonlit views. They also offer two-hour sunset sails in June, July, and August. Reservations are advised. ⊠ *North Cove Marina at World Financial Center, Lower Manhattan, New York* ☎ *212/619–0907* ⊕ *www. manhattanbysail.com* ⌫ *From $39.*

Bus Tours

Big Bus New York. Like its double-decker competitors, Big Bus offers various hop-on, hop-off open-top tours of the city, but its most popular ticket is a two-day pass that includes loops that cover downtown, uptown, and Brooklyn, as well as a night tour and a free sightseeing cruise with Hornblower Cruises from Pier 15 at the South Street Seaport. ⊠ *Ticket desk, B.B. King Blues Club & Grill, 237 W. 42nd St., Midtown West, New York* ☎ *212/685–8687* ⊕ *www.bigbustours.com/newyork* ⌫ *From $49.*

Gray Line New York Sightseeing. Gray Line runs various hop-on, hop-off double-decker bus tours, including a downtown Manhattan loop, an upper Manhattan loop, a Brooklyn loop, and evening tours of the city. Packages include 48-hour and 72-hour options plus entrance fees to attractions. ⊠ *777 8th Ave., between 46th and 47th sts., Midtown West, New York* ☎ *800/669–0051* ⊕ *www. newyorksightseeing.com* ⌫ *From $54.*

Walking Tours

Big Onion Walking Tours. The wisecracking, PhD candidates of Big Onion Walking Tours lead themed tours such as "Upper East Side: A Clash of Titans," "Immigrant New York," and "The Official Gangs of New York," as well as famous multiethnic eating tours and guided walks through neighborhoods from Harlem to the Financial District and Brooklyn. Tours run daily and last about two hours; there's an additional $5 tacked on for tours that include making various stops to eat. ⊠ *New York* ☎ *888/606–9255* ⊕ *www.bigonion.com* ⌫ *$20.*

Levy's Unique New York. With tours that include "Jewish Gangsters of the Lower East Side," "Staten Island: Sailors,

Suburbs & Secrets," and "Graffiti to Galleries: Street Art in NYC," family-run Levy's tours are anything but the usual top attractions hitlist (although you can visit those, too). Guides are knowledgeable and personable, and will cater to specific interests. All tours are private so the more the merrier (and the cheaper!). ⊠ *New York* ⊕ *www.levysuniqueny.com* 🖃 *From $300.*

Like A Local. Walk like a local, talk like a local, and best of all eat like a local with a highly curated tour from Like A Local. Tours include the Flatiron Food tour, which is a lovely walk from the Flatiron District to Union Square with a lot of tasty stops, photo ops, local history, and private kitchen visits along the way. If you're looking to feel like a hip local in Brooklyn, take the Sunday Funday tour of Williamsburg. ⊠ *New York* ⊕ *www. likealocaltours.com* 🖃 *From $42.*

The Municipal Art Society of New York. The Municipal Art Society conducts a series of walking tours that emphasize the architecture, history, and changing faces of particular neighborhoods. Options include "What's New (and Old) in Long Island City," "The Bronx's Urban Art," and "Storefront: the Disappearing Face of New York." An official daily walking tour of Grand Central explores the 100-year-old terminal's architecture, history, and hidden secrets. Tours begin in the main concourse at 12:30 and last 75 minutes. Tickets can be purchased in advance online or from the ticket booth in the main concourse. ⊠ *111 W. 57th St., New York* ☎ *212/935–3960, 212/935–3960 for recorded info* ⊕ *www.mas.org* 🖃 *$20.*

New York City Cultural Walking Tours. Alfred Pommer's walking tours cover such topics as buildings' gargoyles, the TriBeCa

Historic District, and the Upper East Side Millionaire's Mile. Two-hour public tours run on some Sundays from March to December (no reservations needed); private tours can also be scheduled. ⊠ *New York* ☎ *212/979–2388* ⊕ *www.nycwalk. com* 🖃 *$20.*

New York Food Tours. Options from the New York Food walking tours include "The Freakiest and Funniest Food" and a "Tastes of Chinatown" tour. Prices range from $52 for a 2½-hour East Village food and culture tour to $125 for a 3½-hour Multicultural bar-hopping tour. ⊠ *New York* ☎ *347/559–0111* ⊕ *www. foodtoursofny.com* 🖃 *From $52.*

Specialty Tours

Bike and Roll. From Central Park to the Brooklyn Bridge, there's a lot of ground to cover; do yourself a favor and use wheels. Bike and Roll NYC offers guided bike (and Segway) tours of the city with a range of distances and levels of difficulty. The Bike and Boat tour is a scenic ride from Lower Manhattan's Battery Park across the Brooklyn Bridge to Brooklyn Heights. From Brooklyn, there's a NY Water Taxi ride to Midtown Manhattan and then a final bike ride south along the Hudson River. Other tour options include New York at Night, 9/11 Memorial, and Central Park. Rates include bike rentals, helmets, and water. ⊠ *New York* ☎ *212/260–0400* ⊕ *www. bikenewyorkcity.com* 🖃 *From $40.*

Boroughs of the Dead. From tours taking in haunts of the East and West villages to 19th century true-crime tours to Manhattan's only dedicated Edgar Allan Poe walking tour, the Boroughs of the Dead two-hour tours suggest that the inhabitants of this city truly never sleep—even when they're dead. Don't wait for

Halloween to explore the historical crime, gore, and paranormal activities of Manhattan and Brooklyn. No capes, costumes, or gimmicks here: just dark, haunting history. It's a good choice for teens. ⊠ *New York* ☎ *646/932–0680* ⊕ *www. boroughsofthedead.com* ✉ *From $45.*

A Slice of Brooklyn. You can manage fine without a guide to hold your hand through Rockefeller Center and past the decked-out windows of 5th Avenue, but if you're interested in experiencing a more local holiday light tradition, take A Slice of Brooklyn's bus tour to the festive (and blinding) neighborhood light scene that is Brooklyn's Dyker Heights. The 3½-hour tour, offered nightly in December, introduces you to some of Brooklyn's less touristed neighborhoods. Other tours include the Original Brooklyn Pizza Tour, a 4½-hour bus tour of iconic Brooklyn pizza joints, and tours of quintessential Brooklyn neighborhoods. ⊠ *New York* ☎ *212/913–9917* ⊕ *www. asliceofbrooklyn.com* ✉ *From $50.*

Shop Gotham. If you're on a mission to shop till you drop, you won't want to waste time with a map. The fashion-savvy guides at Shop Gotham will save you time and money by guiding you to the best boutiques of SoHo and NoLIta and elsewhere, getting you exclusive shop discounts, and also offering styling advice. Tours last 2 to 3 hours. Private tours are available, too. ⊠ *New York* ☎ *212/209–3370* ⊕ *www.shopgotham.com* ✉ *From $38.*

Free Tours

Big Apple Greeter. This free volunteer-led tour service pairs visitors with knowledgeable locals who share insights and tips and cater tours to specific interests. It's like having a friend in town who squires you around and pays for his or her own lunch! Request a greeter at least three weeks before your visit by filling in the online form. ⊠ *New York* ☎ *212/669–8159* ⊕ *www.bigapplegreeter.org* ✉ *Free.*

Central Park Conservancy. The Central Park Conservancy offers free one- to two-hour guided tours that provide an introduction to the different areas of Central Park: its woodlands, romantic vistas, Conservatory garden, Seneca Village, and secret corners and off-the-beaten-path walks. Volunteer-led Welcome Tours meet at different points in the park, so check the website for details. Premier tours are ticketed ($15) and provide a more in-depth experience. ⊠ *New York* ☎ *212/794–6564* ⊕ *www.centralparknyc.org* ✉ *Free.*

Free Tours by Foot. The walking, photography, food, and biking tours of Manhattan and Brooklyn hosted by Free Tours by Foot are technically free (you pay what you feel the tour was worth, if anything, upon completion) but there is a rental fee for bike and bus tours—still significantly cheaper than most other bike and bus tours. (Reservations are required.) Highlights include a sunset walking tour of the High Line, a Harlem food tour, and a journey through the storied past of the East Village. ⊠ *New York* ☎ *646/450–6831* ⊕ *www.freetoursbyfoot.com* ✉ *Free (suggested donation).*

THE STATUE OF LIBERTY AND ELLIS ISLAND: GATEWAY TO THE NEW WORLD

A quintessential part of a visit to New York, the trip to the Statue of Liberty and Ellis Island takes up the better part of a day. It involves a ferry ride, long lines, security checks, and ultimately, the rare opportunity to appreciate some of the most powerful symbols of America right up close. It's worth the effort. It's no overstatement to say that these two sights have played defining roles in American culture.

THE STATUE OF LIBERTY

Impressive from the shore, the Statue of Liberty is even more majestic up close. For millions of immigrants, the first glimpse of America was Lady Liberty, growing from a vaguely defined figure on the horizon into a towering, stately colossus. Visitors approaching Liberty Island on the ferry from Battery Park may experience a similar sense of wonder as they approach.

What's Here

The 152-foot-tall **statue** of Liberty, officially named *La Liberté éclairant le monde* ("Liberty Enlightening the World") was a gift from the people of France to the United States. It was designed by French sculptor Frédéric Auguste Bartholdi, built in France, and shipped to America where it was assembled. The statue stands atop an 89-foot-tall **pedestal** designed by American architect Richard Morris Hunt. The lines of Emma Lazarus's sonnet "The New Colossus" ("Give me your tired, your poor, your huddled masses yearning to breathe free...") are inscribed on a plaque inside the pedestal.

Inside the pedestal is an informative and entertaining **museum**. Highlights include the torch's original glass flame (the current flame is 24-karat gold and lit at night by floodlights), full-scale copper replicas of Lady Liberty's face and one of her giant feet, Bartholdi's alternative designs for the statue, and a model of the interior framework designed by Gustave Eiffel)of Eiffel Tower fame).

The **observatory platform** at the top of the pedestal is a great place for a photo op; it's 16 stories high, and you'll have all of Lower Manhattan spread out in front of you. The observatory platform is accessible via elevator if you don't want to climb the stairs.

The **crown** is the statue's highest accessible point. It's reached by stairs (154 of them; about a 20 minute journey) from the observatory platform.

Liberty Island has a nice shop and café.

Know Before You Go

Buy your tickets in advance. There are a limited number of same-day standby tickets available at ferry ticket offices, where you catch the ferry but we strongly advise planning early. Once you reach the island, there are no tickets available, and without a ticket there is absolutely no admittance into the pedestal or the museum.

You have three choices when buying your ticket to the Statue of Liberty:

A. You can just buy a ferry ticket. This will get you to Liberty Island and Ellis Island but it does not get you *into* the Statue of Liberty—either the pedestal or the crown. The ferry ticket does include a self-guided audio tour of Liberty Island (there's an adult version and a kids version). Pick up your audio guide when you exit the ferry at Liberty Island.

B. You can buy your ticket with pedestal access; there is no extra charge but you should do this in advance. Pedestal access includes access to the Liberty Island Museum.

C. For crown access, plan *far* in advance, as there are only 320 spots available each day and they sell out months in advance. There is a small extra fee.

Liberty Highlights

■ The surreal chance to stand next to, and be dwarfed by, the original glass torch and the copper cast of Lady Liberty's foot.

■ The vistas of New York from the observatory platform.

ALTERNATIVE VIEWS

■ The free Staten Island Ferry offers a great view of New York Harbor and of the Statue of Liberty from a distance (see Chapter 2).

■ Webcams placed around the statue's torch allow you to see what Lady Liberty sees—wide views of the New York City skyline, the Hudson River, and ships in the harbor—from your computer or phone.

■ Liberty Helicopters has sightseeing tours that fly over the crown and torch (see Chapter 1).

Liberty helicopters

FAST FACT: To move the Statue of Liberty from its initial home on a Paris rooftop to its final home in the New York Harbor, the statue was broken down into 350 individual pieces and packed in 214 crates. It took four months to reassemble it.

FAST FACT: The face of Lady Liberty is actually a likeness of sculptor Frederic-Auguste Bartholdi's mother—quite a tribute.

FAST FACT: Lady Liberty has formidable proportions. Her face is more than 8 feet tall, she has a 35-foot waistline, and she weighs 225 tons (450,000 pounds). Her crown has 7 rays, to represent the 7 continents; each is 9-feet long and weighs about 150 pounds.

Foundation of the pedestal to torch: 305′6″

Heel to top head: 111′6″

ELLIS ISLAND

Chances are you'll be with a crowd of international tourists as you disembark at Ellis Island. Close your eyes and imagine the jostling crowd 100 times larger. Now imagine that your journey has lasted weeks at sea and that your day pack contains all your worldly possessions. You're hungry, tired, jobless, and homeless. This scenario just begins to set the stage for the story of the millions of immigrants who passed through Ellis Island. Between 1892 and 1924, approximately 12 million men, women, and children first set foot on U.S. soil at the Ellis Island federal immigration facility. By the time the facility closed in 1954, it had processed the ancestors of more than 40% of Americans living today.

WHAT'S HERE

The island's main building, now a national monument, is now known as the **Ellis Island National Museum of Immigration**, and tells the story not just of Ellis Island but also of immigration from the colonial era to the present day through numerous galleries containing artifacts, photographs, and recorded oral histories. Visitors enter the museum into the **Baggage Room**, with general information and displays including the **American Flag of Faces**, an interactive display filled with images of immigrants submitted online (submit yours at FlagofFaces.org). At the **American Family Immigration Center**, you can search immigration records for information about your own ancestors.

The museum is divided into three sections: before Ellis Island, while Ellis Island was used to process prospective immigrants, and after Ellis Island was closed.

On the ground floor are the pre–Ellis Island "**Peopling of America**" exhibits, which explore stories of the earliest arrivals to America, from the Native Americans through Colonial and Victorian periods, up until 1892, when Ellis Island opened. It explores themes like how and why people made the journey to America. Also on the ground floor is the post–Ellis Island "**New Eras of Immigration**" wing, with interpretative graphics and poignant audio stories that give first-hand accounts of the immigrant journey in the modern era.

On the second floor is the centerpiece of the museum, the **Registry Room** (also known as the Great Hall). It feels dignified and cavernous today, but photographs show that it took on many configurations through the years, always packed with humanity. Here and on the third floor are exhibits about what immigrants experienced coming through Ellis Island, including **Through America's Gate and Treasures from Home**, with displays of possessions that people brought with them from their homeland.

Outside is the **American Immigrant Wall of Honor**, which has the names of more than 600,000 immigrant Americans against the backdrop of the Manhattan skyline.

MAKING THE MOST OF YOUR VISIT

Because there's so much to take in, it's a good idea to use the museum's interpretive tools. The audio tour (included in the price of your ferry ticket) takes you through the exhibits, providing thorough, engaging commentary interspersed with recordings of immigrants recalling their experiences. Make time for the moving 25-minute *Island of Hope, Island of Tears* film, which takes viewers through an immigrant's journey from the troubled conditions of European life, to their arrival at Ellis Island, and their introduction to American cities. Check at the visitor desk in the Baggage Room for tour times, movie showing times, and other special programs.

IN FOCUS THE STATUE OF LIBERTY AND ELLIS ISLAND: GATEWAY TO THE NEW WORLD

IMMIGRANT HISTORY TIMELINE

Starting in the 1880s, troubled conditions throughout Europe persuaded both the poor and the persecuted to leave their family and homes to embark on what were often gruesome journeys to come to the golden shores of America.

1880s 5.7 million immigrants arrive in U.S.

1892 Federal immigration station opens on Ellis Island in January.

1901–1910 8.8 million immigrants arrive in U.S.; 6 million processed at Ellis Island.

1907 Highest number of immigrants (860,000) arrives in one year, including a record 11,747 on April 17.

1910 75% of the residents of New York, Chicago, Detroit, Cleveland, and Boston are now immigrants or children of immigrants.

1920s Federal laws set immigration quotas based on national origin.

1954 Ellis Island immigration station is closed.

New arrivals line up to have their eyes inspected.

FAST FACT: Some immigrants who passed through Ellis Island later became household names. A few include Charles Atlas (1903, Italy); Irving Berlin (1893, Russia); Frank Capra (1903, Italy); Bob Hope (1908, England); Knute Rockne (1893, Norway); and Baron Von Trapp and his family (1938, Germany).

FAST FACT: In 1897, a fire destroyed the original pine immigration structure on Ellis Island, including all immigration records dating back to 1855.

FAST FACT: The first test that immigrants had to pass was known as the "six-second medical exam." As they entered the Great Hall, they were watched by doctors; if anyone seemed disabed, their clothing was marked with chalk and they were sent for a full exam.

Four immigrants and their belongings, on a dock, look out over the water; view from behind.

PLANNING

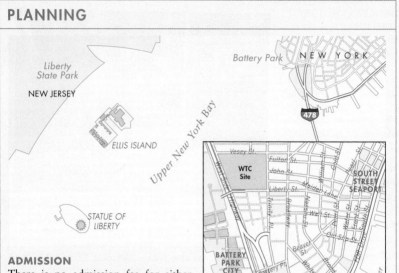

ADMISSION

There is no admission fee for either the Statue of Liberty or Ellis Island, but the ferry ride (which goes round-trip from Battery Park to Liberty Island to Ellis Island) costs $18. Ferries leave from Battery Park (see Ch. 2) every 30 to 40 minutes, depending on the time of year. There are often long lines, so arrive early, especially if you have a reserved-time ticket. (Oversize bags and backpacks aren't permitted onboard.) Reserve tickets online—you'll still have to wait in line, both to pick up the tickets (or print your tickets at home) and to board the ferry, but you'll be able to pick up a Monument Pass for access to the pedestal, the museum, and the statue's interior. There is no fee for the Monument Pass, but you cannot enter the Statue of Liberty without it.

WHERE TO CATCH THE FERRY

Broadway and Battery Pl., Lower Manhattan Ⓜ Subway: 4, 5 to Bowling Green.

PLANNING TIPS

Buy tickets in advance. This is the only way to assure that you'll have tickets to actually enter the Statue of Liberty museum and observatory platform.

Be prepared for intense security. At the ferry security check, you will need to remove your coat; at the statue, you will need to remove your coat as well as your belt, watch, and any metal accessories. At this writing, no strollers, large umbrellas, or backpacks are allowed in the statue.

Check ferry schedules in advance. Before you go, check www.statuecruises.com.

Keep in mind that even though the last entry time for the monument is at 4:30 PM, **the last ferry to the Statue of Liberty and Ellis Island is at 3:30 PM.** You need to arrive by at least 3 PM (to allow for security checks and lines) if you want to make the last ferry of the day.

LOWER
MANHATTAN

GETTING ORIENTED

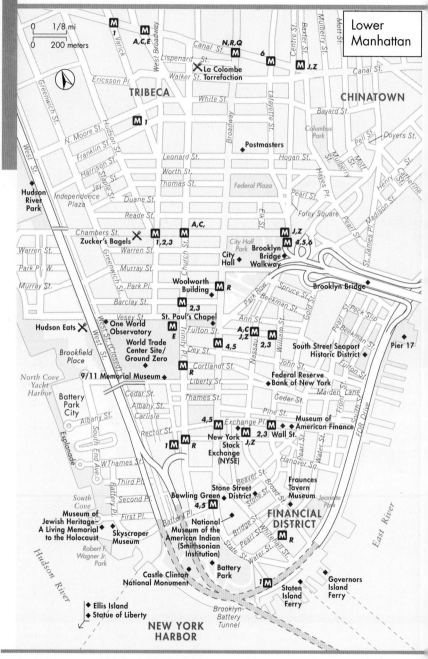

MAKING THE MOST OF YOUR TIME

Visit the Financial District during the weekend and you might feel like a lone explorer in a canyon of buildings; even on weeknights the decibel level of the neighborhood reduces significantly after about 6. Weekdays, however, the sidewalks bustle so much that you can expect to be jostled if you stand still too long. End your visit by watching the sunset over the Hudson River.

The sights of the New York Harbor are some of the most quintessential of New York, but be prepared for long lines for Ellis Island and the Statue of Liberty, especially on weekends. TriBeCa is one of the quieter neighborhoods in Manhattan, being mostly residential. There are pleasant shops, restaurants, and local bars, but the neighborhood tends not to be a tourist attraction unless the film festival is going on.

COFFEE AND QUICK BITES

Hudson Eats at Brookfield Place. The food court and terrace in the Brookfield Place complex has the best of NYC's casual food options ranging from Blue Ribbon Sushi to Black Seed Bagels to Dos Toros Tacos. ⊠ *West St. between Vesey and Liberty Sts., Financial District* ⊕ *www.brookfieldplaceny. com* Ⓜ *E to World Trade Center; R to Cortlandt St.*

La Colombe Torrefaction. In this loftlike space just below Canal Street, expect excellent espresso drinks and impressive latte art. Unlike other coffee shops plagued by laptops and customers clad in headphones, La Colombe does not have Wi-Fi. ⊠ *319 Church St., at Lispenard St., TriBeCa* ☎ *212/343–1515* ⊕ *www.lacolombe.com* Ⓜ *A, C, E to Canal St.*

Zucker's Bagels. This is one of the few places left in the city that still serves hand-rolled, kettle-boiled New York bagels, baked throughout the day. Coffee is from La Colombe. ⊠ *146 Chambers St., Financial District* ☎ *212/608–5844* ⊕ *www. zuckersbagels.com* Ⓜ *1, 2, 3 to Chambers St.*

TOP EXPERIENCES

Visiting the National 9/11 Memorial

Riding the Staten Island Ferry

Touring Ellis Island and the Statue of Liberty

Snapping a photo in front of Wall Street's bull

Strolling through Hudson River Park

BEST FOR KIDS

Castle Clinton and Battery Park

South Street Seaport Museum

GETTING HERE

Many subway lines connect to the Financial District. The Fulton Street station is serviced by eight different subway lines (2, 3, 4, 5, A, C, J, Z) and puts you within walking distance of City Hall, South Street Seaport, and the World Trade Center site (*Ground Zero feature in this chapter*). To get to the Brooklyn Bridge, take the 4, 5, or 6 to Brooklyn Bridge–City Hall.

For sights around New York Harbor, take the R to Whitehall Street, or the 4 or 5 to Bowling Green. (Note that you can also reach the Harbor area via the 1 train to South Ferry; it also stops in the heart of TriBeCa, at Franklin Street.)

2

Sightseeing
★★★★★
Nightlife
★★
Dining
★★★★
Lodging
★★
Shopping
★★

Lower Manhattan, or "all the way downtown" in the parlance of New Yorkers emphatically giving directions to tourists, has long been where the action—and transaction—is. Originally the Dutch trading post called New Amsterdam (1626–47), this neighborhood is home to historic, cobblestone streets next to soaring skyscrapers. This mix of old and new, the bustle of Wall Street, and a concentration of city landmarks all lure visitors to the southern tip of Manhattan.

FINANCIAL DISTRICT

Updated by
Jessica Colley

Little from Manhattan's colonial era is left in Lower Manhattan (apart from a precious few structures built in the 1700s), but you can still sense history in the South Street Seaport's 19th-century brick facades and in pedestrianized Stone Street's picnic tables. There's life to be found within the skyscraper canyons of Wall Street and lower Broadway, as locals move into the neighborhood and fill the barstools in candlelit watering holes. Bounded by the East and Hudson rivers to the east and west, respectively, and by Chambers Street and Battery Park to the north and south, the Financial District is best appreciated by getting lost in its streets.

You'll want to see what's here, but above all you'll want to see what's not, most notably in that empty gulf among skyscrapers: the World Trade Center site where two 1-acre pools represent the footprints of the fallen Twin Towers.

TOP ATTRACTIONS

9/11 Memorial Museum. To one side of the reflecting pools of the 9/11 Memorial is the glass atrium of the Memorial Museum. The museum descends some 70 feet down to the bedrock the Twin Towers were built on, and displays a collection of donated artifacts, memorabilia, photographs, and various recordings, as well as an exhibition that takes visitors through the history of events leading up to the attack and its aftermath. There's also a memorial wall with portraits of those who died, pieces of the Towers' structural columns and foundation, and remnants of the "Survivors Stairs," which allowed hundreds of people to escape the buildings. Current access the museum and the Memorial is from the intersection of Liberty and Greenwich streets, the intersection of Liberty and West, or the intersection of West and Fulton. Admission to the museum includes the 9/11 Memorial. ⊠ *180 Greenwich St., Financial District* ☎ *212/266–5211* ⊕ *www.911memorial.org/museum* ✐ *$24 (free Tues. 5–8 pm)* ☉ *Sun.–Thurs. 9–8, Fri. and Sat. 9–9* Ⓜ *1 to Rector St.; R to Rector St.; 2, 3, 4, 5, A, C, J, Z to Fulton St.; E to World Trade Center.*

FAMILY **Battery Park.** Jutting out at the southernmost point of Manhattan, tree-filled Battery Park is a respite from the narrow, winding, and (on weekdays) jam-packed streets of the Financial District. Even if you don't plan to stay for long, carve out a few minutes of sightseeing time to sit on a bench and take in the view, which includes the Statue of Liberty and Ellis Island. On clear days you can see all the way to Port Elizabeth's cranes, which seem to mimic Lady Liberty's stance; to Governors Island, a former Coast Guard installation now managed by the National Park Service; a hilly Staten Island in the distance; and the old railway terminal in Liberty State Park, on the mainland in Jersey City, New Jersey. Looking away from the water and toward Lower Manhattan's skyscrapers, there's a feeling that you're at the beginning of the city, and a sense of all the possibility it possesses just a few blocks in.

The park's main structure is **Castle Clinton National Monument,** the ticket office site and takeoff point for ferries to the Statue of Liberty and Ellis Island. This monument was once 200 feet off the southern tip of the island located in what was called the Southwest Battery, and was erected during the War of 1812 to defend the city. (The East Battery sits across the harbor on Governors Island.) As dirt and debris from construction were dumped into the harbor, the island expanded, eventually engulfing the landmark. Later, from 1855 to 1890, it served as America's first official immigration center (Ellis Island opened in 1892).

Inside Battery Park are several monuments and statues, including *The Sphere,* which for three decades stood on the plaza at the World Trade Center as a symbol of peace. Damaged but still intact after the collapse of the towers, it serves as a temporary memorial to those who lost their lives.

The southern link in a chain of parks connecting Battery Park north to Chambers Street, Robert F. Wagner Jr. Park has a flat, tidy lawn and wide benches from which to view the harbor or the stream of runners and in-line skaters on the promenade. A brick structure at the southeast section of Battery Park has public bathrooms and a restaurant with additional views from its flat roof. ⊠ *Battery Park* ☎ *212/417–2000* ⊕ *www.nycgovparks.org/parks/batterypark* Ⓜ *4, 5 to Bowling Green; 1 to South Ferry.*

Fodor's Choice ★ **Brooklyn Bridge.** "A drive-through cathedral" is how the journalist James Wolcott described the Brooklyn Bridge, one of New York's noblest and most recognized landmarks, perhaps rivaling Walt Whitman's comment that it was "The best, most effective medicine my soul has yet partaken." The bridge stretches over the East River, connecting Manhattan and Brooklyn. A walk across its promenade—a boardwalk elevated above the roadway, shared by pedestrians, in-line skaters, and cyclists—takes about 40 minutes and delivers exhilarating views. If you start from Lower Manhattan, you'll end up in the heart of Brooklyn Heights (you can also take the subway to the Brooklyn side and walk back towards Manhattan). It's worth noting that on weekends when the weather is nice, the path can get pretty congested; it's most

> ### BROOKLYN BRIDGE FACTS
>
> ■ Overall length: 6,016 feet
>
> ■ Span of twin Gothic-arch towers: 1,595½ feet
>
> ■ Distance from top of towers to East River: 272 feet
>
> ■ Distance from roadway to the water: 133 feet
>
> ■ Number of times the line "If you believe that, I've got a bridge to sell you" is used referring to the Brooklyn Bridge: infinite

magical, and quietest, early in the morning or during sunset when the city lights come to life. ⊠ *East River Dr., Lower Manhattan* Ⓜ *4, 5, 6 to Brooklyn Bridge–City Hall; J, Z to Chambers St.; A, C to High St. (in Brooklyn).*

New York Stock Exchange (NYSE). Unfortunately you can't tour it, but it's certainly worth ogling. At the intersection of Wall and Broad streets, the exchange is impossible to miss. The Neoclassical building, designed by architect George B. Post, opened on April 22, 1903. It has six Corinthian columns supporting a pediment with a sculpture titled *Integrity Protecting the Works of Man,* featuring a tribute to the then-sources of American prosperity: Agriculture and Mining to the left of Integrity; Science, Industry, and Invention to the right. The Exchange was one of the world's first air-conditioned buildings. ⊠ *11 Wall St., Financial District* ☎ *212/656–3000* ⊕ *www.nyse.com* Ⓜ *1 to Rector St.; R to Rector St.; 2, 3, 4, 5 to Wall St.; J, Z to Broad St.*

FAMILY **One World Observatory.** Be whisked to the top of the tallest building in the Western Hemisphere, in the world's fastest elevators (the trip to the 102nd floor takes less than 60 seconds) for incredible panoramic views of Manhattan, Brooklyn, and beyond. The observatory occupies three floors of One World Trade Center and the experience includes exhibits and personal stories about the construction and bedrock of this monumental building, a dramatic 2-minute video of time-lapse photography and bird's-eye views. There are three dining options on the 101st floor, including a casual café and a sit-down restaurant. ⊠ *One World Trade Center, 285 Fulton St., Financial District* ☎ *844/698–1776* ⊕ *www. oneworldobservatory.com* ☞ *$32* ⊗ *May–Labor Day, daily 9 am– midnight; Labor Day–May, daily 9–8* Ⓜ *E to World Trade Center; R to Cortlandt St.*

South Street Seaport Historic District. Had this charming cobblestone corner of the city not been declared a historic district in 1977, the city's largest concentration of early-19th-century commercial buildings would have been destroyed. Today, the area is largely filled with tourists, and if you've been to Boston's Quincy Market or Baltimore's Harborplace, you may feel a flash of déjà vu—the same company leased, restored, and adapted the existing buildings, with the result being the blend of a quasi-authentic historic district with a slightly homogenous shopping mall.

At the intersection of Fulton and Water streets, the gateway to the seaport, is the *Titanic* Memorial, a small white lighthouse that commemorates the sinking of the RMS *Titanic* in 1912. Beyond the lighthouse, Fulton Street turns into a busy pedestrian mall. On the south side of Fulton is the seaport's architectural centerpiece, Schermerhorn Row, a red-brick terrace of Georgian- and Federal-style warehouses and countinghouses built from 1811 to 1812. Some upper floors house gallery space, and the ground floors are occupied by shops, bars, and restaurants. Cross South Street, once known as the Street of Ships, runs under an elevated stretch of FDR Drive to Pier 16, where historic ships are docked, including the *Pioneer*, a 102-foot schooner built in 1885; the *Peking*, the second-largest sailing bark in existence; the iron-hulled *Wavertree*; and the lightship *Ambrose*. The Pier 16 ticket booth provides information and sells tickets to the museum, ships, tours, and exhibits. Pier 16 is the departure point for various seasonal cruises.

To the north is Pier 17, a former multilevel dockside shopping mall that is currently undergoing redevelopment and is expected to open in 2016 with a new rooftop space, restaurants, outdoor bars, and an amphitheater. Pier 17 used to be the home of the Fulton Fish Market, which first opened in South Manhattan in 1807; starting in 1939 it was housed in the New Market Building, just north of the Seaport, but that closed in 2005 when operations were moved to a new 400,000-square-foot facility in Hunt's Point in the Bronx. ✉ *South Street Seaport* ☎ *212/732–8257 for event and shopping info* ⊕ *www.southstreetseaport.com* Ⓜ *2, 3, 4, 5, A, C, J, Z to Fulton St.*

Stone Street Historic District. Amid skyscrapers, the low-rise, two-block oasis of bars and restaurants along historic Stone Street feels more like a village than the center of the financial universe. In the summer, tables spill out into the cobblestone street and the mood is convivial, especially on Thursday and Friday nights. This was Manhattan's first paved street and today the cluster of buildings along here, with South William and Pearl streets, and Coenties Alley, make up the Stone Street Historic District. ✉ *Stone, S. William, and Pearl sts., and Coenties Alley, Financial District* Ⓜ *R to Whitehall St.; 4,5 to Bowling Green.*

World Trade Center Site (Ground Zero). *See highlighted feature in this chapter.*

WORTH NOTING

Bowling Green. Perhaps most recognized as the home of Arturo Di Modica's 7,000-pound, bronze *Charging Bull* statue (1989), Bowling Green, at the foot of Broadway, became New York's first public park in 1733. Legend has it that before that, this was the site upon which Peter Minuit purchased the island of Manhattan from the Native Americans, in 1626, supposedly for what amounted to 24 U.S. dollars. On July 9,

Continued on page 60

A GLIMPSE OF THE WORLD TRADE CENTER

An illuminated antenna reaches to 1,776 feet to commemorate America's founding.

Tower 2
Designed by Norman Foster. Ground was broken in 2010.

Tower 1
Designed by David Childs. At a height of 1,776 feet (and 104 stories) it is the tallest building in the United States.

Tower 3
Designed by Richard Rogers. Ground was broken in 2010; when complete it will stand 80 stories with five levels of retail shops.

7 World Trade Center
Designed by David Childs. Opened in 2006.

Performing Arts Center
Funding still to be worked out. To be designed by Frank Gehry.

Transportation Hub
Designed by Santiago Calatrava.

9/11 Museum
Street-level pavilion by Snøhetta; designed by Aedas.

Tower 4
Designed by Fumihiko Maki. To be 72 stories tall when it's complete.

National September 11 Memorial
Entitled *Reflecting Absence*. Designed by Michael Arad and Peter Walker. Opened on 9/11/11.

WORLD TRADE CENTER SITE
GROUND ZERO

A decade after September 11, 2001, the 9/11 Memorial opened, giving thousands of annual visitors a solemn place to reflect and think about that brutal day. After delays, its accompanying underground museum opened in 2014, on the same bedrock once used by the Twin Towers' foundation. It is a fitting place to display artifacts from 9/11 and its aftermath. As you plan your visit, set aside time to visit other key parts of the story, such as St. Paul's Chapel and the "Ten House" firehouse on Liberty Street.

(above) President Obama, Michelle Obama, former President George W. Bush, and Laura Bush at the National 9/11 Memorial. (below) Names on the 9/11 Memorial; (opposite) Rendition of the future WTC site.

THE TOWERS

The World Trade Towers, each 110 stories tall, were an impressive feat of engineering. Construction began in 1968, and the Twin Towers officially opened in 1973. Avoiding the typical construction used at the time, the architects gave each building an exterior skeleton made up of 244 slim steel columns and an inner "core" tube that supported the weight of the tower.

Approximately 50,000 people worked in the north tower (1 World Trade Center) and south tower (2 World Trade Center), and another 40,000 people visited the 16-acre complex every day. Beneath the towers was a multi-level mall with nearly 100 stores and restaurants.

The Twin Towers prior to 9/11

EVENTS OF THE DAY On September 11, 2001, terrorist hijackers steered two jets into the World Trade Center's Twin Towers, demolishing them and five outlying buildings.

- The first hijacked jet, American Airlines Flight 11, crashed into the north tower, 1 World Trade Center, at 8:46 AM, cutting through floors 93 to 99. The tower collapsed at 10:28 AM. Cantor Fitzgerald, a brokerage firm headquartered between the 101st and 105th floors, lost 658 of its 1,050 employees. At the Windows on the World restaurant (floors 106 and 107), 100 patrons and 72 staff members died.

- The second hijacked jet, United Airlines Flight 175, hit the south tower, 2 World Trade Center, at 9:03 AM, crashing through the 77th to 85th floors. The plane banked as it hit, so portions of the building remained undamaged on impact floors. Consequently, one stairwell initially remained passable from at least the 91st floor down. The tower collapsed at 9:58 AM.

- The attack killed 2,753 people. (Deaths are still being counted; casualties after the fact included Jerry J. Borg who died in late 2010 from pulmonary sarcoidosis, a lung disease caused by inhaling toxins from the dust cloud that formed when the towers collapsed.) The fenced-in 16-acre work site that emerged from the rubble, almost immediately dubbed Ground Zero, came to symbolize the personal, political, and historical impact of September 11.

(above) Towers burning after attack.

THE DAMAGE

Why *did* the towers fall? A three-year federal study revealed several reasons. The two airplanes used in the attack, both Boeing 767s, hit their respective towers at roughly 500 mph. They both damaged the exterior columns, destroying core supports for at least three of the north tower's floors and up to six of the south tower's floors. Ensuing fires, fed by tens of thousands of gallons of jet fuel, further weakened the buildings. The collapse of the most heavily damaged floors then triggered a domino effect, causing the towers to crumple at an estimated speed of about 125 mph.

Many other area buildings suffered collateral damage. The Brookfield Place office complex, to the west of Ground Zero, has as its centerpiece the 10-story glass-domed Winter Garden. After having nearly all its glass blown out in the attacks, the atrium reopened in September 2002 after repairs that included the installation of 2,000 windows and 1.2 million pounds of stone.

The 47-story 7 World Trade Center, to the north of Ground Zero, was struck by large chunks of falling debris from the north and south towers. The building remained standing at first, but subsequent fires caused it to collapse later that afternoon. A new 52-story 7 World Trade Center opened in May 2006 with a much smaller footprint than its predecessor.

St. Paul's Chapel, across the street from Ground Zero, sustained no major dam-

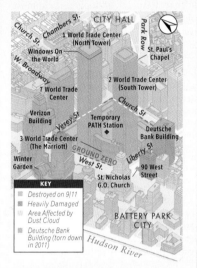

age; staff there credit a huge sycamore that toppled over during the attack. Its gigantic root system, now above ground, helped to shield the building and the headstones in its attached cemetery from falling debris.

Although the New York Stock Exchange's building wasn't physically harmed during the attacks, the market remained closed for six days (including 9/11). When trading resumed on September 17, the Dow Jones industrial average dropped 684.81 points, or 7.13 percent. The American Stock Exchange (Amex), however, sustained some damage on 9/11, and for two weeks Amex stocks and exchange-traded funds were traded on the NYSE floor.

(above) A New York City fire fighter looks up at what remains of the World Trade Center after its collapse; a 9/11 memorial wreath; the "Tribute in Light" memorial on the fifth anniversary of 9/11.

A vision of the future Manhattan skyline

It may have taken longer than most observers could have imagined, but a new World Trade Center is now a reality, at least partially. Following the master plan laid down by the architect Daniel Libeskind, the footprints of the original towers have been made into pools, their rushing waterfalls part of a powerful memorial. When all the work is finished—and there's still more to do—the World Trade Center will include office buildings, a transit hub, and a performing arts center.

NATIONAL SEPTEMBER 11 MEMORIAL

The architect Michael Arad, working in partnership with the landscape architect Peter Walker, won the international contest to design the memorial. It is entitled "Reflecting Absence," and it takes up about half of the 16-acre complex. It opened on the tenth anniversary of 9/11.

No buildings are in the space where the Twin Towers once stood. In their place are recessed waterfalls cascading thirty feet down into two subterranean reflecting pools that limn the Twin Towers' original footprints (each roughly an acre in size). The water then tumbles down into smaller square holes at the center of each pool. The effect manages to be both moving and solemn but not sentimental. In the words of Paul Goldberger, the *New Yorker's* architecture critic, "Arad figured out how to express the idea that what were once the largest solids in Manhattan are now a void, and he made the shape of this void into something monumental."

Future downtown skyline at dusk

Surrounding each waterfall on the plaza level is a low bronze wall with the names of the 2,887 victims of the 9/11 attacks (including those at the Pentagon and on flights 11, 77, 93, and 175), and the six people who died in the first World Trade Center bombing, in 1993. The names are sorted by affiliation, so that names lie etched near those of people they worked with or otherwise knew. Kiosks on the edge of the site help with finding out which panel holds a particular name or group (the information can also be found online, at *www.911memorial.org*, and through a smartphone app). Surrounding the waterfalls is a stark plaza punctuated with hundreds of swamp white-oak saplings, which some day will be 70 feet tall. Joining them is the so-called "survivor tree," a Callery pear tree that was plucked from the rubble, nursed back to health elsewhere, and replanted on the site as a symbol of resilience.

One World Trade Center towering over Lower Manhattan.

Fumihiko Maki, Larry Silverstein, and Norman Foster

Standing at an angle to the memorial's pools is the small center that serves as the entrance to the memorial's accompanying **9/11 Memorial Museum**. From here, visitors walk down a ramp to the bedrock the towers were built on, 71 feet below. One exhibit is the "last column," the last piece of steel to be removed from the site, which was covered with slogans and memorials from rescue crews and others.

ONE WORLD TRADE CENTER

Known for a time as the Freedom Tower, this 104-story skyscraper has a roof that's 1,368 feet tall—identical to that of the taller of the Twin Towers. An illuminated antenna further increases the building's height to 1,776 feet to commemorate America's founding (and making it the country's tallest building). Designed by David Childs of Skidmore, Owings & Merrill, the new 1 WTC was finished in 2014. **One World Observatory**, on the 100th, 101st, and 102nd floors of 1 WTC opened in 2015. The three other office buildings on the site (all at various stages of construction) are each by a different prominent architect: Fumihiko Maki, Richard Rogers, and Norman Foster.

TRANSPORTATION HUB

Intended to connect New Jersey's PATH train with 13 of New York's subway lines, this transportation hub was designed by the Spanish architect Santiago Calatrava. Inspired by the image of a child releasing a dove, the massive glass-roofed building is likely to be awe-inspiring once it's finished, but soaring costs and a complicated design mean that completion has been delayed.

For more information on the new structures, visit www.lowermanhattan.info and www.911memorial.org.

A GROUND ZERO WALK

Names on the 9/11 Memorial Wall.

This tour starts near the WTC Tribute Center, which runs its own well-regarded walking tours that include the memorial and other sites important to the history of 9/11. If you're just doing this walking tour, you can do it in any order.

1 One place to start your walk is at the corner of Liberty and Greenwich streets, just a short distance from where the World Trade Center's South Tower once stood. This is Ten House, a firehouse named for the number of its engine and ladder

Inspired by the giant sycamore that fell under the rubble and helped protect old headstones in St. Paul's graveyard, the *Trinity Root* sculpture, a 9/11 memorial pictured here, can be seen at Trinity Church

companies. On 9/11, the station was nearly destroyed, and six of its members lost their lives after responding to the disaster. The station's restored exterior is now covered with a 56-foot bronze bas-relief "dedicated to those who fell and to those who carry on." The Tribute WTC Visitor Center, a project of the September 11th Families' Association, is next-door. Its exhibits give a heartbreaking picture of the many lives lost on that day.

2 Head around the corner to the National 9/11 Memorial, which incorporates the footprints of the Twin Towers into two pools of water. Make sure to visit the 9/11 Museum. Its 110,000 square feet, nearly all of them underground, take up the seven stories of space that were once occupied by the stores and parking garage under the original Twin Towers.

3 After you've finished paying your respects, head south to exit the memorial, making a quick stop at the nearby 9/11 Memorial Visitor Center, at 90 West Street. From here, take the next left (onto Albany Street) and walk over to Trinity Place (which turns into Church Street), turn left (north) and continue until you reach the churchyard behind St. Paul's, the Episcopal chapel that became a dormitory, mess hall, and medical center in the months after 9/11.

The firefighters' memorial.

Even George Washington's pew was called back into service for the exhausted rescue workers. Across the street, at 20 Vesey Street, is the 9/11 Memorial Preview Site, which has models of what the entire World Trade Center will look like once it's completed. It also has a good selection of books and other items about 9/11 and its aftermath.

The Tribute WTC Visitor Center

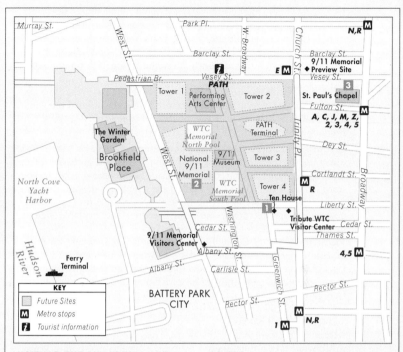

KEY

- Future Sites
- Metro stops
- Tourist information

VISITING THE MEMORIAL AND THE MUSEUM

There is airport-like security at the memorial, and no large bags are allowed, there's no bag storage, and there are no bathrooms. Entry is free. Allow at least two hours to visit the 9/11 Memorial (daily 7:30am–9pm) and the 9/11 Memorial Museum (see full listing in chapter), more at a busy times of the year.

VISITOR CENTERS

An **information booth** on Vesey Street has maps of the area. The **9/11 Memorial Visitor Center** (✉ 90 West St., ☎ 212/225–1009, ⊕ www.911memorial.org) is open daily, 7:30 am–9 pm. The 9/11 Memorial Preview Site (✉ 20 Vesey St., ☎ 212/267–2047, ✉ free) is open daily, 10–7:30 early Mar.–early Oct. and around Thanksgiving and Christmas, and 9–7 other times. The **Tribute WTC Center** (✉ 120 Liberty St., ☎ 866/737–1184, ⊕ www. tributewtc.org, ✉ $20) is open 10–6, Mon.–Sat., 10–5 on Sun.

TOURS

The Tribute WTC Center leads hour-long walking tours that include the National September 11 Memorial and nearby sites. The $22 cost ($5 if you've already paid to see the exhibits; keep your receipt) includes admission to the Tribute WTC Center exhibits ($12 for just the tour). You don't need to book in advance. Booking a tour with the Tribute WTC Visitor Center saves you having to get your own timed ticket for the 9/11 memorial.

GETTING THERE

Subway: ❶, N, R to Rector St.; ❷,❸,❹,❺,Ⓐ,Ⓒ,Ⓙ,Ⓩ to Fulton St./Broadway-Nassau; Ⓔ to World Trade Center/Church St.

PATH: Any line to World Trade Center.

1776, a few hours after citizens learned about the signing of the Declaration of Independence, rioters toppled a statue of British King George III that had occupied the spot for 11 years; much of the statue's lead was melted down into bullets. In 1783, when the occupying British forces fled the city, they defiantly hoisted a Union Jack on a greased, uncleated flagpole so it couldn't be lowered; patriot John Van Arsdale drove his own cleats into the pole to replace the flag with the Stars and Stripes. The copper-top subway entrance here is the original one, built in 1904–05. ⊠ *Broadway at Whitehall St., Financial District* Ⓜ *4, 5 to Bowling Green.*

City Hall. What once marked the northernmost point of Manhattan today houses the office of the mayor and serves as a gathering place for demonstrators voicing concerns and the news crews that cover their stories. This is the oldest City Hall in the country, a striking (but surprisingly small) building dating back to 1803. If the history of local politics and architecture is your thing, free tours are available (sign up in advance online). Tours begin outside. Indoors, highlights include the Victorian-style City Council Chamber, the Rotunda where President Lincoln lay in state in 1865 under a soaring dome supported by 10 Corinthian columns, and the Governor's Room, an elegantly preserved space with intricate portraits of historic figures and a writing table that George Washington used in 1789 when New York was the U.S. capital. If nothing else, take a moment to snap a photo of the columned exterior and see the small but lovely City Hall Park, bound by Broadway to the west and Chambers Street to the north. This park is an underrated place to stop and take a breath away from the typical congestion of Lower Manhattan. ⊠ *City Hall Park, Financial District* ☎ *212/788–2656 for tour reservations* ⊕ *www.nyc.gov/html/artcom/html/tours/city_hall. shtml* 🆓 *Free* ☉ *Tours available some weekdays (reserve online or by phone)* Ⓜ *2, 3 to Park Pl.; R to City Hall; 4, 5, 6 to Brooklyn Bridge– City Hall; A, C to Chambers St.; J, Z to Chambers St.*

Federal Reserve Bank of New York. With its imposing mix of sandstone, limestone, and ironwork, the Federal Reserve looks the way a bank ought to: strong and impregnable. The gold ingots in the subterranean vaults here are worth roughly $350 billion—reputedly a third of the world's gold reserves. Forty-five-minute tours (conducted twice a day and requiring reservations made at least five days in advance) include a visit to the gold vault, the trading desk, and "FedWorks," a multimedia exhibit center where you can track hypothetical trades. Visitors must show an officially issued photo ID, such as a driver's license or passport, and pass through scanning equipment to enter the building. The Fed advises arriving 20 minutes before your tour to accommodate security screening. Photography is not permitted. ⊠ *33 Liberty St., between William and Nassau sts., Financial District* ☎ *212/720–6130* ⊕ *www. newyorkfed.org* ☉ *Tours weekdays at 1 and 2 (reservations required)* Ⓜ *2, 3, 4, 5, A, C, J, Z to Fulton St.*

Fraunces Tavern Museum. This former tavern, where General George Washington celebrated the end of the Revolutionary War in 1783, is now a museum covering two floors above a restaurant and bar. Here, in his pre-presidential days, Washington bid an emotional farewell to

The Gangs of Five Points

In the mid-19th century, the Five Points area was perhaps the city's most notorious and dangerous neighborhood. The confluence of five streets—Mulberry, Anthony (now Worth), Cross (now Park), Orange (now Baxter), and Little Water (no longer in existence)—had been built over a drainage pond that had been filled in the 1820s. When buildings began to sink into the mosquito-filled muck, middle-class residents abandoned their homes. Buildings were then chopped into tiny apartments that were rented to the poorest of the poor, who at this point were newly emancipated slaves and Irish immigrants fleeing famine. Newspaper accounts at the time tell of daily robberies and other violent crimes. With corrupt political leaders like William Marcy "Boss" Tweed more concerned with lining their pockets than patrolling the streets, keeping order was left to the club-wielding hooligans portrayed in *Gangs of New York*. The neighborhood, finally razed in the 1880s to make way for Columbus Park, has left a lasting legacy: In the music halls where different ethnic groups grudgingly came together, the Irish jig and the African-American shuffle combined to form a new type of fancy footwork called tap dancing. Today, this is the heart of Chinatown. Residents gather in Columbus Park for Tai Chi in the morning and rowdy board games in the afternoon.

his officers upon the British evacuation of New York. Today, this historic landmark has two fully furnished period rooms—including the Long Room, site of Washington's address—and other modest displays of 18th- and 19th-century American history. You'll find more tourists and Wall Street types than revolutionaries in the tavern and restaurant on the ground floor these days, but a cozy colonial atmosphere and decent hearty meal are also available. ⊠ *54 Pearl St., at Broad St., Financial District* ☎ *212/425–1778* ⊕ *www.frauncestavernmuseum.org* ⊠ *$7* ⊘ *Daily noon–5* Ⓜ *R to Whitehall St.; 4, 5 to Bowling Green; 1 to South Ferry; J, Z to Broad St.*

Museum of American Finance. Pre-9/11, a visit to the New York Stock Exchange was the ultimate high; the energy of the floor and the proximity to so much power couldn't be beat. Post-9/11 security prohibits tours of the Exchange but you can still get a feel—albeit a less exhilarating feel—for what makes the financial world go 'round (and sometimes down) by visiting this museum. Located in the grandiose former banking hall of the Bank of New York, this Smithsonian affiliate is home to artifacts of the financial market's history; interactive exhibits on the financial markets, banking, entrepreneurship, and Alexander Hamilton; and well-executed temporary exhibits. ⊠ *48 Wall St., at William St., Financial District* ☎ *212/908–4110* ⊕ *www.moaf.org* ⊠ *$8* ⊘ *Tues.– Sat. 10–4* Ⓜ *2, 3 to Wall St.*

Museum of Jewish Heritage—A Living Memorial to the Holocaust. In a granite 85-foot hexagon at the southern end of Battery Park City, this museum pays tribute to the 6 million Jews who perished in the Holocaust. Architects Kevin Roche and John Dinkeloo built the museum in the shape of

DID YOU KNOW?

Liberty Enlightening the World, as the Statue of Liberty is officially named, was given by France to the United States in 1886 to mark the U.S. centennial.

a Star of David, with three floors of exhibits demonstrating the dynamism of 20th-century Jewish culture. Visitors enter through a gallery that provides context for the early-20th-century artifacts on the first floor: an elaborate screen hand-painted for the fall harvest festival of Sukkoth, tools used by Jewish tradesmen, and wedding invitations. Original documentary films play throughout the museum. The second floor details the rise of Nazism and anti-Semitism, and the ravages of the Holocaust. A gallery covers the doomed final voyage of the SS *St. Louis,* a ship that crossed the Atlantic twice in 1939, carrying German Jewish refugees in search of safe haven. Signs of hope are also on display, including a trumpet that Louis Bannet (the "Dutch Louis Armstrong") played for three years in the Auschwitz-Birkenau inmate orchestra. The third floor covers postwar Jewish life. Recent temporary exhibits explore the history of American Jews who tried to rescue European Jews leading up to and during the Holocaust, as well as the rich Jewish history of Oswiecim, the town the Germans called Auschwitz. The museum's east wing has a theater, memorial garden, library, galleries, and café. A free audio guide, with narration by Meryl Streep and Itzhak Perlman, is available at the admissions desk. ⊠ *36 Battery Pl., Battery Park City, Financial District* ☎ *646/437–4202* ⊕ *www.mjhnyc. org* ⌫ *$12 (free Wed. 4–8)* ☉ *Thurs. and Sun.–Tues. 10–5:45, Wed. 10–8, Fri. and eve of Jewish holidays 10–3* Ⓜ *4, 5 to Bowling Green; 1 to Rector St.; R to Rector St.*

National Museum of the American Indian (Smithsonian Institution). Massive granite columns rise to a pediment topped by a double row of statues at the impressive Beaux Arts Alexander Hamilton U.S. Custom House (1907), which is home to the New York branch of this Smithsonian museum (the other branch is in Washington, D.C.). Inside, the egg-shape stairwell and rotunda embellished with shipping-theme murals (completed in the 1930s) are also worth a pause. The permanent exhibit, "Infinity of Nations," is an encyclopedic survey of Native cultures from throughout the Americas, with 700 objects from ancient times to present day. The venue also presents changing exhibits, videos and films, dance, music, and storytelling programs. ⊠ *1 Bowling Green, between State and Whitehall sts., Financial District* ☎ *212/514–3700* ⊕ *www.nmai.si.edu* ⌫ *Free* ☉ *Mon.–Wed. and Fri.–Sun. 10–5, Thurs. 10–8* Ⓜ *4, 5 to Bowling Green; 1 to Rector St.; R to Whitehall St.; J, Z to Broad St.; 4, 5 to Wall St.*

Skyscraper Museum. Why get a crick in your neck—or worse, risk looking like a tourist—while appreciating New York City's famous skyline, when you can visit the Skyscraper Museum instead? At this small museum that shares a building with the Ritz Carlton in Battery Park City, you can appreciate highly detailed hand-carved miniature wood models of Midtown and Lower Manhattan; explore the past, present, and future of the skyscraper—from New York City's Empire State Building to Dubai's Burj Khalifa (taller than the Empire State Building and Chicago's Sears Tower combined); and examine both the history of the Twin Towers at the World Trade Center and the ongoing reconstruction at Ground Zero. Expect models of current or future buildings, videos, drawings, floor plans, talks, and exhibits that reveal the influence of history, real estate, and individuals on shaping city skylines. ✉ *39 Battery Pl., across from Museum of Jewish Heritage, Financial District* ☎ *212/968–1961* ⊕ *www.skyscraper.org* 💲 *$5* ⊙ *Wed.–Sun. noon–6* Ⓜ *4, 5 to Bowling Green.*

St. Paul's Chapel. For more than a year after the World Trade Center attacks, the chapel's fence served as a shrine for visitors seeking solace. People from around the world left tokens of grief and support, or signed one of the large dropcloths that hung from the fence. After serving as a 24-hour refuge where rescue and recovery workers could eat, pray, rest, and receive counseling, the chapel, which amazingly suffered no damage, reopened to the public in fall 2002. The powerful ongoing exhibit, titled "Unwavering Spirit: Hope & Healing at Ground Zero," honors the efforts of rescue workers in the months after September 11 with photos, drawings, banners, and other items sent to them as memorials. Open since 1766, St. Paul's is the oldest public building in continuous use in Manhattan. ✉ *209 Broadway, at Fulton St., Financial District* ☎ *212/602–0800* ⊕ *www.trinitywallstreet.org/about/st-pauls* ⊙ *Mon.–Sat. 10–6, Sun. 7 am–9 pm* Ⓜ *2, 3, 4, 5, A, C, J, Z to Fulton St.; E to World Trade Center.*

NEW YORK HARBOR

The southern tip of Manhattan has often served as a microcosm for a city that offers as many first shots as it does second chances, so it's appropriate that the key point of departure for the Statue of Liberty and Ellis Island is here. This experience should never be dismissed as too touristy. Unlike any other, the excursion is a reminder that New York is a city of immigrants and survivors.

TOP ATTRACTIONS

Fodor'sChoice ★ **Ellis Island.** ⇨ *See highlighted feature at the end of Chapter 1. Free; ferry $18 round-trip (includes Liberty Island); Daily 9–5:15; last ferry at 3:30 (extended hrs in summer); 212/561–4588 for Ellis Island; 212/561–4500 for Wall of Honor info; 877/523–9849 for ferry info; www.ellisisland.org.*

FAMILY Fodor'sChoice ★ **Governors Island.** Governors Island is open to the public from May to October: get there via a short, free ferry ride. It's essentially a big, charming park that looks like a small New England town—it's popular with locals for biking and running trails, festivals, art shows, concerts, and family programs. Wouter Van Twiller, a representative for Holland, supposedly purchased the island for his private use, in 1637, from Native Americans for two ax heads, a string of beads, and a handful of nails. It was confiscated by the Dutch a year later, and for the next decade its ownership switched back and forth between the Dutch and British until the Brits gained firm control of it in the 1670s. The island was officially named in 1784 for His Majesty's Governors and used by the American military until the 1960s, when the Coast Guard took it over. After their facilities were abandoned in 1995, the island was purchased by the public in 2002 and started welcoming visitors in 2003. The ferry to the island departs from the Battery Maritime Building. It is

On a typical weekday, five ferries make roughly 110 trips back and forth between Staten Island and Manhattan, transporting about 70,000 passengers.

a favorite summertime excursion for New Yorkers. ⊠ *Battery Maritime Building (for ferry), 10 South St., Financial District* ⊕ *www.govisland. com* ✉ *Free* ⊗ *May–Oct., Fri. 10–5, weekends 10–7* Ⓜ *1 to South Ferry; 4, 5 to Bowling Green; R to Whitehall St.*

Fodor's Choice ★ **Staten Island Ferry.** Every day, some 70,000 people ride the free ferry to Staten Island, one of the city's outer boroughs, and you should be one of them. Without paying a cent, you get phenomenal views of the Lower Manhattan skyline, the Statue of Liberty, and Ellis Island during the 25-minute boat ride across New York Harbor. You also pass tugboats, freighters, and cruise ships—a reminder that this is very much still a working harbor. The boat embarks every 15 to 30 minutes from the Whitehall Terminal at Whitehall and South streets, near the east end of Battery Park. You must disembark once you reach the opposite terminal, but you can just get back in line to board again if you don't plan to stay. ⊠ *Battery Park, Financial District* ☎ *212/639–9675* ⊕ *www.siferry.com* ✉ *Free* Ⓜ *1 to South Ferry; R to Whitehall St.; 4, 5 to Bowling Green.*

Fodor's Choice ★ **Statue of Liberty.** ⇨ *See highlighted feature at the end of Chapter 1. Free; ferry $18 round-trip (includes Ellis Island), crown tickets $3 extra; 212/363–3200; Daily 9:30–5; last ferry at 3:30(extended hrs in summer); www.libertyellisfoundation.org.*

TRIBECA

Tucked on the west side, south of Canal Street, residential TriBeCa (the *Tri*angle *Be*low *Ca*nal Street) has a quieter vibe than most other Manhattan neighborhoods. Walk the photogenic streets, especially the stretch of Federal row houses on Harrison Street, and you'll understand why so many celebrities own apartments here. The two-block-long Staple Street, with its connecting overhead walkway, is a favorite of urban cinematographers. Although TriBeCa's money is often hidden behind grand cast-iron facades, you can get a taste of it at posh neighborhood restaurants, cocktail bars, and boutiques, or at the star-studded TriBeCa Film Festival in spring.

WORTH NOTING

FAMILY

Fodor's Choice

★

Hudson River Park. The quiet places of New York City are treasured by locals, and one of the best options is Hudson River Park, a 5-mile path from Battery Place to 59th Street. This riverside stretch has been renovated into a landscaped park, incorporating the piers that jut out into the Hudson, with walking and cycling paths, a seasonal minigolf course, dog runs, and skate parks. The TriBeCa portion consists of Piers 25 and 26 and has picnic spaces, playgrounds, and a sand volleyball court. The areas adjacent to the West Village (Piers 45 and 46) and near Chelsea (Piers 63 and 64) are equally attractive, with lots of green spaces. ⊠ *TriBeCa* 🕾 *212/627–2020* ⊕ *www.hudsonriverpark.org* Ⓜ *1 to Franklin St. for TriBeCa section of the park.*

Postmasters. This gallery shows new and established conceptual artists. Past exhibits have included Claude Wampler's *Pomerania*—a series of photographs, sculptures, video, and drawings examining the artist's relationship with her pet Pomeranian. ⊠ *54 Franklin St., between Broadway and Lafayette Ave., TriBeCa* 🕾 *212/727–3323* ⊕ *www. postmastersart.com* 🖾 *Free* ⊗ *Tues.–Sat. 11–6, Thurs. 11–8* Ⓜ *6, J, N, Q, R, Z to Canal St.*

3

SOHO, NOLITA, LITTLE ITALY, AND CHINATOWN

GETTING ORIENTED

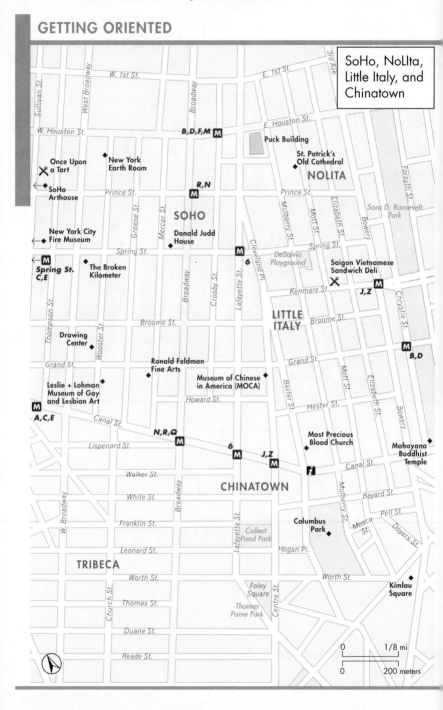

SoHo, NoLIta, Little Italy, and Chinatown

W. 1st St.
E. 1st St.
Sullivan St.
West Broadway
Broadway
3rd Ave.
W. Houston St.
E. Houston St.
B,D,F,M
Puck Building
St. Patrick's
Old Cathedral
Once Upon
a Tart
New York
Earth Room
NOLITA
Forsyth St.
SoHo
Arthouse
Prince St.
Prince St.
R,N
Elizabeth St.
Mott St.
Mulberry St.
Bowery
Sara D. Roosevelt
Park
SOHO
New York City
Fire Museum
Greene St.
Mercer St.
Donald Judd
House
Spring St.
Spring St.
Cleveland Pl.
DeSalvio
Playground
Saigon Vietnamese
Sandwich Deli
Spring St.
C,E
The Broken
Kilometer
6
Kenmare St.
J,Z
Chrystie St.
Thompson St.
Wooster St.
Broadway
Crosby St.
Lafayette St.
LITTLE
ITALY
Broome St.
Broome St.
Drawing
Center
Grand St.
Ronald Feldman
Fine Arts
Grand St.
B,D
Leslie + Lohman
Museum of Gay
and Lesbian Art
Museum of Chinese
in America (MOCA)
Baxter St.
Mott St.
Elizabeth St.
Bowery
A,C,E
Howard St.
Hester St.
Canal St.
N,R,Q
Lispenard St.
6
J,Z
Most Precious
Blood Church
Canal St.
Mahayana
Buddhist
Temple
Walker St.
CHINATOWN
W. Broadway
White St.
Broadway
Bayard St.
Mulberry St.
Pell St.
Franklin St.
Lafayette St.
Collect
Pond Park
Columbus
Park
Mosco
St.
Dovers St.
Leonard St.
Hogan Pl.
TRIBECA
Worth St.
Foley
Square
Centre St.
Worth St.
Kimlau
Square
Church St.
Thomas St.
Thomas
Paine Park
Duane St.
0   1/8 mi
Reade St.
0   200 meters

MAKING THE MOST OF YOUR TIME

If you're coming to SoHo and NoLIta to shop, there's no need to rush out the door—most shops don't open until 10 or 11 am, and many stay open until the early evening. If art is your thing, avoid Sunday, because most galleries are closed. SoHo, with national chains lining its section of Broadway, is almost always a madhouse on weekend afternoons (unless it's raining), but weekdays are somewhat less frenetic. NoLIta, with less traffic, fewer chains, and more boutiques, is calmer and less crowded.

Little Italy is a small area nowadays, having lost ground to a growing Chinatown. Note that foodwise, most of the checkered-tablecloth spots in Little Italy itself are touristy, with mediocre food.

If you're visiting New York in mid-September, you'll time it right for the the Feast of San Gennaro—a huge street fair in honor of the patron saint of Naples—along with thousands of others, who enjoy exploring the many food and souvenir booths and playing games of chance. Given that few Italian Americans live in the area anymore, it's not exactly like visiting old Napoli, but it is a fun way to spend an hour or two.

Chinatown bustles with local shoppers pretty much any time of day, but there are more tourists on the weekends, when it gets so busy there isn't much room on the sidewalk.

TOP EXPERIENCES

Browsing boutiques and people-watching in SoHo and NoLIta

Ogling the out-of-the-ordinary produce and seafood in Chinatown

Gallery hopping in SoHo

Eating dim sum in Chinatown

Sipping a cocktail in NoLIta

GETTING HERE AND AROUND

SoHo (*South of Houston*) is bounded by Houston Street, Canal Street, 6th Avenue, and Lafayette Street. To the east, NoLIta (*North of Little Italy*) is contained by Houston, the Bowery, Kenmare, and Lafayette. Plenty of subways service the area: take the 6, C, or E to Spring Street; the N or R to Prince Street; or the B, D, F, or M to Broadway–Lafayette Street. For Chinatown, farther south, take the 6, J, N, Q, R, or Z to Canal Street, or the B or D to Grand Street.

COFFEE AND QUICK BITES

Once Upon a Tart. A place with a great name that has the goods to back it up. At lunch the sweet items on the menu are joined by soups, sandwiches, and savory tarts. ⊠ *135 Sullivan St., between W. Houston and Prince Sts.* ☎ *212/387–8869* ⊕ *www.onceuponatart.com* Ⓜ *C, E to Spring St.*

Saigon Vietnamese Sandwich Deli. Predating the banh mi craze by perhaps a decade, this storefront keeps hungry gallery-hoppers, shoppers, and locals happy with its complicated and delicious sandwiches, all served on baguettes. Try the No. 1: pâté, cucumbers, a tangy sauce, peppers, and shredded vegetables. It's one of the best deals in town. ⊠ *369 Broome St., between Mott and Elizabeth Sts.* ☎ *212/219–8341* ⊕ *www.vietnamese-sandwich.com* Ⓜ *J, Z to Bowery; 6 to Spring St.; B, D to Grand St.*

Sightseeing
★★★
Nightlife
★★★
Dining
★★★★
Lodging
★★★
Shopping
★★★★★

SoHo, NoLIta, Little Italy, and Chinatown are all jam-packed with humanity, all the more perfect for people-watching as you shop, nibble, and wander. Parts of SoHo and NoLIta are destinations for super-trendy shopping as well as popular chains and department stores: the boutiques are often over-priced but undeniably glamorous (and sometimes you can snag a great sale). Little Italy and Chinatown are more about local shopping and Instagram-worthy food shops and stalls.

SOHO

Updated by
Jessica Colley

Once the epicenter of the New York art scene, SoHo today is now more synonymous with shopping. A bit of bohemia still exists on the cobblestone side streets, where there are charming restaurants with sidewalk seating and some of the art galleries that haven't scattered elsewhere. The main thoroughfares tend to have sidewalks full of tables with handmade jewelry, leather belts, hats, and purses. If you take the time to look, there's a local vibe here beneath the glitzy boutiques—elderly residents speaking Italian on the corners around Sullivan Street and Thompon Street reveal the neighborhood's Italian past.

WORTH NOTING

Donald Judd House. A 5-story cast-iron building from 1870, 101 Spring Street was the New York home and studio of artist Donald Judd. While the neighborhood used to be home to many single-use, cast-iron build-ings, this is the only one that remains—and is a designated historic building. Judd bought it in 1968, and today, guided 90-minute tours explore Judd's living and working spaces and include art installations as they were arranged by Judd prior to his death in 1994 (note: climb-ing stairs is required). ⊠ *101 Spring St.* ☎ *212/219–2747* ⊕ *www. juddfoundation.org* ☎ *$25* ⊘ *Tues.–Sat., by guided tour only* Ⓜ *N, R to Prince St.; 6 to Spring St.*

Drawing Center. At this nonprofit organization the focus is on drawings—contemporary and historical. Works shown in the three galleries often push the envelope on what's considered drawing; many projects are commissioned by the center. ✉ *35 Wooster St., between Broome and Grand Sts., SoHo* ☎ *212/219–2166* ⊕ *www.drawingcenter.org* 🎫 *$5* ⊙ *Wed. and Fri.–Sun. noon–6, Thurs. noon–8* Ⓜ *1 to Canal St.; A, C, E to Canal St.; 6, J, N, Q, R, Z to Canal St.*

Leslie + Lohman Museum of Gay and Lesbian Art. Founded in the late 1980s, this museum has roots in the collection of its founders, Charles Leslie and Fritz Lohman. The well-curated exhibits are usually photographic, with much of it sexually charged or at least homoerotic. ✉ *26 Wooster St., between Grand and Canal Sts., SoHo* ☎ *212/431–2609* ⊕ *www.leslielohman.org* 🎫 *Free* ⊙ *Tues.–Sun. noon–6 (Thurs. until 8)* Ⓜ *1 to Canal St.; A, C, E to Canal St.; 6, J, N, Q, R, Z to Canal St.*

New York City Fire Museum. In the former headquarters of Engine 30, a handsome Beaux Arts building dating from 1904, retired firefighters volunteer their time in the morning and early afternoon to answer visitors' questions. The collection of firefighting tools from the 18th century to the present includes hand-pulled and horse-drawn engines, speaking trumpets, pumps, and uniforms. A memorial exhibit with photos, paintings, children's artwork, and found objects relating to the September 11 attacks is also on view—a poignant reminder and tribute to the 343 firefighters who died on 9/11. ✉ *278 Spring St., between Hudson and Varick Sts., SoHo* ☎ *212/691–1303* ⊕ *www.nycfiremuseum.org* 🎫 *$8* ⊙ *Daily 10–5* Ⓜ *C, E to Spring St.; 1 to Houston St.*

New York Earth Room. Noted "earthworks" artist Walter De Maria's 1977 avant-garde installation consists of 140 tons of gently sculpted soil (22 inches deep). It fills 3,600 square feet of a second-floor gallery maintained by the Dia Art Foundation since 1980. As the *New York Times* put it in 1999, "a loamy smell definitely permeates the space." You can't touch or walk on the dirt, nor can you take its photo. If you like this installation, check out De Maria's equally odd and impressive work, *The Broken Kilometer,* an 18.75-ton installation that consists of five columns of a total of 1,000 meter-long brass rods, which cover the wood floors of an open loft space. It's a few blocks away at 393 West Broadway, and has the same hours as the Earth Room. ✉ *141 Wooster St., 2nd fl., between W. Houston and Prince Sts., SoHo* ☎ *212/989–5566* ⊕ *www.diaart.org/sites/main/earthroom* 🎫 *Free* ⊙ *Mid-Sept.–mid-June, Wed.–Sun. noon–3 and 3:30–6* Ⓜ *N, R to Prince St.; B, D, F, M to Broadway–Lafayette St.*

Ronald Feldman Fine Arts. Founded in 1971 and in SoHo since the 1980s, this gallery represents more than 30 international contemporary artists;

CLOSE UP

SoHo and NoLIta Architecture

There are plenty of beautiful people in SoHo and NoLIta, but tilt your eyes up, beyond the turn-of-the-20th-century lampposts adorned with cast-iron curlicues, and discover some of New York's most impressive architecture. SoHo has one of the world's greatest concentrations of cast-iron buildings, created in response to fires that wiped out much of Lower Manhattan in the mid-18th century. Look down, and see Belgian brick cobblestones lining some of the streets. Along Broadway and the neighboring streets of SoHo, you see "vault lights" in the sidewalk: starting in the 1850s, these glass lenses were set into sidewalks to permit daylight to reach basements.

The **King of Greene Street,** at 72–76 Greene, between Grand and Canal, is a five-story, Renaissance-style 1873 building with a magnificent projecting porch of Corinthian columns and pilasters. These days it's unmistakably painted in high-gloss ivory. Over at 28–30 Greene Street is the **Queen of Greene Street,** a graceful 1873 cast-iron beauty that exemplifies the Second Empire style with its dormers, columns, window arches, projecting central bays, and roof.

The **Haughwout Building,** at 488–492 Broadway, north of Broome, is best known for what's no longer inside—the world's first commercial passenger elevator, invented by Elisha Graves Otis. The building's exterior is worth a look, though: nicknamed the "Parthenon of Cast Iron," the five-story, Venetian palazzo–style structure was built in 1857 to house department-store merchant E. V. Haughwout's china, silver, and glassware store. Each window is framed by Corinthian columns and rounded arches.

Built in 1904, the **Little Singer Building,** at 561 Broadway, is a masterpiece of cast-iron styling, its delicate facade covered with curlicues of wrought iron. The L-shape building's second facade is around the corner on Prince Street.

Charlton Street, not technically in SoHo but across 6th Avenue in the West Village, is Manhattan's longest stretch of Federal-style red-brick row houses from the 1820s and '30s. The high stoops, paneled front doors, leaded-glass windows, and narrow dormer windows are all intact. King and Vandam streets also have historic houses. Much of this area was the site of a mansion called Richmond Hill, and in the late 18th century the surrounding area was a beautiful wild meadow from where you could see the nearby "hamlet" of Greenwich Village.

Over in Little Italy/NoLIta, the magnificent old **Police Headquarters** building at 240 Centre Street, between Broome and Grand, might be familiar from Martin Scorsese's *Gangs of New York.* The 1909 Edwardian baroque–style structure with its striking copper dome was the headquarters of the New York City Police Department until 1973. Designed to "impress both the officer and the prisoner with the majesty of the law," it was converted into luxury condos in 1988 and is known today as the Police Building Apartments.

The 1885 Romanesque Revival **Puck Building,** at 295 Lafayette Street, on the southeast corner of Houston, is a former magazine headquarters and now a busy event space—look for the statue of Puck just over the door.

The stark, simple interior of OK Harris Works of Art exemplifies the typical gallery space in SoHo.

exhibits include contemporary painting, sculpture, installations, drawings, and prints. The space also hosts performances and has a large selection of Andy Warhol prints, paintings, and drawings. ⊠ *31 Mercer St., between Grand and Canal Sts., SoHo* ☎ *212/226–3232* ⊕ *www. feldmangallery.com* ✉ *Free* ⊙ *Winter, Tues.–Sat. 10–6; summer, Mon.– Thurs. 10–6, Fri. 10–3* Ⓜ *1 to Canal St.; A, C, E to Canal St.; 6, J, N, Q, R, Z to Canal St.*

SoHo Arthouse. This contemporary gallery represents some of the artistic spirit of old SoHo: walk down this pretty stretch of Sullivan Street on any given evening and you may find a film screening, fashion show, or photography exhibition inside. This multipurpose space is also home to a 75-seat theater and hosts events showcasing film, fashion, and art in many forms. Check the online calendar for event details. ⊠ *138 Sullivan St., between Prince and W. Houston Sts.* ☎ *212/228–2810* ⊕ *www. sohodigart.com* ⊙ *Tues.-Sat. 1-5* Ⓜ *C, E to Spring St.; 1 to Houston St.*

NOLITA

Many locals would say that the spirit of old SoHo is somewhat alive in NoLIta, a charming neighborhood with an artistic spirit, independently run boutiques and restaurants, and a local vibe. The streets here are less frantic and crowded than either SoHo or Chinatown, and each block could provide hours of fun shopping in small shops, nursing a cappuccino at a sidewalk café, or lingering over a meal surrounded by creative New Yorkers. This is downtown, so the prices aren't cheap, but the quality is high and the experience unique.

WORTH NOTING

St. Patrick's Old Cathedral. If you've seen *The Godfather*, you've had a peek inside New York's first Roman Catholic cathedral—the interior shots of the infamous baptism scene were filmed here. Dedicated in 1815, this church lost its designation as the seat of New York's bishop when the current St. Patrick's opened uptown, in 1879. The unadorned exterior of the cathedral gives no hint of the splendors within, which include an 1868 Henry Erben pipe organ. The interior dates from the 1860s, after a large fire gutted most of the original design. The enormous marble altar surrounded by hand-carved niches (*reredos*) houses an extraordinary collection of sacred statuary and other Gothic exuberance. Sunday Mass in English is at 9:15 and 12:45. ⊠ *263 Mulberry St., corner of Mott and Prince Sts., NoLIta* ☎ *212/226–8075* ⊕ *www.oldcathedral.org* ☯ *Daily 8–5 (hrs vary)* Ⓜ *N, R to Prince St.; 6 to Bleecker St.*

LITTLE ITALY

Just east of Broadway, the tangle of pedestrian-friendly blocks surrounding Mulberry Street between NoLIta and bustling Canal Street are still a cheerful salute to all things Italian, although Little Itay has been whittled down by the spread of nearby Chinatown. There are red, green, and white street decorations on permanent display and specialty grocers and cannelloni makers dish up delights, though it's all a bit touristy these days and if it's a great Italian meal you want, look elsewhere. Still, Little Italy is fun to walk around, and several of the classic food stores on Grand Street are worth a stop if you're after an edible souvenir. If you're looking for a bigger and more bustling Little Italy, head up to Arthur Avenue in the Bronx(⇨ *Chapter 15*) and you'll find several good, affordable restaurants and a cornucopia of authentic Italian goods, all of them marketed to New Yorkers and tourists alike.

Every September, Mulberry Street becomes the giant Feast of San Gennaro, a crowded 11-day festival that sizzles with the smell of sausages and onions (don't miss John Fasullo's braciole, an iconic sandwich filled with filet of pork roasted over a coal pit and topped with peppers and onions).

WORTH NOTING

Most Precious Blood Church. The National Shrine of San Gennaro, a replica of the grotto at Lourdes, is the high point of Most Precious Blood Church's richly painted interior. The church becomes a focal point during the annual Feast of San Gennaro. Sunday Mass is in English at 9 and noon. ⊠ *113 Baxter St., between Canal and Hester Sts., Little Italy* ☎ *212/226–6427* Ⓜ *6, J, N, Q, R, Z to Canal St.*

CHINATOWN

Chinatown is a living, breathing, anything-but-quiet ethnic enclave with vibrant streets full of food shops selling vegetables and fish (some still alive and squirming), Chinese restaurants and bakeries, massage

Some of the storefronts and signage in Chinatown are bilingual—but some are just in Chinese.

parlors, Buddhist temples, herbalists, and barbershops. A quarter of the city's nearly 700,000 Chinese residents live here, in a neighborhood that started as a 7-block area, but now covers some 40-plus blocks above and below Canal Street (encroaching on what was once a thriving Little Italy). Head to **Mott Street,** south of Canal, Chinatown's main thoroughfare, where the first Chinese immigrants (mostly men) settled in tenements in the late 1880s. Walk carefully, as the sidewalks can be slick from the ice underneath the eels, blue crabs, snapper, and shrimp that seem to look back at you as you pass by. You can create a movable feast here with soup dumplings, Peking duck, a yellow custard cake, and a jasmine bubble tea—each at a different place in the neighborhood. A city tourist-information kiosk on a traffic island where Canal, Baxter, and Walker streets meet can help you with tours, and also has a map that's very useful for unraveling the tangled streets in the area.

WORTH NOTING

Columbus Park. People-watching is the thing to do in this park. If you swing by in the morning, you'll see men and women practicing tai chi; the afternoons bring intense games of mahjong. In the mid-19th century the park was known as Five Points—the point where Mulberry Street, Anthony (now Worth) Street, Cross (now Park) Street, Orange (now Baxter) Street, and Little Water Street (no longer in existence) intersected—and was notoriously ruled by dangerous Irish gangs. In the 1880s a neighborhood-improvement campaign brought about the park's creation. ⊠ *Chinatown* ⊕ *www.nycgovparks.org/parks/M015* Ⓜ *6, J, N, Q, R, Z to Canal St.*

Kimlau Square. Ten streets converge at this labyrinthine intersection criss-crossed at odd angles by pedestrian walkways. Standing on an island in this busy area is the **Kimlau Arch,** named for Ralph Kimlau, a bomber pilot who died in World War II; the arch is dedicated to all Chinese Americans who "lost their Lives in Defense of Freedom and Democracy." A statue on the square's eastern edge pays tribute to a Qing Dynasty official named Lin Zxeu, the Fujianese minister who sparked the Opium War by banning the drug. ⊠ *Chatham Sq., Bowery and E. Broadway, Chinatown* ⊕ *www.nycgovparks.org/parks/kimlausquare* Ⓜ *4, 5, 6 to Brooklyn Bridge–City Hall; J, Z to Chambers St.*

Mahayana Buddhist Temple. This pleasant and bright Buddhist temple is at a very busy corner, at the foot of the Manhattan Bridge Arch on the Bowery. There's an excellent gift shop on the second floor. Before its reincarnation as a place of worship in 1997, this was the Rosemary, a movie theater showing a mix of kung fu and porn. ⊠ *133 Canal St., at the Bowery, Chinatown* ☎ *212/925–8787* ⊕ *en.mahayana.us* 🖃 *Donations accepted* ☉ *Daily 8–6* Ⓜ *B, D to Grand St.*

The Museum of Chinese in America (MOCA). Founded in 1980, this museum is dedicated to preserving and presenting the history of the Chinese people and their descendants in the United States. Its current building, which opened in 2009 near the boundary between Chinatown and Little Italy (technically, many would say it's in Little Italy), was designed by Maya Lin, architect of the Vietnam Veterans Memorial in Washington, D.C. MOCA's permanent exhibit on Chinese American history,"With a Single Step: Stories in the Making of America," includes artworks, personal and domestic artifacts, historical documentation, and films. Chinese laundry tools, a traditional general store, and antique business signs are some of the unique objects on display. Rotating exhibits, some of which examine the sometimes turbulent relations between Asian Americans and the rest of the country, are on display in the second gallery. MOCA sponsors workshops, walking tours, lectures, and family events. ⊠ *215 Centre St., between Grand and Howard Sts., Chinatown* ☎ *212/619–4785* ⊕ *www.mocanyc.org* 🖃 *$10* ☉ *Tues., Wed., and Fri.–Sun. 11–6, Thurs. 11–9* Ⓜ *6, J, N, Q, R, Z to Canal St.*

THE EAST VILLAGE AND THE LOWER EAST SIDE

GETTING ORIENTED

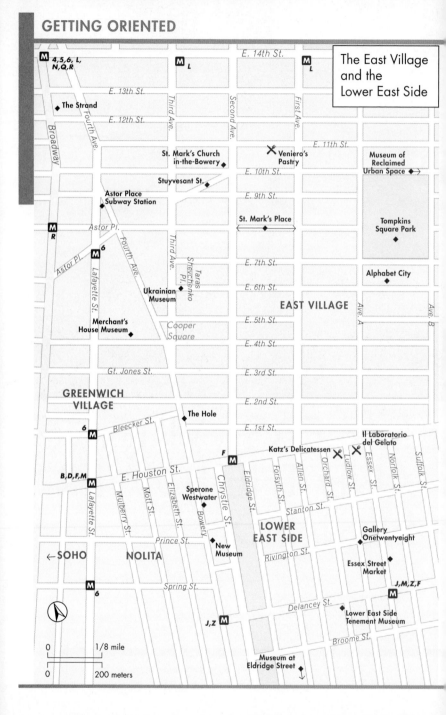

The East Village and the Lower East Side

MAKING THE MOST OF YOUR TIME

Houston Street runs east–west and neatly divides the East Village (north of Houston) and the Lower East Side (south of Houston). The eastern boundary of the East Village and Lower East Side is the East River; the western boundary is 4th Avenue and the Bowery. So many communities converge in these neighborhoods that each block seems like a neighborhood unto itself.

The East Village lets loose on weekend nights, when nightlife-seekers converge on the area, filling up the bars and spilling out onto the sidewalks. Weekday evenings are less frenetic, with more of a local vibe—although the term "local" around here always means a large number of students from New York University. Daytime is great for shopping in local boutiques, and brunch on weekends around here generally means lines for hot spots like Prune and Back Forty, which fill with patrons lingering over coffee.

The Lower East Side does not tend to be an early-riser destination any day of the week. Although there's plenty to see during the day, nightfall offers a more exciting vision: blocks that were previously empty rows of pulled-down gates transform into clusters of throbbing bars. On the trendy streets around Rivington and Stanton, stores, bars, and cafés buzz all week.

GETTING HERE AND AROUND

For the East Village, take the N or R subway line to 8th Street–New York University (NYU), the 6 to Astor Place, or the L to 3rd Avenue. To reach Alphabet City, take the L to 1st Avenue or the F to 2nd Avenue. For the Lower East Side, head southeast from the 2nd Avenue stop on the F, or take the F, M, J, or Z to the Delancey Street–Essex Street stop.

TOP EXPERIENCES

People-watching on St. Marks Place or at Tompkins Square Park

Shopping at boutiques and vintage clothing stores

Visiting the Lower East Side Tenement Museum

COFFEE AND QUICK BITES

Il Laboratorio del Gelato. Seasonal flavors make this gelato la crème de la crème. There are 48 flavors offered each day. ⊠ *188 Ludlow St., at E. Houston St., Lower East Side* ☎ *212/343-9922* ⊕ *www. laboratoriodelgelato.com* Ⓜ *F to 2nd Ave.*

Katz's Delicatessen. Given Katz's location and its equally lost-in-time vibe, this deli goes as well with visits to the Tenement Museum as a Cel-Ray soda goes with pastrami. ⊠ *205 E. Houston St., at Ludlow St., Lower East Side* ☎ *212/254-2246* ⊕ *www.katzsdelicatessen. com* Ⓜ *F to 2nd Ave.*

Veniero's Pastry. This Italian bakery has been churning out cookies, coffee, and elaborate cakes and tarts since 1894— and the late hours it keeps only sweetens the deal. The fruit-topped mini cheesecakes are always a good idea. ⊠ *342 E. 11th St., between 1st and 2nd aves., East Village* ☎ *212/674-7070* ⊕ *www.venierospastry. com* Ⓜ *L to 1st Ave.*

4

Sightseeing
★★

Nightlife
★★★★★

Dining
★★★★★

Lodging
★★

Shopping
★★★★

Vibant, bold, and bohemian: the streets of the East Village and the Lower East Side are some of the most electric in New York City. Both neighborhoods have a deep immigrant past, and have evolved into nighttime destinations where you can dance until dawn any day of the week. This area of downtown is tamer than it used to be (as the arrival of Whole Foods and several glass-and-chrome condos attests), but there's definitely still a gritty edge in the dive bars, sultry live music venues, and experimental restaurants. Spend some time wandering these bohemain side streets, and you'll be struck by the funky pastiche of ethnicities whose imprints are visible in the neighborhood's restaurants, shops, and of course, people.

EAST VILLAGE

Updated by
Jessica Colley

Many opposites coexist peacefully in the East Village: dive bars and craft cocktail dens, Ukranian diners and the latest chef-driven restaurant, stylish boutiques and counterculture stores. Known for its nightlife, the East Village has become increasingly more upscale in recent years with St. Marks Place trading in its gritty scene for a hodgepodge of students, well-earning postgrads, and Japanese expats. At its roots, the neighborhood is a community of artists, activists, and social dissenters—and though this is still the essential vibe here, the finish is much more polished these days.

East of 1st Avenue is Alphabet City, once the city's seedy drug haunt but now an ever more gentrified neighborhood. There is still a young, artistic vibe in and around Tompkins Square Park.

Keep Your Eyes Peeled

The East Village's reputation for quirkiness is evinced not only by its residents and sites but also in the many incongruous structures that somehow coexist so easily that they often go unnoticed. Keep your eyes open as you explore the streets. You never know what might turn up: the Hells Angels' Headquarters, for example, tucked into a residential block of 3rd Street between 1st and 2nd avenues, surrounded by a bevy of show-stopping bikes; the architectural "joke" on New York City atop the Red Square building on Houston Street at Norfolk, where a statue of Lenin points to the sky and a clock has lost its notion of time; or the shingled Cape Cod–style house perched on the apartment building at the northwest corner of Houston and 1st Avenue, one of the city's many unique rooftop retreats (it's best viewed from the east). Two privately owned, nearly hidden but airy "marble" cemeteries (New York Marble Cemetery and the New York City Marble Cemetery) established in the 1830s on 2nd Avenue between 2nd and 3rd streets hold the remains of thousands in underground, marble-lined vaults thought to prevent the spread of disease in a time marked by cholera epidemics. The gardens are surrounded by 12-foot walls made of Tuckahoe marble, and are entered through wrought-iron gates. Although rarely open to the public, they can be visited by appointment.

TOP ATTRACTIONS

Alphabet City. The north–south avenues east of 1st Avenue, from Houston Street to 14th Street, are all labeled with letters, not numbers, which gives this area its nickname: Alphabet City. Avenues A, B, and C are full of restaurants, cafés, stores, and bars that run from the low-rent and scruffy to the pricey and polished—the streets are more mixed than in other neighborhoods downtown. Parts of avenues A and B run along Tompkins Square Park. A close-knit Puerto Rican community makes its home around Avenue C, also called "Loisaida" (a Spanglish creation meaning "Lower East Side"). Although it's still filled with many Latino shops and bodegas, it's also now home to some trendy restaurants and bars. Avenue D remains rough around the edges—in part because of the uninterrupted row of projects that are on its east side. The East River Park, farther east, provides some nice views of Williamsburg and other parts of Brooklyn. To reach the park, cross Avenue D and take one of the pedestrian bridges that crosses FDR Drive at East 10th or East 5th Street, or cross the road at East Houston Street. ⊠ *East Village* Ⓜ *L to 1st Ave.; F to 2nd Ave.*

St. Marks Place. The longtime hub of the edgy East Village, St. Marks Place is the name given to idiosyncratic East 8th Street between 3rd Avenue and Avenue A. During the 1950s, beatniks Allen Ginsberg and Jack Kerouac lived and wrote in the area; the 1960s brought Bill Graham's Fillmore East (nearby, at 105 2nd Avenue), and Andy Warhol's Dom and the Electric Circus nightclub (both at nos. 19–25), where the Velvet Underground performed. The studded, pink-haired, and shaved-head punk scene followed, and there's a good chance of still seeing some pierced rockers and teenage Goths on the block. Trash & Vaudeville, the punk store at No. 4, is the real deal—it's been open since 1971. Farther down, at No. 33, is where the punk store Manic Panic first foisted its lurid hair dyes and make-up on the world. At No. 57 stood the short-lived Club 57, a church basement that attracted such 80s stalwarts as Keith Haring, Ann Magnuson, Klaus Nomi, Kenny Scharf, and Fab Five Freddy.

These days, there's not much cutting edge left. Some of the grungy facades lead to luxury condos, and the area has become a Little Japan, with several ramen and dumpling shops, some sake bars, and lots of young Japanese students. The blocks between 2nd and 3rd avenues can feel like a shopping arcade, crammed with body-piercing and tattoo salons, and shops selling cheap jewelry, sunglasses, incense, and out-there sloganed T-shirts. The cafés and bars from here over to Avenue A attract customers late into the night—prices for a drink are lower than in other downtown neighborhoods. ⊠ *8th St., between 3rd Ave. and Ave. A, East Village* Ⓜ *6 to Astor Pl.; N, R to 8th St.–NYU.*

FAMILY **Tompkins Square Park.** This leafy park fills up with locals year-round, partaking in picnics and drum circles, and making use of the playground and the dog run. Free Wi-Fi (strongest on the north side of the park) joins the shade, benches, and an elegant 1891 water fountain (donated by a teetotaling benefactor) as some of the best amenities here. There are movie screenings and music gatherings throughout the summer, a year-round farmers market on Sunday, and an annual Halloween dog costume event. But it wasn't always so rosy in the park: in 1988, police followed then-mayor David Dinkins's orders to evict the many homeless who had set up makeshift homes here, and homeless rights and anti-gentrification activists fought back with sticks and bottles. The park was reclaimed and reopened in 1992 with a midnight curfew, still in effect today. ⊠ *From 7th to 10th St., between Aves. A and B, East Village* ⊕ *www.nycgovparks.org/parks/tompkinssquarepark* Ⓜ *6 to Astor Pl., L to 1st Ave.*

WORTH NOTING

Astor Place Subway Station. At the beginning of the 20th century almost all of the city's Interborough Rapid Transit (IRT) subway entrances resembled the one here—an ornate cast-iron replica of a Beaux Arts kiosk marking the subway entrance for the uptown 6 train. This traffic-island entrance, which was—and still is—the stop to get to the venerable Cooper Union college, is now on the National Register of Historic Places. Inside, plaques of beaver emblems line the tiled station walls, a reference to the fur trade that contributed to John Jacob Astor's fortune. Milton Glaser, the Cooper Union graduate who originated the "I [heart] NY" logo, designed the station's murals. ⊠ *Traffic island at 8th St. and 4th Ave., East Village* Ⓜ *6 to Astor Pl.*

The Hole. Run by Kathy Grayson, the former director of the highly influential Deitch Projects, this contemporary-arts gallery generally hosts two simultaneous shows a month. Its artists lean more toward the up-and-coming rather than the establishment. The on-site Hole Shop carries lots of quirky zines, posters, books, and art objects. ✉ *312 Bowery, between Bleecker and E. Houston sts., East Village* ☎ *212/466–1100* ⊕ *www.theholenyc.com* ☼ *Wed.–Sun. noon–7* Ⓜ *6 to Bleecker St.; B, D, F, M to Broadway–Lafayette St.*

Merchant's House Museum. Built in 1832, this red-brick house, combining Federal and Greek Revival styles, provides a glimpse into the domestic life of the period 30 years before the Civil War. Retired merchant Seabury Tredwell and his descendants lived here from 1835 until 1933. The home became a museum in 1936, with the original furnishings and architectural features preserved; family memorabilia are also on display. The fourth-floor servants' bedroom, where the Tredwell family's Irish servants slept and did some of their work, offers a rare and intimate look at the lives of Irish domestics in the mid-1800s. A guided tour is offered at 2pm. ✉ *29 E. 4th St., between the Bowery and Lafayette St., East Village* ☎ *212/777–1089* ⊕ *www.merchantshouse.org* ✆ *$10* ☼ *Thurs.–Mon. noon–5; guided tours Thurs.–Mon. at 2* Ⓜ *N, R to 8th St.–NYU; 6 to Astor Pl.; B, D, F, M to Broadway–Lafayette St.*

Museum of Reclaimed Urban Space. Opened in late 2012, this self-described "living archive of urban activism" covers the vexatious postwar period in New York, during which the city's public housing was often woefully mismanaged and hundreds of apartments lay abandoned and crumbling. Zines, photographs, and videos fill the small exhibit space inside a tenement's storefront and its basement. Squatters, community gardens, the Tompkins Square riots, and the renaissance of bicycling in the city are all given their due, as is Occupy Wall Street. Tours of community gardens, activist landmarks, and other squats, both legal and otherwise, are also run by the museum. ✉ *C-Squat, 155 Ave. C, between 9th and 10th sts., East Village* ☎ *973/818–8495* ⊕ *www.morusnyc.org* ✆ *$5 suggested donation; tours $20* ☼ *Thurs.–Sun. and Tues. 11–7* Ⓜ *L to 1st Ave.*

St. Mark's Church in-the-Bowery. This charming 1799 fieldstone country church, which is Episcopalian, stands on what was once Governor Peter Stuyvesant's *bouwerie*, or farm. It's Manhattan's second-oldest church, and both Stuyvesant and Commodore Matthew Perry are buried in vaults here. Check out the gorgeous modern stained-glass windows on the balcony, which replaced the more traditional windows (like those on the ground level) after a fire in the late '70s. Over the years St. Mark's has hosted many avant-garde arts events, including readings by poet Carl Sandburg and dance performances by Martha Graham and Merce Cunningham. The tradition of art partnerships has continued with Danspace, the Poetry Project, New York Theatre Ballet, and LocoMotion, which give performances throughout the year. Services are held Sunday at 11. ✉ *131 E. 10th St., at 2nd Ave., East Village* ☎ *212/674–6377* ⊕ *www.stmarksbowery.org* Ⓜ *6 to Astor Pl.; L to 3rd Ave.; N, R to 8th St.-NYU.*

Stuyvesant Street. This diagonal slicing through the block bounded by 2nd and 3rd avenues and East 9th and 10th streets is unique in Manhattan: it's the oldest street laid out precisely along an east–west axis. Among the handsome 19th-century red-brick rowhouses are the

Federal-style **Stuyvesant-Fish House** at No. 21, built as a wedding gift for a great-great-granddaughter of the Dutch governor Peter Stuyvesant, and **Renwick Triangle,** an attractive group of Anglo-Italianate brick and brownstone residences, that face Stuyvesant and East 10th streets. ☒ Ⓜ *6 to Astor Pl; N, R to 8th St.-NYU.*

Ukrainian Museum. From the late 19th century through the end of World War II, tens of thousands of Ukrainians made their way to New York City—and particularly to "Little Ukraine," as much of the East Village was known. This museum, which opened in 2005, examines Ukrainian Americans' dual heritage, with a permanent collection made up of folk art, fine art, and documentary materials about the immigrants' lives. Ceramics, jewelry, hundreds of brilliantly colored Easter eggs, and an extensive collection of Ukrainian costumes and textiles are the highlights. If you're feeling like a little Ukrainian food to continue the experience, the nearby Veselka diner awaits. ☒ *222 E. 6th St., between 2nd and 3rd aves., East Village* ☏ *212/228–0110* ⊕ *www.ukrainianmuseum. org* 🖃 *$8* ⊗ *Wed.–Sun. 11:30–5* Ⓜ *6 to Astor Pl.; N, R to 8th St.-NYU.*

LOWER EAST SIDE

The Lower East Side (or simply LES) is a center of all things cool: arts and nightlife, restaurants and cafés, boutiques and cool hair salons. What was once the "Gateway to America" (and home of waves of Irish, German, Jewish, Hispanic, and Chinese immigrants) is now a quickly gentrifying neighborhood where modern high-rises, the ultra-contemporary New Museum, and low-key restaurants exist in the same corner of Manhattan.

On Saturday night, the scene can be as raucous as in a college town, especially on Rivington and Orchard streets, but Ludlow Street, one block east of Orchard, has become the main drag for twentysomethings with attitude, its boutiques wedged between bars and small restaurants.

The best time to experience the neighborhood's past is by day. The excellent Lower East Side Tenement Museum movingly captures the immigrant legacy of tough times and survival instincts. You might not find many pickles being sold from barrels anymore, but this remains a good place to nosh on typical Jewish food from Katz's Delicatessen or Russ & Daughters.

TOP ATTRACTIONS

FAMILY **Lower East Side Tenement Museum.** Step back in time and into the par-
Fodor'sChoice tially restored 1863 tenement building at 97 Orchard Street, where
★ you can squeeze through the preserved apartments of immigrants, learn about the struggles of past generations, and gain historical perspective on the still contentious topic of immigration. This is America's first urban living-history museum dedicated to the life of immigrants. The museum itself is only accessible by guided tour, each run at various times each day and limited to 15 people, so it's a good idea to buy tickets in advance. The building tour called "Hard Times" visits the homes of Natalie Gumpertz, a German-Jewish dressmaker (dating from 1878), and Adolph and Rosaria Baldizzi, Catholic immigrants

from Sicily (1935). "Sweatshop Workers" visits the Levines' garment shop/apartment and the home of the Rogarshevsky family from Eastern Europe (1918). "Irish Outsiders" explores the life of the Moores, an Irish American family living in the building in 1869, and shows a re-created tenement backyard. "Shop Life" looks at the various businesses run on the street level here, including a German-style bar, a kosher butcher, an auctioneer, and, in the 1970s, a discount underwear store. A two-hour extended experience tour with a chance for in-depth discussion is given every day, as are walking tours of the neighborhood. Note that most tours don't allow kids under 5. ⊠ *103 Orchard St., at Delancey St., Lower East Side* ☎ *212/982–8420* ⊕ *www.tenement.org* ⊡ *Most tours $25* ⊙ *Fri.–Wed. 10–6:30, Thurs. 10–8:30; last tour at 5* Ⓜ *B, D to Grand St.; F to Delancey St.; J, M, Z to Essex St.*

WORTH NOTING

Gallery Onetwentyeight. Inside this narrow space, artist Kazuko Miyamoto directs crisp and provocative group shows. ⊠ *128 Rivington St., between Essex and Norfolk sts., Lower East Side* ☎ *212/674–0244* ⊕ *www. galleryonetwentyeight.org* Ⓜ *F to Delancey St.; J, M, Z to Essex St.*

International Center of Photography. Founded in 1974 by photojournalist Cornell Capa (photographer Robert Capa's brother), this top-notch photography museum and school has a collection of over 150,000 original prints spanning the history of photography from daguerreotypes to large-scale pigment prints. The museum left it's Midtown space in early 2015 to move downtown, but at press time there were no further details. Check the website for updates. ⊠ *Lower East Side* ☎ *212/857–0000* ⊕ *www.icp.org.*

Museum at Eldridge Street. The exterior of this Orthodox synagogue, the first to be built by the many Eastern European Jews who settled in the Lower East Side in the late 19th century, is a striking mix of Romanesque, Gothic, and Moorish motifs. Inside is an exceptional hand-carved ark of mahogany and walnut, a sculptured wooden balcony, jewel-tone stained-glass windows, vibrantly painted and stenciled walls, and an enormous brass chandelier. The synagogue can be viewed as part of an hour-long tour, which begins at the small museum downstairs where interactive "touch tables" teach all ages about Eldridge Street and the Lower East Side. The crowning piece of the synagogue's decades-long restoration is a stained-glass window by artist Kiki Smith and architect Deborah Gans, which weighs 6,000 pounds and has more than 1,200 pieces of glass. ⊠ *12 Eldridge St., between Canal and Division sts., Lower East Side* ☎ *212/219–0302* ⊕ *www.eldridgestreet.org* ⊡ *$12* ⊙ *Sun.–Thurs. 10–5, Fri. 10–3; tours on the hr* Ⓜ *F to East Broadway; B, D to Grand St.*

New Museum. This seven-story, 60,000-square-foot structure—a glimmering metal mesh–clad assemblage of off-center squares—caused a small neighborhood uproar when it was built in 2007, with some residents slow to accept the nontraditional building. Not surprisingly, given the museum's name and the building, shows are all about contemporary art: previous exhibitions have included the popular "Carsten Höller: Experience," with a slide connecting the fourth and second floors, and a sensory deprivation tank, among other things. Studio 231, the museum's adjacent, ground-floor space at 231 Bowery, gives emerging artists the opportunity to create work outside the confines of the main museum building in a studiolike space. If you're visiting on the weekend, check out the seventh-floor "sky room" and its panoramic view of Lower Manhattan. From 10 to noon on the first Saturday of every month, the museum runs free family-oriented programs and events designed for kids age 3 to 10. Thursday's pay-what-you-wish night always brings a fun-loving, hipster-heavy crowd out of the woodwork. ⊠ *235 Bowery, at Prince St., Lower East Side* ☎ *212/219–1222* ⊕ *www.newmuseum. org* ⟲ *$16 (pay-what-you-wish Thurs. 7–9)* ☉ *Tues.–Sun. 11–6 (Thurs. until 9)* Ⓜ *6 to Spring St., F to 2nd Ave.*

Sperone Westwater. Founded in 1975 in SoHo, and after spending nearly a decade in Chelsea, Sperone Westwater now finds itself a major part of the "artification" of the Lower East Side. In 2010, the gallery moved into this nine-story building, which it commissioned for itself—a vote of confidence in both its Bowery surroundings and the continued importance of its artists, which have included Bruce Nauman, William Wegman, Gerhard Richter, and a host of blue-chip minimalists. The narrow building, designed by Norman Foster, rivals the New Museum (a few doors down) for crisp poise: in 2011 New York's Municipal Art Society deemed it the best new building of the year. Its Big Red Box, essentially a huge roomlike freight elevator, is a major contributor to the building's good looks. ⊠ *257 Bowery, between E. Houston and Stanton sts., Lower East Side* ☎ *212/999–7337* ⊕ *www.speronewestwater.com* Ⓜ *6 to Spring St., F to 2nd Ave.*

5

GREENWICH VILLAGE AND THE WEST VILLAGE

GETTING ORIENTED

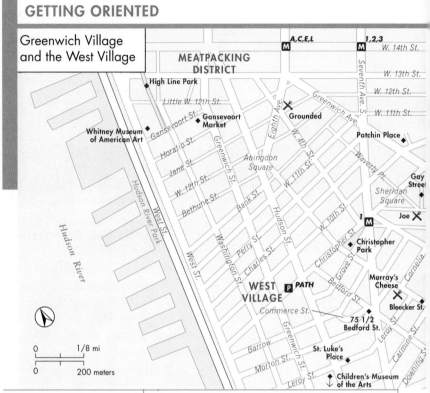

Greenwich Village
and the West Village

MEATPACKING
DISTRICT

A,C,E,L
Ⓜ

1,2,3
Ⓜ   W. 14th St.

W. 13th St.

W. 12th St.

High Line Park

Little W. 12th St.

Gansevoort
Market

Grounded

W. 11th St.

Patchin Place

Whitney Museum
of American Art

Gansevoort St.

Horatio St.

Jane St.

W. 12th St.

Bethune St.

Greenwich St.

Abingdon
Square

W. 4th St.

W. 11th St.

W. 10th St.

Waverly Pl.

Patchin Place

Gay
Street

Sheridan
Square

Joe

Hudson River Park

West St.

Bank St.

Perry St.

Charles St.

Hudson St.

Washington St.

Christopher St.

Ⓜ

Christopher
Park

Hudson River

West St.

WEST
VILLAGE

Commerce St.

Ⓟ PATH

Grove St.

Bedford St.

Murray's
Cheese

Bleecker St.

Cornelia

Barrow

Greenwich St.

Morton St.

St. Luke's
Place

75 1/2
Bedford St.

Leroy St.

Carmine St.

Leroy St.

Children's Museum
of the Arts

Downing St.

0   1/8 mi

0   200 meters

TOP EXPERIENCES	MAKING THE MOST OF YOUR TIME
People-watching in Washington Square Park	A visit to Washington Square Park is a must for people-watching and relaxing on a bench (you might also catch some live music performances). There are lots of restaurants and shops in the neighborhood, though they do tend to be touristy or cater primarily to students.
Strolling and window-shopping along the pretty streets of the West Village	The West Village—basically from 7th Avenue to the Hudson River—is more residential, and tends to be pretty quiet, with carefully tended, tree-lined streets that are pleasant for a stroll. Upscale boutiques line Bleecker Street and Greenwich Avenue (note that, confusingly, there is also a Greenwich Street in this neighborhood).
Relaxing in one of the many cafés	
Walking along Hudson River Park by the water	The windy streets of the West Village often seem mazelike, even to locals, because most of the streets here are named rather than numbered and they're not organized on a grid system. Assume that you're going to get a little bit lost— that's part of the fun—but don't hesitate to ask for directions.
Eating your way along Bleecker Street	

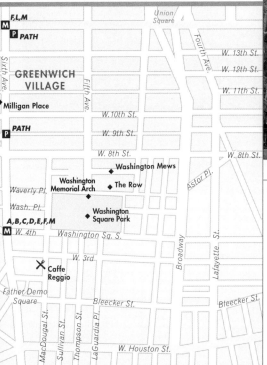

GETTING HERE AND AROUND

The West 4th Street subway stop—serviced by the A, B, C, D, E, F, and M lines—puts you in the center of Greenwich Village. Farther west, the 1 train has stops at Houston Street and at Christopher Street–Sheridan Square. The L stops at 8th Avenue, and the A, C, and E trains stop at 14th Street, which is the northern boundary of the West Village.

BEST FOR KIDS

Hudson River Park

Washington Square Park

Taking time out for pizza or dessert

COFFEE AND QUICK BITES

Caffe Reggio. Usually packed, this café dates back to the 1920s, making it one of the oldest coffeehouses in the city. The enormous espresso machine, which may have introduced cappuccino to New York, has served many a Beat poet, politician, folk singer, artist, activist, tourist, and student since then. ✉ *119 MacDougal St., between W. 3rd and Carmine sts.* ☎ *212/475–9557* ⊕ *www.caffereggio.com* Ⓜ *A, B, C, D, E, F, M to W. 4th St.*

Grounded. At this welcoming café, both the pastries and the people-watching are a cut above. ✉ *28 Jane St., between 8th and Greenwich aves., West Village* ☎ *212/647–0943* ⊕ *www.groundedcoffee.com* Ⓜ *A, C, E to 14th St.; L to 8th Ave.; 1, 2, 3 to 14th St.*

Joe (West Village). The coffee is exquisitely prepared at this small corner café, the first of what is now a small chain. ✉ *141 Waverly Pl., at Gay St., Greenwich Village* ☎ *212/924–6750* ⊕ *www.joenewyork.com* Ⓜ *A, B, C, D, E, F, M to W. 4th St.; 1 to Christopher St.–Sheridan Sq.*

Sightseeing
★★★
Nightlife
★★★★
Dining
★★★★★
Lodging
★★★
Shopping
★★★★

The charming, tree-lined streets of the Village are beloved by New Yorkers (whether they can afford to live there or not) for their cozy restaurants and cafés, chic cocktail bars, and inviting boutiques. Long the home of writers, artists, bohemians, and bon vivants, the Village is made up of Greenwich Village proper (the area surrounding Washington Square Park) and the West Village, between 7th Avenue and the Hudson River. Greenwich Village, in prime New York University (NYU) territory, has lots of young people, while the West Village is primarily residential, with lots of well-to-do couples and families and a substantial community of older gay men and some lesbians. Both sections have a relaxed, downtown vibe and a distinctly New York spin in their bookstores, corner bars, and trendy restaurants.

GREENWICH VILLAGE

Updated by
Jessica Colley

Many would argue that Washington Square Park is still the beating heart of downtown, a magnet for all kinds of life—people come here to listen to live music performances, stretch out on a picnic blanket, let the pooch loose at the dog run, or play with kids on the playground, This park is at the core of Greenwich Village, where you can find just about every sort of person imaginable lounging on a summer day, from skateboarders and students to people who look like they've lived in the park for years, playing chess and checkers at the stone tables. This is also a historic part of the neighborhood, with the grand Washington Memorial Arch looking north to two blocks of lovingly preserved Greek Revival and Federal-style townhouses known as "the Row."

Halloween in the Village

All things weird and wonderful, all creatures great and small, all things witty and fantastical, New York City has them all—and on All Hallows' Eve they strut through the streets in New York's Halloween parade. White-sheeted ghouls feel dull compared with fishnets and leather, sequins and feathers posing and prancing along 6th Avenue in this vibrant display of vanity and insanity.

In 1973 mask-maker and puppeteer Ralph Lee paraded his puppets from house to house, visiting friends and family along the winding streets of his Greenwich Village neighborhood. His merry march quickly outgrew its original, intimate route and now, decades later, it parades up 6th Avenue, from Spring Street to 21st Street, attracting 90,000 creatively costumed exhibition-ists, artists, dancers, and musicians, hundreds of enormous puppets, scores of bands, and more than 2 million spectators. Anyone with a costume can join in, no advance registration required, although the enthusiastic

interaction between participants and spectators makes it just as much fun simply to watch. It's a safe "street event" for families and singles alike (though, be aware you will be enter-ing very dense crowds), and a joyful night unlike any other.

The parade lines up along 6th Avenue between Canal and Spring streets from 6:30 to 8:30 pm. The walk actually starts at 7, but it takes about two hours to leave the staging area. It's best to arrive from the south to avoid the crush of strollers and participants. Get there a few hours early if possible. Costumes are usually handmade, clever, and outrageous, and revelers are happy to strike a pose. The streets are crowded along the route, with the most congestion below 14th Street. Of course, the best way to truly experience the parade is to march, but if you're not feeling the face paint, it's possible to volunteer to help carry the puppets. For informa-tion visit ⊕ www.halloween-nyc.com.

—Jacinta O'Halloran

Bountiful doesn't even begin to describe Greenwich Village's yield of creative genius. In the late 1940s and early 1950s, abstract expression-ist painters Franz Kline, Jackson Pollock, Mark Rothko, and Willem de Kooning congregated here, as did Beat writers Jack Kerouac, Allen Ginsberg, and Lawrence Ferlinghetti. The 1960s brought folk musicians and poets, notably Bob Dylan and Joan Baez. Its bohemian days may be long gone, but there is still a romantic allure lingering along tree-lined streets and at the back of the cafés, behind the frenetic clamor of NYU students and the professional veneer of multimillion-dollar townhouses.

TOP ATTRACTIONS

Bleecker Street. Walking the stretch of Bleecker Street between 5th and 7th avenues provides a smattering of just about everything synony-mous with Greenwich Village these days: NYU buildings, used-record stores, Italian cafés and food shops, pizza and takeout joints, some nightclubs, and funky boutiques. A lazy afternoon here may consist of sampling some of the city's best pizza, grabbing an espresso, and people-watching. Notable along the Greenwich Village length of the street is Our Lady of Pompeii Church, at Bleecker and Carmine, where Mother Cabrini, a naturalized Italian immigrant who became the first American citizen to be canonized, often prayed. Foodies love the blocks between 6th and 7th avenues for the specialty purveyors like Murray's Cheese (at No. 254). West of 7th Avenue, where Bleecker crosses the border into the West Village, things get more upscale, with fashion and home-furnishings boutiques featuring antiques, eyeglasses, handbags, shoes, and designer clothing. ⊠ *Greenwich Village* Ⓜ *A, B, C, D, E, F, M to W. 4th St.*

FAMILY
Fodor's Choice
★

Washington Square Park. NYU students, street musicians, skateboarders, jugglers, chess players, and those just watching the grand opera of it all generate a maelstrom of activity in this physical and spiritual heart of Greenwich Village. The 9¾-acre park had inauspicious beginnings as a cemetery, principally for yellow-fever victims—an estimated 10,000–22,000 bodies lie below (a headstone was actually unearthed in 2009). At one time, plans to renovate the park called for the removal of the bodies, but local resistance prevented this from happening. In the early 1800s the park was a parade ground and the site of public executions; bodies dangled from a conspicuous Hanging Elm that still stands at the northwest corner of the square. Today that gruesome past is all but forgotten, as playgrounds attract parents with tots in tow, dogs go leash-free inside the popular dog runs, and everyone else seems drawn toward the large central fountain.

The triumphal European-style **Washington Memorial Arch** stands at the square's northern flank, marking the start of 5th Avenue. The original wood-and-papier-mâché arch, originally situated a half block north, was erected in 1889 to commemorate the 100th anniversary of George Washington's presidential inauguration. The arch was reproduced in Tuckahoe marble in 1892, and the statues—*Washington as General Accompanied by Fame and Valor* on the left, and *Washington as Statesman Accompanied by Wisdom and Justice* on the right—were added in 1916 and 1918, respectively. ⊠ *5th Ave., between Waverly Pl. and 4th St., Greenwich Village* Ⓜ *A, B, C, D, E, F, M to W. 4th St.*

WORTH NOTING

Gay Street. A curved, one-block lane lined with small rowhouses, Gay Street was probably named after an early landowner and definitely had nothing to do with gay rights. In the 1930s this tiny thoroughfare and nearby Christopher Street became famous nationwide after Ruth McKenney began to publish somewhat zany autobiographical stories based on what happened when she and her sister moved to No. 14 from Ohio. The stories, first published in the *New Yorker,* birthed many adaptations, including the 1953 Broadway musical *Wonderful Town* (revived in 2004) and the 1942 and 1955 movies *My Sister Eileen.* ⊠ *Between Christopher St. and Waverly Pl., Greenwich Village* Ⓜ *1 to Christopher St.–Sheridan Sq.; A, B, C, D, E, F, M to W. 4th St.*

Patchin Place. This little cul-de-sac off West 10th Street between Greenwich and 6th avenues has 10 diminutive 1848 rowhouses. Around the corner on 6th Avenue is a similar dead-end street, **Milligan Place,** with five small houses completed in 1852. The houses in both quiet enclaves

Out and On Display: George Segal's sculptures of two gay couples in Christopher Park embody gay pride in Greenwich Village.

were originally built for waiters who worked at 5th Avenue's high-society Brevoort Hotel, long since demolished. Later Patchin Place residents included writers Theodore Dreiser, e. e. cummings, Jane Bowles, and Djuna Barnes. Milligan Place became popular among playwrights, including Eugene O'Neill. ✉ *Greenwich Village* Ⓜ *A, B, C, D, E, F, M to W. 4th St.*

The Row. Built from 1833 through 1837, this series of Greek Revival and Federal rowhouses along Washington Square North, between University Place and MacDougal Street, once belonged to merchants and bankers, then to writers and artists such as John Dos Passos and Edward Hopper. Many are now owned by NYU and used for housing and offices. Although the facades remain beautifully preserved, the interiors have been drastically altered over the years. ✉ *1–13 and 19–26 Washington Sq. N, between University Pl. and MacDougal St., Greenwich Village* Ⓜ *A, B, C, D, E, F, M to W. 4th St.*

Washington Mews. A rarity in Manhattan, this pretty, brick-covered street—really a glorified alley—is lined on one side with the former stables of the houses on the Row on Washington Square North. Although the street is private and owned by New York University, which uses many of the stables for offices, it's open to pedestrian traffic from 7 am to 11 pm and is a lovely, historic strip for a stroll. ✉ *From Washington Sq. N to 8th St., between 5th Ave. and University Pl., Greenwich Village* Ⓜ *A, B, C, D, E, F, M to W. 4th St.; N, R to 8th St.–NYU.*

Bleecker Street's Little Italy

Little Italy can be besieged by slow-moving crowds, touristy shops, and restaurant hosts hollering invitations to dine inside. Bleecker Street between 6th and 7th avenues, on the other hand, with its crowded cafés, bakeries, pizza parlors, and old-world merchants, offers a more pleasurable, equally vital alternative to the traditional tourist trap.

For an authentic Italian bakery experience, stop by Pasticceria Rocco (No. 243) for wonderful cannoli, cream puffs, and cookies packed up, or order an espresso and linger over the treats.

Step into the past at the old-style (and now high-end) butcher shops, such as Ottomanelli & Sons (No. 285) and Faicco's Pork Store (No. 260), where locals have bought their sausage and custom-cut pork since 1900.

The sweet (or stinky) smell of success is nowhere more evident than at Murray's Cheese (No. 254). The original shop, opened in 1940 by Murray Greenberg (not Italian), was not much larger than the display case that stocked the stuff. Now it's a fromage-fiend's emporium, with everything from imported crackers and bamboo cutting boards to a full-service sandwich counter. Samples of cheese, salami, gelato, and other goodies are frequently served. Educational cheese tasting classes are also held in the upstairs classroom (sign up online in advance).

There are also a few popular pizzerias along this strip; Kesté Pizza & Vino (No. 271) serves Neapolitan pies that some would argue give even Da Michele in Naples a run for its money. It is also the official location in the United States for the Associazione Pizzaiuoli Napoletani, whose mission is to promote pizzas made in the Neapolitan tradition, using Neapolitan products. Brick-oven favorite John's Pizzeria (No. 278) is a classic New York pizza joint—pies only, no slices!

WEST VILLAGE

Small curving streets, peculiar alleys, and historic townhouses—it's easy to see why the tree-lined streets of the West Village (which are primarily residential) are in such high demand. A stroll here reveals charming cafés, carefully disheveled celebrities out and about, and well-dressed children playing in the parks. Visitors come here to feel like a local, to daydream about a life in New York. Unlike 5th Avenue or SoHo, the pace is slower, allowing shoppers to enjoy the peaceful streets and small-scale stores. This is the place to come for unusual finds as well as global-brand goods. The West Village section of Bleecker Street is a particularly good place to indulge all sorts of shopping appetites; high-fashion foragers prowl the stretch between West 10th Street and 8th Avenue. Hudson Street and Greenwich Avenue are also prime boutique-browsing territories.

Christopher Street has long been the symbolic heart of New York's gay and lesbian community, though places like Chelsea, Hell's Kitchen, and parts of Brooklyn attract more gay and lesbian residents these days. On Christopher Street, among cafés, lifestyle boutiques, and clothing shops, is one of the city's most acclaimed Off-Broadway theaters, the Lucille Lortel, where major playwrights like David Mamet, Eugene Ionesco, and Edward Albee have their own markers in the sidewalk. Nearby, at 51–53 Christopher Street, is the site of the Stonewall Inn and the historic Stonewall riots, one of the signal events in the gay rights movement. Across the street is a green triangle named Christopher Park, where there are commemorative statues of two gay and lesbian couples.

TOP ATTRACTIONS

Hudson River Park. ⇨ *See the listing in the TriBeCa section of Chapter 2.*

WORTH NOTING

75½ Bedford Street. Rising real-estate prices inspired the construction of New York City's narrowest house—just 9½ feet wide and 32 feet deep—in 1873. Built on a lot that was originally a carriage entrance of the Isaacs-Hendricks House next door, this sliver of a building's past residents include actor John Barrymore and poet Edna St. Vincent Millay. ⊠ *75½ Bedford St., between Commerce and Morton sts., West Village* Ⓜ *A, B, C, D, E, F, M to W. 4th St.*

FAMILY   **Children's Museum of the Arts.** The CMA encourages children ages 1 to 15 to get creative through a variety of mediums. Along with the requisite children's museum offerings like pencils, chalk, and paint, you'll find a clay bar; a media lab with mounted cameras and a recording studio; a small slide and colorful ball pond that kids can play in; an airy exhibition space with rotating exhibits (and workshops inspired by exhibits); a permanent collection of children's art from more than 50 countries; and classes in ceramics, origami, animation, filmmaking, and more. Check the website for a busy calendar of events. ⊠ *103 Charlton St., between Hudson and Greenwich Sts., West Village* ☎ *212/274–0986* ⊕ *www. cmany.org* ⊠ *$11* ☼ *Mon. and Wed. noon–5, Thurs. and Fri. noon–6, weekends 10–5* Ⓜ *C, E to Spring St.; 1 to Houston St.*

Christopher Park. You might have to share a bench in this tiny park with George Segal's life-size sculptures of a lesbian couple. The painted bronzes, cast in 1980 and titled *Gay Liberation,* also include a gay male couple, captured mid-chat nearby. ⊠ *Bordered by W. 4th, Grove, and Christopher Sts., West Village* Ⓜ *1 to Christopher St.–Sheridan Sq.; A, B, C, D, E, F, M to W. 4th St.*

CHELSEA AND THE MEATPACKING DISTRICT

GETTING ORIENTED

Hudson River Park

Nancy Hoffman Gallery
Galerie Lelong
Cheim & Read
Marlborough Chelsea

Robert Miller Gallery
Pace Gallery

W. 26th St.
W. 25th St.

CHELSEA

W. 27th St.

Eighth Ave.

W. 24th St.

Gladstone Gallery
Metro Pictures
Gagosian Gallery
Luhring Augustine Gallery
Mary Boone Gallery
Matthew Marks Gallery
Andrea Rosen Gallery

M C,E

Eleventh Ave.

High Line Park

Chelsea Piers

Matthew Marks Gallery
Paula Cooper Gallery

Tanya Bonakdar Gallery

303 Gallery
David Zwirner
Jack Shainman Gallery

Cushman Row

W. 19th St.

Ninth Ave.

Eighth Ave.

Hauser & Wirth

W. 18th St.

W. 17th St.

Hudson River

West Side Hwy.

Eleventh Ave.

Chelsea Market

Ninth St. Espresso

Blue Bottle Coffee

A,C,E,L

W. 14th St.

M

High Line Park Access Point

MEATPACKING DISTRICT

0   1/2 mile

Little   W. 12th St.

Gansevoort St.

Hudson St.

Horatio St.

Eighth Ave.

W. 4th St.

0   800 meters

Whitney Museum of American Art

Gansevoort Market

Jane St.

GETTING HERE AND AROUND	MAKING THE MOST OF YOUR TIME

The A, C, E, L, 1, 2, and 3 trains stop at 14th Street for both the Meatpacking District and Chelsea. The latter neighborhood is further served by the C, E, F, M, and 1 lines at 23rd Street and by the 1 train at 28th Street. PATH trains also stop at 14th Street and 23rd Street.

Plan your visit to the High Line around food: work up an appetite first by walking downtown along the High Line from 34th Street and then to Chelsea Market, Gansevoort Market, or the food carts peppering the southern reaches of the park (from 15th to 17th Street) for a bite, or pick up food on your way to the High Line for a picnic there. There are also seasonal food vendors on the High Line for impromptu snacking.

Chelsea has a dual life: typical gallery hours are Tuesday to Saturday 10–6, but at night the neighborhood changes into a party town, with bars (gay and straight) and high-profile nightclubs that don't rev up until after 11.

To truly appreciate the Meatpacking District, make a 9 pm or later dinner reservation at a hot restaurant, then hit the bars to see the glitterati.

If shopping is your pleasure, weekdays are great; come after noon, though, or find most spots shuttered.

Casey Kaplan

Museum at FIT

W. 26th St.

W. 25th St.

W. 24th St.

Seventh Ave.

Sixth Ave.

W. 23rd St. **M** *F,M*

W. 22nd St.

W. 21st St.

W. 20th St.

W. 19th St.

W. 18th St.

M *1*

W. 17th St.

Rubin Museum of Art

W. 16th St. **M** *F,M*

W. 15th St.

✕ Donut Pub

W. 14th St. **M** *L*

W. 13th St.

Madison Square Park

Madison Ave.

Broadway

Fifth Ave.

Union Square Park

N,Q,R,4,5,6,L **M**

Greenwich Ave.

W. 12th St.

W. 11th St.

W. 10th St.

Sixth Ave.

Fifth Ave.

rd Arsenam

Chelsea and the Meatpacking District

COFFEE AND QUICK BITES

Blue Bottle Coffee. If you're serious about coffee, fresh-baked pastries, eco-friendly practices, and good old-fashioned service, stop in at this trendy coffee shop, or its seasonal outpost on the High Line. ✉ *450 W. 15th St., Chelsea* ⊕ *www. bluebottlecoffee.com* Ⓜ *A, C, E to 14th St.; L to 8th Ave.*

Donut Pub. Care for an apple fritter, a red-velvet doughnut, or an old-fashioned cruller with your coffee? A 5 am sugar fix after a night clubbing in the Meatpacking District? Pull up a stool—it's open 24/7. ✉ *203 W. 14th St., at 7th Ave., Chelsea* ☏ *212/929–0126* ⊕ *www. donutpub.com* Ⓜ *1, 2, 3 to 14th St.; A, C, E to 14th St.; L to 8th Ave.*

Ninth Street Espresso. The Chelsea Market outpost of Ninth Street Espresso is popular all day, though the lines in the morning are longest. The lattes here are liquid gold. ✉ *Chelsea Market, 9th Ave., between 15th and 16th sts., Chelsea* ☏ *212/228–2930* ⊕ *www. ninthstreetespresso.com* Ⓜ *A, C, E to 14th St.; L to 8th Ave.*

TOP EXPERIENCES

Gallery-hopping in Chelsea

Walking along the High Line

Exploring the Whitney Museum of American Art: the new building has light-filled galleries and wonderful views from the terraces.

Checking out the Meatpacking District's nightlife

Eating your way through Chelsea Market or Gansevoort Market

Shopping the ultrachic boutiques in the Meatpacking District

BEST FOR KIDS

Chelsea Piers

The High Line

Hudson River Park

Chelsea long ago usurped SoHo as the epicenter of New York contemporary art galleries, but the opening of the High Line above 10th Avenue gave a new life to this part of the city. Rising rents have meant fewer small galleries but the opening of the new Whitney Museum of American Art firmly solidifies the area as a major art hub that also has exciting restaurants and boutiques.

MEATPACKING DISTRICT

Updated
by Jacinta
O'Halloran

Concentrated in a few blocks of what is essentially the West Village, between the Hudson River and 9th Avenue, from Little West 12th Street to about West 17th Street, the Meatpacking District used to be the center of the wholesale meat industry for New York City. There are few meat markets left in this now rather quaint, cobblestone area but it's definitely a figurative meat market at night, when the city's trendiest frequent the equally trendy restaurants and bars here. The area is also home to some of the city's swankiest retailers, with high-profile fashion designers and labels like Christian Louboutin, Diane von Furstenberg, Catherine Malandrino, and Honor, as well as lesser known boutiques like Owen, Kilian, and Elizabeth Charles.

TOP ATTRACTIONS

Gansevoort Market. Named after a food market that existed here in the 1800s, this 8,000-square-foot food hall—with its carefully curated list of vendors and vine-covered, skylit dining space—is like the younger, cooler, lesser known sister of nearby tourist-mobbed Chelsea Market. Opened in late 2014, the market is slowly filling up with a mix of artisan purveyors selling everything from overstuffed lobster rolls, sweet and savory stuffed brioche-muffin hybrids, and American-style macarons to tacos served from a VW van, homemade bread from Gansevoort Bakery, and a variety of pork-fare from the Pig Guy. When weather permits, the garage door facade rolls up to expose the market to the cobblestone streets outside. ⊠ *52 Gansevoort St., between Greenwich* *and Washington sts., Meatpacking District* ☎ *212/247–1701* ⊕ *www. gansmarket.com* ⊙ *Daily 9–9* Ⓜ *A, C, E, to 14th St.; L to 8th Ave.*

CHELSEA

Most of Chelsea's art galleries are found from about 20th to 27th streets, primarily between 10th and 11th avenues. The range of contemporary art on display includes almost every imaginable medium and style; if it's going on in the art world, it'll be in one of the 300 or so galleries here.

TOP ATTRACTIONS

FAMILY **Chelsea Market.** This former Nabisco plant—where the first Oreos were baked in 1912—now houses more than three-dozen vendors carrying everything from gourmet food and wine, to oils, vinegars, teas, spices, gift baskets, and kitchen supplies; there's also an Anthropologie store, wine bar, barbershop, shoeshine stand, and one of New York City's last independent book stores (Posman Books). Renowned specialty purveyors including L'Arte del Gelato, Fat Witch Bakery, Amy's Bread, Jacques Torres Chocolate, and Ninth Street Espresso flank the interior walkway that stretches between 9th and 10th avenues. Be sure to wander into the 15th Street Arcade, where a bunch of great new kiosks sell everything from fresh mini doughnuts to Korean soups with Japanese noodles, Brooklyn-made caramels, and authentic Mexican street food. The market's funky industrial design—a tangle of glass and metal for an awning, a factory pipe converted into an indoor waterfall—complements the eclectic assortment of shops. There is some seating inside but if the weather's nice, take your goodies to the High Line. ⊠ *75 9th Ave., between 15th and 16th sts., Chelsea* ☎ *212/652–2117* ⊕ *www.chelseamarket.com* ⊙ *Mon.–Sat. 7–9, Sun. 8–8* Ⓜ *A, C, E to 14th St.; L to 8th Ave.*

David Zwirner. In 2013, Zwirner further solidified his commitment to contemporary art, and his place in the ranks of the most successful galleries in the art world, with this vast, purpose-built, five-story exhibition and project space, created to complement the programming of the gallery's three existing West 19th Street locations a block away. Zwirner's galleries show works in all mediums by artists like Dan Flavin, Donald Judd, Blinky Palermo, Jeff Koons, Gordon Matta-Clark, Doug Wheeler, and Yayoi Kusama. In 2015, Zwirner presented a large-scale new sculpture created by Richard Serra. ⊠ *537 W. 20th St., between 10th and 11th aves., Chelsea* ☎ *212/517–8677* ⊕ *www.davidzwirner.com* ▨ *Free* ⊙ *Tues.–Sat. 10–6* Ⓜ *C, E to 23rd St.*

Gagosian Gallery. This enterprising modern gallery has two large Chelsea branches (the other is at 522 West 21st Street, between 10th and 11th avenues) and three galleries on the Upper East Side, as well as nine more outposts in cities around the world. Perhaps the most powerful dealer in the business, Gagosian Gallery shows works by heavy hitters such as Pablo Picasso, Jean-Michel Basquiat, Urs Fischer, Richard Serra, and pop-art icon Roy Lichtenstein. ⊠ *555 W. 24th St., at 11th Ave., Chelsea* ☎ *212/741–1111* ⊕ *www.gagosian.com* ▨ *Free* ⊙ *Tues.–Sat. 10–6* Ⓜ *C, E to 23rd St.*

6

WHITNEY MUSEUM OF AMERICAN ART

✉ *99 Gansevoort St., between Washington St. and 10th Ave., Meatpacking District* ☎ *212/570–3600* ⊕ *www.whitney.org* ✍ *$22* ⊘ *Mon., Wed., Sun. 10:30–6, Thurs.– Sat. 10:30–10* Ⓜ *A, C, E to 14th St.; L to 8th Ave.*

TIPS

■ Free tours of the collection and current exhibitions are offered daily; check the website for more information.

■ The Untitled restaurant on the ground floor and the Studio Cafe on the 8th floor are run by Danny Meyer's Union Square Hospitality Group.

■ After 7pm on Friday the price of admission is pay-what-you-wish.

In early 2015, the Whitney opened the doors of its fabulous new Renzo Piano–designed building in the Meatpacking District, between the High Line (New York's beloved elevated park) and the Hudson River.

Founder Gertrude Vanderbilt Whitney's talent and taste were accompanied by the money of two wealthy families, and the Whitney Museum of Art's collection has always been known for its bold works of 20th- and 21st-century contemporary American art. The new museum has 8 floors (6 accessible to the public) with more than 50,000 square feet of state-of-the-art gallery space, as well as 13,000 square feet of outdoor space with views of the Hudson River, Downtown, and the Meatpacking District. After the opening of the Whitney's new building, the Metropolitan Museum of Art will present exhibitions and special programs at the Whitney's old location for at least eight years.

Highlights

The galleries house rotating exhibitions of postwar and contemporary works from the permanent collection by artists such as Jackson Pollock, Jim Dine, Jasper Johns, Mark Rothko, Chuck Close, Cindy Sherman, and Roy Lichtenstein.

Notable pieces often on view include Hopper's *Early Sunday Morning* (1930), Bellows's *Dempsey and Firpo* (1924), Alexander Calder's beloved *Circus,* and several of Georgia O'Keeffe's dazzling flower paintings.

The outdoor terraces on floors 6, 7, and 8 are connected by exterior stairs and have rotating exhibits as well as stunning views.

Gladstone Gallery. The international roster of artists at this gallery's two Chelsea locations includes painter Ahmed Alsoudani, sculptor Anish Kapoor, photographer Sharon Lockhart, and multimedia artists Matthew Barney and Cecilia Edefalk. The other location is 530 West 21st Street, between 10th and 11th avenues. ⊠ *515 W. 24th St., between 10th and 11th aves., Chelsea* ☎ *212/206–9300* ⊕ *www.gladstonegallery.com* 🖾 *Free* ◷ *Tues.–Sat. 10–6* Ⓜ *C, E to 23rd St.*

Hauser & Wirth. On the site of the former Roxy nightclub and roller rink on West 18th Street, this Hauser & Wirth gallery is the opposite of its narrow townhouse location on the Upper East Side. The space is huge (23,000 square feet), cavernous, and begs for sprawling exhibits and large-scale works. Emerging and established contemporary artists in the powerful Hauser & Wirth fold that show here include Dieter Roth, Paul McCarthy, Eva Hesse, and Jason Rhoades. ⊠ *511 W. 18th St., between 10th and 11th aves., Chelsea* ☎ *212/790–3900* ⊕ *www.hauserwirth. com* 🖾 *Free* ◷ *Tues.–Sat. 10–6* Ⓜ *C, E to 23rd St.*

Hudson River Park. ⇨ *See the listing in the TriBeCa section of Chapter 2.*

Marlborough Chelsea. With galleries in London, Monaco, and Madrid, the Marlborough empire also operates two of the largest and most influential galleries in New York City, as well as a shared annex on the Lower East Side. The Chelsea location (the other is on 57th Street) shows the latest work of modern artists, with a focus on sculptural forms, such as the boldly colorful paintings of Andrew Kuo. Red Grooms, Richard Estes, and Fernando Botero are just a few of the 20th-century luminaries represented. ⊠ *545 W. 25th St., between 10th and 11th aves., Chelsea* ☎ *212/463–8634* ⊕ *www.marlboroughgallery.com* 🖾 *Free* ◷ *Tues.–Sat. 10–6* Ⓜ *C, E to 23rd St.*

Mary Boone Gallery. Based in SoHo in the late seventies, when it was a hot showcase for younger artists, the Mary Boone Gallery relocated to midtown (745 5th Avenue, near 58th Street) in 1996 and then opened this additional branch in a former garage in Chelsea in 2000. The Chelsea space allows for large-scale works and dramatic installations. Over the years, Boone has shown and represented artists including Jean-Michel Basquiat, Jeff Koons, Julian Schnabel, Ross Bleckner, and Ai Weiwei. Boone continues to show established artists such as Barbara Kruger, Pierre Bismuth, and Eric Fischl, as well as relative newcomers such asJacob Hashimoto, and Hilary Harkness. ⊠ *541 W. 24th St., between 10th and 11th aves., Chelsea* ☎ *212/752–2929* ⊕ *www. maryboonegallery.com* 🖾 *Free* ◷ *Tues.–Sat. 10–6* Ⓜ *C, E to 23rd St.*

Matthew Marks Gallery. A hot venue for both the New York and international art crowd, openings at any of the four Matthew Marks galleries are always an interesting scene—there are three other locations along 22nd Street between 10th and 11th avenues. Swiss artist Ugo Rondinone made his U.S. debut here, as did Andreas Gursky. Luigi Ghirri, Darren Almond, Robert Adams, Nan Goldin, Ellsworth Kelly, and a cast of illustrious others also show here. ⊠ *523 W. 24th St., between 10th and 11th aves., Chelsea* ☎ *212/243–0200* ⊕ *www.matthewmarks. com* 🖾 *Free* ◷ *Tues.–Sat. 10–6* Ⓜ *C, E to 23rd St.*

THE HIGH LINE

✉ *10th Ave., from Gansevoort St. to 34th St., Chelsea* ☎ *212/206–9922* ⊕ *www. thehighline.org* ◷ *Dec.–Mar., daily 7–7; Apr., May, Oct., and Nov., daily 7 am–10 pm; June–Sept., daily 7 am–11 pm* Ⓜ *A, C, E to 14th St.; L to 8th Ave.; 1, 2, 3 to 14th St.; 1 to 23rd St. or 28th St.*

TIPS

■ The best way to fully appreciate the High Line is to walk the full length of the elevated park in one direction (preferably from Gansevoort Street uptown so that you can end with stunning views) and then make the return journey at street level, taking in the Chelsea neighborhood, and eats, below.

■ This is an elevated park so you need to look for elevator points along the route if you are traveling with wheelchairs or strollers.

■ Chelsea Market and Gansevoort Market are convenient places to pick up fixings for a picnic lunch.

■ Well-maintained restrooms are available at 16th Street and Gansevoort.

■ The new Whitney Museum of Art is located at the Gansevoort Street base of the High Line; the two make an excellent combination, along with lunch in the area.

Once a railroad track carrying freight trains, this elevated space—running from Gansevoort Street in the Meatpacking District (at the Whitney Museum of Art) to West 34th Street—has been transformed into a wonderful retreat from the hubbub of the city. A long, landscaped "walking park" with plants, curving walkways, picnic tables and benches, public art installations, and views of the Hudson River and the Manhattan skyline, the High Line is now one of the most visited parks in New York City.

Highlights

One of the main draws of the High Line is the landscaping, which is carefully choreographed and yet wild and untamed at the same time. Visitors can see many of the original species that grew in the rail beds, as well as shrubs, trees, grasses, and perennials chosen for their hardiness and sustainability. The landscape is always changing; check the website before you visit to see what's in bloom.

Chelsea Market Passage, between 15th and 16th streets, is accented with Spencer Finch's stained glass art and home to public art displays, video programs, music performances, and sit-down events.

A particularly popular feature that illustrates the High Line's greatest achievement—the ability to see the city with fresh eyes—is the 10th Avenue Square (between 16th and 17th streets). This viewing window with stadium seating and large picture windows frames the ever-moving and -changing city below as art, encouraging viewers to linger, watch, pose, and engage with the city in a new way.

The 25-by-75-foot billboard located within a parking lot next to the High Line at 18th Street and 10th Avenue presents a series of art installations on view for a month at a time.

You never know what you might see in Chelsea's galleries: new works by well-known artists like Alexander Calder, or pieces by up-and-coming artists.

Fodor's Choice ★ **Museum at FIT.** What this small, three-gallery museum housed in the Fashion Institute of Technology (FIT) lacks in size, staging, and effects, it more than makes up for in substance and style. You don't find interactive mannequins, elaborate displays, or overcrowded galleries at the self-declared "most fashionable museum in New York City," but you do find carefully curated exhibits, an impressive permanent collection that includes more than 50,000 garments and accessories from the 18th century to the present, and dedicated followers and students sketching and leaning in to wow over seams and sequins. The Fashion and Textile History Gallery, on the main floor, provides ongoing historical context with a rotating selection of historically and artistically significant objects from the museum's permanent collection (exhibits change every six months), but the real draw here is the special exhibitions in the lower level gallery. Recent examples include "Faking It: Originals, Copies, and Counterfeits"; "Yves Saint Laurent + Halston: Fashioning the 70s," and "Lauren Bacall: The Look." Gallery FIT, also located on the main floor, is dedicated to student and faculty exhibitions. ⊠ 227 W. 27th St., at 7th Ave., Chelsea ☎ 212/217–4558 ⊕ www.fitnyc.edu/museum ☑ Free ⊗ Tues.–Fri. noon–8, Sat. 10–5 Ⓜ N, R to 28th St.

Pace Gallery. The impressive roster of artists represented by the Pace Gallery includes a variety of upper-echelon artists, sculptors, and photographers, including Alexander Calder, Tara Donovan, Chuck Close, Sol LeWitt, and Robert Rauschenberg. Pace has three spaces along West 25th Street in Chelsea (in addition to this one, there is No. 508 and No. 510), as well as a Midtown location (at 32 East 57th Street). ⊠ 534 W. 25th St., between 10th and 11th aves., Chelsea ☎ 212/929–7000 ⊕ www.thepacegallery.com ☑ Free ⊗ Tues.–Sat. 10–6 Ⓜ C, E to 23rd St.

Chelsea Galleries 101

Good art, bad art, edgy art, downright disturbing art—it's all here waiting to please and provoke in the contemporary art capital of the world. For the uninitiated, the concentration of nearly 300 galleries within a seven-block radius can be overwhelming, and the sometimes cool receptions on entering and the deafening silence, intimidating. Art galleries are not exactly famous for their customer service, but you don't need a degree in art appreciation to stare at a canvas or installation.

There's no required code of conduct, although most galleries are library-quiet and cell phones are seriously frowned-on. Don't worry, you won't be pressured to buy anything; staff will probably be doing their best to ignore you.

Galleries are generally open Tuesday through Saturday from 10 to 6. Gallery hop on a Saturday afternoon—the highest-traffic day—if you want company. You can usually find a binder with the artist's résumé, examples of previous work, and exhibit details (usually including prices) at the front desk;if not, ask. Also ask whether there's information you can take with you.

You can't see everything in one afternoon, so if you have specific interests, plan ahead. Find gallery information and current exhibit details by checking the listings in the *New Yorker* or the weekend section of the *New York Times*. Learn more about the galleries and the genres and artists they represent at ⊕ *www.artincontext.org.*

—Jacinta O'Halloran

Paula Cooper Gallery. SoHo pioneer Paula Cooper moved to Chelsea in 1996 and enlisted architect Richard Gluckman to transform a warehouse into a dramatic space with tall ceilings and handsome skylights. There are now two galleries (the other is at 521 West 21st Street) that showcase the minimalist works of artists such as Carl Andre, Sam Durant, Hans Haacke, Donald Judd, and Dan Flavin. ⊠ *534 W. 21st St., between 10th and 11th aves., Chelsea* ☎ *212/255–1105* ⊕ *www.paulacoopergallery.com* ⊠ *Free* ⊗ *Tues.–Sat. 10–6* Ⓜ *C, E to 23rd St.*

Ryan Lee Gallery. In 2014, the Ryan Lee Gallery moved from its year-old, street-level location a few doors down to this new third-floor, 8,000-square-foot space, thereby doubling its physical space and—thanks to its elevated exhibition space, RLWindow, which can be viewed from the High Line—increasing its visibility by millions. RLWindow shows innovative and experimental projects by contemporary artists; recent exhibits turning heads on the High Line have included video installations from Martín Gutierrez and Zachary Fabri. ⊠ *515 W. 26th St., between 10th and 11th aves., Chelsea* ☎ *212/397–0742* ⊕ *www.ryanleegallery.com* ⊠ *Free* ⊗ *Tues.–Sat. 10–6* Ⓜ *C, E to 23rd St.*

WORTH NOTING

303 Gallery. International cutting-edge artists shown here include up-and-coming New York artist Jacob Kassay, photographer Doug Aitken, and installation artists Karen Kilimnik and Jane and Louise Wilson. In 2013, the gallery moved from its home on West 21st Street to a spot under the

High Line at 24th Street, with plans to move back to 21st Street to anchor a new Norman Foster high-rise in late 2015; 303 may retain both locations, so be sure to call and confirm before you visit. ⊠ *507 W. 24th St., between 10th and 11th aves., Chelsea* ☎ *212/255–1121* ⊕ *www.303gallery.com* 🔖 *Free* ☉ *Tues.–Sat. 10–6; closed Aug.* Ⓜ *C, E to 23rd St.*

Andrea Rosen Gallery. Artists on the cutting edge, such as Felix Gonzalez-Torres, video-artists Ryan Trecartin and Lizzie Fitch, sculptor Andrea Zittel, and painter and installation artist Matthew Ritchie, are on view here. Rosen has a second space, Gallery 2 (at 544 West 24th Street), just down the street from the gallery headquarters, with more experimental shows that place less emphasis on commercial appeal or success. ⊠ *525 W. 24th St., between 10th and 11th aves., Chelsea* ☎ *212/627–6000, 212/627–6100 for Gallery 2* ⊕ *www.andrearosengallery.com* 🔖 *Free* ☉ *Tues.–Sat. 10–6* Ⓜ *C, E to 23rd St.*

Casey Kaplan. While many galleries are fleeing Chelsea's high rents for less pricey and more artist-friendly neighborhoods like the Lower East Side or the Upper East Side, Casey Kaplan chose to mark its 20th anniversary in 2015 by moving just a few blocks, into a new 10,000-square-foot, two-story storefront space on West 27th Street. Kaplan gallery represents contemporary artists from Europe and the Americas. ⊠ *121 W. 27th St., between 6th and 7th aves., Chelsea* ☎ *212/645–7335* ⊕ *www.caseykaplangallery.com* 🔖 *Free* ☉ *Tues.–Sat. 10–6* Ⓜ *1 to 28th St.*

Cheim & Read. This prestigious gallery represents artists such as Louise Bourgeois, William Eggleston, Joan Mitchell, Jenny Holzer, Donald Baechler, and Jack Pierson. ⊠ *547 W. 25th St., between 10th and 11th aves., Chelsea* ☎ *212/242–7727* ⊕ *www.cheimread.com* 🔖 *Free* ☉ *Tues.–Sat. 10–6* Ⓜ *C, E to 23rd St.*

FAMILY **Chelsea Piers.** This sports-and-entertainment complex along the Hudson River between 17th and 23rd streets, a phenomenal example of adaptive reuse, is the size of four 80-story buildings laid out flat. There's pretty much every kind of sports activity going on both inside and out, including golf (check out the multitier, all-weather, outdoor driving range), sailing classes, ice-skating, rock climbing, soccer, bowling, gymnastics, and basketball. Plus there's a spa, elite sport-specific training, and film studios. Chelsea Piers is also the jumping-off point for some of the city's various boat tours and dinner cruises. ⊠ *Piers 59–62, Hudson River from 17th to 23rd sts. (entrance at 23rd St.), Chelsea* ☎ *212/336–6666* ⊕ *www.chelseapiers.com* Ⓜ *C, E to 23rd St.*

Cushman Row. Built in 1840 for merchant and developer Don Alonzo Cushman, this string of red-brick beauties between 9th and 10th avenues represents some of the country's best examples of Greek Revival rowhouses. Original details include small wreath-encircled attic windows, deeply recessed doorways with brownstone frames, and striking iron balustrades and fences. Note the pineapples, a traditional symbol of welcome, on top of the black iron newels in front of No. 416. ⊠ *406–418 W. 20th St., between 9th and 10th aves., Chelsea* Ⓜ *C, E to 23rd St.*

Galerie Lelong. This large gallery presents challenging installations, including work by many Latin American artists. Look for art by Yoko Ono, Alfredo Jaar, Andy Goldsworthy, Cildo Meireles, Ana Mendieta,

Hélio Oiticica, Nalini Malani, and Petah Coyne. ⊠ *528 W. 26th St., between 10th and 11th aves., Chelsea* ☎ *212/315–0470* ⊕ *www. galerielelong.com* ⊠ *Free* ☉ *Tues.–Sat. 10–6* Ⓜ *C, E to 23rd St.*

Luhring Augustine Gallery. Owners Lawrence Luhring and Roland Augustine have been working with established and emerging artists from Europe, Japan, and America since 1985. In 2012, Luhring Augustine opened a Brooklyn outpost (at 25 Knickerbocker Avenue in Bushwick) for large-scale installations and long-term projects. ⊠ *531 W. 24th St., between 10th and 11th aves., Chelsea* ☎ *212/206–9100* ⊕ *www. luhringaugustine.com* ⊠ *Free* ☉ *Tues.–Sat. 10–6* Ⓜ *C, E to 23rd St.*

Metro Pictures. The hottest talent in contemporary art shown here includes Cindy Sherman, Olaf Breuning, Louise Lawlor, Trevor Paglen, T. J. Wilcox, and B. Wurtz. ⊠ *519 W. 24th St., between 10th and 11th aves., Chelsea* ☎ *212/206–7100* ⊕ *www.metropicturesgallery.com* ⊠ *Free* ☉ *Tues.–Sat. 10–6* Ⓜ *C, E to 23rd St.*

Nancy Hoffman Gallery. Contemporary painting, sculpture, drawing, photography, and video works by an impressive array of international artists are on display in this light-filled space with high ceilings and a sculpture garden. Artists range from Viola Frey, known for her heroic-scale ceramic male and female figures, to well-established artists and a strong group of young artists embarking on their first solo shows. ⊠ *520 W. 27th St., between 10th and 11th aves., Chelsea* ☎ *212/966–6676* ⊕ *www.nancyhoffmangallery.com* ⊠ *Free* ☉ *Sept.–July, Tues.–Sat. 10–6; Aug., weekdays 10–5* Ⓜ *C, E to 23rd St.*

Robert Miller Gallery. Robert Miller was a titan of the New York art world, and he founded this gallery in 1977 (he passed away in 2011). It continues to represent some of the biggest names in modern painting and photography, including Diane Arbus, Patti Smith, and the estates of Lee Krasner and Alice Neel. ⊠ *524 W. 26th St., between 10th and 11th aves., Chelsea* ☎ *212/366–4774* ⊕ *www.robertmillergallery.com* ⊠ *Free* ☉ *Sept.–June, Tues.–Sat. 10–6; July, weekdays 10–6; Aug., by appointment only* Ⓜ *C, E to 23rd St.*

Rubin Museum of Art. This sleek and serene museum spread over six floors is the largest in the Western Hemisphere dedicated to the art of the Himalayas, India, and neighboring regions. The pieces shown here include paintings on cloth, metal sculptures, and textiles dating from the 2nd century onward. Many of the works from areas such as Tibet, Nepal, southwest China, and India relate to Buddhism, Hinduism, Bon, and other eastern religions. A pleasant café and gift shop is on the ground floor. ■**TIP➔** **Admission is free Friday 6–10 pm.** ⊠ *150 W. 17th St., near 7th Ave., Chelsea* ☎ *212/620–5000* ⊕ *www.rmanyc.org* ⊠ *$15* ☉ *Mon. and Thurs. 11–5, Wed. 11–9, Fri. 11–10, weekends 11–6* Ⓜ *1 to 18th St.*

Tanya Bonakdar Gallery. Contemporary artists such as Olafur Eliasson, Uta Barth, Ernesto Neto, and Sarah Sze, who represented the United States at the 55th Venice Biennale, are shown here. ⊠ *521 W. 21st St., between 10th and 11th aves., Chelsea* ☎ *212/414–4144* ⊕ *www. tanyabonakdargallery.com* ⊠ *Free* ☉ *Tues.–Sat. 10–6* Ⓜ *C, E to 23rd St.*

UNION SQUARE, THE FLATIRON DISTRICT, AND GRAMERCY PARK

GETTING ORIENTED

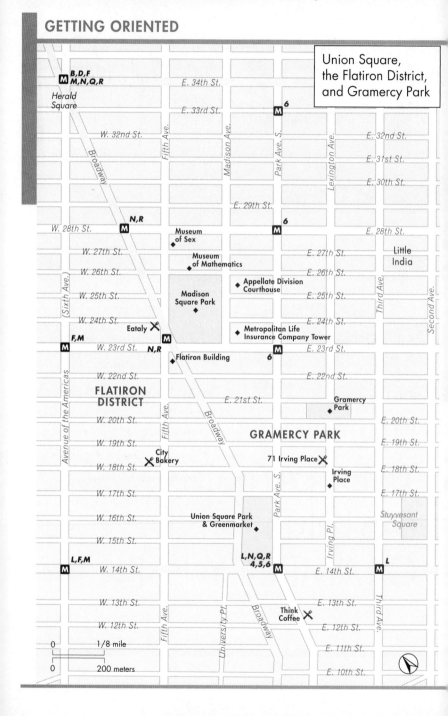

Union Square, the Flatiron District, and Gramercy Park

M B,D,F
M,N,Q,R
Herald
Square

E. 34th St.

E. 33rd St.

M 6

W. 32nd St.

E. 32nd St.

Broadway

Fifth Ave.

Madison Ave.

Park Ave. S.

Lexington Ave.

E. 31st St.

E. 30th St.

E. 29th St.

M N,R

W. 28th St.

M 6

E. 28th St.

Little
India

W. 27th St.

Museum
of Sex

E. 27th St.

W. 26th St.

Museum
of Mathematics

E. 26th St.

(Sixth Ave.)

W. 25th St.

Appellate Division
Courthouse

E. 25th St.

Third Ave.

Second Ave.

Madison
Square Park

W. 24th St.

Eataly ✕

E. 24th St.

M F,M

W. 23rd St. **M** N,R

Metropolitan Life
Insurance Company Tower

M 6 E. 23rd St.

W. 22nd St.

Flatiron Building

E. 22nd St.

**FLATIRON
DISTRICT**

Avenue of the Americas

E. 21st St.

Gramercy
Park

W. 20th St.

Fifth Ave.

Broadway

E. 20th St.

W. 19th St.

GRAMERCY PARK

E. 19th St.

W. 18th St.

City
Bakery ✕

71 Irving Place ✕

E. 18th St.

Irving
Place

W. 17th St.

Park Ave. S.

E. 17th St.

W. 16th St.

Union Square Park
& Greenmarket

Stuyvesant
Square

W. 15th St.

Irving Pl.

M L,F,M

W. 14th St.

M L,N,Q,R
4,5,6

E. 14th St.

M L

Third Ave.

W. 13th St.

E. 13th St.

Fifth Ave.

University Pl.

Broadway

Think
Coffee ✕

E. 12th St.

W. 12th St.

E. 11th St.

0   1/8 mile

0   200 meters

E. 10th St.

MAKING THE MOST OF YOUR TIME

Union Square seems like it's busy at just about every time of day and night, with people hanging out on the steps, eating lunch, or watching street performers, but market days—Monday, Wednesday, Friday, and Saturday—are even busier. Early weekday mornings are quietest, before the market is set up, though without all the people, the area loses some of its allure.

This is definitely an area for strolling, shopping, and eating, so plan your visit around a meal—or several.

If you're planning to eat at the Shake Shack in Madison Square Park, come before noon to avoid long lines.

COFFEE AND QUICK BITES

71 Irving Place. Steps from Union Square, this cozy little café roast their own beans—always a good sign—and serves good people-watching along with sandwiches, muffins, and snacks. ✉ *71 Irving Pl., Gramercy Park* ☎ *212/995–5252* ⊕ *www.irvingfarm.com/locations/gramercy-cafe* Ⓜ *4, 5, 6, L, N, Q, R to 14th St.–Union Sq.*

Eataly. There are multiple restaurants, take-out shops, and cafés, as well as a rooftop brewery at Mario Batali's Italian food emporium. You can also shop for gourmet Italian chocolates, coffees, gelati, and pastries. ✉ *200 5th Ave., at 23rd St., Flatiron District* ☎ *212/229–2560* ⊕ *www.eataly.com* Ⓜ *N, R to 23rd St.*

TOP EXPERIENCES

Strolling in Union Square Park and checking out the produce and other goodies at the greenmarket

Browsing the miles of books in the Strand bookstore

Strolling from Irving Place to Gramercy Park, and around the perimeter of this historic, private park

GETTING HERE AND AROUND

Union Square is a major subway hub, with the 4, 5, 6, L, N, Q, and R lines all converging here. For Madison Square Park and the Flatiron District, take the N or R train to 23rd Street (this lets you out on Broadway). The 6 stops at 23rd and 28th streets (on Park Avenue South).

7

SEASONAL HIGHLIGHTS

Union Square Holiday Market. From Thanksgiving to Christmas, this outdoor market has more than 150 vendors selling unique, often locally made products. Nosh on sweet and savory treats and sip hot apple cider as you shop for holiday gifts and cool NYC souvenirs. ⊕ *www.urbanspacenyc.com*

Madison Square Eats. This month-long pop-up food market happens twice a year (spring and fall) across the street from Madison Square Park, and includes popular vendors like the Red Hook Lobster Pound, Soul Lee Korean BBQ, the Hong Kong Street Cart, and Roberta's Pizza. ⊕ *www.madisonsquarepark.org/mad-sq-eats*

Sightseeing
★★★★

Nightlife
★

Dining
★★★

Lodging
★★★

Shopping
★★★★

Union Square is a hub of seemingly neverending activity and people-watching, which anchors the quieter neighborhoods of Gramercy and the Flatiron District. When that certain brand of New Yorker says they don't like to travel above 14th Street, they're usually thinking about Union Square as the cut-off.

UNION SQUARE

Updated
by Jacinta
O'Halloran

The energy of Union Square reaches its peak during greenmarket days (Monday, Wednesday, Friday, and Saturday), when more than 140 regional farmers and food purveyors set up shop on the square's north and west sides to peddle everything from produce to meat and fresh fish to baked goods. The market is a great place to rub elbows with—and get elbowed by—local shoppers and chefs and a great source for tasty souvenirs (locally produced honeys, jams, pickles, and cheeses) as well as lunch. Find a bench in the park to savor your goodies and take in the scene. Political rallies sometimes happen here, too.

Even on a non-market day, Union Square regularly has vendors of all kinds, selling everything from art to jewelry to T-shirts. New York University students, nannies with their charges, visitors, and other local gather in this open space that can at times feel more like an outdoor version of Grand Central Terminal than a park. Just south of Union Square, on Broadway at 12th Street, is the Strand, a giant bookstore that attracts booklovers like a magnet.

On September 5, 1882, Labor Day was born when more than 10,000 New York City unionized workers took an unpaid day off to march from City Hall to Union Square.

TOP ATTRACTIONS

Union Square Park and Greenmarket. A park, farmers' market, meeting place, and the site of rallies and demonstrations, this pocket of green space sits in the center of a bustling residential and commercial neighborhood. The name "Union" originally signified that two

DID YOU KNOW?

In 1976 the Union Square Greenmarket began as a handful of farmers selling their goods. Now, in peak season, more than 70 vendors sell everything from wine to wool.

main roads—Broadway and 4th Avenue—crossed here. It took on a different meaning in the late 19th and early 20th centuries, when the square became a rallying spot for labor protests; many unions, as well as fringe political parties, moved their headquarters nearby.

Union Square is at its best on Monday, Wednesday, Friday, and Saturday (8–6), when the largest of the city's greenmarkets gathers farmers and food purveyors from the tri-state area. Browse the stands

> **TIME OUT!**
>
> Union Square's most love-it-or-hate-it feature is the *Metronome* sculpture with its bank of cascading numbers. Half art installation, half timepiece, it sits above Nordstrom Rack, and is actually a clock that counts both time elapsed and time remaining in the day. At noon and midnight huge bursts of steam emerge.

of fruit and vegetables, flowers, plants, fresh-baked pies and breads, cheeses, cider, New York State wines, fish, and meat. Between Thanksgiving and Christmas, there is a popular market where artisans sell gift items and food in candycane–stripe booths toward the square's southwest end.

New York University dormitories, theaters, and cavernous commercial spaces occupy the handsomely restored 19th-century commercial buildings that surround the park, along with chain coffee shops and restaurants. The run of diverse architectural styles on the Decker Building at 33 Union Square West is as imaginative as its former contents: this was once home to Andy Warhol's studio. The building at 17th Street and Union Square East, now housing the New York Film Academy and the Union Square Theater, was the final home of Tammany Hall, an organization famous in its day as a corrupt and powerful political machine. Statues in the park include those of George Washington, Abraham Lincoln, Mahatma Gandhi (often wreathed in flowers), and the Marquis de Lafayette (sculpted by Frederic Auguste Bartholdi, designer of the Statue of Liberty). Plaques in the sidewalk on the southeast and southwest sides chronicle the park's history from the 1600s to 1800s. After years of legal battles, the once-crumbling pavilion in the northern end of the park was reincarnated in summer 2014 as an upscale, seasonal restaurant: The Pavilion. The restaurant provides alfresco dining, pricey brunches, and much-needed tables and seating—open to diners and non-diners alike. ⊠ *From 14th to 17th St., between Broadway and Park Ave. S, Flatiron District* Ⓜ *4, 5, 6, L, N, Q, R to 14th St.–Union Sq.*

FLATIRON DISTRICT

The Flatiron District—anchored by Madison Square Park on the north and Union Square to the south—is one of the city's busiest neighborhoods, particularly along 5th Avenue and Park Avenue South. Once known as Ladies' Mile because of the fashionable row of department stores where women routinely shopped, the area is still a favorite for lady-spotting because of the number of modeling agencies and photography studios here. Lovely Madison Square Park, a pleasant green space hemmed in by the neighborhood's notable architecture—from the

The wedge-shape Flatiron Building got its nickname because of its resemblance to the shape of a clothes iron; its original name is the Fuller Building.

triangular Flatiron to the dazzling, gold pyramid–topped New York Life Building and Metropolitan Life Tower, with its elegant clock face—is the best place to savor the view. Sit and admire the scene with a burger and shake from the park's always-busy Shake Shack, or takeout from the mother (or "mamma mia") of all Italian markets, Eataly, across the street from the west side of the park.

TOP ATTRACTIONS

Flatiron Building. When completed in 1902, the Fuller Building, as it was originally known, caused a sensation. Architect Daniel Burnham made ingenious use of the triangular wedge of land at 23rd Street, 5th Avenue, and Broadway, employing a revolutionary steel frame that allowed for the building's 22-story, 286-foot height. Covered with a limestone and white terra-cotta facade in the Italian Renaissance style, the building's shape resembled a clothing iron, hence its nickname. When it became apparent that the building generated strong winds, gawkers would loiter at 23rd Street hoping to catch sight of ladies' billowing skirts. Local traffic cops had to shoo away the male peepers—one purported origin of the phrase "23 skidoo." There is a small display of historic building and area photos in the lobby, but otherwise you have to settle for appreciating this building from the outside, at least for now; the building may be converted to a luxury hotel when current occupant leases expire in 2018. ⊠ *175 5th Ave., bordered by 22nd and 23rd sts., 5th Ave., and Broadway, Flatiron District* Ⓜ *N, R to 23rd St.*

FAMILY **Madison Square Park.** The benches of this elegant tree-filled park afford great views of some of the city's oldest and most charming skyscrapers—the Flatiron Building, the Metropolitan Life Insurance Tower, the gold-crowned New York Life Insurance Building, and the Empire State Building—and serve as a perfect vantage point for people-, pigeon-, and dog-watching. Add free Wi-Fi, the newly renovated Shake Shack, temporary art exhibits, and summer and fall concerts, and you realize that a bench here is definitely the place to be. New York City's first baseball games were played in this 7-acre park in 1845 (though New Jerseyans are quick to point out that the game was actually invented across the river in Hoboken, New Jersey). On the north end of the park, an imposing 1881 statue by Augustus Saint-Gaudens memorializes Civil War naval hero Admiral David Farragut. An 1876 statue of Secretary of State William Henry Seward (the Seward of the term "Seward's Folly," coined when the United States purchased Alaska from the Russian Empire in 1867) sits in the park's southwest corner, though it's rumored that the sculptor placed a reproduction of the statesman's head on a statue of Abraham Lincoln's body. ⊠ *From 23rd to 26th St., between 5th and Madison aves., Flatiron District* 🕾 *212/538–1884* ⊕ *www.madisonsquarepark.org* Ⓜ *N, R to 23rd St.*

WORTH NOTING

Appellate Division Courthouse. Sculpted by Frederick Ruckstull, figures representing Wisdom and Force flank the main portal of this imposing Beaux Arts courthouse, built in 1899. Melding the structure's purpose with artistic symbolism, statues of great lawmakers line the roof balustrade, including Moses, Justinian, and Confucius. In total, sculptures by 16 artists adorn the ornate building, a showcase of themes relating to the law. This is one of the most important appellate courts in the country: it hears more than 3,000 appeals and 6,000 motions a year, and also admits approximately 3,000 new attorneys to the bar each year. Inside the courtroom is a stunning stained-glass dome set into a gilt ceiling. The main hall and the courtroom are open to visitors weekdays from 9 to 5. All sessions, which are generally held Tuesday to Thursday at 2pm, are open to the public (visitors can call the main number ahead of time to be sure court is in session). ⊠ *27 Madison Ave., entrance on 25th St., Flatiron District* 🕾 *212/340–0400* ⊕ *www.courts.state.ny.us/ courts/ad1* ⊗ *Weekdays 9–5* Ⓜ *N, R, 6 to 23rd St.*

Metropolitan Life Insurance Company Tower. When it was added to the original building on this site in 1909, the 700-foot tower resembling the campanile of St. Mark's in Venice made this 1893 building the world's tallest; it was surpassed in height a few years later (by the Woolworth Building). It was stripped of much of its classical detail during renovations in the early 1960s but remains a prominent feature of the Midtown skyline today. The clock's four faces are each three stories high, and their minute hands weigh half a ton each. If the view from the park doesn't quite cut it, you can now reserve a room in the skyline itself: in early 2015, Marriott International and Ian Schrager opened a 355 luxury hotel, the New York Edition Hotel, in the long-vacant clocktower portion of the building. ⊠ *1 Madison Ave., between 23rd and 24th sts., Flatiron* Ⓜ *N, R, 6 to 23rd St.*

FAMILY **Museum of Mathematics** (*MoMath*). There's no exact formula to get kids excited about math, but the sleek, two-floor Museum of Mathematics (MoMath)—the only cultural institution devoted to math in all of

North America—comes close to finding the perfect fun-to-math ratio. Kids can ride square-wheel trikes, create human fractal trees, build virtual 3-D geometric shapes (which can be printed out on a 3-D printer for a fee), use lasers to explore cross-sections of objects, solve dozens of puzzles, and generally bend their minds while they unknowingly multiply brain cells (sshh!). MoMath's newest exhibition, Robot Swarm, allows kids to explore swarm robotics and interact with two-dozen small (Roomba-like), glowing robots, using simple math rules. Exhibits are best suited to kids ages six and up but preschoolers can still enjoy many of the interactive exhibits, like the Math Square, a light-up floor programmed with math games, simulations, and patterns. The museum closes at 2:30 pm the first Wednesday of every month. Save $1 by ordering tickets in advance online. ⊠ *11 E. 26th St., between 5th and Madison aves., Flatiron District* ☎ *212/542–0566* ⊕ *www.momath.org* ✉ *$16* ⊙ *Daily 10–5* Ⓜ *N, R to 28th St.*

Museum of Sex. Ponder the profound history and cultural significance of sex at this 14,000-square-foot museum while staring at vintage pornographic photos, S&M paraphernalia, antimasturbation devices from the 1800s, explicit film clips, vintage condom tins, and a collection of artwork. Recent exhibits have included a puppet show of shady half-beast, half-human characters from Peruvian artist Ety Fefer, an interactive selection of carnival attractions, and probes of such topics as desire on the Internet and the sex lives of animals. The subject matter is given serious curatorial treatment, though the gift shop is full of fun sexual kitsch. Only patrons over 18 are admitted. After visiting the museum's exhibitions, sate your appetite with a kinky cocktail or gourmet coffee and pastry in the museum's Play bar and Nice & Sweet café. ⊠ *233 5th Ave., Flatiron* ☎ *212/689–6337* ⊕ *www.museumofsex.com* ✉ *$17.50* ⊙ *Sun.–Thurs. 10–8, Fri. and Sat. 10–9* Ⓜ *N, R to 28th St.*

7

GRAMERCY PARK

The haste and hullabaloo of the city calms considerably in the residential neighborhood of Gramercy Park. Dignified Gramercy Park, named for its 1831 gated garden ringed by historic buildings and private clubs, is an early example of the city's best creative urban planning. Just north of the park is Ian Schrager's reincarnation of the Gramercy Park Hotel on Lexington Avenue. South of the park, running north to south from 14th Street, is Irving Place, a short street honoring Washington Irving, which feels calm, green, exclusive, and has a combination of old and new eateries, stores, and architecture. Pete's Tavern (⇨ *Nightlife*), on Irving Place since 1864, maintains its claim as the oldest original bar in the city. Two famous writers, O. Henry (*Gift of the Magi*) and Ludwig Bemelmans (*Madeline*), were "inspired" here, probably by the amazing eggnog or Pete's House Ale.

TOP ATTRACTIONS

Gramercy Park. You may not be able to enter this private park (the only truly private park in Manhattan—only those residing around it have keys), but a look through the bars in the wrought-iron fence that encloses it is worth your time, as is a stroll around its perimeter. The beautifully planted 2-acre park, designed by developer Samuel B. Ruggles, dates from 1831, and is flanked by grand examples of early-19th-century architecture and permeated with the character of its many celebrated occupants.

When Ruggles bought the property, it was known as Krom Moerasje ("little crooked swamp"), named by the Dutch settlers. He drained the swamp and set aside 42 lots for a park to be accessible exclusively to those who bought the surrounding lots in his planned London-style residential square. The park is still owned by residents of the buildings surrounding the square, although neighbors from the area can now buy visiting privileges. Guests of the Gramercy Park Hotel also enjoy coveted access to this private park. In 1966 the New York City Landmarks Preservation Commission designated Gramercy Park a historic district. Notable buildings include No. 15, a Gothic Revival brownstone with black granite trim designed by Calvert Vaux, was once home to Samuel Tilden, governor of New York. A secret passageway to 19th Street permitted Tilden to evade his political enemies. It is now home to the 100-year-old National Arts Club. Next door at No. 16 Gramercy Park South lived the actor Edwin Booth, perhaps most famous for being the brother of Lincoln's assassin. In 1888 he turned his Gothic-trim home into the Players Club, a clubhouse for actors and theatrical types who were not welcome in regular society. A bronze statue of Edwin Booth as Hamlet has pride of place inside the park. ■TIP→ Alexander Calder's iconic, monumental outdoor sculpture *Janey Waney* (1969) is installed inside the park and can be viewed through the railings. ⊠ *Lexington Ave. and 21st St., Gramercy Park* Ⓜ *4, 5, 6, L, N, Q, R to 14th St.–Union Sq.; 6 to 23rd St.*

MIDTOWN EAST

GETTING ORIENTED

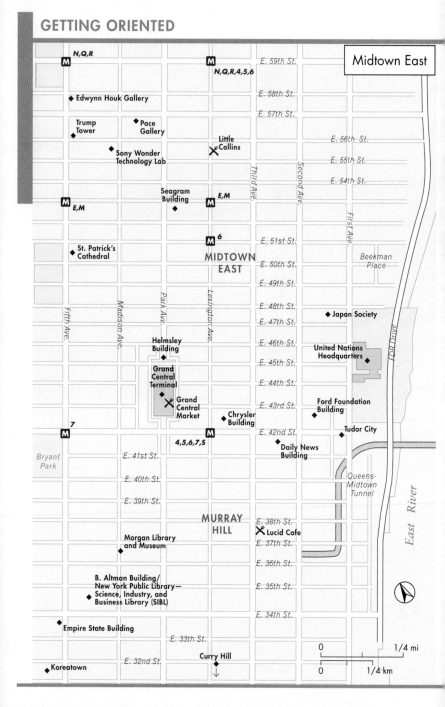

Midtown East

N,Q,R

N,Q,R,4,5,6

E. 59th St.

E. 58th St.

E. 57th St.

♦ Edwynn Houk Gallery

Trump Tower ♦

♦ Pace Gallery

E. 56th St.

E. 55th St.

E. 54th St.

Little ✕ Collins

♦ Sony Wonder Technology Lab

Third Ave.

Second Ave.

First Ave.

Seagram Building ♦

E,M

E,M

⁶

E. 51st St.

MIDTOWN EAST

E. 50th St.

E. 49th St.

♦ St. Patrick's Cathedral

Beekman Place

Fifth Ave.

Madison Ave.

Park Ave.

Lexington Ave.

E. 48th St.

E. 47th St.

♦ Japan Society

E. 46th St.

Helmsley Building ♦

E. 45th St.

United Nations Headquarters ♦

FDR Drive

Grand Central Terminal ♦

E. 44th St.

E. 43rd St.

Grand ✕ Central Market

♦ Chrysler Building

Ford Foundation Building ♦

♦ Tudor City

⁷

4,5,6,7,S

E. 42nd St.

✕ Daily News Building

Bryant Park

E. 41st St.

E. 40th St.

E. 39th St.

Queens-Midtown Tunnel

East River

MURRAY HILL

E. 38th St. ✕ Lucid Cafe

E. 37th St.

Morgan Library and Museum ♦

E. 36th St.

E. 35th St.

B. Altman Building/ New York Public Library— Science, Industry, and Business Library (SIBL) ♦

E. 34th St.

♦ Empire State Building

E. 33rd St.

E. 32nd St.

Curry Hill ↓

0   1/4 mi

0   1/4 km

♦ Koreatown

MAKING THE MOST OF YOUR TIME

The east side of Midtown is somewhat more laid-back than the west side, but there's still lots to keep you busy. Wherever you're headed, try to make sure you at least pass through Grand Central Terminal, which celebrated its 100th birthday in 2013—it's a madhouse on weekday mornings or in the early evening, right after work, but extremely quiet on weekends, an ideal time to visit.

If you're planning to visit the Empire State Building, try to do so either early or late in the day—morning is the least crowded time, and late at night the city lights are dazzling. Allow at least two hours for a visit to the observation deck.

It's also worth making time for a quick trip out of the United States to visit the "international zone" of the United Nations; take a tour of the newly renovated buildings and mail a postcard with a unique U.N. stamp.

TOP EXPERIENCES

Standing in the center of Grand Central Terminal's main concourse and taking in the fiber-optic map of the constellations overhead

Strolling down 5th Avenue, where some of the world's top luxury brands have flagship stores, especially around the holidays when store windows are dressed to impress

Viewing rare manuscripts at the Morgan Library

Enjoying panoramic views of the city at dusk from the top of the Empire State Building

Soaking in peace and serenity while ogling the neo-Gothic architecture, stained glass, and sculptures at iconic St. Patrick's Cathedral

Dining with locals in Koreatown and Curry Hill

GETTING HERE

To get to the east side of Midtown, take the 4, 5, 6, or 7 to Grand Central. The S, or Shuttle, travels back and forth between Grand Central and Times Square.

You can reach the Empire State Building via the B, D, F, M, N, Q, and R trains to 34th Street or the 6 to 33rd Street. The 6 also stops at 23rd and 28th streets.

COFFEE AND QUICK BITES

Grand Central Market. The lower level of Grand Central is a cornucopia of gourmet eating options, including Ciao Bella Gelato, Murray's Cheese, and Joe the Art of Coffee. ✉ *Grand Central Terminal main entrance, 42nd St., at Park Ave., Midtown East* ⊕ *www.grandcentralterminal.com/market* Ⓜ *4, 5, 6, 7, S to Grand Central–42nd St.*

Little Collins. This Australian import pays as much attention to what it puts on your plate— try the avocado and feta on toast—as what it pours in your coffee mug. ✉ *667 Lexington Ave., near 56th St., Midtown East* ☎ *212/308–1969* ⊕ *www.littlecollinsnyc.com* Ⓜ *4, 5, 6 to 59th St.; N, Q, R to Lexington Ave./59th St.; E, M to Lexington Ave./53rd St.*

Lucid Cafe. A tiny coffee spot in Murray Hill has excellent coffee, espresso, and Belgian hot chocolate, as well as tasty pastries. ✉ *311 Lexington Ave., at 38th St., Midtown East* ☎ *212/867–3490* Ⓜ *4, 5, 6, 7, S to Grand Central–42nd St.*

8

Sightseeing
★★★★★

Nightlife
★★

Dining
★★★★

Lodging
★★★★★

Shopping
★★★★★

Fifth Avenue is Manhattan's dividing line, marking the division of east and west sides, but the avenue itself seems to connote so much of what the city's East Side is all about. This is where some of the city's most iconic buildings are found, including the Empire State Building, in the Murray Hill neighborhood.

MIDTOWN EAST

Updated
by Jacinta
O'Halloran

In terms of architecture, Midtown East has some of the city's most notable gems, including the stately Chrysler Building, considered an Art Deco triumph, and the bustling Beaux Arts masterpiece, Grand Central Terminal. At night the streets here are relatively quiet, but the restaurants are filled with expense-account diners celebrating successes. Some of the most formal dining rooms and expensive meals in town can be found here. The lower section of 5th Avenue is also a shopper's paradise, home to megabrand flagships such as Louis Vuitton, Yves Saint Laurent, and Chanel, and some of the world's most famous jewelry stores, including Tiffany, Van Cleef & Arpels, and Harry Winston. Upscale department stores like Bloomingdale's and Saks Fifth Avenue are also around here.

TOP ATTRACTIONS

Chrysler Building. A monument to modernity and the mighty automotive industry, the former Chrysler headquarters wins many New Yorkers' vote for the city's most iconic and beloved skyscraper (and the world's tallest for 40 days, until the Empire State Building stole the honor). Architect William Van Alen, who designed this 1930 Art Deco masterpiece, incorporated car details into its form: American eagle gargoyles made of chromium nickel sprout from the 61st floor, resembling hood ornaments used on 1920's Chryslers; winged urns festooning the 31st floor reference the car's radiator caps. Most breathtaking is the pinnacle, with tiered crescents and spiked windows that radiate out like a magnificent steel sunburst. View it at sunset to catch the light gleaming off the tip. Even better, observe it at night, when its peak illuminates the sky. The inside is sadly off-limits, apart from the amazing time-capsule lobby replete with chrome "grillwork," intricately patterned wood elevator doors, marble walls and floors, and an enormous ceiling mural saluting transportation and human endeavor. ⊠ *405 Lexington Ave., at 42nd St., Midtown East* Ⓜ *4, 5, 6, 7, S to 42nd St./Grand Central.*

Fodor's Choice **Grand Central Terminal.** Grand Central is not only the world's largest (76 ★ acres) and the nation's busiest railway station—nearly 700,000 commuters and subway riders use it daily—but also one of the world's most magnificent, majestic public spaces. Past the glimmering chandeliers of the waiting room is the jaw-dropping **main concourse,** 200 feet long, 120 feet wide, and 120 feet (roughly 12 stories) high, modeled after an ancient Roman public bath. In spite of it being completely cavernous, Grand Central manages to evoke a certain sense of warmth rarely found in buildings its size. Overhead, a twinkling fiber-optic map of the constellations covers the robin's egg–blue ceiling. To admire it all with some sense of peace, avoid visiting at rush hour.

To escape the crowds, head up one of the sweeping staircases at either end, where three upscale restaurants occupy the balcony space. Any would make an enjoyable perch from which to survey the concourse, but for a real taste of the station's early years, head beyond the western staircase to the **Campbell Apartment,** a clubby cocktail lounge housed in the restored private offices and salon of 1920's tycoon John W. Campbell. Located around and below the main concourse are fantastic shops and eateries—this is, of course, home to the eponymous Grand Central Oyster Bar—making this one of the best, if somewhat labyrinthine, "malls" in the city.

To best admire Grand Central's exquisite Beaux-Arts architecture, start with its ornate south face on East 42nd Street, modeled after a Roman triumphal arch. Crowning the facade's Corinthian columns and 75-foot-high arched windows, a graceful clock keeps time for hurried commuters. In the central window stands an 1869 bronze statue of Cornelius Vanderbilt, who built the station to house his railroad empire. Also noteworthy is the 1½-ton, cast-iron bald eagle displaying its 13-foot wingspan atop a ball near the corner of 42nd Street and Vanderbilt Avenue.

Grand Central still functions primarily as a railroad station, and might resemble its artless crosstown counterpart, Penn Station, were it not for Jacqueline Kennedy Onassis's 1975 public information campaign to save it as a landmark. Underground, more than 60 ingeniously integrated railroad tracks carry trains upstate and to Connecticut via Metro-North Commuter Rail. The subway connects here as well. The **Municipal Art Society** (*212/935–3960; www.mas.org/tours*) leads an official daily walking tour to explore the 100-year-old terminal's architecture, history, and hidden secrets. Tours begin in the main concourse at 12:30 and last 75 minutes. Tickets ($20) can be purchased in advance online (*www.docentour.com/gct*) or from the ticket booth in the main concourse. ⊠ *Main entrance, 42nd St. and Park Ave., Midtown East*

8

Irish pride takes to the streets and sweeps up 5th Avenue in the annual St. Patrick's Day Parade.

☎ 212/935–3960 ⊕ *www.grandcentralterminal.com* Ⓜ *4, 5, 6, 7, S to Grand Central–42nd St.*

St. Patrick's Cathedral. This Gothic edifice—the largest Catholic cathedral in the United States, seating approximately 2,400 people—is among Manhattan's most striking churches, with its double spires topping out at 330 feet. "St. Pat's," as locals call it, holds a special place in the hearts of many New Yorkers and provides a calm and quiet refuge in the heart of buzzy Midtown. Despite the throngs of tourists (the cathedral receives more than 5½ million visitors annually) and ongoing renovations.

The church dates back to 1858–79 and over has been undergoing an extensive $177 million rehabilitation project that is expected to finally be completed in December of 2015. The cathedral remains open during renovations: the Fifth Avenue facade was finished in December 2014, and the stone faces of the 80-foot spires that tower above 5th Avenue have been cleaned and caulked and the copper crosses that crown them polished. Inside, there might still be some scaffolding but try to get a glimpse of the organ loft and the famous rose window (considered stained-glass artist Charles Connick's greatest work). Also check out the statues in the alcoves around the nave, including a modern depiction of the first American-born saint, Mother Elizabeth Ann Seton. Don't miss the ornately carved bronze double doors on your way in and out: each weighs 9,200 pounds and features sculptures of saints.

The church's Pieta sculpture is three times larger than the Pieta in St. Peter's Rome. Construction does not interfere with daily masses or the free guided tours held at 10 am most days (call ahead to confirm). ⊠ *5th*

Ave., between 50th and 51st sts., Midtown East ☎ *212/753–2261 for rectory* ⊕ *www.saintpatrickscathedral.org* ⊙ *Daily 6:30 am–8:45 pm* Ⓜ *E, M to 5th Ave./53rd St.*

FAMILY **Sony Wonder Technology Lab.** Have kids in tow? The free Sony Wonder Technology Lab in the Sony Building lets them program robots, remix songs, perform virtual heart surgery, learn about new technologies inspired by nature, and see their dance moves performed by favorite Sony-animated characters in real time through motion capture. A fascinating evolutionary timeline explores how technology keeps getting faster, sharper, smaller, and more portable. The lab also shows classic and contemporary films for both young and adult audiences in its HD theater on Thursday and Saturday. Admission is free, but reservations are strongly recommended; they can be made a minimum of seven days and up to three months from the time of visit. A limited number of same-day tickets are available on a first-come, first-served basis. ⊠ *550 Madison Ave., at 56th St., Midtown East* ☎ *212/833–8100* ⊕ *www.sonywondertechlab.com* ⊙ *Tues.–Sat. 9:30–5:30* Ⓜ *E, M to 5th Ave./53rd St.*

United Nations Headquarters. Officially an "international zone" and not part of the United States, the U.N. Headquarters is a working symbol of global cooperation. Built between 1947 and 1961, the headquarters sit on a lushly landscaped, 18-acre tract on the East River, fronted by flags of member nations. The United Nations celebrated its 70th anniversary in 2015 with the completion of a seven-year overhaul that retained the 1950's look and feel (and in some cases, green carpet) of the complex, while incorporating state-of-the-art technology to upgrade the heat, sound, and security systems and to improve its overall performance. The $2.1 billion renovation returns the historic campus to its original design, in the process addressing contemporary concerns, like accessibility, energy efficiency, and blast-proofing, as well as adding some not exactly *new* conveniences, like sprinklers. The General Assembly Building reopened in early 2015 after its 16-month renovation, which included replacing the gold-leafed background of the iconic U.N. emblem that had become caked with tar and nicotine—as had the walls and ceiling of the hall—after decades of cigar and cigarette smoke (city law did not apply here, so smoking was not outlawed until 2008). The only way to enter the U.N. Headquarters is the 45-minute guided tour (given in 20 languages; reservations can be made through the website), which includes the **General Assembly** and major council chambers. While the tour covers a lot of educational ground, it does not cover a lot of physical ground; council chambers may be closed on any given day, and you cannot enter the Secretariat building. Also, you can no longer wander the grounds, rose garden, or riverside promenade. Arrive 30 minutes before the start of your tour for security screening. If you ordered tickets online, be sure to bring your print-out. The newly renovated Conference Building, which includes the original chambers of the Security Council, the Trusteeship Council, and the Economic and Social Council, as well as gifts from U.N. Member States, like the mosaic representation of Norman Rockwell's *Golden Rule,* are all back on public display. The tour also includes displays on war, peacekeeping, nuclear nonproliferation, human rights, and refugees, and passes corridors overflowing with imaginatively diverse artwork. Free tickets to assemblies are sometimes available on a first-come, first-served basis before sessions begin; pick them up in the General Assembly lobby. The complex's buildings (the slim, 505-foot-tall green-glass **Secretariat Building**; the much smaller, domed **General Assembly Building**; and the **Dag Hammarskjöld Library**) evoke the influential French modernist Le Corbusier (who was on the team of architects that designed the complex), and the surrounding park and plaza remain visionary. The public concourse has a gift shop, a bookstore, and a post office where you can mail postcards with U.N. stamps; you can also get your passport stamped with the U.N. stamp. ⊠ *Visitor entrance, 1st Ave. at 47th St., Midtown East* ☎ *212/963–8687* ⊕ *visit.un.org* ✉ *Tour $18 (plus $2 online surcharge)* ⊗ *Tours weekdays 9:15–4:15 (tours in English leave every 30 mins; for other languages, check schedule online)* ☞ *Children under 5 not admitted* Ⓜ *4, 5, 6, 7, S to Grand Central–42nd St.*

WORTH NOTING

Daily News Building. The landmark lobby of this Art Deco tower contains an illuminated 12-foot globe that revolves beneath a black glass dome. Around it, spreading across the floor like a giant compass and literally positioning New York at the center of the world, bronze lines indicate mileage to various international destinations. Movie fans may recognize the building as the offices of the fictional newspaper *The Daily Planet* in the original *Superman* movie. On the wall behind the globe you can check out a number of meteorological gauges, which read New York City's weather—especially fun on a windy day when the meters are whipping about. The *Daily News* hasn't called this building home since the mid-1990s;only the lobby is open to the public (but that's enough). ■TIP➔ The globe was last updated in 1967 so part of the fun here is seeing how our maps have changed; note Manchuria and East and West Germany. ⊠ *220 E. 42nd St., between 2nd and 3rd aves., Midtown East* ☎ *212/210–2100* Ⓜ *4, 5, 6, 7, S to Grand Central–42nd St.*

Edwynn Houk Gallery. The impressive stable of 20th-century photographers represented and shown here includes Sally Mann, Robert Polidori, Man Ray, Lalla Essaydi, Annie Leibovitz, Herb Ritts, Mona Kuhn, and Elliott Erwitt. The gallery also has prints by masters Edward Weston and Alfred Stieglitz. ⊠ *745 5th Ave., 4th fl., between 57th and 58th sts., Midtown East* ☎ *212/750–7070* ⊕ *www.houkgallery.com* ✉ *Free* ⊗ *Tues.–Sat. 11–6* Ⓜ *N, R, Q to 5th Ave./59th St.*

Ford Foundation Building. While most Midtown office lobbies remain off limits to visitors, the Ford Foundation Building's is a welcome respite from high-trafficked Midtown sidewalks and nearby attractions like Grand Central Station and the United Nations Headquarters. Built in 1967 as the Ford Foundation's New York City headquarters, and designed by Kevin Roche John Dinkeloo and Associates (also responsible for several galleries and wings at the Metropolitan Museum of Art, the renovation of the Central Park Zoo, and many other iconic attractions), this landmark, 12-story transparent glass cube is one of Midtown's most notable buildings, thanks to its open, C-shape office floors overlooking an incredibly lush, secret—but public—garden.

While most office buildings fulfill their green quota with a few potted plants and maybe a fountain in the courtyard, this light-filled atrium is a veritable oasis, complete with soaring trees, cascading plants, walking paths, three tiers of plantings, and a small pool. Whether you're an urban gardener or just a weary visitor, pause in this rare patch of quiet in the heart of the city—you'll likely have this tropical scene to yourself. The atrium can be accessed from the 42nd or 43rd Street entrance during office hours (10–4). ⊠ *320 E. 43rd St., between 1st and 2nd aves., Midtown East* ☎ *212/573–5000* ⊕ *www.fordfoundation.org* Ⓜ *4, 5, 6, 7, S to Grand Central–42nd St.*

Helmsley Building. This Warren & Wetmore–designed 1929 landmark was intended to match neighboring Grand Central Terminal in bearing, and succeeded, with a gold-and-copper roof topped with an enormous lantern (originally housing a 6,000-watt light) and distinctive dual archways for traffic on Park Avenue. The building's history gets quirky. When millionaire real estate investor Harry Helmsley purchased the building in 1977, he changed its name from the New York Central Building to the New York General Building in order to save money by replacing only two letters in the facade (only later did he rename it after himself). During a renovation the following year, however, he actually gilded the building, applying gold paint even to limestone and bronze—it was removed by a succeeding owner. In 2010, after a $100 million renovation, the Helmsley Building, no longer under Helmsley ownership (so technically 230 Park, or "the building formerly known as the Helmsley Building and informally still known as the Helmsley Building"), became the first prewar office tower to receive LEED Gold certification for energy efficiency. Despite being blocked from view from the south by the MetLife Building (originally, the Pan Am Building), the Helmsley Building remains a defining—and now "green," as opposed to gold—feature of one of the world's most lavish avenues. ⊠ *230 Park Ave., between 45th and 46th sts., Midtown East* Ⓜ *4, 5, 6, 7, S to 42nd St./Grand Central.*

8

Japan Society. The stylish, serene lobby of the Japan Society has interior bamboo gardens linked by a second-floor waterfall. Works by well-known Japanese artists are exhibited in the second-floor gallery. Past shows have included the first American retrospective of Sakai Hōitsu, a samurai aristocrat turned Buddhist monk who dedicated his life to art and poetry; a display of artwork created by children from Tōhoku after Japan's 2011 earthquake; and the dramatic "Garden of Unearthly Delights"—a collection of paintings, digital works, and installations from contemporary Japanese artists that harkens back to the traditions of the master craftsmen. In July, the museum hosts an annual film festival, Japan Cuts, showcasing contemporary Japanese cinema. ⊠ *333 E. 47th St., between 1st and 2nd aves., Midtown East* ☎ *212/832–1155* ⊕ *www.japansociety.org* ☞ *Gallery $12* ☉ *Gallery Tues.–Thurs. 11–6, Fri. 11–9, weekends 11–5; building hrs vary* Ⓜ *4, 5, 6, 7, S to Grand Central–42nd St.; E, M to Lexington Ave./53rd St.; 6 to 51st St.*

Pace Gallery (Midtown). This leading contemporary art gallery—with three outposts in Chelsea, two in London, and one each in Beijing and Hong Kong—focuses on such modern and contemporary artists as

Julian Schnabel, Mark Rothko, James Turrell, and New York School painter Ad Reinhardt. ⊠ *32 E. 57th St., 2nd fl., between Park and Madison aves., Midtown East* ☎ *212/421–3292* ⊕ *www.thepacegallery.com* ⬚ *Free* ☉ *Tues.–Sat. 10–6* Ⓜ *N, Q, R to 5th Ave./59th St.*

Seagram Building. Ludwig Mies van der Rohe, a pioneer of modern architecture, built this boxlike bronze-and-glass tower in 1958. The austere facade belies its wit: I-beams, used to hold buildings up, here are merely attached to the surface, representing the *idea* of support. The Seagram Building's innovative ground-level plaza, extending out to the sidewalk, has since become a common element in urban skyscraper design, but at the time it was built, it was a radical announcement of a new, modern era of American architecture. Most visitors are distracted by more elaborate figures in the city skyline, but the Seagram is a must-visit for architecture buffs. With its two giant fountains and welcoming steps, it's also a popular lunch spot with Midtown workers. Visit late in the afternoon to avoid crowds. ⊠ *375 Park Ave., between 52nd and 53rd sts., Midtown East* ⊕ *www.375parkavenue.com* Ⓜ *6 to 51st St.; E, M to Lexington Ave./53rd St.*

Trump Tower. The tallest all-glass building in Manhattan when it was completed in 1983, this skyscraper's ostentatious atrium flaunts that decade's unbridled luxury, with three well-trafficked dining options (a café, grill, and bar), expensive boutiques (including Ivanka Trump's Fine Jewelry store), and gaudy brass everywhere. You half-expect the pleasant-sounding waterfall streaming down to the lower-level food court to flow with champagne. These days, the building is best known for its appearances on TV reality show *Celebrity Apprentice,* where Donald Trump hires and fires celebrities. ⊠ *725 5th Ave., at 56th St., Midtown East* ☎ *212/832–2000* ⊕ *www.trump.com* Ⓜ *N, Q, R to 5th Ave./59th St.; E, M to 5th Ave./53rd St.*

Tudor City. Before Donald Trump, there was Fred F. French. In 1925 the prominent real-estate developer became one of the first to buy up a large number of buildings—more than 100, in fact, most of them tenements—and join their properties into a single new development. He designed a collection of nine apartment buildings and two parks in the "garden city" mode, which placed a building's green space not in an enclosed courtyard, but in the foreground. French also elevated the entire development 70 feet (40 stone steps) above the river and built a 39-by-50-foot "Tudor City" sign, best viewed from 42nd Street walking east, atop one of the 22-story buildings. The development's residential towers opened between 1927 and 1930, borrowing a marketable air of sophistication from Tudor-style stonework, stained-glass windows, and lobby design flourishes. An official city landmark, Tudor City has featured in numerous films, and its landmark gardens—sometimes compared to Gramercy Park, but without the key—remain a popular lunch spot among office workers. The neighborhood was designated a historic district in 1988. ⊠ *From 40th to 43rd St., between 1st and 2nd aves., Midtown East* Ⓜ *4, 5, 6, 7, S to Grand Central–42nd St.*

The restoration and cleaning of Grand Central in the late 1990s uncovered the elaborate astronomical design on the ceiling of the main concourse.

MURRAY HILL

Murray Hill stretches roughly from 30th to 40th Street between 5th and 3rd avenues and is a mix of high-rises, restaurants, and bars filled mostly with a postcollege crowd. The small but solid enclave of Little India (also known as "Curry Hill"), primarily around Lexington and 28th Street, is a good area to sample authentic cuisine and shop for traditional clothing and other goods in a handful of boutiques. Farther north, a few side streets are tree-lined and townhouse-filled with some high-profile haunts, including the Morgan Library and Museum with its vast book stacks and rare manuscripts. Probably the biggest reason to visit this neighborhood is to see New York's biggest icon, the Empire State Building.

TOP ATTRACTIONS

FAMILY

Fodor'sChoice

★

Empire State Building. With a pencil-slim silhouette, recognizable virtually worldwide, the Empire State Building is an Art Deco monument to progress, a symbol for New York City, and a star in some great romantic scenes, on- and off-screen. Its cinematic résumé—the building has appeared in more than 250 movies—means that it remains a fixture of popular imagination, and many visitors come to relive favorite movie scenes. You might just find yourself at the top of the building with *Elf* lookalikes or even the building's own *King Kong* impersonator.

Built in 1931 at the peak of the skyscraper craze, this 103-story limestone giant opened after a mere 13 months of construction. The

The view from Midtown over the East River and into Queens

framework rose at an astonishing rate of 4½ stories per week, making the Empire State Building the fastest-rising skyscraper ever built.

Unfortunately, your rise to the observation deck might not be quite so record-breaking. There are three lines to get to the top of the Empire State Building; a line for tickets, a line for security, and a line for the elevators. Save time by purchasing your tickets in advance online. You can't skip the security line, but you can skip to the front of both the ticket line and the line for elevators by purchasing an Express ticket ($50). If you don't want to pony up for express service, do yourself a favor and skip that last elevator line at the 80th floor by taking the stairs.

If this is your first visit, keep yourself entertained during your ascent by renting a headset with an audio tour by Tony, a fictional but "authentic" native New Yorker (available in eight languages).

The 86th-floor observatory (1,050 feet high) has both a glass-enclosed area (heated in winter and cooled in summer) and an outdoor deck spanning the building's circumference. Don't be shy about going outside into the wind (even in winter), or you'll miss half the experience. Also, don't be deterred by crowds; there's an unspoken etiquette when it comes to sharing the views and backdrop, and there's plenty of city to go around. Bring quarters for the high-powered binoculars—on clear days you can see up to 80 miles—or bring binoculars of your own so you can get a good look at some of the city's rooftop gardens. If it rains, the deck will be less crowded and you can view the city between the clouds or watch the rain travel sideways around the building from the shelter of the enclosed walkway.

The Lights of the Empire State Building

At night the Empire State Building lights up the Manhattan skyline with a colorful view as awe-inspiring from a distance as the view from the top. The colors at the top of the building are changed regularly to reflect seasons, events, and holidays, so New Yorkers and visitors from around the world always have a reason to look at this icon in a new light.

The building's first light show was in November 1932, when a simple searchlight was used to spread the news that New York–born Franklin Delano Roosevelt had been elected president of the United States. Douglas Leigh, sign designer and mastermind of Times Square's kinetic billboard ads, tried to brighten up prospects at the "Empty State Building" after the Depression by negotiating with the Coca-Cola Company to occupy the top floors. He proposed that Coca-Cola could change the lights of the building to serve as a weather forecast and then publish a small guide on its bottles to decipher the colors. Coca-Cola loved this idea, but the deal fell through after the bombing at Pearl Harbor, when the U.S. government needed office space in the building.

In 1956 the revolving "freedom lights" were installed to welcome people to America; then in 1964 the top 30 floors of the building were illuminated to mark the New York World's Fair. Douglas Leigh revisited the lights in 1976, when he was made chairman of City Decor to welcome the Democratic Convention. He introduced the idea of color lighting, and so the building's tower was ablaze in red, white, and blue to welcome the convention and mark the celebration of the American Bicentennial. The color lights were a huge success, and they remained red, white, and blue for the rest of the year.

Leigh's next suggestion of tying the lights to different holidays, a variation on his weather theme for Coca-Cola, is the basic scheme still used today. In 1977 the lighting system was updated to comply with energy conservation programs and allow for a wider range of colors. Leigh further improved this new system in 1984 by designing an automated color-changing system so vertical fluorescents in the mast could be changed.

The Empire State Building's LED light system can produce intensely saturated full-color light and dimmable cool white light, allowing for an astonishing and flexible range of dramatic or subtle lighting effects.

For a full lighting schedule, visit ⊕ www.esbnyc.com.

—Jacinta O'Halloran

8

The views of the city from the 86th-floor deck are spectacular, but the views from 16 stories up on the 102nd-floor observatory are even more so—and yet, fewer visitors make it this far. Instead of rushing back to elevator lines, ask yourself when you'll be back again and then head up to the enclosed 102nd floor. The ticket for both the 86th-floor and 102nd-floor decks costs $44, but you will be rewarded with peaceful, bird's-eye views of the entire city. Also, there are fewer visitors angling for photo ops, so you can linger a while and really soak in the city and experience. (Combination tickets are available with the NY Skyride.)

Even if you skip the view from up top, be sure to step into the lobby and take in the ceiling, beautifully restored in 2009. The gilded gears and sweeping Art Deco lines, long hidden under a drop ceiling and decades of paint, are a romantic tribute to the machine age and part of the original vision for the building. ⊠ *350 5th Ave., at 34th St., Murray Hill* ☎ *212/736–3100, 877/692–8439* ⊕ *www.esbnyc.com* ✉ *$27; $44 for 86th–fl. and 102nd–fl. decks* ☉ *Daily 8 am–2 am; last elevator up leaves at 1:15 am* Ⓜ *B, D, F, M, N, Q, R to 34th St.–Herald Sq.; 6 to 33rd St.*

Morgan Library and Museum. The treasures inside this museum, gathered by John Pierpont Morgan (1837–1913), one of New York's wealthiest financiers, are exceptional: medieval and Renaissance illuminated manuscripts, old master drawings and prints, rare books, and autographed literary and musical manuscripts. Other crowning achievements on paper include letters penned by John Keats and Thomas Jefferson; a summary of the theory of relativity in Einstein's own elegant handwriting; three Gutenberg Bibles; drawings by Dürer, Leonardo da Vinci, Rubens, Blake, and Rembrandt; the only known manuscript fragment of Milton's *Paradise Lost*; Thoreau's journals; and original manuscripts and letters by Charlotte Brontë, Jane Austen, Thomas Pynchon, and many others.

The library shop is housed within an 1852 Italianate brownstone, once the home of Morgan's son, J. P. Morgan Jr. Outside on East 36th Street, the sphinx in the right-hand sculptured panel of the original library's facade is rumored to wear the face of architect Charles McKim. ⊠ *225 Madison Ave., at 36th St., Murray Hill* ☎ *212/685–0008* ⊕ *www.themorgan.org* ✉ *$18 (free Fri. 7–9)* ☉ *Tues.–Thurs. 10:30–5, Fri. 10:30–9, Sat. 10–6, Sun. 11–6* Ⓜ *B, D, F, M, N, Q, R to 34th St.–Herald Sq.; 6 to 33rd St.*

FAMILY **NY SKYRIDE.** Although some parents blanch when they discover both how much it costs and how it lurches, the second-floor NY SKYRIDE, New York's only aerial-tour simulator, is a favorite of children and much cheaper than an actual aerial tour of New York. Narrated by actor Kevin Bacon, the ride takes a 30-minute virtual tour of New York, soaring by the Brooklyn Bridge, the Statue of Liberty, Central Park, Times Square, Yankee Stadium, and other top attractions along the way. There's also a brief but poignant trip back in time to visit the World Trade Center's Twin Towers—a sight sure to drive you straight into the arms of the first "I [Heart] NY" T-shirt vendor you see after leaving the building. It's a fun way to get a sense of the city's highlights, though teenagers may find the technology a little dated. When you purchase a SKYRIDE–Empire State Building combo ticket, you visit the SKYRIDE first, then join the line for the observation deck at the elevators, skipping up to half the wait. ⊠ *Empire State Building, 33rd St. entrance, Murray Hill* ☎ *212/279–9777, 888/759–7433* ⊕ *www.skyride.com* ✉ *$42; $59 combo Skyride and observatory* ☉ *Daily 8 am–10 pm* Ⓜ *B, D, F, M, N, Q, R to 34th St.–Herald Sq.; 6 to 33rd St.*

WORTH NOTING

FAMILY **B. Altman Building/New York Public Library–Science, Industry, and Business Library (SIBL).** In 1906, department-store magnate Benjamin Altman gambled that his fashionable patrons would follow him uptown from his popular store in the area now known as the Ladies' Mile Historic District. His new store, one of the first of the grand department stores on 5th Avenue, was designed to blend in with the mansions nearby. Note in particular the beautiful entrance on 5th Avenue. In 1996 the New York Public Library (NYPL) set up a high-tech library here. A 33-foot-high atrium unites the building's two floors: the lending library off the lobby and the research collections below. Downstairs, a wall of electronic ticker tapes and TVs tuned to business-news stations beams information and instructions to patrons. As part of the controversial Central Library Plan, the NYPL had planned to sell this library and its Mid-Manhattan circulating library to fund renovations to the iconic Schwarzman Building on 42nd Street and 5th Avenue, but the sale was delayed and ultimately abandoned due to public outcry. A free hour-long tour is given Thursday at 2; meet at the reception desk. ✉ *188 Madison Ave., between 34th and 35th sts., Murray Hill* ☎ *917/275–6975* ⊕ *www.nypl.org* ⊗ *Mon., Fri., and Sat. 11–6, Tues.–Thurs. 10–8* Ⓜ *B, D, F, M, N, Q, R to 34th St.–Herald Sq.; 6 to 33rd St.*

Curry Hill. An affectionate play on the name of the neighborhood, Curry Hill is an aromatic three-block cluster of Indian restaurants and one of the city's most exciting dining destinations. There are nearly 25 Indian restaurants peppered (or is it spiced?) around Lexington Avenue between 26th and 28th streets, and while the neighborhood is popular with in-the-know New Yorkers, it is decidedly off the beaten tourist track. You'll find culinary offerings from a variety of regional cuisines, be it a filling *biryani* or a quick *chaat* (savory snack).Highlights include a *saag paneer* (spinach dish with cheese) or a bowl of curry at one of the neighborhood's founding restaurants, Curry in a Hurry (28th and Lex); sweet-and-sour *bamia kuhta* (lamb stew) or potato-and-beet fritters at Jewish-Indian restaurant Haldi (Lexington between 27th and 28th); and *kati* rolls (meat or veggie filling wrapped in flatbread) and other urban Indian street snacks at Desi Galli (Lexington between 27th and 28th). Don't leave the neighborhood without sampling a *dosa*, a fermented crêpe often filled with spiced potato and served with dipping sauces, and shopping the spice markets. Too full to walk? Curry Hill is a great place to score a ride as Indian cab drivers regularly stop here for food. ✉ *Lexington Ave., between 26th and 28th sts., Murray Hill* Ⓜ *6 to 28th St.; N, R to 23rd St.*

Koreatown. Despite sitting in the shade of the Empire State Building, and within steps of Herald Square, Koreatown (or "K-Town," as it's locally known) is not a tourist destination. In fact, it feels decidedly off-the-beaten-track and insulated, as though locals wryly planted their own place to eat, drink, be merry, and get a massage—right under the noses of millions of tourists. Technically, Koreatown runs from 31st to 36th Street between 5th and 6th avenues, though the main drag is

8

32nd Street between 5th and Broadway. Labeled Korea Way, this strip is home to 24/7 Korean barbecue joints, karaoke bars, and spas, all piled on top of each other. Fill up on *kimchi* (spicy pickled cabbage), *kimbap* (seaweed rice), and red bean doughnuts (delicious), try some authentic Asian karaoke, and then top off your Koreatown experience by stepping into a jade igloo sauna (at Juvenex Spa, 25 West 32nd Street). Expect a big bang for your buck, to rub elbows with locals, and bragging rights over visitors who followed the crowds to Chinatown. ⊠ *From 31st to 36th St., between 5th and 6th aves., Murray Hill* Ⓜ *B, D, F, M, N, Q, R to 34th St.–Herald Sq.; 6 to 33rd St.*

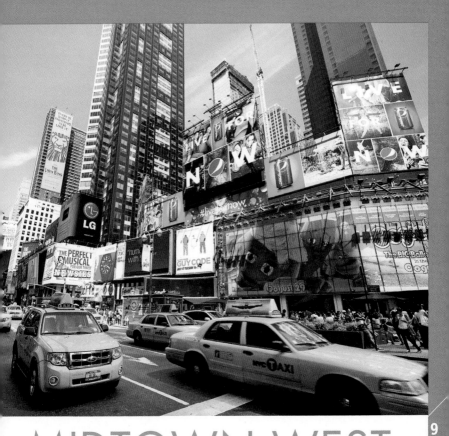

MIDTOWN WEST

GETTING ORIENTED

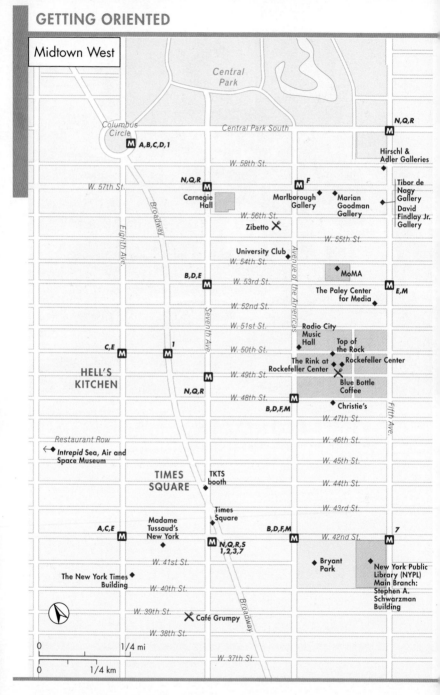

Midtown West

Central Park

Columbus Circle

M A,B,C,D,1

Central Park South

W. 58th St.

N,Q,R

M

Hirschl &
Adler Galleries

N,Q,R

M

W. 57th St.

Broadway

Eighth Ave.

Carnegie
Hall

Marlborough
Gallery

F

Marian
Goodman
Gallery

Tibor de
Nagy
Gallery

David
Findlay Jr.
Gallery

W. 56th St.

Zibetto ✕

W. 55th St.

University Club

W. 54th St.

B,D,E

M

W. 53rd St.

Seventh Ave.

Avenue of the Americas

MoMA

The Paley Center
for Media

E,M

M

W. 52nd St.

W. 51st St.

Radio City
Music
Hall

Top of
the Rock

Rockefeller Center

C,E

M

1

M

W. 50th St.

The Rink at
Rockefeller Center ✕

HELL'S
KITCHEN

M

W. 49th St.

Blue Bottle
Coffee

N,Q,R

M

W. 48th St.

B,D,F,M

M

Christie's

W. 47th St.

Restaurant Row

W. 46th St.

← ◆ **Intrepid** Sea, Air and
Space Museum

W. 45th St.

W. 44th St.

TKTS
booth

TIMES
SQUARE

W. 43rd St.

Times
Square

Madame
Tussaud's
New York

B,D,F,M

M

A,C,E

M

W. 42nd St.

7

M

N,Q,R,S
1,2,3,7

M

Fifth Ave.

W. 41st St.

Bryant
Park

New York Public
Library (NYPL)
Main Branch:
Stephen A.
Schwarzman
Building

The New York Times
Building ◆

W. 40th St.

W. 39th St.

✕ Café Grumpy

W. 38th St.

0 _____ 1/4 mi

0 _____ 1/4 km

W. 37th St.

MAKING THE MOST OF YOUR TIME

Most people think of Times Square when they think of Midtown, but there's a lot more going on here. The Museum of Modern Art (MoMA) is one of the neighborhood's top attractions and definitely worth a visit, as is Bryant Park, a cool oasis for Midtown's workers and locals. If you have enough time, hop in a cab and head over to 12th Avenue to visit the space shuttle *Enterprise* at the *Intrepid* Sea, Air & Space Museum.

Times Square is almost always a frenetic mass of people, staring up at the lights and the giant televisions. If you're in a hurry to get somewhere, try to avoid walking—or cabbing—through here. If staying in Midtown, you can take advantage of the prime location and rise early to be first in line at landmarks, museums, or the TKTS booth for discount day-of theater tickets (⇨ *Chapter 20: Performing Arts*).

TOP EXPERIENCES

Summer film screenings at dusk in Bryant Park

Skating at Rockefeller Center

Checking out the views from the Top of the Rock; opinions vary on whether the better views are from here or from the Empire State Building. Either way, if you go at night, the city spreads out below in a mesmerizing blanket of lights.

Soaking in the art and serenity of MoMA's sculpture garden

GETTING HERE

You can get to Midtown via (almost) all the subways; many make numerous stops throughout the area. For Midtown West, the 1, 2, 3, 7, A, C, E, N, Q, and R serve Times Square and West 42nd Street. The S, or Shuttle, travels back and forth between Times Square and Grand Central Station. The B, D, F, and M trains serve Rockefeller Center.

COFFEE AND QUICK BITES

Blue Bottle Coffee. Known for their meticulous brewing, freshly roasted organic beans (prepared in a Brooklyn roastery), and delicious treats and pastries (also rushed in fresh from Brooklyn), the Rock Center outpost of this cult California coffee favorite is the perfect refueling spot amid the chaos of Midtown. ✉ *1 Rockefeller Plaza, Concourse level, Midtown West* ☎ *510/653-3394* ⊕ *www. bluebottlecoffee.com/cafes/ rockefeller-center* Ⓜ *B, D, F, M to 47–50th Sts./Rockefeller Center; E, M to 5th Ave./53rd St.*

Café Grumpy. Stop by this Garment District outlet of the New York minichain and turn any sign of grumpiness into a smile with coffee roasted at the Greenpoint, Brooklyn, location. All pastries are baked at the Lower East Side branch: the black pepper and cardamom banana bread is a standout. ✉ *200 W. 39th St., Midtown West* ☎ *646/499-8749* ⊕ *www. cafegrumpy.com* ⊟ *No credit cards* Ⓜ *1, 2, 3, 7, N, Q, R, S to Times Sq.–42nd St.*

Zibetto Espresso Bar. You won't find any seats, but you will find arguably the best espresso in New York. ✉ *1385 6th Ave., at 56th St., Midtown West* ⊕ *www.zibettoespressobar.com* Ⓜ *F to 57th St.*

9

Sightseeing
★★★★★

Nightlife
★★★

Dining
★★★★★

Lodging
★★★★★

Shopping
★★★★★

Big is the buzz in Times Square, where giant TV screens, towering skyscrapers, and Broadway theaters play starring roles alongside megastores like Hershey's and Toys "R" Us. Love it or hate it, Times Square is the flashy and flashing heart of Midtown. A visit to New York demands a photo op in Times Square. Just don't forget that there's also a lot more to see and experience on this side of Midtown.

Updated
by Jacinta
O'Halloran

Luckily, you needn't go far from Times Square to get away from the crowds. Head over to 9th Avenue—also known as Hell's Kitchen (where the food is heavenly)—and calmer side streets, home to a mixed bag of locals, many of whom work in the theater industry. There are lots of eclectic restaurants, pre-theater dining options, and cute boutiques for shopping. Head over to the Avenue of the Americas (6th Avenue), and discover Bryant Park's zen green space, stretched out like a yoga mat at the backdoor of the New York Public Library (another refuge from Midtown madness).

You can score good seats to some of the hottest Broadway and Off-Broadway shows for half the going rate at the TKTS booth in Duffy Square at 47th Street and Broadway (⇨ *Performing Arts*). Although people think of Broadway as the heart of the theater scene, few theaters actually line the thoroughfare. For some of the grandes dames, head west on 45th Street. There are several Broadway beauties here, including the **Booth,** the **Schoenfeld,** the **Jacobs,** the **Music Box,** and the **Imperial.** On the southern side of 45th Street there's the pedestrians-only **Shubert Alley,** distinguished by colorful posters advertising the latest hit plays and musicals, and the **Shubert Theatre,** one of Broadway's most lustrous gems. Head west along 44th Street to see the **Helen Hayes,** the **Broadhurst,** the **Majestic,** and the **St. James.**

You might be surprised to learn that Chelsea is not the only gallery hub in the city; 57th Street between 5th and 6th avenues is home to some of the city's most prestigious galleries, including Marian Goodman, the Pace Gallery, and Tibor de Nagy Gallery.

TOP ATTRACTIONS

FAMILY **Bryant Park.** This lovely green space spread out among landmarks and skyscrapers is one of Manhattan's most popular parks. Tall London plane trees line the perimeter of the sunny central lawn, overlooking stone terraces, formal flower beds, gravel pathways, and a smattering of kiosks selling everything from sandwiches to egg creams (in season). The garden tables scattered about fill with lunching office workers and folks enjoying the park's free Wi-Fi (signs show you how to log on). In summer you can check out free live jazz and "Broadway in Bryant Park" musical theater performances, as well as author readings. Most popular of all is the Summer Film Festival: locals leave work early to snag a spot on the lawn for the outdoor screenings each Monday at dusk. At the east side of the park, near a squatting bronze cast of Gertrude Stein, is the stylish Bryant Park Grill, which has a rooftop garden, and the adjacent open-air Bryant Park Café, open seasonally. The 5th Avenue terrace is home to a different food truck at lunchtime every day during the week. On the south side of the park is an old-fashioned carousel ($3) where kids can ride fanciful rabbits and frogs instead of horses, and attend storytellings and magic shows. Big kids can play with the park's selection of lawn and tabletop games, which includes everything from Quoits and Scrabble to Chinese Checkers and Scandinavian Kubb. Come November the park rolls out the artificial frozen "pond" (*Nov.–Mar., daily 8 am–10 pm; skate rental $15–$19*) for ice skating. Surrounding the ice rink are the Christmas market–like stalls of the Holiday Shops, selling handcrafted goods and local foods. ⊠ *6th Ave. between 40th and 42nd sts., Midtown West* ☎ *212/768–4242* ⊕ *www. bryantpark.org* ⊗ *Hrs vary by month; see website for exact times* Ⓜ *B, D, F, M to 42nd St.–Bryant Park; 7 to 5th Ave.*

FAMILY **Intrepid Sea, Air & Space Museum.** The centerpiece of the *Intrepid* Sea, Air & Space Museum complex is the 900-foot *Intrepid* aircraft carrier, Manhattan's only floating museum. The carrier's most trying moment of service, the day it was attacked in World War II by kamikaze pilots, is recounted in a multimedia presentation. The museum faced its own trying period when forced to close for several months due to extensive flooding after 2012's Superstorm Sandy. Fortunately, the *Intrepid*'s unparalleled collection of aircraft was not damaged in the storm. The museum reopened in late December 2012 with a reinforced home for the space shuttle *Enterprise*, NASA's first prototype orbiter, which joined the Intrepid in July 2012. *Enterprise* is temporarily housed in a climate-controlled bubble tent on the flight deck of the *Intrepid,* but visitors can check out plans for its eventual permanent home, on the interactive wall outside the Space Shuttle Pavilion. While *Enterprise* never flew in space, it is presented in a dramatic darkened display with blue lighting to evoke the atmosphere of flight. Images and displays share the shuttle's history and that of NASA's 30-year space shuttle program.

The interactive Exploreum contains 18 hands-on exhibits. You can experience a flight simulator, transmit messages in Morse code, and see what it was like to live aboard the massive carrier. Docked alongside the *Intrepid*, and also part of the museum, is the *Growler*, a strategic-missile submarine. Ticket booths and gift shops have been relocated to the museum's plaza while the visitor Welcome Center is being rebuilt. ■TIP→ **Before you visit, download the Intrepid's new, free Explore Enterprise app to unlock additional trivia, history, and behind-the-scenes video at trigger points in exhibits throughout the museum. There are also frequent ticket discounts if you purchase through the museum website.** ✉ *Pier 86, 12th Ave. at 46th St., Midtown West* ☎ *212/245–0072, 877/957–7447* ⊕ *www.intrepidmuseum.org* ☞ *$24; $31 combo ticket with Space Shuttle* ☉ *Apr.–Oct., weekdays 10–5, weekends 10–6; Nov.–Mar., daily 10–5; last admission 1 hr before closing* Ⓜ *A, C, E to 42nd St.–Port Authority.*

Radio City Music Hall. ⇨ *See the listing in Chapter 20: Performing Arts.*

Rockefeller Center. If Times Square is New York's crossroads, Rockefeller Center is its communal gathering place, where the entire world converges to snap pictures, skate on the ice rink, peek in on a taping of the *Today* show, shop, eat, and take in the monumental Art Deco structures and public sculptures from the past century. Totaling more than 100 shops and 50 eateries (including Thomas Keller's Bouchon Bakery), the complex runs from 47th to 52nd streets between 5th and 7th avenues. Special events and huge pieces of art dominate the central plazas in spring and summer. In December an enormous twinkling tree towers above the ice-skating rink, causing huge crowds of visitors from across the country and the globe to shuffle through with necks craned and cameras flashing. The first official tree-lighting ceremony was held in 1933.

The world's most famous ice-skating rink *(The Rink at Rockefeller Center)* occupies Rockefeller Center's sunken lower plaza October through April and converts to a café in summer. The gold-leaf statue of the fire-stealing Greek hero Prometheus—Rockefeller Center's most famous sculpture—hovers above, forming the backdrop to zillions of photos. Carved into the wall behind it, a quotation from Aeschylus reads, "Prometheus, teacher in every art, brought the fire that hath proved to mortals a means to mighty ends." The lower plaza also provides access to the marble-lined corridors underneath Rockefeller Center, which houses restaurants, a post office, and clean public restrooms—a rarity in Midtown.

Rising from the Lower Plaza's west side is the 70-story (850-foot-tall) Art Deco GE Building, a testament to modern urban development. Here Rockefeller commissioned and then destroyed a mural by Diego Rivera (upon learning that it featured Vladimir Lenin). He replaced it with the monumental *American Progress* by José María Sert, still on view in the lobby, flanked by additional murals by Sert and English artist Frank Brangwyn. Up on the 65th floor is the landmark Rainbow Room, a glittering big-band ballroom dating to 1934; they serve a showy and very expensive brunch on Sunday, and dinner and entertainment on Monday nights. Higher up, Top of the Rock has what many consider the finest panoramic views of the city. ✉ *30 Rockefeller Plaza, Midtown West* ⊕ *www.rockefellercenter.com* Ⓜ *B, D, F, M to 47th–50th Sts./Rockefeller Center; E, M to 5th Ave./53rd St.*

The iconic marquee at Radio City Music Hall

FAMILY **The Rink at Rockefeller Center.** Set in the shadow of the giant Rockefeller Center Christmas Tree, the city's most iconic ice-skating rink is a quintessential experience for visitors and a longstanding tradition for many locals. Skaters swoop or stumble across the ice while crowds gather at street level to watch the spins and spills. General admission skating is on a first-come, first-served basis, so it is best to come early, and on weekdays, to avoid crowds. First Skate tickets ($45–$55, reserved online) allow 7 am access to the rink, followed by a complimentary hot chocolate/coffee and pastry or breakfast. VIP Skate packages ($60–$120) allow guests to skate past the long lines and include skate rental, 90 minutes of ice time, and hot chocolate and cookies. Other packages include Sky Skate ($48), which includes admission to the rink, skate rental, and admission to the Top of the Rock Observation Deck; and Engagement on Ice packages ($350–$1,000), which provide exclusive ice time, a romantic backdrop, and a variety of romantic add-ons to seal the deal. The rink is a café in summer. ⊠ *30 Rockefeller Plaza, Midtown West* ⊕ *www.therinkatrockcenter.com* ⊡ *$27–$30; $12 skate rental* ⊙ *Oct.–Apr., daily 8:30 am–midnight* Ⓜ *B, D, F, M to 47th–50th Sts./ Rockefeller Center; E, M to 5th Ave./53rd St.*

Times Square. Hands down, this is the most frenetic part of New York City, a cacophony of flashing lights and shoulder-to-shoulder crowds that many New Yorkers studiously avoid. Originally named after the *New York Times* (whose headquarters have since relocated nearby), the area has seen many changes since the first subway line, which included a 42nd Street station, opened in 1904. You won't find speakeasies and unsavory clubs around here nowadays; it's a vibrant, family-friendly

Ice-skating under the sculpture of Prometheus, at Rockefeller Center, is a winter ritual for many local and visiting families.

destination, with a newly resurfaced pedestrianized stretch of Broadway with granite benches, and stadium seating behind discount theater ticket seller TKTS, all under the glare of brand names like MTV and M&Ms. If you like sensory overload, the chaotic mix of huge underwear billboards, flashing digital displays, on-location television broadcasts, naked cowboys, and Elmo clones will give you your fix. The focus of the entertainment may have shifted over the years, but showtime is still the heart of New York's theater scene, and there are forty Broadway theaters nearby. The Times Square Visitor Center closed its doors in 2014 but you can still learn about Broadway's history and architecture with a 90-minute walking tour ($30) of the area by Manhattan Walking Tours; the guided Broadway Walking tour (*daily at 9:30, 11:30, and 2; www.walkinbroadway.com*) includes audio headsets and 30 stops, and leaves from the Actor's Chapel on West 49th Street, between Broadway and 8th Avenue. ⊠ *Broadway between 42nd and 44th sts., Midtown West* ☎ *212/768–1560* ⊕ *www.timessquarenyc.org* Ⓜ *1, 2, 3, 7, N, Q, R, S to Times Sq.–42 St.*

Fodor's Choice **Top of the Rock.** Rockefeller Center's multifloor observation deck, the
★ Top of the Rock, on the 69th and 70th floors of the building, provides views that rival those from the Empire State Building (some would say they're even better because the views include the Empire State Building). Arriving just before sunset affords a view of the city that morphs before your eyes into a dazzling wash of colors, with a bird's-eye view of the tops of the Empire State Building, the Citicorp Building, and the Chrysler Building, and sweeping views northward to Central Park and south to the Statue of Liberty. Timed-entry ticketing eliminates long

Art in Rockefeller Center

Art and Office Space

The mosaics, murals, and sculptures that grace Rockefeller Center—many of them Art Deco masterpieces—were part of John D. Rockefeller Jr.'s plans. In 1932, as the steel girders on the first of the buildings soared heavenward, he put together a team of advisers to find artists who could make the project "as beautiful as possible." Some artists scoffed at the idea of decorating an office building: Picasso declined to meet with Rockefeller, and Matisse replied that busy businessmen wouldn't be in the "quiet and reflective state of mind" needed to appreciate his art. Those who agreed to contribute, including muralists Diego Rivera and José María Sert, were relatively unknown, though a group of American artists protested Rockefeller's decision to hire "alien" artists. More than 50 artists were commissioned for 200 works.

Controversy and Highlights

As Rockefeller Center neared completion in 1932, Rockefeller still needed a mural for the lobby of the main buildings and he wanted the subject to be grandiose: "human intelligence in control of the forces of nature." He hired Rivera. *Man at the Crossroads*, with its depiction of massive machinery moving mankind forward, seemed exactly what Rockefeller wanted—until it was realized that a portrait of Soviet Premier Vladimir Lenin surrounded by red-kerchiefed workers occupied a space in the center. Rockefeller, who was building what was essentially a monument to capitalism, was less than thrilled. When Rivera was accused of propagandizing, he famously replied, "All art is propaganda."

Rivera refused to remove the offending portrait and, in early 1934, as Rivera was working, representatives for Rockefeller informed him that his services were no longer required. Within a half hour, tar paper had been hung over the mural. Despite negotiations to move it to the Museum of Modern Art, Rockefeller was determined to get rid of the mural once and for all. Not content to have it painted over, he ordered ax-wielding workers to chip away the entire wall. He commissioned a less offensive one (by Sert) instead.

Rivera had the last word, though: he re-created the mural in the Palacio de Bellas Artes in Mexico City, adding a portrait of Rockefeller among the Champagne-swilling swells ignoring the plight of the workers.

The largest of the original artworks that remains is Lee Lawrie's two-ton sculpture, *Atlas*. Its building also stirred up controversy, as it was said to resemble Italy's fascist dictator, Benito Mussolini. The sculpture, depicting a muscle-bound man holding up the world, drew protests in 1936. Some even derided Paul Manship's golden *Prometheus*, which soars over the ice-skating rink, when it was unveiled the same year. Both are now considered to be among the best public artworks of the 20th century.

Lawrie's sculpture *Wisdom*, over the main entrance of 20 Rockefeller Plaza, is another gem. Also look for Isamu Noguchi's stainless-steel plaque *News* over the entrance of the Bank of America Building at 50 Rockefeller Plaza and Attilio Piccirilli's 2-ton glass-block panel *Youth Leading Industry* over the entrance of the International Building.

9

lines. Indoor exhibits include films of Rockefeller Center's history and a model of the building. Glass elevators lift you to the 67th-floor interior viewing area, and then an escalator leads to the outdoor deck on the 69th floor for sightseeing through nonreflective glass safety panels. Then, take another elevator or stairs to the 70th floor for a 360-degree outdoor panorama of New York City on a deck that is only 20 feet wide and nearly 200 feet long. Especially interesting is a Plexiglas screen on the floor with footage showing Rock Center construction workers dangling on beams high above the streets; the brave can even "walk" across a beam to get a sense of what it might have been like to erect this skyscraper. A Sun & Stars ticket ($42) allows you to visit twice and see the city as it rises and sets in the same day. ⊠ *30 Rock-efeller Plaza, 50th St. entrance, between 5th and 6th aves., Midtown West* 🕾 *212/698–2000, 212/698–2000* ⊕ *www.topoftherocknyc.com* ⊠ *$29* ⊙ *Daily 8–midnight; last elevator at 11 pm* Ⓜ *B, D, F, M to 47th–50th Sts./Rockefeller Center; E, M to 5th Ave./53rd St.*

WORTH NOTING

Christie's. One of the first items to be auctioned at the New York outpost of this infamous auction house, when it opened in 2000, was the "Happy Birthday" dress worn by Marilyn Monroe when she sang to President Kennedy (it sold for more than $1.2 million, in case you were wondering). Yes, the auction house has come a long way since James Christie launched his business in England by selling two chamber pots, among other household goods, in 1766. You could easily spend an hour or more wandering the free, museumlike galleries, where on any given day, you find impressive works of art, estate jewelry, furniture, and other rarely displayed letters and objects of interest that are usually housed in (and most likely, soon to be returned to) private collections. The lobby's specially commissioned abstract Sol LeWitt mural alone makes it worth visiting the 310,000-square-foot space. Hours vary by sale, so call ahead to confirm. ⊠ *20 Rockefeller Plaza, 49th St. between 5th and 6th aves., Midtown West* 🕾 *212/636–2000* ⊕ *www. christies.com* ⊙ *Weekdays 9:30–5, weekend hrs vary; hrs vary for specific exhibits* Ⓜ *B, D, F, M to 47th–50th Sts./Rockefeller Center; E, M to 5th Ave./53rd St.*

David Findlay Jr. Gallery. This well-established gallery concentrates on contemporary and 20th-century American artists from Whistler to Herman Cherry, Byron Brown, and David Aronson, and specializes in the New York School. ⊠ *724 5th Ave., 8th fl., between 56th and 57th sts., Midtown West* 🕾 *212/486–7660* ⊕ *www.davidfindlayjr.com* ⊠ *Free* ⊙ *Mon.–Sat. 10–5:30* Ⓜ *N, Q, R to 5th Ave./59th St.*

Hirschl & Adler Galleries. Although this gallery has a selection of European works, it's best known for American paintings, prints, and decorative arts. The celebrated 19th- and 20th-century artists whose works are featured include Stuart Davis, Childe Hassam, Camille Pissarro, and John Singleton Copley. Each year, the gallery presents up to a dozen special exhibits exploring historical themes of works culled from its collection. ⊠ *730 5th Ave., 4th fl., at 57th St., Midtown West* 🕾 *212/535–8810* ⊕ *www.hirschlandadler.com* ⊠ *Free* ⊙ *Tues.–Fri. 9:30–5:15, Sat. 9:30–4:45* Ⓜ *N, Q, R to 5th Ave./59th St.*

FAMILY **Madame Tussauds New York.** Sit in the Oval Office with President Obama, strike a fierce pose alongside *Hunger Games* heroine Katniss Everdeen, croon with Lady Gaga and Taylor Swift, pucker up to your favorite heartthrob, be it Justin Bieber or Justin Timberlake, or enjoy a royal chat with the Duke and Duchess of Cambridge, William and Kate. Much of the fun here comes from photo opportunities—you're encouraged to pose with and touch the over 200 realistic replicas of the famous, infamous, and downright super. The Marvel 4D Experience includes wax likenesses of heroes like the Hulk, Captain America, Ironman, and Thor, as well as a short animated movie shown on a 360-degree screen that surrounds the viewer. Other interactive options at the museum include a karaoke café, a celebrity walk down the red carpet, and a haunted town populated with both wax figures and real people. Closing hours vary during peak seasons, so call ahead to verify. ⊠ *234 W. 42nd St., between 7th and 8th aves., Midtown West* ☎ *866/841–3505* ⊕ *www.madametussauds.com* ✉ *$37 (discounts available online)* ☾ *Sun.–Thurs. 10–8, Fri. and Sat. 10–10* Ⓜ *1, 2, 3, 7, N, Q, R, S to Times Sq.–42nd St.; A, C, E to 42nd St.–Port Authority.*

Marian Goodman Gallery. Perhaps the most respected contemporary art dealer in town, the Marian Goodman Gallery has been introducing top European artists to American audiences for over thirty years. The stable of excellent contemporary artists in the Goodman fold includes Gerhard Richter, Jeff Wall, John Baldessari, William Kentridge, Thomas Schutte, and Steve McQueen. ⊠ *24 W. 57th St., between 5th and 6th aves., Midtown West* ☎ *212/977–7160* ⊕ *www.mariangoodman.com* ✉ *Free* ☾ *Mon.–Sat. 10–6* Ⓜ *F to 57th St.*

Marlborough Gallery (Midtown). The Marlborough Gallery has an international reputation, representing modern artists such as Magdalena Abakanowicz, Zao Wou-Ki, Red Grooms, and photorealist Richard Estes. Look for sculptures by Tom Otterness, whose whimsical bronzes are found in several subway stations. There is also a branch in Chelsea. ⊠ *40 W. 57th St., between 5th and 6th aves., Midtown West* ☎ *212/541–4900* ⊕ *www.marlboroughgallery.com* ✉ *Free* ☾ *Mon.–Sat. 10–5:30* Ⓜ *F to 57th St.*

New York Public Library Main Branch. In 2011 the "Library with the Lions" celebrated its centennial as a masterpiece of Beaux Arts design and as one of the great research institutions in the world, with more than 6 million books, 12 million manuscripts, and 3 million pictures. Expect changes, if not to the look, then to the feel, of the building as it attempts to become more welcoming and useful without selling its soul. The marble staircase at the library's grand 5th Avenue entrance is an excellent perch for people-watching, before or after you explore the opulent interior.

The library's bronze front doors open into Astor Hall, which leads to several special exhibit galleries and, to the left, a stunning periodicals room with wall paintings of New York publishing houses. Ascend the sweeping double staircase to a second-floor balconied corridor overlooking the hall, with panels highlighting the library's development. Make sure to continue up to the recently restored, magisterial Rose

THE MUSEUM OF MODERN ART (MOMA)

✉ *11 W. 53rd St., between 5th and 6th aves., Midtown West* ☎ *212/708–9400* ⊕ *www. moma.org* 💲 *$25* ⊙ *Sat.– Thurs. 10:30–5:30, Fri. 10:30–8* Ⓜ *E, M to 5th Ave./53rd St.; F to 57th St.; B, D, E to 7th Ave.*

TIPS

■ MoMA's Audio+ app allows visitors to listen to audio commentaries and access, share, and save additional content. Audio+ iPods can be rented at the museum, or the app can be downloaded from MoMA's website.

■ Tickets are available online (www.moma.org) at a reduced price. Entrance between 4 and 8 pm on Friday is free, but expect long lines. Free Wi-Fi service within the museum allows you to listen to audio tours (log on to www.moma.org/wifi with your smartphone).

■ Film passes to the day's screenings are included with the price of admission. Tickets to MoMA also include free admission to its affiliate PS1 in Queens; save your ticket and you can go in for free any time within 30 days of your original purchase.

■ Grab a quick bite at one of MoMA's two cafés—Cafe 2 and Terrace 5, or dine leisurely at the upscale Modern. In summer there is gelato in the Sculpture Garden.

Art enthusiasts and novices alike are often awestruck by the masterpieces they find at the MoMA, including Picasso's *Les Demoiselles d'Avignon* and Van Gogh's *Starry Night.* Plans for an expansion into the space next door (which, controversially, meant tearing down the American Folk Art Museum) include additional gallery space, a retractable glass wall, an expanded lobby, and the opening of its entire first floor, including the sculpture garden, as a free public space. Construction is already underway with an expected completion date in 2019.

Highlights

In addition to the artwork, one of the main draws of MoMA is the building itself. A maze of glass walkways permits art viewing from many angles.

The 110-foot atrium entrance (accessed from the museum's lobby on either 53rd or 54th Street) leads to movie theaters and the main-floor restaurant, Modern, with Alsatian-inspired cuisine.

A favorite resting spot is the Abby Aldrich Rockefeller Sculpture Garden. Designed by Philip Johnson, it features Barnett Newman's *Broken Obelisk* (1962–69). The glass wall lets visitors look directly into the surrounding galleries from the garden, where there's also a reflecting pool and trees.

Contemporary art (1970 to the present) from the museum's seven curatorial departments shares the second floor of the six-story building, and the skylighted top floor showcases an impressive lineup of changing exhibits.

Main Reading Room—297 feet long (almost two full north–south city blocks), 78 feet wide, and just over 51 feet high; walk through to best appreciate the rows of oak tables and the extraordinary ceiling. Several additional third-floor galleries show rotating exhibits on print and photography (past exhibits have included old New York restaurant menus and a 1455 Gutenberg Bible). Free hour-long tours leave Monday–Saturday at 11 and 2, and Sunday at 2 from Astor Hall. Women's bathrooms are on the ground floor and third floor, and there's a men's bathroom on the third floor. ⊠ *5th Ave., between 40th and 42nd sts., Midtown West* ☏ *212/930–0800 for exhibit info* ⊕ *www.nypl.org* ⊗ *Mon. and Thurs.–Sat. 10–6, Sun. 1–5, Tues. and Wed. 10–8; exhibitions until 6* Ⓜ *B, D, F, M to 42nd St.–Bryant Park; 7 to 5th Ave.*

The New York Times Building. This 52-story building with its distinctive, ladderlike ceramic rods is a testament to clean-lined modernism. The architect, Renzo Piano, extended the ceramic rods beyond the top of the building so that it would give the impression of dissolving into the sky. One of the skyscraper's best features—and the one that's open to the public—is the building's lobby atrium, which includes an open-air moss garden with 50-foot paper birch trees and a wooden footbridge; a 560-screen media art installation titled *Moveable Type*, streaming a mix of the newspaper's near–real time and archival content; and the New York flagship store of minimalist home goods designer MUJI. You never know which famous journalists you'll spy on the coffee line in Dean & DeLuca. Unfortunately, tours are not offered. ⊠ *620 8th Ave., between 40th and 41st sts., Midtown West* ☏ *212/984–8128* ⊕ *www. newyorktimesbuilding.com* Ⓜ *A, C, E to 42nd St.–Port Authority; 1, 2, 3, 7, N, Q, R, S to Times Sq.–42nd St.*

The Paley Center for Media. With three galleries of photographs and artifacts that document the history of broadcasting, a computerized catalog of more than 150,000 television and radio programs, and public seminars, lectures, and programs, the Paley Center for Media examines the past and constantly evolving present state of media. The past is the main draw here. If you want to see a performance of "Turkey Lurkey Time" from the 1969 Tony Awards, for example, type the name of the song, show, or performer into a computer terminal, then proceed to one of the semiprivate screening areas to watch your selection. People nearby might be watching classic comedies from the '50s, miniseries from the '70s, or news broadcasts from the '90s. Possibly the most entertaining part of these TV shows from yesteryear is the fact that the original commercials are still embedded in many of the programs. If ads are your thing, you can also skip the programming altogether and watch compilations of classic commercials. ⊠ *25 W. 52nd St., between 5th and 6th aves., Midtown West* ☏ *212/621–6800* ⊕ *www.paleycenter.org* ⌑ *$10* ⊗ *Wed., Fri., and weekends noon–6, Thurs. noon–8* Ⓜ *E, M to 5th Ave./53rd St.; B, D, F, M to 47th–50th Sts./Rockefeller Center.*

9

Tibor de Nagy Gallery. Founded in 1950, this gallery shows works by 20th-century artists such as Biala, Nell Blaine, Jane Freilicher, and Shirley Jaffe. Instrumental in bringing many of America's finest abstract expressionist artists to public attention in the mid-20th century, the gallery now shows abstract and realistic work. ⊠ *724 5th Ave., 12th fl., between 56th and 57th sts., Midtown West* ☎ *212/262–5050* ⊕ *www.tibordenagy.com* ☉ *Tues.–Sat. 10–5:30* Ⓜ *N, Q, R to 5th Ave./59th St.*

THE UPPER
EAST SIDE

GETTING ORIENTED

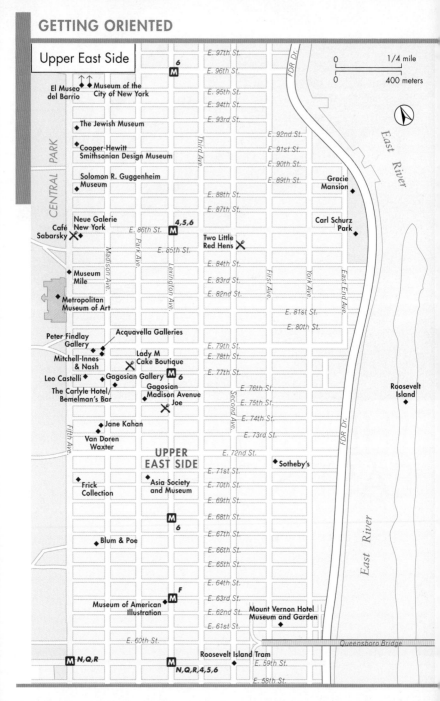

Upper East Side

0   1/4 mile
0   400 meters

El Museo del Barrio
Museum of the City of New York
The Jewish Museum
Cooper-Hewitt Smithsonian Design Museum
Solomon R. Guggenheim Museum
Neue Galerie New York
Café Sabarsky
Museum Mile
Metropolitan Museum of Art
Peter Findlay Gallery
Acquavella Galleries
Mitchell-Innes & Nash
Lady M Cake Boutique
Leo Castelli
Gagosian Gallery
The Carlyle Hotel/ Bemelman's Bar
Gagosian Madison Avenue
Joe
Jane Kahan
Van Doren Waxter
Frick Collection
Asia Society and Museum
Blum & Poe
Museum of American Illustration

CENTRAL PARK
Madison Ave.
Park Ave.
Fifth Ave.
Lexington Ave.
Third Ave.
Second Ave.
First Ave.
York Ave.
East End Ave.
FDR Dr.

E. 97th St.
E. 96th St.
E. 95th St.
E. 94th St.
E. 93rd St.
E. 92nd St.
E. 91st St.
E. 90th St.
E. 89th St.
E. 88th St.
E. 87th St.
E. 86th St.
E. 85th St.
E. 84th St.
E. 83rd St.
E. 82nd St.
E. 81st St.
E. 80th St.
E. 79th St.
E. 78th St.
E. 77th St.
E. 76th St.
E. 75th St.
E. 74th St.
E. 73rd St.
E. 72nd St.
E. 71st St.
E. 70th St.
E. 69th St.
E. 68th St.
E. 67th St.
E. 66th St.
E. 65th St.
E. 64th St.
E. 63rd St.
E. 62nd St.
E. 61st St.
E. 60th St.
E. 59th St.
E. 58th St.

Gracie Mansion
Carl Schurz Park
Two Little Red Hens

UPPER EAST SIDE

Sotheby's
Roosevelt Island
Mount Vernon Hotel Museum and Garden
Queensboro Bridge
Roosevelt Island Tram

East River

N,Q,R
N,Q,R,4,5,6

F
6
4,5,6
6
6

MAKING THE MOST OF YOUR TIME

The Upper East Side lends itself to a surprising variety of simple but distinct itineraries: exploring the landmarks on Museum Mile; languorous gallery grazing; window shopping on Madison Avenue; or bar hopping for just-out-of-college kids on 2nd Avenue. If it's the museums you're after, make sure to plan at least a few hours per museum—with some snack or coffee breaks. There's a lot to see, so we advise not more than one museum a day.

The Upper East Side's townhouses, boutiques, consignment stores, and hidden gardens are easy to miss unless you take some time to wander. If all that walking wears you out, you can always recharge in one of the nail salons and indulge in a neighborhood stereotype of the pampered Upper East Sider. A well-deserved post–Museum Mile foot rub and mani/pedi are surprisingly reasonably priced.

GETTING HERE

Take the Lexington Avenue 4 or 5 express train to 59th or 86th Street. The 6 local train also stops at 59th, 68th, 77th, 86th, and 96th streets. If coming from Midtown, the F train lets you out at Lexington Avenue at 63rd Street, where you can transfer to the 4, 5, or 6 after a short walk (and free transfer). From the Upper West Side, take one of the crosstown buses, the M66, M72, M79, M86, or M96. You can also take the N or R train to 59th Street and Lexington Avenue.

TOP EXPERIENCES

Exploring any of the world-class museums here, followed by a relaxing, restorative lunch

Gallery-hopping the UES's so-unhip-it's-now-hip art scene (plus they're free)

Window-shopping on Madison Avenue

Appreciating the views from the cable car on the ride to the recently opened Four Freedoms Park on Roosevelt Island

COFFEE AND QUICK BITES

Joe (Upper East Side). One of the city's best coffee chains, Joe has the kind of quality caffeine and sweets to fuel you up and down Museum Mile (and maybe even around the park). ⊠ *1045 Lexington Ave., between 74th and 75th sts., Upper East Side* ☎ *212/988–2500* ⊕ *www.joenewyork.com/locations/lexington* Ⓜ *6 to 77th St.*

Lady M Cake Boutique. The signature here is the Mille Crepes cake: twenty crêpes stacked together with a delicious cream filling. Thank us later. ⊠ *41 E. 78th St., at Madison Ave., Upper East Side* ☎ *212/452–2222* ⊕ *www.ladym.com* Ⓜ *6 to 77th St.*

Two Little Red Hens. With first-rate coffee and delicious cupcakes, cheesecake, and cookies to match, this little bakery is a legend with locals. ⊠ *1652 2nd Ave., at 86th St., Upper East Side* ☎ *212/452–0476* ⊕ *www.twolittleredhens.com* Ⓜ *4, 5, 6 to 86th St.*

10

Sightseeing
★★★
Nightlife
★
Dining
★★
Lodging
★★
Shopping
★★★★

To many New Yorkers, the Upper East Side connotes old money and high society. Alongside Central Park, between 5th and Lexington avenues, up to East 96th Street, the trappings of wealth are everywhere apparent: posh buildings, Madison Avenue's flagship boutiques, and doormen in braided livery. It's also a key destination for visitors, because some of the most fantastic museums in the country are here.

Updated
by Jacinta
O'Halloran

There's a reason this stretch of Manhattan is called "Museum Mile": this is where you'll find the **Metropolitan Museum of Art**, the **Solomon R. Guggenheim Museum**, the **Cooper Hewitt, Smithsonian Design Museum**, as well as a number of art galleries. For a local taste of the luxe life, catwalk down Madison Avenue for its lavish boutiques; strolling the platinum-card corridor between 60th and 82nd street is like stepping into the pages of a glossy magazine. Many fashion houses have their flagships here and showcase their lush threads in exquisite settings.

Venture east of Lexington Avenue and encounter a less wealthy—and more diverse—Upper East Side, inhabited by couples seeking some of the last (relatively) affordable places to raise a family south of 100th Street, as well as recent college grads getting a foothold in the city (on weekend nights 2nd Avenue resembles a miles-long fraternity and sorority reunion). One neighborhood particularly worth exploring is northeast-lying Yorkville, especially between 78th and 86th streets east of 2nd Avenue. Once a remote hamlet with a large German population, its several remaining ethnic food shops, 19th-century rowhouses, and—one of the city's best-kept secrets—**Carl Schurz Park,** make for a good half-day's exploration, as does catching a glimpse of the most striking residence there, **Gracie Mansion.**

If art galleries appeal, there are some elegant ones on the Upper East Side. In keeping with the tony surroundings, the emphasis here is on works by established masters.

TOP ATTRACTIONS

Asia Society and Museum. The Asian art collection of Mr. and Mrs. John D. Rockefeller III forms the core of this museum's holdings, which span from Pakistan to Java and date back to the 11th century BC, including Hindu stone sculpture, Tibetan Buddhist paintings, Vietnamese ceramics, Han Dynasty bronzes, and Japanese woodblock prints. Founded in 1956, the society has a regular program of lectures, films, and performances, in addition to changing exhibitions of traditional and contemporary art. Trees grow in the glass-enclosed, skylighted Garden Court Café, which serves an eclectic Asian lunch menu and weekend brunch. Call ahead to reserve afternoon tea service, available 2–5 pm. Admission is free Friday 6–9 pm (September to July). A free audio tour is included with admission, or you can take a free guided tour at 2 daily and 6:30 Friday. ⊠ *725 Park Ave., at 70th St., Upper East Side* ☎ *212/288–6400* ⊕ *www.asiasociety.org/ny* 🎟 *$12* ☉ *Tues.–Sun. 11–6 (Fri. until 9 Sept.–June)* Ⓜ *6 to 68th St.–Hunter College.*

Blum & Poe New York. This contemporary art gallery may be a relative newbie on the Upper East Side art scene (it opened in Spring 2014), but as one of L.A.'s top art galleries, Blum & Poe was very quick to settle into its renovated townhouse on East 66th Street—a cozy space compared to its sprawling, 21,000-square-foot L.A. counterpart—and to establish itself in the New York art world. Recent exhibits have featured artists including Hugh Scott-Douglas, Kishio Suga, Henry Taylor, and Penny Slinger. ⊠ *19 E. 66th St., at 5th Ave., Upper East Side* ☎ *212/249–2249* ⊕ *www.blumandpoe.com* ☉ *Tues.–Sat. 10–6* Ⓜ *6 to 68th St.–Hunter College.*

Cooper Hewitt, Smithsonian Design Museum. Reopened in late 2014, after a three-year, $81 million overhaul, the Cooper Hewitt, Smithsonian Design Museum is a slick, 21st-century museum in a century-old mansion. It marries old and new, digital and physical, and the result is an ornate, historic home (once the residence of industrialist Andrew Carnegie) outfitted with the latest technologies and amenities for a highly interactive experience. You don't just *look* at design here; you play with it, engage it, and then take it home. On arrival at the museum, visitors receive a digital pen that acts as a key to the museum's entire collection of more than 200,000 objects, everything from antique cutlery and Japanese sword fittings to robotics and animation. Museum highlights include a giant touchscreen tables where visitors can summon random-yet-relevant items from the museum's collection by drawing a squiggle or a shape; the Immersion Room, where visitors can view and save their favorite wallpapers from the museum's incredible collection or create their own designs (which can be projected onto the gallery walls); and the Process Lab where visitors get hands-on to solve design dilemmas and enhance everyday design objects. The focus on design and discovery extends to "SHOP," where limited-edition objects created in collaboration with contemporary designers and influenced by exhibitions are for sale. There is a café, too. Guided tours run daily at 11 and 1. Admission is pay-what-you-wish Saturday evening from 6 to 9. ⊠ *2 E. 91st St., at 5th Ave., Upper East Side* ☎ *212/849–8400* ⊕ *www.cooperhewitt.org* 🎟 *$18 ($16 online)* ☉ *Sun.–Fri. 10–6, Sat. 10–9* Ⓜ *4, 5, 6 to 86th St.*

10

El Museo del Barrio. *El barrio* is Spanish for "the neighborhood" and the nickname for East Harlem, a largely Spanish-speaking Puerto Rican and Dominican community. El Museo del Barrio, on the edge of this neighborhood, focuses on Latin American and Caribbean art, with some 10 percent of its collection concentrated on works by self-taught artists from New York, Puerto Rico, the Caribbean, and Latin America. The more than 6,500-object permanent collection includes over 400 pre-Columbian artifacts, sculpture, photography, film and video, and traditional art from all over Latin America. The collection of 360 *santos,* carved wooden folk-art figures from Puerto Rico, is popular. El Museo hosts performances, lectures, films, and cultural events, including a month-long Día de los Muertos celebration. ■TIP→ **Admission to El Museo del Barrio gains you free entrance to the neighboring Museum of the City of New York.** ⊠ *1230 5th Ave., between 104th and 105th sts., Upper East Side* ☎ *212/831–7272* ⊕ *www.elmuseo.org* ⬚ *$9 suggested donation* ۞ *Tues.–Sat. 11–6* Ⓜ *6 to 103rd St.*

Fodor'sChoice
★

Frick Collection. Henry Clay Frick made his fortune amid the soot and smoke of Pittsburgh, where he was a coke (a coal fuel derivative) and steel baron, but this lovely museum, once Frick's private New York residence, is decidedly removed from soot. With an exceptional collection of works from the Renaissance through the late 19th century that includes Édouard Manet's *The Bullfight* (1864), a Chinard portrait bust (1809), three Vermeers, three Rembrandts, works by El Greco, Goya, Van Dyck, Hogarth, Degas, and Turner, as well as sculpture, decorative arts, and 18th-century French furniture, everything here is a highlight. The Portico Gallery, an enclosed portico along the building's 5th Avenue garden, houses the museum's growing collection of sculpture. Be sure to take in the Frick's green spaces while you can; in 2014, the museum announced plans to build a six-story addition to allow for educational programs and conservation facilities, and to accommodate its increased attendance and growing collection. The plan met with immediate outcry, in part because it will carve into the museum's beautiful viewing garden (a garden that is intended to be appreciated from the street or museum windows—as a work of art in itself), designed by landscape architect Russell Page, but also because it could potentially ruin the intimacy of this house museum. If a proposal is approved, the expansion is expected to begin in 2017(the museum will remain open during renovations). An audio guide, available in several languages, is included with admission, as are the year-round temporary exhibits. The tranquil indoor garden court is a magical spot for a rest. Children under 10 are not admitted, and those ages 10–16 with an adult only. ⊠ *1 E. 70th St., at 5th Ave., Upper East Side* ☎ *212/288–0700* ⊕ *www.frick.org* ⬚ *$20* ۞ *Tues.–Sat. 10–6, Sun. 11–5* Ⓜ *6 to 68th St.–Hunter College.*

Gagosian Madison Avenue. If you are looking for ambitious works by the world's most acclaimed artists in a gallery that easily competes with the city's top museums, you have to visit Gagosian. Perhaps the most powerful art dealer in the world, Larry Gagosian has galleries in London, Paris, Rome, Athens, and Hong Kong, as well as five galleries in New York (three of which are on the Upper East Side). The Madison Avenue location, the contemporary art empire's headquarters, is a multifloor gallery that has shown works by big names like Warhol, Pollock, Miró, Calder, Twombly, and Hirst. Because Gagosian likes to dominate the real estate market the way he dominates the art market, he also has spaces at nearby 976 Madison Avenue, as well as it newest uptown outpost (with a decidedly downtown feel)—a storefront space on Park Avenue and 75th Street. ✉ *980 Madison Ave., near 76th St., Upper East Side* ☎ *212/744–2313* ⊕ *www.gagosian.com* ⊗ *Tues.–Sat. 10–6* Ⓜ *6 to 77th St.*

Gracie Mansion. The official mayor's residence, Gracie Mansion was built in 1799 by shipping merchant Archibald Gracie, and enlarged in 1966. Nine mayors have lived here since it became the official residence in 1942, though Michael Bloomberg broke with tradition and chose to stay in his own 79th Street townhouse during his three terms as mayor. He poured millions into renovations at Gracie Mansion without spending a single night there. In January 2014, the newly prepped, polished, and spruced-up mansion became home to newly elected Mayor Bill de Blasio and his family. The resident first family of New York City do not appreciate visitors traipsing through their living room so the "People's House"—with all its history and colorful rooms furnished over centuries and packed with American objets d'art—is not currently open to the people. Privacy and security appear to be a concern; in addition to closing the house to tours, there is a new 10-foot-high fence surrounding the property. ■TIP➔ **The mayor's office has indicated that tours of the impressive interior could resume mid-2015, so it's worth calling or emailing before you visit; you might get lucky.** ✉ *Carl Schurz Park, East End Ave. at 88th St., Upper East Side* ☎ *212/570–4778* ✍ *gracietours@ cityhall.nyc.gov* Ⓜ *4, 5, 6 to 86th St.*

The Jewish Museum. In a Gothic-style 1908 mansion, the Jewish Museum draws on a large collection of art and ceremonial objects to explore Jewish identity and culture spanning more than 4,000 years. The two-floor permanent exhibition "Culture and Continuity: The Jewish Journey" displays nearly 800 objects complemented by interactive media. The wide-ranging collection includes a 3rd-century Roman burial plaque, 20th-century sculpture by Elie Nadelman, and contemporary art from artists such as Marc Chagall and Man Ray. Russ & Daughters—an almost century-old Jewish specialty store and an NYC institution downtown—is set to open an outpost in the Jewish Museum in summer 2015. ✉ *1109 5th Ave., at 92nd St., Upper East Side* ☎ *212/423–3200* ⊕ *www.jewishmuseum.org* 🎫 *$15 (free Sat., pay-what-you-wish Thurs. 5–8)* ⊗ *Sat.–Tues. 11–5:45, Thurs. 11–8, Fri. 11–4 (Fri. until 5:45 Mar.– Nov.)* Ⓜ *6 to 96th St.*

10

Fodor's Choice ★ **Metropolitan Museum of Art.** *See highlighted listing in this chapter. 1000 5th Ave., at at 82nd St.; $25 suggested donation; $7 for audio guide; Sun.–Thurs. 10–5:30, Fri. and Sat. 10–9; 212/535–7710; 4, 5, 6 to 86th St.*

Museum of the City of New York. In a Colonial Revival building designed for the museum in the 1930s, the city's history and many quirks are revealed through engaging exhibits here. The museum stages rotating exhibitions on subjects such as architecture, fashion, history, and

SOLOMON R. GUGGENHEIM MUSEUM

✉ *1071 5th Ave., between 88th and 89th sts., Upper East Side* ☎ *212/423–3840, 212/423–3500* ⊕ *www.guggenheim.org* 🎟 *$25* ☉ *Sun.–Wed. and Fri. 10–5:45, Sat. 10–7:45* Ⓜ *4, 5, 6 to 86th St.*

TIPS

■ The museum's free app enhances your visit before, during, and after. Features include detailed floor maps, multimedia guides to exhibits, interviews with artists, and access to the permanent collection.

■ The museum often runs special programs—including lectures, conversations, and film screenings—in conjunction with major exhibitions. Check the museum's website for details of upcoming events.

■ Escape the crowded lobby by taking the elevator to the top and working your way down the spiral.

■ The museum is pay-what-you-wish on Saturday from 5:45 to 7:45. Lines can be long, so arrive early. The last tickets are handed out at 7:15.

■ Eat before you visit; restaurants on Lexington Avenue have more affordable options than the museum's elegant Wright restaurant, and more varied fare than the small Café 3 espresso and snack bar on the third floor.

Frank Lloyd Wright's landmark nautilus-like museum building is renowned as much for its famous architecture as for its superlative collection of art and well-curated shows. Opened in 1959, shortly after Wright's death, the Guggenheim is acclaimed as one of the greatest buildings of the 20th century. Inside, under a 96-foot-high glass dome, a ramp spirals down, past the artworks of the current exhibits (the ramp is just over a quarter mile long, if you're wondering). The museum has strong holdings of Wassily Kandinsky, Paul Klee, Marc Chagall, Pablo Picasso, and Robert Mapplethorpe.

Highlights

Wright's design was criticized by some who believed that the distinctive building detracted from the art within, but the interior nautilus design allows artworks to be viewed from several different angles and distances. Be sure to notice not only what's in front of you but also what's across the spiral from you.

Even if you aren't planning to eat, stop at the museum's modern American restaurant, the Wright (at 88th Street), for its stunning design by Andre Kikoski. If planning to eat, note that hours are limited and prices high.

On permanent display, the museum's Thannhauser Collection is made up primarily of works by French Impressionists and Post-Impressionists Van Gogh, Toulouse-Lautrec, Cézanne, Renoir, and Manet. Perhaps more than any other 20th-century painter, Wassily Kandinsky, one of the first "pure" abstract artists, has been closely linked to the museum's history: beginning with the acquisition of his masterpiece *Composition 8* (1923) in 1930, the collection has grown to encompass more than 150 works.

politics. "Saving Place: Fifty Years of New York City Landmarks" and "Folk City: New York and the American Folk Music Revival" provided unique perspectives of the everchanging city–exploring the architectural struggles in the periods before and after the Landmarks Law of 1965 as well as the cultural and political changes—playing out against a soundtrack of folk music—in Greenwich Village in the 50s and 60s. Don't miss *Timescapes,* a 25-minute media projection that innovatively illustrates New York's physical expansion and population changes, or "Activist New York," an ongoing exploration of the city's history of social activism. You can also find New York–centric lectures, films, and walking tours here. The museum is currently in the last phase of a three-part, $95 million renovation that will upgrade and modernize the entire facility. Improvements to date include a new climate-control system, new flooring, an updated lobby and terrace, a redesigned gift shop, and restored historical elements throughout the building. The third phase of the modernization includes the addition of a state-of-the-art auditorium and a new café. The museum remains open during renovations, which are expected to be completed in early 2016. When finished touring the museum, cross the street and stroll through the Vanderbilt Gates to enter the Conservatory Garden, one of Central Park's hidden gems. ⊠ *1220 5th Ave., at 103rd St., Upper East Side* ☎ *212/534–1672* ⊕ *www.mcny.org* ✉ *$14 suggested donation* ☉ *Daily 10–6* Ⓜ *6 to 103rd St.*

Neue Galerie New York. Early-20th-century German and Austrian art and design are the focus here, with works by Gustav Klimt, Wassily Kandinsky, Paul Klee, Egon Schiele, Josef Hoffmann, and other designers from the Wiener Werkstätte taking center stage. The Neue Galerie was founded by the late art dealer Serge Sabarsky and cosmetics heir and art collector Ronald S. Lauder. It's in a 1914 wood- and marble-floored mansion designed by Carrère and Hastings, which was once home to Mrs. Cornelius Vanderbilt III. An audio guide is included with admission. Children under 12 are not admitted, and teens 12–16 must be accompanied by an adult. Café Sabarsky, in an elegant, high-ceiling space on the first floor, is a destination in its own right for Viennese coffee, cakes, strudels, and Sacher tortes. Admission is free 6–8 pm on the first Friday of the month. ⊠ *1048 5th Ave., at 86th St., Upper East Side* ☎ *212/628–6200* ⊕ *www.neuegalerie.org* ✉ *$20* ☉ *Thurs.–Mon. 11–6* ☞ *Children under 12 not admitted* Ⓜ *4, 5, 6 to 86th St.*

10

WORTH NOTING

Acquavella Galleries. The 19th- and 20th-century museum-quality art inside this five-story, marble-floored French Neolassical mansion tends to be big-name, from Impressionists through Pop Artists, including Picasso, Lucian Freud, Jean-Michel Basquiat, James Rosenquist, and Wayne Thiebaud. ⊠ *18 E. 79th St., between 5th and Madison aves., Upper East Side* ☎ *212/734–6300* ⊕ *www.acquavellagalleries.com* ✉ *Free* ☉ *Weekdays 10–5* Ⓜ *6 to 77th St.*

FAMILY **Carl Schurz Park.** Facing the East River, this park, named for a German immigrant who was a prominent newspaper editor in the 19th century, is so tranquil you'd never guess you're directly above the FDR Drive.

Continued on page 167

THE METROPOLITAN MUSEUM OF ART

If the city held no other museum than the colossal Metropolitan Museum of Art, you could still occupy yourself for days roaming its labyrinthine corridors. Because the Metropolitan Museum has more than 2 million works of art representing 5,000 years of history, you're going to have to make tough choices. Looking at everything here could take a week.

Mesmerizing carvings in the ancient Egyptian Temple of Dendur.

Before you begin exploring, check the museum's floor plan, available at all entrances, for location of the major wings and collections. The museum's free app, The Met, offers details of the current exhibitions and events as well as lists of must-sees, hidden treasuresm and staff picks. Google Maps will help you find your way through the museum. The service guides you through exhibits, across floors, and to bathrooms and exits.

The posted adult admission, though only a suggestion, is one that's strongly encouraged. Whatever you choose to pay, admission includes all special exhibits and same-day entrance to the Cloisters (see Chapter 12). The Met's audio guide costs an additional $7, and if you intend to stay more than an hour or so, it's worth it.

If you want to avoid the crowds, visit weekday mornings. Also good are Friday and Saturday evenings, when live classical music plays from the Great Hall balcony. If the Great Hall (the main entrance) is mobbed, avoid the chaos by heading to the street-level entrance to the left of the main stairs, near 81st Street. Ticket lines and coat checks are much less ferocious here.

What to see? Check out the museum highlights on the following pages.

Left, Great Hall

MUSEUM HIGHLIGHTS

Egyptian Art

A major star is the **Temple of Dendur** (circa 15 BC), in a huge atrium to itself and with a moatlike pool of water to represent its original location near the Nile. The temple was commissioned by the Roman emperor Augustus to honor the goddess Isis and the sons of a Nubian chieftain. Look for the scratched-in graffiti from 19th-century Western explorers on the inside. Egypt gave the temple as a gift to the U.S. in 1965; it would have been submerged after the construction of the Aswan High Dam.

Temple of Dendur

The Egyptian collection as a whole covers 4,000 years of history, with papyrus pages from the Egyptian Book of the Dead, stone sarcophagi inscribed with hieroglyphics, and tombs. The galleries should be walked through counterclockwise from the Ancient Kingdom (2650–2150 BC), to the period under Roman rule (30 BC–400 AD). In the latter, keep an eye out for the enormous, bulbous **Sarcophagus of Horkhebil**, sculpted from basalt.

Greek and Roman Art

Today's tabloids have nothing on ancient Greece and Rome. They had it all—sex, cults, drugs, unrelenting violence, and, of course, stunning art. The recently redone Greek and Roman galleries encompass 6,000 works of art that reveal aspects of everyday life in these influential cultures.

The urnlike terracotta kraters were used by the Greeks for mixing wine and water at parties and other events. Given that, it's not surprising that most depict slightly racy scenes. Some of the most impressive can be found in the gallery covering 5th century BC.

On the mezzanine of the Roman galleries, the Etruscan bronze chariot from 650 BC depicts scenes from the life of Achilles. Notice how the simplistic Etruscan style in combination with the Greek influence evolved into the naturalistic Roman statues below.

The frescoes from a bedroom in the Villa of P. Fannius Synistor preserved by the explosion of Mt. Vesuvius in 79 AD give us a glimpse into the stylistic achievement of perspective in Roman painting.

ART TO TAKE HOME

You don't have to pay admission to get to the mammoth gift shop on the first floor. One of the better souvenirs here is also one of the more reasonable: the Met's own **illustrated guide** to 869 of the best items in its collection ($19.95).

Engelhard Court

An artifact from ancient Greece.

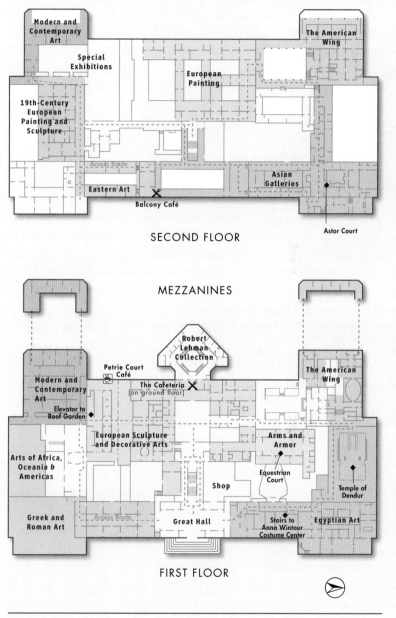

SECOND FLOOR

Modern and Contemporary Art

Special Exhibitions

European Painting

The American Wing

19th-Century European Painting and Sculpture

Access Route

Eastern Art

Balcony Café

Asian Galleries

Astor Court

MEZZANINES

Robert Lehman Collection

Petrie Court Café

The Cafeteria (on ground floor)

Modern and Contemporary Art

The American Wing

Elevator to Roof Garden

European Sculpture and Decorative Arts

Arms and Armor

Arts of Africa, Oceania & Americas

Equestrian Court

Shop

Temple of Dendur

Greek and Roman Art

Access Route

Great Hall

Stairs to Anna Wintour Costume Center

Egyptian Art

FIRST FLOOR

5th Avenue

The American Wing of the Metropolitan Museum of Art.

American Wing

After years of extensive renovations, the Met's revitalized **New American Wing Galleries for Paintings, Sculpture, and Decorative Arts** reopened in 2012 with 30,000 square feet of skylit space to showcase one of the best and largest collections of American art in the country.

There's much to see, from Colonial furniture to the works of the great masters, including John Singleton Copley, Gilbert Stuart, Thomas Cole, Frederic Edwin Church, Winslow Homer, and Thomas Eakins, among others. The highlight of the new installation is Emanuel Gottlieb Leutze's magnificent 1851 painting, *Washington Crossing the Delaware*. Hung in an immense gilded frame (recreated from an 1864 photograph of the painting), Leutze's iconic work is displayed just as it was at a fundraiser for Union soldiers in 1864—flanked by Frederic Church's *Heart of the Andes* and Albert Bierstadt's *Rocky Mountains*.

Also not to be missed are John Singer Sargent's *Madame X*, a once-scandalous portrait of a Parisian socialite; the recreation of the entrance hall of the 18th Century Van Rensselaer Manor House in Albany, New York; and the collection of portrait miniatures—detailed watercolors to be carried or gifted as tokens of love.

Tiffany

Arms and Armor

The **Equestrian Court,** where the knights are mounted on armored models of horses, is one of the most dramatic rooms in the museum. For a bird's-eye view, check it out again from the balconies in the Musical Instruments collection on the second floor.

European Sculpture and Decorative Arts

Among the many sculptures in the sun-filled Petrie Court, *Ugolino and His Sons* still stands out for the despairing poses of its subjects. Ugolino, a nobleman whose family's tragic story is told in Dante's *Inferno,* was punished for treason by being left to starve to death with his grandsons and sons in a locked tower. (It's not clear if putting such a sculpture so near the Petrie Court's café is some curator's idea of a joke or not.) By the way, the redbrick and granite wall on the court's north side is the museum's original entrance.

The newly renovated Wrightsman Galleries for French Decorative Arts on the first floor displays the opulence that caused Louis the XVI to lose his head. The blindingly golden Boiserie from the Hotel de Cabris, a remnant of French 18th century Neo-classical interiors, represents the finest collection of French decorative arts in the country.

Anna Wintour Costume Center

In May 2014, the Met's Costume Institute reopened with a newly designed 4,200-square-foot main gallery, an updated costume conservation laboratory, expanded study and storage facilities, and a new name—the Anna Wintour Costume Center. Named for the legendary *Vogue* editor-in-chief and Met Trustee (responsible for the annual Met Gala), and housing one of the most comprehensive costume collections in the world, the new Costume Center (on the ground floor), with its fashion-focused exhibits and tours— is a huge draw for fashion lovers.

European Paintings

On the second floor, the 13th- to 18th-century paintings are grouped at the top of the Great Hall's stairs.

Recently, the Met spent about $45 million to buy Duccio di Buoninsegna's **Madonna and Child,** painted circa 1300. The last remaining Duccio in private hands, this painting, the size of a piece of typewriter paper, is unimpressive at first glance. The work, though rigid, represents a revolution in Byzantine art. The humanity reflected in the baby Jesus grabbing his mother's veil changed European painting.

IN FOCUS THE METROPOLITAN MUSEUM OF ART

10

Equestrian Court (1930)

Rembrandt's masterful **Aristotle with a Bust of Homer** (1653) shows a philosopher contemplating worldly gains versus values through its play of light and use of symbols. Around Aristotle is a gold medal of Alexander the Great, one of the philosopher's students.

In the room dedicated to **Monet** you can get to all his greatest hits—poplar trees, haystacks, water lilies, and the Rouen Cathedral. The muted tones of Pissaro are followed by a room full of bright and garish colors announcing works by Gauguin, Matisse, and Van Gogh.

Vincent van Gogh, *Wheatfield with Cypresses*

Islamic Galleries

In late 2011, after an eight-year renovation, the Met reopened its Islamic galleries, a suite of 15 galleries housing one of the world's premier collections of Islamic art. Now known as the "Art of the Arab Lands, Turkey, Iran, Central Asia, and Later South Asia," the collection comprises more than 12,000 works of art and traces the course of Islamic Civilization over a span of 13 centuries. Highlights include an 11-foot-high 14th century mihrab, or prayer niche, decorated with glazed ceramic tiles; the recently restored Emperor's Carpet—a 16th century Persian carpet that was presented to the Hapsburg Emperor Leopold I by Peter the Great of Russia; the Damascus Room—a Syrian Ottoman reception room decorated with poetic verses; and glass, ceramics, and metalwork from Egypt, Syria, Iraq, and Iran.

Asian Galleries

The serene **Astor Court**, which has its own skylight and pond of real-life koi (goldfish), is a model of a scholar's court garden in Soochow, China.

The Han dynasty (206 BC–220 AD) introduced the practice of sending the dead on to the afterlife with small objects to help them there. Keep an eye out for these **small clay figures,** which include farm animals (enclosed in barnyards) and dancing entertainers.

On display in a glass case in the center of an early-Chinese gallery is a complete set of 14 **bronze altar vessels.** Dating 1100 BC—800 AD, these green and slightly crusty pieces were used for worshipping ancestors. The Met displays some of its finest **Asian stoneware and porcelain** along the balcony overlooking the Great Hall.

The teak dome and minature balconies from a **Jain meeting hall** in western India were carved in the 16th century. Just about the entire surface is covered with musicians, animals, gods, and servants.

Standing eight-armed Avalokiteshvara

Walk along the promenade, where you can take in views of the river and the Roosevelt Island Lighthouse across the way. To the north are Randall's and Wards Islands and the RFK Bridge (aka the Triborough Bridge)—as well as the more immediate sight of locals pushing strollers, riding bikes, or walking their dogs. If you use the 86th Street entrance, you'll find yourself near the grounds of a Federal-style wood-frame house that belies the grandeur of its name: Gracie Mansion. ⊠ *From 84th to 90th St., between East End Ave. and the East River, Upper East Side* ☎ *212/459–4455* ⊕ *www.carlschurzparknyc.org* Ⓜ *4, 5, 6 to 86th St.*

Castelli Gallery. One of the most influential dealers of the 20th century, Leo Castelli helped foster the careers of many important artists, including one of his first discoveries, Jasper Johns. Castelli died in 1999, but the gallery continues to show works by Roy Lichtenstein, Andy Warhol, Ed Ruscha, Jackson Pollock, Robert Morris, and other heavies. ⊠ *18 E. 77th St., between 5th and Madison aves., Upper East Side* ☎ *212/249–4470* ⊕ *www.castelligallery.com* ⊠ *Free* ⊙ *Tues.–Sat. 10–6* Ⓜ *6 to 77th St.*

Jane Kahan. This welcoming gallery represents some lofty works. In addition to tapestries by modern masters like Pablo Picasso, Joan Miró, and Alexander Calder—one of this gallery's specialties—works by late-19th- and early-20th-century modern artists like Fernand Léger and Marc Chagall are showcased. ⊠ *922 Madison Ave., 2nd fl., between 73rd and 74th sts., Upper East Side* ☎ *212/744–1490* ⊕ *www.janekahan. com* ⊠ *Free* ⊙ *Labor Day–Memorial Day, Tues.–Sat. 10–6; Memorial Day–Labor Day, weekdays 11–5* Ⓜ *6 to 77th St.*

Mitchell-Innes & Nash. This sleek spot represents the estates of Roy Lichtenstein, Alberto Burri, Nancy Graves, and Jack Tworkov as well as other Impressionist, modern, and contemporary masters. ⊠ *1018 Madison Ave., between 78th and 79th sts., Upper East Side* ☎ *212/744–7400* ⊕ *www.miandn.com* ⊠ *Free* ⊙ *Weekdays 10–5* Ⓜ *6 to 77th St.*

FAMILY **Mount Vernon Hotel Museum and Garden.** Built in 1799, this former carriage house became a day hotel (a sort of country club) in 1826. Now restored and owned by the Colonial Dames of America, it provides a glimpse of the days when the city ended at 14th Street and this area was a country escape for New Yorkers. A 45-minute tour (the only way to see the museum and garden) passes through the eight rooms that display furniture and artifacts of the Federal and Empire periods. Many rooms have real artifacts such as clothes, hats, and fans that children can handle. There is a lovely adjoining garden, designed in an 18th-century style. Tours are on demand and can be geared to specific interests. Arrive at least a half hour before closing time to allow for tour. ⊠ *421 E. 61st St., between York and 1st aves., Upper East Side* ☎ *212/838–6878* ⊕ *www.mvhm.org* ⊠ *$8* ⊙ *Tues.–Sun. 11–4* Ⓜ *4, 5, 6 to 59th St.; N, Q, R to Lexington Ave./59th St.*

Museum of American Illustration. Founded in 1901, the museum of the Society of Illustrators presents its annual "Oscars," a juried international competition, from January to March. The best in children's book illustration is showcased October through November. In between are

10

eclectic exhibitions on science fiction, fashion, politics, and history illustrations. In 2012, the Society of Illustrators incorporated the holdings of the Museum of Comic and Cartoon Art (MoCCA) into its collections. MoCCA's collection is housed in its own gallery on the second floor and continues its workshops, programs, and comic festival (MoCCA Fest). ■TIP→ Admission is free on Tuesday 5–8. ⊠ *128 E. 63rd St., between Lexington and Park aves., Upper East Side* ☎ *212/838–2560* ⊕ *www.societyillustrators.org* ✉ *$10* ⊗ *Tues. 10–8, Wed.–Fri. 10–5, Sat. noon–4* Ⓜ *F to Lexington Ave./63rd St.; 4, 5, 6 to 59th St.; N, Q, R to Lexington Ave./59th St.*

Peter Findlay Gallery. Covering 19th- and 20th-century works by European artists, this gallery shows pieces by Mary Cassatt, Paul Klee, and Alberto Giacometti. ⊠ *16 E. 79th St., 2nd fl., Upper East Side* ☎ *212/644–4433* ⊕ *www.findlay.com* ⊗ *Weekdays 1:30–5* Ⓜ *6 to 77th St.*

FAMILY **Roosevelt Island.** The 2-mile-long East River slice of land that parallels Manhattan from 48th to 85th streets is now a quasi-suburb of more than 12,000 people, and the vestiges of its infamous asylums, hospitals, and prisons make this an offbeat trip for the historically curious. At its southern tip are the eerie ruins of a Smallpox Hospital, built in 1854 in a Gothic Revival style by the prominent architect James Renwick Jr. (Among many other works, Renwick also designed St. Patrick's Cathedral.) Neighboring the hospital ruins is the recently opened Four Freedoms Park, a memorial to Franklin Delano Roosevelt designed by famed architect Louis I. Kahn. The monument to President Roosevelt is essentially a large, open granite box with a giant bust of FDR, and a wall inscribed with the words of the wartime Four Freedoms speech. Visitors can stroll the stone walkways and the symmetrical tree-lined pebble paths that run along the manicured lawn and enjoy unique views of the United Nations and East River. Free guided walking tours of FDR Four Freedoms Park are available weekends at 1 pm on a first-come, first-served basis. At the island's north tip, is a small park with a lighthouse built in 1872 by island convicts. You can get to the island by subway, but why would you when you can take the five-minute ride on the Roosevelt Island Tramway, the only commuter cable car in North America, which lifts you 250 feet in the air for impressive views of Queens and Manhattan. A visitor center (open May to September), made from an old trolley kiosk, stands to your left as you exit the tram. Free red buses service the island. ⊠ *Tramway entrance, 2nd Ave. between 59th and 60th sts., Upper East Side* ☎ *212/688–4836 for visitor center* ⊕ *www.fdrfourfreedomspark.org* ✉ *$2.75 (one-way subway fare)* ⊗ *Park Wed.–Mon. 9–5. Tram Sun.–Thurs. 6 am–2 am, Fri. and Sat. 6 am–3:30 am; leaves approximately every 15 mins* Ⓜ *F to Roosevelt Island.*

Van Doren Waxter. The gallery formerly known as the Greenberg Van Doren Gallery changed its name and moved to this historic townhouse on a tree-lined street, just a block from the Met Museum's new outpost at the former Whitney Museum. Solo and group shows of postwar artists as well as emerging young artists are exhibited here. ⊠ *23 E. 73rd St., between Madison and 5th aves., Upper East Side* ☎ *212/445–0444* ⊕ *www.vandorenwaxter.com* ✉ *Free* ⊗ *Tues.–Sat. 10–6* Ⓜ *6 to 77th St.*

11

Central Park

WORD OF MOUTH

"Central Park was fabulous! I love that this busy, bustling city has such a huge expanse of peaceful parkland."

— cathies

OUR BACKYARD

HOW A SWAMP BECAME AN OASIS

1855 Using the power of eminent domain, New York City acquires 843 acres of undeveloped swamp for the then-obscene sum of $5 million, displacing 1,600 people living there.

1857 The landscape architect Frederick Law Olmsted becomes superintendent of a park that does not yet exist. He spends days clearing dirt and evicting squatters and evenings working with architect Calvert Vaux on what will become the Greensward plan. The plan is the winning entry in the city's competition to develop a design for the park.

While the Panic of 1857 creates widespread unemployment, thousands of workers begin moving five million cubic yards of dirt and planting more than five million trees and plants. Beleaguered by bureaucrats, Olmsted and Vaux unsuccessfully submit resignations several times.

1873 The Greensward plan is completed. It has been the basic blueprint for Central Park ever since.

More than thirty-eight million people visit Central Park each year; on an average summer weekend day, a quarter of a million children and adults flood these precincts, frolicking in the 21 playgrounds and 26 ballfields, and collapsing on more than 9,000 benches, which would span seven miles if you lined them up. There are more than 55 monuments and sculptures in the park, and countless ways to have fun.

⟨30⟩ THINGS WE LOVE TO DO IN CENTRAL PARK

1 Take a rowboat out on the lake

2 Clap for the sea lions at the zoo

3 Jog around the Reservoir

4 Ice-skate at Trump Wollman Rink

5 Watch rollerbladers show off

6 Go bird-watching at the Ramble

7 Doze in Sheep Meadow

8 Rent a bike at the Boathouse

9 Sit on the hill behind the Met Museum

10 See a free concert or play

11 Catch a softball game

12 Bask in fall foliage

13 Remember John Lennon at Strawberry Fields

14 Take a Central Park Conservancy Tour

15 Rent a gondola and a gondolier

16 Cross the park on the bridle path

17 Stand under the 72nd Street Wisteria Pergola

18 Hear the Delacorte Clock's musical chimes

19 Crunch the snow before anyone else

20 Pilot a model boat at Conservatory Water

21 Stroll through Shakespeare Garden

22 Fish at Harlem Meer

23 Sunbathe on Hernshead

24 Smell the Conservatory Garden tulips

25 Shoot photos from Bow Bridge

26 Ride the Carousel

27 People-watch at Bethesda Fountain

28 Picnic on the Great Lawn

29 Pet the bronze Balto statue

30 Climb to the top of Belvedere Castle

(top left) Monarch butterfly pollinates at Conservatory Garden (top center) Bethesda Fountain (top right) Chrysanthemums near Sheep Meadow (center) The skyline with some of the park's 26,000 trees (bottom) Park skaters in the 1860s.

PARK BASICS

Several entrances lead into the park. You can enter from the east, west, south, and north by paved pedestrian walkways, just off Fifth Avenue, Central Park North (110th St.), Central Park West, and Central Park South (59th St.).

Four roads, or transverses, cut through the park from east to west—66th, 79th, 86th, and 96th streets. The East and West drives are both along the north–south axis; Center Drive enters the south edge of the park at Sixth Avenue and connects with East Drive around 66th Street.

There are five Visitor Centers—the Dairy (just south of the 66th St. transverse), Belvedere Castle (just north of the 79th Street transverse), the Chess & Checkers House (mid-park at 64th St.), and the Charles A. Dana Discovery Center (at the top of the park at Central Park North) and the North Meadow Recreation Center (mid-park, near 96th St.)—that have directions, park maps, event calendars, and volunteers who can guide you.

TOURS

The **Central Park Conservancy** gives several different free and ticketed walking tours of the park based on the season. Most tours are 60 to 90 minutes and explore the park's history, ecology, and design. Custom tours are also available. If you'd rather go it alone, the free Central Park app offers an audio guide with celebrity tours of popular park locations. The app also offers a GPS-enabled map and updated listings. For more information, see *centralparknyc.org*.

WHERE AM I?

Along the main loop and some paths, lampposts are marked with location codes. Posts bear a letter—always "E" (for east) or "W" (for west)—and four numbers. The first two numbers tell you the nearest cross street. The second two tell you how far you are from either 5th Ave. or Central Park West (depending on whether it's an "E" or "W" post). Download the free Central Park app (www.centralparknyc.org/digital); with its interactive GPS-enabled map, event calendar, and site info and you'll never get lost in the park again.

PERFORMERS AND THE PARK: SOULMATES

It was inevitable that Central Park, conceived to give so much and ask little in return, would attract artists and art lovers who feel the same way.

Be they superstars like Paul Simon, Diana Ross, or Elton John or one of the amateur musicians, animal handlers, or jugglers who delight passersby, they all share the urge to entertain and give back to the city, the park, and its visitors.

Information on scheduled events is provided, but if you can't catch one, don't fret: you'll be rewarded by the serendipitous, particularly on summer and autumn days. Just keep your ears peeled for the music, applause, and laughter. The Central Park Conservancy, in cooperation with other arts patrons, organizes a series of free events, including the Harlem Meer Performance Festival and the Great Lawn performances by the New York Philharmonic. SummerStage has yielded a cornucopia of international performers.

Perhaps the brass ring of park performances is Shakespeare in the Park, which celebrated its 50th year in 2012. Every summer's performances of works by the Bard (and others) wow as many as 90,000 New Yorkers and visitors. Free tickets (two per person) are given out starting at noon for the performance that evening, but you need to line up by midmorning or earlier, depending on the show. Tickets are also distributed via online lottery on the show day at *www.publictheater.org*. Either way, the trouble is worth it, as casts are often studded with stars like Meryl Streep, Oliver Platt, Natalie Portman, Morgan Freeman, Denzel Washington, and Kevin Kline.

GOINGS ON

Central Park Conservancy Film Festival: Five nights at end of summer; Rumsey Playfield, near E. 72nd St. entrance.

Global Citizen: VIPs of rock and roll join 60,000 fans to raise their voices for change in this one-day annual concert in late Sept.

Harlem Meer Performance Festival: Late June–early Sept., Sun.; at Dana Discovery Center, near Lenox Ave. entrance.

Ice Festival: Artists use chainsaws to transform ice into art. Naumberg Band Shell, mid-Feb.

New York Philharmonic: Two performances in the summer; Great Lawn.

Shakespeare in the Park: June–early Aug., Tues.–Sun. evenings.

Storytelling: June–Sept., Sat. 11 AM; Hans Christian Andersen Statue at 72nd St. and 5th Ave.

SummerStage: Late May or June–early Sept.; Rumsey Playfield.

Swedish Cottage Marionette Theatre: Since 1947, puppeteers have entertained in this 1876 Swedish schoolhouse.

(center) N.Y. Philharmonic associate conductor Xian Zhang (right) Shakespeare's *Much Ado About Nothing*

FROM 59TH TO 72ND ST.

The busy southern section of Central Park is where most visitors get their first impression; it's also where most of the park's child-friendly attractions are centered. Artists line the entrances off Central Park South, and horse carriages await passengers. But no matter how many people gather here, you can always find a spot to picnic, ponder, or just take in the beauty, especially on a sunny day.

At the southeast corner of the park, you will come upon one of its prettiest areas, the **Pond.** Swans and ducks cruise on its calm waters, and if you follow the shore line to Gapstow Bridge and look southward, you'll see much of New York City's skyline: to the left (east) are the peak-roofed Sherry-Netherland Hotel, the black-and-white GM Building, the Chippendale-style top of the Sony Building, and the black-glass Trump Tower. In front of you is the château-style Plaza Hotel.

Opening in late October, **Trump Wollman Skating Rink** sits inside the park against a backdrop of Central Park South skyscrapers. You can rent skates, buy snacks, and have a perfect city-type outing. There's a

lively feeling here with lots of great music playing and a terrace so you can watch if you're not into skating.

The **Friedsam Memorial Carousel,** also known as the Central Park Carousel, was built in 1908. It has 58 nearly life-size hand-carved horses and remains a favorite among young and old. Its original Wurlitzer organ plays calliope waltzes, polkas, and standards. Even if you don't need visitor infomation, the **Dairy** is worth a stop for its Swiss-chalet exterior.

If you saw the film *Madagascar,* you may recognize the **Central Park Zoo.** Here, the polar bears play at the Polar Circle, monkeys frolic in the open-air Temperate Territory, and the Rain Forest showcases flora and fauna that you wouldn't expect to see in Manhattan. An unusual exhibit is the ant colony—even New York City's zoo has a sense of humor. Stick around to see the sea lion feedings (call for times) and to watch the animal statues dance to a variety of nursery rhymes at the **Delacorte Musical Clock** just outside, on the hour and half-hour from 8 AM to 5 PM.

Wedged between the zoo and the clock is **The Arsenal,** the second-oldest building in the park. Inside are rotating

exhibits that often cover park history and landscape art.

North of the clock is **Tisch Children's Zoo,** where kids can pet and feed sheep, goats, rabbits, cows, and pigs. Enter through the trunk of a make-believe tree and arrive at The Enchanted Forest, filled with huge "acorns,"

a climbable "spider web," and hoppable "lily pads."

Perhaps more pettable than any of the zoo's occupants is a decidely more inert creature, perched on a rockpile at East Drive and 67th Street: **Balto.** Shiny in places from constant touching, this bronze statue commemorates a real-life sled dog who led a team of huskies that carried medicine for 674 mi across perilous

ice to Nome, Alaska, during a 1925 diphtheria epidemic.

The Mall, at the intersection of Central Drive and East Drive, is arguably the most elegant area of Central Park. In the beginning of the 20th century, it was the place to see and be seen. Today, these formal walkways are still a wonderful place to stroll, meander, or sit and take in the "parade" under a canopy of the largest col-

lection of American elms in North America. The mall's southern end, known as **Literary Walk,** is lined with statues of authors and artists such as Robert Burns and William Shakespeare.

(from left to right) Riding on the outside track (recommended) of the Carousel; Getting in a workout on a park drive loop; The Mall, where Dustin Hoffman's character famously teaches his son to ride a bike in *Kramer vs. Kramer*.

The large expanse to the west of the Mall is known as the **Sheep Meadow**, the only "beach" that some native New Yorkers have ever known. Join in on a Frisbee or football game, admire the tenacity of kite flyers, or indulge simultaneously in the three simplest meadow pleasures of them all—picnicking, sunbathing, and languorously reading a book or magazine.

There's a reason why the ornate **Bethesda Fountain**, off the 72nd Street transverse, shows up in so many movies set in New York City: the view from the staircase above is one of the most romantic in the city. The statue in the center of the fountain, **The Angel of the Waters**, designed by Emma Stebbins, is surrounded by four figures symbolizing Temperance, Purity,

Health, and Peace. There's a good amount of New York–style street entertainment here, too, with break dancers, acrobats, and singers all vying for your spare change. It's also a great place to meet, sit, and admire the beautiful lake with its swans. For a glimpse of the West Side skyline, walk slightly west to **Cherry Hill.** Originally a watering area for horses, this circular plaza

has a small wrought-iron-and-gilt fountain. It's particularly beautiful in the spring when the cherry trees are in full pink-and-white bloom. Farther west are the Oak Bridge and the lovely Ladies Pavilion, emblematic of the park's past.

Across from the Dakota apartment building on Central Park West is **Strawberry Fields**, named for the Beatles' 1967 classic, "Strawberry Fields Forever." Sometimes called the "international garden of peace," this spot draws fans who come to reflect among its shrubs, trees, and flower beds, and lay flowers on the black-and-white "Imagine" mosaic. On December 8, hundreds of Beatles fans mark the anniversary of Lennon's death by gathering here.

(top from left to right) Bethesda Fountain; Artist painting the oft-rendered Gapstow bridge, which spans the northeast end of the Pond; Cutting through the park is a classic midday timesaver and post-work respite; Seals at the Central Park Zoo (center left); Nighttime at Wollman Rink serves up twinkling skyscrapers and skaters of all abilities (center right); The late John Lennon and his widow, Yoko Ono, often visited the site of what would become Strawberry Fields.

FROM 72ND ST.
TO THE RESERVOIR

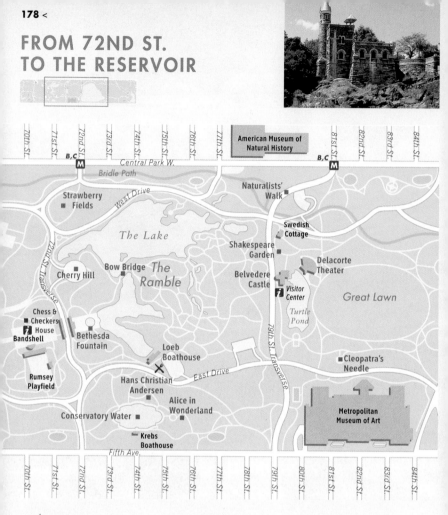

Playgrounds, lawns, jogging and biking paths, and striking buildings populate the midsection of the park. You can soak up the sun, have a picnic, or even play in a pick-up basketball or baseball game by the Great Lawn; get your cultural fix at the Metropolitan Museum of Art; or train for the next New York City Marathon along the Reservoir.

A block from Fifth Avenue, just north of the 72nd Street entrance, is a peaceful section of the park where you'll find the **Conservatory Water**, named for a conservatory that was never built. Generations of New Yorkers have grown up racing radio-controlled model sailboats here. It's a tradition that happens each Saturday at 10 AM from April through Oct. During those months smaller boats are available for rent

daily. At the north end is the **Alice in Wonderland** statue; on the west side of the pond, a bronze statue of **Hans Christian Andersen**, the Ugly Duckling at his feet, is the site of Saturday story-telling hours during summer.

At the neo-Victorian **Loeb Boathouse** on the park's 18-acre Lake, you can rent a rowboat, kayak, bike, or ride in an authentic Venetian gondola. The attached café is a worthy pit stop.

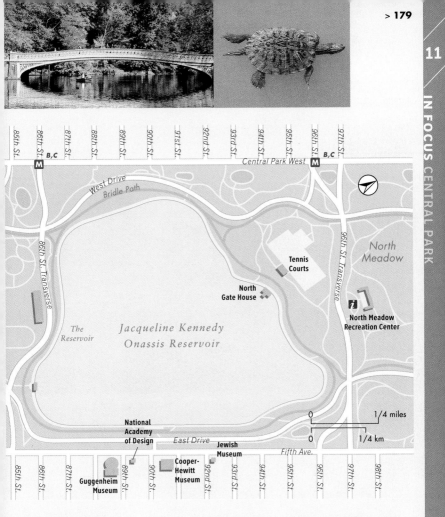

Designed to resemble upstate New York's Adirondack Mountain region, the **Ramble** covers 38 acres and is laced with twisting, climbing paths. This is prime bird-watching territory, since it's a rest stop along a major migratory route and a shelter for many of the more than 230 species of birds that have been sighted in the park; bring your binoculars. Because the Ramble is so dense and isolated,

however, don't wander here alone, or after dark. Head south through the Ramble and you'll come to the beautiful cast-iron **Bow Bridge**, spanning part of the Lake between the Ramble and Bethesda Fountain. From the center of the bridge, you can get a sweeping view of the park as well as of the apartment buildings on both the East Side and the West Side.

North of the Ramble atop Vista Rock, **Belvedere Castle** is the second-highest natural point in the park. If you can't get tickets for Delacorte Theater, you can climb to one of the castle's

(from left to right) Belvedere means "beautiful view" in Italian, a clue to why we climb to the top of Belvedere Castle; Birders, photographers, and couples of all ages are drawn to Bow Bridge; Red-eared slider turtles frolic in Turtle Pond, at the base of Belvedere Castle.

three terraces and look down on the stage. You'll also get a fantastic view of the Great Lawn—it's particularly beautiful during the fall foliage months—and of the park's myriad bird visitors. Since 1919 the castle has served as a U.S. Weather Bureau station, and meteorological instruments are set on top of the tower. If you enter the Castle from the lower level, you can visit the Henry Luce Nature Observa-tory, which has nature exhibits, children's workshops, and educational programs.

Somewhat hidden behind Belvedere Castle, **Shake-speare Garden** is an informal jumble of flowers, trees, and pathways, inspired by the flora mentioned in Shakespeare's plays and poetry. Bronze plaques throughout the garden bear the bard's lines mentioning the plants.

The Great Lawn hums with action on weekends, on warm days, and on most summer evenings, when its baseball fields and picnic grounds fill with city folks and visitors alike. Its 13 acres have endured millions of footsteps, thousands of ball games, hundreds of downpours, dozens of concerts, fireworks displays, and even a papal mass. On a beautiful day, everyone seems to be here.

Chancing upon the 70-ft-tall **Cleopatra's Needle** always feels a bit serendipitous and delightfully jarring, even to the most cynical New Yorkers. This weathered hieroglyphic-covered obelisk began life in Heliopolis, Egypt, around 1500 BC, but has only a little to do with Cleopatra—it's just New York's nickname for the work. It was eventually carted off to Alexandria by the Romans in 12 BC, and

it landed here on January 22, 1881, when the khedive of Egypt made it a gift to the city.

At the southwest corner of the Great Lawn is the fan-shaped **Delacorte Theater**, home to the summer Shakespeare in the Park festival.

If you want to take in several sites in a single brisk jaunt, consider walking the **Naturalists' Walk.** On this path you can wind your way

toward the Swedish Cottage, the Shakespeare Garden, and Belvedere Castle on a landscaped nature

(top, from left to right) A female Canada goose and goslings on Turtle Pond; Cyclists make good use of the bike paths; Bikers as well as joggers boost their egos by outpacing the hansom carriages; Racing boats at Conservatory Water (center) In the 1930s, a flock of sheep was evicted from what would later be known as the Sheep Meadow.

walk with spectacular rock outcrops, a stream that attracts bird life, a woodland area with various native trees, stepping-stone trails, and, thankfully, benches.

North of the Great Lawn and the 86th Street transverse is a popular gathering place for New Yorkers and visitors alike, the **Jacqueline Kennedy Onassis Reservoir**. Rain or shine, you'll see runners of all ages and paces heading counterclockwise around the 1.58-mi dirt path that encircles the water. The path in turn is surrounded by hundreds of trees that burst into color in the spring and fall. The 106-acre reservoir, finished in 1862, was a source of fresh water for Manhattanites. It holds more than a billion gallons, but it's no longer used for drinking water; the city's main reservoirs are upstate. From the top of the stairs at 90th Street just off 5th Avenue you have a 360-degree panorama of the city's exciting skyscrapers and often-brilliant sunsets. On the south side, there are benches so you can rest and recharge.

FROM THE RESERVOIR TO 110TH ST.

 More locals than tourists know about the wilder-looking, less-crowded northern part of Central Park, and there are hidden gems lurking here that enable even the most tightly wound among us to decompress, at least for a short while.

Walking along Fifth Avenue to 105th Street, you'll see a magnificent wrought-iron gate—once part of the 5th Avenue mansion of Cornelius Vanderbilt II—that marks the entrance to the **Conservatory Garden**. As you walk through it, you enter a different world, a quiet place that's positively idyllic for reading and slowing down. The Italian-style **Central Garden** is a beauty, with an expansive lawn, a strikingly simple fountain, and a wisteria-draped pergola that just oozes romance.

The French-inspired **North Garden** is a colorful place with plants placed into elaborate patterns. Springtime is magical—thousands of tulips come to life in a circle around the garden's striking Untermyer Fountain and its three bronze dancers; in the fall, chrysanthemums take their place. The English-style **South Garden** conjures up images from the classic children's book *The Secret Garden*. The garden is a beautiful hodgepodge of trees, bushes, and flowers that bloom year-round. A free tour is conducted on Saturday at 11 AM, from April through October.

At **Harlem Meer**, the third-largest body of water in Central Park, you can borrow fishing poles (identification required) from mid-April through October and try your hand at catching (and releasing) the largemouth bass, catfish, golden shiners, and bluegills that are stocked in the water's 11 acres. You can also learn about the upper park's geography, ecology, and history at the Victorian-style **Charles A. Dana Discovery Center**.

Although only a shell of this stone building remains, **Blockhouse #1** serves as a historical marker: the structure was built in 1814 as a cliffside fortification against the British. The area is deserted and dense with trees, so go as a group here, and avoid it at night.

(left) A pensive raccoon in the park's northern reaches; (center) A jogger makes her counterclockwise progress along the reservoir; (right) Inside the Central Park Conservancy Garden.

CONTACT INFORMATION

Central Park Conservancy
☎ 212/310–6600
⊕ www.centralparknyc.org

Central Park SummerStage
☎ 212/360–2777
⊕ www.summerstage.org

Central Park Wildlife Center (Central Park Zoo)
☎ 212/439–6500
⊕ www.centralparkzoo.org

Central Park Visitor Centers
☎ 212/794–6564 (Dairy)
⊕ www.nycgovparks.org

Charles A. Dana Discovery Center
☎ 212/860–1370

Loeb Boathouse, Boathouse Restaurant
☎ 212/517–2233
⊕ www.thecentral parkboathouse.com

Shakespeare in the Park
☎ 212/539–8500 (Public Theater)
⊕ www.publictheater.org

Swedish Cottage Marionette Theatre
☎ 212/988–9093
⊕ www.cityparks foundation.org

Trump Wollman Rink
☎ 212/439–6900
⊕ www.wollmanskating rink.com

THE UPPER
WEST SIDE

GETTING ORIENTED

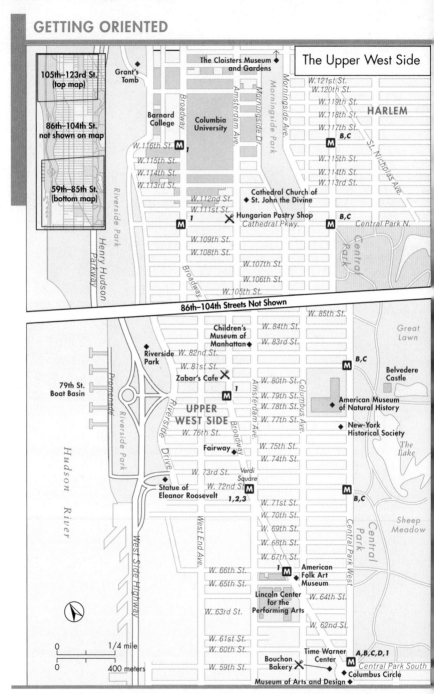

The Upper West Side

105th–123rd St.
(top map)

86th–104th St.
not shown on map

59th–85th St.
(bottom map)

The Cloisters Museum and Gardens

Grant's Tomb

Barnard College

Columbia University

Riverside Park

Henry Hudson Parkway

Broadway

Amsterdam Ave.

Morningside Dr.

Morningside Park

W. 121st St.
W. 120th St.
W. 119th St.
W. 118th St.
W. 117th St.
B, C
W. 115th St.
W. 114th St.
W. 113th St.

HARLEM

St. Nicholas Ave.

W. 116th St.
W. 115th St.
W. 114th St.
W. 113rd St.

W. 112nd St.
W. 111st St.
Cathedral Church of St. John the Divine
Hungarian Pastry Shop
Cathedral Pkwy.
B, C
Central Park N.

W. 109th St.
W. 108th St.
W. 107th St.
W. 106th St.
W. 105th St.

Central Park

86th–104th Streets Not Shown

W. 85th St.

Great Lawn

Children's Museum of Manhattan
W. 84th St.
W. 83rd St.

Riverside Park
W. 82nd St.
W. 81st St.
Zabar's Cafe
W. 80th St.
B, C
Belvedere Castle

79th St. Boat Basin

UPPER WEST SIDE
W. 79th St.
W. 78th St.
W. 77th St.
American Museum of Natural History

New-York Historical Society

W. 76th St.
Amsterdam Ave.
Columbus Ave.

Promenade

Riverside Drive

W. 75th St.
W. 74th St.

The Lake

Fairway
W. 73rd St.
Verdi Square
W. 72nd St.
Statue of Eleanor Roosevelt
1, 2, 3
B, C

Hudson River

W. 71st St.
W. 70th St.
W. 69th St.
W. 68th St.
W. 67th St.

Sheep Meadow

West End Ave.

West Side Highway

W. 66th St.
American Folk Art Museum
W. 65th St.
Lincoln Center for the Performing Arts
W. 64th St.
W. 63rd St.
W. 62nd St.

Central Park West

Central Park

0   1/4 mile
0   400 meters

W. 61st St.
W. 60th St.
W. 59th St.
Bouchon Bakery
Time Warner Center
A, B, C, D, 1
Central Park South
Columbus Circle
Museum of Arts and Design

MAKING THE MOST OF YOUR TIME

Broadway is one of the most walkable and interesting thoroughfares on the Upper West Side because of its broad sidewalks and aggressive mix of retail stores, restaurants, and apartment buildings. If you head north from the Lincoln Center area (around 65th Street) to about 81st Street (about 1 mile), you'll get a feel for the neighborhood's local color, particularly above 72nd Street. Up here you'll encounter residents of every conceivable age and ethnicity either shambling or sprinting, street vendors hawking used and newish books, and such beloved landmarks as the 72nd Street subway station, the Beacon Theater, the produce mecca Fairway (the cause of perhaps the most perpetually congested block), and Zabar's (a food spot that launches a memorable assault on all five of your senses—and your wallet). The Upper West Side's other two main avenues—Columbus and Amsterdam—are more residential but also have myriad restaurants and shops.

If you're intrigued by having the city's only Ivy League school close at hand, hop the 1 train to 116th Street and emerge on the east side of the street, which puts you smack in front of Columbia University and its Graduate School of Journalism. Pass through the gates and up the walk for a look at a cluster of buildings so elegant you'll understand why it's an iconic NYC setting.

GETTING HERE

The A, B, C, D, and 1 subway lines take you to Columbus Circle. From there, the B and C lines run along Central Park. The 1 train runs up Broadway, making local stops. The 2 and 3 are express trains that also go along Broadway.

TOP EXPERIENCES

Strolling through Riverside Park past the boat basin

12

Exploring Central Park (⇨ *See Chapter 11*)

Standing below the gigantic blue whale at the American Museum of Natural History

Taking in the views, gardens, and medieval masterpieces at the Cloisters Museum and Gardens

COFFEE AND QUICK BITES

Bouchon Bakery. In Columbus Circle's busy Time Warner shopping center, this little bakery serves excellent sandwiches, quiches, pastries, and coffee. ⊠ *Time Warner Center, 10 Columbus Circle, 3rd fl., Upper West Side* ☎ *212/823–9366* ⊕ *www.thomaskeller.com* Ⓜ *1, A, B, C, D to 59th St.–Columbus Circle.*

Hungarian Pastry Shop. Linger over a danish and bottomless cups of coffee with the Columbia kids and professors at this old-world (cash only) café and bakery. ⊠ *1030 Amsterdam Ave., at 111th St., Upper West Side* ☎ *212/866–4230* Ⓜ *1 to Cathedral Pkwy.–110th St.*

Zabar's Cafe. Fast-track the Zabar's experience with a gourmet coffee and sandwich, pickled lox, or slice of cheesecake. ⊠ *2245 Broadway, at 80th St., Upper West Side* ☎ *212/787–2000* ⊕ *www.zabars.com* Ⓜ *1 to 79th St.*

Sightseeing
★★★

Nightlife
★★

Dining
★★

Lodging
★

Shopping
★★★★

Updated
by Jacinta
O'Halloran

The Upper West Side is one of the city's quieter, more residential neighborhoods, with wide sidewalks and a (relatively) slower pace. The Cloisters, in Inwood, has the Metropolitan Museum's medieval collection.

The tree-lined side streets of the Upper West Side are lovely, with high stoops leading up to stately brownstones. Central Park, of course, is one of the main attractions here, no matter the season or time of day, though locals know that Riverside Park, along the Hudson River, can be even more appealing, with smaller crowds.

The Upper West Side also has its share of cultural institutions, from the 16-acre **Lincoln Center** complex, to the impressive and quirky collection at the **New-York Historical Society,** to Columbus Circle's **Museum of Arts and Design** and the much-loved **American Museum of Natural History.**

Most people think the area north of 106th Street and south of 125th Street on the West Side is just an extension of the Upper West Side. Technically it's Morningside Heights, largely dominated by Columbia University along with a cluster of academic, religious, and medical institutions, including Barnard College and the **Cathedral Church of St. John the Divine.**

TOP ATTRACTIONS

Fodor'sChoice **American Museum of Natural History.** *See highlighted feature in this chap-*
★ *ter.* ⊠ *Central Park W at 79th St.* ☎ *212/769–5100* ⊕ *www.amnh.org*
✉ *$22 suggested donation, includes admission to Rose Center for Earth and Space; $27 includes an IMAX or planetarium show* ⊙ *Daily 10–5:45* Ⓜ *B, C to 81st St.–Museum of Natural History.*

Cathedral Church of St. John the Divine. The largest Gothic-style cathedral in the world, even with its towers and transepts still unfinished, this divine behemoth comfortably asserts its bulk in the country's most vertical city. The seat of the Episcopal diocese in New York, it acts as a sanctuary for all, giving special services that include a celebration of New York's gay and lesbian community as well as the annual Blessing of the Bikes (mid-April), when cyclists of all faiths bring their wheels for a holy-water benediction. Built in two long spurts starting in 1892, the cathedral remains only two-thirds complete. What began as a Romanesque Byzantine–style structure under the original architects, George Heins and Christopher Grant Lafarge, shifted upon Heins's death in 1911 to French Gothic under the direction of Gothic Revival purist Ralph Adams Cram. You can spot the juxtaposition of the two medieval styles by comparing the finished Gothic arches, which are pointed, with the still-uncovered arches, which are rounded in the Byzantine style.

To get the full effect of the cathedral's size, approach it from Broadway along 112th Street. Above the 3-ton central bronze doors is the intricately carved Portal of Paradise, which depicts St. John witnessing the Transfiguration of Jesus, and 32 biblical characters. Step inside to the cavernous nave: more than 600 feet long, it holds some 5,000 worshippers, and the 162-foot-tall dome crossing could comfortably contain the Statue of Liberty (minus its pedestal). The Great Rose Window is the largest stained-glass window in the United States; it's made from more than 10,000 pieces of colored glass.

At the end of the nave, surrounding the altar, are seven chapels expressing the cathedral's interfaith tradition and international mission—with menorahs, Shinto vases, and dedications to various ethnic groups. The Saint Saviour Chapel contains a three-panel bronze altar in white gold leaf with religious scenes by artist Keith Haring (his last work before he died in 1990). Outside in the cathedral's south grounds is the eye-catching Peace Fountain. It depicts the struggle of good and evil in the form of the archangel Michael decapitating Satan, whose head hangs from one side. Encircling it are whimsical animals cast in bronze from pieces sculpted by children.

On the first Sunday of October, in honor of St. Francis of Assisi, the patron saint of animals, the church holds its usual Sunday service with a twist: the service is attended by men, women, children, dogs, cats, rabbits, hamsters, and the occasional horse, sheep, or ant farm. In past years upward of 3,500 New Yorkers have shown up to have their pets blessed. A procession is led by such guest animals as elephants, camels, llamas, and golden eagles. Sunday services are at 8, 9, 11, and 4. "Highlight Tours" and "Vertical Tours" are offered throughout the week; check the website for details and to reserve. ⊠ *1047 Amsterdam Ave., at 112th St., Upper West Side* ☎ *212/316–7540, 866/811–4111 for tour reservations* ⊕ *www.stjohndivine.org* ⊒ *$10 suggested donation; tours $8–$17* ⊙ *Daily 7:30–6; Visitor Center daily 9–5; tours Mon. at 11 and 2, Tues.–Sat. at 11 and 1, Sun. at 1* Ⓜ *1 to Cathedral Pkwy.–110th St.*

Fodor'sChoice **Central Park.** ⇨ *See Chapter 11.*
★
FAMILY

Fodor'sChoice **Lincoln Center for the Performing Arts.** ⇨ *See the listing in Chapter 20*
★

New-York Historical Society. Manhattan's oldest (and perhaps most under-the-radar) museum, founded in 1804, boasts one of the city's finest research libraries in addition to a contemporary glass facade, sleek interactive technology, a children's museum, restaurant, and inventive exhibitions that showcase the museum's eclectic collections and unique

Continued on page 198

AMERICAN MUSEUM ᵒₓ NATURAL HISTORY

Theodore Roosevelt
Memorial Hall

The largest natural history museum in the world is also one of the most impressive sights in New York. Four city blocks make up its 45 exhibition halls, which hold more than 33 million artifacts and wonders from the land, the sea, and outer space. With all those wonders, you won't be able to see everything on a single visit, but you can easily hit the highlights in half a day.

Before you begin, plan a route before setting out. Be sure to pick up a map when you pay your admission. The museum's four floors (and lower level) are mazelike.

Visitors can use the free AMNH Explorer app to navigate the museum. It tracks your location, has turn-by-turn directions, profiles of iconic museum objects, and tours, and guides you to bathrooms and exits. There are free companion apps to support special exhibits; check the website. The museum has devices you can borrow if you don't have an app-friendly phone.

Enter the museum at the below-street-level entrance connected to the 81st Street subway station for the shortest lines (look for the subway entrance to the left of the museum's steps). The entrance on Central Park West, where the vast steps lead up into the impressive, barrel-ceilinged Theodore Roosevelt Rotunda, is central and a good starting place for exploring.

The Rose Center for Earth and Space is attached to the museum. Enter from West 81st Street, where a path slopes down to the entrance, after which elevators and stairs descend to the ticket line on the lower level.

What to see? Check out the museum highlights on the following pages.

Left, Spectrum of Life Wall

MUSEUM HIGHLIGHTS

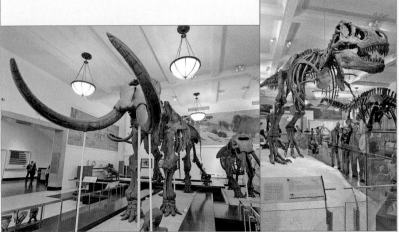

Left, Woolly Mammoth
Above, Tyrannosaurus rex

Dinosaurs and Mammals

An amazing assembly of dinosaur and mammal fossils covers the entire fourth floor. The organization can be hard to grasp at first, so head to the **Wallace Orientation Center,** where a short film explains how each of the Fossil Halls lead into each other. You'll want to spend at least an hour here—the highlights include a *T. rex,* an *Apatosaurus* (formerly called a Brontosaurus), and the *Buettneria,* which resembles a modern-day crocodile.

The specimens are not in chronological order; they're put together based on their shared characteristics. Key branching-off points—a watertight egg, a grasping hand—are highlighted in the center of rooms and surrounded by related fossil groups. Check out the touch screens here; they make a complex topic more comprehensible.

Reptiles and Amphibians

Head for the Reptiles and Amphibians Hall on the third floor to check out the Komodo Dragon lizards and a 23-foot-long python skeleton. The weirdest display is the enlarged model of the Suriname toad *Pipa pipa,* whose young hatch from the female's back. The Primates Hall carries brief but interesting comparisons between apes, monkeys, and humans. Also on the third floor is the upper gallery of the famed Akeley Hall of African Mammals.

SPECIAL SHOWS AND NEW EXHIBITS

Special exhibits, the IMAX theater, and the Space Show cost extra. The timed tickets are available in advance at the museum's Web site and are sold same day at the door. Between October and May, don't miss the warm, plant-filled Butterfly Conservatory, where blue morphos, monarchs, and other butterflies flit and feed. Ten minutes is probably enough time to enjoy it.

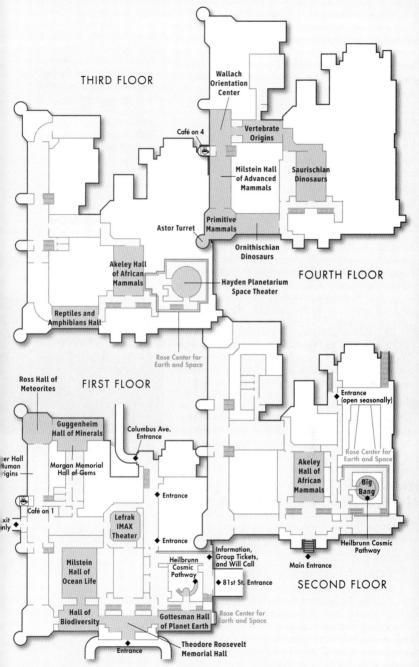

THIRD FLOOR

Wallach
Orientation
Center

Café on 4

Vertebrate
Origins

Milstein Hall
of Advanced
Mammals

Saurischian
Dinosaurs

Astor Turret

Primitive
Mammals

Ornithischian
Dinosaurs

FOURTH FLOOR

Akeley Hall
of African
Mammals

Hayden Planetarium
Space Theater

Reptiles and
Amphibians Hall

Rose Center for
Earth and Space

FIRST FLOOR

Ross Hall of
Meteorites

Entrance
(open seasonally)

Guggenheim
Hall of Minerals

Columbus Ave.
Entrance

Rose Center for
Earth and Space

ter Hall
luman
rigins

Morgan Memorial
Hall of Gems

Akeley
Hall of
African
Mammals

Big
Bang

Café on 1

Entrance

xit
nly

Lefrak
IMAX
Theater

Entrance

Heilbrunn Cosmic
Pathway

Milstein
Hall of
Ocean Life

Heilbrunn
Cosmic
Pathway

Information,
Group Tickets,
and Will Call

Main Entrance

81st St. Entrance

SECOND FLOOR

Hall of
Biodiversity

Gottesman Hall
of Planet Earth

Rose Center for
Earth and Space

Entrance

Theodore Roosevelt
Memorial Hall

Theodore Roosevelt Memorial

After a $40 million renovation, the two-story Theodore Roosevelt Memorial re-opened in late 2012. It includes the restored Central Park West entrance, the Theodore Roosevelt Rotunda, and the Theodore Roosevelt Memorial Hall. Highlights are a new bronze statue of a seated Roosevelt, celebratory murals honoring the Conservation President, touch-screen timelines, and film footage. The Hall of North American Mammals was also restored as part of the memorial to Roosevelt; the hall originally opened in 1942 and many of its displays feature scenes from National Parks that were signed into being by the president.

Akeley Hall of African Mammals

Opened in 1936, this hall on the third floor, its 28 dramatically lighted dioramas is one of the most beloved parts of the museum.

The hall was the life's work of the explorer Carl Akeley, who came up with the idea for the hall, raised the funds for the expeditions, gathered specimens, and sketched landscape studies for what would become the stunning backgrounds. (The backgrounds themselves were painted by James Perry Wilson, whose works can be found throughout the museum.)

Akeley died a decade before the hall opened on an expedition in what's now Rwanda. His gravesite is near the landscape portrayed in the gorilla diorama, completed after his death as a memorial to him and his work.

Hall of Human Origins

The Spitzer Hall of Human Origins on the first floor is a comprehensive exhibit that allows visitors to draw their own conclusions about human evolution by presenting both the scientific methods and the material evidence that goes into evolutionary theory.

The exhibit then traces the evolution of our species over six million years of fossil record and spells out our ancestors' physical and intellectual advancements. Highlights include casts of our famous hairy relative "Lucy," who walked the plains of Africa over 1.8 million years ago.

Hall of Biodiversity

The small **Hall of Biodiversity** on the first floor includes a shady replica of a Central African Republic rain forest. Nearby, the **Spectrum of Life Wall** showcases 1,500 specimens and models, helping show just how weird life can get. The wall opens into the gaping Milstein Hall of Ocean Life, designed to give it an underwater glow and to show off the 94-foot model of a **blue whale** that's suspended from the ceiling.

ROSE CENTER FOR EARTH AND SPACE

The vast expanses of space and time involved in the creation of the universe can be hard to grasp even with the guiding hand of a museum, so you may want to visit the center when you're at your sharpest. The stunning glass building's centerpiece is the aluminum-clad Hayden Sphere, 87 feet in diameter. Enclosed within are the planetarium, called the Space Theater, and an audiovisual Big Bang presentation consisting of four minutes of narration by Maya Angelou, indistinct washes of color, and frightening bursts of sound. The rock-filled **Hall of Planet Earth** is particularly timely given the earthquakes and other natural disasters of recent years: one section uses a working earthquake monitor to help explain just what causes such seismic violence.

The Space Theater

At the Space Theater, the stage is the dome above you and the actors, heavenly projections. One of the world's largest virtual reality simulators, the theater uses surround sound and slight vibrations in the seats, to immerse you in scenes of planets, star clusters, and galaxies. *Dark Universe* puts Hollywood effects to shame as it explores the cosmos and just how little we know about it.

Tip: The Museum's Cosmic Discoveries app allows you to take the universe, and all its galaxies and planets, with you when you leave. The app offers images, findings, and bulletins all culled from the museum's archives and curated by the museum's astrophysicists. ⊕ *www.amnh.org/apps*

TIME TO EAT?

Inside the museum:
The **main food court** on the lower level serves sandwiches, pizza, hamburgers and global street food. The animal- and planet-shaped cookies are draws for kids; adults should check out the barbecue station.

The small **Café on 4**, in a turret next to the fossil halls, offers garden views and sells premade sandwiches and salads, soup, yogurt, and desserts.

The über-white **Café on 1**, tucked away beside the Hall of Human Origins, sells warm sandwiches, soup, salads, beer and wine at New York prices.

TIME TO PLAY

In addition to family-friendly "Night at the Museum" events, the museum hosts adults-only sleepovers, as well as the Rose Center's monthly One Step Beyond series, featuring live bands, DJs, VJs, and cocktails. Get tickets at amnh.org/plan-your-visit/one-step-beyond.

TIME TO WATCH

Each October, the AMNH hosts the Margaret Mead Film & Video Festival, the longest-running premiere showcase for international documentaries in the United States. Tickets are made available one month prior to the festival, and online at www.amnh.org/mead

AMNH TALKS TO FODOR'S

Rose Center for Earth and Space

Interview with Ellen V. Futter, President of the American Museum of Natural History, conducted by Michelle Delio.

If You Only Have an Hour: The American Museum of Natural History has the world's finest collection of dinosaur fossils, so a visit to the fourth-floor's Fossil Halls, where more than 600 specimens are on display, is a must. An extraordinarily high percentage of the specimens on view—85%—are real fossilized bones as opposed to casts. At most museums those percentages are reversed, so here visitors have the chance to see the real thing including T. rex, velociraptor, and triceratops.

What to Hit Next? The museum also is renowned for its habitat dioramas, which are considered among the finest examples in the world. Visits to the Akeley Hall of African Mammals, the Hall of North American Mammals, and the Sanford Hall of North American Birds provide an overview of the diorama arts—pioneered and advanced at the museum—while allowing visitors to come face-to-face with some glorious and beautiful animals depicted in their natural habitats—habitats which in many cases no longer exist in such pristine conditions.

If You're Looking to Be Starstruck: Even if you don't have time to take in a space show in the Hayden Planetarium, the Rose Center for Earth and Space has lots of fascinating exhibits describing the vast range of sizes in the cosmos; the 13-billion-year history of the universe; the nature of galaxies, stars, and planets; and the dynamic features of our own unique planet Earth—all enclosed in a facility with spectacular award-winning architecture.

Hidden gems

The museum consists of 45 exhibition halls in 25 interconnected buildings so there are gems around every corner. Some lesser-known treasures include:

Star of India: The 563-carat Star of India, the largest and most famous star sapphire in the world, is displayed in the Morgan Memorial Hall of Gems.

ID PLEASE!

Once a year (usually in May or June—check website for details), the museum invites visitors to share rocks, teeth, shells, insects, feathers, and other curiosities with their scientists and anthropologists. Previous Identification Days have yielded rocks from the Jurassic Period, a fossilized walrus skull, and a 5,000-year-old stone spear point from Morocco. Lines can be long, but it's *so* interesting.

Black Smokers: These sulfide chimneys—collected during groundbreaking museum expeditions to the Pacific Ocean—are the only such specimens exhibited anywhere. Black smokers form around hot springs on the deep ocean floor and support a microbial community that does not live off sunlight but instead on the chemical energy of the Earth. Some of these microbes are considered the most ancient forms of life on Earth and may offer clues to the development of life here and the possibility of life elsewhere. See them in the Gottesman Hall of Planet Earth.

Spectrum of Life: The Hall of Biodiversity aims to showcase the glorious diversity of life on Earth resulting from 3.5 billion years of evolution. The impressive "Spectrum of Life" display is a 100-foot-long installation of more than 1,500 specimens and models—microorganisms and mammals, bacteria and beetles, fungi and fish. Use the computer workstations to learn more about the species depicted in each area.

Dodo: One of the museum's rarest treasures is the skeleton of a dodo bird, displayed along with other endangered or extinct species in the "Endangered Case" in the Hall of Biodiversity.

Small Dioramas: Tucked along the sides of the Hall of North American Mammals are two easy-to-miss corridors displaying a number of exquisitely rendered dioramas. In these jewel-box-like displays, some a mere 3 feet deep, you will see the smaller animals such as wolves galloping through a snowy night, a Canada lynx stalking a snowshoe hare, and a spotted skunk standing on its hands, preparing to spray a cacomistle, to name just a few of the evocative scenes.

Dinosaur Eggs: In 1993 museum scientists working in the Gobi Desert of Mongolia were the first to unearth fossilized embryos in dinosaur eggs, as well as the fossil of an adult oviraptor in a brooding posture over its nest. This discovery provided invaluable information about dinosaur gestation and revolutionized thinking about dinosaur behavior. Look for the display in the museum's Fossil Halls on the fourth floor.

Ross Terrace: In warmer months the Ross Terrace, with its fountains and cosmic theme, offers a wonderful outdoor spot for resting and reflecting, while providing a spectacular view of the Rose Center for Earth and Space.

Star of India

A diorama featuring a Komodo Dragon, the largest and most powerful lizard in the world.

MOST INTERESTING OBJECT?

What's most interesting about the American Museum of Natural History is not any single object on exhibit, but the sheer range and scope of what you can experience here. Think of it is a field guide to the natural world, the universe, and the cultures of humanity—all under one roof. The experience of visiting the museum is ultimately about awakening a sense of discovery, wonder, awe, and stewardship of this Earth we call home.

voice. While the permanent collection of more than 6 million pieces of art, literature, and memorabilia sheds light on America's history, art, and architecture, the special exhibitions showcase the museum's fresh—and often surprising—insight on all things New York. The Henry Luce III Center for the Study of American Culture (due to reopen in late 2016) will include a new Center for the Study of Women's History, with permanent and rotating exhibits that examine and celebrate New York's central role in women's history, especially for New Yorkers like Eleanor Roosevelt, Zora Neale Hurston, and Margaret Sanger. The DiMenna Children's History Museum on the lower level invites children to become "history detectives" and explore New York's past through interactive displays, hands-on activities, and the stories of iconic New York children through the centuries. The Historical Viewfinder allows kids to see how certain New York sites have changed over time. Unlike most other childrens' museums, this museum is geared to mature elementary and middle schoolers, not toddlers. Caffé Storico, the light-filled restaurant on the first floor (with a separate entrance), serves upscale Italian food at lunch and dinner and is open for weekend brunch. ⊠ *170 Central Park W, Upper West Side* ☏ *212/873–3400* ⊕ *www.nyhistory.org* ⊠ *$19 (pay-as-you-wish Fri. 6–8 pm)* ⊗ *Tues.–Thurs. and Sat. 10–6, Fri. 10–8, Sun. 11–5* Ⓜ *B, C to 81st St.–Museum of Natural History.*

WORTH NOTING

American Folk Art Museum. After a near–death, or rather, near- *debt* experience in late 2011, the American Folk Art Museum left its home of 10 years on 53rd Street(since overtaken by MoMA) and returned to its humble rental near Lincoln Center. Here, the focus returns to its incredible collection of contemporary self-taught artists of the 20th and 21st centuries, including the single largest collection of reclusive Chicago artist Henry Darger, known for his painstakingly detailed collage paintings of fantasy worlds. Past exhibitions have included "Folk Couture: Fashion and Folk Art," which featured the work of 13 established and emerging designers who created an original ensemble comprising paintings, sculptures, photographs, quilts, and furniture from the museum's collection. The gift shop has an impressive collection of handcrafted items. ⊠ *2 Lincoln Sq., Columbus Ave. at 66th St., Upper West Side* ☏ *212/595–9533* ⊕ *www.folkartmuseum.org* ⊠ *Free* ⊗ *Tues.–Thurs. and Sat. 11:30–7, Fri. noon–7, Sun. noon–6* Ⓜ *1 to 66th St.–Lincoln Center; A, B, C, D to 59th St.–Columbus Circle.*

FAMILY **Children's Museum of Manhattan.** In this five-story exploratorium, children ages 1–7 are invited to paint their own masterpieces, float boats down a "stream" (weather permitting), rescue animals with Dora and Diego (in an exhibition created in collaboration with Nickelodeon), and walk through giant interactive organs to explore the connections between food, sleep, and play. Special exhibits are thoughtfully put together and fun. Seasonal programs include a Grinch Holiday workshop. Art workshops, science programs, and storytelling sessions are held daily. Admission is free 5–8 pm on the first Friday of every month. ⊠ *212 W. 83rd St., between Broadway and Amsterdam Ave., Upper West Side* ☏ *212/721–1223* ⊕ *www.cmom.org* ⊠ *$11* ⊗ *Tues.–Fri. and Sun. 10–5, Sat. 10–7* Ⓜ *1 to 79th St.*

Columbus Circle. This busy traffic circle at Central Park's southwest corner anchors the Upper West Side and makes a good starting place for exploring the neighborhood if you're coming from south of 59th Street. The central 700-ton granite monument (capped by a marble statue of Christopher Columbus) serves as a popular meeting place. To some people, Columbus Circle is synonymous with the Time Warner Center building (*212/823–6300; www.theshopsatcolumbuscircle.com*) and its several floors of shops and restaurants, including takeout-friendly Bouchon Bakery and Whole Foods—both perfect places to pick up picnic fixings to take to Central Park. It's also home to the Rose Hall performing arts complex, part of Jazz at Lincoln Center. ⊠ *Broadway at 58th St. to 60th St., Upper West Side* Ⓜ *1, A, B, C, D to 59 St.–Columbus Circle.*

The Dakota. One of the first residences built on the Upper West Side, the château-style Dakota (1884) remains an architectural fixture with its lovely gables, gaslights, copper turrets, and central courtyard. Celebrity residents have included Boris Karloff, Rudolf Nureyev, José Ferrer, Rosemary Clooney, Lauren Bacall, Leonard Bernstein, Gilda Radner, and Connie Chung, but none more famous than John Lennon, who in 1980 was shot and killed at the Dakota's gate by a deranged fan. ⊠ *1 W. 72nd St., at Central Park W, Upper West Side* Ⓜ *B, C to 72nd St.*

Grant's Tomb (*General Grant National Memorial*). Walk through upper Riverside Park and you're sure to notice this towering granite mausoleum (1897), the final resting place of Civil War general and two-term president Ulysses S. Grant and his wife, Julia Dent Grant. As the old joke goes, who's buried here? Nobody—they're *entombed* in a crypt beneath a domed rotunda, surrounded by photographs and Grant memorabilia. Once a more popular sight than the Statue of Liberty, this pillared Classical Revival edifice feels more like a relic of yesteryear, but it remains a moving tribute. The words engraved on the tomb, "Let Us Have Peace," recall Grant's speech to the Republican convention upon his presidential nomination. Surrounding the memorial are the so-called "rolling benches," which are swoopy and covered with colorful mosaic tiles that bring to mind the works of architect Antoni Gaudí's Park Güell, in Barcelona. Made in the 1970s as a public art project, they are now as beloved as they are incongruous with the grand memorial they surround. Free public talks are available in the visitor center (across the street from the tomb), Thursday through Monday at 11:15, 1:15, and 3:15. ⊠ *Riverside Dr. at 122nd St., Upper West Side* ☎ *212/666–1640* ⊕ *www.nps.gov/gegr* ᠅ *Free* ☉ *Wed.–Sun. 9–5* Ⓜ *1 to 116th St. St.*

Museum of Arts and Design (*MAD*). In a funky-looking white building across from the Time Warner Center, the Museum of Arts and Design celebrates joyful quirkiness and personal, sometimes even obsessive, artistic visions. The art is human-scale here, much of it neatly housed in display cases rather than hanging on the walls, with a strong focus on contemporary jewelry, glass, ceramic, fiber, wood, and mixed-media works. Thursday evening is pay-what-you-wish. ⊠ *2 Columbus Circle, 59th St. at 8th Ave., Upper West Side* ☎ *212/299–7777* ⊕ *www.madmuseum.org* ᠅ *$16* ☉ *Tues., Wed., and weekends 10–6, Thurs. and Fri. 10–9* Ⓜ *1, A, B, C, D to 59th St.–Columbus Circle.*

FAMILY   **Riverside Park.** Surrounded by concrete and skyscrapers in Manhattan, you might not realize that there is an expansive green space running along the water just blocks away. Riverside Park—which, along with the Riverside Park South extension, runs along the Hudson from 58th to 156th streets—dishes out a dose of tranquillity. The original sections of Riverside Park, designed by Frederick Law Olmsted and Calvert Vaux of Central Park fame and laid out between 1873 and 1888, have a waterfront bike and walking paths. There are several access points to the park, including one at West 72nd Street and Riverside Drive (look for the statue of Eleanor Roosevelt), where you reach the waterfront path by an underpass beneath the West Side Highway. You can then head north along the Hudson River, past the 79th Street Boat Basin, where a flotilla of houseboats bobs in the water. Above it, a ramp leads to the Rotunda, home in summer to the Boat Basin Café, a dog-friendly open-air café that serves lunch and dinner in the warmer months (from March-ish through October). The 91st Street Garden, planted by community gardeners, explodes with flowers in most seasons and is a level up from the water: leave the riverside path near 92nd Street by taking another underpass and then heading up the path on the right. ⊠ *From 58th to 156th St., between Riverside Dr. and the Hudson River, Upper West Side* ⊕ *www.nycgovparks.org/parks/riversidepark* Ⓜ *1, 2, 3 to 72nd St.*

INWOOD

Well north of Harlem, at the very northern tip of Manhattan, Inwood is essentially the upper Upper West Side, with Fort Tryon Park lying just to it's south.

TOP ATTRACTIONS

The Cloisters Museum and Gardens. Perched on a wooded hill in Fort Tryon Park, near Manhattan's northwestern tip, the Cloisters Museum and Gardens houses the medieval collection of the Metropolitan Museum of Art and is a scenic destination in its own right. Colonnaded walks connect authentic French and Spanish monastic cloisters, a French Romanesque chapel, a 12th-century chapter house, and a Romanesque apse. One room is devoted to the 15th- and 16th-century Unicorn Tapestries, which date to 1500—a must-see masterpiece of medieval mythology. The tomb effigies are another highlight. Two of the three enclosed gardens shelter more than 250 species of plants similar to those grown during the Middle Ages, including flowers, herbs, and medicinals; the third is an ornamental garden planted with both modern and medieval plants, providing color and fragrance from early spring until late fall. Concerts of medieval music are held here regularly (concert tickets include same-day admission to the museum). The outdoor Trie Café is open 10 to 4:15 Tuesday through Sunday, from April to October, and serves sandwiches, coffee, and snacks. Admission includes same-day entry to the Metropolitan Museum of Art's main building on 82nd Street. ⊠ *99 Margaret Corbin Dr., Fort Tryon Park, Upper West Side* ☎ *212/923–3700* ⊕ *www.metmuseum.org* ✍ *$25 suggested donation* ☉ *Mar.–Oct., daily 10–5:15; Nov.–Feb., daily 10–4:45* Ⓜ *A to 190th St.*

HARLEM

GETTING ORIENTED

Highbridge Park

Morris-Jumel
Mansion

C M   B,D

Hispanic Society
of America Museum
and Library

Sugar Hill

W. 155th St.

W. 153rd St.

W. 152nd St.

W. 151st St.

Gitler &

W. 150th St.

W. 149th St.

W. 148th St.

W. 147th St.

W. 146th St.

M 3

W. 145th St.   3

M

A,B,C,D

Hamilton
Terrace

W. 144th St.

W. 143rd St.

W. 142nd St.

The Butcher's
Daughter

Manhattanville
Coffee

W. 141st St.

Hamilton Grange
Nat'l Memorial

Strivers'
Row

W. 140th St.

City College

W. 139th St.

W. 138th St.

Tatiana Pagés
Gallery

W. 137th St.

M 1

W. 136th St.

M 2,3

W. 135th St.

B,C

W. 134th St.

W. 133rd St.

Levain Bakery

Sugar Hill
Market

W. 132nd St.

W. 131st St.

W. 130th St.

W. 129th St.

W. 129th St.

W. 128th St.

M 1

W. 127th St.

W. 128th St.

Apollo
Theater

W. 127th St.

A,B,C,D   M

African Sq.

W. 126th St.

2,3

125th St-
Metro North

Dr. Martin Luther King Jr. Blvd. (125th St.)

Studio Museum
in Harlem

HARLEM

W. 124th St.

Marcus
Garvey
Park

W. 123rd St.

W. 122nd St.

W. 121st St.

Barnard
College

Columbia
University

W. 120th St.

W. 119th St.

E. 119th St.

W. 118th St.

E. 118th St.

Levain Bakery

W. 117th St.

E. 117th St.

B,C   M

Masjid Malcolm
Shabazz

M 2,3

E. 116th St.

W. 116th St.

Malcom Shabazz
Harlem Market

E. 115th St.

W. 114th St.

W. 112nd St.

Cathedral Church
of St. John the Divine

W. 113th St.

M 1

Cathedral Pkwy.

B,C

W. 111th St.

Central Park North   2,3

W. 109th St.

CENTRAL
PARK

Harlem
Meer

THE
BRONX

Harlem River

Riverside
Park

Riverside Dr.

Henry Hudson Pkwy

Broadway

Amsterdam Ave.

Convent Ave.

St. Nicholas Ave.

Jackie Robinson Park

Edgecombe Ave.

Frederick Douglass Blvd.

Harlem River Dr.

145 St. Bridge

Fifth Ave.

Madison Ave. Bridge

Park Ave.

E. 135th St.

E. 131st St.

E. 129th St.

St. Nicholas Park

Adam Clayton Powell Jr. Blvd.

Lenox Ave. (Malcolm X Blvd.)

Morningside Park

Dr. Martin Luther King Jr. Blvd.

Columbus Ave.

Amsterdam Ave.

Broadway

Central Park W.

(7th Ave.)

(8th Ave.)

(Sixth Ave.)

Mt. Morris Park West

St. Nicholas Ave.

Fifth Ave.

Madison Ave.

Harlem

0 ————— 1/4 mile

0 ————— 400 meters

MAKING THE MOST OF YOUR TIME

Harlem's simplest pleasures are free. Take time to walk the areas around Strivers' Row, Hamilton Heights, Sugar Hill, and 116th Street to see some impressive—and often fanciful—architecture. Hear the sweet sounds of a choir practice as you stroll by any of Harlem's churches (which number in the hundreds). See well-curated exhibits showcasing the work of contemporary artists of African descent at the Studio Museum in Harlem (open Thursday–Sunday), or visit the Morris-Jumel Mansion for a trip back in time to colonial New York.

GETTING HERE AND AROUND

The 2 and 3 subway lines stop on Lenox Avenue; the 1 goes along Broadway, to the west; and the A, B, C, and D trains travel along St. Nicholas and 8th avenues. And yes, as the song goes, the A train is still usually "the quickest way to Harlem."

The city's north–south avenues take on different names in Harlem: 6th Avenue is called both Malcolm X Boulevard *and* Lenox Avenue; 7th Avenue is Adam Clayton Powell Jr. Boulevard (named for the influential minister and congressman); and 8th Avenue is Frederick Douglass Boulevard. West 125th Street, the major east–west street and Harlem's commercial center, is also known as Dr. Martin Luther King Jr. Boulevard.

TOP EXPERIENCES

Shopping at the monthly Sugar Hill Market

Visiting the Studio Museum in Harlem

COFFEE AND QUICK BITES

Levain Bakery. From coffee and cakes to breads and scones, this bakery has something for every sweet tooth. It's the cookies, however, that make them famous. Choose from varieties such as chocolate chip walnut and dark-chocolate chocolate chip; they're big enough to share, but after one bite you may not want to. ⊠ *2167 Frederick Douglass Blvd., between 116th and 117th sts., Harlem* ☎ *646/455–0952* ⊕ *www.levainbakery.com* Ⓜ *B, C to 116th St.*

Manhattanville Coffee. It may be on a quiet corner, but this coffee shop is always buzzing. The vintage-inspired space appeals to laptop-toting locals with a large communal table, tufted leather couches, and free Wi-Fi. The super-friendly staff, Intelligentsia coffee, and gourmet pastries make this a neighborhood favorite. ⊠ *142 Edgecombe Ave., at 142nd St., Harlem* ☎ *646/781–9900* ⊕ *www.manhattanvillecoffee. com* Ⓜ *A, B, C, D to 145th St.; B, C to 135th St.*

Sightseeing
★★
Nightlife
★★★★
Dining
★★★
Lodging
★★
Shopping
★★

Harlem is known throughout the world as a center of African American culture, music, and life. The neighborhood invites visitors to see historic jewels such as the Apollo Theater, architecturally splendid churches, cultural magnets like the Studio Museum in Harlem and the Schomburg Center for Research in Black Culture, as well as an ongoing list of new and renovated sites and buildings.

Updated by
Anuja Madar

Harlem's 125th Street is at the heart of the neighborhood. Bill Clinton's New York office is at 55 West 125th Street, and the legendary Apollo Theater stands at No. 253. A large number of chains (Starbucks, Red Lobster, H&M) makes it hard to distinguish 125th Street from the city's other heavily commercialized areas, but there are still a few things that set it apart: an energy created by sidewalk vendors hawking bootleg DVDs, incense, and African shea butter; impromptu drum circles; and some of the best people-watching in Manhattan.

To get a feel for Harlem, spend time visiting its past and present. On 116th Street, particularly between St. Nicholas and Lenox avenues (Malcolm X Boulevard), you'll find some of the area's most interesting religious buildings, from ornate churches to a green-domed mosque.

Along Lenox Avenue and Frederick Douglass Boulevard, between 110th and 130th streets are restaurants, bars, and a few boutiques offering everything from bespoke cocktails and live music to Harlem-inspired gifts and high-end menswear.

TOP ATTRACTIONS

Apollo Theater. ⇨ *See the listing in Chapter 20 Performing Arts.*

Hamilton Heights. To taste this neighborhood's Harlem Renaissance days, walk down tree-lined Convent Avenue and cross over to Hamilton Terrace to see a time capsule of elegant stone rowhouses in mint condition. One of the neighborhood's most beautiful blocks, it's popular with film and TV crews. The Hamilton Grange National Memorial, founding father Alexander Hamilton's Federal-style mansion, resides at the southern end of the block, on 141st Street. Turn west and continue

CLOSE UP

D.I.Y. Harlem Gospel Tours

For the past decade, the popularity of Sunday gospel tours has surged. While some in the community see it as an opportunity to broaden horizons and encourage diversity, others find tours disruptive and complain that tourists take seats away from regular parishioners (churches regularly fill to capacity). If you plan on attending a service, here are some tips:

Most churches have Sunday services at 11, but you may need to arrive as much as two hours early (depending on the church) to get in. Dress nicely (no shorts, sneakers, or jeans); be as quiet as possible; do not leave in the middle of the service; and do not take photos or videos or use your cell phone. Most important, remember that parishioners do not consider the service, or themselves, tourist attractions or entertainment.

A bus tour is generally an inauthentic (and more expensive) way to experience Harlem. Explore the neighborhood and churches on your own, or join a small tour like those led by **Harlem Heritage Tours** (*212/280-7888; www.harlemheritage.com*). Their tours ($39) get high marks from past clients and are run by guides who were born and raised in Harlem. Groups are no larger than 25 people.

The following are some of the uptown churches with Sunday services:

Abyssinian Baptist Church (*132 W. 138th St., between Adam Clayton Powell Jr. Blvd. and Lenox Ave.; 212/862-7474; www.abyssinian.org*) is one of the few churches that does not allow tour groups. Service for visitors is at 11; arrive at least two hours ahead of time. **Canaan Baptist Church of Christ** (*132 W. 116th St., between Malcolm X and Adam Clayton Powell Jr. blvds.; 212/866-0301; www.cbccnyc.org*) has service at 10. **Convent Avenue Baptist Church** (*420 W. 145th St., between Convent and St. Nicholas aves.; 212/234-6767; www.conventchurch.org*) has services at 8, 11, and 5. **First Corinthian Baptist Church** (*1912 Adam Clayton Powell Jr. Blvd., at 7th Ave.; 212/864-5976; www.fcbcnyc.org*) has services at 7:30, 9:30, and 11:30.

Greater Refuge Temple (*2081 Adam Clayton Powell Jr. Blvd., at 124th St.; 212/866-1700; www.greaterrefugetemple.org*) has services at 11, 4, and 7:30. **Memorial Baptist Church** (*141 W. 115th St., between Malcolm X and Adam Clayton Powell Jr. blvds.; 212/663-8830; www.mbcvisionharlem.org*) has service at 11.

13

---

down Convent Avenue to see the looming Gothic spires (1905) of City College. The stately Oxford-inspired buildings here are New York to the core: they are clad with the schist rock unearthed when the city was building the IRT line (1 train). Next, head southwest to visit Strivers' Row. ⊠ *Convent Ave., between 138th and 150th sts., Harlem* Ⓜ *A, B, C, D to 145th St.*

FAMILY **Morris-Jumel Mansion.** During the Revolutionary War, General Washington used this wooden, pillared 8,500-square-foot house (1765) as his headquarters, and when he visited as president in 1790, he brought along John Quincy Adams, Thomas Jefferson, and Alexander Hamilton. Inside are rooms furnished with period decorations; upstairs, keep an eye out for the hand-painted wallpaper (original to the house) and a "commode chair," stuck in a corner of the dressing room. Outside, behind the house, is a Colonial-era marker that says it's 11 miles to New York—a reminder of what a small sliver of Manhattan the city was at that time. East of the house is the block-long Sylvan Terrace, a row of crisp two-story clapboard houses built in 1882. ⊠ *65 Jumel Terr., north of 160th St., between St. Nicholas and Edgecome aves., Harlem* 🕾 *212/923–8008* ⊕ *www.morrisjumel.org* ✉ *$5; guided tour $6* ۞ *Tues.–Sun. 10–4; guided tours Sat. at noon* Ⓜ *C to 163rd St.*

Strivers' Row. This block of gorgeous 1890s Georgian and Italian Renaissance Revival homes earned its nickname in the 1920s from less affluent Harlemites who felt its residents were "striving" to become well-to-do. Some of the few remaining private service alleys, used when deliveries arrived via horse and cart, lie behind these houses and are visible through iron gates. Note the gatepost between nos. 251 and 253 on 138th Street that reads, "Private Road. Walk Your Horses." These houses were built by the contractor David H. King Jr., whose works also include the base for the Statue of Liberty and the oldest parts of the Cathedral Church of St. John the Divine. When they failed to sell to whites, the properties on these blocks were sold to African American doctors, lawyers, and other professionals; composers and musicians W. C. Handy and Eubie Blake were also among the residents. If you have the time, detour a block north to see the palazzo-style group of houses designed by Stanford White, on the north side of 139th Street. ⊠ *138th and 139th sts., between Adam Clayton Powell Jr. and Frederick Douglass blvds., Harlem* Ⓜ *B, C to 135th St.*

Fodor'sChoice
★

Studio Museum in Harlem. Contemporary art by African American, Caribbean, and African artists is the focus of this small museum with a light-filled sculpture garden. Three artists in residence present their works each year, and summer hosts the lively Uptown Fridays! featuring DJs, cocktails, and a fashionable crowd. The gift shop is small but packs a lot of punch; don't miss its fantastic collection of coffee table books. ⊠ *144 W. 125th St., between Lenox Ave. and Adam Clayton Powell Jr. Blvd., Harlem* 🕾 *212/864–4500* ⊕ *www.studiomuseum.org* ✉ *$7 suggested donation (free Sun.)* ۞ *Thurs. and Fri. noon–9, Sat. 10–6, Sun. noon–6* Ⓜ *2, 3 to 125th St.*

Fodor'sChoice
★

Sugar Hill Market. This monthly market, held on the ground floor of an art gallery's brownstone space, features a mostly consistent roster of Harlem-based designers. Expect to find handmade items including vegan soaps, pottery, gourmet jams, and clothing fusing modern silhouettes with Ghanaian fabrics. The market's founder (who happens to have a fashion background) creates limited-edition Harlem T-shirts that make great souvenirs. ⊠ *La Maison d'Art, 259 W. 132nd St., between Frederick Douglass and Adam Clayton Powell Jr. blvds.* ⊹ *Located on the ground floor of a brownstone; look for the sandwich board on the sidewalk* ⊕ *sugarhillmarketnyc.blogspot.com* ۞ *Date and location of market varies, so check the website before visiting* Ⓜ *A, B, C, 2, 3 to 135th St.*

The Studio Museum, in Harlem

WORTH NOTING

The Butcher's Daughter. After five years in Detroit, Monica Bowman (yes, she really is a butcher's daughter) moved her gallery to this quiet block in Harlem. The glass-front space is minimal, allowing the exhibits, which change every six weeks and showcase emerging and established fine artists from across the U.S., to really shine. ✉ *318 W. 142nd St., between Edgecombe Ave. and Frederick Douglass Blvd.* ☎ 917/634–1354 ⊕ *www.thebutchersdaughtergallery.com* 🎟 *Free* ⏲ *Tues.–Sat. 11–6* Ⓜ *A, B, C, D to 145th St.*

Gitler & ____. This sliver of a gallery gets its name from owner and curator Avi Gitler, who uses the tight space to showcase up-and-coming artists from around the world and across genres. ✉ *3629 Broadway, between 149th and 150th sts.* ☎ *No phone* 📧 *info@gitlerand.com* ⊕ *www.gitlerand.com* 🎟 *Free* ⏲ *Weekends 1–6, Mon. 3–8* Ⓜ *1 to 145th St.*

FAMILY **Hamilton Grange National Memorial.** Founding father Alexander Hamilton and his wife raised eight kids in this Federal-style country home, which he called his "sweet project." Located on Hamilton's 32 acres, the Grange, named after his father's childhood home in Scotland, has moved three times since it was built in 1802. It now stands in St. Nicholas Park and gives a lesson in Hamilton's life, from his illegitimate birth in the West Indies and his appointment as the nation's first Secretary of Treasury to his authorship on *The Federalist Papers* and his death following a duel with Vice President Aaron Burr. The house's ground floor, formerly servants quarters, hosts an interactive exhibit that includes a short film on Hamilton's life. Upstairs a parlor, study, dining room,

Harlem's Jazz Age

It was in Harlem that Billie Holiday got her first singing job, Duke Ellington made his first recording, and Louis Armstrong was propelled to stardom. Jazz was king during the Harlem Renaissance in the 1920s and '30s, and though Chicago and New Orleans may duke it out for the "birthplace of jazz" title, New York was where jazz musicians came to be heard.

In the 1920s, socialites made the trek uptown to Harlem's Cotton Club and Connie's Inn (131st Street and 7th Avenue) to hear "black" music. Both clubs were white-owned and barred blacks from entering, except

as performers. (The rules changed years later.) Connie's introduced New Yorkers to Louis Armstrong. The Cotton Club—Harlem's most popular nightspot by far—booked such big names as Fletcher Henderson, Coleman Hawkins, Duke Ellington, Cab Calloway, and Ethel Waters. After shows ended at the paying clubs, musicians would head to after-hours establishments with black patrons, such as Small's Paradise, Minton's Playhouse (which reopened in 2013), and Basement Brownies, where they'd hammer out new riffs into the wee hours.

and two guest rooms are open to view; note the beautiful piano, which belonged to his daughter Angelica. ⊠ *414 W. 141st St., between St. Nicholas and Convent aves., Harlem* ☎ *646/548–2310* ⊕ *www.nps.gov/hagr/index.htm* ☞ *Free* ☉ *Wed.–Sun. 9–5* ☞ *Self-guided tours of the furnished rooms 9–10, noon–1, and 3–4 only; 30-min ranger-led tours at 10, 11, 2, and 4* Ⓜ *1 to 137th St.–City College; A, B, C, D to 145th St.*

FAMILY

Fodor'sChoice

★

The Hispanic Society of America Museum and Library. This is the best collection of Hispanic and Spanish art outside El Prado in Madrid, with paintings, sculptures, textiles, manuscripts, music, and decorative arts from ancient Iberia through the 20th century. On the first floor, Joaquín Sorolla y Bastida's *Vision of Spain* fills the entire Sala Bancaja; stand in the middle and admire the 13 massive, colorful paintings, capturing everything from Holy Week penitents to fishermen in Catalonia. A smaller room houses intricately carved marble pieces from bishops' tombs. Upstairs, there's a room filled with antique iron doorknockers, two rooms of earthenware from Spain and Mexico, and notable pieces by Goya, El Greco, Murillo, Velázquez, and Zurbarán. The entrance is on Broadway, between 155th and 156th streets, up the steps to the left. ⊠ *Audubon Terr., 613 W. 155th St., Harlem* ☎ *212/926–2234* ⊕ *www.hispanicsociety.org* ☞ *Free* ☉ *Tues.–Sat. 10–4:30, Sun. 1–4* Ⓜ *1 to 157th St.*

Masjid Malcolm Shabazz (*Mosque*). Talk about religious conversions. In the mid-'60s, the Lenox Casino was transformed into this house of worship and cultural center, and given bright yellow arches and a huge, green onion dome that loudly proclaims its presence in a neighborhood of churches. Once functioning as Temple No. 7 under the Nation of Islam with a message of pro-black racism, the mosque was bombed after the assassination of Malcolm X, who had preached here. It was then rebuilt and renamed in honor of the name Malcolm took at the end of his life, El-Hajj Malik Shabazz; its philosophy now is one of inclusion. These days the Sunni congregation has a large proportion of immigrants from Senegal, many of whom live in and around 116th Street. Next door is Graceline Court, a 16-story luxury condominium building that cantilevers somewhat awkwardly over the mosque. Farther east on 116th Street is the outdoor Malcolm Shabazz Harlem Market, where you can find African and African-inspired jewelry, art, clothing, and fabrics. On weekends with nice weather more vendors open. ✉ *102 W. 116th St., at Malcolm X Blvd., Harlem* ☎ *212/662–2200* ⊕ *www. masjidmalcolmshabazz.com* Ⓜ *2, 3 to 116th St.*

Sugar Hill. Standing on the bluff of Sugar Hill overlooking Jackie Robinson Park, outside the slightly run-down 409 Edgecombe Ave., you'd never guess that here resided such influential African Americans as NAACP founder W.E.B. DuBois and Supreme Court Justice Thurgood Marshall, or that farther north at 555 Edgecombe (known as the "Triple Nickel"), writers Langston Hughes and Zora Neale Hurston and jazz musicians Duke Ellington, Count Basie, and others lived and played. It's also here that for nearly 20 years musician Marjorie Eliot has been hosting jazz concerts in her apartment, 3F, at 3:30 pm every Sunday. Farther down, at No. 345, you can't miss the Benzinger House with its flared mansard roof. Amid all this history, the modern-looking Sugar Hill Children's Museum of Art & Storytelling, at 155th Street and St. Nicholas Avenue, is set to open in spring 2015. Its design has earned it the nickname "the Sugar Cube Building." ✉ *From 145th to 155th sts., between Edgecombe and St. Nicholas aves., Harlem* Ⓜ *A, B, C, D to 145th St.*

Tatiana Pagés Gallery. This Chilean-born, Dominican Republic–raised designer and collector doesn't have a long commute to work—she lives next door to her namesake gallery. Set on an unsuspecting corner near Strivers' Row, the gallery (Pagés's first) exhibits contemporary art and design, with an emphasis on Caribbean and Latin American art, ✉ *2605 Frederick Douglass Blvd., at 139th St.* ☎ *646/415–8093* ⊕ *www.tatianapagesgallery.com* 🎟 *Free* ☉ *Tues.–Fri. 11–7, Sat. 12–7* Ⓜ *A, B, C, D to 145th St.; B, C to 135th St.*

BROOKLYN

GETTING ORIENTED

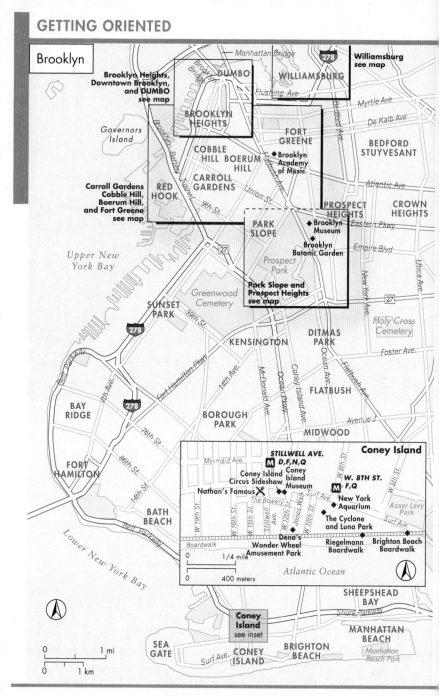

Brooklyn

**Brooklyn Heights,
Downtown Brooklyn,
and DUMBO
see map**

Manhattan Bridge

278 **Williamsburg
see map**

DUMBO

WILLIAMSBURG

Flushing Ave

Myrtle Ave

**BROOKLYN
HEIGHTS**

FORT
GREENE

De Kalb Ave

BEDFORD
STUYVESANT

*Governors
Island*

COBBLE
HILL BOERUM
HILL

◆ **Brooklyn
Academy
of Music**

CARROLL
GARDENS

Atlantic Ave

**Carroll Gardens
Cobble Hill,
Boerum Hill,
and Fort Greene
see map**

RED
HOOK

Union St.

PROSPECT
HEIGHTS

CROWN
HEIGHTS

9th St.

PARK
SLOPE

◆ **Brooklyn
Museum**

Eastern Pkwy

*Upper New
York Bay*

27

*Prospect
Park*

◆ **Brooklyn
Botanic Garden**

Empire Blvd

Ulica Ave.

27

*Greenwood
Cemetery*

**Park Slope and
Prospect Heights
see map**

*Holy Cross
Cemetery*

SUNSET
PARK

39th St.

KENSINGTON

DITMAS
PARK

Foster Ave.

278

Ocean Ave.

Flatbush Ave.

FLATBUSH

Fort Hamilton Pkwy

14th Ave.

McDonald Ave.

Ocean Pkwy

Coney Island Ave.

BAY
RIDGE

278

76th St.

BOROUGH
PARK

Avenue J

MIDWOOD

FORT
HAMILTON

86th St.

14th Ave.

Coney Island

BATH
BEACH

STILLWELL AVE.

Ⓜ **D,F,N,Q**

Mermaid Ave.

W. 8th St.

**Coney Island
Circus Sideshow**

**Coney
Island
Museum**

W. 8TH ST.

Ⓜ **F,Q**

Nathan's Famous ✕

◆◆

The Bowery

Surf Ave.

◆ **New York
Aquarium**

*Asser Levy
Park*

Bell Parkway

Jones Walk

*Stillwell
Ave.*

W 12th St.

W 15th St.

W 16th St.

W 19th St.

◆ **The Cyclone
and Luna Park**

Surf Ave.

Lower New York Bay

Dena's

**Wonder Wheel
Amusement Park**

Boardwalk

**Riegelmann
Boardwalk**

**Brighton Beach
Boardwalk**

◆

0   1/4 mile

0   400 meters

Atlantic Ocean

SHEEPSHEAD
BAY

Shore Parkway

**Coney
Island
see inset**

MANHATTAN
BEACH

SEA
GATE

Surf Ave.

CONEY
ISLAND

BRIGHTON
BEACH

*Manhattan
Beach Park*

0   1 mi

0   1 km

TOP EXPERIENCES

Eating and bar-hopping in Williamsburg

Screaming at the top of the Cyclone roller coaster in Coney Island

Smelling the roses, and everything else, at the Brooklyn Botanic Garden

Catching a show at BAM or Barclay's Center

Walking across the Brooklyn Bridge

Picnicking in Brooklyn Bridge Park

Being awestruck by architecture in Brooklyn Heights

GETTING HERE

Brooklyn is very accessible by subway from Manhattan; check the listings for subway info. Brooklyn Heights, Downtown Brooklyn, DUMBO, and Williamsburg are the closest neighborhoods to Manhattan. Coney Island and Brighton Beach are the farthest; budget about an hour each way if you're traveling from Midtown.

MAKING THE MOST OF YOUR TIME

The best way to get to Brooklyn is by its most majestic bridge. Walking along the wooden pedestrian path of the Brooklyn Bridge—a classic New York experience—takes about 30 minutes, worth it for the panoramic views of the skylines and the harbor. On summer weekends the path is crowded, unless you go early in the morning. Exit the bridge onto Cadman Plaza on the Brooklyn side, then walk southwest to get to Brooklyn Heights, a charming neighborhood of 19th-century brownstone homes, or walk north into the hip neighborhood of DUMBO.

COFFEE AND QUICK BITES

Almondine Bakery. The best French bakery this side of Montmartre is on Water Street. Chef Herve P. helms this neighborhood favorite, baking on-site daily chocolate raspberry croissants, mille feuille, macarons, and pear tarts, as well as baguettes, quiche, and sandwiches. These are perfect snacks to take to the park. ⊠ *85 Water St., DUMBO* ☎ *718/797–5056* ⊕ *www.almondinebakery.com* Ⓜ *F to York St.*

Jacques Torres Chocolate. French-born Torres is New York's adopted Willy Wonka. Here, he dishes out drool-worthy truffles and bonbons, and hot chocolate rich enough to make a Swiss miss blush. Festively wrapped bars and baskets make sweet souvenirs but the shop also has a café with marble-top tables for those whose chocolate cravings simply cannot wait. ⊠ *66 Water St., DUMBO* ☎ *718/875–1269* ⊕ *www.mrchocolate.com* Ⓜ *A, C to High St.; F to York St.*

14

Sightseeing
★★★

Nightlife
★★★★

Dining
★★★★ ★

Lodging
★ ★

Shopping
★★★

Updated by
Laura Itzkowitz,
Kristin Iversen,
Christina Knight,
Megan Eileen
McDonough,
Marisa Meltzer,
Chris Molanphy,
Matt Rodbard,
Emily Saladino,
and Sarah
Spagnolo

Hardly Manhattan's sidekick, Brooklyn is a destination in its own right, with many diverse neighborhoods and a seemingly endless number of compelling sights and fabulous places to eat and drink and shop.

Across the East River from Manhattan, on Long Island's western edge, Brooklyn is one of New York City's five boroughs. At 71 square miles, it's more than three times the size of Manhattan, and with more than 2½ million people, if it were a city it would be the fourth largest in the United States, in terms of population.

Brooklyn *was* a city until the end of the 19th century, with its own widely circulated newspaper (*The Brooklyn Eagle*), its own expansive park (Prospect Park), and its own baseball team that would eventually be called the Brooklyn Dodgers. In 1883 it also got its own bridge: the Brooklyn Bridge, which drew the attention of the entire country.

Today **Brooklyn Heights** and **DUMBO** are easily accessible from Manhattan by subway or via the Brooklyn Bridge; both neighborhoods have compelling but very different architecture (brownstones versus 19th-century warehouses), and fabulous views of Manhattan. **Carroll Gardens, Cobble Hill, Boerum Hill,** and **Fort Greene** all have plenty of lovely streets to stroll, thriving restaurant and bar scenes. The latter also has the Brooklyn Academy of Music. **Williamsburg** is the epicenter of trendsetting Brooklyn, which is overflowing into up-and-coming **Bushwick** and **East Williamsburg. Park Slope** and **Prospect Park** welcome with laid-back, family-friendly activities, while **Prospect Heights** and **Crown Heights** are home to heavy hitters like the Barclays Center, the Brooklyn Botanic Gardens, Weeksville Heritage Center, and the Brooklyn Children's Museum. **Coney Island** and **Brighton Beach** have Brooklyn's subway-accessible beaches, boardwalks, and amusement parks, including the legendary Cyclone roller coaster.

Brooklyn Is Book Country

Brooklyn has been a mecca for writers and literature since the days of *Uncle Tom's Cabin*, written by a preacher's daughter in Brooklyn Heights. Since then writers have flocked here for the cheap rent and quiet streets. Henry Miller, Norman Mailer, Truman Capote, Arthur Miller (with Marilyn Monroe), Paul and Jane Bowles, Carson McCullers, James Purdy, and Walt Whitman created more than one masterpiece here.

Today, amid the gentrification, Brooklyn continues to lure famous and near-famous writers and musicians from all over the world.

Perhaps reflecting the plethora of writers in the neighborhood, the borough has a relatively high density of both used and new bookstores, and also several small presses, including Melville House, a publisher with a storefront.

And with all these writers so close by, it only makes sense that Brooklyn has a fabulous book festival, to boot. The Brooklyn Book Festival happens every year at Borough Hall, on the third weekend in September. Authors gather for readings and signings, and independent publishers display their wares.

14

BROOKLYN HEIGHTS

Brooklyn Heights is quintessential "brownstone Brooklyn." It's the oldest neighborhood in the borough, and the original village of Brooklyn; almost the entire neighborhood is part of the Brooklyn Heights Historic District. This is still very much the neighborhood of shady lanes, cobblestone streets, centuries-old rowhouses, and landmark buildings that Walt Whitman rhapsodized about, and the magnificent postcard views of of the Manhattan skyline and the Brooklyn Bridge have inspired countless artists and photographers since. In the early to mid-20th century, Brooklyn Heights was a bohemian haven, home to such writers as Arthur Miller, Truman Capote, Henry Miller, Alfred Kazin, Carson McCullers, Paul Bowles, Marianne Moore, Norman Mailer, and W.E.B. DuBois.

The majestic **Brooklyn Bridge** has one foot in Brooklyn Heights, near DUMBO, and a walk across it either to or from Lower Manhattan is one of the classic New York experiences.

TOP ATTRACTIONS

Brooklyn Bridge. (⇨ *Chapter 2*) *4, 5, 6 to Brooklyn Bridge–City Hall; J, Z to Chambers St.; A, C to High St.*

FAMILY

Fodor's Choice

★

Brooklyn Bridge Park. What started as a scenic but small hilltop park beneath the Manhattan Bridge has turned into a sweeping feat of green urban renewal stretching from the Manhattan Bridge in DUMBO to the Brooklyn Bridge and south all the way to Pier 5, carpeting old industrial sites along the waterfront with scenic esplanades and lush meadows. The park has playgrounds, sports fields, food concessions, a beach, a pop-up pool, and lots of grass for lounging. You can access the park at various points, including Main Street, for the Main Street Playground;

Old Dock Street, off Water Street, for the wonderfully restored **Jane's Carousel** (*see full listing in DUMBO*); Old Fulton Street, for the popular Fulton Ferry Landing and Pier 1; Old Squibb Park Bridge, off Columbia Heights, for piers 1 and 2; Montague Street, for Pier 5; and Joralemon Street, for piers 5 and 6. ⊠ *Brooklyn waterfront, between Manhattan Bridge and Pier 6, Brooklyn Heights* ☎ *718/222–9939* ⊕ *www.brooklynbridgepark.org* Ⓜ *2, 3 to Clark St.; A, C to High St.; F to York St.*

FAMILY
Fodor'sChoice
★

Brooklyn Heights Promenade. Strolling this mile-long path, famous for its magnificent Manhattan views, you might find it surprising to learn that its origins were purely functional: the promenade was built as a sound barrier to protect nearby brownstones from highway noise. Find a bench and take in the skyline, the Statue of Liberty, and the Brooklyn Bridge; the setting is especially impressive in the evening, when the lights of the city sparkle across the East River. Below are the Brooklyn–Queens Expressway and Brooklyn Bridge Park. ⊠ *Between Remsen and Cranberry Sts., Brooklyn Heights* Ⓜ *2, 3 to Clark St.; A, C to High St.; R to Court St.*

"Fruit" Streets. Brooklyn Heights is filled with stately brownstones and brick homes, and the quiet blocks of Pineapple, Cranberry, and Orange streets contain some of the most picturesque ones. A few homes made of wood still exist, too, although they've been banned in the Brooklyn Heights area since the mid-19th century because of the fire hazard. The wood-frame house at 24 Middagh Street, a typical example built in the Federal style, dates to the 1820s. Middagh Street was named for the ancestors of one Lady Middagh, who, so the legend goes, thought that naming streets after wealthy families was pretentious. Milady removed the existing street signs and installed her own fruit-themed ones. The city confiscated them, but she kept replacing the city's signs until her choices were made official. To ponder the irony that despite her initiative Middagh Street still exists, repair west (toward the East River) on Orange or Cranberry to the Fruit Street Sitting Area, the connector between Brooklyn Heights Promenade and Columbia Heights. ⊠ *Pineapple, Orange, and Cranberry Sts., Brooklyn Heights* Ⓜ *2, 3 to Clark St.; A, C to High St.*

FAMILY
Fodor'sChoice
★

New York Transit Museum. Step down into an old 1930s subway station to experience this entertaining museum's displays of vintage trains and memorabilia. You can wander through trains and turnstiles and sit behind the wheel of a former city bus (it's not only the kids who do this). Original advertising, signage, and upholstery make this feel like a trip back in time. The gift shop carries subway-line socks, decorative tile reproductions, and other fun stuff. ⊠ *Boerum Pl., at Schermerhorn St., Brooklyn Heights* ☎ *718/694–1600* ⊕ *www.mta.info/museum* ⊡ *$7* ⊙ *Tues.–Fri. 10–4, weekends 11–5* Ⓜ *2, 3, 4, 5 to Borough Hall; A, C, G to Hoyt–Schermerhorn Sts.; A, C, F, R to Jay St.–MetroTech; R to Court St.*

Brownstones in Brooklyn Heights

WORTH NOTING

Brooklyn Borough Hall. Built in 1848 as Brooklyn's city hall, this Greek Revival landmark, adorned with Tuckahoe marble, is one of the borough's handsomest buildings. The statue of Justice atop its cast-iron cupola was part of the original plan but wasn't installed until 1988. Today the building serves as the office of Brooklyn's borough president and the home of the Brooklyn Tourism & Visitors Center (weekdays 10–6; 718/802—3846). ⊠ *209 Joralemon St., between Court and Adams Sts., Brooklyn Heights* Ⓜ *2, 3, 4, 5 to Borough Hall; R to Court St.; A, C, F, R to Jay St.–MetroTech.*

Fodor'sChoice ★ **Brooklyn Historical Society.** Four centuries' worth of art and artifacts bring Brooklyn's story to life at this marvelous space. Housed in an 1881 Queen Anne–style National Historic Landmark building—one of the neighborhood's gems—the society surveys the borough's changing identity through permanent exhibits that include interactive displays, landscape paintings, photographs of the area, portraits of prominent Brooklynites, and fascinating memorabilia. Check the website for details about the stellar lineup of temporary exhibitions. ⊠ *128 Pierrepont St., at Clinton St., Brooklyn Heights* ☎ 718/222–4111 ⊕ *www.brooklynhistory.org* ⊐ *$10 suggested donation* ☉ *Wed.–Sun. noon–5* Ⓜ *2, 3, 4, 5 to Borough Hall; R to Court St.; A, C, F to Jay St.–MetroTech.*

SHOPPING

Fodor'sChoice ★ **Sahadi's.** Inhale the aromas of spices and dark-roast coffee beans as you enter this Middle Eastern trading post that's been selling bulk foods in Brooklyn since 1948. Bins and jars and barrels hold everything from

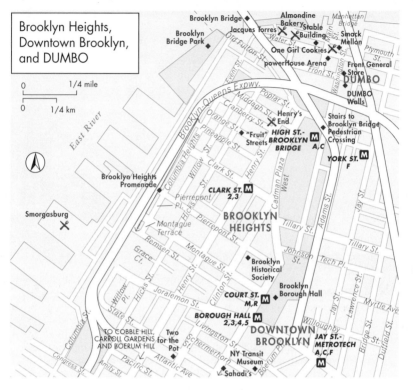

Brooklyn Heights,
Downtown Brooklyn,
and DUMBO

nuts, dried fruit, olives, and pickled vegetables to cheeses, chocolate, candy, those intoxicating coffees, and all manner of spices. There's a large selection of prepared food and groceries as well. ✉ *187 Atlantic Ave., Brooklyn Heights* ☎ *718/624–4550* ⊕ *www.sahadis.com* ⊗ *Closed Sun.* Ⓜ *2, 3, 4, 5 to Borough Hall; R to Court St.; A, C, F to Jay St.–MetroTech.*

Two for the Pot. The name of this narrow shop refers to the indulgent practice of adding two extra scoops of coffee grounds to every pot you brew, and if you're at all fond of indulging your coffee or tea tastes, you must stop in here. The wide selection of top-quality coffees and teas is complemented by brewing paraphernalia, artisanal honey, and hard-to-find brands of UK sweets and other comestibles. Helpful staff members have kept customers coming back since the shop opened in 1973. ✉ *200 Clinton St., Brooklyn Heights* ☎ *718/855–8173* ⊗ *Closed Mon.* Ⓜ *2, 3, 4, 5 to Borough Hall; R to Court St.; A, C, F to Jay St.–MetroTech.*

DOWNTOWN BROOKLYN

Downtown Brooklyn is modern and bustling, and other than a few notable restaurants, there isn't much to attract visitors—but it's convenient to the Brooklyn Bridge and Brooklyn Heights, and walking distance to neighborhoods like Cobble Hill, Boerum Hill, and DUMBO.

DUMBO

For sheer jaw-dropping drama, few city walks are as cinematic as strolling the DUMBO waterfront. The photogenic area pairs turn-of-the-century warehouses and refurbished industrial buildings on cobblestone streets with rumbling trains and soaring bridges overhead. (The latter gives the district its name, an acronym of Down Under the Manhattan Bridge Overpass.) Across the East River, the glittering Manhattan skyline provides epic views and popular backdrops for wedding proposals, fashion shoots, and innumerable selfies. Major galleries and performance hubs imbue the neighborhood with artistic élan, and an influx of technology start-ups bring 21st-century swagger in vintage sneakers.

An integral part of DUMBO is the Brooklyn Bridge Park, and the stroller set and nine-to-five lunch crowds flock to its benches and green spaces, as do brides galore, posing for wedding pictures with the perfect background.

TOP ATTRACTIONS

Fodor'sChoice ★ **The Stable Building.** Many Brooklynites mourned the Galapagos Art Space when they closed shop and moved to Detroit; fortunately the site continues its arts legacy, and the building now houses four first-floor gallery spaces, which were previously part of the 111 Front Street gallery collective. Minus Space shows artists specializing in "reductive abstract art" (simple materials, precise craftsmanship, monochromatic or limited color, repetition of shapes). United Photo Industries (UPI) shows work by emerging photographers and those working in new photography styles. The Klompching Gallery focuses on fine-art photography. Masters Projects represents artists working in all sorts of media, including paint, mixed media, street art, photography, and installations. Gallery hours vary, but weekday and Saturday afternoons are your best bet to visit; most are closed Monday. ⊠ *16 Main St., at Water St., DUMBO* ⊙ *Gallery hrs vary* Ⓜ *2, 3 to Clark St.; A, C to High St.; F to York St..*

QUICK BITES ✕ **Smorgasburg Dumbo.** One hundred of New York City's best and brightest cooks and culinary artisans unite along the East River to form the city's hottest foodie flea market. This bazaar has launched countless culinary crazes (ramen burger, anyone?), and most vendors are small-scale, homegrown operators. An offshoot of the Brooklyn Flea, there is also an outpost on the Williamsburg waterfront. Smorgasburg is open Sundays, 11 to 6, from April to November. It's cash-only, but there are ATMs at the entrance. ⊠ *Brooklyn Bridge Park, Pier 5, DUMBO* ✛ *Enter near Pierrepont and Furman sts.* ⊕ *www.brooklynflea.com/markets/smorgasburg-dumbo* ⊙ *Closed Mon.–Sat. and Dec.–Mar.* Ⓜ *2, 3 to Clark St.; A, C to High St.; N, R to Court St.*

14

WORTH NOTING

DUMBO Walls. Keep your eyes on the wall under and around the Manhattan Bridge and the BQE, where eight walls display artwork by big names including CAM, Shepard Fairey and MOMO. The project is sponsored by the DUMBO Improvement District and Two Trees Management Co, along with the New York City Department of Transportation Urban Art Program and the Jonathan LeVine Gallery. ⊠ *DUMBO* ⊕ *www. dumbo.is/itineraries/667* Ⓜ *F to York St.*

Smack Mellon. The transformation of an industrial boiler house into an edgy arts compound is quintessential DUMBO. The 12,000-square-foot structure now hosts large-scale, avant-garde exhibitions. They also run a prestigious residency program. Don't be surprised if you pass a binder-clutching bride-to-be on your way in: the 5,000-square-foot gallery is also a popular wedding venue. ⊠ *92 Plymouth St., DUMBO* ☎ *718/834–8761* ⊕ *www.smackmellon.org* ⊙ *Wed.–Sun. noon–6* Ⓜ *A, C to High St.; F to York St.*

QUICK
BITES **One Girl Cookies.** Snag a window seat overlooking cobblestone Main Street and tuck into a variety of whoopie pies, cakes, and cookies in flavors like chocolate-cinnamon ganache and Thai-ginger oatmeal, served with Stumptown Coffee. ⊠ *33 Main St., DUMBO* ☎ *347/338–1268* ⊕ *www. onegirlcookies.com/dumbo* Ⓜ *F to York St.; A, C to High St.*

SHOPPING

Fodor'sChoice
★ **Front General Store.** Outfitting DUMBO's cool kids since 2011, this shop sells his-and-hers vintage Ralph Lauren blazers, 1940s Royal Stetson hats, and other curated odds 'n' ends, including antique Mexican glassware and Chesterfield-esque leather armchairs. The store also hosts pop-up sidewalk shops by local artisans and designers. ⊠ *143 Front St., DUMBO* ☎ *347/693–5328* ⊕ *www.facebook.com/frontgeneralstore* Ⓜ *A, C to High St.; F to York St.*

Fodor'sChoice
★ **powerHouse Arena.** Edgy art-book publisher powerHouse is a vision in concrete and steel at this bright showroom that sells illustrated titles, children's books, and works by authors from Joseph Mitchell to Gary Shteyngart. The space also hosts publishing parties, book launches, readings, and discussion groups. ⊠ *37 Main St., DUMBO* ☎ *718/666–3049* ⊕ *www.powerhousearena.com* Ⓜ *A, C to High St.; F to York St.*

CARROLL GARDENS

Traditionally an Italian neighborhood, Carroll Gardens began gentrifying as far back as the 1960s, then really started to pick up in th 70s and 80s and never looked back. While many old-school vestiges remain—bakeries and butcher shops and others that harken to the 1950s—particularly along Court Street, a recent influx of Manhattanites and French expats has given the neighborhood a leafy and refined Parisian–West Village vibe. With that has come an exciting mix of cutting-edge restaurants and bistros, handsome cocktail lounges and craft beer bars, and boutiques selling the most current styles.

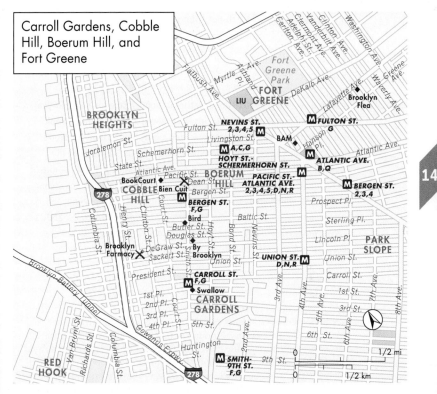

Carroll Gardens, Cobble Hill, Boerum Hill, and Fort Greene

14

SHOPPING

Fodor'sChoice **Bird.** Looking for the chic-est womenswear in Brooklyn? You found
★ it. Kaleidoscopic Tsumori Chisato knit sweater dresses, buttery Alexander Wang boots, A.P.C. cardigans, smart Edun tunics, 3.1 Phillip Lim frocks, Isabel Marant motorcycle jackets, Rachel Comey statement shoes, and delicate gold jewelry share the cozy space in this beloved boutique known for its indie designers and high prices. There are a few items for men as well. ⊠ *220 Smith St., at Butler St., Carroll Gardens* ☎ *718/797–2774* ⊕ *www.shopbird.com* Ⓜ *F, G to Bergen St.*

Fodor'sChoice **By Brooklyn.** The name says it all. This is the borough's prime purveyor of
★ dry goods, gifts, and comestibles conceived of and created in Brooklyn. Fill a Maptote denim tote bag stamped "Brooklyn" (of course) with jewelry by Natural Abstract, Morris Kitchen's ginger syrup (to create the perfect cocktail), and Apotheke soap. Other top picks include *The New Brooklyn Cookbook* featuring favorite recipes by some of the chefs and restaurants that have made Brooklyn's dining scene so buzzed-about, and the reclaimed Brooklyn slate cheeseboard by Brooklyn Slate Company. ⊠ *261 Smith St., Carroll Gardens* ☎ *718/643–0606* ⊕ *www. bybrooklyn.com* Ⓜ *F, G to Bergen St. or Carroll St.*

Fodor'sChoice **Swallow.** If you're looking for a gift or a special trinket for that hard-
★ to-shop-for friend or family member who has exquisite taste and an

appreciation for the finer things found in nature, head to Swallow. Delicate daguerreotypes, vases, anatomy-inspired jewelry, and other objets d'art and curiosities are just some of the offerings. Browsing here is a bit like traveling down the rabbit hole into a grown-up's houseware wonderland. ⊠ *361 Smith St., at 2nd St., Carroll Gardens* ☎ *718/222–8201* ⊕ *www.dearswallow.com* Ⓜ *F, G to Carroll St.*

QUICK BITES

Brooklyn Farmacy. In 2010 an industrious couple reopened this 100-year-old soda fountain that had been closed for about a dozen years. A book deal, national television appearances, and a couple thousand children's birthday parties since have definitely spelled success. Visit during the week, when you can score a seat at the counter for an egg cream or one of the Farmacy's seasonal sundaes. The sleeper hit, though, is the ice cream sandwiches, which are made daily using freshly churned ice cream and homemade wafers. ⊠ *513 Henry St., Carroll Gardens* ☎ *718/522–6260* ⊕ *www.brooklynfarmacyandsodafountain.com* ⌂ *Reservations not accepted* Ⓜ *F, G t~ Carroll St.*

COBBLE HILL

Cobble Hill stands out for its 19th-century architecture and leafy, compact parks. Dutch residents called the area Cobleshill in reference to a Revolutionary War–era land mound, which was flattened by British soldiers to prevent strategic use by George Washington's troops. These days, most of the 22-block neighborhood is landmarked as Brooklyn's second-oldest district, a mix of brick townhouses, brownstones, and Victorian schoolhouses, where only the Gothic Revival churches exceed a 50-foot height limit. Historically working-class, the neighborhood has adopted all the trappings of haute Brooklyn, especially along busy Court Street.

SHOPPING

Fodor's Choice ★ **BookCourt.** This wonderful, family-run shop has been a star on Court Street for more than 30 years. The tables and shelves are filled with books to browse, and the staff is happy to recommend titles. The shop stocks works by the neighborhood's many local writers, who often appear for readings and signings. ⊠ *163 Court St., Cobble Hill* ☎ *718/875–3677* ⊕ *www.bookcourt.com* Ⓜ *2, 3, 4, 5 to Borough Hall; F, G to Bergen St.*

BOERUM HILL

Understated elegance defines Boerum Hill, where red-brick townhouses and brownstones line quiet, leafy thoroughfares from 4th Avenue to Smith Street and Schermerhorn to Warren. The neighborhood saw an influx of immigrants in the late 1800s, with completion of the Brooklyn Bridge and the emergence of trolley cars, but fell into disrepair after World War II. Now fully gentrified, the setting is laden with beautiful cafés that are worth a visit. Despite its air of sophistication, Boerum Hill presents moments of levity, namely artist Susan Gardner's sparkly mosaic-covered brownstone at 108 Wyckoff Street.

**QUICK
BITES**

Bien Cuit. Locally ground flour, hand-mixed doughs, and European recipes are among this artisanal bakery and café's secrets to success. Some regulars drop by to stock up on classic challah, French *pain de mie* (a sweet bread good for sandwiches or to toast) and baguettes, and Italian Pugliese loaves, but others come for the pastries. It's hard to choose among the cranberry danishes, fruit tarts, chocolate pecan tortes, or the flawless croissants, the latter served plain or with chocolate. Bien Cuit makes sandwiches and quiches, too. ⊠ *120 Smith St., Boerum Hill* ☏ *718/852–0200* ⊕ *www.biencuit.com* ⊙ *No dinner* Ⓜ *F, G to Bergen St.*

FORT GREENE

Art institutions, flatteringly lit cafés, and the sort of show-stopping architecture that sends real estate agents into early retirement make Fort Greene irresistible. Bookended by the Pratt Institute and the Williamsburg Savings Bank—a four-sided clock tower that was once the borough's tallest building and remains a local landmark—the neighborhood has a central location and an illustrious past. Everyone from Walt Whitman to Spike Lee has called these leafy streets home, and the grassy hills of Fort Greene Park might just inspire you to write the Great American Novel. (Hey, it worked for Richard Wright, author of *Native Son*.)

TOP ATTRACTIONS

Fodor'sChoice
★

Brooklyn Flea. The country's chic-est flea market is a collection of antiques dealers, artisanal woodworkers, culinary craftsmen (try the roasted garlic achaar!), vintage clotheshorses, and so much more. Held Saturdays, April through October, in an outdoor lot in Fort Greene, and on Sundays in Williamsburg, the Flea has launched many brick-and-mortar businesses throughout New York City. It's also spawned an all-culinary offshoot, **Smorgasburg**, along the waterfront in of Williamsburg and on Brooklyn Bridge Park, as well as the **Ber g'n** food hall. November through March, the Flea has an indoor space in Crown Heights (1000 Dean St.). ⊠ *176 Lafayette Ave., Fort Greene* ⊕ *www.brooklynflea.com* ⊙ *Weekends (different locations)* Ⓜ *C to Lafayette Ave., G to Clinton–Washington Aves.*

WILLIAMSBURG

These days, it's impossible to walk through North Brooklyn without encountering something new. Fabulous boutiques, vintage shops, and forward-thinking restaurants crop up constantly, lending an energy that verges on overwhelming. The neighborhood has certainly glossed itself up in recent years, evinced by pricey cocktail bars, high-rise waterfront condos, and expensive boutiques. But Williamsburg's past is also endlessly intriguing: for much of the 20th century this industrial area on the East River was home to a mix of working-class Americans. Rising Manhattan rents in the 1990s sent an influx of East Village artists and musicians onto the L train, and since then the area has rapidly, albeit creatively, gentrified. And while some side streets may appear graffitied

14

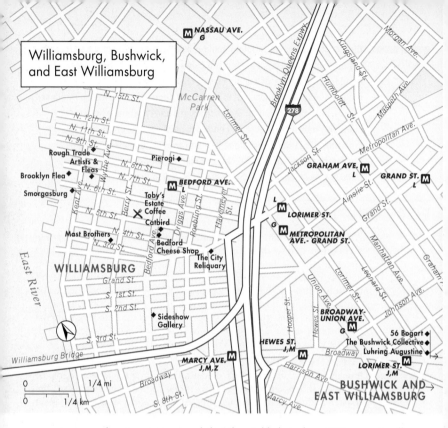

and creepy, rest assured that there's likely to be a DIY concert-gallery space in one of those seemingly abandoned factories.

Williamsburg's 70-plus galleries are distributed randomly, with no single main drag. Plan your trip ahead of time using the online **Brooklyn Art Guide** at ⊕ *www.wagmag.org*. (You can also pick up a copy at neighborhood galleries and some cafés.) Hours vary widely, but most are open weekends (call ahead). Although serendipitous poking is the best way to sample the art, two longtime galleries—Sideshow and Pierogi—are must-sees.

TOP ATTRACTIONS

FAMILY

Fodor's Choice

★

City Reliquary. Subway tokens, Statue of Liberty figurines, antique seltzer bottles, and other artifacts you might find in a time capsule crowd the cases of this museum that celebrates New York City's past and present. Temporary exhibits here have included one about doughnut shops and another about Jewish gangsters of the Lower East Side. ✉ *370 Metropolitan Ave., Williamsburg* ☎ *718/782–4842* ⊕ *www.cityreliquary.org* 🎫 *$5* ⊙ *Wed.–Sun. noon–7* Ⓜ *L to Lorimer St., G to Metropolitan Ave.*

WORTH NOTING

Pierogi Gallery. Nope, it's not a restaurant; it's a hip art gallery showcasing multimedia artists. Virtual visitors can browse the Flat Files, an online collection of the portfolios of more than 900 young artists. The Boiler, an affiliated space nearby (*191 N. 14th St.; 718/599–2144*), has more limited hours. ✉ *177 N. 9th St., between Bedford and Driggs aves., Williamsburg* ☎ *718/599–2144* ⊕ *www.pierogi2000.com* ⊘ *Pierogi, Tues.–Sun. 11–6; The Boiler, Thurs.–Sun. noon–6* Ⓜ *L to Bedford Ave.*

✕**Toby's Estate.** With four cafés in New York City, Toby's Estate is expanding quickly, a mini coffee empire that started in Brooklyn. The spacious location on North 6th Street is perennially packed, so you might have to wait for a seat to open up—but it's worth it, especially for a prime spot on the long, comfy couch. Light streaming in through large windows gives the place a bright, airy feel. The coffee drinks are outstanding, as are the made-to-order sandwiches (think egg on a roll with espresso-lacquered bacon) and salads. ✉ *125 N. 6th St., between Bedford Ave. and Berry St., Williamsburg* ☎ *347/457–6160* ⊕ *www.tobysestate.com* Ⓜ *L to Bedford Ave.*

14

SHOPPING

For Shopping, there are boutiques along Bedford Avenue, but you'll also find stores along Grand Street, and on many side streets, especially North 6th.

Fodor's Choice ★ **Artists & Fleas.** Hands-down the best place to lay eyes on the latest cool creations from Brooklyn-based artists and designers, this huge warehouse lures canny connoisseurs seeking one-of-a-kind items. Every weekend, nearly 100 vendors sell everything from handmade jewelry and objets d'art to custom clocks made from old hardcover books and T-shirts with vintage cartoons. ✉ *70 N. 7th St., Williamsburg* ☎ *917/488–4203* ⊕ *www.artistsandfleas.com* ⊘ *Closed weekdays* Ⓜ *L to Bedford Ave.*

Fodor's Choice ★ **Bedford Cheese Shop.** A cheese lover's dream, this small fromagerie sells everything needed for a gourmet antipasto. The more than 200 artisanal cheeses are arranged by style—hard, soft, Bries and other bloomy-rind cheeses, blues, et cetera. Dry goods include crackers, biscuits, premium olive oils, small-batch jams, and chocolates. Prosciutto di Parma and Serrano ham are among the cured meats; you'll also find foie gras, quail eggs, marinated artichokes, and other comestibles. Overwhelmed by the choices? Expert cheesemongers will help you navigate the offerings. ✉ *229 Bedford Ave., at N. 4th St., Williamsburg* ☎ *718/599–7588* ⊕ *www.bedfordcheeseshop.com* Ⓜ *L to Bedford Ave.*

Fodor's Choice ★ **Catbird.** Known for its trademark stackable rings, the tiny store also sells soft cashmere hats, candles, and gift items, all curated with an emphasis on area designers. Any gift you buy here—for a friend or for yourself—will be cherished. ✉ *219 Bedford Ave., near N. 5th St., Williamsburg* ☎ *718/599–3457* ⊕ *www.catbirdnyc.com* Ⓜ *L to Bedford Ave.*

Fodor's Choice ★ **Mast Brothers.** The elegantly wrapped bars of Brooklyn's artisanal bean-to-bar chocolatiers may be ubiquitous in New York City, but to experience the magic as it transpires, head to the Mast flagship on North 3rd Street, where you can tour the factory and sample the goodies ($16, register online). The all-natural, single-origin chocolate bars are known for their earthy, barely sweet flavor. Two doors down at Brew Bar, cocoa beans are brewed like coffee—the taste is like nothing you've tried before. ⊠ *111 N. 3rd St., Williamsburg* ☎ *718/388–2625* ⊕ *www. mastbrothers.com* Ⓜ *L to Bedford Ave.*

Rough Trade Records. This cavernous, London-based store sells LPs, CDs, and books, and doubles as a 250-seat concert venue and art gallery (event listings at *www.roughtradenyc.com*). The shop's cool, of-the-moment design incorporates recycled shipping containers. ⊠ *64 N. 9th St., Williamsburg* ☎ *718/388–4111* ⊕ *www.roughtrade.com/pages/ about* Ⓜ *L to Bedford Ave.*

BUSHWICK

Bushwick is young and hip and cool and still very industrial—working factories make everything from wontons to plastic bags—but it's definitely where to go if you're interested in street art: check out the Bushwick Collective and the streets surrounding it. The neighborhood also has pockets of cafés and restaurants, including Roberta's, one of the buzziest restaurants around.

TOP ATTRACTIONS

Fodor's Choice ★ **The Bushwick Collective.** For evidence of art's ability to transform individuals and their surroundings, visit this colorful outdoor street-art gallery curated by Joseph Ficalora. The Bushwick native came of age during the neighborhood's period of decline, which he experienced firsthand in the early 1990s when his father was murdered. Following his mother's death in 2011, he channeled his grief over both losses into developing this space where street artists are commissioned to create temporary works of art. Pixel Pancho of Turin and Baltimore-based Gaia are among the established artists whose contributions have helped turn urban streets into an arts destination. Many works are also by up-and-comers. ⊠ *Troutman St. at St. Nicholas Ave., Bushwick* Ⓜ *L to Jefferson St.*

EAST WILLIAMSBURG

Industrial East Williamsburg, between Williamsburg and Bushwick, has become an enclave of street art, up-and-coming art galleries, cafés, and restaurants.

TOP ATTRACTIONS

56 Bogart (The BogArt). Many young Bushwick galleries showcase edgy and experimental work—visiting this converted warehouse is an easy way to see a lot of art, of varying quality, in one shot. The BogArt, as the space is commonly known, contains large studios for working artists, and more than a dozen galleries on the main and lower levels. Standouts include Robert Henry Contemporary, Theodore: Art, Fresh Window, Momenta Art, and NurtureArt. You can also hang out and browse the books and other materials at Mellow Pages, an independently run library and reading room. Gallery hours vary, but the best time to visit is on Friday and weekends, when most of them are open. ⊠ *56 Bogart St., East Williamsburg* ☎ *718/599–0800 ext. 12* ⊕ *www.56bogartstreet. com* ▣ *Free* ☉ *Library: Wed.—Sun. noon—7* Ⓜ *L to Morgan Ave.*

Luhring Augustine. Probably the neighborhood's most established gallery, this annex of the Chelsea original is worth a stop to see whatever show is up and to appreciate the soaring space and its cantilevered ceiling. ⊠ *25 Knickerbocker Ave., East Williamsburg* ☎ *718/386–2746* ⊕ *www.luhringaugustine.com* ☉ *Sept.–June, Thurs.–Sun. 11–6; July–Aug., Thurs.–Sun. 11–5:30* Ⓜ *L to Morgan Ave.*

PARK SLOPE

Full of young families, well-dressed dog walkers, and impeccably curated shops, the neighborhood that literally slopes down from Prospect Park can feel like a veritable Norman Rockwell painting. Add to all that a slew of laptop-friendly coffeehouses and turn-of-the-20th-century brownstones—remnants of the days when Park Slope had the nation's highest per-capita income—and it's no surprise that academics and writers have flocked here. Park Slope's busiest drags, 5th and 7th avenues, present plenty of shopping and noshing opportunities. Head to the elegant, 585-acre Prospect Park for long strolls or bicycle rides past lazy meadows, shady forests, and lakes designed by Olmsted and Vaux of Central Park fame (look out for free summertime concerts). Adjacent is Brooklyn Botanic Garden, which features a variety of public classes and the springtime Cherry Blossom Festival. Also perched on the park is the Brooklyn Museum, lauded for collections of American, Egyptian, and feminist art.

TOP ATTRACTIONS

LeFrak Center at Lakeside. The highlight of this restored 26-acre space in Prospect Park is the all-season ice- and roller-skating rinks; also check out the new walkways, the reconstructed esplanade near the lake, and the Music Island nature reserve, all of which were part of the original Olmsted and Vaux plans. Themed roller-skating night takes place on Friday, July through October; in winter, the rink hosts hockey and curling clinics for all ages. There's also a café and snack bar. ⊠ *Prospect Park, 171 East Dr., Prospect Park* ☎ *718/ 462–0100* ⊕ *www.lakesidebrooklyn. com* ⊠ *Skating $6 weekdays, $8 weekends; rentals $6* ☉ *Tues.–Thurs. 11–6, Fri. 11–8, Sat. 10–9, Sun. 10–6.* Ⓜ *B, Q, S to Prospect Park; Q to Parkside Ave.*

FAMILY
Fodor's Choice
★
Prospect Park. Brooklyn residents are passionate about Prospect Park, and with good reason: lush green spaces, gently curved walkways, summer concerts, vivid foliage in autumn, and an all-season skating rink make it a year-round getaway. In 1859 the New York Legislature decided to develop plans for a park in the fast-growing city of Brooklyn. After landscape architects Frederick Law Olmsted and Calvert Vaux completed the park in the late 1880s, Olmsted remarked that he was prouder of Prospect Park than of any of his other works—Manhattan's Central Park included. Many critics agree that this is their most beautiful work. On weekends, those not jogging the 3.35-mile loop gravitate to the tree-ringed Long Meadow to fly kites, picnic, or play cricket, flag football, or frisbee. The park's north entrance is at Grand Army Plaza, where the Soldiers' and Sailors' Memorial Arch (patterned on the Arc

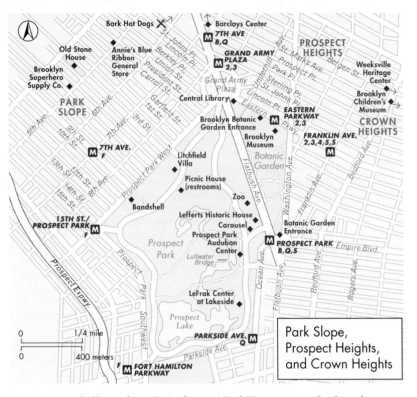

Park Slope, Prospect Heights, and Crown Heights

de Triomphe in Paris) honors Civil War veterans. On Saturdays year-round, a greenmarket at the plaza throngs with shoppers.

A good way to experience the park is to walk the Long Meadow and then head to the eastern side, where you'll find the lake and most attractions, including the Lefferts Historic House, Prospect Park Audubon Center, and the LeFrak Center. The extravagant Prospect Park Carousel, built in 1912, still thrills the kids. The annual Celebrate Brooklyn! festival takes place at the Prospect Park Bandshell from early June through mid-August. Films are occasionally shown on a 50-foot-wide outdoor screen, one of the world's largest. ⊠ *450 Flatbush Ave., Prospect Park* ☎ *718/965–8951* ⊕ *www.prospectpark.org* ⊠ *Carousel $2 per ride* ☉ *Carousel: Apr.–June, Sept., and Oct., Thurs.–Sun. noon–5; July–Labor Day, Thurs.–Sun. noon–6* Ⓜ *2, 3 to Grand Army Plaza; F, G to 7th Ave.; B, Q to 7th Ave.*

QUICK BITES

✕ **Bark Hot Dogs.** The locally sourced and sustainable ingredients used in the burgers, hot dogs, and sausages served here, along with sides like brussels sprouts and kale salad, make this fast food without the guilt. Feeling too healthy? Order some cheddar fries.) Sixpoint beer is on tap, or choose from cider, milkshakes, and Dr. Brown's sodas. Seating is at tall, communal tables, and there's usually a game on TV. Make sure to sort your recyclables after your meal. ⊠ *474 Bergen St., between Flatbush and 5th aves., Park Slope* ☎ *718/789–1939* ⊕ *www.barkhotdogs.com* Ⓜ *2, 3 to Bergen St.*

WORTH NOTING

FAMILY **Lefferts Historic House.** A visit to this Dutch Colonial farmhouse, built in 1783 and moved from nearby Flatbush Avenue to Prospect Park in 1918, is a window into how Brooklynites lived in the 19th century, when the area was predominately farmland. Rooms are furnished with antiques and reproductions from the 1820s, when the house was last redecorated. ⊠ *Prospect Park, 452 Flatbush Ave., at Empire Blvd., Prospect Park* ☎ *718/789–2822* ⊠ *$3 suggested donation* ☺ *Apr.–June and Sept.–Oct., Thurs.–Sun. noon–5; July and Aug., Thurs.–Sun. noon–6; Nov.–Dec., Thurs.–Sun. noon–4; Jan.–Mar. call for hrs.*

14

FAMILY **Old Stone House.** The original of this reconstructed Dutch farmhouse was built in 1699 and survived until the 1890s. It played a central role in the Battle of Brooklyn, one of the largest battles of the Revolutionary War and the small museum here focuses on the events of that week in 1776. The museum also depicts the early life of Dutch setters in the area and the years of British occupation in New York, until 1783. Music, art, plays, and other events take place year-round, including a ball game to celebrate the Brooklyn Baseball Club, which started here and gave rise to the Brooklyn Dodgers. ⊠ *Washington Park/J.J. Byrne Playground, 336 3rd St., between 4th and 5th aves., Park Slope* ☎ *718/768–3195* ⊕ *www.theoldstonehouse.org* ⊠ *$3 suggested donation* ☺ *Weekends 11–4 and by appt.* Ⓜ *R to Union St.*

SHOPPING

Park Slope's main shopping drags are 7th Avenue and 5th Avenue.

FAMILY
Fodor's Choice
★
Annie's Blue Ribbon General Store. The perfectly giftable, Brooklyn-made products at this variety store include Apotheke candles and diffusers, Bellocq teas, Brooklyn Slate Co. cheese boards, Claudia Pearson's brownstone tea towels, and Alexandra Ferguson's felt pillows and accessories. Brooklyn-theme tchotchkes, eco-friendly cleaning supplies, stationery, and toys round out the selection. You can't go wrong gifting the mass-produced prank kit to any kid between the ages of 4 and 10. ⊠ *232 5th Ave., between President and Carroll sts., Park Slope* ☎ *718/522–9848* ⊕ *www.blueribbongeneralstore.com* Ⓜ *R to Union St.*

FAMILY
Fodor's Choice
★
Brooklyn Superhero Supply Co. If you can't crack a smile in this store—where all proceeds from superhero costumes, gear, and secret identity kits benefit 826NYC's writing and tutoring programs for kids—step immediately into its Devillainizer cage. Once cleansed, browse the invisibility, dark matter, and cloning tools sold in plastic jugs and fake paint cans. The clever labels listing "ingredients" and "warnings" are worth every ounce of the tongue-in-cheek superpower products. ⊠ *372 5th Ave., between 5th and 6th Sts., Park Slope* ☎ *718/499–9884* ⊕ *www.superherosupplies.com* Ⓜ *F, G to 4th Ave.; R to 9th St.*

PROSPECT HEIGHTS

An influx of creative young professionals and impressive eats has lifted Prospect Heights out from the shadow of nearby Park Slope. Swing by on a Saturday to hit the borough's flagship farmer's market, Grand Army Plaza Greenmarket, where cooking demos and fresh produce entice the food-loving hoards. Vanderbilt Avenue and Washington Avenue are the main thoroughfares for restaurants and bars.

TOP ATTRACTIONS

FAMILY **Barclays Center.** This rust-tinted spaceship of an arena houses two sports franchises—basketball's Brooklyn Nets and, as of Fall 2015, ice hockey's New York Islanders. With a capacity rivaling Madison Square Garden, Barclays is now a regular stop for national tours, from circuses and ice capades to glossy pop stars and bearded indie-rockers. Also impressive are the Barclays food vendors: a solid roster of local restaurateurs, including L&B Spumoni Gardens, Habana Outpost, and Calexico. ⊠ *620 Atlantic Ave., at Flatbush Ave., Prospect Heights* ☎ *917/618—6100* ⊕ *www.barclayscenter.com* Ⓜ *2, 3, 4, 5, B, D, N, Q, R to Atlantic Ave.–Barclays Ctr.*

FAMILY **Brooklyn Botanic Garden.** A gem even among New York's superlative
Fodor's Choice botanical sites, this verdant 52-acre oasis charms with its array of "gar-
★ dens within the garden"—an idyllic Japanese Hill-and-Pond garden, a nearly century-old rose garden, and a Shakespeare garden. The Japanese cherry arbor turns into a breathtaking cloud of pink every spring, and the Sakura Matsuri two-day cherry blossom festival is the largest public-garden event in America. There are entrances on Eastern Parkway, next to the subway station, and on Washington Avenue, behind the Brooklyn Museum. Free garden tours meet at the front gate weekends at 1 pm. ⊠ *150 Eastern Pkwy., Prospect Heights* ☎ *718/623–7200* ⊕ *www.bbg.org* ⊠ *$12 (free all day Tues., Sat. before noon, and weekdays mid-Nov.–mid-Feb.)* ⊗ *Mar.–Oct.: grounds Tues.–Fri. 8–6, weekends 10–6; conservatory Tues.–Sun. 10–5:30. Nov.–Feb.: grounds Tues.–Fri. 8–4:30, weekends 10–4:30; conservatory Tues.–Sun. 10–4. Closed Mon. except major holidays* Ⓜ *2, 3 to Eastern Pkwy.–Brooklyn Museum; 2, 3, 4, 5 to Franklin Ave.; S to Botanic Garden; B, Q to Prospect Park.*

FAMILY **Brooklyn Museum.** First-time visitors may well gasp at the vastness of
Fodor's Choice New York's second-largest museum (after Manhattan's Metropolitan
★ Museum of Art) and one of the largest in America at 560,000 square feet of exhibition space. Along with changing exhibitions, the colossal Beaux-Arts structure houses one of the best collections of Egyptian art in the world and impressive collections of African, pre-Columbian, and Native American art. It's also worth seeking out the museum's works by Georgia O'Keeffe, Winslow Homer, John Singer Sargent, George Bellows, Thomas Eakins, and Milton Avery—all stunners in a collection that ranges from Egyptian antiquities to Colonial paintings with very contemporary, cutting-edge special exhibits. The monthly (except for September) "First Saturday" free-entry night is a neighborhood party of art, music, and dancing, with food vendors and several cash bars. ⊠ *200 Eastern Pkwy., at Washington Ave., Prospect Heights* ☎ *718/638–5000*

⊕ *www.brooklynmuseum.org* ✉ *$16 suggested donation (free 1st Sat. of month), $23 combo ticket with Brooklyn Botanic Garden* ⊙ *Wed., Fri., and weekends 11–6, Thurs. 11–10; 1st Sat. of month 11–11* Ⓜ *2, 3 to Eastern Pkwy.–Brooklyn Museum.*

CROWN HEIGHTS

Diverse Crown Heights, and Bedford-Stuyvesant (known as Bed-Stuy), next door, have a lot going on. Crown Heights is walking distance from the Brooklyn Museum and is home to the Brooklyn Children Museum and Weeksville Heritage Center.

TOP ATTRACTIONS

14

FAMILY · Fodor'sChoice · ★   **Brooklyn Children's Museum.** What's red, yellow, and green, and shaped like a spaceship? The Brooklyn Children's Museum. Nestled in a residential area and abutting a pretty city park, the attention-grabbing exterior suits this interactive space designed for kids—one of a few places in New York City where "little people" can run and touch and play with abandon indoors. Exhibits range from a working greenhouse to Totally Tots, where daily afternoon programming includes art experiences for kids five and under. The cornerstone is World Brooklyn, a warren of rooms dedicated to various NYC cultures—from an Italian pizza shop to a Hispanic bakery—and a replica MTA bus for fun photo ops. Feel free to bring strollers and heavy coats: the museum may be a long walk from the subway, but the coat check takes everything free of charge. ✉ *145 Brooklyn Ave., at St. Marks Ave., Crown Heights* ☎ *718/735–4400* ⊕ *www.brooklynkids.org* ✉ *$9* ⊙ *Tues.–Sun. 10–5* Ⓜ *C to Kingston–Throop Aves.; 3 to Kingston Ave.; A, C to Nostrand Ave.*

FAMILY · Fodor'sChoice · ★   **Weeksville Heritage Center.** Devoted to honoring the history of the 19th-century African American community of Weeksville, one of the first communities of free blacks in New York (founded by James Weeks), this Crown Heights museum comprises a new industrial-modern building by Caples Jefferson Architects, botanical gardens, and three houses that date as far back as 1838. The restored homes, located along historic, gravel Hunterfly Road, are now period re-creations depicting African American family life in the 1860s, 1900s, and 1930s. Tours (Wed., Thurs., Fri., at 3pm, and select Sat. from 10–3; $5;) lead visitors through bedrooms, kitchens, and sitting rooms accented by objects such as original clothing irons and ceramics found in the area at student-led archeological digs. Throughout the year, the venue hosts exhibits that honor the neighborhood's history; in 2015 there will be a program in partnership with the Brooklyn Historical Society. ✉ *158 Buffalo Ave., Crown Heights* ☎ *718/756–5250* ⊕ *www.weeksvillesociety.org* ⊙ *Tues.–Fri. 9–5* Ⓜ *A, C to Utica Ave.; 3, 4 to Crown Heights–Utica Ave.*

CONEY ISLAND

Coney Island is practically synonymous with the sounds, smells, and sights of a New York City summer: hot dogs and ice cream, suntan lotion, roller coasters, excited crowds, and weathered old men fishing.

Strolling on the boardwalk at Coney Island

Named Konijn Eiland (Rabbit Island) by the Dutch for its wild rabbit population, the Coney Island peninsula has a boardwalk, a 2½-mile-long beach, amusement parks, and the **New York Aquarium**, still partially closed after sustaining damage from Hurricane Sandy. Nathan's Famous (*1310 Surf Ave.*) is the quintessential hot dog spot.

Among the other entertainments out here are the freakish attractions at **Coney Island Circus Sideshow** and the heart-stopping plunge of the granddaddy of all roller coasters—the **Cyclone**. The minor-league baseball team, the Cyclones, plays at MCU Park, where music concerts are held in summer. The area's banner day is during the raucous Mermaid Parade, held in June. A fireworks display lights up the sky Friday night from late June through Labor Day.

TOP ATTRACTIONS

FAMILY **The Cyclone.** This historic wooden roller coaster first thrilled riders in 1927 and it'll still make you scream. Anticipation builds as the cars slowly clack up to the first unforgettable 85-foot plunge—and the look on your face is captured in photos that you can purchase at the end of the ride. The Cyclone may not have the speed or the twists and turns of more modern rides, but that's all part of its rickety charm. It's one of two New York City landmarks in Coney Island: the other is Deno's Wonder Wheel. ⊠ *Luna Park, 834 Surf Ave., at W. 10th St., Coney Island* ☎ *718/373—5862* ⊕ *www.lunaparknyc.com* ✉ *$9* ◷ *Seasonal hrs vary, but generally Mar.–May, weekends only (plus daily Apr. 3–12); June–Aug., daily* Ⓜ *F, Q to W. 8th St.–NY Aquarium; D, F, N, Q to Coney Island–Stillwell Ave.*

FAMILY
Fodor'sChoice
★

New York Aquarium. The oldest continually operating aquarium in the United States is run by the Wildlife Conservation Society; their mission is to save wildlife and wild places worldwide through science, conservation action, and education. The aquarium occupies 14 acres of beachfront property and is home to 266 aquatic species. At the Sea Cliffs, you can watch penguins, sea lions, sea otters, seals, and walrus frolic: the best action is at feeding time. The Conservation Hall and Glovers Reef building is home to marine life from Belize, Fiji, and all over the world, including angel fish, eels, rays, and piranhas. The new Ocean Wonders: Sharks! exhibit, will bring hundreds more species, including nurse sharks, to the aquarium when it opens in 2016. ✉ *502 Surf Ave., at W. 8th St., Coney Island* ☎ *718/265–3474* ⊕ *www.nyaquarium.com* ☜ *$11.95* ☉ *Sept.–May, 10–4:30; June–Sept., 10–6* Ⓜ *F, Q to W. 8th St.–NY Aquarium; D, F, N, Q to Coney Island–Stillwell Ave.*

14

QUICK
BITES

Nathan's Famous. Nathan Handwerker, a Polish immigrant, founded this Coney Island hot dog stand in 1916, and what followed can only be described as a quintessential American success story. With a $300 loan and his wife's Ida's secret spice recipe, Nathan set up shop and his success was almost instantaneous—Al Capone, Jimmy Durante, and Cary Grant became regulars early on, President FDR served Nathan's dogs to the King and Queen of England, local girl Barbra Streisand had them delivered to London, and Walter Matthau asked that they be served at his funeral. The century-old recipe still works: the hot dogs have good, firm texture and a snap when you bite. The light smoky, spicy flavor is reminiscent of the ball park on a summer evening. Buns are soft and the crinkle fries are hot, crispy, and perfectly creamy on the inside. ✉ *1310 Surf Ave., at Stillwell Ave., Coney Island* ☎ *718/946–2705* ⊕ *www.nathansfamous.com* Ⓜ *D, F, N, Q to Coney Island–Stillwell Ave.* ✛ *7:G6.*

FAMILY
Fodor'sChoice
★

Riegelmann Boardwalk. Built in 1923 this famous, wood-planked walkway is better known as the Coney Island Boardwalk and in summer it seems like all of Brooklyn is out strolling along the two-and-a-half mile stretch. The quintessential walk starts at the end of the pier in Coney Island, opposite the Parachute Jump—you can see the whole shoreline stretched out before you, a beautiful confluence of nature and city. From here to Brighton Beach is a little over a mile and should take about a half hour at a leisurely amble. Those modernistic, rectangular structures perched over the beach are the new bathrooms and lifeguard stations. ✉ *Coney Island* Ⓜ *D, F, N, Q to Coney Island–Stillwell Ave.; F, Q to W. 8th St.–NY Aquarium; B, Q to Brighton Beach; Q to Ocean Pkwy.*

WORTH NOTING

Fodor'sChoice
★

Coney Island Circus Sideshow. The cast of talented freaks and geeks who keep Coney Island's carnival tradition alive include sword swallowers, fire eaters, knife throwers, contortionists, and Serpentina the snake dancer. Every show is an extravaganza, with 10 different acts to fascinate and impress. ✉ *Sideshows by the Seashore, 1208 Surf Ave., at W. 12th St., Coney Island* ☎ *718/372–5159* ⊕ *www.coneyisland.com/*

sideshow.shtml ✉ *$10* ⏱ *Apr.–Sept.* Ⓜ *F, Q to W. 8th St.–NY Aquar-
ium; D, F, N, Q to Coney Island–Stillwell Ave.*

FAMILY

Fodor's Choice

★

Deno's Wonder Wheel Amusement Park. The star attraction at Deno's is the
towering, 150-foot tall Wonder Wheel. The Ferris wheel first opened
in 1920, making it the oldest ride in Concy Island, and the spectacular
views from the top take in a long stretch of the shoreline. Other rides
for tots here, include the Dizzy Dragons, the Pony Carts, and a brightly
painted carousel. ✉ *3059 W. 12th St., Coney Island* ☎ *718/372–2592*
⊕ *www.wonderwheel.com* ✉ *$7 per ride (4 rides for $25)* ⏱ *Late Mar.–
Oct., hrs vary* Ⓜ *F, Q to W. 8th St.–NY Aquarium; D, F, N, Q to Coney
Island–Stillwell Ave.*

BRIGHTON BEACH

A pleasant stroll just down the boardwalk from Coney Island is Brighton Beach, named after Britain's beach resort. In the early 1900s Brighton Beach was a resort in its own right, with seaside hotels that catered
to rich Manhattan families visiting for the summer. Since the 1970s and
'80s Brighton Beach has been known for its 100,000 Soviet émigrés.
To get to the heart of "Little Odessa" from Coney Island, walk about
a mile east along the boardwalk to Brighton 1st Place, then head up to
Brighton Beach Avenue. To get here from Manhattan directly, take the
B or Q train to the Brighton Beach stop; the trip takes about an hour
from Midtown Manhattan.

TOP ATTRACTIONS

FAMILY

Fodor's Choice

★

Brighton Beach. Just steps from the subway; this stretch of golden sand
is the showpiece of Brooklyn's oceanside playground. Families set up
beach blankets, umbrellas, and coolers, and pick-up games of beach
volleyball and football add to the excitement. Calm surf, a lively boardwalk, and a handful of restaurants for shade and refreshments complete
the package. That spit of land in the distance is the Rockaway Peninsula, in Queens. ✉ *Brighton Beach, between Ocean Pkwy. and Brighton
14th St., Brighton Beach* Ⓜ *B, Q to Brighton Beach; Q to Ocean Pkwy.*

Brighton Beach Avenue. The main thorough fare of "Little Odessa" can
feel more like Kiev than Manhattan. Cyrillic shop signs advertise everything from salted tomatoes and pickled mushrooms to Russian language
DVDs and Armani handbags. When the weather's good, local bakeries
sell sweet honey cake, cheese-stuffed *vatrushki* danishes, and chocolatey
rugelach from sidewalk tables. ✉ *Brighton Beach Ave., between Ocean
Pkwy. and Brighton 6th St., Brighton Beach* Ⓜ *B, Q to Brighton Beach.*

SHOPPING

Fodor's Choice

★

Williams Candy. Selling homemade candy apples, marshmallow sticks,
popcorn, nuts, and giant lollipops for more than 75 years, this old-
school, corner candy shop with the yellow awning is a Coney Island
mainstay. Owner Peter Agrapides used to visit the store with his mother
when he was a kid; he's been the proud owner for 30 years. ✉ *1318
Surf Ave., at W. 15th St., Coney Island* ☎ *718/372–0302* ⊕ *www.
candytreats.com* Ⓜ *D, F, N, Q to Coney Island–Stillwell Ave.*

QUEENS, THE BRONX, AND STATEN ISLAND

GETTING ORIENTED

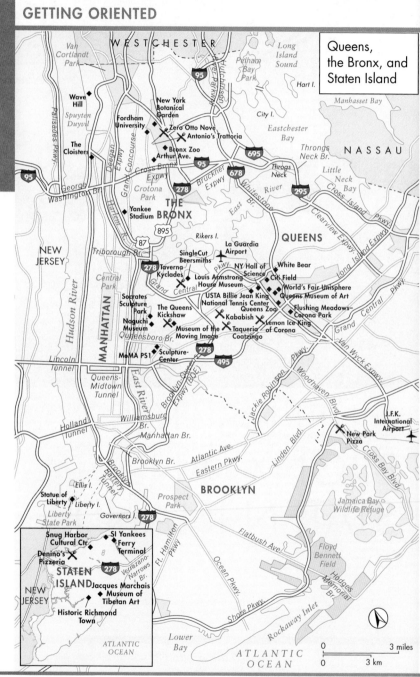

Queens, the Bronx, and Staten Island

WESTCHESTER

Van Cortlandt Park

Long Island Sound

Pelham Bay Park

Hart I.

Manhasset Bay

Wave Hill

Spuyten Duyvil

Fordham University

New York Botanical Garden

Zero Otto Nove
Antonio's Trattoria

City I.

Eastchester Bay

Throgs Neck Br.

NASSAU

The Cloisters

Bronx Zoo
Arthur Ave.

Throgs Neck

Throgs Neck

Little Neck Bay

Cross Island Pkwy.

George Washington Br.

Deegan Expwy

Grand Concourse

Cross Bronx Expwy

Bruckner Expwy

East River

Whitestone

Clearview Expwy

NEW JERSEY

Crotona Park

THE BRONX

Yankee Stadium

Rikers I.

La Guardia Airport

QUEENS

Long Island Expwy

Hudson River

Central Park

Triborough Br.

Harlem River

Grand Central Pkwy

SingleCut Beersmiths

Taverna Kyclades

NY Hall of Science

Louis Armstrong House Museum

White Bear

Citi Field

World's Fair Unisphere
Queens Museum of Art

Grand Central Pkwy.

Van Wyck Expwy

Socrates Sculpture Park

The Queens Kickshaw

Noguchi Museum

MANHATTAN

Queensboro Br.

USTA Billie Jean King National Tennis Center

Kababish

Queens Zoo

Flushing Meadows–Corona Park

Lemon Ice King of Corona

Taqueria Coatzingo

Woodhaven Blvd.

MoMA PS1

Sculpture Center

Museum of the Moving Image

Lincoln Tunnel

Queens–Midtown Tunnel

East River

Brooklyn-Queens Expwy (BQE)

Jackie Robinson Pkwy

Linden Blvd.

J.F.K. International Airport

New Park Pizza

Cross Bay Blvd.

Holland Tunnel

Williamsburg Br.

Manhattan Br.

Brooklyn Br.

Atlantic Ave.

Eastern Pkwy.

BROOKLYN

Jamaica Bay Wildlife Refuge

Battery Tunnel

Ellis I.

Statue of Liberty

Liberty I.

Liberty State Park

Governors I.

Prospect Park

Floyd Bennett Field

Hodges Memorial Br.

Snug Harbor Cultural Ctr.

SI Yankees
Ferry Terminal

Denino's Pizzeria

STATEN ISLAND

Jacques Marchais Museum of Tibetan Art

Historic Richmond Town

NEW JERSEY

Ft. Hamilton Pkwy

Verrazano-Narrows Br.

Flatbush Ave.

Ocean Pkwy

Shore Pkwy.

Rockaway Inlet

ATLANTIC OCEAN

Lower Bay

ATLANTIC OCEAN

0   3 miles
0   3 km

MAKING THE MOST OF YOUR TIME

Queens is rich with museums. An afternoon in Long Island City and Astoria enables you to take in the PS1 Contemporary Art Center, the Museum of the Moving Image, and the Noguchi Museum. Then jump on the 7 train and have dinner in Jackson Heights or Flushing.

It's easy to spend a full day at either of the Bronx's treasures: the New York Botanical Garden or the Bronx Zoo. To visit both, start early and plan a late lunch or early dinner in the Arthur Avenue area.

Many tourists' only sight of Staten Island is during a round-trip ride on the ferry, but the borough also holds unexpected offerings in its small museums and historic villages. Set aside a few hoursto explore Snug Harbor and St. George, or venture deeper into the island for a visit to Historic Richmond Town and the Museum of Tibetan Art.

GETTING HERE

Queens is served by many subway lines. To get to Astoria, take the N or Q train. For Long Island City, take the E, M, G or 7 train. To get to Jackson Heights, take the 7 train to the 74th Street–Broadway stop. You can also take the E, F, M, or R train to Jackson Heights–Roosevelt Avenue.

The Bronx is serviced by the 1, 2, 4, 5, 6, B, and D trains. The attractions in the Bronx are spread out across the borough, though, so you need to take different lines to get where you want to go, and it's not necessarily convenient to make connections across town. The B, D, and 4 trains all go to Yankee Stadium, and the B and D continue uptown to the vicinity of Arthur Avenue. The 2 and 5 trains take you to the Bronx Zoo and Arthur Avenue.

From the scenic (and free) Staten Island Ferry you can catch a local bus to attractions. Tell the driver where you're going, and ask about the return schedule.

CRAFT BEER AND QUICK BITES

SingleCut Beersmiths. Named for a body style of guitar, this craft brewery has a tap room that also serves food, free tours, and weekly live music. ✉ *19-33 37th St., Astoria* ✛ *Brewery is slightly less than a mile from subway* ☎ *718/606–0788* ⊕ *www.singlecutbeer.com* ☾ *Closed Mon.–Wed.* ☞ *Free tours weekends at 3 and 4* Ⓜ *N, Q to Astoria–Ditmars Blvd.*

Taqueria Coatzingo. Order an al pastor taco and take a seat among the locals in this authentic Mexican taquería. ✉ *7605 Roosevelt Ave., Jackson Heights* ☎ *718/424–1977* Ⓜ *7 to 74th St.–Broadway; E, F, M, R to Jackson Heights–Roosevelt Ave.*

White Bear. The wontons at this tiny hole-in-the-wall are worth the trek to New York's other Chinatown, in Flushing. Order the No. 6: a dozen wontons with hot sauce for $4.50. ✉ *135-02 Roosevelt Ave. (entrance on Prince St.), Flushing* ☎ *718/961–2322* ☾ *Closed Wed.* Ⓜ *7 to Flushing–Main St.*

15

Many tourists miss out on Queens, the Bronx, and Staten Island—the three boroughs of New York City other than the biggies, Manhattan and Brooklyn—and that's a shame. There are some noteworthy restaurants, museums, and attractions, and the subway's handful of express trains means that they're closer than you might think.

QUEENS

Updated by
Josh Rogol

Just for the museums and restaurants alone, a short 15-minute trip from Midtown on the 7, E or M train to **Long Island City** or a slightly longer ride on the N or Q train to **Astoria** is truly worth it. In Long Island City, major must-sees are **MoMA PS1** and the **Noguchi Museum.** No trip to Astoria—once nicknamed "Little Athens"—is complete without sampling some of the city's finest Greek and Mediterranean fare and a stop at the **Museum of the Moving Image.**

Jackson Heights boasts a diverse cornucopia of culture and cuisine and is home to one of the city's largest Indian populations. It's a wonderful place to spend an afternoon browsing shops and dining in one of the many authentic ethnic restaurants.

Top reasons to trek out to **Flushing** and **Corona** include seeing a ballgame at the New York Mets' stadium, **Citi Field,** spending time at the expansive **Flushing Meadows–Corona Park,** especially if traveling with kids, and devouring a wide array of Asian dim sum in downtown Flushing's Chinatown.

ASTORIA

Head to Astoria for authentic Greek restaurants, shops, and grocery stores. Here you can buy kalamata olives and salty sheep's milk feta from storeowners who can tell you where to go for the best gyro or spinach pie. Taverna Kyclades is well known for its classic Greek seafood dishes that attract diners from all five boroughs, while just a few

TIPS FOR QUEENS ADDRESSES

Addresses in Queens can seem confusing at first. Not only is there 30th Street and 30th Avenue, but also 30th Place and 30th Road, all next to one another. Then there are those hyphenated building numbers. But the system is actually logical. Sequentially numbered avenues run east-to-west, and sequentially numbered streets run north-to-south. If there are any smaller roads between avenues, they have the same number as the nearest avenue and are called roads or drives.

Similarly, smaller side roads between streets are called places or lanes. Thus, 30th Place is one block east of 30th Street. Most buildings have two pairs of numbers, separated by a hyphen. The first pair indicates the nearest cross street, and the second gives the location on the block. So 47-10 30th Place is 10 houses away from the corner of 47th Avenue and 30th Place. Logical, right? If this all still seems confusing to you, there's good news: locals are used to giving directions to visitors.

blocks up the road, SingleCut Beersmiths run free brewery tours and pour some tasty ales and lagers. Astoria, named for John Jacob Astor—America's first multimillionaire—was the center of Greek immigrant life in New York City for more than 60 years. Today substantial numbers of Arab, Asian, Eastern European, Irish, and Latino immigrants also live in Astoria. The heart of what remains of the Greek community is on Broadway, between 31st and Steinway streets. Thirtieth Avenue is another busy thoroughfare, with almost every kind of food store imaginable. Astoria is also home to the nation's only museum devoted to the art, technology, and history of film, TV, and digital media. The Museum of the Moving Image has countless hands-on exhibits that allow visitors to edit, direct, and step into favorite movies and television shows.

TOP ATTRACTIONS

Fodor'sChoice ★ **Museum of the Moving Image.** Like switching to a widescreen television, the Museum of the Moving Image is twice as nice as it was before the 2011 expansion and renovation. The Thomas Lesser design includes a three-story addition and a panoramic entrance to this museum full of Hollywood and television memorabilia. Exhibitions range from "Behind the Screen," which demonstrates how movies are produced and shot, to watching the live editing of Mets baseball games as they happen on SportsNet New York. Classic family films are shown as matinees on Saturday and Sunday, while the museum also has a section devoted to video artists for visitors looking for some culture. Film buffs love the film retrospectives, lectures, and other special programs. ✉ *36-01 35th Ave., at 37th St., Astoria* ☎ *718/777–6888* ⊕ *www.movingimage. us* ✉ *$12 (free Fri. after 4)* ⊙ *Wed. and Thurs. 10:30–5, Fri. 10:30–8, weekends 11:30–7* Ⓜ *M, R to Steinway St.; N, Q to 36th Ave.*

QUICK BITES

The Queens Kickshaw. Run by a local husband and wife team, the menu at this cozy spot uses fresh, high-quality ingredients in every recipe. Come here for specialty coffee, a vast variety of grilled cheese sandwiches, and craft ales. It's close to the Museum of the Moving

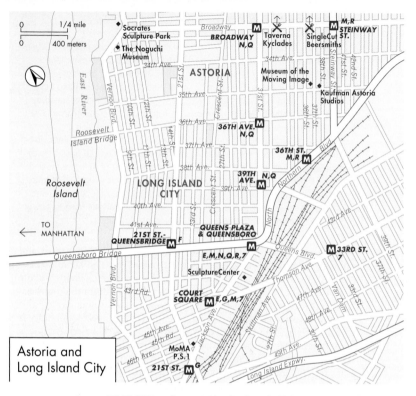

Astoria and
Long Island City

Image. ✉ 40-17 Broadway, at 41st St., Astoria ☎ 718/777–0913 ⊕ www.
thequeenskickshaw.com Ⓜ M, R to Steinway St.

LONG ISLAND CITY

Long Island City (LIC) is the outer-borough art capital, with MoMA
PS1, which presents experimental and innovative work; the Noguchi
Museum, showcasing the work of Japanese American sculptor Isamu
Noguchi in a large, peaceful garden and galleries; and the Socrates
Sculpture Park.

TOP ATTRACTIONS

Fodor'sChoice **MoMA PS1.** A pioneer in the "alternative-space" movement, PS1 rose
★ from the ruins of an abandoned school in 1976 as a sort of community
arts center for the future. MoMA PS1 focuses on the work of currently
active experimental and innovative artists. Long-term installations
include work by Sol LeWitt, James Turrell, and Pipilotti Rist. Every
available corner of the enormous 100-room building is used; discover
art not only in galleries but also on the rooftop, in the boiler room, and
even in some bathrooms. Also inside the museum is M. Wells Dinette,
a café designed to resemble a school classroom, with daily specials
listed on the chalkboard and lunch served at your "desk." On summer

Saturdays, MoMA PS1 presents "Warm Up," an outdoor dance party series that attracts a hip art-school crowd, held in the courtyard noon–9. Similarly, their "Sunday Sessions" are held in the Dome and include various artistic installations, scholarly lectures, and special performances. ⊠ *22–25 Jackson Ave., at 46th Ave., Long Island City* 🕾 *718/784–2084* ⊕ *www.momaps1.org* ⊡*$10 suggested donation (free with MoMA entrance ticket, within 14 days of visit); Warm Up $18 in advance, $20 at the door* ⊙ *Thurs.–Mon. noon–6* ⊂ *M. Wells Dinette closed Tues. and Wed.* Ⓜ *7 to Court Sq.; E, M to Court Sq.–23rd St.; G to 21st St.*

The Noguchi Museum. In 1985 the Japanese American sculptor Isamu Noguchi (1904–88) transformed this former photo-engraving plant into a place to display his modernist and earlier works. A peaceful central garden is surrounded by gallery buildings, and there are more than 250 pieces in stone, metal, clay, and other materials on display. Temporary exhibits have examined his collaborations with others, such as industrial designer Isamu Kenmochi. The museum is about a mile from subway stops; check the website for complete directions. ⊠ *9-01 33rd Rd., at Vernon Blvd., Long Island City* 🕾 *718/204–7088* ⊕ *www.noguchi. org* ⊡*$10 (free 1st Fri. of month)* ⊙ *Wed.–Fri. 10–5, weekends 11–6* Ⓜ *N, Q to Broadway.*

WORTH NOTING

SculptureCenter. Founded by artists in 1928 to exhibit innovative contemporary work, SculptureCenter now occupies a former trolley repair shop renovated by artist Maya Lin and architect David Hotson, not far from MoMA PS1. Indoor and outdoor exhibition spaces sometimes close between shows; call ahead before visiting. ⊠ *44-19 Purves St., at Jackson Ave., Long Island City* 🕾 *718/361–1750* ⊕ *www.sculpture-center.org* ⊡*$5 suggested donation* ⊙ *Thurs.–Mon. 11–6* Ⓜ *7, G to Court Sq.; E, M to Court Sq.–23rd St.; N, Q to Queensboro Plaza.*

FAMILY **Socrates Sculpture Park.** In 1986 local artist Mark di Suvero and other residents rallied to transform what had been an abandoned landfill and illegal dump site into this 4½-acre waterfront park devoted to public art. Today a superb view of the East River and Manhattan frames changing exhibitions of contemporary sculptures and multimedia installations. Free public programs include art workshops and an annual outdoor international film series (Wednesday evenings in July and August). Socrates is open 365 days a year, but the best time to visit is during warmer months. Check online for a list of current and upcoming exhibitions. ⊠ *32-01 Vernon Blvd., at Broadway, Long Island City* ⊕ *From subway, walk about 8 blocks west on Broadway* 🕾 *718/956–1819* ⊕ *www.socratessculpturepark.org* ⊡*Free* ⊙ *10 am–sunset* ⊂ *On weekends May–Sept. 12–6 pm, the LIC Art Bus provides free shuttle service between Socrates, the Noguchi Museum, SculptureCenter, and MoMA PS1* Ⓜ *N, Q to Broadway.*

JACKSON HEIGHTS

Much more than just a hub for traditional Indian delicacies, Jackson Heights resembles a giant international food court. Even in the diverse borough of Queens, it stands out for being a true multicultural neighborhood. In just a few blocks surrounding the three-way intersection of Roosevelt Avenue, 74th Street, and Broadway are shops and restaurants catering to the area's strong Tibetan, Bangladeshi, Colombian, Mexican, and Ecuadorian communities. Built as a planned "garden community" in the late 1910s, the area boasts many prewar apartments with elaborate block-long interior gardens as well as English-style homes. Celebs who grew up in the area include Lucy Liu and Gene Simmons. It's also the birthplace of the board game Scrabble.

QUICK BITES

✕ **Kababish.** For freshly baked *naan* (Indian style flat bread) and grilled kebabs, pop in to this wee New York City eatery. Kababish churns out authentic Indian, Pakistani, and Bangladeshi take-out. Everything is made to order, so consider calling ahead to avoid a wait. ⌧ *70-64 Broadway* ☎ *718/565–5131* ◷ *Daily 9–5* ☞ *Take-out only* Ⓜ *7 to 74th St.–Broadway; E, F, M, R to Jackson Heights–Roosevelt Ave.*

FLUSHING AND CORONA

To New Yorkers, making the trip to Flushing usually means catching a baseball game at Citi Field or hunting down the best the Far East has to offer in NYC's "other" Chinatown. The historic town of Flushing is a microcosm of a larger city, including a bustling downtown area, fantastic restaurants, and the bucolic Flushing Meadows–Corona Park nearby. Flushing may seem like a strange name for a town, but it's an English adaption of the original (and hard-to-pronounce) Dutch name Vlissingen. The Dutch named it for a favorite port city in the Netherlands.

Next door, quiet Corona could easily be overlooked, but that would be a mistake. Here you find two huge legacies: the music of Satchmo and the cooling simplicity of an Italian Ice.

TOP ATTRACTIONS

FAMILY
Fodor's Choice
★

Citi Field. Opened in 2009, the Mets' newest stadium was designed to hark back to Ebbets Field (where the Dodgers played in Brooklyn until 1957), with a brick exterior and plenty of bells and whistles, from a batting cage and Wiffle-ball field to the original giant apple taken from the team's old residence, Shea Stadium. Even those who aren't Mets fans but simply love baseball should come to see the Jackie Robinson Rotunda, a soaring multistory entrance and history exhibit dedicated to the Dodgers player who shattered baseball's color barrier. While here, don't miss the chance to taste your way through the more-than-fabulous food court behind center field, where you find Shake Shack burgers, Blue Smoke ribs, close to 40 beer varieties at the Big Apple Brews stand, and even lobster rolls and tacos. Though it seats fewer people than Shea by about 15,000, tickets are not hard to come by, especially later in the season. Still feeling nostalgic for the old Shea? Stop by the Mets Hall of Fame & Museum, or pay your respects at the plaque in the parking lot. ⌧ *123-01 Roosevelt Ave., 126th St. and Roosevelt Ave., Flushing* ☎ *718/507–8499* ⊕ *newyork.mets.mlb.com* Ⓜ *7 to Mets–Willets Point.*

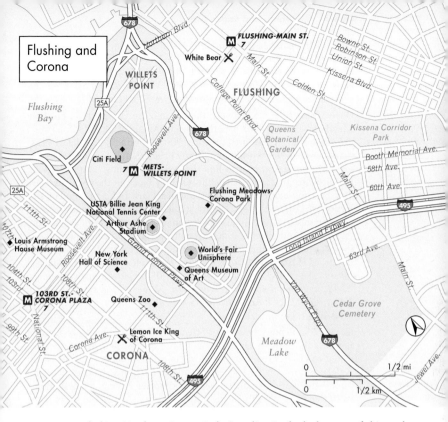

Flushing and Corona

FLUSHING-MAIN ST.
7

White Bear ✕

WILLETS
POINT

FLUSHING

Flushing
Bay

25A

Citi Field

7 M METS-
WILLETS POINT

Flushing Meadows-
Corona Park

USTA Billie Jean King
National Tennis Center

Arthur Ashe
Stadium

Louis Armstrong
House Museum

New York
Hall of Science

World's Fair
Unisphere

Queens Museum
of Art

103RD ST.-
CORONA PLAZA
7

Queens Zoo

Lemon Ice King
✕ of Corona

CORONA

Queens
Botanical
Garden

Kissena Corridor
Park

Booth Memorial Ave.
58th Ave.
60th Ave.

495

63rd Ave.

Cedar Grove
Cemetery

Meadow
Lake

678

0   1/2 mi

0   1/2 km

FAMILY **Flushing Meadows–Corona Park.** Standing in the lush grass of this park, you'd never imagine that it was once a swamp and dumping ground. But the gleaming Unisphere (an enormous 140-foot-high steel globe) might tip you off that this 897-acre park was also the site of two World's Fairs. Take advantage of the park's barbecue pits and sports fields, but don't forget that there's an art museum, petting zoo, golf and minigolf course, and even a model-airplane field. There's way too much to see here to pack into a day, so aim to hit a few primary spots, noting that while several are clustered together on the northwest side of the park, visitors should be prepared for long peaceful walks in between. The flat grounds are ideal for family biking; rent bikes near the park entrance or Meadow Lake from March to October. Although the park is great in daytime, avoid visiting once it gets dark; there has been some crime in this area. ⊠ *Between 111th St./Grand Central Pkwy. and Van Wyck Expressway at 44th Ave., Flushing* ⊕ *www.nycgovparks.org/parks/fmcp* Ⓜ *7 to 111th St. or Mets–Willets Point.*

FAMILY **New York Hall of Science.** At the northwestern edge of Flushing Meadows–Corona Park, the New York Hall of Science has more than 400 hands-on exhibits that make science a playground for inquisitive minds of all ages. Climb aboard a replica of John Glenn's space capsule, throw a fastball and investigate its speed, or explore Charles and Ray Eames's classic Mathematica exhibition. ✉ *47-01 111th St., Flushing* ✥ *From subway, walk 4 blocks south* ☎ *718/699–0005* ⊕ *www.nysci.org* 🖃 *$11 (free Fri. 2–5 and Sun. 10–11 Sept.–June)* ⊙ *Weekdays 9:30–5, weekends 10–6* ⌁ *3-D Theater, Rocket Park Mini Golf, and Science Playground require additional admission fee* Ⓜ *7 to 111th St.*

Queens Museum of Art. Between the zoo and the Unisphere in Flushing Meadows–Corona Park lies the Queens Museum of Art. Don't miss the astonishing Panorama, a nearly 900,000-building model of NYC made for the 1964 World's Fair. Many unsuspecting park visitors looking for a bathroom instead find themselves spending hours exploring the intricate structures that replicate every block in the city. There are also rotating exhibitions of contemporary art and a permanent collection of Louis Comfort Tiffany stained glass. The museum recently doubled in size after a major expansion project, which resulted in more exhibitions and education departments, a café, bookstore, and places for children's activities. There are free guided tours on Sunday afternoons. ✉ *Flushing Meadows–Corona Park, New York City Building, Flushing* ☎ *718/592–9700, 718/592–9700* ⊕ *www.queensmuseum.org* 🖃 *$8 suggested donation* ⊙ *Wed.–Sun. 12–6; call for extended hrs in July and Aug.* ⌁ *Free guided tours Sun. afternoon* Ⓜ *7 to 111th St. or Mets–Willets Point.*

FAMILY   **Queens Zoo.** Behind the Hall of Science in Flushing Meadows–Corona Park lies the intimate Queens Zoo, whose small scale is especially well-suited to easily tired young visitors. In only 11 acres you find North American animals such as bears, mountain lions, bald eagles, and *pudu*—the world's smallest deer. Buckminster Fuller's geodesic dome from the 1964 World's Fair is now the aviary. Across the street is the tri-state's largest petting zoo. ✉ *53-51 111th St., at 53rd Ave., Flushing* ✥ *From subway, walk south to park; from bus, walk east to 111th St.* ☎ *718/220–5100* ⊕ *www.queenszoo.com* 🖃 *$8* ⊙ *Apr.–Oct., weekdays 10–5, weekends and holidays 10–5:30; Nov.–Mar., daily 10–4:30. Last ticket sold 30 mins before closing* Ⓜ *7 to 111th St., Q58 to Corona Ave.*

USTA Billie Jean King National Tennis Center. Each August, 700,000 fans come here for the U.S. Open, which claims the title of highest-attended annual sporting event in the world. The rest of the year, the 34 courts (19 outdoor and 12 indoor, all DecoTurf, plus 3 stadium courts) are open to the public for $24–$68 hourly. Make reservations up to two days in advance. ✉ *Flushing Meadows–Corona Park, Flushing* ☎ *718/760–6200* ⊕ *www.ntc.usta.com* ⊙ *Daily 6 am–midnight; closed major holidays and 1 month around U.S. Open* Ⓜ *7 to Mets–Willets Point.*

WORTH NOTING

Louis Armstrong House Museum. For the last 28 years of his life the famed jazz musician lived in this modest three-story house in Corona with his wife Lucille. Take a 40-minute guided tour, and note the difference between the rooms vividly decorated by Lucille in charming midcentury style and Louis's dark den, cluttered with phonographs and reel-to-reel tape recorders. Although photographs and family mementos throughout the house impart knowledge about Satchmo's life, it's in his den that you really begin to understand his spirit. ✉ *34-56 107th St., at*

37th Ave. ☎ *718/478–8274* ⊕ *www.louisarmstronghouse.org* ☜ *$10, includes guided house tour* ☉ *Tues.–Fri. 10–5, weekends 12–5; tours hourly (last tour at 4 pm)* Ⓜ *7 to 103rd St.–Corona Plaza.*

NEED A BREAK?

Lemon Ice King of Corona. If you're looking for an authentic Queens experience, there are few as true as eating an Italian ice from the Lemon Ice King of Corona on a hot summer day. There are no seats and the service can often be gruff at this neighborhood institution of more than 60 years, but none of that matters after your first taste. And yes, there are plenty of flavors other than lemon. ⊠ *52-02 108th St., at 52nd Ave.* ☎ *718/699–5133* ⊕ *www.thelemonicekingofcorona.com* ☉ *Daily 11–8* Ⓜ *7 to 111th St.*

THE BRONX

Whether you're relaxing at a ballgame, indulging in fresh mozzarella and cannoli on Arthur Avenue, or scoping out exotic species at the zoo, there's plenty of fun to be had here. Named for the area's first documented Europen settler Jonas Bronck, the Bronx is often the city's most misunderstood borough. Its reputation as a gritty, down-and-out place is a little outdated, and there's lots of beauty if you know where to look. There is more parkland in the Bronx than in any other borough, as well as one of the world's finest botanical collections, the largest metropolitan zoo in the country, and, of course, Yankee Stadium.

TOP ATTRACTIONS

FAMILY
Fodor's Choice
★

The Bronx Zoo. When it opened its gates in 1899, the Bronx Zoo had only 843 animals. But today, with 250 acres and more than 4,000 animals (of more than 650 species), it's the largest metropolitan zoo in the United States. Get up close and personal with exotic creatures in outdoor settings that re-create natural habitats; you're often separated from them by no more than a moat or wall of glass. Don't miss the Congo Gorilla Forest, a 6½-acre re-creation of a lush African rain forest with two troops of lowland gorillas, as well as white-bearded DeBrazza's monkeys, okapis, and red river hogs. At Tiger Mountain an open viewing shelter lets you get incredibly close to Siberian tigers, who frolic in a pool, lounge outside (even in cold weather), and enjoy daily "enrichment sessions" with keepers. As the big cats are often napping at midday, aim to visit in the morning or evening. In the $62 million exhibit Madagascar!, the formality of the old Lion House has been replaced with a verdant re-creation of one of the most threatened natural habitats in the world. Here you see adorable lemurs and far-from-adorable hissing cockroaches.

Go on a mini safari via the Wild Asia Monorail, May through October, weather permitting. As you wend your way through the forest, see Asian elephants, Indo-Chinese tigers, Indian rhinoceroses, *gaur* (the world's largest cattle), Mongolian wild horses, and several deer and antelope species. Try to visit the most popular exhibits, such as Congo Gorilla Forest, early to avoid lines later in the day. In winter the outdoor exhibitions have fewer animals on view, but there are also fewer crowds, and plenty of indoor exhibits to savor. Also note that there is an extra charge

15

Two bronze rhinoceros statues stand at the entrance to the Keith W. Johnson Zoo Center at the Bronx Zoo. They're modeled after a rhino named Bessie, who lived at the zoo from 1923 to 1962.

for some exhibits. If you want to see everything, you'll save money by purchasing the Total Experience ticket. ⊠ *2300 Southern Blvd., near 187th St.* ☎ *718/220–5100* ⊕ *www.bronxzoo.com* ✉ *General admission $16.95–$19.95 (extra charge for some exhibits); Total Experience $23.95–$33.95; free entry Wed. ($15 suggested donation). Parking: $15 cars, $18 buses* ⊗ *Apr.–Oct., weekdays 10–5, weekends and holidays 10–5:30; Nov.–Mar., daily 10–4:30 Last ticket sold 30 mins before closing* ☞ *Check website for seasonal discounts available when purchasing tickets online* Ⓜ *2, 5 to West Farms Sq.–E. Tremont Ave., then walk 2 blocks up Boston Rd. to Asia entrance; 2, 5 to Pelham Pkwy. or BxM11 express bus to Bronx River entrance. Metro-North (Harlem line) to Fordham, then Bx9 bus to 183rd St. and Southern Blvd.*

FAMILY
Fodor's Choice
★

The New York Botanical Garden. Considered one of the leading botany centers in the world, this 250-acre garden is one of the best reasons to make a trip to the Bronx. Built around the dramatic gorge of the Bronx River, the Garden is home to lush indoor and outdoor gardens and acres of natural forest, and offers classes, concerts, and special exhibits. Be astounded by the captivating fragrance of the Peggy Rockefeller Rose Garden's 4,000 plants of more than 650 varieties; see intricate orchids that look like the stuff of science fiction; relax in the quiet of the forest or the calm of the Conservatory; or take a jaunt through the Everett Children's Adventure Garden: a 12-acre, indoor-outdoor museum with a boulder maze, giant animal topiaries, and a plant discovery center.

The Garden's roses bloom in June and September, but there's plenty to see year-round. The Victorian-style Enid A. Haupt Conservatory houses re-creations of misty tropical rain forests and arid African and North

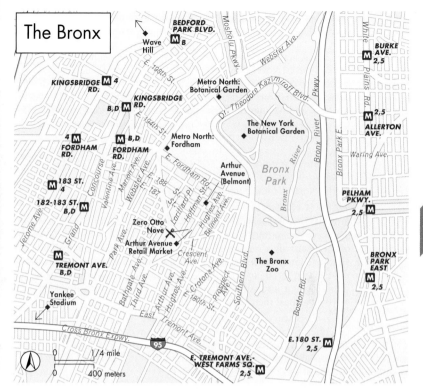

American deserts, as well as exhibitions such as the annual Holiday Train Show and Orchid Show. The All-Garden Pass ($20–$28) gives you access to the Conservatory, Rock Garden, Native Plant Garden, Tram Tour, Everett Children's Adventure Garden, and exhibits in the library.

The most direct way to the Garden is via Metro-North Railroad (*www.mta.info/mnr*) from Grand Central Terminal (Harlem Local Line, Botanical Garden stop). Round-trip tickets are $12.50–$16.50, depending on time of day. A cheaper alternative is to take the B, D or 4 train to Bedford Park Boulevard, then walk southeast. ✉ *2900 Southern Blvd.* ☎ *718/817–8700* ⊕ *www.nybg.org* ✉ *Grounds only $13 (free Sat. 9–10 and all day Wed.); All-Garden Pass $20 ($28 during special events). Parking $12 weekdays, $15 weekends and during special events* ⊙ *Tues.–Sun. 10–6 (mid-Jan.–Feb. 10–5); some holiday Mon. 10–6 (check online)* Ⓜ *B, D to Bedford Park Blvd.; 4 to Bedford Park Blvd.–Lehman College; then walk about 8 blocks downhill to the Garden (or take the Bx26 bus). Metro-North (Harlem local line) to Botanical Garden.*

FAMILY

Fodor's Choice

★

Yankee Stadium. Fans are still nostalgic for the original, legendary Yankee Stadium, which saw its last season in 2008. The new $1.5 billion Yankee Stadium, however—right across the street from "the House that Ruth Built"—got off to a good start, with the Yankees winning the

World Series in its inaugural year. Tickets can be pricey, but the experience is like watching baseball in a modern-day coliseum. It's incredibly opulent and over-the-top: a traditional white frieze adorns the stadium's top; inside, limestone-and-marble hallways are lined with photos of past Yankee greats; lower-level seats have cushions, cup holders, and easy access to a boffo meatery, NYY Steak. Like the team, amenities don't come cheap. History buffs and hardcore fans should visit the Yankees Museum and Monument Park (closes 45 minutes prior to first pitch), with plaques of past Yankee legends, by center field—it survived from its original left-field location at the old stadium. Aside from the subway, you can also get here by taking Metro-North to the Yankees–E. 153rd Street Station. ⊠ *1 E. 161st St., at River Ave.* ☎ *718/293–6000* ⊕ *newyork.yankees.mlb.com* Ⓜ *4, B, D to 161st St.–Yankee Stadium; Metro-North (Hudson line) to Yankees–E. 153rd St.*

WORTH NOTING

Arthur Avenue (Belmont). Manhattan's Little Italy is sadly overrun with mediocre restaurants aimed at tourists, but Belmont, the Little Italy of the Bronx, is a real, thriving Italian-American community. Unless you have family in the area, the main reason to come here is for the food: eating it, buying it, or looking at it fondly through windows. A secondary(but just as important) reason is chatting with shopkeepers so you can steal their recipes.

Nearly a century after pushcarts on Arthur Avenue catered to Italian American workers constructing the zoo and Botanical Garden, the area teems with meat markets, bakeries, and cheese makers. There are long debates about which store or restaurant is the "best," but thanks to generations of Italian grandmothers, vendors here don't dare serve anything less than super fresh, handmade foods.

Although the area is no longer solely Italian—many Latinos and Albanians share this neighborhood now—Italians dominate the food scene. The covered Arthur Avenue Retail Market is a terrific starting point. It houses more than a dozen vendors. Regulars mostly shop on Saturday afternoon; many stores are shuttered on Sunday and after 6 pm. ⊠ *Arthur Ave. between Crescent Ave./184th St. and 188th St., and 187th St. between Lorillard Pl. and Hughes Ave., Belmont* ⊕ *www.arthuravenuebronx.com* Ⓜ *4, B, D to Fordham Rd., then Bx12 bus east; 2, 5 to Pelham Pkwy., then Bx12 bus west. Metro-North (Harlem local line) to Fordham, then 15-min walk.*

OFF THE
BEATEN
PATH

Wave Hill. Drawn by stunning views of the Hudson River and New Jersey's dramatic Palisades, 19th-century Manhattan millionaires built summer homes in the Bronx suburb of Riverdale. One of the most magnificent, Wave Hill, is now a 28-acre public garden and cultural center that attracts green thumbs from all over the world. Along with exquisite gardens, grand beech and oak trees tower above wide lawns, while an elegant pergola overlooks the majestic river view, and benches on curving pathways provide quiet respite. Wave Hill House (1843) and Glyndor House (1927) now host art exhibitions, Sunday concerts, and gardening workshops. Even England's Queen Mother stayed here during a visit. It's worth the schlep. ⊠ *Independence Ave., at W. 249th St.,*

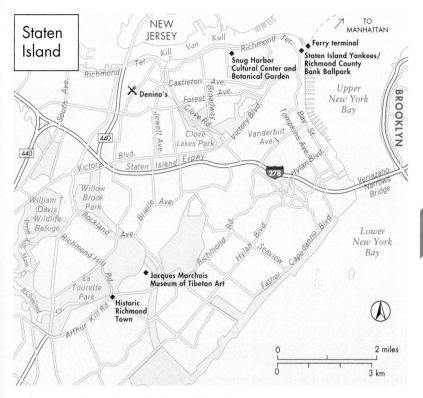

Staten
Island

NEW
JERSEY

TO
MANHATTAN

Ferry terminal

Staten Island Yankees/
Richmond County
Bank Ballpark

Snug Harbor
Cultural Center and
Botanical Garden

Denino's

Upper
New York
Bay

BROOKLYN

Clove
Lakes Park

Vanderbilt
Ave.

Staten Island Expwy.

278

Verrazano-
Narrows
Bridge

Willow
Brook
Park

William T.
Davis
Wildlife
Refuge

Lower
New York
Bay

Jacques Marchais
Museum of Tibetan Art

La
Tourette
Park

Historic
Richmond
Town

15

0   2 miles
0   3 km

Riverdale ☎ *718/549–3200* ⊕ *www.wavehill.org* ✍ *$8 (free Tues. and
Sat. 9–noon)* ◷ *Mid-Mar.–Oct., Tues.–Sun. 9–5:30; Nov.–mid-Mar.,
Tues.–Sun. 9–4:30; closed Mon. except holidays. Free garden tours
Sun. at 2* ☞ *On-site parking $8* Ⓜ *1 to Van Cortlandt Park–242nd
St. (free hourly shuttle service between 9:10 am and 3:10 pm); 1 to
231st St., then Bx7 or Bx10 bus to 252nd St. and Riverdale Ave.; A
to Inwood–207th St., then Bx7 or Bx20 bus to W. 252nd St. Metro-
North (Hudson line) to Riverdale (free hourly shuttle service between
9:45 am and 3:45 pm).*

STATEN ISLAND

A free 25-minute ferry voyage from the southern tip of Manhattan to
Staten Island provides one of the city's best views of the Statue of Liberty and the downtown Manhattan skyline. Upon arrival, it's hard to
miss the Richmond County Bank Ballpark at St. George, the home of
the Staten Island Yankees, where minor leaguers in pinstripes affection-
ately known as "baby bombers" dream of one day playing in the Bronx.
When venturing beyond the borough's northernmost tip, you will find
that Staten Island is full of surprises. Along with suburban sprawl, there
are wonderful small museums, including a premier collection of Tibetan

DID YOU KNOW?

Many New Yorkers consider the Staten Island Ferry the ultimate inexpensive date. Its decks provide romantic waterfront views of the Statue of Liberty and Lower Manhattan without costing a cent (and beer is a bagain).

art; walkable woodlands; and a historic village replicating New York's rural past. From the ferry terminal, grab an S40 bus to the **Snug Harbor Cultural Center** (about 10 minutes) or take the S74 and combine visits to the **Tibetan Museum** and **Historic Richmond Town.**

Legally part of New York City since 1898, Staten Island is in many ways a world apart. The "Forgotten Borough," as some locals refer to it, is geographically more separate, less populous, politically more conservative, and ethnically more homogeneous than the rest of the city.

TOP ATTRACTIONS

FAMILY

Fodor'sChoice

★

Snug Harbor Cultural Center and Botanical Garden. Once part of a sprawling farm, this 83-acre community is now a popular spot to see maritime art, frolic in the Children's Museum (*www.sichildrensmuseum.org*), or take a stroll through lush gardens.

Made up of 26 mostly restored historic buildings, Snug Harbor's center is a row of mid-19th-century Greek Revival temples. Main Hall—the oldest building on the property—is home to the Eleanor Proske Visitors Center (*$5, including Newhouse Center*), which has exhibits on art and Snug Harbor's history. The adjacent Newhouse Center for Contemporary Art (*718/425–3524; $5, includes visitor center*) shows multidisciplinary videos, mixed media, and performances. Next door at the Noble Maritime Collection (*718/447–6490; www.noblemaritime. org; suggested donation*) an old seamen's dormitory is now a museum of ocean-inspired artwork.

From the Staten Island Ferry terminal, take the S40 bus 2 miles (about seven minutes) to the Snug Harbor Road stop. Otherwise grab a car service at the ferry terminal (the ride should cost $5–$8.) ⊠ *1000 Richmond Terr., between Snug Harbor Rd. and Tysen St.* ☎ *718/425–3504* ⊕ *www.snug-harbor.org* 🎟 *Grounds and gardens free; $5 New York Chinese Scholar's Garden, $5 art galleries, $8 Chinese Scholar's Garden and gallery combo ticket; $6 Children's Museum* ☉ *Grounds and Botanical Gardens daily dawn–dusk; Chinese Scholar's Garden Tues.–Sun. 10–4; visitor center and galleries Tues.–Sun. 10–5; Noble Maritime Thurs.–Sun. 1–5 or by appt.; Children's Museum school days noon–5, summer, weekends, and holidays 10–5. Check website for more info* ☞ *Packing a picnic is recommended.*

Jacques Marchais Museum of Tibetan Art. At the top of a hill sits this replica of a Tibetan monastery containing one of the largest collections of Tibetan and Himalayan sculpture, paintings, and artifacts outside Tibet. Meditate with visiting Buddhist monks, or just enjoy the peaceful views from the terraced garden. ⊠ *338 Lighthouse Ave.* ☎ *718/987–3500* ⊕ *www.tibetanmuseum.org* 🎟 *$6* ☉ *Apr.–Dec. 22, Wed.–Sun. 1–5; Feb.–Mar., Fri.–Sun. 1–5; Jan., by appt. only* Ⓜ *S74 bus to Lighthouse Ave. (30- to 45-min ride from Ferry Terminal) and walk uphill 15 mins.*

WORTH NOTING

FAMILY **Historic Richmond Town.** Think of a small-scale version of Virginia's Colonial Williamsburg (the polar opposite of Brooklyn's scene-y Williamsburg), and you'll understand the appeal of Richmond Town. This 100-acre village, constructed from 1695 to the 19th century, was the site of Staten Island's original county seat. Fifteen of the site's 27 historic

15

buildings are open to the public; more than $12 million has been raised for ongoing renovations to many of the structures. Highlights include the Gothic Revival Courthouse, the one-room General Store, and the Voorlezer's House, one of the oldest buildings on the site. It served as a residence, place of worship, and elementary school. Also on-site is the Staten Island Historical Society Museum, built in 1848 as the second county clerk's and surrogate's office, which now houses Staten Island artifacts plus changing exhibits about the island. Audio tours are free with admission.

You may see staff in period dress demonstrate Early American crafts and trades such as tinsmithing or basket making, though the general era meant to be re-created is 1820–1860. December brings a month-long Christmas celebration. Take the S74–Richmond Road bus (30–45 minutes) or a car service (about $25) from the ferry terminal. ⊠ *441 Clarke Ave.* ☎ *718/351–1611* ⊕ *www.historicrichmondtown.org* 🎫 *$8 (free Fri.)* ☽ *Wed.–Sun. 1–5; guided tours Wed.–Fri. at 2:30, weekends at 2 and 3:30* ☞ *Free parking; if visiting from Midtown by public transportation, expect about 90 mins of travel time each way* Ⓜ *S74 bus to St. Patrick's Pl.*

WHERE TO EAT

Updated by
David Farley

Ready to take a bite out of New York? Hope you've come hungry. In a city where creativity is expressed in innumerable ways, the food scene takes center stage, with literally thousands of chances to taste what Gotham is all about. Whether lining up at street stands, gobbling down legendary deli and diner grub, or chasing a coveted reservation at the latest celebrity-chef venue, New Yorkers are a demanding yet appreciative audience.

Every neighborhood offers temptations high, low, and in between, meaning there's truly something for every taste, whim, and budget. No matter how you approach dining out here, it's hard to go wrong. Planning a day of shopping among the glittering flagship boutiques along 5th and Madison? Stop into one of the Upper East Side's storied restaurants for a repast among the "ladies who lunch." Clubbing in the Meatpacking District? Tuck into a meal at eateries as trendy as their patrons. Craving authentic ethnic? From food trucks to hidden joints, there are almost more choices than there are appetites. Recent years have also seen entire food categories, from ramen to meatballs to mac 'n' cheese, riffed-upon and fetishized, and at many restaurants you find an almost religious reverence for seasonal, locally sourced cuisine.

And don't forget—New York is still home to more celebrity chefs than any other city. Your chances of running into your favorite cookbook author, Food Network celeb, or paparazzi-friendly chef are high, adding even more star wattage to a restaurant scene with an already through-the-roof glamour quotient. Newfound economic realities, however, have revived appreciation for value, meaning you can tap into wallet-friendly choices at every level of the food chain. Rest assured, this city does its part to satisfy your appetite. Ready, set, eat.

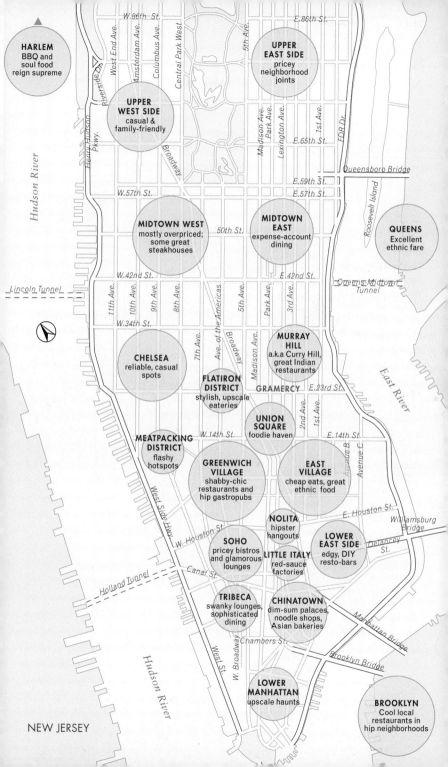

HARLEM
BBQ and soul food reign supreme

UPPER WEST SIDE
casual & family-friendly

UPPER EAST SIDE
pricey neighborhood joints

W. 86th St.

E. 86th St.

West End Ave.

Amsterdam Ave.

Columbus Ave.

Central Park West

5th Ave.

Riverside Dr.

Henry Hudson Pkwy.

Broadway

Madison Ave.

Park Ave.

Lexington Ave.

1st Ave.

FDR Dr.

E. 65th St.

Queensboro Bridge

E. 59th St.

E. 57th St.

W. 57th St.

Roosevelt Island

MIDTOWN WEST
mostly overpriced; some great steakhouses

50th St.

MIDTOWN EAST
expense-account dining

QUEENS
Excellent ethnic fare

Hudson River

Lincoln Tunnel

W. 42nd St.

E. 42nd St.

Queens-Midtown Tunnel

11th Ave.

10th Ave.

9th Ave.

8th Ave.

7th Ave.

Ave. of the Americas

5th Ave.

Broadway

Madison Ave.

Park Ave.

3rd Ave.

2nd Ave.

1st Ave.

W. 34th St.

East River

CHELSEA
reliable, casual spots

MURRAY HILL
a.k.a Curry Hill, great Indian restaurants

FLATIRON DISTRICT
stylish, upscale eateries

GRAMERCY

E. 23rd St.

UNION SQUARE
foodie haven

MEATPACKING DISTRICT
flashy hotspots

W. 14th St.

E. 14th St.

GREENWICH VILLAGE
shabby-chic restaurants and hip gastropubs

EAST VILLAGE
cheap eats, great ethnic food

Avenue B

Avenue C

West St.

WMH

E. Houston St.

Williamsburg Bridge

W. Houston St.

NOLITA
hipster hangouts

SOHO
pricey bistros and glamorous lounges

LITTLE ITALY
red-sauce factories

LOWER EAST SIDE
edgy, DIY resto-bars

Delancey St.

Canal St.

Holland Tunnel

TRIBECA
swanky lounges, sophisticated dining

CHINATOWN
dim-sum palaces, noodle shops, Asian bakeries

Manhattan Bridge

West St.

W. Broadway

Chambers St.

Brooklyn Bridge

Hudson River

LOWER MANHATTAN
upscale haunts

BROOKLYN
Cool local restaurants in hip neighborhoods

NEW JERSEY

BEST BETS FOR NEW YORK CITY DINING

With thousands of restaurants to choose from, how do you decide where to eat? Fodor's writers and editors have selected their favorite restaurants by price, cuisine, and experience in the Best Bets lists below.

Fodor's Choice ★

Babbo, $$$

Back Forty West, $$

Bar Boulud, $$$

The Breslin Bar and Dining Room, $$$

Burger Joint, $

Café Sabarsky, $$

Candle 79, $$

The City Bakery, $

Clinton St. Baking Co., $$

Co., $$

Daniel, $$$$

Danji, $$

Edi & the Wolf, $$

Eleven Madison Park, $$$$

Empellón Taqueria, $$

Emporio, $$

Estela, $$$

The Fat Radish, $$

Fatty Crab, $$

Freemans, $$

Gotham Bar & Grill, $$$$

Ivan Ramen, $$

Katz's Delicatessen, $

Le Bernardin, $$$$

M. Wells Dinette, $$

Marea, $$$

Marta, $$

Momofuku Ko, $$$$

Momofuku Noodle Bar, $

The NoMad, $$$

Northern Spy Food Co., $$

Osteria Morini, $$$

Per Se, $$$$

Reynard, $$$

Roberta's, $$

Saxon & Parole, $$

Shake Shack, $

Best by Price

$

Burger Joint

The City Bakery

Gray's Papaya

Katz's Delicatessen

Legend

Mile End

Momofuku Noodle Bar

Shake Shack

Somtum Der

Tía Pol, $

$$

Arturo's

Bubby's

Café Sabarsky

Candle 79

Emporio

Fatty Crab

M. Wells Dinette

Northern Spy Food Co.

Roberta's

$$$

ABC Kitchen

Babbo

Balthazar

Bar Boulud

Marea

Minetta Tavern

The NoMad

Osteria Morini

The Standard Grill

$$$$

Craft

Eleven Madison Park

Jean Georges

Le Bernardin

The Modern and Bar Room

Per Se

Best by Cuisine

AMERICAN

ABC Kitchen

Cookshop

Craft

Eleven Madison Park

Gramercy Tavern

Hundred Acres

Northern Spy Food Co.

Per Se

The Red Cat

CHINESE

Grand Sichuan

Great New York Noodletown

Joe's Shanghai

Legend

Shun Lee Palace

Tasty Hand-Pulled Noodles

Xi'an Famous Foods

FRENCH

Bar Boulud

Daniel

Jean Georges

Lafayette Grand Café & Bakery

Le Bernardin

The Modern and Bar Room

GREEK

Kefi

Pylos

Snack

INDIAN

Tamarind

ITALIAN

Babbo

Emporio

Lupa

Marea

Osteria Morini

JAPANESE

Ippudo
Kuruma Zushi
Sushi Nakazawa
Sushi of Gari
Sushi Yasuda

MEDITERRANEAN

Aldea
Il Buco
The NoMad
Picholine

MEXICAN

Empellón Taqueria
Maya
Mission Cantina
Toloache

PIZZA

Arturo's
Co.
Esca
Keste Pizza & Vino
Lombardi's

SEAFOOD

Grand Central Oyster
Bar & Restaurant
The John Dory
Marea
Mary's Fish Camp
Pearl Oyster Bar

SPANISH

Boqueria
Casa Mono
Tía Pol

STEAKHOUSE

BLT Prime
BLT Steak
Peter Luger's
Porter House New
York
Sparks Steakhouse

Best by Experience

BRUNCH

Balthazar
Bubby's
Cookshop
Hundred Acres
Sarabeth's Kitchen

CELEB-SPOTTING

ABC Kitchen
Balthazar
The Breslin Bar and
Dining Room
Café Boulud
DBGB Kitchen & Bar
The Four Seasons
Minetta Tavern
Nobu
The Standard Grill

CHILD-FRIENDLY

Bubby's
Carmine's
The City Bakery
Joe's Shanghai
Lombardi's
Odeon

GREAT VIEW

Asiate
Marea
Michael Jordan's The
Steakhouse NYC
Per Se
Porter House New
York

LATE-NIGHT DINING

Balthazar
The Breslin Bar and
Dining Room
DBGB Kitchen & Bar
Emporio
Fatty Crab
Minetta Tavern
Osteria Morini
The Standard Grill

16

EAT LIKE A LOCAL

A handful of foods are associated with New York City: apples (big ones, obviously), pizza, pastrami, hot dogs, bagels—the list of earthly delights is long and delicious. These, generally speaking, are what the locals tend to talk about.

Food Trucks

The food-truck movement is officially on. It seems there's a special truck for everything from ethnic eats to fresh-baked sweets. The southern end of Washington Square, near NYU, is a prime location, with trucks lined up serving the cuisines of Holland, Colombia, Cambodia, and Mexico, but you can find food trucks parked all over town, some with legendary followings and Twitter feeds to help you find them. Thompson Hotels, which has several properties in New York, even has a Food Truck Concierge.

Pizza

There are few things more Big Apple than a slice of pizza, its bottom crust crispy from the coal oven. There are take-out joints for slices and sit-down restaurants that only serve pies; some are thin-crust, some are thick, some even have fried dough, and everyone has a favorite. There's no question that pizza will always be synonymous with New York, but the crust is being elevated to a real art form these days. Some people say the reason the pizza here is so good is because of the excellent quality of the New York water.

Soul Food in Harlem

Sylvia Woods, the "Queen of Soul Food" and proprietor of the eponymous Harlem restaurant, may have ascended to that great soul food restaurant in the sky, but the cuisine lives on in this historic neighborhood—in fact, more now than ever, since celeb-chef Marcus Samuelsson moved into the area, opening the Red Rooster, a global eatery that gives a big nod to soul food.

Chinese Food

There's Chinese food and then there's New York's downtown Chinatown Chinese food, which some visitors might find head-scratchingly unfamiliar. That's because Chinatown boasts a diverse population from China's many regions, which means menus are going to look deliciously foreign to the uninitiated. Go ahead, point and order something you've never heard of. Restaurants serving dim sum, which are basically different kinds of small fried or steamed dumplings, are popular for weekend breakfast.

Burgers

Hamburgers will forever be a part of the Big Apple dining landscape. But it so happens that it's never been a better time to be a burger eater, and nearly every restaurant—American or not—has some kind of burger on its menu. If you're a discriminating burger lover, look for the name Pat LaFrieda, a meat purveyor

par excellence. Just don't expect to save any money; it's not unusual to see a $20 hamburger on a menu.

Gastropubs

The gastropub phenomenon, imported from London, began with the Spotted Pig in the West Village, and within a few years, every neighborhood had one. And why not? Blending a casual pub atmosphere with way-better-than-average pub grub is a fun and tasty combination that's hard to beat.

Banh Mi Sandwiches

The banh mi sandwich has grabbed the attention of Big Apple eaters in recent years and has not let go. This French-influenced Vietnamese sandwich consists of pork, pâté, carrots, cilantro, and jalapeño peppers stuffed into a baguette. This is a delicacy worth seeking out, so check the menus at our top Asian restaurant picks.

Locavore

The focus on local food and beverages has definitely taken hold at NYC restaurants. Menus flaunt the nearby provenance of their meat and produce, whether it's from upstate New York or from the restaurant's rooftop garden. Wine lists frequently include excellent Long Island wines, as well as bourbon and other spirits brewed as close as the Brooklyn Navy Yards or the Hudson Valley.

16

PLANNING

CHILDREN

Although it's unusual to see children in the dining rooms of Manhattan's most elite restaurants, dining with youngsters in New York does not have to mean culinary exile. Many of the restaurants reviewed in this chapter are excellent choices for families, and are marked as such.

RESERVATIONS

It's always a good idea to plan ahead. Some renowned restaurants like Per Se, Daniel, Brooklyn Fare, and Momofuku Ko are booked weeks or even months in advance. If that's the case, you can get lucky at the last minute if you're flexible—and friendly. Most restaurants keep a few tables open for walk-ins and VIPs. Show up for dinner early (5:30) or late (after 10), and politely inquire about any last-minute vacancies or cancellations.

Occasionally, an eatery may take your credit-card number and ask you to call the day before your scheduled meal to reconfirm: don't forget or you could lose out, or possibly be charged for your oversight.

WHAT TO WEAR

New Yorkers like to dress up, and so should you. Whatever your style, dial it up a notch. Have some fun while you're at it. Pull out the clothes you've been saving for a special occasion and get glamorous. Unfair as it is, the way you look can influence how you're treated—and where you're seated. Generally speaking, jeans and a button-down shirt suffice at most table-service restaurants in the $ to $$ range. In reviews, we note dress only when a jacket or jacket and tie are required. If you have doubts, call the restaurant and ask.

TIPPING AND TAXES

In most restaurants, tip the waiter 15%–20%. (To figure out a 20% tip quickly, just move the decimal point one place to the left on your total and double that amount.) Tip at least $1 per drink at the bar, and $1 for each coat checked. Never tip the maître d' unless you're out to impress your guests or expect to pay another visit soon.

SMOKING

Smoking is prohibited in all enclosed public spaces in New York City, including restaurants and bars.

HOURS

New Yorkers seem ready to eat at any hour. Many restaurants stay open between lunch and dinner, some have late-night seating, and still others serve around the clock. Restaurants that serve breakfast often do so until noon or later. Restaurants in the East Village, Lower East Side, SoHo, TriBeCa, and Greenwich Village are likely to remain open late, whereas Midtown spots and those in the Theater and Financial districts and uptown generally close earlier. Unless otherwise noted, the restaurants listed in this guide are open daily for lunch and dinner.

PRICES

Be sure to ask the price of the daily specials recited by the waiter; the charge for specials at some restaurants is noticeably out of line with the other prices on the menu. Beware of the $10 bottle of water; ask for tap water instead, and always review your bill.

If you eat early or late, you may be able to take advantage of a prix-fixe deal not offered at peak hours. Most upscale restaurants have great lunch deals.

Credit cards are widely accepted, but many restaurants (particularly smaller ones downtown) accept only cash. If you plan to use a credit card, it's a good idea to confirm that it is acceptable when making reservations or before sitting down to eat.

Prices in the reviews are the average cost of a main course at dinner or, if dinner is not served, at lunch.

WHAT IT COSTS AT DINNER

	$	$$	$$$	$$$$
RESTAURANTS	under $13	$13–$24	$25–$35	over $35

Price per person for a median main course or equivalent combination of smaller dishes. Note: If a restaurant offers only prix-fixe (set-price) meals, it has been given the price category that reflects the full prix-fixe price.

CHECK BEFORE YOU GO

The nature of the restaurant industry means that places open and close in a New York minute. It's always a good idea to phone ahead and make sure your restaurant is still turning tables.

RESTAURANT REVIEWS

Listed alphabetically within neighborhoods. Use the coordinate (1:B2) at the end of each listing to locate a property on the corresponding map at the end of the chapter.

LOWER MANHATTAN

FINANCIAL DISTRICT

The southern tip of the island, once skyscraper-laden and nightlife-starved, has been getting buzzier in the last few years. Exciting new bars and restaurants have opened, but the old dependable steakhouses and bistros are still here.

$$ ITALIAN FAMILY

✕ **Adrienne's Pizza Bar.** It's hip to be square at this downtown pizzeria. Father-and-son team Harry and Peter Poulakakos's square (also known as Grandma) pies are worth the trek and a convenient stop en route to the Statue of Liberty. They also do a mean traditional round pizza, and first-timers should opt for the signature Old Fashioned: thin, crispy crust loaded with tangy tomato sauce, fresh mozzarella, and Parmesan cheese. Salads and pasta are on the menu, too. Service has never been Adrienne's forte, so be flattered if you get someone to crack a smile. [$] *Average main: $17* ✉ *54 Stone St., near Hanover Sq., Financial*

District ☎ 212/248–3838 🌐 www.adriennespizzabarnyc.com [M] R to Whitehall St.; 4, 5 to Bowling Green ✣ 1:E4.

$$$$ STEAKHOUSE 🍴 **Delmonico's.** The oldest continually operating restaurant in New York City (since 1837), austere Delmonico's is steeped in cultural, political, and culinary history. Lobster Newburg and Baked Alaska were invented here—and are still served. Inside the stately mahogany-panel dining room, tuck into the classic Delmonico's steak, a 20-ounce boneless ribeye smothered with frizzled onions, and don't forget to order creamed spinach on the side. The cheesy spaetzle with pancetta is also sinfully sublime. The dining room gets busy early with an after-work Wall Street crowd, making reservations essential. [$] *Average main: $37 ✉ 56 Beaver St., at William St., Financial District ☎ 212/509–1144 🌐 www.delmonicosny.com ⏲ No lunch weekends ✍ Reservations essential [M] 2, 3 to Wall St.; R to Whitehall St.; 4, 5 to Bowling Green; J, Z to Broad St. ✣ 1:D4.*

$ CAFÉ 🍴 **Financier Patisserie.** On the cobblestone pedestrian street that has become the Financial District's restaurant row, this charming pâtisserie serves excellent pastries and delicious savory foods, like mushroom bisque, salads, and hot or cold sandwiches (we have cravings for the panini pressed with prosciutto, fig jam, mascarpone, and arugula). After lunch, relax with a cappuccino and a *financier* (almond tea cake), or an elegant pastry. In warm weather, perch at an outdoor table and watch Manhattanites buzz by. There are locations all over town. [$] *Average main: $7 ✉ 62 Stone St., between Mill La. and Hanover Sq., Financial District ☎ 212/344–5600 🌐 www.financierpastries.com ⏲ No dinner ✍ Reservations not accepted [M] 2, 3 to Wall St.; 4, 5 to Bowling Green; J, Z to Broad St. ✣ 1:E4.*

$$$ STEAKHOUSE 🍴 **Harry's Café and Steak.** Its noise-dampening acoustics and maze of underground nooks combine to make Harry's Steak—the fine-dining half of the restaurant (Harry's Café is more casual, but the menu is the same)—one of the city's most intimate steakhouses. Settle into a leather booth and start with a classic shrimp cocktail or the tomato trio, starring thick beefsteak slices topped with bacon and blue cheese, mozzarella and basil, and shaved onion with ranch dressing. The star attraction—prime aged porterhouse for two—is nicely encrusted with sea salt and a good match for buttery mashed potatoes infused with sweet roasted shallots and thick steak sauce spooned from Mason jars. Weekend brunch is popular, too. [$] *Average main: $35 ✉ 1 Hanover Sq., between Stone and Pearl sts., Financial District ☎ 212/785–9200 🌐 www.harrysnyc.com ⏲ Closed Sun. ✍ Reservations essential [M] 4, 5 to Bowling Green; 2, 3 to Wall St.; J, Z to Broad St. ✣ 1:E4.*

$ AMERICAN 🍴 **Ulysses'.** Squeezed between skyscrapers and the towering New York Stock Exchange, Stone Street is a two-block restaurant oasis that feels more like a village than the center of the financial universe. After the market closes, Wall Streeters head to Ulysses', a popular pub with 12 beers on tap and more than 50 bottled beers. Hungry? There are decent pub-grub options, like mini cheeseburgers, fried oysters, nachos, and wings. [$] *Average main: $9 ✉ 95 Pearl St., near Hanover Sq., Financial District ☎ 212/482–0400 🌐 www.ulyssesnyc.com [M] R to Whitehall St.; J, Z to Broad St.; 2, 3 to Wall St. ✣ 1:E4.*

TRIBECA

TriBeCa and its restaurants are a playground for the rich and famous. Fortunately, glamorous dining rooms in converted warehouses have been joined in the last few years by more casual spots.

$$$ ✕ **Blaue Gans.** Chef Kurt Gutenbrunner, one of the most lauded Austrian
AUSTRIAN chefs in New York, runs this sprawling brasserie like an all-day club-
FAMILY house. Pop in for a late-morning or early-afternoon snack—the coffee comes topped with *schlag*, the doughnuts filled with apricot jam. Or swing by in the evening for Central European standards like sausage, schnitzel, potato dumplings, and beef goulash. Wash it all down with a hoppy Austrian brew. $ *Average main: $25* ✉ *139 Duane St., near West Broadway, TriBeCa* ☎ *212/571–8880* ⊕ *www.kg-ny.com* Ⓜ *1, 2, 3, A, C to Chambers St.* ✛ *1:C1.*

$$ ✕ **Bubby's.** Neighborhood crowds clamoring for coffee and freshly
AMERICAN squeezed juice line up for brunch at this TriBeCa mainstay, but Bubby's
FAMILY is good for lunch and dinner, too, if you're in the mood for comfort food like mac 'n' cheese or fried chicken. The dining room is homey and cozy, with big windows; in summer, patrons sit at tables outside with their dogs. Brunch options include just about everything, including homemade granola, sour-cream pancakes with bananas and strawberries, and *huevos rancheros* with guacamole and grits. $ *Average main: $18* ✉ *120 Hudson St., at N. Moore St., TriBeCa* ☎ *212/219–0666* ⊕ *www.bubbys.com* Ⓜ *1 to Franklin St.* ✛ *1:C1.*

$$ ✕ **Kitchenette.** This small, comfy restaurant lives up to its name with
AMERICAN tables so close together, you're likely to make new friends. Indeed, the
FAMILY dining room pretty much feels like a breakfast nook, and the food tastes like your mom made it—provided she's a great cook. Think comfort food: fried chicken, barbecue brisket with mashed potatoes, and even a turkey dinner. There are no frills here, just solid cooking, friendly service, and a long line at peak times. At brunch don't miss the peach pancakes or the baked cinnamon-swirl French toast. $ *Average main: $15* ✉ *156 Chambers St., near Greenwich St., TriBeCa* ☎ *212/267–6740* ⊕ *www.kitchenetterestaurant.com* Ⓜ *1, 2, 3, A, C to Chambers St.* ✛ *1:C2.*

$$$ ✕ **Locanda Verde.** Chef Andrew Carmellini, first an acolyte of Daniel
ITALIAN Boulud, and then a chef with a half a dozen restaurants in his culinary arsenal, has definitely made a name for himself in New York City. This Robert De Niro–backed restaurant is still one of his best. The space at Locanda Verde is warm and welcoming, with accents of brick and wood and large windows that open to the street, weather permitting, while the menu is full of inspired Italian comfort food that hits the mark. Standouts include small plates like blue crab crostino with jalapeños and the pumpkin agnolotti in brown sage butter that diners reminisce about. Several draft beers, along with more than a dozen wines by the glass, make an already hopping bar scene even more of a draw. $ *Average main: $26* ✉ *377 Greenwich St., at N. Moore St., TriBeCa* ☎ *212/925–3797* ⊕ *www.locandaverdenyc.com* ⌂ *Reservations essential* Ⓜ *1 to Franklin St.* ✛ *1:B1.*

$$$ ✕ **Marc Forgione.** Restaurant success runs in Chef Marc Forgione's
AMERICAN blood—his father was one of the New York food scene megastars with

16

his 1980's restaurant, An American Place—but he more than holds his own at this neighborhood restaurant that continues to attract crowds for the ambitious, creative New American cuisine. The menu changes frequently, but whatever you order will be bold, flavorful, and inventive without a hint of preciousness. Meat dishes are excellent and well-prepared, but Forgione has a special way with seafood. His chili lobster appetizer, a take on a dish you find all over Asia, comes with Texas toast for mopping up the spicy, buttery sauce. Tartare (perhaps kingfish, hamachi, or salmon, depending on the day) is accented with avocado in a pool of sweet, soy-lashed sauce. $ *Average main: $30* ⊠ *134 Reade St., between Hudson and Greenwich sts., TriBeCa* ☎ *212/941–9401* ⊕ *www.marcforgione.com* ☽ *No lunch* ⌣ *Reservations essential* Ⓜ *1, 2, 3 to Chambers St.* ✛ *1:C1.*

$$$$ ✕ **Nobu.** At this large, bustling TriBeCa dining room (or its sister loca-
JAPANESE tion uptown), you might just spot a celeb or two. New York's famed Japanese restaurant has gained a lot of competition in recent years, but this is still the destination for the innovative Japanese cuisine Nobu Matsuhisa made famous (though he's rarely in attendance these days). Dishes like fresh yellowtail sashimi with jalapeño, rock shrimp tempura, or miso-marinated Chilean sea bass continue to draw huge crowds. Put yourself in the hands of the chef by ordering the tasting menu, or *omakase,* and specify how much you want to spend, then let the kitchen do the rest. Can't get reservations? Try your luck at the first-come, first-served Nobu Next Door (literally next door), with a similar menu plus a sushi bar. $ *Average main: $37* ⊠ *105 Hudson St., at Franklin St., TriBeCa* ☎ *212/219–0500* ⊕ *www.myriadrestaurantgroup.com* ☽ *No lunch weekends* ⌣ *Reservations essential* Ⓜ *1 to Franklin St.* ✛ *1:B1.*

$$$ ✕ **Odeon.** New Yorkers change hangouts faster than they can speed-dial,
FRENCH but this spot has managed to maintain its quality and flair for more
FAMILY than 30 years. It still feels like *the* spot in TriBeCa to get a late-night bite. The neo–Art Deco room is still packed nightly with revelers, and the pleasant service and well-chosen wine list are always in style. Bistro menu highlights include frisee *aux lardons* (with bacon) with poached farm egg, grilled NY strip steak, and slow-cooked cod with baby leeks and fennel confit. $ *Average main: $28* ⊠ *145 West Broadway, between Duane and Thomas sts., TriBeCa* ☎ *212/233–0507* ⊕ *www. theodeonrestaurant.com* Ⓜ *1, 2, 3, A, C to Chambers St.* ✛ *1:C1; 2:D6.*

$$$ ✕ **Tamarind.** Many consider Tamarind to be Manhattan's best Indian
INDIAN restaurant and the elegant atmosphere makes it a different experience from many other NYC Indian restaurants. Forsaking the usual brass, beads, sitar, and darkness, the dining room is airy and modern. Welcoming host, owner Avtar Walia, practically reinvents charm. The busy kitchen prepares multiregional dishes, some familiar (tandoori chicken, a searing lamb vindaloo), some unique (succulent venison chops in a vigorously spiced cranberry sauce, she-crab soup with saffron, nutmeg, and ginger juice). The more intriguing a dish sounds, the better it turns out to be. $ *Average main: $25* ⊠ *99 Hudson St., at Franklin St., TriBeCa* ☎ *212/674–7400* ⊕ *www.tamarindrestaurantsnyc.com* Ⓜ *1 to Franklin St.; A, C, E to Canal St.* ✛ *2:C6.*

SOHO, NOLITA, LITTLE ITALY, AND CHINATOWN

SOHO

Sure, eating in SoHo may not feel very low-key, with mostly pricey eateries full of fashionistas and the "see and be seen" crowd. But the restaurants here are too hot to dampen any hungry spirits and worth the fight for a table.

$$$
SEAFOOD

✕ **Aquagrill.** A SoHo standard for fresh seafood, this lively neighborhood eatery also make their own pastries and baked goods—including the bread for their brunchtime challah French toast with cinnamon apples and pecan butter. Fans rave about the lunchtime $24.50 prix-fixe Shucker Special—a half-dozen oysters with homemade soup or chowder and a salad. Dinner specialties include roasted Dungeness crab–cake Napoleon with sun-dried tomato oil, and falafel-crusted salmon. Desserts are excellent, too, especially the chocolate tasting plate with its molten chocolate cake, milk-chocolate ice cream, and white chocolate mousse. Service is warm and welcoming. $ *Average main: $28* ✉ *210 Spring St., at 6th Ave., SoHo* ☎ *212/274–0505* ⊕ *www.aquagrill.com* ⚑ *Reservations essential* Ⓜ *C, E to Spring St.* ✛ *2:D4.*

$$
AMERICAN
Fodor's Choice
★

✕ **Back Forty West.** Chef Peter Hoffman has been doing sustainable farm-to-table fare long before it became a near-obligatory restaurant trend in the Big Apple. The original Back Forty was in the East Village but the current location just makes it more convenient for neighborhood denizens and shoppers to access the well-executed comfort food. The menu changes with the season, but expect dishes like coconutmilk–spiked scallop ceviche, pumpkin hummus, a very good grass-fed burger, and grilled trout from the Catskills, served alongside quality cocktails and a short but excellent list of beer and wine. Add in rustic, homey décor, and feel like you're hundreds of miles from that shopping mecca known as SoHo. $ *Average main: $18* ✉ *70 Prince St., at Crosby St., SoHo* ☎ *212/219–8570* ⊕ *www.backfortynyc.com* ☾ *No dinner Sun.* Ⓜ *B, D, F, M to Broadway–Lafayette St.; N, R to Prince St.; 6 to Spring St.* ✛ *2:E3.*

$$$
FRENCH

✕ **Balthazar.** Even with long waits and excruciating noise levels, most out-of-towners agree that it's worth making reservations to experience restaurateur Keith McNally's flagship, a painstakingly accurate reproduction of a Parisian brasserie with an insider New York feel. Like the décor, entrées recreate French classics: Gruyère-topped onion soup, steak frites, and icy tiers of crab, oysters, and other pristine shellfish. Brunch is still one of the toughest tables in town. The best strategy to experience this perennial fave is to go at off-hours or on weekdays for breakfast to miss the crush. $ *Average main: $28* ✉ *80 Spring St., between Broadway and Crosby St., SoHo* ☎ *212/965–1414* ⊕ *www. balthazarny.com* ⚑ *Reservations essential* Ⓜ *6 to Spring St.; N, R to Prince St.; B, D, F, M to Broadway–Lafayette St.* ✛ *2:E4.*

$$
BAKERY

✕ **Balthazar Bakery.** Follow the beguiling scent of fresh-baked bread to Balthazar Bakery, next door to Keith McNally's always-packed Balthazar restaurant. Choices include fresh-baked baguettes and other varieties of French breads, as well as gourmet sandwiches, soups, and memorable pastries to take out (there is no seating). Try the berry noisette tart or

16

coconut cake, or keep it simple with an eggy canelé or a buttery lemon or chocolate madeleine. $ *Average main: $23* ⊠ *80 Spring St., near Crosby St., SoHo* ☎ *212/965–1785* ⊕ *www.balthazarbakery.com* ☽ *No dinner* ⚄ *Reservations not accepted* Ⓜ *6 to Spring St.; N, R to Prince St.; B, D, F, M to Broadway–Lafayette St.* ✛ *2:E4.*

$$$ ✕ **Blue Ribbon.** After 20-plus years, Blue Ribbon still has a reputation
MODERN   not just as an eclectic, top-notch seafood joint, but also as a serious
AMERICAN   late-night foodie hangout. Join the genial hubbub for midnight nosh-ing, namely the beef marrow with oxtail marmalade and renowned raw-bar platters. Trustafarians, literary types, chefs, designers—a good-looking gang—generally fill this dark box of a room until 4 am. The menu appears standard at first blush, but it's not. Try the duck club sandwich or matzo ball soup; the latter is a heady brew filled with the sacrilegious combo of seafood and traditional Jewish dumplings. $ *Average main: $32* ⊠ *97 Sullivan St., between Prince and Spring sts., SoHo* ☎ *212/274–0404* ⊕ *www.blueribbonrestaurants.com* ☽ *No lunch* ⚄ *Reservations not accepted* Ⓜ *C, E to Spring St.; N, R to Prince St.* ✛ *2:D3.*

$$$ ✕ **Blue Ribbon Sushi.** Sushi, like pizza, attracts plenty of opinionated
JAPANESE   fanatics, and Blue Ribbon Sushi gets consistent raves for their überfresh sushi and sashimi. Stick to the excellent raw fish and specials here if you're a purist, or branch out and try one of the experimental rolls: the Blue Ribbon—lobster, *shiso* (Japanese basil), and black caviar—is popular. The dark, intimate nooks, minimalist design, and servers with downtown attitude attract a stylish crowd who don't mind waiting for a table or chilled sake. Given the quality and the location, it's not cheap. $ *Average main: $25* ⊠ *119 Sullivan St., between Prince and Spring sts., SoHo* ☎ *212/343–0404* ⊕ *www.blueribbonrestaurants.com* ⚄ *Reservations not accepted* Ⓜ *C, E to Spring St.; N, R to Prince St.* ✛ *2:D3.*

$$$ ✕ **The Dutch.** Perpetually packed with the "see and be seen" crowd, Chef
AMERICAN   Andrew Carmellini's homage to American cuisine is really an encapsula-tion of recent food and dining trends: there's an excellent burger (and at $22 it should be), a Kentucky-size bourbon collection behind the bar, greenmarket-driven comfort food dishes like fried chicken, and bacon paired with things you would have not likely seen a couple decades ago (in this case, scallops with bacon jam). And it all works well at this SoHo restaurant—so much so, you might consider returning for weekend brunch when the housemade bologna sandwich or cornmeal flapjacks appear on the menu. $ *Average main: $28* ⊠ *131 Sullivan St., at Prince St., SoHo* ☎ *212/677–6200* ⊕ *www.thedutchnyc.com* ⚄ *Reservations essential* Ⓜ *C, E to Spring St.* ✛ *2:D3.*

$$$ ✕ **Hundred Acres.** Set on a quiet block of Greenwich Village, the rustic,
MODERN   farmhouse-slash-greenhouse that is Hundred Acres is a lovely place to
AMERICAN   while away a long lunch or quiet dinner. The market-driven creative comfort food keeps the neighborhood patrons and out-of-towners-in-the-know coming back. The menu is loaded with all the items you'd expect from a farm-to-table affair: oysters, deviled eggs, broccoli rabe, and, yes, kale. Mains run the gamut from fish to meat: think a luscious pork shank with polenta and rhubarb chutney; shrimp and grits; or a classic burger made from pasture-raised beef, topped with Vermont

cheddar and served with fries and Vidalia onion mayonnaise. Weekend brunch stands out, with variations on a bloody mary theme, and treats like a country pâté sandwich and goat cheese–sage bread pudding. [$] *Average main: $26* ✉ *38 MacDougal St., between Houston and Prince sts., SoHo* ☎ *212/475–7500* 🌐 *www.hundredacresnyc.com* [M] *1 to Houston St.; C, E to Spring St.; N, R to Prince St.* ⊕ *2:D3.*

$$ BISTRO 🍴 **Lucky Strike.** Whether you're lucky enough to nab a table at this scene-y SoHo bistro at 1 pm or 1 am, Lucky Strike always seems like the place to be. Bedecked in classic bistro trappings—hammered-copper stools, mirrors with menu items scrawled on them—the restaurant would look just as perfect in the Bastille neighborhood of Paris as it does in this swanky part of the Big Apple. The kitchen offerings are straightfoward: croque monsieur, grilled salmon, and salade niçoise are old standbys, with a turkey burger thrown in to accommodate the *Americain* palate. [$] *Average main: $18* ✉ *59 Grand St., between West Broadway and Wooster St., SoHo* ☎ *212/941–0772* 🌐 *www.luckystrikeny.com* 💳 *No credit cards* [M] *1, A, C, E to Canal St.* ⊕ *2:D4.*

$$$ SEAFOOD 🍴 **Lure Fishbar.** Decorated like the clubby interior of a sleek luxury liner, Lure serves oceanic fare in multiple culinary styles. From the sushi bar, feast on options like the Lure House Roll—a shrimp tempura roll crowned with spicy tuna and Japanese tartar sauce—or opt for creative dishes from the kitchen, like steamed branzino with oyster mushrooms, scallions, and ponzu sauce, or Manila clams over pancetta-studded linguine. For an all-American treat, you can't go wrong with a classic lobster roll on brioche. The dark subterranean bar is a good spot for cocktails and a snack. Brunch is served on weekends. [$] *Average main: $29* ✉ *142 Mercer St., at Prince St., SoHo* ☎ *212/431–7676* 🌐 *www.lurefishbar.com* [M] *B, D, F, M to Broadway–Lafayette St.; N, R to Prince St.* ⊕ *2:E3.*

16

$ CAFÉ FAMILY 🍴 **MarieBelle.** Practically invisible from the front of the chocolate emporium, the back entry to the Cacao Bar opens into a sweet, high-ceiling, 12-table hot-chocolate shop. Most people order the Aztec, European-style (that's 60% Colombian chocolate mixed with hot water—no cocoa powder here!). The first sip is startlingly rich but not too dense; American-style, made with milk, is sweeter. Not to worry if you're visiting in spring or summer: you can opt for Aztec iced chocolate—the warm-weather version of the decadent cacao elixir—or the house-made chocolate gelato. For more substantial snacking, choose a salad or sandwich from the dainty lunch menu . [$] *Average main: $12* ✉ *484 Broome St., between West Broadway and Wooster St., SoHo* ☎ *212/925–6999* 🌐 *www.mariebelle.com* 🕒 *No dinner* ✍ *Reservations not accepted* [M] *6 to Spring St.; A, C, E to Canal St.* ⊕ *2:D4.*

$$$ ASIAN FUSION 🍴 **The Mercer Kitchen.** Part of Alsatian superchef Jean-Georges Vongerichten's culinary empire, the celebrity-laden front room of this SoHo spot in the Mercer Hotel is as much about scene as cuisine, which isn't a bad thing. Dishes here look toward Asia (as is the proclivity of Mr. Vongerichten), using simple ingredients and pairings. Think scallops with lentils and pancetta or crispy squid with black-olive tartar sauce. It's all good enough to make you feign disinterest over the A-list celeb who just walked in. [$] *Average main: $30* ✉ *Mercer Hotel, 99 Prince*

St., at Mercer St., SoHo ☎ *212/966–5454* 🌐 *www.jean-georges.com* ▭ *No credit cards* Ⓜ *6 to Spring St.; N, R to Prince St.; B, D, F, M to Broadway–Lafayette St.* ✣ *2:E3.*

$$$ ITALIAN Fodor's Choice ★ ✕ **Osteria Morini.** Less formal than Chef Michael White's other renowned Italian restaurants (like Marea in Midtown West), the atmosphere at Osteria Morini is lively and upbeat, with communal tables at the center and a rock 'n' roll soundtrack. The food nevertheless steals the show. Start with a selection of cheeses and cured meats, then move on to hearty pastas—a lusty ragù Bolognese or garganelli with prosciutto and truffle butter, for example—and main courses like oven-baked polenta accompanied by either sausage or mushrooms. Waits can be long, so try to come early or late, or grab one of the few bar seats for an inventive cocktail or a glass of Italian wine. Brunch is served weekends. $ *Average main: $25* ✉ *218 Lafayette St., between Spring and Broome sts., SoHo* ☎ *212/965–8777* 🌐 *www.osteriamorini.com* ⏲ *No lunch weekends* ✍ *Reservations essential* Ⓜ *6 to Spring St.* ✣ *2:E4.*

$$$ FRENCH ✕ **Raoul's.** One of the first trendy spots in SoHo, this arty French restaurant has yet to lose its touch, either in the kitchen or atmosphere. Expect a chic bar scene—especially late at night—filled with polished PYTs, amazing photos on every piece of available wall space, and a lovely back room that you reach through the kitchen. The winding stairs to the upstairs dining room are narrow and a bit treacherous if wearing your highest heels. Foodwise, it's bistro-inspired, with oysters and salads to start, and pastas, fish, and meat options for mains. $ *Average main: $29* ✉ *180 Prince St., between Sullivan and Thompson sts., SoHo* ☎ *212/966–3518* 🌐 *www.raouls.com* ▭ *No credit cards* ⏲ *No lunch* Ⓜ *C, E to Spring St.* ✣ *2:D3.*

$$ GREEK ✕ **Snack.** This SoHo cubbyhole may look like just another drop-in café, but the food served inside transports diners to Greece. Typical mezes like tzatziki, taramosalata, hummus, and skordalia are several notches better than what you'd get elsewhere, but the menu options go beyond snacks: pop in at lunch for a braised-lamb sandwich or spinach pie, or linger in the evenings over votive-lighted tables and pastitsio or stuffed peppers. The light-filled West Village location, Snack Taverna, is somewhat roomier and also serves breakfast daily and brunch on weekends. $ *Average main: $19* ✉ *105 Thompson St., near Prince St., SoHo* ☎ *212/925–1040* 🌐 *www.snacksoho.com* ✍ *Reservations not accepted* Ⓜ *C, E to Spring St.* ✣ *2:D3.*

$$ AMERICAN ✕ **Spring Street Natural.** When this SoHo spot first fired up its burners in 1973, restaurants emphasizing organic, whole, and natural ingredients were mostly limited to San Francisco and college towns. The dining landscape may have caught up, but Spring Street Natural is still going strong, powered by a loyal clientele who come here for healthy food that actually tastes good. Start with the creamy organic hummus (and warm pita bread) before moving on to pan-roasted free-range chicken (accompanied by sweet potato–poblano pepper gratin) or the pancetta-laced pumpkin ravioli. If too full for dessert, order a glass of organic wine, sit back and stare out the floor-to-ceiling windows, gawking at the occasional celebrity and the SoHo shoppers. $ *Average main:*

$18 ⊠ 62 Spring St., at Lafayette St., SoHo ☎ 212/966–0290 ⊕ www. springstreetnatural.com ▭ No credit cards Ⓜ 6 to Spring St. ✛ 2:E4.

NOLITA

In NoLIta, SoHo's trendy next-door neighborhood, the spirit of old, pre–chainstore SoHo prevails. Diminutive eateries, squeezed between up-and-coming designer boutiques, flank the narrow streets of this atmospheric neighborhood.

$ ✕ Black Seed Bagels. New York is known for bagels, which tend to be large and doughy and delicious. Montreal-style bagels, which is what you'll find at Black Seed, have a denser, sweeter dough. The "toppings" (sesame, poppy seed, salt, everything) are more generous than on the New York bagels. The all-day menu here includes sandwich options with cream cheese, smoked salmon, whitefish salad, or baked eggs; the lunch menu adds a BLT with spicy mayo, roast beef with horseradish cream cheese, and a tuna melt to the mix, among others. Order at the counter and eat in if you can get a seat: the dark-wood-paneled café make this one of the classiest bagel joints around. Ⓢ *Average main: $9 ⊠ 170 Elizabeth St., NoLIta ☎ 212/730—1950 ⊕ www. blackseedbagels.com ☽ No dinner Ⓜ 6 to Spring St. ✛ 2:F4.*

$$ ✕ Café Gitane. Specializing in simple salads, sandwiches, and a selection
FRENCH of hot mains, this French-Moroccan café draws models and model-gazers to its rather cramped NoLIta location. Both the clientele and the waitstaff seem to have wandered in fresh off the runway. The scene is quietest in the morning, when there are flaky croissants and big bowls of café au lait. There's a larger branch on the far edge of the West Village. Ⓢ *Average main: $15 ⊠ 242 Mott St., near Prince St., NoLIta ☎ 212/334–9552 ⊕ www.cafegitanenyc.com ⌫ Reservations not accepted ▭ No credit cards Ⓜ 6 to Spring St.; N, R to Prince St.; J, Z to Bowery ✛ 2:F3.*

$ ✕ Café Habana. The Mexican-style grilled corn, liberally sprinkled with
MEXICAN chili powder, lime, and cotija cheese is undoubtedly worth getting your
FAMILY hands dirty at this crowded, hip luncheonette. Follow up with a classic Cuban sandwich (roast pork, ham, Swiss cheese, pickles, and chipotle mayo), fish tacos, or one of the innovative salads. Be prepared for a wait at lunchtime or on weekend afternoons. The cocktails are good, too. There's a take-out shop with a few seats down the street at 229 Elizabeth Street. Ⓢ *Average main: $13 ⊠ 17 Prince St., at Elizabeth St., NoLIta ☎ 212/625–2001 ⊕ www.cafehabana.com ⌫ Reservations not accepted Ⓜ 6 to Spring St.; N, R to Prince St.; J, Z to Bowery ✛ 2:F3.*

$$$ ✕ Cherche Midi. Restaurateur Keith McNally's signature is restaurants
FRENCH that become perpetually hip"see-and-be-seen" spots (cases in point: Odeon, Minetta Tavern, Balthazar, Schiller's Liquor Bar, etc.). This French bistro opened in 2014 but fits in so well with the neighborhood that it seems like it's been anchored on this corner for decades. The menu of classic French fare blends well with the rustic décor: as with most McNally restaurants, the culinary wheel is not being re-invented. Expect the classics—pan-roasted foie gras, steak tartare, steak frites, and lobster ravioli—-executed very well. The wine list, French and Italian, includes ample amounts of affordable but delicious options. Ⓢ *Average main: $25 ⊠ 282 Bowery, NoLIta ☎ 212/226–3055 ⊕ www.*

16

cherchemidiny.com Ⓜ *6 to Bleecker St.; B, D, F, M to Broadway–Lafayette St.; F to 2nd Ave.* ✛ *2:F3.*

$$ ✕ **Emporio.** The brick-lined front room of this homey Roman eatery
ITALIAN in NoLIta is a gathering spot for early-evening happy hour at the
Fodor'sChoice bar, where you'll find an appetizing selection of free small bites like
★ frittata, white-bean salad, and ham-and-spinach *tramezzini* (finger
sandwiches). The centerpiece of the large, skylighted back room is a
wood-fired oven that turns out crisp, thin-crust pizzas topped with
quality ingredients like prosciutto and buffalo mozzarella. Service
is solicitous but not speedy, so you can linger over a bottle of wine
from the copious selection. House-made pastas like garganelli with
pork sausage and house ragù, and entrées like whole roasted fish
with grilled lemon, are also excellent. ⓈAverage main: $22 ⊠ 231
Mott St., between Prince and Spring sts., NoLIta ☎ 212/966–1234
⊕ www.emporiony.com Ⓜ B, D, F, M to Broadway–Lafayette St.; N,
R to Prince St.; 6 to Bleecker St. ✛ 2:F3.

$$$ ✕ **Estela.** Long before Mr. and Mrs. Obama ate dinner here in late 2014,
MEDITERRANEAN this second-floor restaurant had been on the map for those in the know.
Fodor'sChoice Ignacio Mattos is the commader-in-chief and his creations have a ten-
★ dancy to sneek up on the diner: Is that rye matzo bread under the
mashed salt cod? And are those sunchoke chips folded into the sumptuous beef tartare? Are scallops and lardo a good paring on the plate?
The answer is "yes" to all of the above. The wine list is compact yet
sprinkled with some great off-the-radar European gems. The minimalist room is a fitting space for the deceptively simple cooking going on
here. ⓈAverage main: ⊠ 47 E. Houston St., NoLIta ☎ 212/219–7693
⊕ www.estelanyc.com ☽ No lunch weekdays ⌂ Reservations essential
Ⓜ 6 to Bleecker St.; B, D, F, M to Broadway–Lafayette St. ✛ 2:F3.

$$ ✕ **Gato.** When an orange cat crossed celebrity chef Bobby Flay's path
MEDITERRANEAN while he was waiting for the real estate agent to show him this space, he
decided right then to call this restaurant Gato(Spanish for cat). And a sly
cat it is. Despite the name, the menu goes beyond Spain to cover large
culinary swaths of the Mediterranean. Sit at the bar and nosh on roasted
octopus deliciously paired with bacon, garlicbread–topped crab risotto,
and Brussels sprouts sprinkled with pomegrantes and pistachios. It all
makes you feel like one lucky cat. ⓈAverage main: $20 ⊠ 324 Lafayette
St., NoLIta ☎ 212/334–6400 ⊕ www.gatonyc.com ☽ No lunch Ⓜ 6 to
Bleecker St.; B, D, F, M to Broadway–Lafayette St. ✛ 2:E3.

$$ ✕ **La Esquina.** Anchoring a downtown corner under a bright neon sign,
MEXICAN La Esquina looks like nothing more than a fast-food taquería, with
cheap tacos sold to-go until 2 in the morning. Just around the corner,
though, is a modestly priced café serving those same tacos along with
more ambitious fare like *chiles rellenos* (stuffed peppers) and *carne
asada* (grilled meat). The real draw, however, is hidden from sight: the
basement brasserie, like a Mexican speakeasy, is accessible by reservation only, through an unmarked door just inside the ground-floor
taquería. Inside, discover a buzzy subterranean scene with pretty people
drinking potent margaritas and dining on upscale Mexican fare. Prices
downstairs are high, but portions are large. ⓈAverage main: $20 ⊠ 106

Kenmare, between Cleveland Pl. and Lafayette St., NoLIta ☎ *646/613–7100* 🌐 *www.esquinanyc.com* [M] *6 to Spring St.* ✥ *2:E4.*

$$ PIZZA FAMILY 🍴 **Lombardi's Pizza.** Brick walls, red-and-white-checker tablecloths, and the aroma of thin-crust pies emerging from the coal oven set the mood for dining on some of the best pizza in Manhattan. Lombardi's has served pizza since 1905 (though not in the same location), and business doesn't seem to have died down one bit. The mozzarella is always fresh, resulting in a nearly greaseless slice, and the toppings, such as meatballs, pancetta, or imported anchovies, are also top-quality. The clam pizza, with freshly shucked clams, garlic oil, pecorino-romano cheese, and parsley, is well-known among aficionados. [$] *Average main: $16* ✉ *32 Spring St., at Mott St., NoLIta* ☎ *212/941–7994* 🌐 *www.firstpizza.com* ✍ *Reservations not accepted* 💳 *No credit cards* [M] *6 to Spring St.; J, Z to Bowery; N, R to Prince St.* ✥ *2:F4.*

$$$ ITALIAN 🍴 **Peasant.** The crowd at this rustic restaurant is stylishly urban. Inspired by the proverbial "peasant" cuisine where meals were prepared in the kitchen hearth, chef-owner Frank DeCarlo cooks all of his wonderful food in a bank of wood- or charcoal-burning ovens, from which the heady aroma of garlic perfumes the room. Don't fill up on the crusty bread and fresh ricotta or you'll miss out on flavorful Italian fare like sizzling sardines that arrive in terra-cotta pots, or spit-roasted leg of lamb with bitter *trevisano* lettuce and polenta. [$] *Average main: $25* ✉ *194 Elizabeth St., between Spring and Prince sts., NoLIta* ☎ *212/965–9511* 🌐 *www.peasantnyc.com* 🕒 *Closed Mon. No lunch* ✍ *Reservations essential* [M] *6 to Spring St.; J, Z to Bowery; N, R to Prince St.* ✥ *2:F3.*

$$$ ECLECTIC 🍴 **Public.** To start with, the space here is complex and sophisticated, with soaring ceilings and whitewashed brick walls, skylights, fireplaces, three dining areas, and a vast bar. You've come for the food, though, and you won't be disappointed. The menu flaunts its nonconformity, and dishes like Australian *barramundi* fish, served with vanilla-celeriac purée and braised garlic greens, demonstrate a light yet adventurous touch. Brunch at Public is a local favorite, with exotic dishes like coconut pancakes topped with fresh ricotta, mango, and lime syrup, and a juicy venison burger. Standout desserts include a chocolate mousse with tahini ice cream and sesame candy. [$] *Average main: $25* ✉ *210 Elizabeth St., between Prince and Spring sts., NoLIta* ☎ *212/343–7011* 🌐 *www.public-nyc.com* 🕒 *No lunch weekdays* [M] *6 to Spring St.; N, R to Prince St.; J, Z to Bowery* ✥ *2:F3.*

$$ ITALIAN 🍴 **Rubirosa.** Named for a jet-setting Dominican playboy, this Rubirosa is only Latin and lascivious in name. Owner Angelo "A. J." Pappalardo created an exciting Italian-American eatery that locals have shown an insatiable appetite for (so be prepared to wait). The kitchen isn't trying to reinvent anything here; they simply serve high-quality classic Italian dishes, from pasta with red sauce or a fork-tender veal chop Milanese to the thin-crust pizza (the recipe for the latter comes from Mr. Pappalardo's parents who have run the popular Staten Island pizza joint, Joe &Pat's, since anyone can remember). You don't have to be a jet-setter or a playboy to love this place. Just come hungry. [$] *Average main: $18* ✉ *235 Mulberry St., between Prince and Spring sts., NoLIta*

16

☎ *212/965–0500* ⊕ *www.rubirosanyc.com* ▭ *No credit cards* Ⓜ *6 to Spring St.; N, R to Prince St.* ✛ *2:F3.*

$$ ⤫ **The Smile.** Subterranean and almost hidden, the Smile turns frowns
AMERICAN upside down, if you like hipsters and celebrities, and, most especially, hipster celebrities. Lounge among the fashionably conscious clientele (who are trying oh-so-hard to not look that way) and munch on breakfast-y items (served until 4:30 pm) like chunky granola, or go for one of the giant sandwiches or spaghetti with heirloom-tomato sauce. Dinner options, like whole trout, brisket, hanger steak, or roasted chicken, are more ambitious. Just be sure you wear shoes that scream "this season." Ⓢ *Average main: $15* ⊠ *26 Bond St., between Lafayette St. and the Bowery, NoLIta* ☎ *646/329–5836* ⊕ *www.thesmilenyc. com* ▭ *No credit cards* Ⓜ *B, D, F, M to Broadway–Lafayette St.; 6 to Bleecker St.* ✛ *2:E2.*

$$ ⤫ **Uncle Boon's.** If you're looking for quality Thai in Manhattan, a good
THAI choice is Uncle Boon's in NoLIta. The chefs are a husband-and-wife team who originally met in the kitchen at Michelin-starred Per Se. You'd have to look underneath the layers to find evidence of über-haute cuisine here—but that just means that the simple, tasty Thai fare here is very good. Skip the green papaya salad—usually a must, but somehow bland here—and go right for hearty entrées, such as the *khao soi*, an ultra-tender chicken leg doused in a delciously tangy yellow curry, or anything that's grilled. Ⓢ *Average main: $22* ⊠ *7 Spring St., near Elizabeth St., NoLIta* ☎ *646/370–6650* ⊕ *www.uncleboons.com* ▭ *No credit cards* Ⓜ *J, Z to Bowery; 6 to Spring St.* ✛ *2:F3.*

LITTLE ITALY

These days Little Italy is a tourist trap of pasta factories that just aren't very good. Don't despair, though: there is seriously yummy Italian food in just about every other neighborhood in the city—including nearby NoLIta.

CHINATOWN

Chinatown beckons adventurous diners with restaurants representing numerous regional cuisines of China, including Cantonese, Szechuan, Hunan, Fujian, Shanghai, and Hong Kong–style cooking. Malaysian and Vietnamese restaurants also have taken root here, and the neighborhood continues to grow rapidly, encroaching into what was Little Italy.

$ ⤫ **456 Shanghai Cuisine.** Come to this Chinatown eatery for above-
CHINESE average Chinese fare, such as General Tso's chicken, pork buns, and cold sesame noodles, but do yourself a favor and order soup dumplings (*xiao long bao*) as soon as you sit down. You won't regret it. The dumplings, doughy and thin on the outside, encase morsels of crab swimming in a bold porky broth, truly a wonder of the culinary world—and 456 does them as well as (or better than) anyone in the city. Ⓢ *Average main: $14* ⊠ *69 Mott St., between Canal and Bayard sts., Chinatown* ☎ *212/964–0003* ▭ *No credit cards* Ⓜ *6, J, N, Q, R, Z to Canal St.* ✛ *2:F5.*

$ ⤫ **Great New York Noodletown.** Although the soups and noodles are
CHINESE unbeatable at this no-frills restaurant, what you should really order
FAMILY are the window decorations—the hanging lacquered ducks and roasted pork, listed on a simple board hung on the wall and superbly served

with pungent garlic-and-ginger sauce on the side. Seasonal specialties like duck with flowering chives and salt-baked soft-shell crabs are excellent. So is the *congee,* or rice porridge, available with any number of garnishes. Solo diners may end up at a communal table. Noodletown is open late—till 4 am on Friday and Saturday. $ *Average main: $11* ✉ *28 Bowery, at Bayard St., Chinatown* ☎ *212/349–0923* ▭ *No credit cards* Ⓜ *6, J, N, Q, R, Z to Canal St.; B, D to Grand St.; F to East Broadway* ✛ *2:G5.*

$$　✕ **Jing Fong.** On weekend mornings people pack this vast dim sum pal-
CHINESE　ace, so be prepared to wait. Once your number is called, take the escala-
FAMILY　tor up to the carnivalesque third-floor dining room, where servers push carts crammed with tasty goodness. Expect to be plied with delights like steamed dumplings, crispy spring rolls, barbecue pork buns, and shrimp balls. For adventurous eaters, there's chicken feet, tripe, and snails. Arrive early for the best selection, and save room for mango pudding. $ *Average main: $16* ✉ *20 Elizabeth St., 2nd fl., between Bayard and Canal sts., Chinatown* ☎ *212/964–5256* ⊕ *www.jingfongny.com* Ⓜ *6, J, N, Q, R, Z to Canal St.; B, D to Grand St.* ✛ *2:F5.*

$　✕ **Joe's Shanghai.** Joe opened his first Shanghai restaurant in Queens
CHINESE　in 1995, but buoyed by the accolades showered on his steamed soup
FAMILY　dumplings—filled with a rich, fragrant broth and ground pork or a pork-crabmeat mixture—several Manhattan outposts soon followed. The trick is to take a bite of the dumpling and slurp out the soup, then eat the rest. There's almost always a wait, but the line moves fast. The soup dumplings are a must, but you can fill out your order from the extensive menu. There's another Joe's Shanghai in Midtown, at 24 West 56th Street, between 5th and 6th avenues (where credit cards are accepted). $ *Average main: $16* ✉ *9 Pell St., between the Bowery and Mott St., Chinatown* ☎ *212/233–8888* ⊕ *www.joeshanghairestaurants. com* ▭ *No credit cards* Ⓜ *6, J, N, Q, R, Z to Canal St.; B, D to Grand St.* ✛ *2:F5.*

$$　✕ **New Malaysia.** This Malaysian restaurant is a real find. Literally. You
MALAYSIAN　could stroll right by it and never know it existed. That's because it's in a passageway between the Bowery and Elizabeth Street. It's worth the trouble, though, as the menu is loaded with Malaysian favorites like roti flatbread with curry and delicious red-bean and coconut-milk drinks. The atmosphere is casual and table service is relaxed, which means you might need to flag down your server. $ *Average main: $14* ✉ *48 Bowery, near Canal St., Chinatown* ☎ *212/964–0284* ⊕ *www. newmalaysiarestaurant.com* Ⓜ *6, J, N, Q, R, Z to Canal St.; B, D to Grand St.* ✛ *2:G5.*

$$　✕ **Peking Duck House.** This Chinatown institution is the place to go in
CHINESE　New York for authentic Peking duck. Although the restaurant serves a full Chinese menu, everyone—and we mean everyone—orders the duck. Begin, as most tables do, with an order of Shanghai soup dumplings, then move on to the bird. It's carved tableside with plenty of fanfare—crisp burnished skin separated from moist flesh. Roll up the duck, with hoisin and scallions, in tender steamed pancakes. The menu at the Midtown location (236 East 53rd Street) is a bit pricier. $ *Average main: $19* ✉ *28 Mott St., at Mosco St., Chinatown* ☎ *212/227–1810*

16

⊕ *www.pekingduckhousenyc.com* Ⓜ *6, J, N, Q, R, Z to Canal St.; B, D to Grand St.* ✛ *2:F5.*

$ ✕ **Tasty Hand-Pulled Noodles.** The name says it all. The open kitchen
CHINESE   at this salt-of-the-earth Chinatown restaurant (located on charming, curved Doyers Street) means you can watch the noodle-slinger in
action while awaiting your bowl of, um, tasty hand-pulled noodles.
Just choose your ingredients—beef, pork, oxtail, eel, chicken, lamb, or
shrimp, among others—and prepare to eat the most delicious bowl of
$5 noodles since that last trip to Shanghai. The restaurant is small so be
prepared to possibly share a table with a fellow diner. Ⓢ *Average main:
$5* ⊠ *1 Doyers St., at Bowery, Chinatown* ☎ *212/791–1817* ⊕ *www.
tastyhandpullednoodles.com* ▭ *No credit cards* Ⓜ *6, J, N, Q, R, Z to
Canal St.; B, D to Grand St.* ✛ *2:F6.*

$ ✕ **Vanessa's Dumpling House.** One of the best deals in Chinatown can
CHINESE   be found here. Sizzling pork-and-chive dumplings are four for a buck.
There are also vegetarian options. The restaurant is very casual: order
at the counter and then grab a table, if you can find one. Vanessa's is
especially popular with Lower East Side revelers looking to pad their
stomachs before the night's debauchery. Ⓢ *Average main: $8* ⊠ *118
Eldridge St., near Broome St., Chinatown* ☎ *212/625–8008* ⊕ *www.
vanessasdumplinghouse.com* ⇗ *Reservations not accepted* Ⓜ *B, D to
Grand St.* ✛ *2:G4.*

$ ✕ **Xe Lua.** A good Vietnamese restaurant in Manhattan is hard to find,
VIETNAMESE   which is why you should seek out Xe Lua, in Chinatown just below
Little Italy. Quick service and the marathon-length menu should satisfy any palate but the real standouts are the clay pot dishes: cooked
and served in—you guessed it—a clay pot, the pork, chicken, veggies,
or whatever you order become slightly caramelized, giving a subtle
sweetness to the dish. The *pho* (the soupy national dish of Vietnam)
is also a good bet, as the broth has a bolder flavor here than at other
places. Ⓢ *Average main: $11* ⊠ *86 Mulberry St., between Canal and
Bayard sts., Chinatown* ☎ *212/577–8887* ⊕ *www.xeluarestaurantnyc.
com* ▭ *No credit cards* Ⓜ *6, J, N, Q, R, Z to Canal St.; B, D to Grand
St.* ✛ *2:F5.*

$ ✕ **Xi'an Famous Foods.** Serving the very underrepresented cuisine of west-
CHINESE   ern China, Xi'an Famous Foods serves food like you might not have
tasted before. The restaurant first made a name for itself at its original location, in the dingy basement food court of a mall in Flushing,
Queens, but this spot—shinier, brighter, and cleaner—serves the same
exciting fare. First-timers should try the spicy cumin lamb burger, which
is mouthwateringly delicious. Some of the dishes challenge the bounds
of adventurousness in eating (lamb offal soup, anyone?), but don't
let that scare you off. It's cheap enough to experiment, so tuck into
that bowl of oxtail noodle soup and enjoy. Ⓢ *Average main: $10* ⊠ *67
Bayard St., between Mott and Elizabeth sts., Chinatown* ☎ *212/608–
4170* ⊕ *www.xianfoods.com* ▭ *No credit cards* Ⓜ *6, J, N, Q, R, Z to
Canal St.; B, D to Grand St.* ✛ *2:F5.*

GETTING CAFFEINATED IN NYC

There might be a chain coffee shop on every corner in New York City, but you won't find many locals there. The so-called "city that never sleeps" is fueled with coffee, but not just any coffee. We're a bit particular, some might say downright snobbish, about coffee, so—even if we're in a rush, which, of course, we are—we'll wait those few extra minutes for the best freshly roasted beans and pour-over brews. If you want to join discerning locals, look for outposts of Blue Bottle Coffee, Everyman Espresso, Joe Coffee, La Colombe, Ninth Street Espresso (which has locations other than 9th Street), Stumptown, and Third Rail Coffee all over Manhattan (and Brooklyn). Most spots offer the added bonus of homemade baked goods, and some also have light snackes, but don't expect that it'll be easy to find a seat.

EAST VILLAGE AND LOWER EAST SIDE

EAST VILLAGE

This neighborhood, once a grungy ghetto for punk rockers and drug addicts, has gotten itself into shape, with great restaurants on every block—from amazing, inexpensive Asian spots to Michelin-starred destinations. St. Mark's Place is the center of New York's downtown Little Tokyo, and East 6th Street is its Indian Row.

$$ AMERICAN 🍴 **Alder.** Chef Wylie Dufresne, whoran the show for years at acclaimed avant-garde eatery wd-50, until it shuttered at the end of 2014, is the wizard in the kitchen at this modern gastropub. As Dufresne has demonstrated in the past, looks can be deceiving, and there is more than meets the eye(and the mouth) here. The rye pasta with toasted caraway and pastrami is an ingenious re-imagining of the classic New York deli sandwich. The crackers in the New England clam chowder are made from puréed oysters and pack a flavorful punch. Pair anything with the carefully selected craft beers or innovative cocktails. Sunday brunch is also fun: try the bacon, egg, and cheese gyoza or the pastrami hash, with one of the unique bloody marys. [$] *Average main: $18* ✉ *157 2nd Ave., near 10th St., East Village* ☎ *212/539–1900* 🌐 *www.aldernyc.com* 💳 *No credit cards* 🕒 *No brunch Mon.–Sat.* ✍ *Reservations essential* [M] *L to 3rd Ave.* ✣ *3:G5.*

$ PIZZA FAMILY 🍴 **Artichoke Pizza.** Grab a gargantuan slice at this popular take-out joint, or order whole pies in the small, adjacent no-frills dining room. In the wee hours, lines often snake out the door for the artichoke-spinach slice, which tastes like cheesy dip on thick, crusty crackers. Those in the know opt for the less greasy margherita slice. Make sure you're hungry, and be prepared to stand in line a while. For shorter lines, stop into the Greenwich Village location at 111 MacDougal Street. Or try the more formal Artichoke outpost underneath the High Line at 114 10th Avenue. [$] *Average main: $5* ✉ *328 E. 14th St., between 1st and 2nd aves., East Village* ☎ *212/228–2004* 🌐 *www.artichokepizza.com* 💳 *No credit cards* ✍ *Reservations not accepted* [M] *L to 1st Ave.* ✣ *3:H4.*

$$ MOROCCAN 🍴 **Cafe Mogador.** An East Village dining institution if there ever was one, Cafe Mogador is a frequent stop for locals and, for some, a hip place

Restaurant Chains Worth a Taste

When you're on the go or don't have time for a leisurely meal, there are several very good chain restaurants and sandwich bars that have popped up around New York City. Those listed below are usually reasonably priced and the best in their category.

Dos Toros. Fresh and inexpensive tacos, burritos, and salads are the calling card at this local minichain with several locations in Manhattan and one in Brooklyn. The brothers who run the joint moved to NYC from San Francisco and were disappointed with the taquería options here, so they took matters into their own hands. Order at the counter and grab a seat. ⊕ *www.dostoros.com.*

Le Pain Quotidien. Part bakery, part café, this Belgian chain with locations throughout the city serves fresh salads and sandwiches at lunch and is great for breakfast. You can grab a snack to go or stay and eat breakfast, lunch, or dinner with waiter service. There are more than 20 locations throughout Manhattan,

including one in Central Park. ⊕ *www. lepainquotidien.com.*

Pret A Manger. This sandwich shop started in London in 1986 and opened their first American outpost in 2000. These days you can find them in various locations around NYC—there are several in Midtown, catering to the bustling lunch crowds. The sandwiches are excellent, and the salads are good, too. ⊕ *www.pret.com.*

Shake Shack. This homegrown chain has expanded across the United States and beyond, but it got it start in Madison Square Park. There are multiple locations in Manhattan and Brooklyn to enjoy burgers, hot dogs, and shakes. ⊕ *www.shakeshack.com.*

'wichcraft. Tom Colicchio may be best known these days as head judge of Bravo's *Top Chef*, but his fine-dining restaurants Craft and Craftbar are also well known around Manhattan and beyond. At 'wichcraft, the sandwich shop he started with several partners back in 2003, the creations have his deliciously distinctive touch. ⊕ *www. wichcraftnyc.com.*

---

to be seen. Since 1983, the restaurant has been serving above-average Morrocan cuisine in a date-friendly candlelit atmosphere. Finish off that creamy hummus before the chicken tagine arrives, nurse that glass of Italian wine, and ponder the fact that most of the people around you were barely walking when this family-run restaurant first fired up its couscous-cooking burners. $ *Average main: $16* ⊠ *101 St. Marks Pl., near 2nd Ave., East Village* 🕾 *212/677–2226* ⊕ *www.cafemogador.com* 🖃 *No credit cards* Ⓜ *L to 1st Ave.* ✛ *2:G1.*

$
FAST FOOD
FAMILY
✕ **Crif Dogs.** Gluttony reigns at Crif Dogs, where you can indulge in creative—and delicous—hot dog creations. Try the Chihuahua, bacon-wrapped and layered with avocado and sour cream, or the Tsunami, bacon-wrapped with pineapple and teriyaki. (There are vegetarian dogs, too.) The tater tots banish all memories of the high school cafeteria. And that phone booth in the corner? Use that to enter secret, chic cocktail bar PDT (where there are more hot dogs available to pair with craft

cocktails). $ *Average main: $5* ✉ *113 St. Marks Pl., at Ave. A, East Village* ☎ *212/614–2728* ⊕ *www.crifdogs.com* Ⓜ *L to 1st Ave.* ✛ *3:H5.*

$$$ ✕ **DBGB Kitchen & Bar.** The downtown arm of Daniel Boulud's New
FRENCH York City restaurant fleet, DBGB forgoes the white tablecloths, formal service, and steep prices found at the famed chef's fancier digs, and instead pays homage to the grittier, younger feel of its Lower East Side location. (The name is a wink at the legendary rock club CBGB.) Lined with shelves of pots, plates, and pans (not to mention copperware donated by renowned chefs from around the world), the dining room gives way to a partially open kitchen where you can catch the chefs preparing Boulud's take on French- and German-inspired pub fare. The menu features 14 different varieties of sausages, decadent burgers (the aptly named "piggy" burger, a juicy beef patty topped with a generous portion of pulled pork, jalapeño mayonnaise, and mustard-vinegar slaw on a cheddar bun), and classic entrées like steak frites and lemon-and-rosemary roasted chicken. $ *Average main: $27* ✉ *299 Bowery, between Houston and 1st sts., East Village* ☎ *212/933–5300* ⊕ *www.dbgb.com* ⌦ *Reservations essential* Ⓜ *F to 2nd Ave.* ✛ *2:F2.*

$$ ✕ **Edi & the Wolf.** For those who have always wanted to spend an evening
AUSTRIAN in a countryside Austrian pub—and who hasn't?—but can't hop on a
Fodor's Choice plane to Vienna, there's Edi &the Wolf, an outstanding restaurant deep
★ in the section of the East Village called Alphabet City. The rustic interior (usually crammed with stylish thirtysomethings) is the perfect venue to sample dishes like honey-and-beer-accented ribs, pork belly–laced poached eggs, and, of course, Wienerschnitzel, which is supertender and refreshingly free of grease. The well-curated beer selection focuses on Central Europe. Try the dark Czech brew, Krusovice (pronounced Kroo-sho-veetzay) $ *Average main: $22* ✉ *102 Ave. C, at 7th St., East Village* ☎ *212/598–1040* ⊕ *www.ediandthewolf.com* ▬ *No credit cards* ⊗ *No lunch weekdays* Ⓜ *F to 2nd Ave., L to 1st Ave.* ✛ *2:H1.*

$$ ✕ **Gemma.** There's something almost formulaic about this restaurant
ITALIAN on the ground floor of the hip Bowery Hotel: from the rustic, wood-bedecked interior to the see-and-be-seen crowd who frequent the place and the menu of above-average Italian staples (from pizza to pastas and heartier mains). But the food here is good, the service is attentive, and nabbing an outside table may make you feel cooler than you are for a couple of hours, so what difference does it make? Answer: no difference, until it's time to pay the bill. Weekend brunch is also a good bet. $ *Average main: $20* ✉ *335 Bowery, at 3rd St., East Village* ☎ *212/505–9100* ⊕ *www.theboweryhotel.com* ▬ *No credit cards* ⌦ *Reservations not accepted* Ⓜ *F to 2nd Ave., 6 to Bleecker St.* ✛ *2:F2.*

$$ ✕ **Gnocco.** Owners Pierluigi Palazzo and Gianluca Giovannetti named
ITALIAN their restaurant not after gnocchi but a regional Italian specialty—deep-fried dough bites typically served with Northern Italian sliced meats like capicola, salami, and aged prosciutto. The *gnocci* are certainly good, but the menu has so many other options you'll be forgiven if you skip them in favor of the house-made pasta specials; pizza topped with mozzarella, truffles, and mushrooms; hearty entrées like pork tenderloin in a balsamic emulsion with flakes of Grana Padano cheese; and salads—preferably all enjoyed in the roomy, canopied garden out back.

16

$ *Average main: $20* ✉ *337 E. 10th St., between Aves. A and B, East Village* ☎ *212/677–1913* ⊕ *www.gnocco.com* ☺ *No lunch weekdays* Ⓜ *L to 1st Ave., 6 to Astor Pl.* ✛ *2:H1.*

$$
CHINESE

✕ **Grand Sichuan.** Yes, it's a local Chinese chainlet, and no, you don't come here for the ambience, but the food—like fiery Sichuan *dan dan* noodles, kung pao chicken, double-cooked pork, or crab soup dumplings—is good and inexpensive. Check the website for other locations around town. $ *Average main: $18* ✉ *19–23 St. Marks Pl., near 3rd Ave., East Village* ☎ *212/529–4800* ⊕ *www.grandsichuanstmarks.com* Ⓜ *6 to Astor Pl.* ✛ *2:F1.*

$$
MEXICAN

✕ **Hecho en Dumbo.** "Made in Dumbo"—referring to the restaurant's former location in Brooklyn—specializes in *antojitos,* or "little cravings." The result is something equivalent to Mexican comfort food for the hip thirtysomethings who frequent this restaurant on the Bowery. Variations on a taco theme may dominate the menu, but Hecho shines with house dishes like roasted kid and wine-braised oxtail served over Oaxacan mole sauce. Pair your meal with one of their delicious margaritas (no bottled mix used here), sangria, or perhaps a *michelada*—beer and tomato juice on ice with lime and a salted rim. $ *Average main: $17* ✉ *354 Bowery, between Great Jones and 4th sts., East Village* ☎ *212/937–4245* ⊕ *www.hechoendumbo.com* ▭ *No credit cards* Ⓜ *6 to Astor Pl.; N, R to 8th St.–NYU* ✛ *2:F2.*

$$$
ITALIAN

✕ **Il Buco.** The unabashed clutter of vintage kitchen gadgets and tableware harks back to Il Buco's past as an antiques store and affects a romantic country-house feel with excellent food—this is a favorite for a cozy, intimate meal. The menu focuses on meat and produce from local farms, with several excellent pasta choices, and a variety of Mediterranean tapas-like appetizers. Call ahead to book the intimate wine cellar for dinner. Il Buco Alimentari & Vineria, around the corner at 53 Great Jones Street, is a more casual setting, with a small market up front selling gourmet cheese and house-cured meats, and a wine bar in the back. $ *Average main: $28* ✉ *47 Bond St., between the Bowery and Lafayette St., East Village* ☎ *212/533–1932* ⊕ *www.ilbuco.com* ☺ *No lunch Sun.* Ⓜ *6 to Bleecker St.; B, D, F, M to Broadway–Lafayette St.* ✛ *2:F2.*

$$
JAPANESE

✕ **Ippudo.** Crowds wait hours for the ramen noodles at Ippudo, the first American branch of the Japanese chain. Loyal patrons say it's all about the rich, pork-based broth—there is a vegetarian version available but it lacks the depth of flavor. Those really in the know, though, make sure to order sleeper-hit appetizers like the peppery chicken wings or pork buns. It's not a hole-in-the-wall ramen spot, so although a meal here is relatively inexpensive, it's not dirt-cheap. There's a newer Ippudo outpost in Midtown at 321 West 51st Street. $ *Average main: $16* ✉ *65 4th Ave., between 9th and 10th sts., East Village* ☎ *212/388–0088* ⊕ *www.ippudony.com* ⚐ *Reservations not accepted* Ⓜ *6 to Astor Pl.; N, R to 8th St.–NYU* ✛ *3:G5.*

$$$$
JAPANESE

✕ **Jewel Bako.** Arguably the best sushi restaurant in the East Village, this tiny space gleams in a minefield of cheap, often inferior sushi houses. The futuristic bamboo tunnel of a dining room is gorgeous, but try to nab a place at the sushi bar and put yourself in the hands of sushi master Yoshi Kousaka. The five-course *omakase,* or chef's menu, starts at $125. (A less expensive sushi or sashimi omakase is $75.) You are served only what's freshest and best. [$] *Average main: $50* ✉ *239 E. 5th St., between 2nd and 3rd aves., East Village* ☎ *212/979–1012* 🌐 *www.jewelbakosushi.com* 🕒 *Closed Sun. No lunch* ✍ *Reservations essential* [M] *6 to Astor Pl.; N, R to 8th St.–NYU* ✥ *3:G6.*

$$ FRENCH 🍴 **Lafayette Grand Cafe & Bakery.** Food media darling, Chef Andrew Carmellini (of Locanda Verde, Bar Primi, and the Dutch) goes Gallic here. After nearly a decade of Italian dominance on the Big Apple restaurant scene, French is back in vogue again, and Lafayette is a return to Carmellini's roots: the kitchens of his mentor the great Daniel Boulud. There's no culinary trickery happening here, just straightforward and very satisfying bistro fare. Creamy duck confit–spiked pumpkin risotto, a silky beef tartare, and steak frites are all excellent. So is the people-watching at this "see-and-be-seen" spot. [$] *Average main: $24* ✉ *380 Lafayette St., at 4th St., East Village* ☎ *212/533–3000* 🌐 *www.lafayetteny.com* [M] *6 to Bleecker St.; B, D, F, M to Broadway–Lafayette St.; N, R to 8th St.–NYU* ✥ *3:F6.*

$ MIDDLE EASTERN FAMILY 🍴 **Mamoun's Falafel.** This hole-in-the-wall institution, bustling day and night, is the place to go for speedy, hot, supercheap, and delicious Middle Eastern food. Tahini-topped pitas are packed with fresh, green-on-the-inside falafel balls. Be warned: the hot sauce is incendiary. The small space has a few tables, but this is food you can easily eat on the go. Best of all, it's open every night until at least 4 am. The original Mamoun's is still on MacDougal Street, near Washington Square Park in Greenwich Village. [$] *Average main: $7* ✉ *22 St. Marks Pl., between 2nd and 3rd aves., East Village* ☎ *212/387–7747* 🌐 *www.mamouns.com* ✍ *Reservations not accepted* 💳 *No credit cards* [M] *6 to Astor Pl.; N, R to 8th St.–NYU* ✥ *3:G5.*

$ DELI 🍴 **Mile End.** Named for a neighborhood in Montréal where the city's famed bagel bakeries exist, Mile End became the darling of the city's fooderati when it opened in January 2010 in Brooklyn. By the time this NoHo location began rolling out its light, chewy, and slightly sweet Montréal bagels in May 2012, the place was already an institution. The bagels are authentic, but the real reason to come here is for the impressive deli fare, including pastrami, roast beef, and smoked-meat sandwiches. The *poutine*—french fries with cheese curds and gravy—is a delicious mess. Once standing-room only, there's now seating in the long, narrow room, as well as dinner service. Dinner is also served at the original Brooklyn location in Boerum Hill, at 97A Hoyt Street. [$] *Average main: $10* ✉ *53 Bond St., near the Bowery, East Village* ☎ *212/529–2990* 🌐 *www.mileenddeli.com* 💳 *No credit cards* 🕒 *No dinner Sun. and Mon.* [M] *6 to Bleecker St.; B, D, F, M to Broadway–Lafayette St.* ✥ *2:F2.*

$ JAPANESE 🍴 **Minca.** It may have received less fanfare than some other East Village noodle bars, but the ramen at this tiny, cramped spot is among the best in the city; the fact that visiting Japanese students eat here is a good sign. Try to get a seat at the bar, where you can watch the chefs prepare your food. Start with homemade *gyoza* dumplings, then dive your spoon and chopsticks into one of the many types of ramen. The *shoyu* (soy sauce) Minca ramen is unfailingly good, but anything with pork is also a good

16

bet. $\boxed{\$}$ *Average main: $13* $\boxtimes$ *536 E. 5th St., between Aves. A and B, East Village* $\boxtimes$ *212/505–8001* ⊕ *www.newyorkramen.com* ⌧ *Reservations not accepted* ⊟ *No credit cards* $\boxed{M}$ *F to 2nd Ave.* ✛ *2:H2.*

$$$$ ✕ **Momofuku Ko.** After a move to this quaint alleyway near where the

ASIAN Bowery and 1st Street meet, Momofuku Ko is still firing on all cylinders.

Fodor'sChoice There are no more tables at James Beard Award–winning chef David

★ Chang's most formal dining option; diners sit at the bar to see Ko's chefs in action or opt for a standalone table. The menu is prix-fixe only: 20 courses for $175. And it's worth it for the complex flavor strata that Chang builds. Reservations can be made online only, no more than 15 days ahead for dinner, and are extremely difficult to get. Log on at 10 am (a credit card number is required just to get into the system), when new reservations are available, and keep hitting reload. $\boxed{\$}$ *Average main: $100* $\boxtimes$ *8 Extra Pl., at 1st St., East Village* $\boxtimes$ *212/203–095* ⊕ *www.momofuku.com* ⊘ *Closed Mon. and Tues. No lunch* ⌧ *Reservations essential* $\boxed{M}$ *F to 2nd Ave.* ✛ *3:H5.*

$ ✕ **Momofuku Milk Bar.** This combination bakery, ice cream parlor, and

CAFÉ sandwich shop boasts quick-serve access to Chef David Chang's cult-

FAMILY ish pork buns, along with some truly psychedelic treats by pastry whiz Christina Tosi. Swing by for a kimchee croissant and glass of "cereal" milk, or for treats like the curiously flavored soft-serve ice cream (cerealmilk, lemon verbena), "candy bar pie" (a sweet bomb of caramel, peanut-butter nougat, and pretzels atop a chocolate-cookie crust), one of the addictive cookies (try the "compost" cookies, with pretzels, chocolate chips, and whatever inspires the bakers that day), or any of the intriguing savories (the "volcano" is a cheese and potato pastry that is impossible to eat daintily). $\boxed{\$}$ *Average main: $6* $\boxtimes$ *251 E. 13th St., East Village* $\boxtimes$ *347/577–9504* ⊕ *www.milkbarstore.com* ⌧ *Reservations not accepted* $\boxed{M}$ *L to 3rd Ave.* ✛ *3:G4.*

$$ ✕ **Momofuku Noodle Bar.** Chef and owner David Chang has created a

ASIAN shrine to ramen with this stylish 70-seat restaurant. His riff on the

Fodor'sChoice Japanese classic features haute ingredients like Berkshire pork, free-

★ range chicken, and organic produce—though there are plenty of other innovative options on the menu. His modern take on pork buns with cucumber and scallions is phenomenal—alone worth the trip. You'll probably have to wait if you go at regular meal times, but seats at the long counter open up fairly quickly, and the lively atmosphere is part of the fun. The excellent fried-chicken meal includes both triple-fried Korean-style and Old Bay southern-style chicken with a variety of accoutrements, and feeds four-to-eight people(available by special reservations only on the website). $\boxed{\$}$ *Average main: $17* $\boxtimes$ *171 1st Ave., between 10th and 11th sts., East Village* $\boxtimes$ *212/777–7773* ⊕ *www. momofuku.com* ⌧ *Reservations not accepted* $\boxed{M}$ *L to 1st Ave.* ✛ *3:H5.*

$$ ✕ **Momofuku Ssäm Bar.** New York foodies have been salivating over

ASIAN Chef David Chang's Asian-influenced fare since he opened Noodle Bar in 2004. Ssäm Bar, with a more extensive menu, is equally worth the raves. The restaurant is packed nightly with downtown diners cut from the same cloth as the pierced and tattooed waitstaff and cooks. The no-reservations policy (except for large parties or special dinners) means having to wait in line for a chance to try Chang's truly inventive flavor combinations. The menu is constantly changing but the not-to-be-missed riff on the classic Chinese steamed pork bun is almost always available. Have a nightcap at Chang's inventive cocktail bar, Booker & Dax, around the corner. $ *Average main: $24* ⊠ *207 2nd Ave., at 13th St., East Village* ☎ *212/254–3500* ⊕ *www.momofuku.com/ssam* Ⓜ *L to 1st Ave.* ✛ *3:G4.*

$$ ✕ **Motorino Pizza.** The Manhattan branch of the Williamsburg origi-
PIZZA nal has brought its impossibly high standards—and long lines—to a new borough. The authentic Neapolitan pies are made with glutinous, dough-friendly double-zero flour and San Marzano tomatoes, and the crusts are lightly charred. You can't go wrong with any of the signature traditional pizzas, like marinara; margherita with fresh tomatoes, mozzarella, and basil; or a pie with spicy sopressata, sausage and garlic; but the seasonal selections are also tempting. Check out the brunch pizza (with egg and pancetta) on weekends. Antipasti like octopus and fingerling potato salad with celery-chili oil, and cockle-clam crostini round out the menu. The weekday, lunchtime prix-fixe means pizza and salad is a bargain at $12 per person. $ *Average main: $16* ⊠ *349 E. 12th St., at 1st Ave., East Village* ☎ *212/777–2644* ⊕ *www.motorinopizza.com* ⌦ *Reservations not accepted* Ⓜ *L to 1st Ave.* ✛ *3:H4.*

16

$$ ✕ **Northern Spy Food Co.** A gem in the East Village, named for an apple
AMERICAN variety, Northern Spy is run by two San Francisco transplants with a
Fodor's Choice West Coast perspective on the farm-to-table movement. Start your meal
★ with the freekeh risotto, a traditional dish made with a quirky little-known grain, or a giant mound of shredded kale tossed with cheddar, pecorino, and toasted almonds. Main courses are winners, too—choose tender meatballs in marinara sauce, roast chicken for two, or baked polenta, eggs, and mushrooms topped with crème fraîche. There is also an interesting, reasonably priced list of wines and beers, and a selection of housemade desserts like chocolate cake with sea salt and caramel. $ *Average main: $22* ⊠ *511 E. 12th St., between 1st Ave. and Ave. A, East Village* ☎ *212/228–5100* ⊕ *www.northernspyfoodco.com* ⌦ *Reservations not accepted* Ⓜ *L to 1st Ave.* ✛ *3:H4.*

$ ✕ **Pinche Taqueria.** Offshoots of a popular Tijuana taco shop established
MEXICAN in 1973 and still going strong, these slim taquerías (the word "pinche"
FAMILY can be translated as "tiny") do fish tacos the West Coast way, with lightly battered fish, crunchy cabbage, and a dollop of cilantro *crema*. The tacos *al pastor*—filled with succulent pork slow-roasted on a rotating spit, are of a similarly superior caliber, stuffed into warm, house-made corn tortillas and generously anointed with fresh guacamole. There's another location just around the corner at 227 Mott Street (near Prince) and at 103 West 14th Street; all these spots get busy at prime meal times. $ *Average main: $6* ⊠ *333 Lafayette St., near Bleecker St., NoHo* ☎ *212/343–9977* ⊕ *www.pinchetaqueria.us* ⊟ *No credit cards* ⌦ *Reservations not accepted* Ⓜ *B, D, F, M to Broadway–Lafayette St.; 6 to Bleecker St.* ✛ *2:E2.*

$ ✕ **Porchetta.** Super-succulent Italian roast pork—dusted in fennel pol-
ITALIAN len and covered in crisp cracklin' skin—is the star attraction here. It is, in fact, just about the only thing on the menu of this tiny spot. Order your pork in a sandwich or as a platter with stewed greens and roasted

potatoes. There's not much room for dining on-site, but the benches out front are ideal when the weather cooperates. $ *Average main: $11* ✉ *110 E. 7th St., near 1st Ave., East Village* ☎ *212/777–2151* ⊕ *www. porchettanyc.com* ⏴ *Reservations not accepted* Ⓜ *6 to Astor Pl.; L to 1st Ave.* ✛ *3:H5.*

$$
AMERICAN

✗ **Prune.** There's just something very right-on about the food at Prune, a cozy treasure of a restaurant serving eclectic, well-executed American food from cult Chef Gabrielle Hamilton. The choices change with the season, but you might find braised rabbit legs in vinegar sauce, whole grilled fish with fennel oil and chunky sea salt, or roasted marrow bones with parsley salad and toast points. If they're on the menu, try the pillowy, fried sweetbreads. There's usually a wait, and quarters are very cramped, so don't expect to feel comfortable lingering at your rickety wooden table. Desserts, like ricotta ice cream with salted-caramel croutons, are irresistible, and on weekends lines form early for the restaurant's deservedly popular brunch. $ *Average main: $22* ✉ *54 E. 1st St., between 1st and 2nd aves., East Village* ☎ *212/677–6221* ⊕ *www. prunerestaurant.com* ⏴ *Reservations essential* Ⓜ *F to 2nd Ave.* ✛ *2:G2.*

$$$
GREEK

✗ **Pylos.** The perfect setting for a relaxed dinner or an intimate special occasion, this tastefully refined, light-filled East Village restaurant emphasizes rustic cooking from all over Greece. There are delicious versions of hearty comfort food dishes like pastitsio and moussaka on the menu but the lighter dishes—especially fish—let the flavors shine through. There is an extensive selection of interesting hot and cold mezes—start with the traditional trio of tzatziki, *taramosalata* (lemony fish roe dip), and *melitzanosalata* (an eggplant-based dip) and explore from there. Accompany your meal with some *vino* from the all-Greek wine list; the light white Atlantis wine from the island of Santorini is particularly enjoyable—and affordable. $ *Average main: $25* ✉ *128 E. 7th St., near Ave. A, East Village* ☎ *212/473–0220* ⊕ *www. pylosrestaurant.com* ▭ *No credit cards* ☾ *No lunch Mon. and Tues.* Ⓜ *F to 2nd Ave.; L to 1st Ave.* ✛ *3:H5.*

$$
MODERN
AMERICAN
Fodor'sChoice
★

✗ **Saxon & Parole.** One of the hottest spots on this burgeoning stretch of the Bowery, this eatery may be named for two 19th-century racehorses but the food—and the extremely good-looking crowd—is nothing you'd find in a barnyard. Settle into this cozy, sceney spot, order a cocktail, and peruse a menu loaded with the Zeitgeist dishes of New York dining: roasted bone marrow, Brussels sprouts, pork belly, chicken liver mousse, and, of course, an overpriced but excellent burger. The kitchen executes it all to complete deliciousness. The bar scene is lively, so come early for a cocktail. $ *Average main: $22* ✉ *316 Bowery, at Bleecker St., East Village* ☎ *212/254–0350* ⊕ *www.saxonandparole.com* ▭ *No credit cards* ☾ *No lunch* Ⓜ *B, D, F, M to Broadway–Lafayette St.; 6 to Bleecker St.; F to 2nd Ave.* ✛ *2:F2.*

$$
THAI
Fodor'sChoice
★

✗ **Somtum Der.** Once upon a time, New Yorkers had to venture to Queens to get good Thai food, but that's no longer the case. Not only have a handful of great Thai restaurants opened in Manhattan in recent years, but many of them hail from Isaan, a region in northeast Thailand that emphasizes light, spicy fare. Somtum Der, originally based in Bangkok, is one of the best. Start with the namesake somtum, a palate-singeing green papaya salad, before moving on to the *larb moo,* a mound of minced pork mixed with veggies and chilis. Also worth trying is the fried chicken, which makes you question the southern United States' monopoly on crispy bird. The restaurant is small and can get quite noisy. Ⓢ *Average main: $15* ⊠ *85 Ave. A, East Village* ☎ *212/260–8570* ⊕ *www.somtumder.com* ⊟ *No credit cards* Ⓜ *F to 2nd Ave.; L to 1st Ave.* ✚ *3:H6.*

$ ✕ **Veniero's Pasticceria.** Since 1894, this bustling bakery-café has sold every kind of Italian *dolce* (sweet), from cherry-topped cookies to creamy cannoli and flaky *sfogliatelle* (shell-shape, filled pastry). Cheesecake-lovers rejoice in Veniero's ricotta-based version. In all, a hungry visitor with a serious sweet tooth can choose from more than 150 different types of desserts. A wine license means you can top off your evening with a bottle of red. Veniero's is worth a look—check out the pressed-tin ceiling, marble floors, and stained glass—even if you're not hungry. Ⓢ *Average main: $5* ⊠ *342 E. 11th St., near 1st Ave., East Village* ☎ *212/674–7070* ⊕ *www.venierospastry.com* ⌕ *Reservations not accepted* Ⓜ *6 to Astor Pl.; L to 1st Ave.* ✚ *3:H5.*

CAFÉ
FAMILY

$ ✕ **Veselka.** Potato pierogies are available 24 hours a day at this East Village stalwart, which opened in 1954. The name means "rainbow" in Ukrainian. The authentic Ukrainian-slash-diner food is the perfect stick-to-your-ribs ending to a night on the town—or beginning to a new day, as the restaurant serves a full array of breakfast staples. It's a neighborhood experience, with tables of families sharing space with the hipsters. The spacious, sunny interior, with giant wall paintings to please the eye, is great for people-watching; don't take the servers' studied indifference personally. Ⓢ *Average main: $11* ⊠ *144 2nd Ave., at 9th St., East Village* ☎ *212/228–9682* ⊕ *www.veselka.com* ⊟ *No credit cards* ⌕ *Reservations not accepted* Ⓜ *6 to Astor Pl.; N, R to 8th St.–NYU; L to 1st Ave.* ✚ *3:H5.*

EASTERN
EUROPEAN
FAMILY

Westville East. *Branch location at 173 Avenue A, near 11th Street. See West Village for full review.*

$$ ✕ **Zum Schneider.** Located in Alphabet City, this garrulous Teutonic spot teaches the ABCs of beer drinking and hearty eating. Grab a table outside when the weather's nice, among the young hipsters who frequent the spot, and get ready for some kraut-laden fun. After quaffing a liter-size stein of the sudsy stuff, you may crave food, and the menu, naturally, is a veritable sausage-palooza. In addition to the usual meaty fare, such as Wiener schnitzel and goulash, there are, well, more sausages. The crispy potato pancakes are a good bet, too. Ⓢ *Average main: $16* ⊠ *107 Ave. C, at 7th St., East Village* ☎ *212/598–1098* ⊕ *www. zumschneider.com* ⊟ *No credit cards* ☽ *No lunch* Ⓜ *L to 1st Ave.; F to 2nd Ave.* ✚ *2:H1.*

GERMAN

LOWER EAST SIDE

The Lower East Side, home to generations of immigrant newcomers, has become quite the culinary hub over the last 15 years, with everything from molecular gastronomy to hipster Chinese cuisine. You can't walk a block without hitting a place that makes your stomach growl.

16

$$ AMERICAN Fodor's Choice ★ 🍴 **Clinton St. Baking Co.** There was a time when this Lower East Side restaurant was *the* place to come for brunch. Specifically, it was *the* place to eat blueberry pancakes, which many regulars professed were the best in the city, if not the state, or the whole country. But all that changed when owners Neil Kleinberg and DeDe Lahman added lunch and dinner to the menu. Oh, it's still a great place for brunch but now you can eat those pancakes (along with a good Black Angus burger or crab-cake sandwich) anytime. February is pancake month when, in addition to the blueberry, every weekday brings a special incarnation of the pancake. [$] *Average main: $19* ✉ *4 Clinton St., near Houston St., Lower East Side* ☎ *646/602–6263* 🌐 *www.clintonstreetbaking.com* 💳 *No credit cards* 🕒 *No dinner Sun.* [M] *F to 2nd Ave.; J, M, Z to Essex St.* ✣ *2:H2.*

$$ CHINESE 🍴 **Congee Village.** Don't be put off by the name—this boisterous Chinatown icon serves much more than the eponymous rice porridge. Indeed, the menu is enormous, covering an encyclopedic range of unusual Cantonese classics. The bamboo-cloaked dining room is great with a group of people, but being wedged in at a communal table with a boisterous family is part of the experience. If feeling adventurous, try the duck tongues in XO sauce or salt-and-pepper frog, or stick to familiar classics. Either way, the congee is a great way to start. [$] *Average main: $15* ✉ *100 Allen St., near Delancey St., Lower East Side* ☎ *212/941–1818* 🌐 *www.congeevillagerestaurants.com* [M] *F to Delancey St.; J, M, Z to Essex St.; B, D to Grand St.* ✣ *2:G3.*

$$$ FRENCH 🍴 **Dirty French.** Rich Torrisi and Mario Carbone, the chefs who created a small empire of Italian-American restaurants (Parm, Carbone, ZZ's Clam Bar) go Gallic at this Lower East Side bistro in the Ludlow Hotel. The name says it all: while the fare from the kitchen is French, the team put their own spin on it, taking many of the dishes on a tour of places like North Africa and Louisiana before they land on your table. Porgy is dusted wth Cajun spices and the duck à l'orange is spiked with Moroccan *ras el hanout* spice blend. The long, all-French wine list includes some nice bottles from off-the-radar regions. [$] *Average main: $30* ✉ *Ludlow Hotel, 180 Ludlow St., Lower East Side* ☎ *212/254–3000* 🌐 *www.dirtyfrench.com* [M] *F to 2nd Ave.* ✣ *2:G3.*

$ CAFÉ FAMILY 🍴 **Doughnut Plant.** If the cupcake craze is getting you down, head to the Doughnut Plant, where the all-American junk food staple is elevated to high art. Fresh seasonal ingredients go into these decadent treats, with real fruit and imported chocolate mixed into the batter. Traditionalists croon over the vanilla-bean doughnut, but there are plenty of exotic flavors to tempt tastebuds: the dense, fudgy Blackout is covered in crumb topping; carrot cake doughnuts have a cream-cheese filling. The Lower East Side location is open every day from 6:30 am to 8 pm ('til 9 pm Friday and Saturday). There's a second location in Chelsea, next to the Chelsea Hotel; doughnuts are also available around the city at Dean & DeLuca and Zabar's. [$] *Average main: $5* ✉ *379 Grand St., Lower East Side* ☎ *212/505–3700* 🌐 *www.doughnutplant.com* ✍ *Reservations not accepted* 💳 *No credit cards* [M] *F to Delancey St.; J, M, Z to Essex St.; B, D to Grand St.* ✣ *2:G4.*

$$ ✕ **The Fat Radish.** The phrase "seasonal British" might have once seemed
BRITISH puzzling but with seasonal ingredients very much in vogue and British
Fodor'sChoice cuisine making a name for itself, this handsome, hip, and sceney Lower
★ East Side (almost Chinatown) restaurant is worth a visit. The menu is
eclectic but full of excellent choices. Expect to be confronted by a lot of
kale and other en-vogue ingredients. Green curried monkfish, a cheese-
burger served with duck-fat fries, pork sausage and mussel stew, and
roasted Peking duck breast are just a few of the menu showstoppers.
Match that with quality craft British brews and potent cocktails and
you'll be championing English cuisine in no time. $ *Average main: $21*
✉ *17 Orchard St., near Canal St., Lower East Side* ☎ *212/300–4053*
⊕ *www.thefatradishnyc.com* ⊗ *No lunch Mon.* Ⓜ *F to East Broadway*
✛ *2:G5.*

$$ ✕ **Freemans.** It's hard to believe now, but there was once a time when
AMERICAN New York restaurant interiors were trying hard not to look cool, with
Fodor'sChoice no taxidermy or ironic tchotchkes littered around the room, or lodge-ish
★ dishes like hunters stew, potted pork, and grilled trout on the menu. But
we have Freemans to thank for the change, and their equally inspired
cocktails menu. Down a little-used alleyway on the Lower East Side,
trendsetting Freemans is as hip and popular as when it opened in 2004.
Just don't try too hard to look cool. $ *Average main: $20* ✉ *End of*
Freeman Alley, near Rivington St., Lower East Side ☎ *212/420–0012*
⊕ *www.freemansrestaurant.com* ⚼ *Reservations not accepted* Ⓜ *F to*
2nd Ave.; J, Z to Bowery ✛ *2:F3.*

$ ✕ **Ivan Ramen.** Ivan Orkin's improbable but true story is one of the
JAPANESE many layers that make New York City's restaurant scene so exciting,
Fodor'sChoice authentic, and delicious: the self-described "Jewish kid from Long
★ Island" moved to Tokyo and became a ramen-making master, achiev-
ing near legendary status in the Japanese capital. In 2014 he opened this
Lower East Side temple to ramen and it's been packed since day one.
First-timers should try the triple pork, triple garlic mazemen, a type of
near-brothless ramen. The spicy red-chili ramen, filled to the rim with
chicken broth, a smashed egg, minced pork, and rye noodles, lives up to
its name. It all goes well with a pint of craft beer or a can of sake. $ *Av-*
erage main: $16 ✉ *25 Clinton St., Lower East Side* ☎ *646/678–3859*
⊕ *www.ivanramen.com* Ⓜ *F to 2nd Ave.; J, M, Z to Essex St.* ✛ *2:G3.*

$$ ✕ **Katz's Delicatessen.** Everything and nothing has changed at Katz's since
DELI it first opened in 1888, when the neighborhood was dominated by Jew-
Fodor'sChoice ish immigrants. The rows of Formica tables, the long self-service coun-
★ ter, and such signs as "Send a salami to your boy in the army" are all
completely authentic. The lines still form on the weekends for giant, suc-
culent hand-carved corned beef and pastrami sandwiches, soul-warming
soups, juicy hot dogs, and crisp half-sour pickles. Weeknights are more
laid-back. You get a ticket when you walk in and then get it punched at
the various stations where you pick up your food; don't lose it or you'll
have to pay the lost ticket fee. $ *Average main: $15* ✉ *205 E. Houston*
St., at Ludlow St., Lower East Side ☎ *212/254–2246* ⊕ *www.katzdeli.*
com Ⓜ *F to 2nd Ave.* ✛ *2:G2.*

16

$$ ✕**Loreley Restaurant & Biergarten.** Beer gardens once dotted the New York
GERMAN City landscape in the way that Starbucks does now, but after World
War I and Prohibition, most of these outdoor drinking spots vanished.
Then in 2003 came Loreley (which eventually kicked off a new beer
garden craze in the city). Don't mistake this Lower East Side hotspot
for a place where geriatrics in lederhosen swing their plus-size steins of
beer to polka music. Instead, there's a better-than-good chance of find-
ing a gaggle of hipsters nursing German craft beers while bobbing their
heads to the new Radiohead album and munching on plates of sausage,
meatballs, or schnitzel. The space out back may be more concrete than
garden, but it's a pleasure on a mild evening. $ *Average main: $17*
✉ *7 Rivington St., near the Bowery, Lower East Side* ☎ *212/253–7077*
⊕ *www.loreleynyc.com* ⊟ *No credit cards* Ⓜ *J, Z to Bowery; B, D to
Grand St.; F to 2nd Ave.* ✛ *2:F3.*

$ ✕**The Meatball Shop.** New York's first full-service meatball restaurant has
ITALIAN a pedigree chef, a professional waitstaff, a wine list, and a hip crowd.
FAMILY And the meatballs, oh, the meatballs: choose beef, pork, chicken, veg-
gie, or "special" ball options that range from chili cheese to Greek lamb
and Buffalo chicken; then decide if you want them served simple as is,
in sliders or a hero, as a salad, or a platter—all with an appropriate
choice of sauce and cheese. The meatball concept quickly caught on,
and there are now six locations: five in Manhattan and one in Wil-
liamsburg. Mix 'n' match ice-cream sandwiches—choose your flavor
and cookie—are worth saving room for. $ *Average main: $10* ✉ *84
Stanton St., near Allen St., Lower East Side* ☎ *212/982–8895* ⊕ *www.
themeatballshop.com* ⌕ *Reservations not accepted* Ⓜ *F to 2nd Ave.; J,
Z to Bowery* ✛ *2:G3.*

$ ✕**Mission Cantina.** Chef Danny Bowien rocked the New York dining
MEXICAN scene when he imported his San Francisco hit Mission Chinese Food
here a few years ago. He has another local favorite in this Mexican eat-
ery. The menu changes seasonally but expect adventurous taco creations
with creative ingredient pairings: beef tongue sprinkled with peanuts,
and fresh tuna with wasabi are standouts. There are also huge burritos
stuffed with chorizo, lamb, and rotisserie chicken. In the morning, the
restaurant morphs into a Vietnamese eatery serving Southeast Asian
breakfast staples like chicken pho and lamb-spiked rice porridge. The
floor-to-ceiling windows are excellent for people-watching. $ *Aver-
age main: $13* ✉ *172 Orchard St., Lower East Side* ☎ *212/254–2233*
⊕ *www.missioncantinany.com* Ⓜ *F to 2nd Ave.*

$$ ✕**Schiller's Liquor Bar.** It may not be as hard to get in as it was back in
BISTRO 2003, when Keith McNally first opened this sceney hangout on the
FAMILY Lower East Side, but it still has the allure, with excellent bistro fare, sexy
cocktails, and the kind of atmosphere that is as comfortable for celebrities as for parents with strollers. This is vintage Parisian à la McNally:
verdigris mirrored panels, forever-in-style subway tiles, a tin ceiling,
and a checkered floor, while Cuban sandwiches and steak frites reveal
a steady hand in the kitchen. This is also the place for a late-night bite,
since the kitchen is open until midnight every night (until 3 am Friday
and Saturday). Breakfast is served weekdays until 4 pm, with brunch
on weekends. $ *Average main: $20* ✉ *131 Rivington St., at Norfolk*

St., Lower East Side ☏ *212/260–4555* ⊕ *www.schillersny.com* Ⓜ *F to Delancey St.; J, M, Z to Essex St.* ✛ *2:G3.*

$$
ECLECTIC
FAMILY

✕ **Shopsin's.** Don't ask for substitutions or sauce on the side at New York's most eccentric eatery, because Kenny Shopsin, owner and chef, may really toss you out or ban you for life; somehow the attitude is part of the appeal here. Though the eclectic menu runs to literally hundreds of items—from pumpkin pancakes to chilaquiles, and from chili cheeseburgers to lamb-curry soups—even the strangest foods conjured up in his tight diner kitchen taste pretty great. The mac 'n' cheese pancakes have loyal followers (they're even better with hot sauce). The space in the Essex market is tiny, so expect to wait. Parties of more than four aren't accepted. Ⓢ *Average main: $17* ⊠ *Essex Market, 120 Essex St., near Rivington St., Lower East Side* ☏ ⊕ *www.shopsins.com* ☻ *Closed Mon. and Tues. No dinner* ⟍ *Reservations not accepted* ⊟ *No credit cards* Ⓜ *F to Delancy St.; J, M, Z to Essex St.* ✛ *2:G3.*

$$
ECLECTIC

✕ **The Stanton Social.** This swanky Lower East Side favorite lures crowds with an expansive and eclectic small-plates menu, accompanied by a perfectly calibrated cocktail list. Come before 7 if you want to be able to hear your companion speak, but the people-watching and shared dishes are good at any hour. Try the gooey, Gruyère-topped onion soup dumplings, juicy Kobe beef sliders, and wasabi-crusted salmon. Downstairs feels like a more traditional dining room, whereas the second level features a buzzy bar. The late-night lounge area, decorated with cherry-blossom wallpaper and red leather upholstery, turns more nightclubby the later it gets. Brunch—with options like spicy lobster Benedict—might blow your mind. Whatever time you come, save room for the fresh doughnuts. Ⓢ *Average main: $20* ⊠ *99 Stanton St., between Ludlow and Orchard sts., Lower East Side* ☏ *212/995–0099* ⊕ *www. thestantonsocial.com* ☻ *No lunch* ⟍ *Reservations essential* Ⓜ *F to 2nd Ave.; J, M, Z to Essex St.* ✛ *2:G3.*

$
CAFÉ
FAMILY

✕ **Sugar Sweet Sunshine.** The brainchild of two former Magnolia Bakery employees, Sugar Sweet's cupcakes are far superior; try the chocolate-almond Gooey Gooey, or the cream cheese frosting–topped pumpkin flavor. The real showstopper? Swoon-inducing banana pudding, with slices of ripe fruit and crumbled Nilla wafers suspended in decadent vanilla pudding. Cupcakes are the perfect on-the-go treat, but if you prefer to hang out, there are cozy couches. Ⓢ *Average main: $5* ⊠ *126 Rivington St., between Essex and Norfolk sts., Lower East Side* ☏ *212/995–1960* ⊕ *www.sugarsweetsunshine.com* ⟍ *Reservations not accepted* Ⓜ *F to Delancy St.; J, M, Z to Essex St.* ✛ *2:G3.*

16

GREENWICH VILLAGE AND THE WEST VILLAGE

GREENWICH VILLAGE

Greenwich Village's bohemian days may have faded, but the romantic allure of its tiny bistros, bars, and cafés remains. Around New York University, shabby-chic eateries and take-out joints cater to students, but there is a growing number of more sophisticated dining spots, too. Avoid the generally schlocky restaurants on Bleecker Street.

$$$ ITALIAN

🍴 **All'onda.** While this stylish restaurant bills itself as serving "modern Venetian cuisine," it's more as if Japanese chefs quietly invaded Venice and begin updating the dishes. Chef Chris Jaeckle sneaks Asian elements into the otherwise Italian menu, emboldening the dishes to the tune of utter deliciousness. Truffle risotto has sake mash, crab-loaded garganelli has just the right touch of yuzu, and thick bucatini noodles are interlaced with fresh uni. There is, of course, more to the Japanese-accented Italian menu than just pasta: the juicy porchetta (laced with a seaweed salsa verde, naturally) and the tender short rib, paired with saffron risotto, are winning entrées. You'll want to say "*grazie*" or perhaps "*arigato*" to the chef on your way out. [$] *Average main: $26* ✉ *22 E. 13th St.* ☎ *212/231-2236* 🌐 *www.allondanyc.com* 🕓 *Closed Mon.* [M] *4, 5, 6, L, N, Q, R to 14th St.–Union Square* ✣ *3:F4.*

$$ PIZZA FAMILY

🍴 **Arturo's.** Few guidebooks list this classic New York pizzeria, but the jam-packed room and pleasantly smoky scent foreshadow a satisfying meal. There's a full menu of Italian classics, but don't be fooled: pizza is the main event. The thin-crust beauties are cooked in a coal-fired oven, and emerge sizzling with simple toppings like pepperoni, sausage, and eggplant. Monday through Thursday, you can call ahead to reserve a table; weekends, be prepared to wait and salivate. If you like the whimsical paintings that plaster the walls, ask the waiter the price: they're for sale. [$] *Average main: $18* ✉ *106 W. Houston St., near Thompson St., Greenwich Village* ☎ *212/535–4480* 🕓 *No lunch weekends* [M] *1 to Houston St.; B, D, F, M to Broadway–Lafayette St.* ✣ *2:D3.*

$$$ ITALIAN Fodor's Choice ★

🍴 **Babbo Ristorante.** It shouldn't take more than one bite of the ethereal homemade pasta or tender barbecue squab with roast beet farrotto for you to understand why it's so hard to get a reservation at Mario Batali's casually elegant restaurant. The menu strays widely from Italian standards and hits numerous high points, in particular with the "mint love letters": ravioli filled with pureed peas, ricotta, and fresh mint, finished with spicy lamb sausage ragout; and rabbit with Brussels sprouts, house-made pancetta, and carrot vinaigrette. This is the perfect spot for a raucous celebratory dinner with flowing wine and festive banter. But be forewarned: if anyone in your party is hard of hearing, or bothered by loud rock music, choose someplace more sedate. [$] *Average main: $30* ✉ *110 Waverly Pl., between MacDougal St. and 6th Ave., Greenwich Village* ☎ *212/777–0303* 🌐 *www.babbonyc.com* 🕓 *No lunch Sun. and Mon.* ✍ *Reservations essential* [M] *A, B, C, D, E, F, M to W. 4th St.* ✣ *2:C1.*

$$$ MODERN AMERICAN

🍴 **Blue Hill.** This tasteful, sophisticated den of a restaurant—formerly a speakeasy—on a quiet side street maintains an impeccable reputation for excellence and consistency under the leadership of Chef Dan Barber. The Obamas even stopped here for dinner, shutting down the street for one of their "date nights." Part of the slow-food, sustainable agriculture movement, Blue Hill mostly uses ingredients grown or raised within 200 miles, including the Four Season Farm at Stone Barns Center for Food and Agriculture, Barber's second culinary project in nearby Westchester County. The chefs produce precisely cooked and elegantly constructed food such as wild striped bass with potato-and-clam chowder and house-cured *guanciale* (pork jowl), and a smoked-tomato soup with

American caviar. $ *Average main: $31* ✉ *75 Washington Pl., between Washington Sq. W and 6th Ave., Greenwich Village* ☎ *212/539–1776* ⊕ *www.bluehillfarm.com* ⊗ *No lunch* ⌕ *Reservations essential* Ⓜ *A, B, C, D, E, F, M to W. 4th St.* ✛ *2:C1.*

$$$$
ITALIAN
✕**Carbone.** It seems like Mario Carbone and Rich Torrisi can do no wrong. Case in point: Carbone. The achingly popular place not only sticks to the Italian-American formula that has won it (and their earlier restaurant Torrisi) acclaim, but goes one step further: the white-tableclothed Greenwich Village restaurant successfully emulates the Big Apple Italian restaurants of the 1950s, with revived dishes like veal marsala, ribeye Diana, and baked clams. It's not cheap, but portions are generous. $ *Average main: $45* ✉ *181 Thompson St., between Bleecker and Houston sts., Greenwich Village* ☎ *212/254–3000* ⊕ *www. carbonenewyork.com* ⊗ *No lunch weekends* ⌕ *Reservations essential* Ⓜ *A, B, C, D, E, F, M to W. 4th St.* ✛ *2:D2.*

$$$
ITALIAN
Fodor's Choice
★
✕**Charlie Bird.** Perpetually packed since the day it opened in the spring of 2013, Charlie Bird is the love child of sommelier Robert Bohr, who was in charge of wine at vino-mad Cru, and Chef Ryan Hardy, who made a name for himself at Little Nell in Aspen and, more recently, sharpened his skills as private chef for food-loving Jay-Z and Beyoncé—it's no coincidence the restaurant has a hip-hop theme (expect old-school and '90's rap on the hi-fi). The Italian-leaning menu is divided into small and large plates, vegetables, a "raw" section, and pasta. The uni-loaded duck-egg spaghetti marries surf 'n' turf in a deeply satisfying way, while the scallops are subtly laced with lardo, giving them an umami boost. $ *Average main: $32* ✉ *5 King St., at 6th Ave., Greenwich Village* ☎ *212/235–7133* ⊕ *www.charliebirdnyc.com* ⊟ *No credit cards* ⌕ *Reservations essential* Ⓜ *C, E to Spring St.; 1 to Houston St.* ✛ *2:C3.*

$
INDIAN
✕**Kati Roll Company.** You can think of a kati roll as a South Asian taco: griddled parathas stuffed with savory-spiced grilled meat, shrimp, paneer, chickpea mash, or spiced mashed potato. They're the only things sold at this tiny, popular lunch spot cheerfully festooned with Bollywood posters. This is an excellent and inexpensive lunch option, but be warned that lines often form at weekday lunch, and there are only a few seats, so a good plan is to take your kati roll to a nearby park bench. There are also locations at 39th Street and 6th Avenue, and 53rd Street and 3rd Avenue. $ *Average main: $6* ✉ *99 MacDougal St., near Bleecker St., Greenwich Village* ☎ *212/730–4280* ⊕ *www. thekatirollcompany.com* ⌕ *Reservations not accepted* Ⓜ *A, B, C, D, E, F, M to W. 4th St.* ✛ *2:D2.*

$$
ITALIAN
✕**Lupa.** Even the most hard-to-please connoisseurs have a soft spot for Lupa, Mario Batali and Joseph Bastianich's "downscale" Roman trattoria. Rough-hewn wood, great Italian wines, and simple preparations with top-quality ingredients define the restaurant, along with the "gentle" prices. People come repeatedly for dishes such as ricotta gnocchi with sweet-sausage ragout, house-made salumi, and sardines with golden raisins and pine nuts. The restaurant is split into two rooms: a boisterous space up front, with plenty of natural light, where walk-ins are welcome; and for those with reservations, an intimate back room, like a culinary cocoon in the best sense. $ *Average main: $22* ✉ *170*

16

Thompson St., between Bleecker and Houston sts., Greenwich Village ☎ *212/982–5089* ⊕ *www.luparestaurant.com* Ⓜ *A, B, C, D, E, F, M to W. 4th St.* ✛ *2:D3.*

$$ ✕ **Mermaid Oyster Bar.** If you're craving a great raw bar, lobster roll, or SEAFOOD soft-shell crab sandwich (in season), Mermaid Oyster Bar gives nearby classics Mary's Fish Camp and Pearl Oyster Bar a run for their money. Almost every dish is a winner here, but the lobster bisque laced with Manzanilla sherry and toasted pumpkin seeds, the blackened striped bass with roasted squash and Swiss chard, and the spicy seafood bucatini fra diavolo are all standouts. From the bar, try something from the list of perfect-pitch cocktails, like a Dark and Stormy, made with black rum and ginger beer, or a Pimm's Cooler with refreshing pieces of cucumber. There are two other locations in Manhattan: on the Upper West Side and in the East Village. Ⓢ *Average main: $23* ✉ *79 MacDougal St., at Houston St., Greenwich Village* ☎ *212/260–0100* ⊕ *www. themermaidnyc.com* ⊘ *No lunch* Ⓜ *1 to Houston St.; A, B, C, D, E, F, M to W. 4th St.* ✛ *2:D2.*

$$$ ✕ **Minetta Tavern.** By converting a moribund 80-year-old Italian res-
MODERN taurant into a cozy hot spot, restaurateur Keith McNally created yet
AMERICAN another hit. Try early and often to score reservations, so that you can sample creations like buttery trout meunière, bone marrow on toast, expertly aged steaks, and the celebrated Black Label burger, a gorgeous assembly of meat topped with caramelized onions and—for the brave— an added layer of cheese. The bar room, with its original details intact, is great for people-watching. Landing a table in the back room, with its original mural depicting West Village life and wall-to-wall photos of famous and infamous customers from eras gone by, makes sweet-talking the reservationist a worthy endeavor. Ⓢ *Average main: $27* ✉ *113 MacDougal St., between Bleecker and 3rd sts., Greenwich Village* ☎ *212/475–3850* ⊕ *www.minettatavernny.com* ⊘ *No lunch Mon. and Tues.* ⌖ *Reservations essential* Ⓜ *A, B, C, D, E, F, M to W. 4th St.* ✛ *2:D2.*

$ ✕ **Peanut Butter & Co. Sandwich Shop.** For a childhood classic kicked up a
AMERICAN notch, head to Peanut Butter & Co. Sandwich Shop. You can go with
FAMILY a standard PB&J, or explore any of the menu's 20 options, including the Elvis (grilled with peanut butter, bananas, and honey), the Pregnant Lady (peanut butter and pickles), or the sandwich of the week, with expertly paired ingredients such as cherry jam, cream cheese, and Crunch Time peanut butter. Try a milkshake—there are traditional flavors as well as more innovative combos. And of course there are peanut butter cookies for dessert, as well as sundaes. Ⓢ *Average main: $8* ✉ *240 Sullivan St., near 3rd St., Greenwich Village* ☎ *212/677–3995* ⊕ *iwww.lovepeanutbutter.com* ⌖ *Reservations not accepted* Ⓜ *A, B, C, D, E, F, M to W. 4th St.* ✛ *2:D2.*

$ ✕ **Umami Burger.** Known as the "sixth taste," *umami* is the sensation
BURGER on our palate when we eat something savory. It's also the name of this restaurant minichain whose New York location serves one of the best burgers in the city. The signature burger looks like any other (except for the "u" branded into the top of the buns) but looks are deceiving. Dig, if you will, the umami-building process: caramelized onions are

doused with star anise, the sweet-accented ketchup is made in-house, and the patty is sprinkled with sea kelp powder and bonito flake, then sprayed with an oyster extract. The Manly Burger goes a step further, adding beer cheddar and bacon lardons. Starters include salads, fries, truffle fries, sweet potato fries, and onion rings. $ *Average main: $13* ⊠ *432 6th Ave., near 10th St., Greenwich Village* ☎ *212/677–8626* ⊕ *www.umami.com* ▭ *No credit cards* Ⓜ *A, B, C, D, E, F, M to W. 4th St.* ✛ *3:D5.*

WEST VILLAGE

The West Village has mastered the art of destination restaurants that feel like neighborhood eateries. Places here are homey, yet remarkable enough to attract diners from all over the city.

$$$
ASIAN

✕**Annisa.** "Annisa" may mean "the women" in Arabic, but the top-notch food at this sedate West Village restaurant is inspired by Asia. Chef Anita Lo, one of the most underrated chefs in New York, cooks up miraculous dishes like foie gras soup dumplings, barbeque squid with basil and peanuts, and Japanese curry-spiked rabbit. Be sure to save room for dessert: the pecan and salted butterscotch beignets with bourbon ice cream are good enough to make you want to come back a second or third time. $ *Average main: $30* ⊠ *13 Barrow St., between 4th St. and 7th Ave. S, West Village* ☎ *212/741–6699* ⊕ *www. annisarestaurant.com* ▭ *No credit cards* ☾ *No lunch* Ⓜ *1 to Christopher St.–Sheridan Sq.; A, B, C, D, E, F, M to W. 4th St.* ✛ *2:C2.*

$$
ITALIAN

✕**Barbuto.** Chef Jonathan Waxman made a name for himself with his French-inspired California cuisine. Barbuto specializes in rustic preparations with bright flavors, like house-made duck sausage with creamy polenta, redwine–braised short ribs, and pasta carbonara, though the menu changes daily, depending on what's available. The chef's acclaimed roasted chicken is usually on the menu in one form or another. The airy, sophisticated space continues to get busy so make a reservation. The restaurant is particularly pleasant in nice weather when the giant garagedoor–like windows open onto the street to watch the neighborhood go by. $ *Average main: $18* ⊠ *775 Washington St., between Jane and 12th sts., West Village* ☎ *212/924–9700* ⊕ *www. barbutonyc.com* Ⓜ *A, C, E to 14th St.; L to 8th Ave.; 1 to Christopher St.–Sheridan Sq.* ✛ *3:B5.*

$$
ISRAELI

✕**Bar Bolonat.** Chef Einat Admony who runs the show at Taïm and Balaboosta has devised an intriguing menu at this sleek West Village spot that serves dishes that represent the Jewish diaspora around the Mediterranean. Sit at the bar and watch the kitchen in action or dine at a two-top in the dark-hued dining room—either way you can munch on tender lamb neck wading in a chickpea purée or the palate-tantalizing yellow Yemonite curry bobbing with shrimp. The wine list goes beyond the diaspora, but there are some interesting bottles from Israel and Morocco. $ *Average main: $20* ⊠ *611 Hudson St., West Village* ☎ *212/390–1545* ⊕ *www.barbolonatny.com* ☾ *No lunch* Ⓜ *A, C, E to 14th St.; L to 8th Ave.* ✛ *3:B5.*

$
PIZZA
FAMILY

✕**Bleecker Street Pizza.** Flavor reigns at this bustling corner pizzeria. It's the perfect place to stop for a stand-up slice at the counter, particularly to soak up some suds late at night. The thin-crusted Nonna

16

Maria is topped with garlicky marinara, grated and fresh mozzarella, and freshly grated Parmesan, and worth the trek to the West Village. If not smitten with "Grandma Maria," there are also Sicilian slices and whole white (that's no tomato sauce) pies available. $ *Average main: $4* ✉ *69 7th Ave. S, at Bleecker St., West Village* ☎ *212/924–4466* ⊕ *www. bleekerstreetpizza.net* ⚲ *Reservations not accepted* Ⓜ *1 to Christopher St.–Sheridan Sq.; A, B, C, D, E, F, M to W. 4th St.* ✛ *2:C2.*

$$$ ✕ **Blue Ribbon Bakery.** A neighborhood standard for good, if expensive,
ECLECTIC   food, this outpost of the Blue Ribbon empire has an eclectic menu with substantial sandwiches on homemade bread (freshly baked in the oven downstairs), small plates, legendary bread pudding, and entrées that span the globe, from hummus to grilled catfish with sautéed collards and sweet potatoes. The cavelike basement dining room is dark and intimate; upstairs is more open and light-filled, with large windows looking out onto a pretty West Village corner. Brunch is notoriously crowded. $ *Average main: $25* ✉ *35 Downing St., at Bedford St., Greenwich Village* ☎ *212/337–0404* ⊕ *www.blueribbonrestaurants.com* Ⓜ *1 to Houston St.; A, B, C, D, E, F, M to W. 4th St.* ✛ *2:C2.*

$$$$ ✕ **Commerce.** This former speakeasy harks back to days gone by with its
ECLECTIC   Diego Rivera–style murals, vintage sconces, and restored subway tiles, but the crowd really comes for Chef Harold Moore's seasonal cuisine. Appetizers range from a red cabbage, apple, and pecan salad to yuzu-marinated hamachi ceviche. Entrées are just as vibrant: bright, sweet peas offset pristine halibut, and the shareable roast chicken, presented tableside, is served with foiegras bread stuffing. Brunch has a Middle Eastern influence, with scrambled eggs and hummus atop a pillowy pita, and a mean *shakshuka* (baked eggs nestled in a pepper, onion, and tomato sauce). Even the contents of the bread basket are a pleasure here. In an interesting twist, especially given the restaurant's name, only credit cards are accepted. No cash. $ *Average main: $36* ✉ *50 Commerce St., West Village* ☎ *212/524–2301* ⊕ *www.commercerestaurant.com* ⊙ *No lunch Mon.–Thurs.* Ⓜ *1 to Christopher St.–Sheridan Sq.; A, B, C, D, E, F, M to W. 4th St.* ✛ *2:B2.*

$$$ ✕ **dell'anima.** Lines still snake out the door of this neighborhood favor-
ITALIAN   ite, so it's a good idea to make a reservation. Once you're in, check out the open kitchen, where the stylish crowd converges to watch chefs prepare authentic Italian dishes with a modern twist. Starters might include sweetbreads, bone marrow, or charred octopus with chorizo, while traditional first courses like pasta alla carbonara with *speck* (smoked and cured pork), egg, and pecorino are impeccable. The signature *pollo al diavolo* (spicy chicken) is seared with enough smoke and heat for all seasons. Anfora, their wine bar next door, is good for an after-dinner drink, if you want to linger in the area. $ *Average main: $26* ✉ *38 8th Ave., at Jane St., West Village* ☎ *212/366–6633* ⊕ *www.dellanima.com* ⊙ *No lunch weekdays* Ⓜ *1, 2, 3, A, C, E to 14th St.; L to 8th Ave.* ✛ *3:C5.*

$$ ✕ **Ditch Plains.** Named for a surf spot in Montauk, this laid-back neigh-
SEAFOOD   borhood restaurant serves an eclectic bill of beachfront fare—from fish tacos, lobster rolls, and fish 'n' chips to clam chowder and crab dip. There are options for landlubbers and vegetarians, too. It's not quite a beach shack, but the food and setting, with an upbeat rock soundtrack,

are designed for conviviality, and the wine-list prices are extremely friendly, with whole and half bottles sold just above cost. The bloody marys are recommended, too. Breakfast/brunch is served every day from 11 am and dinner served until 2 am nightly. $ *Average main: $18* ✉ *29 Bedford St., near Downing St., West Village* ☎ *212/633–0202* ⊕ *www.ditch-plains.com* ⌂ *Reservations not accepted* Ⓜ *1 to Houston St.* ✛ *2:C3.*

$$ ✕ **Do Hwa.** If anyone in New York is responsible for making Korean
KOREAN food cool and user-friendly, it is the mother-daughter team behind this chic and perennially popular restaurant. Jenny Kwak and her mother, Myung Ja, serve home cooking in the form of *kalbi jim* (braised short ribs), *bibimbop* (a spicy, mix-it-yourself vegetable-and-rice dish), and other favorites that may not be as pungent as in Koreatown but are satisfying nevertheless—in a far more sophisticated atmosphere. The bar area, where movies are projected onto a side wall, gets pretty happening, too. $ *Average main: $23* ✉ *55 Carmine St., between Bedford St. and 7th Ave. S, West Village* ☎ *212/414–1224* ⊕ *www.dohwanyc. com* ☾ *No lunch weekends* Ⓜ *1 to Houston St.; A, B, C, D, E, F, M to W. 4th St.* ✛ *2:C2.*

$$ ✕ **Empellón Taquería.** Chef Alex Stupak worked for years as the wiz-
MEXICAN ardlike pastry chef at wd-50, New York's premier home to molecular
Fodor's Choice gastronomy, so when he left to open—wait for it—a taquería, many
★ Manhattan diners either scratched their heads or wondered if they'd be served deconstructed tacos. Instead, they got simple yet well-executed fare using top-notch ingredients. There are straightforward options— fish tempura, lamb, steak—as well as surprising variations, like tacos with sweetbreads and a chorizo gravy poured over it. There are also several variations on the margarita theme including one using the Japanese citrus, *yuzu.* Empellón isn't really south-of-the-border in its authenticity but when it's this good, who cares? $ *Average main: $23* ✉ *230 W. 4th St., at 10th St., West Village* ☎ *212/367–0999* ⊕ *www.empellon.com* ⊟ *No credit cards* Ⓜ *1 to Christopher St.–Sheridan Sq.* ✛ *2:B1.*

$$ ✕ **Fatty Crab.** This rustic Malaysian cantina showcases the exciting cui-
MALAYSIAN sine of Chef Zak Pelaccio, who spent years cooking at famous French
Fodor's Choice restaurants before escaping to Southeast Asia for a year, where he fell
★ in love with the flavors of the region. Start with the addictive pickled watermelon and crispy pork salad, an improbable combination that's both refreshing and decadent. The can't-miss signature dish is chili crab—cracked Dungeness crab in a pool of rich, spicy chili sauce, served with bread for dipping. It's messy for sure, but worth rolling up your sleeves. The small space fills up quickly, and be warned that the tables are practically on top of each other, but it's lots of fun. $ *Average main: $18* ✉ *643 Hudson St., between Gansevoort and Horatio sts., West Village* ☎ *212/352–3592* ⊕ *www.fattycrab.com* ⌂ *Reservations not accepted* Ⓜ *A, C, E to 14th St.; L to 8th Ave.* ✛ *3:C5.*

$$$ ✕ **Fedora.** Up until 2011, subterranean Fedora was an ancient, little-
ECLECTIC patronized restaurant with an even more ancient owner (for which the restaurant was named). But charming Fedora, the old Italian owner, has left the building and restaurateur Gabe Stulman took it over, vowing to keep the design largely intact. Now "see-and-be-seen" folk cram

16

the long, narrow space, munching on French Canadian–accented fare like garlic cream–topped duck breast and scallops paired with bone marrow, and sipping creatively named (and made) signature cocktails. Fedora (the restaurant) will never be the same and that's maybe a good thing. [$] *Average main: $25* ✉ *239 W. 4th St., between Charles and 10th sts., West Village* ☎ *646/449–9336* 🌐 *www.fedoranyc.com* 💳 *No credit cards* 🕒 *No lunch* [M] *1 to Christopher St.–Sheridan Sq.* ✥ *2:B1.*

$$ ITALIAN 🍴 **Frankies Spuntino.** The Frankies—that is, owners and chefs Frank Falcinelli and Frank Castronovo—have a winning formula at their West Village restaurant: serve hearty not-necessarily-by-the-book Italian-inflected fare using local, organic, and humanely raised ingredients in a laidback atmosphere. Most menu items change seasonally, but expect pasta dishes like pappardelle with mushrooms and chestnuts; black spaghetti with mussels, cockels, and pistachios; and sweet potato gnocchi with oxtail ragout. The large menu also includes crostini, fresh salads, cured meats, and cheese plates. It's a casual, family-friendly, neighborhood spot. [$] *Average main: $18* ✉ *570 Hudson St., at 11th St., West Village* ☎ *212/924–0818* 🌐 *www.frankiesspuntino.com* 💳 *No credit cards* [M] *A, C, E to 14th St.; L to 8th Ave.* ✥ *2:B1.*

$$$ ITALIAN 🍴 **I Sodi.** In a city of what seems like a million Italian restaurants, this minimalist-designed Tuscan-focused eatery in the West Village is a real find. Spikey-haired owner, Rita Sodi, a Florentine who formerly worked in the fashion industry, ensures the traditional fare coming from the kitchen is satisfying. The menu changes weekly based on seasonal ingredients but, expect a bevy of pasta dishes topped with good stuff like duck ragout and artichoke-laced lasagna, as well as not-very-Lipitor-friendly pancetta-wrapped pork and rabbit. Hoist a glass of grappa at the end of the meal, and be happy you're in the right place. [$] *Average main: $26* ✉ *105 Christopher St., between Bleecker and Hudson sts., West Village* ☎ *212/414–5774* 🌐 *www.isodinyc.com* 💳 *No credit cards* 🕒 *No lunch* [M] *1 to Christopher St.–Sheridan Sq.* ✥ *2:B2.*

$$ PIZZA 🍴 **Keste Pizza & Vino.** At the back of the long, narrow Keste Pizza & Vino restaurant is a beautiful, tiled, wood-fired oven that cooks what might be Manhattan's most authentic Neapolitan pies at 1,000 degrees. Blistered and chewy around the edges, the margherita pie gives way to a softer center pooled with San Marzano tomato sauce and house-made mozzarella. There are numerous pizza options, including white pies and gluten-free crusts. This is a definite contender for best pizza in New York. The dining room is casual, and the location means it's almost always busy. [$] *Average main: $16* ✉ *271 Bleecker St., between 6th and 7th aves., West Village* ☎ *212/243–1500* 🌐 *www.kestepizzeria.com* ✍ *Reservations not accepted* [M] *1 to Chrispher St.–Sheridan Sq.; A, B, C, D, E, F, M to W. 4th St.* ✥ *2:C2.*

$$ MODERN AMERICAN 🍴 **The Little Owl.** This tiny neighborhood joint, with seating for 28 people, is exceptionally eager to please—and this attitude, plus the food, is a winning combination. The menu is just as small, which actually makes it easier to decide what you want. And what you want are the pork-veal-beef-pecorino-cheese meatball "sliders," or miniburgers. The unusually juicy pork loin chop, served with Parmesan butter beans and wild dandelion greens, is gigantic and hugely satisfying. Raspberry-filled

beignets, served with a ramekin of warm Nutella, are otherworldly. It's quintessential West Village: quirky and wonderful. Fans of sitcom *Friends* might recognize the apartment building that houses the restaurant. $ *Average main: $24* ⊠ *90 Bedford St., at Grove St., West Village* ☎ *212/741–4695* ⊕ *www.thelittleowlnyc.com* ⚓ *Reservations essential* Ⓜ *1 to Christopher St.–Sheridan Sq.; A, B, C, D, E, F, M to W. 4th St.* ⊕ *3:D6.*

$$ ✕ **Mary's Fish Camp.** Diners still line up down the street before the restaurant opens for dinner to get a table at this small but bustling seafood shack. The result of a split between Pearl Oyster Bar's partners, Mary's is a more intimate space, but the two have similar menus: excellent fried oysters, chowders, and, of course, the sweet lobster roll with crisp fries, all of which have you licking your fingers. The killer hot fudge sundae is worth saving room for. The staff here are warm and friendly, too. This is the kind of place everyone wishes was in their neighborhood. $ *Average main: $21* ⊠ *64 Charles St., at 4th St., West Village* ☎ *646/486–2185* ⊕ *www.marysfishcamp.com* ⚓ *Reservations not accepted* Ⓜ *1 to Christopher St.–Sheridan Sq.* ⊕ *2:B1.*

SEAFOOD

$ ✕ **Moustache.** There's typically a crowd waiting outside for one of the copper-top tables at this casual Middle Eastern neighborhood restaurant. The focal point is the perfect pita that accompanies tasty salads like lemony chickpea and spinach, hearty lentil and bulgur, or falafel. Also delicious is *lahambajin*, spicy ground lamb on a crispy flat crust. For entrées, try the leg of lamb, the juicy baby lamb sandwich, or merguez sausage sandwiches. Service is slow but friendly. There are also locations in the East Village and East Harlem. $ *Average main: $12* ⊠ *90 Bedford St., between Barrow and Grove sts., West Village* ☎ *212/229–2220* ⊕ *www.moustachepitza.com* ◷ *Closed Sun.* ⚓ *Reservations not accepted* ▭ *No credit cards* Ⓜ *1 to Christopher St.–Sheridan Sq.; A, B, C, D, E, F, M to W. 4th St.* ⊕ *2:B2.*

MIDDLE EASTERN

16

$$$ ✕ **Pearl Oyster Bar.** There have been many imitators and few real competitors to this West Village seafood institution. Since 1997, Rebecca Charles has been serving arguably the best lobster roll in New York City in a no-frills space down charming, restaurant-lined Cornelia Street—and expanded next door to accommodate the throngs. But that's not the only reason you should cast your net here. Pan-roasted sea scallops and plus-size crab cakes compete with the legendary lobster roll for your taste buds' attention. Service is very efficient—you might even say rushed. $ *Average main: $25* ⊠ *18 Cornelia St., between 4th and Bleecker sts., West Village* ☎ *212/691–8211* ⊕ *www.pearloysterbar.com* ▭ *No credit cards* ◷ *Closed Sun. No lunch Sat.* Ⓜ *A, B, C, D, E, F, M to W. 4th St.* ⊕ *2:C2.*

SEAFOOD

$$$ ✕ **RedFarm.** Conceived and run by Ed Schoenfeld, an expert on Chinese cuisine, and Joe Ng, known as the dumpling king of New York, this West Village restaurant specializes in—you guessed it—Chinese-style dumplings. At least partly. The menu focuses mostly on *dim sum*—small plates and snacks (often in dumpling form)—as well as Chinese-American dishes like three-chili chicken and chicken in garlic sauce. The lobster dumplings and the crab and pork soup dumplings are culinary wonders and nearly obligatory for first-timers. But come with a wallet

CHINESE

the size of China itself because the dishes add up. Also consider trying the restaurant's duck-themed restaurant, Decoy, in the basement. There's also a location of RedFarm on Broadway and West 76th Street. [$] *Average main: $30* ✉ *529 Hudson St., between 10th and Charles sts., West Village* ☎ *212/792–9700* 🌐 *www.redfarmnyc.com* 💳 *No credit cards* 🕓 *No lunch* [M] *1 to Christopher St.–Sheridan Sq.* ✥ *2:B2.*

Snack Taverna. *Branch location at 63 Bedford Street, at Morton. See SoHo for full review.*

$$ BRITISH 🍴 **The Spotted Pig.** Part cozy English pub, part laid-back neighborhood hangout, part gastronome's lure, the Spotted Pig showcases the impeccable food of the now legendary London Chef April Bloomfield (Mario Batali and his partners consulted). Dishes like arugula salad with tangy radishes and Parmesan, and smoked haddock-and-corn chowder with homemade crackers are studies in texture and flavor contrast. Shoestring potatoes accompany the Roquefort cheeseburger. Chase it with a glass of Old Speckled Hen dripping foam. This neighborhood hangout still packs it in, so come early, or late. The Breslin, at the Ace Hotel, is another of Bloomfield's standout New York restaurants with an über-clubby feel. [$] *Average main: $24* ✉ *314 W. 11th St., at Greenwich St., West Village* ☎ *212/620–0393* 🌐 *www.thespottedpig.com* ✍ *Reservations not accepted* [M] *1 to Christopher St.–Sheridan Sq.; 2, 3 to 14th St.; L to 8th Ave.* ✥ *2:A1.*

$$$$ JAPANESE Fodor's Choice ★ 🍴 **Sushi Nakazawa.** Daisuke dreams of sushi. Fans of the acclaimed 2011 documentary *Jiro Dreams of Sushi* may remember Daisuke Nakazawa, the apprentice to the great Tokyo-based sushi master Jiro Ono, who spent the near-entirety of the film trying to perfect the egg custard. He finally succeeded, just as he has succeeded in wooing even the most finicky New York diners. It's all *omakase* (a tasting menu set by the chef) here, so sit back and enjoy two hours of being fed by one of the best sushi chefs in New York. Mr. Nakazawa practices an old Tokyo style of sushi-making—putting all his highly fresh fish on a thumb-size bundle of rice. (Sorry, sashimi fans.) Reserve at least a month in advance. [$] *Average main: $150* ✉ *23 Commerce St., near Bedford St., West Village* ☎ *212/924–2212* 🌐 *www.sushinakazawa.com* 💳 *No credit cards* 🕓 *Closed Sun. No lunch* ✍ *Reservations essential* [M] *1 to Christopher St.–Sheridan Sq.; A, B, C, D, E, F, M to W. 4th St.* ✥ *3:D6.*

$ MIDDLE EASTERN 🍴 **Taïm.** There's a real chef behind this tiny sliver of a restaurant, New York's only gourmet falafel stand. *Taïm*means "tasty" in Hebrew, and Tel Aviv transplant Einat Admony's fried chickpea balls are delicious, and available in several beguiling flavors (try them infused with spicy harissa sauce) along with a tantalizing display of à la carte salads (the carrots with Moroccan spices is a standout). There's another location in NoLIta, on Spring Street between Mott and Mulberry, as well as a food truck that makes its way around the city (you can find it via Twitter). [$] *Average main: $9* ✉ *222 Waverly Pl., near Perry St., West Village* ☎ *212/691–1287* 🌐 *www.taimfalafel.com* ✍ *Reservations not accepted* [M] *1, 2, 3 to 14th St.; L to 8th Ave.* ✥ *2:B1.*

$$$ AUSTRIAN 🍴 **Wallsé.** The modern Austrian menu at Kurt Gutenbrunner's lovely, light-filled neighborhood restaurant has a strong emphasis on Austrian tradition and urban New York attitude. It's hard to argue with such

dishes as Wiener schnitzel with potato-cucumber salad and lingonberries, or venison goulash with spaetzle and Brussels sprouts, and it's often lighter than you'd think Austrian food would be. Desserts do Vienna proud: apple-walnut strudel is served with apple sorbet. The atmosphere is casual but sophisticated—perfect for either a weeknight dinner or a special occasion. [$] *Average main: $33* ✉ *344 W. 11th St., at Washington St., West Village* ☎ *212/352–2300* 🌐 *www.wallse.com* 🕒 *No lunch Mon.–Sat.* ✍ *Reservations essential* [M] *1 to Christopher St.–Sheridan Sq.; A, C, E to 14th St.; L to 8th Ave.* ✥ *3:B6.*

$ AMERICAN FAMILY

🍴 **Westville.** If New York's neighborhoods were small country towns, they'd all have restaurants just like Westville. These adorable spots—with branches in the East and West Village, Chelsea, and west SoHo—serve simple wholesome fare, at reasonable prices. Salads, grilled chicken, burgers, and chops are all good, but the seasonal sides, which change daily based on what's fresh at the market, are the real star attraction (the "Market Plate" with any three sides is a popular dinner option). Dessert is worth saving room for, too, especially the daily pie selections. Expect a wait on weekend nights. [$] *Average main: $11* ✉ *210 W. 10th St., near Bleecker St., West Village* ☎ *212/741–7971* 🌐 *www.westvillenyc.com* [M] *1 to Christopher St.–Sheridan Sq.* ✥ *3:C6.*

16

CHELSEA AND THE MEATPACKING DISTRICT

CHELSEA

Several big-name chefs have moved to the western part of this neighborhood in recent years, putting Chelsea on the dining map. For a tasty quick bite or a gift for your favorite foodie, stop by **Chelsea Market.**

$$ PIZZA Fodor's Choice ★

🍴 **Co.** "Company," as it's pronounced, took the New York pizza scene by redsauce–scented storm when it opened in early 2009. Bread master Jim Lahey, who made a name for himself at the Sullivan Street Baking Company, crafts simple but memorable pies, the dough and crust of which play a starring role. The simple margherita (tomato sauce, mozzarella, basil) is a good way to sample Co.'s fare, but diners are always tempted by unorthodox pizzas like the carmelized-onion-walnut-purée pie or the béchamel-and-Parmesan-topped version. If you can, take a few friends, and order several pies. But it's not all pizza: the delicious veal meatballs and chicken-liver toast tempt even the most die-hard pizza lover to stray. This casual Chelsea pizzeria is anything but half baked. [$] *Average main: $17* ✉ *230 9th Ave., at 24th St., Chelsea* ☎ *212/243–1105* 🌐 *www.co-pane.com* 💳 *No credit cards* 🕒 *No lunch Mon.* [M] *C, E to 23rd St.* ✥ *3:B2.*

$$$ AMERICAN

🍴 **Cookshop.** One of far-west Chelsea's first hot restaurants, Cookshop manages a casual elegance while focusing on seasonal, farm-fresh cuisine that continues to wow. Outdoor seating on 10th Avenue is quite peaceful in the evening; during the day you can survey a cross-section of gallery-hoppers and shoppers. Divine cocktails, made with fresh fruit juices, are veritable elixirs of well-being. Line up early for brunch; it's worth the wait for dishes like baked eggs over duck and Swiss chard, or the fluffiest pancakes in town. Dinner is also a triumph, with a variety of perfectly prepared dishes like whitefish with lemony asparagus and hen-of-the-woods mushrooms, or a simple roasted chicken. [$] *Average main: $26* ✉ *156 10th Ave., at 20th St., Chelsea* ☎ *212/924–4440* 🌐 *www.cookshopny.com* ⏲ *No breakfast weekends* [M] *A, C, E to 23rd St.* ✥ *3:B3.*

> **WORD OF MOUTH**
>
> "On our last trip one of the highlights was sitting outside on the patio (actually, the sidewalk) of a restaurant in Chelsea, eating and people-watching. We would have sat in that seat for hours if they'd let us!" —Austin

$$ ECLECTIC 🍴 **Coppelia.** Named for a legendary ice cream shop in Havana, Coppelia is neither Cuban nor an ice-cream parlor. At least not strictly speaking. Chef Julian Medina has created a 24-hour pan-Latin diner that works on many levels—for a quick breakfast, casual lunch, or late-night bite. The continent-sized menu emphasizes comfort food, with satisfying dishes like the pork belly–spiked mac 'n' cheese, mountainous nachos, grilled cheese with jalapeño and bacon, and even kimchi-stuffed tacos. If you did have your *corazón* set on ice cream, there's plenty of it on the dessert menu. [$] *Average main: $15* ✉ *207 W. 14th St., between 7th and 8th aves., Chelsea* ☎ *212/858–5001* 🌐 *www.ybandco.com* 💳 *No credit cards* [M] *1, 2, 3, A, C, E, F, M to 14th St.; L to 8th Ave.* ✥ *3:C4.*

$$ CHINESE 🍴 **Legend.** Sure, there's nothing Chinese about the generic name; and the location, on a stretch of 7th Avenue in Chelsea, is flanked by forgettable eating options. But do your taste buds a favor, and eat at this affordable Sichuan spot, whose quiet opening was followed by a lot of buzz among New York's fooderati. The long menu is not for the indecisive but nearly anything is a hit, including the double-cooked bacon, the massive and flaky whole roasted fish, and the ultra-spicy ma po tofu. Dishes here lean toward the fiery side. [$] *Average main: $14* ✉ *88 7th Ave., between 15th and 16th sts., Chelsea* ☎ *212/929–1778* 🌐 *www.legendrestaurant88.com* 💳 *No credit cards* [M] *1, 2, 3, A, C, E, F, M to 14th St.; L to 8th Ave.* ✥ *3:D4.*

$$$ ITALIAN 🍴 **Mulino a Vino.** You can't throw a meatball in New York without hitting an Italian restaurant. But if there's one spot not to miss, it's this subterranean restaurant on 14th Street. The top toque is Davide Scabin, who has received all manner of acclaim for his avant-garde eatery in Italy, Combal. Zero. He tones things down a bit here, the fare balancing between weird and wonderful. The *cacio a pepe* doughnut is a pecorino-cheese-and-pepper stuffed fried ball of dough, and it's revalatory. The San Daniele's Miracle might be the best thing in the menu, though: it's the porkiest prosciutto-and-fried-lardo sandwich you will ever eat. The wine list is long and Italian, and each can be had by the bottle or glass. [$] *Average main: $30* ✉ *337 W. 14th St., Chelsea* ☎ *212/433–0818* 🌐 *www.mulinoavino.com* ⏲ *Closed Mon. No lunch Tues.–Sat.* 💳 *No credit cards* [M] *A, C, E to 14th St.; L to 8th Ave.* ✥ *3:C4.*

$$$ MODERN AMERICAN 🍴 **The Red Cat.** Elegant yet unpretentious, a lovely neighborhood spot *and* a destination restaurant, the Red Cat is a great place to chat awhile with a friend, celebrate an auspicious occasion, have a business dinner, or just an excellent meal. The American-meets-Mediterranean menu changes frequently, based on what's in season, but expect an

eclectic menu of well-executed pastas, burgers, saffron-laced seafood, and meaty numbers. Factor in the affordable wine list and you'll most definitely feel like one lucky cat. [$] *Average main: $25* ✉ *227 10th Ave., between 23rd and 24th sts., Chelsea* ☎ *212/242–1122* 🌐 *www.redcatrestaurants.com* 💳 *No credit cards* [M] *C, E to 23rd St.* ✣ *3:A2.*

$ SPANISH 🍴 **Tía Pol.** It may be sardine-can small and dark, but that doesn't stop this popular tapas bar from being packed most nights. This is one of the best tapas spots in town, with a welcoming vibe, a dozen reasonably priced Spanish wines by the glass, and charm to spare. One of the most original tapas has become a signature here: bittersweet chocolate smeared on a baguette disc and topped with salty Spanish chorizo. *Patatas bravas* (rough-cut potatoes served with spicy aioli) are so addictive, you won't want to share them. The pork loin, piquillo pepper, and mild tetilla cheese sandwich is scrumptious, and so is the Galician octopus terrine. Tía Pol is also a great spot to stop and snack midway through a High Line jaunt. [$] *Average main: $13* ✉ *205 10th Ave., between 22nd and 23rd sts., Chelsea* ☎ *212/675–8805* 🌐 *www.tiapol.com* ✍ *Reservations essential* [M] *C, E to 23rd St.* ✣ *3:A2.*

$$ SOUTHERN 🍴 **Tipsy Parson.** If New York's Chelsea neighborhood were magically transported to the American South, the food might taste something like it does at this hip, southern-accented eatery with a menu of artery-hardening delights. Named for a boozy southern dessert, the Tipsy Parson and its menu are all about comfort in the belly and soul: fried pickles, homemade peanut butter with crackers, bourbon-laced chicken liver mousse, and seafood potpie are designed to make you full and happy. The restaurant's close proximity to the High Line, the elevated park and greenway, means you can walk it all off afterward. [$] *Average main: $24* ✉ *156 9th Ave., between 19th and 20th sts., Chelsea* ☎ *212/620–4545* 🌐 *www.tipsyparson.com* 💳 *No credit cards* [M] *C, E to 23rd St.* ✣ *3:B3.*

$$ SWISS 🍴 **Trestle on Tenth.** Cozy and warm with an inviting exposed brick interior, this Swiss brasserie is a true west Chelsea neighborhood spot. Locals and gallery-hoppers quaff foamy beers and glasses of wine from the reasonable list while awaiting hearty Alpine-inspired dishes. Crispy duck necks, calves' liver with potato *rösti* and butter lettuce with bacon are favorites. It's not art—for that, hit up one of the many galleries in the neighborhood—but it makes you yearn for Alpine landscapes. The location is convenient to the High Line. [$] *Average main: $20* ✉ *242 10th Ave., at 24th St., Chelsea* ☎ *212/645–5659* 🌐 *www.trestleontenth.com* 💳 *No credit cards* [M] *C, E to 23rd St.* ✣ *3:A2.*

$$ SPANISH 🍴 **Txikito.** After being wined and dined at this popular Chelsea Spanish restaurant, you'd never guess that Chef Alexandra Raij is from very un-Spanish Minneapolis. Her husband and business partner is, though, and the duo put on an impressive show. The theme is *cucina vasca,* or Basque cuisine, one of the most exciting regions in Iberia for eating. Raij captures the moment by serving standouts like juicy lamb meatballs in a minty broth, crispy beef tongue, and an addictive crabmeat gratin. The wine list at Txikito (pronounced Chi-kee-toe) is loaded with great bottles of Rioja and other tempranillos, many of which are from Basque winemakers. [$] *Average main: $15* ✉ *240 9th Ave., at 25th St.,*

Chelsea ☎ *212/242–4730* 🌐 *www.txikitonyc.com* 🕒 *No lunch* [M] *C, E to 23rd St.* ✥ *3:B2.*

MEATPACKING DISTRICT

Europeans, models, actors, and the people who love them stroll the sidewalk like they're on a catwalk, going from one hot restaurant to the next in this cobblestone-laden neighborhood, which has become almost too sceney for its own good. There's plenty of great eating here—you just might have to wait a while (or impersonate a celebrity) to get a table.

$$$$ ITALIAN 🍴 **Del Posto.** Much more formal than Babbo, Del Posto is Mario Batali's grown-up venue (in partnership with Lidia and Joe Bastianich), and the dining room—with its sweeping staircase, formal décor, and live music from a baby grand—has the feel of an opulent hotel lobby. This is one of the most consistently dazzling special-occasion spots in the city, and the food is stellar. There are a variety of set menus to choose from ($126 for five courses; $179 for eight), plusà la carte options for parties of four and under. Pitch-perfect risotto is made fresh to order for two people or more, meat dishes like roasted veal chops are standouts, and pastas are ethereal—all with old-world tableside service. For a smaller taste of the experience, come for a cocktail and sample the bargain bar menu. [$] *Average main: $60* ✉ *85 10th Ave., between 15th and 16th sts., Meatpacking District* ☎ *212/497–8090* 🌐 *www.delposto.com* 🕒 *No lunch weekends* ✍ *Reservations essential* [M] *A, C, E to 14th St.; L to 8th Ave.* ✥ *3:A4.*

$$ ASIAN 🍴 **Spice Market.** Set in a cavernous space amid embroidered curtains and artifacts from Burma, India, and Malaysia, Chef Jean-Georges Vongerichten's playful take on Southeast Asian street food keeps you asking the waiters, "What exactly was in that?" Sometimes the playfulness works, sometimes it doesn't, but don't miss the steamed lobster with garlic, ginger, and dried chili, or the squid salad with papaya and cashews. This may not be the hottest new restaurant on the block anymore, but it's still a fun Meatpacking venue with food that doesn't disappoint. [$] *Average main: $23* ✉ *403 W. 13th St., at 9th Ave., Meatpacking District* ☎ *212/675–2322* 🌐 *www.spicemarketnewyork.com* ✍ *Reservations essential* [M] *A, C, E to 14th St.; L to 8th Ave.* ✥ *3:B4.*

$$$ AMERICAN 🍴 **The Standard Grill.** Hotelier Andre Balazs created a scene for celebs, fashion-industry insiders, and the common folk, too, who all cluster at this buzzy restaurant inside the Standard Hotel. In warm weather, the spacious outdoor seating area is perfect for sampling creative cocktails; there's an indoor bar, too, and two dining rooms—a casual one in front and a larger room in back, with a floor whimsically made up of thousands of glittering pennies. The menu is comfort-luxe, with dishes like roast chicken for two in a cast-iron skillet and delicious moist trout with a currant-and-pine-nut relish. For dessert, there's a nearly obscene chocolate mousse that comes with silicone spatulas in lieu of spoons. A late-night menu is served until 4 am. [$] *Average main: $30* ✉ *848 Washington St., between Little W. 12th and 13th sts., Meatpacking District* ☎ *212/645–4100* 🌐 *www.thestandardgrill.com* 💳 *No credit cards* [M] *A, C, E to 14th St.; L to 8th Ave.* ✥ *3:B4.*

UNION SQUARE WITH THE FLATIRON DISTRICT AND GRAMERCY

UNION SQUARE

Once the main spot in New York to go for protests, Union Square is now the stage for another type of communal experience: breaking bread. There is no shortage of appealing options at any price range (including picnic provisions from the wonderful greenmarket, open Monday, Wednesday, Friday, and Saturday).

$$$$ AMERICAN Fodor'sChoice ★ 🍴 **Gotham Bar & Grill.** A culinary landmark, Gotham Bar & Grill is every bit as thrilling as when it opened in 1984. Celebrated chef Alfred Portale, who made the blueprint for "architectural food"—that is, towers of stacked ingredients—builds on a foundation of simple, clean flavors. People come for Portale's transcendent preparations: no rack of lamb is more tender, no seafood salad sweeter. The stellar 20,000-bottle cellar provides the perfect accompaniments—at a price. The three-course $35 greenmarket-driven prix-fixe lunch, served weekdays from noon to 2:15, is a steal, even if it's not as sophisticated as dinner. Take a stroll through the Union Square Greenmarket before or after lunch to see the chef's inspirations. Desserts are also memorable. [$] *Average main: $41* ✉ *12 E. 12th St., between 5th Ave. and University Pl., Union Square* ☎ *212/620–4020* 🌐 *www.gothambarandgrill.com* 🕒 *No lunch weekends* [M] *4, 5, 6, L, N, Q, R to 14th St.–Union Sq.* ✥ *3:E4.*

$ ASIAN 🍴 **Republic.** When Republic first opened, it was one of very few places to get an Asian-style noodle bowl with a stylish edge. Many have followed in its footsteps—and some are better—but for window-shoppers, greenmarketers, and anyone else in the Union Square area, this is a fun stop for a meal. The look is a cross between a downtown art gallery and a Japanese school cafeteria, and the young waitstaff dressed in black T-shirts and jeans hold remote-control ordering devices to accelerate the already speedy service. Sit at the long, bluestone bar or at the picnic-style tables, and order appetizers such as smoky grilled eggplant and luscious fried wontons. Spicy coconut chicken soup and Vietnamese-style barbecue pork are menu standouts. [$] *Average main: $14* ✉ *37 Union Sq. W, between 16th and 17th sts., Union Square* ☎ *212/627–7172* 🌐 *www.thinknoodles.com* ✍ *Reservations not accepted* [M] *4, 5, 6, L, N, Q, R to 14th St.–Union Sq.* ✥ *3:F4.*

$$$ MODERN MEXICAN 🍴 **Rosa Mexicano.** The idea that you can't find good south-of-the-border cuisine in the Big Apple is quickly fading, thanks in part to this Union Square restaurant (there are two other locations, at Lincoln Center and in Midtown East). Although the spacious, colorfully lighted interior might tip you off that authenticity is best sought elsewhere, if you're looking for high-quality, well-executed Mex-flavored fare, step right up, hombre. Start with an order of guac (made tableside), moving on to the pork belly and scallop tacos, soul-comforting chicken tortilla pie, or the crispy pork shank—-all of which taste better with a margarita. The daily happy hour at the bar is a great deal but gets crowded. [$] *Average main: $28* ✉ *9 E. 18th St., between 5th Ave. and Union Sq. W, Union Square* ☎ *212/533–3350* 🌐 *www.rosamexicano.com* 💳 *No credit cards* [M] *4, 5, 6, L, N, Q, R to 14th St.–Union Sq.* ✥ *3:F3.*

$$$ MODERN AMERICAN 🍴 **Tocqueville.** Hidden just steps from busy Union Square, this refined dining oasis is a secret even to many New Yorkers. Enter through the austere reception area, past the heavy curtains and six-seat bar, and find the intimate dining area where chef and owner Marco Moreira's signature starter is the unctuous angel hair sea-urchin carbonara. Main courses are steeped in French tradition, with international flavors like saffron-and-fennel-spiked grilled octopus, and smoked duck breast paired with baby bok choy and Asian pear. The three-course $29 prix-fixe lunch is the ultimate deal. Jacket and tie are recommended. [$] *Average main: $30* ✉ *1 E. 15th St., between 5th Ave. and Union Sq. W, Union Square* ☎ *212/647–1515* 🌐 *www.tocquevillerestaurant.com* 🕘 *Closed Sun.* ✍ *Reservations essential* [M] *4, 5, 6, L, N, Q, R to 14th St.–Union Sq.* ✥ *3:E4.*

FLATIRON DISTRICT

The popular Union Square Greenmarket has done wonders for the dining landscape in the area. Chefs, wanting to be close to the green bounty, have opened up restaurants nearby, particularly in the Flatiron District.

$$$ AMERICAN 🍴 **ABC Kitchen.** Much more than a shopping break, Jean-Georges Vongerichten's popular restaurant, inside posh housewares emporium ABC Carpet and Home, is more like a love letter to greenmarket cuisine. Underneath the exposed concrete beams, a chic crowd devours fresh, flavorful appetizers like the roasted carrot salad with avocado, crème fraîche, and toasted pumpkin seeds, or pretzel-dusted calamari. Winning entrées include roast suckling pig with smoked bacon marmalade and sea bass with chilis and herbs. The restaurant is committed to all the right causes—environmentalism, sustainability, supporting local farmers—all of which are announced in a near manifesto-length list on the back of the menu; thankfully, ABC Kitchen pulls it off without seeming patronizing or preachy. [$] *Average main: $28* ✉ *35 E. 18th St., between Broadway and Park Ave. S, Flatiron* ☎ *212/475–5829* 🌐 *www.abckitchennyc.com* ✍ *Reservations essential* [M] *4, 5, 6, L, N, Q, R to 14th St.–Union Sq.* ✥ *3:F3.*

$$$ PORTUGUESE 🍴 **Aldea.** Bouley alumnus George Mendes's popular restaurant relies on his Portuguese heritage as inspiration, which he elevates to new heights. Although there are no bad seats in this sleek bilevel space decorated with wood, glass, and blue accents, watching Mendes work in his spotless tiled kitchen from one of the seats at the chef's counter in the back is undeniably exciting. *Petiscos* (small bites) like cubes of crisp pork belly with apple cider reveal sophisticated cooking techniques and flavors. A delicate matsutake mushroom broth floated with a slow-poached egg is edged with a subtle brace of pine, while sea-salted cod reveals a deep, satisfying flavor strata. [$] *Average main: $33* ✉ *31 W. 17th St., between 5th and 6th aves., Flatiron District* ☎ *212/675–7223* 🌐 *www.aldearestaurant.com* 🕘 *Closed Sun. No lunch* ✍ *Reservations essential* [M] *4, 5, 6, L, N, Q, R to 14th St.–Union Sq.; F, M to 14th St.* ✥ *3:E3.*

$$ SPANISH 🍴 **Boqueria.** Perenially packed, this convivial tapas spot has leather banquettes lining the main room and a few seats at the bar, but if you want to make friends, opt for the communal table running down the center of the dining room—if you can get a seat. Fried quail eggs and chorizo on roasted bread are even better than they sound, and the mushroom

and ham croquettes are a mainstay. Traditional churros come with a thick hot chocolate for dipping. The original spot in the Flatiron District was so popular it spawned an offshoot in SoHo, at 171 Spring Street. $ *Average main: $19* ⊠ *53 W. 19th St., between 5th and 6th aves., Flatiron District* ☎ *212/255–4160* ⊕ *www.boquerianyc.com* ⌕ *Reservations not accepted* Ⓜ *1 to 18th St.; F, M to 14th St.; L to 6th Ave.; N, R to 23rd St.* ✛ *3:E3.*

$$$ ✕ **The Breslin Bar and Dining Room.** A sceney meatopia inside the ever-
BRITISH   trendy Ace Hotel, the Breslin is not for the Lipitor crowd. English chef
Fodor'sChoice   April Bloomfield, who also runs the John Dory right next door and the
★   excellent Spotted Pig in the West Village, hardens arteries with peanuts fried in pork fat, whipped lardo on pizza bianca, blood sausage accompanied by a fried duck egg, and a delicious feta-topped lamb burger. The dimly lighted, wood-bedecked interior is like a culinary womb, inspiring thoughts of planting yourself there all day or night nursing pints of cask-conditioned ale or scotch-based cocktails—you wouldn't be the first (or last). $ *Average main: $30* ⊠ *16 W. 29th St., at Broadway, Flatiron District* ☎ *212/679–1939* ⊕ *www.thebreslin.com* ▭ *No credit cards* Ⓜ *N, R to 28th St.* ✛ *3:E1.*

$ ✕ **The City Bakery.** This self-service bakery-restaurant has the urban
AMERICAN   aesthetic to match its name. Chef and owner Maury Rubin's baked
FAMILY   goods—giant cookies; addictively flaky, salty-sweet pretzel croissants; elegant caramel tarts—are unfailingly rich and delicious, but another major draw is the salad bar. It may seem overpriced, but the large selection of impeccably fresh food, including whole sides of baked salmon, roasted vegetables, soups, and several Asian-accented dishes, delivers a lot of bang for the buck. Much of the produce comes from the nearby farmers' market. In winter, the bakery hosts a hot-chocolate festival; in summer, it's lemonade time. $ *Average main: $12* ⊠ *3 W. 18th St., between 5th and 6th aves., Flatiron District* ☎ *212/366–1414* ⊕ *www. thecitybakery.com* ☾ *No dinner* ⌕ *Reservations not accepted* Ⓜ *4, 5, 6, L, N, Q, R to 14th St.–Union Sq.; F, M to 14th St.* ✛ *3:E3.*

$$$ ✕ **Cosme.** When Enrique Olvera, chef at Pujol, arguably Mexico's best
MEXICAN   restaurant, announced he was coming north of the border, New York
Fodor'sChoice   foodies went loco. Olvera's haute touch to his native cuisine is magic
★   and, coupled with the sleek design (soft lighting, minimalist décor), Cosme makes for one fine dining experience. Sip an Expat Martini (it comes with a pickled tomatilla pepper floating in it) and peruse the menu of small plates: start with the hamachi crudo, impossibly complex with lime and chili bringing out a charge in the fish; and move on to lobster pibil with chorizo, which beautifully marries the surf and turf concept. $ *Average main: $30* ⊠ *35 E. 21st St., Flatiron District* ☎ *212/913–9659* ⊕ *www.cosmenyc.com* ☾ *No lunch* ⌕ *Reservations essential* Ⓜ *N, R, 6 to 23rd St.* ✛ *3:F3.*

$$$$ ✕ **Craft.** A meal here is like a luscious choose-your-own-adventure
MODERN   game since every delectable dish comes à la carte. Craft is the flag-
AMERICAN   ship of *Top Chef* head judge Tom Colicchio's mini-empire of excellent restaurants around the country, including the upscale Craftbar and Craftsteak brands, as well as grab-and-go sandwich bars called 'wichcraft. Just about everything here is exceptionally prepared with little

16

fuss, from simple yet intriguing starters (like harissa-spiked octopus) and sides (including the justly famous variety of roasted mushrooms, with oysters, trumpets, chanterelles, and hen-of-the-woods) to desserts (warm chocolate tart with buttermilk ice cream, cinnamon custard, and cashews). The serene dining room of burnished dark wood and dangling radiant bulbs is more welcoming than it sounds. $ *Average main: $40* ✉ *43 E. 19th St., between Broadway and Park Ave. S, Flatiron District* ☏ *212/780–0880* ⊕ *www.craftrestaurant.com* ☽ *No lunch* ☖ *Reservations essential* Ⓜ *4, 5, 6, L, N, Q, R to 14th St.–Union Sq.* ✛ *3:F3.*

$$$
MODERN
AMERICAN
✕ **Craftbar.** This casual sibling to Tom Colicchio's Craft is a bargain by comparison but still not cheap, though the food continues to garner raves and the service is consistently excellent. The menu features assertive seasonal cooking similar to what you can find at the upscale flagship just around the corner. The small-plates category on the menu elevates tiny nibbles like sausage-stuffed fried sage leaves or addictive fluffy salt-cod croquettes to temptations that make you forget the main course entirely. The rest of the menu is eclectic enough to satisfy. $ *Average main: $25* ✉ *900 Broadway, between 19th and 20th sts., Flatiron District* ☏ *212/461–4300* ⊕ *www.craftbarnyc.com* ☖ *Reservations essential* Ⓜ *4, 5, 6, L, N, Q, R to 14th St.–Union Sq.* ✛ *3:F3.*

$
BAKERY
FAMILY
✕ **Dough.** There's a reason why these doughnuts in multilicious flavors have become a signature at so many cafés throughout Manhattan and Brooklyn——the dough is the perfect combination of light and airy, with enough substance to not be overwhelmed by toppings. And at the Manhattan outpost of the Bed-Stuy original, you can get them fresh out of the oven. Can't decide what kind? The hibiscus has just the right amount of tart fruitiness to balance the sweetness of the dough; other favorites include passion fruit, salted chocolate, and cinnamon and sugar. The coffee's good and the rustic benches mean you can linger long enough to think about going back for another (they taste good the next day, too). $ *Average main: $3* ✉ *14 W. 19th St., Flatiron District* ☏ *212/243—6844* ⊕ *www.doughdoughnuts.com* Ⓜ *N, R to E. 23rd St.* ✛ *3:E3.*

$$$
ITALIAN
✕ **Eataly.** The cavernous Eataly, from Mario Batali & Co., is a temple to all things Italian. Ignore the overpriced produce market by the front entrance and make a beeline for La Piazza for sandwiches made with meticulously sourced ingredients (you can eat at the stand-up tables nearby). There's also a full-service pizza and pasta restaurant, a raw bar and fish eatery, and a wine bar for quaffing glass pours and beers on tap. Gourmet Italian chocolates, coffees, gelati, and pastries are all delicious for take-away, too, though still not cheap. Upstairs, the covered, rooftop birreria is open in all weather and serves hearty Austrian and German food as well as Italian specialties—and excellent beer, of course. $ *Average main: $25* ✉ *200 5th Ave., at 23rd St., Flatiron District* ☏ *646/398–5100* ⊕ *www.eatalyny.com* ☖ *Reservations not accepted* Ⓜ *N, R, 6 to 23rd St.* ✛ *3:E2.*

$$$$
MODERN
AMERICAN
Fodor's Choice
★
✕ **Eleven Madison Park.** Luxury, precision, and creativity are the driving forces at this internationally renowned restaurant overlooking Madison Park. Swiss-born chef Daniel Humm oversees the kitchen, concocting unexpected dishes that change often. It's entirely prix-fixe, and dishes are kept minimalist, giving Humm and company maximum latitude to

work their magic on the plate. Not that they're resting on their laurels and accolades: the restaurant seems to reinvent itself when you least expect it, and its most recent incarnation focuses on elevated versions of classic New York fare. Think cognac-doused, truffle-sprinkled foie gras and Sichuan peppercorn–encrusted duck. Reservations should be made two months in advance. [$] *Average main: $225* ✉ *11 Madison Ave., at 24th St., Flatiron District* ☎ *212/889–0905* 🌐 *www.elevenmadisonpark.com* 🕓 *No lunch Sun.–Wed.* ✍ *Reservations essential* [M] *N, R, 6 to 23rd St.* ✥ *3:F2.*

$$ SEAFOOD

🍴 **The John Dory.** Chef April Bloomfield and former rock band manager-turned-restaurateur Ken Friedman can do no wrong. After winning tastebuds and palates with gastropub Spotted Pig and the Breslin, the duo turned their attention to the sea. Fish tanks with brightly colored reefs and floor-to-ceiling windows create an eye-pleasing venue for the seafood feast that awaits those who snagged tables at this restaurant off the lobby of the hip Ace Hotel. The menu is dominated by small plates—chorizo-stuffed squid, an excellent lobster roll—but focuses on *crudo* (raw) dishes. The happy-hour special of $2 oysters and half off certain wines and beers is the perfect start to an evening. [$] *Average main: $20* ✉ *1196 Broadway, at 29th St., Flatiron District* ☎ *212/792–9000* 🌐 *www.thejohndory.com* 💳 *No credit cards* ✍ *Reservations not accepted* [M] *N, R to 28th St.* ✥ *3:E1.*

16

$$ FRENCH FAMILY

🍴 **Les Halles.** This local hangout, owned by Philippe Lajaunie since 1990 and benefiting from the celebrity of former executive chef, writer, and TV host Anthony Bourdain (although he has little to do with the restaurant these days), is boisterous and unpretentious—like a true French brasserie. A good bet is steak frites, its fries regarded by some as the best in New York. Other prime choices include crispy duck-leg confit with frisée salad, blood sausage with caramelized apples, and steak tartare, prepared tableside. Another Les Halles is in Lower Manhattan at 15 John Street. [$] *Average main: $22* ✉ *411 Park Ave. S, between 28th and 29th sts., Flatiron District* ☎ *212/679–4111* 🌐 *www.leshalles.net* [M] *6 to 28th St.* ✥ *3:F1.*

$$$ MODERN AMERICAN Fodor's Choice ★

🍴 **The NoMad.** Named for the hotel, which itself is named for the up-and-coming neighborhood north of Madison Square Park, the NoMad is brought to you by Daniel Humm and Will Guidara, the masterminds behind much-lauded Eleven Madison Park. The atmosphere is a blend of lively and sophisticated: plush velvet chairs and drapes for the hip young crowd that frequent the place. The food is similalry vibrant yet simple: seared scalllops are paired with pumpkin, juicy suckling pig goes very nicely with pear confit and mustard. The poached egg and quinoa dish unexpectedly transforms into a stew once the yolks are broken. The restaurant's pièce de résistance is the whole roasted chicken for two, which looks basic until the foie gras and black truffles are uncovered. Have a nightcap in the dimly lit and atmospheric Library Bar, which has floor-to-ceiling bookshelves and comfy chairs. [$] *Average main: $34* ✉ *1170 Broadway, at 28th St., Flatiron District* ☎ *347/472–5660* 🌐 *www.thenomadhotel.com* 💳 *No credit cards* ✍ *Reservations essential* [M] *N, R to 28th St.* ✥ *3:E2.*

$$$
ITALIAN

✕ **SD26.** The charming father-daughter restaurant team of Tony and Marisa May closed uptown's San Domenico to open this more casual yet still impressive Italian spot. The cavernous main dining room, decorated with a constellation of pinpoint lights and ringed with more intimate tables and banquettes, speaks to a fresher, more modern approach than its predecessor took. The food—pappardelle with wild boar ragout, smoked lobster with porcini mushrooms and orange segments—is a refreshing mix of classic and forward-thinking. Expect a personal greeting from either father or daughter before your meal comes to an end. Ⓢ *Average main: $26* ✉ *19 E. 26th St., between 5th and Madison aves., Flatiron District* ☎ *212/265–5959* ⊕ *www.sd26ny.com* ⊙ *Closed Sun.* ⌖ *Reservations essential* Ⓜ *N, R to 23rd St.; 6 to 28th St.* ✛ *3:F2.*

$
AMERICAN
Fodor's Choice
★

✕ **Shake Shack.** Although there are other locations of Danny Meyer's patties 'n' shakes joint around town (including Brooklyn), this is where it all began. Here in Madison Square Park, there's no indoor seating— just snaking outdoor lines. Check the "Shack Cam" from their website to gauge your wait. Fresh Angus beef burgers are ground daily, and a single will run you from $4.60 to $8.80, depending on what you want on it. For a burger on-the-go, they're decidedly tasty. For a few more bucks you can order a double, a stack, or a vegetarian 'Shroom Burger—a super-rich melty Muenster-and-cheddar-stuffed, fried portobello, topped with lettuce, tomato, and Shack sauce. The menu also offers "beef and bird" (chicken) hot dogs, french fries, and a variety of delicious frozen custard desserts, and—of course—shakes! Ⓢ *Average main: $6* ✉ *Madison Square Park, near Madison Ave. and 23rd St., Flatiron District* ☎ *212/889–6600* ⊕ *www.shakeshack.com* Ⓜ *N, R, 6 to 23rd St.* ✛ *3:F2.*

GRAMERCY

This leafy, high-rent neighborhood, which has an old-world, old-money feel, is home to a few gems, tucked away down the long blocks of brownstones. Gramercy is a great place for a stroll before dinner.

$$$$
STEAKHOUSE

✕ **BLT Prime.** A masculine, vivacious space is the showcase for bold, appealing Franco-American cuisine. Menu specials are scrawled on a blackboard. Everything is served à la carte, and prices are high, but so is the quality of every dish. Although there are poultry, veal, and lamb dishes on the menu—from lemon-rosemary chicken to a lamb T-bone— steaks are the main event. The dry-aged USDA prime steaks—pulled from a 30-foot-wide dry-aging room—are broiled at 1,700 degrees, spread lightly with herb butter and served with a choice of sauce (the béarnaise is perfection). Ⓢ *Average main: $40* ✉ *111 E. 22nd St., between Lexington and Park aves., Gramercy Park* ☎ *212/995–8500* ⊕ *www.bltprime.com* ⊙ *No lunch* ⌖ *Reservations essential* Ⓜ *N, R, 6 to 23rd St.* ✛ *3:F2.*

$$
SPANISH

✕ **Casa Mono.** Andy Nusser put in his time cooking Italian under Mario Batali at Babbo before an obsession with Spain landed him his own acclaimed Iberian niche. The perennially cramped and crowded Casa Mono sends patrons to Bar Jamón, the wine-and-ham-bar annex next door, where you can pick at plates of *jamón serrano* while awaiting the main feature. Our favorite seats are at the Casa Mono counter overlooking the chef's open kitchen. Though most menu items are delectably shareable, of particular note are all things seared *à la plancha,* including blistered peppers and garlic-kissed mushrooms. Like his mentor, Nusser has a weakness for the neglected cuts of meat so check your food fears at the door. $ *Average main: $20* ⊠ *52 Irving Pl., at 17th St., Gramercy Park* ☎ *212/253–2773* ⊕ *www.casamononyc.com* ☉ *No Lunch weekdays* Ⓜ *4, 5, 6, L, N, Q, R to 14th St.–Union Sq.* ✢ *3:G3.*

$$$$　✕ **Gramercy Tavern.** Danny Meyer's intensely popular restaurant tops
AMERICAN　many a New Yorker's list of favorite dining spots. In front, the first-come, first-served tavern has a lighter menu—including a value-packed three-course prix-fixe—along with great craft beers and cocktails scrawled on a board at the bar. The more formal dining room has a prix-fixe American menu, where choices include seasonal dishes such as marinated sea scallops with pickled peppers and fresh grapes, and rack of lamb with sunchokes, hazelnuts, and exotic mushrooms. Meyer's restaurants— he owns several well-regarded eateries in the city—are renowned for their food and hospitality, and Gramercy Tavern sets the standard. $ *Average main: $35* ⊠ *42 E. 20th St., between Broadway and Park Ave. S, Gramercy Park* ☎ *212/477–0777* ⊕ *www.gramercytavern.com* ⌂ *Reservations essential* Ⓜ *N, R, 6 to 23rd St.* ✢ *3:F3.*

$$$　✕ **Maialino.** Named for its signature dish—suckling pig—the perpetually
ROMAN　packed restaurant in the Gramercy Park Hotel is what it might look like if Manhattan and Rome collided: fashionable people eating in an Eternal City ambience. If you haven't been to the Italian capital in a while, there's plenty to reintroduce your taste buds to *la dolce vita*: excellent fried artichokes, spaghetti alla carbonara (made with *guanciale,* or pig cheek, just like in Rome), and sausage-studded pasta dish *lumaconi alla Norcia.* It's enough to make a toast to the good life—that is, if your dining companions can hear you over the chatter of the fashion models and bankers at surrounding tables. $ *Average main: $26* ⊠ *2 Lexington Ave., at 21st St., Gramercy Park* ☎ *212/777–2410* ⊕ *www. maialinonyc.com* ▭ *No credit cards* ⌂ *Reservations essential* Ⓜ *6 to 23rd St.* ✢ *3:G3.*

16

MIDTOWN EAST WITH MURRAY HILL

MIDTOWN EAST

Midtown East's streets are relatively quiet at night and on weekends, but during the week, the restaurants are filled with expense-account diners celebrating their successes. Indeed, some of the most formal dining rooms and most expensive meals in town can be found here.

$$$$　✕ **Aquavit and Aquavit Café.** This elegant and refined Scandinavian res-
SCANDINAVIAN　taurant has seen a transition in the kitchen these last few years, going from Marcus Samuelsson to Marcus Jernmark, until he, too, exited. The place is now in steady hands with Emma Bengtsson at the helm. The elegant atmosphere features warm woods and modern Scandinavian design. There are a few options here: a $135 eight-course meal, $85 three-course affair, and a $105 six-course dinner that changes according to the season. Standout dishes include foie gras paired with liquorice, sweetbreads paired with sauerkraut, venison tartare, and for dessert,

smoked vanilla crème brûlée. Head to the sumptuous bar area to sample housemade aquavit. [$] *Average main: $70* ✉ *65 E. 55th St., between Madison and Park aves., Midtown East* ☎ *212/307–7311* 🌐 *www.aquavit.org* ⏲ *Closed Sun. No lunch Sat.* ✍ *Reservations essential* [M] *E, M to 5th Ave./53rd St.* ✥ *4:F2.*

$$$ STEAKHOUSE 🍴 **BLT Steak.** Chef Laurent Tourondel may no longer be involved with his namesake steakhouse, but this classy space, decked out in beige with resin-top black tables, still draws crowds. As soon as you're settled, puffy Gruyère popovers arrive still steaming. The no-muss, no-fuss menu is nonetheless large, and so are the portions of supple crab cakes with celery-infused mayonnaise and luscious ruby tuna tartare with avocado, ramped up with soy-lime dressing. A veal chop crusted with rosemary and Parmesan lends new depth to the meat. Sides and desserts, like a killer peanut butter–chocolate mousse with banana ice cream, are all superior. [$] *Average main: $33* ✉ *106 E. 57th St., between Lexington and Park aves., Midtown East* ☎ *212/752–7470* 🌐 *www.bltsteak.com* ⏲ *No lunch weekends* ✍ *Reservations essential* [M] *4, 5, 6, N, R, Q to 59th St./Lexington Ave.* ✥ *4:F1.*

$$$$ AMERICAN 🍴 **The Four Seasons.** The landmark Seagram Building houses one of America's most famous restaurants, truly an only-in-New-York experience. Owners Alex Von Bidder and Julian Niccolini supervise the seating chart like hawks, placing power players in finance, entertainment, and New York society in prime positions for maximum visibility. The stark Grill Room, birthplace of the power lunch, has one of the best bars in New York (and the $28 two-course bar lunch is a steal). Illuminated trees and a gurgling Carrara marble pool characterize the more romantic Pool Room. The menu changes seasonally; there's a $75 prix-fixe pretheater dinner—a delicious indulgence. You can't go wrong with classic dishes like Dover sole, filet mignon, or crispy duck, but the restaurant moves with the times, so expect seasonal specials featuring luxe ingredients and preparations. [$] *Average main: $60* ✉ *99 E. 52nd St., between Park and Lexington aves., Midtown East* ☎ *212/754–9494* 🌐 *www.fourseasonsrestaurant.com* ⏲ *Closed Sun. No lunch Sat.* ✍ *Reservations essential* 👔 *Jacket required* [M] *E, M to Lexington Ave./53rd St.; 6 to 51st St.* ✥ *4:F2.*

$$$ SEAFOOD 🍴 **Grand Central Oyster Bar & Restaurant.** Deep in the belly of Grand Central Station, the vast Oyster Bar has been a worthy seafood destination since 1913. Sit at the counter for the fried oyster po'boy or to slurp an assortment of bracingly fresh oysters before a steaming bowl of clam chowder, washed down with an ice-cold beer. This is also the place to experience the pleasure of fresh, unadorned seafood, such as lobster with drawn butter or grilled herring in season—generally better options than anything that sounds too complicated, like a cream-smothered seafood pan-roast. [$] *Average main: $30* ✉ *Grand Central Terminal, dining concourse, 42nd St. at Vanderbilt Ave., Midtown East* ☎ *212/490–6650* 🌐 *www.oysterbarny.com* ⏲ *Closed Sun.* [M] *4, 5, 6, 7, S to Grand Central–42nd St.* ✥ *4:F4.*

$$$$ JAPANESE 🍴 **Kurumazushi.** Only a small sign in Japanese indicates the location of this extraordinary restaurant that serves sushi and sashimi exclusively. Bypass the tables, sit at the sushi bar, and put yourself in the

hands of Toshihiro Uezu, the chef and owner. Among the selections are hard-to-find fish that Uezu imports directly from Japan. The most attentive, pampering staff in the city completes the wildly expensive experience. The showstopping chef's *omakase*, priced at whatever the market dictates and the type of fish on offer, could run as much as $300, but it's a multicourse feast you'll never forget. $ *Average main: $175* ⌧ *7 E. 47th St., 2nd fl., between 5th and Madison aves., Midtown East* ☎ *212/317–2802* ⊕ *www.kurumazushi.com* ⊘ *Closed Sun.* ⌕ *Reservations essential* Ⓜ *4, 5, 6, 7, S to Grand Central–42nd St.* ✛ *4:E3.*

$$$$ ✕ **Le Cirque.** Impresario-owner Sirio Maccioni still presides over this
FRENCH   dining room, filled nightly with a "who's who" of politics, business, and society—regulars who've table-hopped from Le Cirque's first incarnation to its latest, in a glass-enclosed aerie on the ground floor of the Bloomberg headquarters. The menu strikes a balance between the creative and classic: Dover sole, filleted tableside, gives way to more avant-garde preparations like foie gras ravioli. Desserts, too, have a split personality, with the menu divided into the "classic" and "new." The foot-tall napoleon that seems to arrive at every second table is an old favorite, but newer creations like the praline tortellini with exotic fruit also satisfy. Though jackets are still required in the dining room, things are more relaxed in the casual wine lounge. $ *Average main: $60* ⌧ *151 E. 58th St., at Lexington Ave., Midtown East* ☎ *212/644–0202* ⊕ *www. lecirque.com* ⊘ *Closed Sun. No lunch Sat.* ⌕ *Reservations essential* Ⓜ *4, 5, 6 to 59th St.; N, Q, R to Lexington Ave./59th St.* ✛ *4:F1.*

$$$ ✕ **Michael Jordan's The Steakhouse NYC.** Don't be dissuaded by the fact
STEAKHOUSE   that this place is technically part of a chain: there's nowhere remotely like it. The handsomely appointed space in Grand Central Terminal, hung with gracious filigree chandeliers, overlooks one of the most famous interiors in America. Start with the stack of soft, toasted bread soldiers in a pool of hot Gorgonzola fondue. Pristine oysters make a great prelude for a prime dry-aged ribeye or a 2½-pound lobster, grilled, steamed, sautéed, or broiled. Sides, like creamy mac 'n' cheese and a crispy rosemary hash-brown cake, are equally tempting. $ *Average main: $32* ⌧ *Grand Central Terminal, West Balcony, 23 Vanderbilt Ave., between 43rd and 44th sts., Midtown East* ☎ *212/655–2300* ⊕ *www.michaeljordansnyc.com* ⊘ *No lunch weekends* ⌕ *Reservations essential* Ⓜ *4, 5, 6, 7, S to Grand Central–42nd St.* ✛ *4:F4.*

$$ ✕ **Mint Restaurant & Lounge.** With a delightful dining room splashed with
INDIAN   bright colors and flattering lighting, and executive chef and owner Gary Sikka's brightly seasoned dishes, Mint has joined the ranks of the best Indian restaurants in town. The large menu includes rarely encountered specialties from Goa and Sikkim. Freshly grilled, moist ground lamb kebabs deliver a slow burn to the palate. Chili heat punctuates other

spices in the lamb vindaloo, resulting in a well-rounded array of savory flavors. Finish with carrot pudding with saffron and coconut flakes. [$] *Average main: $20* ✉ *150 E. 50th St., Midtown East* ☎ *212/644–8888* 🌐 *www.mintny.com* [M] *6 to 51st St.; E, M to Lexington Ave./53rd St.* ✥ *4:G3.*

$$$ STEAKHOUSE 🍴 **The Palm Restaurant.** They may have added tablecloths, but it takes more than that to hide the brusque, no-nonsense nature of this legendary steakhouse. The steak is always impeccable, and the Nova Scotia lobsters are so big—three pounds and up—that there may not be room at the table for classic side dishes like rich creamed spinach, served family-style for two or more. The "half-and-half" side combination of cottage-fried potatoes and fried onions is particularly addictive. There are other locations (the original, Palm One, is on 2nd Avenue at East 58th Street, there's one in the mid-50s, one in TriBeCa, and one at JFK Airport), but because of its perch near the Theater District and Midtown businesses, this is the one with the most action. [$] *Average main: $30* ✉ *837 2nd Ave., between 44th and 45th sts., Midtown East* ☎ *212/687–2953* 🌐 *www.thepalm.com* 🕒 *No lunch weekends* [M] *4, 5, 6, 7, S to Grand Central–42nd St.* ✥ *4:G4; 1:B2.*

$$ AMERICAN 🍴 **P. J. Clarke's.** This East Side institution has been dispensing burgers and beer for more than a century. Despite renovations and several owners over the years, the original P. J. Clarke's (there are offshoots in Lincoln Square and Chelsea) maintains the beveled-glass and scuffed-wood look of an old-time saloon. Many of the bartenders and patrons are as much a part of the décor as the light fixtures. More civilized at lunchtime, the bar area heaves with an after-work mob on weekday evenings. Pull up a stool if you can for superlative bar food, like clams casino and the signature burger smothered in creamy béarnaise. [$] *Average main: $18* ✉ *915 3rd Ave., at 55th St., Midtown East* ☎ *212/317–1616* 🌐 *www.pjclarkes.com* [M] *E, M to 5th Ave./53rd St.; N, Q, R to Lexington Ave./59th St.; 4, 5, 6 to 59th St.* ✥ *4:G2; 1:B3; 5:C5.*

$$$ CHINESE 🍴 **Shun Lee Palace.** If you want inexpensive Cantonese food without pretensions, head to Chinatown. If you prefer to be pampered and don't mind spending a lot of money, then this is the place, which has been elegantly serving classic Chinese fare for more than four decades. Supposedly the dish orange beef was first made here. Indeed, it's certainly worth a sample, but there's so much more. Beijing pan-fried dumplings make a good starter, and rack of lamb Szechuan-style, grilled with scallions and garlic, is a popular entrée. The "Lion's Head," a slow-baked pork dish, is one of the most tender porky things you'll eat. Beijing duck, served tableside with thin pancakes, is a signature dish here—and for good reason. [$] *Average main: $28* ✉ *155 E. 55th St., between Lexington and 3rd aves., Midtown East* ☎ *212/371–8844* ✍ *Reservations essential* [M] *N, Q, R to Lexington Ave./59th St.; 4, 5, 6 to 59th St.* ✥ *4:G2.*

$$$$ STEAKHOUSE 🍴 **Sparks Steakhouse.** Fans of mob history recognize Sparks as the spot where, in 1985, members of the Gambino crime family were gunned down under the orders of John Gotti. Today there's a lot less shooting and a lot more sizzling happening here, but still be sure to bring a wad of cash. Magnums of wines that cost more than most people earn in

a week festoon the large dining rooms of this classic New York steakhouse. Tasty fresh seafood is given more than fair play on the menu, and the extra-thick lamb and veal chops are also noteworthy—but Sparks is really about dry-aged steak. Classic sides of hash browns, creamed spinach, sautéed mushrooms, and grilled onions are all you need to complete the experience—plus maybe a martini. $ *Average main: $40* ✉ *210 E. 46th St., between 2nd and 3rd aves., Midtown East* ☎ *212/687–4855* ⊕ *www.sparkssteakhouse.com* ⊙ *Closed Sun. No lunch Sat.* ⊲ *Reservations essential* Ⓜ *4, 5, 6, 7, S to Grand Central–42nd St.* ✛ *4:G4.*

$$$ ╳ **Sushi Yasuda.** Devotees mourned the return of namesake Chef
JAPANESE Naomichi Yasuda to Japan, but things are in able hands with his hand-picked successor, Mitsuru Tamura. Whether using fish flown in daily from Japan or the creamiest sea urchin, the chef makes sushi so fresh and delicate, it melts in your mouth. A number of special appetizers change daily (crispy fried eel backbone is a surprising treat), and a fine selection of sake and beer complements the lovely food. The sleek bamboo-lined interior is as elegant as the food. Try to sit at the bar, which was hand-crafted by Yasuda out of imported Japanese materials. $ *Average main: $31* ✉ *204 E. 43rd St., between 2nd and 3rd aves., Midtown East* ☎ *212/972–1001* ⊕ *www.sushiyasuda.com* ⊙ *Closed Sun. No lunch Sat.* Ⓜ *4, 5, 6, 7, S to Grand Central–42nd St.* ✛ *4:G4.*

MURRAY HILL

This area has a residential feel with plenty of bistros perfect for a casual meal. Lexington Avenue's "Curry Hill" section between 27th and 29th streets is home to Indian spice shops, cafés, and restaurants.

$$ ╳ **2nd Ave Deli.** It may no longer be on 2nd Avenue, but the most recent
DELI incarnation of this East Village institution—about a mile uptown, in Midtown—still delivers on its longtime traditional matzo-ball soup, overstuffed three-decker sandwiches filled with house-cured pastrami, and other old-world specialties. Hot open-face sandwiches, like juicy beef brisket served with gravy and french fries, may be a heart attack on a plate, but hey, you only live once. Even better, you can now get your fill of *kasha varnishkes*, carrot *tzimmes*, and potato *kugel* until the wee hours of the night. There's also an outpost on the Upper East Side. $ *Average main: $23* ✉ *162 E. 33rd St., between Lexington and 3rd aves., Midtown East* ☎ *212/689–9000* ⊕ *www.2ndavedeli.com* Ⓜ *6 to 33rd St.* ✛ *4:G6.*

$$ ╳ **Marta.** The excellent cracker-thin crust of the Roman-style pizzas at
ITALIAN Marta are a refreshing break from the thicker crust of the Neapolitan
Fodor'sChoice pizzas that have overtaken Manhattan in recent years. And we have
★ beloved restaurateur Danny Meyer to thank for it. The high-ceiling dining room belies the casual fare but the menu is a love letter to salt-of-the-earth Roman food, from the baseball-sized *suppli* (fried rice balls) to fried squash to those excellent thin pizzas topped with tangy tomato sauce and delicious items like *guanciale* (pork jowl) and arugula. $ *Average main: $20* ✉ *29 E. 29th St., at Madison Ave., Murray Hill* ☎ *212/651–3800* ⊕ *www.martamanhattan.com* Ⓜ *6 to 28th St.* ✛ *4:F1.*

16

MIDTOWN WEST

It's true that tourist traps abound on Broadway, but fortunately you needn't head far from Times Square to score a stellar meal. Just move away from the bright lights and unrelenting foot traffic that clogs the area. On calmer side streets and in adjoining Hell's Kitchen there are excellent dining options for budget travelers and expense-account diners alike. Some of the best steakhouses and Italian restaurants are here, and many eateries offer budget pretheater dinners and prix-fixe lunch menus to draw in new business.

$$$$
AMERICAN
✕ **'21' Club.** Tradition's the thing at this townhouse landmark, a former speakeasy that opened in 1929. Chef Sylvain Delpique tries to satisfy everyone with standards like the famous '21' burger and Dover sole with brown butter, as well as more modern dishes, such as sautéed pork belly with butternut squash purée, but the food is almost secondary to the restaurant's storied past. Belongings donated by famous patrons—for example, John McEnroe's tennis racket or Howard Hughes's model plane—hang from the ceiling. Men: jackets are required, but you can leave your ties at home. Ⓢ *Average main: $41 ⊠ 21 W. 52nd St., between 5th and 6th aves., Midtown West* ☎ *212/582–7200* ⊕ *www.21club.com* ⊗ *Closed Sun.* Ⓜ *Jacket required* Ⓜ *E, M to 5th Ave./53rd St.; B, D, F, M to 47th–50th Sts./Rockefeller Center* ✛ *4:D2.*

$$$$
MODERN
AMERICAN
✕ **Aureole.** An island of fine dining just a stone's throw from bustling Times Square, Aureole is the second act of a New York classic from Charlie Palmer and his executive chef, Marcus Gleadow-Ware. From the street, a curved second-story corridor hosting the restaurant's storied wine collection beckons. A welcoming front barroom serves a more casual, yet still refined, menu with dishes like a cheddar-bacon burger with pickled ramp mayonnaise. The dining room, with its abundance of flowers, is the place to hobnob with expense-account diners and pretheater revelers. For dinner, starters like the pumpkin risotto with shrimp is a treat, and the $148 "parallel tasting" has the menu's greatest hits. There is no à la carte option in the main dining room. Ⓢ *Average main: $50 ⊠ 135 W. 42nd St., between Broadway and 6th Ave., Midtown West* ☎ *212/319–1660* ⊕ *www.charliepalmer.com* ⊗ *No lunch weekends* ⌂ *Reservations essential* Ⓜ *B, D, F, M to 42nd St.–Bryant Park; 1, 2, 3, 7, N, Q, R, S to Times Sq.–42nd St.* ✛ *4:D4.*

$$$
SOUTHERN
✕ **Bar Americain.** Celeb chef Bobby Flay's largest Manhattan restaurant is the soaring Bar Americain. The 200-seat, two-story space looks like a dining room on a luxury liner. This is not food for the faint-of-heart: Flay piles on the butter, cream, and endless varieties of bacon. Southern-inflected brasserie fare includes deviled eggs with smoked shrimp, "secret recipe" fried chicken with black pepper biscuit, and duck confit flavored with bourbon-based sauce and fig chutney. Slightly naughtier are the éclairs piped with whiskey-infused pastry cream and burnished with a burnt-sugar glaze. Brunch, featuring dishes like biscuits and cream gravy with sausage and scrambled eggs, is delicious. Ⓢ *Average main: $35 ⊠ 152 W. 52nd St., between 6th and 7th aves., Midtown West* ☎ *212/265–9700* ⊕ *www.baramericain.com* ⌂ *Reservations essential* Ⓜ *B, D, E to 7th Ave.; 1, C, E to 50th St.; N, Q, R to 49th St.* ✛ *4:C2.*

$$ ✗**Becco.** An ingenious concept makes Becco a prime Restaurant Row
ITALIAN choice for time-constrained theatergoers. There are two pricing sce-
narios: one includes an all-you-can-eat selection of antipasti and three
pastas served hot out of pans that waiters circulate around the dining
room; the other adds a generous entrée to the mix. The pasta selection
changes daily, but often includes gnocchi, fresh ravioli, and fettuccine
in a cream sauce. The entrées include braised veal shank, grilled double-
cut pork chop, and rack of lamb, among other selections. $ *Average
main: $24 ⊠ 355 W. 46th St., between 8th and 9th aves., Midtown West
☎212/397–7597 ⊕ www.becco-nyc.com* Ⓜ *A, C, E to 42nd St.–Port
Authority* ✢ *4:B3.*

$$$ ✗**Benoit.** Who needs to go to Paris when the world's most famous
FRENCH French chef, Alain Ducasse, can come to you? The interior of Ducasse's
imported Right Bank bistro—cozy red-velour banquettes and wall
lamps illuminating each table—is plucked straight from the City of
Light. So is the menu, which doesn't reinvent anything as much as it
replicates. And that's okay, especially when the fennel-inflected *loup de
mer* (sea bass) or the tender roasted veal loin are so well executed. It's
not exactly cheap for simple bistro fare. Then again, neither is a round-
trip ticket to Paris. $ *Average main: $27 ⊠ 60 W. 55th St., between 5th
and 6th aves., Midtown West* ☎*646/943–7373 ⊕ www.benoitny.com*
▭ *No credit cards* Ⓜ *N, Q, R to 5th Ave./59th St.; F to 57th St.* ✢ *4:D2.*

$$$ ✗**Brasserie Ruhlmann.** In a plush 120-seat dining room with just enough
BRASSERIE Art Deco touches to harmonize with its Rockefeller Center setting,
sublime French bistro cookery is on display. The room has a refined
air but the staff is so friendly that the place could never be stuffy. The
raw bar, with its selection of pedigreed oysters, is a great way to begin,
or opt for a blue crab salad over mâche with a honey-lime vinaigrette.
If it's on the menu, order braised rabbit nestled in mustard cream on a
bed of fresh pappardelle, sprinkled with pitted cherries. Desserts like
Floating Island—delicately baked meringue floating on a pond of crème
anglaise—are embellished with a flurry of spun sugar. $ *Average main:
$28 ⊠ 45 Rockefeller Plaza, 50th St. between 5th and 6th aves., Mid-
town West* ☎*212/974–2020 ⊕ www.brasserieruhlmann.com* ◷ *No
dinner Sun.* ⌘ *Reservations essential* Ⓜ *B, D, F, M to 47th–50th Sts./
Rockefeller Center; E, M to 5th Ave./53rd St.* ✢ *4:D3.*

$ ✗**Burger Joint.** What's a college burger bar, done up in particleboard
BURGER and rec-room design straight out of *Happy Days*, doing inside a five-
Fodor'sChoice star Midtown hotel? This tongue-in-cheek lunch spot, hidden behind a
★ heavy red velvet curtain in the Parker Meridien hotel, does such boister-
ous midweek business that lines often snake through the lobby (which
means you're best-off coming at noon or earlier). Stepping behind the
curtain, you can find baseball cap–wearing, grease-spattered cooks dis-
pensing paper-wrapped cheeseburgers and crisp, thin fries. Forget Kobe
beef or foie gras—these burgers are straightforward, cheap, and deli-
cious. There's a second location, serving inferior burgers, at 33 West 8th
Street in Greenwich Village. $ *Average main: $8 ⊠ Le Parker Meridien,
119 W. 56th St., between 6th and 7th aves., Midtown West* ☎*212/708–
7414 ⊕ www.burgerjointny.com* Ⓜ *N, Q, R to 57th St.–7th Ave.; F to
57th St.* ✢ *4:D1.*

16

$$ ITALIAN FAMILY 🍴 **Carmine's.** Savvy New Yorkers line up early for the affordable family-style meals at this large, busy Midtown eatery. Family photos line the walls, and there's a convivial feeling amid all the Times Square hubbub. Don't be fooled: Carmine's may be huge, but it fills up with families carbo-loading for a day of sightseeing or a night of theater on Broadway. Hungry diners are rewarded with mountains of such popular, toothsome viands as fried calamari, linguine with white clam sauce, chicken parmigiana, and veal saltimbocca. [$] *Average main: $24* ✉ *200 W. 44th St., between Broadway and 8th Ave., Midtown West* ☎ *212/221–3800* 🌐 *www.carminesnyc.com* [M] *A, C, E to 42nd St.–Port Authority; 1, 2, 3, 7, N, Q, R, S to Times Sq.–42nd St.* ✥ *4:C4; 6:A5.*

$$ KOREAN Fodor's Choice ★ 🍴 **Danji.** Diminutive and dark, Danji is no ordinary Korean restaurant. Helmed by talented chef Hooni Kim, this Hell's Kitchen spot stands out among the rows of restaurants that attract theatergoing tourists in the neighborhood. That's because Kim's take on Korean cuisine is inventive and inspired. The menu is split in two, and both sides contain a number of winning dishes. Start with the scallion and pepper pancake and the trio of kimchi from the "traditional" side, then set your taste buds singing with Korean chicken wings and unctuous pork-belly sliders from the "modern" side of the menu. Then count your blessings that you're not eating a mediocre meal like the rest of the out-of-town visitors in the neighorhood. [$] *Average main: $18* ✉ *346 W. 52nd St., between 8th and 9th aves., Midtown West* ☎ *212/586–2880* 🌐 *www.danjinyc.com* 💳 *No credit cards* 🕘 *Closed Sun. No lunch Sat.* [M] *C, E to 50th St.* ✥ *4:B2.*

$$$ FRENCH 🍴 **db Bistro Moderne.** Daniel Boulud's "casual bistro" (it's neither, actually) consists of two elegantly appointed dining rooms. The menu features classic dishes like Nantucket Bay scallops or hanger steak exquisitely prepared. Ever the trendsetter, Boulud's $35 "db" hamburger stuffed with braised short ribs, foie gras, and black truffles, is the patty credited with kick-starting the whole gourmet burger trend. Although it may not be the trendy destination it once was, it's still a treat and worth every penny. The service is friendly without being overbearing. [$] *Average main: $31* ✉ *55 W. 44th St., between 5th and 6th aves., Midtown West* ☎ *212/391–2400* 🌐 *www.dbbistro.com* ✍ *Reservations essential* [M] *B, D, F, M to 42nd St.–Bryant Park; 7 to 5th Ave.* ✥ *4:D4.*

$$ AMERICAN FAMILY 🍴 **Ellen's Stardust Diner.** If you haven't had enough Broadway singing and dancing, you'll get a kick out of Ellen's, a retro, 1950s-style diner, complete with a singing waitstaff. The menu focuses on all-American classics like meatloaf and chicken potpie, and the waiters and waitresses serenading you on roller skates have the talent to prove this restaurant is right on Broadway. It's the kind of over-the-top family fun you'd expect from the Times Square location, so don't expect a sophisticated—or quiet—dining experience. [$] *Average main: $20* ✉ *1650 Broadway, at 51st St., Midtown West* ☎ *212/956–5151* 🌐 *www.ellensstardustdiner.com* [M] *1 to 50th St.; B, D, E to 7th Ave.* ✥ *4:C3.*

$$$ SEAFOOD 🍴 **Esca.** The name is Italian for "bait," and this restaurant, courtesy of partners Mario Batali, Joe Bastianich, and longtime chef David Pasternack, lures diners in with delectable crudo preparations—such as tilefish with orange and Sardinian oil or pink snapper with a sprinkle of crunchy red clay salt—and hooks them with entrées like whole,

salt-crusted *branzino,* sea bass for two, or *bucatini* pasta with spicy baby octopus. The menu changes daily. Bastianich is in charge of the wine cellar, so expect an adventurous list of Italian bottles. $ *Average main: $33* ✉ *402 W. 43rd St., at 9th Ave., Midtown West* ☎ *212/564– 7272* ⊕ *www.esca-nyc.com* ⊗ *No lunch Sun.* ⌖ *Reservations essential* Ⓜ *A, C, E to 42nd St.–Port Authority* ✛ *4:A4.*

$$ ✕ **Five Napkin Burger.** This perennially packed Hell's Kitchen burger
BURGER place and brasserie has been a magnet for burger lovers since day one. Bottles of Maker's Mark line the sleek, alluringly lighted bar in the back, a collection of antique butcher's scales hangs on a tile wall near the kitchen, and meat hooks dangle from the ceiling between light fixtures. Though there are many menu distractions—deep-fried pickles and warm artichoke dip, to name a few—the main attractions are the juicy burgers, like the original 10-ounce chuck with a tangle of onions, Gruyère cheese, and rosemary aioli. There's a patty option for everyone, including a ground lamb *kofta* and an onion ring–topped ahi tuna burger. For dessert, have an überthick black-and-white malted milkshake. $ *Average main: $16* ✉ *630 9th Ave., at 45th St., Midtown West* ☎ *212/757–2277* ⊕ *www.5napkinburger.com* Ⓜ *A, C, E to 42nd St.–Port Authority* ✛ *4:B4.*

$ ✕ **La Bonne Soupe.** Midtown office workers and in-the-know out-of-
FRENCH towners keep this French restaurant bustling for the ever-popular La Bonne Soupe special—you get a bowl of their excellent soup with bread, salad, a beverage (house wine, beer, soda, or coffee), and dessert for $20.95. À la carte options include bistro classics like crêpes, omelets, salads, quiche, sandwiches, and croques madame and monsieur. It's not the hippest place in town, but you leave satisfied. There's often a line at lunchtime, but there are two floors of tables so you won't go hungry for long. $ *Average main: $17* ✉ *48 W. 55th St., between 5th and 6th aves., Midtown West* ☎ *212/586–7650* ⊕ *www.labonnesoupe.com* Ⓜ *B, D, F, M to 47th–50th Sts./Rockefeller Center* ✛ *4:E2.*

$$$$ ✕ **The Lambs Club.** Restaurateur Geoffrey Zakarian's opulent supper club
MODERN on the ground floor of the Chatwal Hotel has superb Art Deco detailing,
AMERICAN blood-red leather banquettes, and a roaring fireplace. Cocktails are concocted by hipster mixologist Sasha Petraske, who eschews the experimental in favor of classics like the sidecar and the martini, done well. The food is typical Zakarian, meaning New American cuisine with luxe touches in dishes like veal sweetbreads with peppered jus and grilled Treviso lettuce, or seared scallops with porcini mushrooms and Indian-spiced sauce. The lunchtime menu is padded with appealing choices, but the sleeper meal here is breakfast. Dishes like a house-made biscuit with fried egg, bacon, and cheddar, or fluffy lemon-ricotta pancakes, fill you up for the rest of the day. $ *Average main: $36* ✉ *132 W. 44th St., between 6th Ave. and Broadway, Midtown West* ☎ *212/997–5262* ⊕ *www.thelambsclub.com* Ⓜ *1, 2, 3, 7, N, Q, R, S to Times Sq.–42nd St.; B, D, F, M to 47th–50th Sts./Rockefeller Center* ✛ *4:D4.*

$$$$ ✕ **Le Bernardin.** Owner Maguy LeCoze presides over the teak-panel dining
SEAFOOD room at this trendsetting French seafood restaurant, and chef and partner
Fodor's Choice Eric Ripert works magic with anything that swims—preferring at times
★ not to cook it at all. Deceptively simple dishes such as poached lobster

16

in rich coconut-ginger soup or crispy spiced black bass in a Peking duck bouillon are typical of his style. It's widely agreed that there's no beating Le Bernardin for thrilling cuisine, seafood or otherwise, coupled with some of the finest desserts in town and a wine list as deep as the Atlantic. It's prix-fixe only, and there are nonfish options (pasta and meat) available on request. $ *Average main: $155* ⊠ *155 W. 51st St., between 6th and 7th aves., Midtown West* ☎ *212/554–1515* ⊕ *www.le-bernardin.com* ⊗ *Closed Sun. No lunch Sat.* ⌂ *Jacket required* Ⓜ *1 to 50th St.; N, Q, R to 49th St.; B, D, E to 7th Ave.* ✛ *4:C2.*

$ ✕ **Le Pain Quotidien.** This international Belgian chain brings its home-
BAKERY   land ingredients with it, treating New Yorkers to crusty organic breads, jams, chocolate, and other specialty products. You can grab a snack to go or stay and eat breakfast, lunch, or dinner at communal or private tables with waiter service. Come for a steaming latte and croissant in the morning or a tartine (open-faced sandwich) at noon. There are more than 20 locations throughout Manhattan, including in Central Park. $ *Average main: $13* ⊠ *1271 6th Ave., at 50th St., Midtown West* ☎ *646/462–4165* ⊕ *www.lepainquotidien.com* ▭ *No credit cards* Ⓜ *B, D, F, M to 47th–50th Sts./Rockefeller Center; N, Q, R to 49th St.; 1 to 50th St.* ✛ *4:D3.*

$$ ✕ **Lugo Cucina Italiana.** The area around Madison Square Garden is a
ITALIAN   restaurant wasteland with the rare sparkling exception of Lugo Cucina Italiana, founded by an Italian menswear line. Locals rejoiced at the introduction of this spacious Italian "brasserie" serving comfort food with a *Dolce Vita* twist all day long. Stop by for an espresso and pastry in the morning. Later, a single menu presents lunch, *aperitivo*, and dinner options, which include grazing portions of salumi, cheeses, and vegetable dishes like eggplant caponata, Tuscan white-bean salad, and grilled zucchini with pine nuts. Fuller meals of Neapolitan-style pizzas, house-made pastas, and grilled meats and fish also are commendable. $ *Average main: $24* ⊠ *1 Penn Plaza, 33rd St. and 8th Ave., Midtown West* ☎ *212/760–2700* ⊕ *www.lugocaffe.com* ⊗ *No dinner weekdays* Ⓜ *1, 2, 3, A, C, E to 34th St.–Penn Station* ✛ *4:C6.*

$$$ ✕ **Má Pêche.** Starkly decorated in the basement of the Chambers Hotel,
ASIAN   Má Pêche is just blocks from MoMA. As the largest restaurant in David Chang's empire, you've got a decent shot of nabbing a seat. The menus are a bit more refined (and expensive) than those at Momofuku Noodle Bar and Ssäm Bar, with elegantly composed plates that might include lamb shank accompanied by eggplant, raisins, and rice, or seared swordfish with black beans, braised celery, and crisped shallots. On the way out you can pick up sweets from the uptown offshoot of Momofuku Milk Bar, like the addictive, buttery Crack Pie or intriguingly flavored soft-serve. $ *Average main: $28* ⊠ *15 W. 56th St., between 5th and 6th aves., Midtown West* ☎ *212/757–5878* ⊕ *www.momofuku.com/ma-peche* ⊗ *No lunch Sun.* Ⓜ *F to 57th St.; N, Q, R to 5th Ave./59th St.* ✛ *4:E1.*

$$$ ✕ **Marea.** Carefully sourced, meticulously prepared fish and seafood
SEAFOOD   take center stage at this well-pedigreed restaurant. Large picture win-
Fodor'sChoice   dows in the dining room look out to expansive views of Central Park
★   South, and silver-dipped shells on pedestals decorate the dining room.

No expense is spared in importing the very best of the ocean's bounty, beginning with crudo dishes—think scallops with orange, wild fennel, and arugula—that are becoming the restaurant's signature. You'd be remiss, though, if you skipped the pastas that made Chef Michael White famous. They're served here in lusty iterations like rich fusilli with octopus and bone marrow, and spaghetti with sea urchin. Whole fish like roasted turbot and salt-baked snapper are equally showstopping. Service is flawless. Ⓢ *Average main: $25* ⊠ *240 Central Park S, between Broadway and 7th Ave., Midtown West* ☎ *212/582–5100* ⊕ *www.marea-nyc.com* ⚓ *Reservations essential* Ⓜ *1, A, B, C, D to 59th St.–Columbus Circle* ✢ *4:B1.*

$$

MEDITERRANEAN

╳**Marseille.** With great food and a convenient location near several Broadway theaters, Marseille is perpetually packed. The Mediterranean creations are continually impressive, including the bouillabaisse, the signature dish of the region for which the restaurant is named—a mélange of mussels, shrimp, and whitefish in a fragrant broth, topped with a garlicky crouton and served with rouille on the side. Also worth a bite or two is the charred octopus with fennel and tomatoes. Leave room for the spongy beignets with chocolate and raspberry dipping sauces. Ⓢ *Average main: $23* ⊠ *630 9th Ave., at 44th St., Midtown West* ☎ *212/333–2323* ⊕ *www.marseillenyc.com* ⚓ *Reservations essential* Ⓜ *A, C, E to 42nd St.–Port Authority* ✢ *4:B4.*

16

$$$$

FRENCH

╳**The Modern and Bar Room.** Side by side on the ground floor of the New York MoMA are two spots that compete for the title of the country's best museum restaurant. The food is no longer by Alsatian chef Gabriel Kreuther, but restaurateur Danny Meyer will, no doubt, make sure that whoever takes over will keep the kitchens turning out impeccable food. The formal Modern dining room features a view of the museum's sculpture garden while the more accessible and popular Bar Room lies just beyond a partition. Ⓢ *Average main: $45* ⊠ *9 W. 53rd St., between 5th and 6th aves., Midtown West* ☎ *212/333–1220* ⊕ *www.themodernnyc.com* ☽ *Closed Sun.* Ⓜ *E, M to 5th Ave./53rd St.* ✢ *4:D2.*

$$$

SEAFOOD

╳**Oceana.** Entering this restaurant is like walking into the dressy stateroom of a modern luxury ocean liner. Floor-to-ceiling windows look out north and west, and the arrestingly designed raw bar backed with Mediterranean-hue ceramics serves stunningly fresh choices—you would expect gorgeous oysters at a restaurant called Oceana, and you get them. Chef Ben Pollinger has the skill and confidence to serve some of the most vivid and delicious seafood in town. A contemporary appetizer section includes items like marinated cucumber with apple and toasted spices. Grilled whole fish like halibut, swordfish, and crispy wild striped bass, are served with a perfect rotating roster of sauces that includes a classic romesco and a grilled pineapple salsa. Ⓢ *Average main: $34* ⊠ *120 W. 49th St., at 6th Ave., Midtown West* ☎ *212/759–5941* ⊕ *www.oceanarestaurant.com* ☽ *No breakfast or lunch weekends* ⚓ *Reservations essential* Ⓜ *B, D, F, M to 47th–50th Sts./Rockefeller Center* ✢ *4:D3.*

$$$

BRAZILIAN

╳**Plataforma Churrascaria Rodizio.** This sprawling, boisterous shrine to meat, with its all-you-can-eat, prix-fixe menu, is best experienced with a group of ravenous friends. A *caipirinha*, featuring cachaça sugarcane liquor, sugar, and lime, kicks things off nicely. Follow up with a trip to the fabulous salad bar, piled with vegetables, meats, and cheeses—but remember, there's about to be a parade of all manner of grilled meats and poultry, from pork ribs to chicken hearts, delivered to the table on long skewers. Everyone at the table gets a coaster-size disc that's red on one side and green on the other: turn the green side up when you're ready for more. Pace yourself so you can try all the different delicacies; it's definitely a fun evening, but make sure to come hungry. $ *Average main: $34* ⊠ *316 W. 49th St., between 8th and 9th aves., Midtown West* ☎ *212/245–0505* ⊕ *www.plataformaonline.com* ⚓ *Reservations essential* Ⓜ *C, E to 50th St.* ✛ *4:B3.*

$$ ✕ **Plaza Food Hall by Todd English.** At the Plaza Food Hall in the base-
ECLECTIC   ment of the Plaza Hotel, celeb chef Todd English oversees a series of mini-restaurants, each with its own counter and seating ideal for a quick snack or a full-fledged meal. Entry is a little confusing: though the place is made up of individual food concepts, you are seated by a hostess at any available counter. Once settled, get up and survey your choices, then sit down and order from your waiter. There's a glistening raw bar, a burger joint, and a wood-fired pizza station where you can sample some of English's iconic pies, such as fig and prosciutto. It's one of the most varied and affordable daytime food options in an area of town that can still feel like a lunchtime wasteland. $ *Average main: $18* ⊠ *Plaza Hotel, 1 W. 59th St., at 5th Ave., Midtown West* ☎ *212/986–9260* ⊕ *www.theplazany/dining/foodhall.com* Ⓜ *N, Q, R to 5th Ave./59th St.* ✛ *4:E1.*

$$$$ ✕ **Quality Meats.** The handsome design at Quality Meats is inspired by
STEAKHOUSE   classic New York City butcher shops in its use of warm wood, stainless steel, and white marble. Sit at the bar to peruse the extensive menu of wines and single-malt scotches, or sip a classic martini. Then retire to the dining room for memorable fare like the massive chunky crab cake, seared scallops, and sophisticated riffs on steakhouse classics like beef Wellington. The grilled bacon, peanut butter, and apple starter is a must for any first-timer. The wine list emphasizes big bold reds, the perfect companion to a rich chunky steak. $ *Average main: $37* ⊠ *57 W. 58th St., near 6th Ave., Midtown West* ☎ *212/371–7777* ⊕ *www. qualitymeatsnyc.com* ☉ *No lunch weekends* ⚓ *Reservations essential* Ⓜ *F to 57th St.; N, Q, R to 5th Ave./59th St.* ✛ *4:D1.*

$$$ ✕ **Sosa Borella.** This is one of the Theater District's top spots for reliable
ITALIAN   food at a reasonable cost. The bilevel, casual Argentinian-Italian eatery is an inviting and friendly space where diners choose from a wide range of options. The lunch menu features staples like warm sandwiches and entrée-size salads, whereas the dinner menu is slightly gussied up with meat, fish, and pasta dishes (the rich agnolotti with lamb Bolognese sauce, topped with a wedge of grilled pecorino cheese, is a must-try). The freshly baked bread served at the beginning of the meal with pesto dipping sauce is a nice touch. Service can be slow at times, so leave yourself ample time before the show. $ *Average main: $25* ⊠ *832 8th Ave., between 50th and 51st sts., Midtown West* ☎ *212/262–8282* ⊕ *www. sosaborella.com* Ⓜ *1, C, E to 50th St.* ✛ *4:B3.*

$$ MEXICAN 🍴 **Toloache.** Make a quick detour off heavily trafficked Broadway into this pleasantly bustling Mexican cantina for one of the best dining options around Times Square. The bilevel eatery has a festive, celebratory vibe, with several seating options: bar, balcony, main dining room, and ceviche bar. Foodies flock here for three types of guacamole (traditional, fruited, and spicy), a trio of well-executed ceviches, and Mexico City–style tacos with Negra Modelo–braised brisket, and quesadillas studded with black truffle and *huitlacoche* (a corn fungus known as the "Mexican truffle"). There's an extensive tequila selection—upward of 100 brands. Adventurous palates are drawn to tacos featuring chili-studded dried grasshoppers, lobes of seared foie gras, and caramelized veal sweetbreads. There's another location in Greenwich Village. [$] *Average main: $19* ✉ *251 W. 50th St., near 8th Ave., Midtown West* ☎ *212/581–1818* 🌐 *www.toloachenyc.com* [M] *1, C, E to 50th St.; N, Q, R to 49th St.* ⊕ *4:B3.*

$$$$ STEAKHOUSE 🍴 **Uncle Jack's Steakhouse.** Surpassing even its celebrated flagship restaurant in Bayside, Queens, Uncle Jack's soars directly into the pantheon of the best steakhouses in Manhattan. As in most great steakhouses, you can feel the testosterone coursing through the place. The space is vast and gorgeously appointed, and service is swift and focused. USDA prime steaks are dry-aged for 21 days. Australian lobster tails are so enormous, they have to be served carved, yet the flesh is meltingly tender. Humongous pork chops, dripping with juice, are accompanied by chipotle sauerkraut. Desserts include an excellent 18-year Macallan scotch–laced bread pudding. It's hard to go wrong at Jack's. [$] *Average main: $67* ✉ *440 9th Ave., between 34th and 35th sts., Midtown West* ☎ *212/244–0005* 🌐 *www.unclejacks.com* ⏲ *No lunch weekends* ✍ *Reservations essential* [M] *A, C, E to 34th St.–Penn Station* ⊕ *4:B6.*

UPPER EAST SIDE

Long viewed as an enclave of the privileged, the Upper East Side has plenty of elegant, pricey eateries that serve the society "ladies who lunch" and bankers looking forward to a steak and single-malt scotch at the end of the day. However, visitors to Museum Mile and 5th Avenue shopping areas need not be put off. Whether you're looking to celebrate a special occasion or just want to grab a quick bite, there is something here for almost any budget.

$$$$ ITALIAN 🍴 **Alloro.** Italian chef Salvatore Corea and his wife, Gina, a native New Yorker, are living their dream of opening an old-fashioned family-run restaurant on the Upper East Side. It's not Corea's first New York restaurant endeavor—he's opened three other successful venues in the city—but Alloro is his first venture with his wife, and judging by the friendly vibe and the delicious dishes coming out of Corea's *cucina*, it's working swimmingly well. Chef Corea's creative take on traditional, regional Italian cuisine leads the way for delicious dishes, like creamy Parmesan risotto with lambrusco-wine caramel. Both the sliced ribeye over corn puree and the fillet of sole in pumpkin-amaretto crust are fantastic. Gluten-free pasta selections are also available. [$] *Average main:*

$38 ✉ *307 E. 77th St., near 2nd Ave., Upper East Side* ☎ *212/535–2866* 🌐 *www.alloronyc.com* ⏲ *Closed Sun. No lunch* [M] *6 to 77th St.* ✥ *5:H2.*

$$$$ FRENCH 🍴 **Café Boulud.** Manhattan's "who's who" in business, politics, and the art world come to hobnob at Daniel Boulud's café-in-name-only, where the food and service are top-notch. The menu is divided into four parts: under La Tradition are classic French dishes such as roasted duck breast Montmorency with cherry chutney, green Swiss chard, and baby turnips, or Guinea hen terrine with pear, rutabaga, and foie gras; Le Potager tempts with lemon ricotta ravioli; La Saison follows the rhythms of the season; and Le Voyage reinterprets cuisines of the world. Start with a drink at the chic Bar Pleiades. [$] *Average main: $42* ✉ *Surrey Hotel, 20 E. 76th St., between 5th and Madison aves., Upper East Side* ☎ *212/772–2600* 🌐 *www.danielboulud.com* ✍ *Reservations essential* [M] *6 to 77th St.* ✥ *5:F3.*

$$ BRASSERIE 🍴 **Café d'Alsace.** Unusually comfortable burgundy banquettes, huge antique mirrors, and low lighting that makes everyone look fabulous characterize this Alsatian gem. Start with a house cocktail—say, L'Alsacien, in which the aperitif Belle de Brillet meets cognac, pear, and fresh lemon in a happy union. Standouts include the *tarte flambée,* a *fromage-blanc*-topped flatbread scattered with tawny caramelized onions and hunks of bacon. The *choucroute garnie* entrée comes in a cast-iron kettle that keeps it piping hot. Sausages, smoked pork breast, and pork belly are so carefully braised that everything comes out in perfect harmony. Can't decide what to wash it all down with? Let the in-house beer sommelier help you. [$] *Average main: $22* ✉ *1695 2nd Ave., at 88th St., Upper East Side* ☎ *212/722–5133* 🌐 *www.cafedalsace.com* [M] *4, 5, 6 to 86th St.* ✥ *6:G6.*

$$ AUSTRIAN Fodor's Choice ★ 🍴 **Café Sabarsky.** In the Neue Galerie, this stately coffeehouse is meant to duplicate the Viennese café experience and does a good job of it, with Art Deco furnishings, a selection of daily newspapers, and cases filled with cakes, strudels, and Sacher tortes. Museumgoers and locals love to linger here over coffee. In fact, so much so it's sometimes a challenge to find a seat (there's a slightly less aesthetically pleasing outpost of the café in the basement). There is also a menu of heartier fare—created by Michelin-starred Austrian chef Kurt Gutenbrunner—of goulash, sandwiches, smoked pork–stuffed potato dumplings, and variations on a sausage theme. [$] *Average main: $18* ✉ *Neue Galerie, 1048 5th Ave., near 86th St., Upper East Side* ☎ *212/240–9557* 🌐 *www.neuegalerie.org* ⏲ *Closed Tues. No dinner Mon. and Wed.* [M] *4, 5, 6 to 86th St.* ✥ *6:E6.*

$$ VEGETARIAN Fodor's Choice ★ 🍴 **Candle 79.** The Upper East Side may seem like an unlikely place for gourmet vegan fare, but the people behind Candle 79 have found a formula that would work in any neighborhood. The elegant, bilevel space, done in warm, autumnal tones, is far from the health-food stereotype. Appetizers like rice balls with tempeh bacon may sound like hippie throwbacks but taste more like well-executed trattoria fare. Signature dishes include the seitan piccata, which replaces the usual protein with a vegetarian substitute and is so well made that you would never miss the meat. Salads, soups, desserts, and entrées are all fresh and made with local, organic, seasonal produce. There's also an impressive list of organic wines and sakes. [$] *Average main: $22* ✉ *154 E. 79th St., at*

Lexington Ave., Upper East Side ☎ 212/537–7179 🌐 www.candle79.com [M] 6 to 77th St. ✥ 5:G2.

$ MEXICAN
🍴 **Cascabel Taqueria.** Wrestling-theme design sets a whimsical backdrop at this reasonably priced Mexican restaurant. Tacos are inventive without veering too far from the comfort-food norm. The Camaron scatters plump roasted shrimp among fresh oregano, garlic oil, and black beans. The beef tongue is slow braised, then topped with spring onion and serrano chilies. There's also fresh, creamy guacamole with house-fried chips, pert tortilla soup with queso fresco and chicken, and dinner-only platters like adobe-marinated Berkshire pork butt. At lunchtime, sandwiches—like shredded chicken with mango and smashed avocado—hit the spot with a cold Mexican beer. Inside seating is limited, but in temperate weather the outdoor tables expand your possibilities. [$] *Average main: $13 ✉ 1538 2nd Ave., between 80th and 81st sts., Upper East Side ☎ 212/717–8226 🌐 www.nyctacos.com [M] 6 to 77th St. ✥ 5:H2.*

$$$ AMERICAN
🍴 **Central Park Boathouse Restaurant.** There are plenty of pushcarts dispensing hot dogs and sodas, but if you're looking to soak up Central Park's magical ambience in an elegant setting, head for the Central Park Boathouse, which overlooks the gondola lake. There you can relax on the outdoor deck with a glass of wine and a cheese plate, or go for a more formal meal inside the restaurant. In warmer months the restaurant can get crowded, so aim for a late lunch or early evening cocktail. Note that dinner is not served in the winter months. [$] *Average main: $30 ✉ E. 72nd St., at Park Dr. N, Upper East Side ☎ 212/517–2233 🌐 www.thecentralparkboathouse.com ⏲ No dinner Dec.–Mar. ✍ Reservations not accepted [M] 6 to 77th St. ✥ 5:E3.*

$$$$ FRENCH
Fodor's Choice ★
🍴 **Daniel.** Celebrity-chef Daniel Boulud has created one of the most elegant dining experiences in Manhattan. The prix-fixe menu (there are à la carte selections in the elegant lounge and bar) is predominantly French, with such modern classics as turbot on Himalayan salt with an ale-and-gingerbread sauce, and a duo of dry-aged Angus black beef featuring meltingly tender red wine–braised short ribs and seared rib eye with black trumpet mushrooms and Gorgonzola cream. Equally impressive are the serious artwork, professional service, extensive wine list, and masterful cocktails. Don't forget the decadent desserts and overflowing cheese trolley. A three-course vegetarian menu is also available. [$] *Average main: $125 ✉ 60 E. 65th St., between Madison and Park aves., Upper East Side ☎ 212/288–0033 🌐 www.danielnyc.com ⏲ Closed Sun. No lunch ✍ Reservations essential 👔 Jacket required [M] 6 to 68th St.–Hunter College ✥ 5:F5.*

$$$ MEXICAN
🍴 **Maya.** The upscale-hacienda appearance of this justifiably popular restaurant showcases some of the best Mexican food in the city, courtesy of pioneering Mexican chef Richard Sandoval. Begin with a fresh mango mojito, then tuck into delicious roasted corn soup with huitlacoche dumplings, stuffed poblano peppers, and a smoky filet mignon taco with jalapeño escabeche. Next indulge in the tender roasted pork carnitas or the spicy chipotle shrimp. The bottomless margarita brunch on weekends can get loud, but local Upper East Siders still enjoy it. [$] *Average main: $25 ✉ 1191 1st Ave., between 64th and 65th sts.,*

Upper East Side ☎ *212/585–1818* 🌐 *www.modernmexican.com* [M] *4, 5, 6 to 59th St.; N, Q, R to Lexington Ave./59th St.* ✣ *5:H5.*

$$$$ FRENCH 🍴 **Rotisserie Georgette.** The Georgette in question is Georgette Farkas who spent 17 years as Chef Daniel Boulud's marketing and PR person. She's now branched out on her own and is set to show the culinary world how high rotisserie chicken can be elevated. This elegant spot with an altarlike rotisserie in the back of the room might spin the best fowl in the city. For a splurge, orderthe "Poule de Luxe," a whole chicken stuffed with foie gras. The creamy burrata and the smoked salmon with fennel are fine starters. [$] *Average main: $39* ✉ *14 E. 60th St., between 5th and Madison aves., Upper East Side* ☎ *212/390–8060* 🌐 *www.rotisserieg.com* ⏲ *No lunch Sun.* [M] *4, 5, 6 to 59th St.; N, Q, R to 5th Ave./59th St.* ✣ *5:F6.*

$$$ JAPANESE 🍴 **Sushi of Gari.** Options at this popular sushi restaurant range from the ordinary (California roll) to the exotic like tuna with creamy tofu sauce, miso-marinated cod, or Japanese yellowtail with jalapeño. Japanese noodles (udon or soba) and meat dishes such as teriyaki and negimaki (scallions rolled in thinly sliced beef) are well prepared. Some of the inventive nonsushi items on the menu are worth a try, especially the fried cream cheese dumplings. Reservations are recommended. There are other locations, too, including one across the park at 370 Columbus Avenue, in Hell's Kitchen at 347 West 46th Street, and in TriBeCa at 130 West Broadway. [$] *Average main: $25* ✉ *402 E. 78th St., at 1st Ave., Upper East Side* ☎ *212/517–5340* 🌐 *www.sushiofgari.com* ⏲ *No lunch* [M] *6 to 77th St.* ✣ *5:H2.*

UPPER WEST SIDE

The area around Lincoln Center is a fine-dining hub; as you head north you'll find a mix of casual and sophisticated neighborhood spots.

$$$$ ASIAN 🍴 **Asiate.** The unparalleled view is reason enough to visit Asiate's pristine dining room, perched on the 35th floor of the Time Warner Center in the Mandarin Oriental Hotel. Artfully positioned tables and minimalist décor help direct eyes to the windows, which peer over Central Park. At night, crystalline lights reflect in the glass, creating a magical effect. The kitchen turns out contemporary dishes with an Asian influence that pair unlikely ingredients: think foie gras and hazlenut brittle, or branzino and truffles. Professional, attentive service helps foster an atmosphere of dreamlike luxury. The restaurant has prix-fixe menus only, and an illustrious wine collection housing 2,000 bottles. [$] *Average main: $100* ✉ *Mandarin Oriental Hotel, 80 Columbus Circle, 35th fl., at 60th St., Upper West Side* ☎ *212/805–8881* 🌐 *www.mandarinoriental.com* [M] *1, A, B, C, D to 59th St.–Columbus Circle* ✣ *5:C6.*

$$$ FRENCH Fodor's Choice ★ 🍴 **Bar Boulud.** Acclaimed French chef Daniel Boulud, known for upscale New York City eateries Daniel and Café Boulud, shows diners his more casual side with this lively contemporary bistro and wine bar. The long, narrow space accommodates 100 people. The menu emphasizes charcuterie, including terrines and pâtés designed by Parisian charcutier Gilles Verot, who relocated just to work with Boulud, as well as traditional French bistro dishes like steak frites and *poulet rôti à l'ail* (roast

chicken with garlic mashed potatoes). The 500-bottle wine list is heavy on wines from Burgundy and the Rhône Valley. A pretheater three-course menu starts at $45, and weekend brunch has four courses plus coffee for $32. [$] *Average main: $28* ✉ *1900 Broadway, between 63rd and 64th sts., Upper West Side* ☎ *212/595–0303* 🌐 *www.barboulud.com* [M] *1 to 66th St.–Lincoln Center; 1, A, B, C, D to 59th St.–Columbus Circle* ✥ *5:B5.*

$$ AMERICAN 🍴 **Barney Greengrass.** At this Upper West Side landmark brusque waiters send out stellar smoked salmon, sturgeon, and whitefish to a happy crowd packed to the gills at small Formica tables. Split a fish platter with bagels, cream cheese, and other fixings, or get your velvety nova scrambled with eggs and buttery caramelized onions. If still hungry, go for a plate of cheese blintzes or the to-die-for chopped liver. Be warned that the weekend brunch wait can exceed an hour, so you're better off coming during the week. [$] *Average main: $18* ✉ *541 Amsterdam Ave., between 86th and 87th sts., Upper West Side* ☎ *212/724–4707* 🌐 *www.barneygreengrass.com* ⏲ *Closed Mon. No dinner* ✍ *Reservations not accepted* 💳 *No credit cards* [M] *1, B, C to 86th St.* ✥ *6:B6.*

$$ CAFÉ 🍴 **Bouchon Bakery.** Never mind that you're in the middle of a shopping mall under a Samsung sign—soups and sandwiches don't get much more luxurious than this. Acclaimed chef Thomas Keller's low-key lunch spot (one floor down from his extravagant flagship, Per Se) draws long lines for good reason. Share a mason jar of salmon rillettes—an unctuous spread of cooked and smoked salmon folded around crème fraîche and butter—then move on to one of the fork-and-knife open-face tartines, like the tuna niçoise. When a sandwich has this much pedigree, $15 is actually a bargain. Grab dessert, a fresh macaroon or éclair, from the nearby bakery window. [$] *Average main: $16* ✉ *Time Warner Center, 10 Columbus Circle, 3rd fl., Upper West Side* ☎ *212/823–9366* 🌐 *www.bouchonbakery.com* [M] *1, A, B, C, D to 59th St.–Columbus Circle* ✥ *5:C6.*

$$ FRENCH 🍴 **Café Luxembourg.** The old soul of the Lincoln Center neighborhood seems to inhabit the tiled and mirrored walls of this lively, cramped restaurant, where West End Avenue regulars—including lots of on-air talent from nearby ABC News—are greeted with kisses, and musicians and audience members pack the room after a concert. The bar's always hopping, and the menu (served until 11 pm Sunday through Tuesday and until midnight from Wednesday through Saturday) includes classics like steak tartare and lobster roll alongside more contemporary dishes like pan-seared trout with haricots verts, hazelnuts, and tomato-caper compote. [$] *Average main: $22* ✉ *200 W. 70th St., between Amsterdam and West End aves., Upper West Side* ☎ *212/873–7411* 🌐 *www.cafeluxembourg.com* ✍ *Reservations essential* [M] *1, 2, 3, B, C to 72nd St.* ✥ *5:A4.*

$$ ITALIAN FAMILY 🍴 **Carmine's.** Set on a nondescript block of Broadway, this branch of the Italian mainstay is a favorite for families celebrating special occasions, pre-prom groups of teens, and plain old folks who come for the tried-and-true items like fried calamari, linguine with white clam sauce, chicken parmigiana, and veal saltimbocca, all served in mountainous portions. Family photos line the walls, an antipasti table groans under

the weight of savory meats, cheese, and salads, and there's a convivial feeling amid the organized chaos. $ *Average main: $24* ✉ *2450 Broadway, between 90th and 91st sts., Upper West Side* ☎ *212/362–2200* 🌐 *www.carminesnyc.com* [M] *1, 2, 3 to 96th St.* ✥ *6:A6.*

$$$$ AMERICAN 🍴 **Dovetail.** Inside Dovetail, chef and owner John Fraser's subdued townhouse restaurant, cream-color walls and maple panels create a warm, soothing atmosphere. The menu, which changes daily based on seasonal and available ingredients, features refined but hearty dishes. Seek solace from winter temperatures with the earthy gnocchi topped with matsutake mushrooms, poppy seeds, and lemon. Tender lamb is heightened by potatoes, artichokes, and olives. The feast continues with pastry chef Italivi Reboreda's luscious brie crème brûlée paired with buttermilk sherbet. $ *Average main: $40* ✉ *103 W. 77th St., at Columbus Ave., Upper West Side* ☎ *212/362–3800* 🌐 *www.dovetailnyc.com* ⏲ *No lunch* [M] *1 to 79th St.; B, C to 81st St.–Museum of Natural History* ✥ *5:B2.*

$$ CAFÉ 🍴 **Fairway Market Café.** Fairway is a neighborhood institution, living up to its reputation for great prices on gourmet products—and shopping-cart jockeying down the narrow aisles. Upstairs, though, is the respite of Fairway Market Café, a large, brick-walled room with windows overlooking Broadway. Up front you can grab a pastry and coffee to go, but there's a full menu of fairly priced entrées as well. The place is run by Mitchell London, who's known for his juicy, well-marbled steaks—try the ribeye and you may never go back to Brooklyn's Peter Luger steakhouse again. $ *Average main: $23* ✉ *2127 Broadway, between 74th and 75th sts., Upper West Side* ☎ *212/595–1888* 🌐 *www.fairwaymarket.com* [M] *1, 2, 3 to 72nd St.* ✥ *5:A3.*

$$ MEDITERRANEAN 🍴 **Fishtag.** Upper West Siders aren't going to be throwing Chef Michael Psilakis and his Greek-heavy Mediterranean fare back into the water any time soon. At Anthos, a big-box Midtown eatery that shuttered a few years ago, Psilakis was lauded for his prowess on the grill. He brings the same skills to Fishtag with dishes like grilled striped bass or swordfish. Fanatics of Anthos's insanely good lamb burger can breath easy: it's on the menu here. The wine list is long and categorized with subtitles like "Funky & Earthy" and "Explosive & Bold," and brew imbibers declare Fishtag a good catch when they see 20 craft beers on the menu. $ *Average main: $20* ✉ *222 W. 79th St., between Broadway and Amsterdam Ave., Upper West Side* ☎ *212/362–7470* 🌐 *www.michaelpsilakis.com/fishtag* 💳 *No credit cards* ⏲ *No lunch* [M] *1 to 79th St.* ✥ *5:A2.*

$ FAST FOOD 🍴 **Gray's Papaya.** It's a stand-up, take-out dive. And yes, limos do sometimes stop here for these legendary hot dogs—they are delicious, and quite the economical meal. The recession special is two hot dogs and a drink for $5. There are cheap breakfast offerings, too, like the quintessential egg and cheese on a roll. Although there used to be several locations of Gray's Papaya, this is the only one left. $ *Average main: $4* ✉ *2090 Broadway, at 72nd St., Upper West Side* ☎ *212/799–0243* 🌐 *www.grayspapayanyc.com* ✍ *Reservations not accepted* 💳 *No credit cards* [M] *1, 2, 3 to 72nd St.* ✥ *5:B4.*

$$ AMERICAN FAMILY 🍴 **Isabella's.** Set in the shadow of the Museum of Natural History, Isabella's has been a brunch-and-beyond stalwart for decades. Brunchtime is especially busy, even though the restaurant is large; lunch is less crowded, and a great time to try neighborhood-institution salads like the seafood-loaded Cobb or grilled artichoke hearts with Parmesan and lemon-thyme vinaigrette. Another winner: the crab cake sandwich layered with lush avocado. For dinner, don't skip the pine nut–sprinkled mushroom ravioli. Try for a table outside when the weather's nice; it's a great perspective on the neighborhood and great for people-watching. [$] *Average main: $21* ✉ *359 Columbus Ave., at 77th St., Upper West Side* ☎ *212/724–2100* 🌐 *www.isabellas.com* [M] *B, C to 81st St.–Museum of Natural History* ⊕ *5:B3.*

$$$$ FRENCH 🍴 **Jean-Georges.** This culinary temple in the Trump International Hotel and Towers focuses wholly on chef célèbre Jean-Georges Vongerichten's spectacular creations. The chef may now have restaurants sprinkled around the globe, but this is the spot in his culinary empire where you want to be. Some dishes approach the limits of the taste universe, like foie-gras brûlée with spiced fig jam and ice-wine reduction. Others are models of simplicity, like slow-cooked cod with warm vegetable vinaigrette. Exceedingly personalized service and a well-selected wine list contribute to an unforgettable meal. It's prix-fixe only. For Jean-Georges on a budget, try the prix-fixe lunch in the front room, Nougatine. [$] *Average main: $120* ✉ *1 Central Park W, at 60th St., Upper West Side* ☎ *212/299–3900* 🌐 *www.jean-georges.com* ✍ *Reservations essential* 👔 *Jacket required* [M] *1, A, B, C, D to 59th St.–Columbus Circle* ⊕ *5:C6.*

16

$$ GREEK 🍴 **Kefi.** *Kefi* is Greek for the bliss that accompanies a bacchanalia. At Michael Psilakis's Upper West Side eatery—a giant homage to his grandmother's Greek cooking—it's not hard to achieve such a euphoric state. Among the mezes, the meatballs with roasted garlic, olives, and tomato stand out; the flavorful roast chicken with potatoes, red peppers, garlic, and thyme makes for a winning entrée; and the béchamel-rich Kefi mac 'n' cheese is irresistible. Reasonable prices make it easy to stick around for a piece of traditional walnut cake with walnut ice cream. [$] *Average main: $17* ✉ *505 Columbus Ave., between 84th and 85th sts., Upper West Side* ☎ *212/873–0200* 🌐 *www.kefirestaurant.com* [M] *1, B, C to 86th St.* ⊕ *5:B1.*

$ BAKERY FAMILY 🍴 **Levain Bakery.** Completely unpretentious and utterly delicious, Levain Bakery's cookies are rich and hefty. In fact, they clock in at six ounces each! Choose from the chocolate-chip walnut, dark-chocolate chocolate chip, dark-chocolate peanut-butter chip, or oatmeal raisin. Batches are baked fresh daily and taste best when they're warm and melty right out of the oven. Levain's also bakes artisanal breads, including banana chocolate chip and pumpkin ginger spice, sour cream coffee cake, chocolate-chip and cinnamon brioche, sourdough rolls stuffed with Valrhona chocolate, blueberry muffins, a variety of scones, and bomboloncini—their unique jelly doughnuts. [$] *Average main: $9* ✉ *167 W. 74th St., near Amsterdam Ave., Upper West Side* ☎ *212/874–6080* 🌐 *www.levainbakery.com* 🕒 *No dinner* [M] *1, 2, 3 to 72nd St.* ⊕ *5:B3.*

$$$ BISTRO FAMILY 🍴 **Nice Matin.** If the Upper West Side and the French Riviera melded into one, it might look a little bit like Nice Matin. This is a longtime neighborhood favorite, particularly in warm-weather months, when regulars plant themselves at sidewalk tables and gawk at passersby while munching on Gallic fare like monkfish wading in sweet potato purée and garlicky mussels, and, of course, steak frites. The novel-size wine list boasts more than 2,000 bottles, so bring your reading glasses. Be sure to dress for the people-watching, particularly at the popular weekend brunch. [$] *Average main: $25* ✉ *201 W. 79th St., at Amsterdam Ave., Upper West Side* ☎ *212/873–6423* 🌐 *www.nicematinnyc.com* 💳 *No credit cards* [M] *1 to 79th St.* ✥ *5:A2.*

$$$$ AMERICAN Fodor's Choice ★ 🍴 **Per Se.** The New York interpretation of what many consider America's finest restaurant, the Napa Valley's French Laundry, Per Se is Chef Thomas Keller's Broadway stage. The large dining room is understated and elegant, with touches of wood, towering florals, and sweeping windows with views of Central Park. Keller embraces seasonality and a witty playfulness that speaks to his confidence in the kitchen, and some of his dishes are now world-renowned, such as the tiny cones of tuna tartare topped with crème fraîche, and the "oysters and pearls"—tiny mollusks suspended in a creamy custard with tapioca. Dessert service is a multicourse celebration of all things sweet, including a choice of 27 house-made chocolates. Service is sublime, as you'd expect. An à la carte "salon" menu is available in the front bar room, but let's face it: if you manage to snag a reservation, there's nothing else to do but submit to the $310 prix-fixe. It's best to make reservations at least two months in advance. [$] *Average main: $85* ✉ *Time Warner Center, 10 Columbus Circle, 4th fl., at 60th St., Upper West Side* ☎ *212/823–9335* 🌐 *www.perseny.com* 🕓 *No lunch Mon.–Thurs.* ✍ *Reservations essential* 👔 *Jacket required* [M] *1, A, B, C, D to 59th St.–Columbus Circle* ✥ *5:C6.*

$$$$ MEDITERRANEAN 🍴 **Picholine.** Terrance Brennan's classic French restaurant has maintained its dignified atmosphere over the years, as well as the emphasis on contemporary Mediterranean cuisine, sourced from artisanal farmers and food producers. The menu is divided into options for five-course and twelve-course tasting menus. The duck and foie gras rillette, inventively paired with gingerbread, is particularly tasty. So is the caviar-sprinkled sea urchin panna cotta. Whatever you do, don't miss the famous cheese course, which Brennan practically invented here. The atmosphere is refined but not stuffy. [$] *Average main: $47* ✉ *35 W. 64th St., between Broadway and Central Park W, Upper West Side* ☎ *212/724–8585* 🌐 *www.picholinenyc.com* 🕓 *Closed Sun. No lunch* ✍ *Reservations essential* [M] *1 to 66th St.–Lincoln Center* ✥ *5:C5.*

$$$$ STEAKHOUSE 🍴 **Porter House New York.** With clubby interiors by Jeffrey Beers and an adjoining lounge area, Porter House is helmed by veteran chef Michael Lomonaco. Filling the meat-and-potatoes slot in the Time Warner Center's upscale "Restaurant Collection," this masculine throwback highlights American wines and pedigreed supersize meat. The neighborhood, long underserved on the steakhouse front, has warmed to Lomonaco's simple, solid American fare. Begin with his smoky clams casino or rich roasted marrow bones. Steaks are huge and expertly seasoned,

and come with the usual battery of à la carte sides—creamed spinach, roasted mushrooms, and truffle mashed potatoes. [$] *Average main: $45* ✉ *Time Warner Center, 10 Columbus Circle, 4th fl., at 60th St., Upper West Side* ☎ *212/823–9500* 🌐 *www.porterhousenewyork.com* [M] *1, A, B, C, D to 59th St.–Columbus Circle* ✥ *5:C6.*

$ ITALIAN 🍴 **Salumeria Rosi Parmacotto.** This compact space is a temple to cured meats. Chef Cesare Casella has created a showcase for dozens of varieties of prosciutto, coppa, mortadella, and more, carved from a professional slicer for consumption on the spot or as indulgent take-out. There's also a more ambitious menu, including salads and a lusty osso buco over creamy mashed potatoes. If you're lucky, you might catch a glimpse of the avuncular chef with his signature rosemary sprig peeking out from his breast pocket. There's a spin-off with a more elaborate menu on the Upper East Side. [$] *Average main: $13* ✉ *283 Amsterdam Ave., between 73rd and 74th sts., Upper West Side* ☎ *212/877–4800* 🌐 *www.salumeriarosi.com* [M] *1, 2, 3 to 72nd St.* ✥ *5:B3.*

$$ AMERICAN 🍴 **Sarabeth's Kitchen.** Lining up for brunch here is as much an Upper West Side tradition as taking a sunny Sunday afternoon stroll in nearby Riverside Park. Locals love the bric-a-brac-filled restaurant for sweet morning-time dishes like lemon ricotta pancakes and comforting dinners. The afternoon tea includes buttery scones with Sarabeth's signature jams, savory nibbles, and outstanding baked goods. Dinner entrées include chicken potpie and truffle mac 'n' cheese. There are several other locations around town, including one at Chelsea Market on 10th Avenue and West 15th Street. [$] *Average main: $18* ✉ *423 Amsterdam Ave., at 80th St., Upper West Side* ☎ *800/773–7378* 🌐 *www.sarabeth.com* [M] *1 to 79th St.* ✥ *5:B2.*

$$$ AMERICAN 🍴 **Telepan.** The greenmarket-driven menu at Chef Bill Telepan's eponymous eatery is heavy on the veggies (the seasonal vegetable starter wakes your palate right up), but fish lovers and first-timers should hook into the signature starter: smoked trout paired with sweet apple sour cream. Anything on the menu that contains eggs, like the "egg-in-a-hole" served with spinach and hen-of-the-woods mushrooms, is worth a try. There's the usual presence of foie gras and pork belly but Telepan does seafood very well (try the scallops). For dessert, a crunchy peanut-butter and gianduja duo with peanut-brittle ice cream is sublime. [$] *Average main: $30* ✉ *72 W. 69th St., between Columbus Ave. and Central Park W, Upper West Side* ☎ *212/580–4300* 🌐 *www.telepan-ny.com* 🕒 *No lunch Mon. and Tues.* [M] *1 to 66th St.–Lincoln Center; 2, 3 to 72nd St.; B, C to 72nd St.* ✥ *5:B4.*

HARLEM

Harlem culinary renaissance? Yes, indeed. This historic northern neighborhood has seen an infusion of fantastic restaurants in the last five years or so. There are still the standby Southern and soul food restaurants but also newer arrivals, making your journey northward even more worthwhile.

$$$ AFRICAN 🍴 **The Cecil.** You might feel like you've stepped into a private club after a pleasant doorman ushers you into this dimly lit space filled with

16

red-leather banquettes and eye-pleasing art on the walls, but at the same time, the Cecil feels very welcoming. The menu is influenced by the African diaspora, so there's a blend of culinary cultures—expect to be wowed. Heaping bowls of udon noodles are tangled around braised goat and edamame, all of which have been dunked in an African peanut sauce. Oxtail dumplings wade in a green apple curry sauce. A tender lamb shank sits upon coconut-spiked grits. This is a club you want to be a part of. $ *Average main: $29* ⊠ *210 W. 118th St., at St. Nicholas Ave.* ☎ *212/866–1262* ⊕ *www.thececilharlem.com* ⊗ *No lunch weekdays* Ⓜ *2, 3, B, C to 116th St.*

$$
BISTRO
✕ **Chez Lucienne.** French Harlem? Not exactly, but Chez Lucienne is as close as you can get without leaving the comfortable confines of this historic neighborhood. If you can't get into the Red Rooster next door, grab a seat at the baby blue banquette or relax at an outdoor table where locals come to sip coffee or wine, dogs at their side. The menu looks to Lyon with classics like sautéed foie gras and steak au poivre by a chef who logged time in the kitchen with famed Chef Daniel Boulud. $ *Average main: $19* ⊠ *308 Lenox Ave., between 125th and 126th sts., Harlem* ☎ *212/289–5555* ⊕ *www.chezlucienne.com* ▭ *No credit cards* Ⓜ *2, 3 to 116th St.* ✛ *6:D1.*

$$$
AMERICAN
✕ **Red Rooster Harlem.** Marcus Samuelsson, who earned his celebrity chefdom at Aquavit in Midtown for his take on Ethiopian-accented Scandinavian cuisine (fusing the food of his birthplace with that of where he grew up), moved way uptown to Harlem in 2010, where he has created a culinary hot spot for the ages. The comfort food menu jumps all over the place, reflecting the ethnic diversity that is modern-day New York City (and the patrons who regularly come here), from plantain-loaded oxtail to fried chicken to the tender meatballs (with lingonberry sauce) that he served at Aquavit. Expect a wait for Sunday brunch, with its gospel music, boozy cocktails, and modern takes on dishes like chicken and waffles. $ *Average main: $26* ⊠ *310 Lenox Ave., between 125th and 126th sts., Harlem* ☎ *212/792–9001* ⊕ *www. redroosterharlem.com* ▭ *No credit cards* Ⓜ *2, 3 to 125th St.* ✛ *6:D1.*

$$
SOUTHERN
FAMILY
✕ **Sylvia's.** This Harlem mainstay has been serving soul-food favorites like smothered chicken, barbecue ribs, collard greens, and mashed potatoes to a dedicated crowd of locals, tourists, and college students since 1962. Owner Sylvia Woods may have passed on in the summer of 2012, but her restaurant and signature sauces, jarred and sold online and in the restaurant, are more popular than ever. Some say it's overly touristy—as the busloads attest—but it's still worth the experience. For the ultimate experience, come for Sunday gospel brunch: singing and eating were never a more delicious combination. $ *Average main: $24* ⊠ *328 Lenox Ave., near 127th St., Harlem* ☎ *212/996–0660* ⊕ *www. sylviassoulfood.com* Ⓜ *2, 3 to 125th St.* ✛ *6:D1.*

BROOKLYN

BROOKLYN HEIGHTS

Brooklyn may be the place to eat these days, but Brooklyn Heights has always been more pleasing to the eye than to the tastebuds. If you know where to look, there are decent neighborhood restaurants, but nearby Carroll Gardens and Cobble Hill are chock full of edible goodness.

$$
MODERN
AMERICAN
Fodor's Choice
★

✕ **Colonie.** The key to this perpetually popular restaurant's success lies in its use of ultrafresh ingredients, sourced from local purveyors and presented with style in an upscale-casual space that honors its neighborhood's historical roots. There's always an oyster special, along with a selection of small plates like octopus with chorizo, duck egg with farro, and carrots with sunflower and candied garlic. The main courses, among them roast chicken and a sizable pork chop, tend to be hearty, though whole fish, fresh from the market, is on the menu as well. Dessert options include a sticky date cake, Vermont cheeses, and rich, sweet wines. $ *Average main: $20* ⊠ *12 Atlantic Ave., Brooklyn Heights* ☎ *718/855—7500* ⊕ *www.colonienyc.com* ⊗ *No lunch weekdays* Ⓜ *2, 3, 4, 5 to Borough Hall; R to Court St.* ✛ *7:A4.*

$$
AMERICAN

✕ **Henry's End.** This neighborhood institution made its reputation serving wonderful food and excellent wines in an unpretentious, high-ceilinged, brick-exposed dining room. The emphasis is on meat, with several nightly changing preparations of duck and veal—the latter, served with brussels sprouts, pancetta, and sage, is a knockout—but there are fish and pasta dishes as well. The annual Wild Game Festival, which lasts several months, is a showcase of hearty fare, including elk, buffalo, venison, and rabbit. The wine list, favoring California and Oregon vintages, includes noteworthy selections at all price points. $ *Average main: $24* ⊠ *44 Henry St., near Cranberry St., Brooklyn Heights* ☎ *718/834–1776* ⊕ *www.henrysend.com* ⊗ *No lunch* Ⓜ *2, 3 to Clark St.; A, C to High St.* ✛ *7:B3.*

$$
ITALIAN

✕ **Noodle Pudding.** Efficient waiters, consistently outstanding food, and the hum of conversation make a visit to this always bustling Italian restaurant exceedingly pleasant. Squeeze lemon over your calamari, savor gnocchi with sage butter, or tuck into lasagne Bolognese: whether you're in the mood for pasta, risotto, meat, chicken, or seafood, you're bound to leave satisfied. Just be sure to hear about the daily specials before making your decision. The wines here are reasonably priced. $ *Average main: $20* ⊠ *38 Henry St., near Cranberry St., Brooklyn Heights* ☎ *718/625–3737* ⊗ *Closed Mon. No lunch* ▭ *No credit cards* Ⓜ *2, 3 to Clark St.; A, C to High St.* ✛ *7:B3.*

$$$$
MODERN
AMERICAN

✕ **The River Café.** A deservedly popular special-occasion destination, this waterfront institution complements its exquisite Brooklyn Bridge views with memorable top-shelf cuisine served by an unfailingly attentive staff. Lobster, lamb, duck, and strip steak are among the staples of the prix-fixe menu ($120 for dinner, $42 for Saturday lunch, $55 for Sunday brunch). The chocolate Brooklyn Bridge mousse delivers the perfect ending to dinner. Jackets are required for men after 5 pm. $ *Average main: $255* ⊠ *1 Water St., Brooklyn Heights* ☎ *718/522—5200*

16

⊕ *www.therivercafe.com* ⊙ *No lunch weekdays* Ⓜ *2, 3 to Clark St.; A, C to High St.; F to York St.* ✛ *7:B2.*

DOWNTOWN BROOKLYN

Filled with neoclassical courthouse buildings and glass skyscrapers, there isn't much reason to come to downtown Brooklyn—unless, of course, you managed to nab a reservation at the borough's only three-Michelin-starred restaurant, Brooklyn Fare.

$$$$ ✕ **Chef's Table at Brooklyn Fare.** Should you manage to snag one of the
ECLECTIC 18 seats at Brooklyn's only Michelin three-star restaurant, you're in for a treat. Chef Cesar Ramirez prepares 20-plus courses of French- and Japanese-influenced raw and cooked seafood small plates. The extravaganza feels like dining in a secret enclave of sophisticates; note-taking, photography, and mobile phone use are discouraged to keep the focus on the meal, which costs $255 per person, exclusive of wine, tax, and tip. Every Monday at 10:30 am, reservations open for the entire week that's six weeks ahead. Seats fill up very quickly. Jackets are required for men. Ⓢ *Average main: $250* ⊠ *200 Schermerhorn St., near Hoyt St., Downtown Brooklyn* ☎ *718/243–0050* ⊕ *www.brooklynfare.com* ⊙ *Closed Sun. and Mon. No lunch* ⌕ *Reservations essential* Ⓜ *2, 3 to Hoyt St.; 2, 3, 4, 5 to Nevins St.; A, C, G to Hoyt–Schermerhorn Sts.; B, Q, R to DeKalb Ave.* ✛ *7:B4.*

$ ✕ **Junior's.** Famous for its thick slices of cheesecake, Junior's has been
DINER the quintessential Brooklyn diner since 1950. Classic cheeseburgers
FAMILY looming over little cups of cole slaw and thick french fries are first-rate, as are the sweet-potato latkes and pretty much all the breakfast offerings. You haven't truly arrived in the borough until you've sunk into one of the vinyl booths and eaten comforting diner classics in this brightly lit space. Ⓢ *Average main: $10* ⊠ *386 Flatbush Ave. Extension, Downtown Brooklyn* ☎ *718/852—5257* ⊕ *www.juniorscheesecake. com* Ⓜ *2, 3, 4, 5 to Nevins St.; B, Q, R to DeKalb Ave.; A, C, G to Hoyt–Schermerhorn Sts.* ✛ *7:C4.*

DUMBO

Once upon a time, the primary reason for a hungry person to come to DUMBO was to eat pizza at Grimaldi's. The past few years have seen the growing gentrification of these loft-strewn cobblestone streets, though, today sprinkled with toothsome eateries and cute boutiques. Now that the Brooklyn waterfront has been fully developed you can walk off your meal on a romantic stroll.

$$ ✕ **Gran Eléctrica.** Few restaurants are as equally suited to neighborhood
MEXICAN families as to trendy twentysomethings, but Gran Eléctrica pleases
FAMILY all palates. Maybe it's the tequila. The impressive list of bottles and a balanced cocktail menu accompany multiregional, streetfood–centric Mexican fare that regularly earns Michelin Bib Gourmand nods. Order a plate of *albondigas de Juana*—plump pork meatballs served with tortillas for mopping up the smoky chipotle broth—-and you'll quickly see what all the fuss is about. Ⓢ *Average main: $13* ⊠ *5 Front St., DUMBO* ☎ *718/852—2700* ⊕ *www.granelectrica.com* ⊙ *No lunch weekdays* Ⓜ *A, C to High St.; F to York St.* ✛ *7:B3.*

$$ ✕ **Juliana's.** Pizza pioneer Patsy Grimaldi's eponymous pie shops checker
PIZZA the city, but Juliana's is the latest in his thin-crust, coal-fired history.
FAMILY The restaurant is hidden in plain sight alongside neighboring Grimaldi's, where the lines are twice as long and the pizzas half as good.
Patsy himself has severed ties with Grimaldi's, so do like the locals do
and sample his classic white and margherita pies, homemade soups,
and Brooklyn Ice Cream Factory desserts in this bright, bustling space.
Ⓢ *Average main: $20* ✉ *19 Old Fulton St., DUMBO* ☎ *718/596–6700*
⊕ *www.julianaspizza.com* Ⓜ *2, 3 to Clark St.; A, C to High St.; F to
York St.* ✛ *7:B3.*

$$$ ✕ **Vinegar Hill House.** DUMBO's top dining destination is well worth
MODERN the sloping walk up from the waterfront. Those who make the trek
AMERICAN are rewarded with candlelit tables, seasonal menus, and a twinkling
Fodor's Choice rear patio lined with cherry trees. Word gets out about a scene this
★ good, so the wait for one of the 40 tables can be considerable, particularly during weekend brunch. Bide your time at the cozy bar, which
pours potent cocktails, local beer, and wine by the glass. Ⓢ *Average
main: $25* ✉ *72 Hudson Ave., between Front and Water sts., DUMBO*
☎ *718/522–1018* ⊕ *www.vinegarhillhouse.com* ☹ *No lunch weekdays*
Ⓜ *F to York St.* ✛ *7:C2.*

CARROLL GARDENS
Carroll Gardens has standout restaurants, which lure even those Manhattanites who might be loathe to cross the river.

$$ ✕ **Bergen Hill.** Seafood specialist Bergen Hill has earned a cult following
SEAFOOD among the neighborhood's discerning diners (many of the city's top
Fodor's Choice food writers call the neighborhood home). Chef Andrew D'Ambrosi, a
★ memorable *Top Chef* contestant, combines precisely cut raw fish with
nontraditional flavors (perhaps tuna with green olive, currant, and jalapeño, or poached octopus with onion, raisin, and harissa). The toasts
are a must—crunchy bread topped with lobster salad or perfectly seasoned roasted eggplant. The best seat is at the tiny chef's bar, where he
might tell you about a recent trip to Barcelona or slide you a sample of
his latest creation. The wine list is mostly old-world and adventurous;
cocktails lean alternately classic and interpretive. Ⓢ *Average main: $18*
✉ *387 Court St., Carroll Gardens* ☎ *718/858—5483* ⊕ *www.bergenhill.
com* ☹ *No lunch* Ⓜ *F, G to Carroll St.* ✛ *7:A5.*

$$ ✕ **Buttermilk Channel.** *Food Network*–famous fried chicken and waffles
AMERICAN have earned this Southern-accented New American bistro epic brunch
lines and a legion of neighborhood regulars with their kids (the Clown
Sundae is legendary among Carroll Gardens third-graders). But when
day turns to night, Buttermilk Channel transforms into a surprisingly
serious restaurant with an excellent, mostly American wine list and
satisfying entrées including steaks, pan-roasted fish, and an outstanding
warm lamb-shoulder salad. Vegetarians are certainly accommodated at
many Brooklyn restaurants but here they get a special menu. Ⓢ *Average main: $22* ✉ *524 Court St., at Huntington St., Carroll Gardens*
☎ *718/852–8490* ⊕ *www.buttermilkchannelnyc.com* ☹ *No lunch weekdays* Ⓜ *F, G to Smith—9th Sts.* ✛ *7:A5.*

16

$$
ITALIAN
Fodor'sChoice
★

✕**Frankies 457.** When Frank Castronovo and Frank Falcinelli opened this pioneering Italian-American restaurant in a former social club, Carroll Gardens was a culinary backwater. Much has evolved in the decade-plus since but what hasn't changed is the small but well-conceived menu of shareable salads (many with vegetables roasted or marinated with the Frankies' own Sicilian olive oil), handmade pastas like the cavatelli with hot sausage and browned sage butter, and crusty sandwiches that ask to be split and shared. When the weather's nice, try to score a seat in the gravel-lined backyard. $ *Average main: $16* ✉ *457 Court St., near Luquer St., Carroll Gardens* ☎ *718/403–0033* ⊕ *www. frankiesspuntino.com* Ⓜ *F, G to Carroll St. or Smith—9th Sts.* ✛ *7:A5.*

$$
VIETNAMESE
Fodor'sChoice
★

✕**Nightingale 9.** Though it's named after an old Brooklyn telephone code, Nightingale 9 takes its culinary inspiration from "long distance": Vietnam. This smartly designed Smith Street favorite is a must for lemongrass-grilled pork chops or the steamed rice crêpes called *banh cuon*, stuffed with minced pork, chicken pâté, and cucumber. Chef Rob Newton visits Vietnam often and brings back authentic recipes that he sometimes reimagines with his Arkansas childhood in mind, such as smoked pork sausage served with rice cakes and shrimp paste. Catfish is fried with turmeric and spices, and served with a unique combination of dill and peanuts. $ *Average main: $16* ✉ *329 Smith St., Carroll Gardens* ☎ *347/689–4699* ⊕ *www.nightingale9.com* ⊘ *Closed Mon. No lunch* Ⓜ *F, G to Carroll St.* ✛ *7:B5.*

$$$
STEAKHOUSE

✕**Prime Meats.** Steak, sausages, and serious Prohibition-era cocktails: it's a winning combination for Frank Castronovo and Frank Falcinelli, who opened this Frankies offshoot as a tribute to turn-of-the-century New York dining rooms. Try a chilled iceberg-lettuce salad with Maytag blue cheese and a Vesper or dry martini to start, followed by a grilled heritage pork chop or perhaps an order of steak frites—though there are many other options, including a number of Teutonic dishes like herb and Gruyère spätzle and house-made weisswurst. $ *Average main: $25* ✉ *465 Court St., at Luquer St., Carroll Gardens* ☎ *718/254–0327* ⊕ *www.frankspm.com* ⟆ *Reservations not accepted* Ⓜ *F, G to Carroll St. or Smith–9th Sts.* ✛ *7:A5.*

WILLIAMSBURG

Still probably the hippest, happening-est neighborhood in the five boroughs, Williamsburg is also one of the hottest destinations on the culinary landscape. You'll find plenty of decadent twists on farm-to-table cuisine, dressed-up comfort food classics, and killer cocktails.

$$
AMERICAN
Fodor'sChoice
★

✕**Diner.** The word "diner" might evoke a greasy spoon, but this trend-setting restaurant under the Williamsburg Bridge is nothing of the sort. Andrew Tarlow—the godfather of Brooklyn's farm-to-table culinary renaissance—opened it in 1999 and launched an entire movement. The restaurant occupies a 1927 dining car, and foodies cram into the tiny booths to sample the daily changing menu. Your waiter will scrawl the offerings on your paper tablecloth: expect two or three meat options, a fish or two, and veggies (asparagus in spring, delicata squash in fall) from farms in the Greater New York area. $ *Average main: $20* ✉ *85 Broadway, at Berry St., South Williamsburg* ☎ *718/486–3077* ⊕ *www.*

dinernyc.com ⌲ *Reservations not accepted* Ⓜ *J, M, Z to Marcy Ave.* ✛ *7:D2.*

$$ ✕ **Fette Sau.** It might seem odd to go to a former auto-body repair shop

BARBECUE to feast on meat, but the funky building and courtyard are just the right setting for the serious barbecue served here. A huge wood-and-gas smoker delivers brisket, sausages, ribs—even duck—all ordered by the pound. Sides include potato salad, broccoli salad, and baked beans, but meat is the main event. Pair your meal with one of the more than 40 American whiskeys and 10 microbrews. Come early, as tables fill up quickly, and even at 700 pounds of meat a night, the good stuff sometimes runs out by 9. Ⓢ *Average main: $13* ⊠ *354 Metropolitan Ave., at Havemeyer St., North Williamsburg* ☎ *718/963–3404* ⊕ *www. fettesaubbq.com* ☉ *No lunch Mon.–Thurs.* Ⓜ *L to Lorimer St., G to Metropolitan Ave.* ✛ *7:E2.*

$$ ✕ **Isa.** Entering this restaurant on a rather barren block feels like

MEDITERRANEAN walking into a modern farmhouse. Whitewashed walls, wood in

Fodor's Choice geometric patterns, and a terra-cotta floor set the tone for Brooklyn-

★ meets-Mediterranean fare, which means Tuscan-kale caesar salads and wood-fired breakfast pizza with pancetta, fontina, salsa verde, and an egg. The food is sourced as locally as possible, and the wine list features many organic bottles from France and Italy. Ask for a seat near the open kitchen if you want to see what the chefs are up to, or sit on the other side and watch the bartenders shake cocktails using herbs from the rooftop garden. Ⓢ *Average main: $24* ⊠ *348 Wythe Ave., at S. 3rd St., South Williamsburg* ☎ *347/689–3594* ⊕ *www.isa.gg* Ⓜ *L to Bedford Ave.; J, M, Z to Marcy Ave.* ✛ *7:D1.*

$$ ✕ **Le Barricou.** The team behind nearby Maison Premiere operate this

FRENCH Parisian-style brasserie serving escargots, coq au vin, and other French

Fodor's Choice bistro classics. Diners sit at rustic wooden tables, and the walls are

★ collaged with vintage French newspapers. Come for brunch if you've been searching for perfect eggs Benedict: the version here is drizzled with hollandaise and accompanied by salad and home fries (there are no reservations at brunch, so come early or expect to wait). Ⓢ *Average main: $18* ⊠ *533 Grand St., between Lorimer St. and Union Ave., South Williamsburg* ☎ *718/782–7372* ⊕ *www.lebarricouny.com* Ⓜ *L to Lorimer St., G to Metropolitan Ave.* ✛ *7:E2.*

$$ ✕ **Marlow & Sons.** With its green-and-white-striped awning, you might

AMERICAN easily mistake this buzzy bistro for an old-timey grocery store, but this

Fodor's Choice is a wood-panel dining room packed nightly with foodies for remark-

★ able locavore cuisine. Part of the Andrew Tarlow empire, Marlow & Sons serves food that sounds simple until you take that first bite. A starter the menu lists as burrata with radishes, for example, emerges from the kitchen as a complex dish of melt-in-your-mouth cheese with thin slices of the root vegetable and a crunchy topping of golden raisin bread toasted with olive oil. The entrées are equally inspired, thanks to the creative use to which the chefs put fresh, seasonal ingredients. The must-do dessert, the salted chocolate caramel tart, represents decadence at its flawless best. Ⓢ *Average main: $23* ⊠ *81 Broadway, at Berry St., South Williamsburg* ☎ *718/384–1441* ⊕ *www.marlowandsons.com*

16

🍴 *Reservations not accepted* Ⓜ *J, M, Z to Marcy Ave.; L to Bedford Ave.* ✛ *7:D2.*

$$$
MODERN
AMERICAN
Fodor's Choice
★

✕ **Meadowsweet.** Amid Williamsburg's culinary landscape of casual, comfort food–centric bistros with rock-and-roll soundtracks, this restaurant and bar feels thoroughly grown-up. Chef-owner Polo Dobkins serves New American cuisine in an airy space with blond-wood accents. The striking mosaic floor was preserved from the original 1890 building, at one point a kosher cafeteria. The sophisticated dishes might include crispy baby artichokes peeking out of a beautifully arranged mound of arugula and topped with shaved Parmesan; the plancha marina entrée contains impeccably cooked shrimp, scallops, squid, and monkfish served with aioli. Save room for dessert—the pastry chef likes to cut loose, drizzling ice cream with olive oil or sprinkling marcona almonds on a lemon ice cream tart. Ⓢ *Average main: $30* ⊠ *149 Broadway, between Bedford and Driggs aves., South Williamsburg* 🕾 *718/384–0673* ⊕ *www.meadowsweetnyc.com* Ⓜ *J, M, Z to Marcy Ave.* ✛ *7:D2.*

$$$$
STEAKHOUSE

✕ **Peter Luger Steak House.** Steak lovers come to Peter Luger for the exquisite dry-aged meat and the casual atmosphere. You can order individual steaks but the porterhouse is highly recommended and served only for two, three, or four. Make reservations as far ahead as possible as prime dining times fill up more than a month in advance. The lunch-only burger is beloved by those in the know, as is the bacon appetizer, available by the slice. Ⓢ *Average main: $50* ⊠ *178 Broadway, at Driggs Ave., South Williamsburg* 🕾 *718/387–7400* ⊕ *www.peterluger.com* 🍴 *Reservations essential* ▭ *No credit cards* Ⓜ *J, M, Z to Marcy Ave.* ✛ *7:D2.*

$
SOUTHERN

✕ **Pies 'N' Thighs.** Opened by three **Diner** alums, this little restaurant takes its moniker seriously, serving famously delicious fried chicken and pies made with organic and local ingredients. Perched on chairs from an elementary school, diners enjoy Southern-style meals that come with a protein (catfish and pulled pork for those who don't want chicken) and two sides (grits, mac 'n' cheese, and biscuits are favorites). Save room for pie: perhaps guava, key lime, banana cream, bourbon pecan, or many other varieties. Ⓢ *Average main: $12* ⊠ *166 S. 4th St., at Driggs Ave., South Williamsburg* 🕾 *347/529–6090* ⊕ *www.piesnthighs.com* Ⓜ *J, M, Z to Marcy Ave.* ✛ *7:D2.*

$$$
MODERN
AMERICAN
Fodor's Choice
★

✕ **Reynard.** The largest of Andrew Tarlow's Williamsburg restaurants (which include **Diner** and **Marlow & Sons**), Reynard has all the hallmarks of a Tarlow venture. Farm-to-table fare highlights the season's freshest ingredients, and everything is made in-house, even the granola. The grass-fed burger is always available but the rest of the menu changes often enough that you'll want to come back to try it all. Ⓢ *Average main: $26* ⊠ *Wythe Hotel, 80 Wythe Ave., at N. 11th St., Williamsburg* 🕾 *718/460–8004* ⊕ *www.reynardnyc.com* Ⓜ *L to Bedford Ave.* ✛ *7:D1.*

$$
STEAKHOUSE
Fodor's Choice
★

✕ **St. Anselm.** This modest spot grills high-quality meat and fish, all sustainably and ethically sourced, and at very reasonable prices. The sides, ordered à la carte, deserve special attention: the spinach gratin is dependably hearty, and the seasonal special of delicata squash with manchego (cheese from sheep's milk) is divine. Come early or risk a long wait, though you can get a drink from the owners' bar, Spuyten Duyvil, next door. St. Anselm is also open for brunch on weekends. [$] *Average main: $19* ✉ *355 Metropolitan Ave., at Havemeyer St., North Williamsburg* ☎ *718/384–5054* 🌐 *www.stanselm.net* 🕑 *No lunch weekdays* ✍ *Reservations not accepted* [M] *L to Lorimer St., G to Metropolitan Ave.* ✥ *7:E1.*

$$$ JAPANESE Fodor's Choice ★

🍴 **Zenkichi.** Modeled on Tokyo's intimate brasseries, this hidden Japanese restaurant serves no sushi: they specialize in exquisitly composed small plates, best enjoyed as part of the eight-course *omakase* (chef's tasting menu), though you can also order à la carte. Instead of a dining room, guests are seated in private booths separated by bamboo curtains, so other diners are audible but not visible. The gracious waiters can recommend sake to pair with your meal. This might be the closest to Tokyo you can get in Brooklyn. [$] *Average main: $26* ✉ *77 N. 6th St., at Wythe Ave., North Williamsburg* ☎ *718/388–8985* 🌐 *www.zenkichi.com* 🕑 *No lunch* ✍ *Reservations essential* [M] *L to Bedford Ave.* ✥ *7:D1.*

BUSHWICK

$$ BRITISH

🍴 **Dear Bushwick.** You never know what you might find on a Bushwick street, like this twee British gastropub. Innovative salads, vegetable sides, and shareable plates complement the small selection of hearty dinner mains—perhaps a skillet-cooked pork chop or cauliflower hash with curry. The Anglocentric cocktail menu deserves thorough investigation. Weekend brunch is outstanding, whether you're in the mood for a full English breakfast, Yorkshire pudding, or the delectable Farmhouse cottage cheese plate. [$] *Average main: $21* ✉ *41 Wilson Ave., at Melrose St., Bushwick* ☎ *929/234–2344* 🌐 *www.dearbushwick.com* 🕑 *No lunch weekdays* [M] *L to Morgan Ave., M to Central Ave.* ✥ *7:G2.*

$$ AMERICAN

🍴 **Northeast Kingdom.** Husband-and-wife team Paris Smeraldo and Meg Lipke opened this restaurant in 2005, basing their farm-to-table aesthetic on the rural communities of their native Vermont. More than a decade later, the place still has a loyal following. The dishes, which change with the seasons, might include chicken with spaetzle and asparagus or rainbow trout with red quinoa, stinging nettles, and *buerre noisette* (hazelnut butter). The burger, served with Vermont cheddar, housemade mayo, and tobacco onions, is a mainstay. [$] *Average main: $21* ✉ *18 Wyckoff Ave., at Troutman St., Bushwick* ☎ *718/386–3864* 🌐 *www.north-eastkingdom.com* [M] *L to Jefferson St.* ✥ *7:G2.*

EAST WILLIAMSBURG

The big draw in East Williamsburg is Roberta's. The neighborhood is still pretty industrial but there are new restaurants and bars out here creating a scene.

$ ETHIOPIAN Fodor's Choice ★

🍴 **Bunna Cafe.** The best way to sample the diverse flavors, many quite spicy, of Ethiopian cuisine at this stellar resaurant are the combination platters—for one or to share—though you can also order individual dishes. If the delicious, seasonal *duba wot* (spiced pumpkin) is available, definitely include it in your platter. Everything is served with *injera*, the sourdough flatbread diners use to scoop up the various stews. The drink menu includes traditional *t'ej* (honey wine), cocktails, and wine and beer from Ethiopia and elsewhere. The namesake *bunna*—Ethiopian

16

coffee brewed with cardamom and cloves—is worth a try, too. There's a special menu for brunch. $ *Average main: $10* ⊠ *1084 Flushing Ave., at Porter Ave., East Williamsburg* ☎ *347/295–2227* ⊕ *www. bunnaethiopia.net* Ⓜ *L to Morgan Ave.* ✛ *7:G2.*

$$
ITALIAN
Fodor'sChoice
★

✕ **Roberta's.** A neighborhood groundbreaker since it opened in 2008, this restaurant in a former garage is a must-visit, especially for pizza connoisseurs. The menu emphasizes hyperlocal ingredients—there's a rooftop garden—and the wood-fired pizzas have innovative combinations of toppings like fennel, pork sausage, and pistachio. There are also pastas and meaty mains, along with a vegetarian-friendly option or two. In summer service extends to a hip patio tiki bar. Roberta's is wildly popular, so either come early or try for a table at lunch or brunch, which isn't as hectic. **Blanca,** the two-Michelin-starred tasting menu-only ($195, Wed.—Sat., waitlist@blancanyc.com) restaurant on the Roberta's property serves innovative New American food. It's reservations only. $ *Average main: $15* ⊠ *261 Moore St., at Bogart St., Bushwick* ☎ *718/417–1118* ⊕ *www.robertaspizza.com* Ⓜ *L to Morgan Ave.* ✛ *7:F2.*

FORT GREENE

Fort Greene has become one of the most desirable neighborhoods in Brooklyn, the lovely brownstone apartments attracting young professionals and many of the borough's established writers and artists. It's also a garden of culinary delights with restaurants leading the locavore farm-to-table movement. And who knows? Maybe even a famous director or author will be sitting at the table next to you.

$
LATIN AMERICAN
FAMILY

✕ **Habana Outpost.** If the hearty Cuban sandwich and spicy Mexican corn on the cob don't win you over, the exceptionally potent margarita slushies will. An outdoor party scene with democratic appeal, Habana Outpost's spacious corner lot is popular with families, first dates, and the occasional raucous-but-friendly group of revelers. Everyone chows down on crowd-pleasing Latin American fare, served from the window of a repurposed truck–turned–kitchen counter. On Sunday nights, May through October, the restaurant screens free movies like *Purple Rain, Heathers,* and neighborhood mainstay Spike Lee's *Crooklyn.* $ *Average main: $9* ⊠ *757 Fulton St., Fort Greene* ☎ *718/858–9500* ⊕ *www. habanaoutpost.com* ☉ *Closed Nov.—Mar.* ▭ *No credit cards* Ⓜ *C to Lafayette Ave., G to Fulton St.* ✛ *7:C4.*

$$
SOUTH AFRICAN

✕ **Madiba.** Opened in 1999, America's first South African restaurant remains a swinging good time. Whether you come for an alfresco brunch, late-night cocktail, or a hearty dinner of spicy chicken livers and oxtail stew, Madiba's is always buzzing. On "Wine Wednesdays," the restaurant pours half-price bottles of renowned South African Indaba wine and has specials on wines by the glass. $ *Average main: $20* ⊠ *195 DeKalb Ave., Fort Greene* ☎ *718/855–9190* ⊕ *www.madibarestaurant. com* Ⓜ *C to Lafayette Ave., G to Fulton St.* ✛ *7:C4.*

$$
MODERN
AMERICAN

✕ **No. 7.** Perch at the marble-top bar or lounge at one of the banquettes in the back at this buzzy neighborhood bistro lighted up by Edison bulbs. The frequently changing menu puts a global spin on American classics. The result is nouveau fusion that pulls in droves of local diners and makes vegetarians happy. Highlights might include anything from crispy eggplant with tofu in a tomato vinaigrette to skirt steak with baked potato, Chinese sausage, and chimichurri sauce. Brunch dishes are similarly innovative but delicious—think fried eggs with nachos and jalapeños, or pork loin with fried eggs, buttermilk pancake, and pineapple maple syrup. On Monday night, the dining room is closed but the bar is still open. [$] *Average main: $20* ✉ *7 Greene Ave., Fort Greene* ☎ *718/522–6370* 🌐 *www.no7restaurant.com* ⏲ *No lunch weekdays; no dinner Mon.* [M] *C to Lafayette Ave.; 2, 3, 4, 5, B, Q to Atlantic Ave.* ⊕ *7:C4.*

$$$ ITALIAN Fodor's Choice ★ 🍴 **Roman's.** Part of an all-star Brooklyn restaurant group that includes Williamsburg favorites Diner and Marlowe & Sons, this seasonally-focused eatery has an Italian accent. Menus change daily and include farm-fresh fare like wintry fennel salads or pork meatballs *in brodo*, or delicacies like artichoke-studded house-made spaghetti in summer. When weather permits, request one of the candlelit, alfresco tables: There's no better perch from which to soak up the Fort Greene scene. [$] *Average main: $26* ✉ *243 Dekalb Ave., near Vanderbilt Ave., Fort Greene* ☎ *718/622–5300* 🌐 *www.romansnyc.com* ⏲ *No lunch weekdays* [M] *C to Lafayette Ave., G to Clinton–Washington Aves.* ⊕ *7:D4.*

16

$$ MODERN AMERICAN 🍴 **Stonehome Wine Bar and Restaurant.** Just down the street from BAM, Stonehome is the place to go before or after a show for sophisticated food and wine at reasonable prices. This dimly lighted basement hideaway has excellent tasting flights—three samples for $18—and 38 wines by the glass, perfect to pair with cheese, charcuterie, and house-made pâtés. The small and uncomplicated menu focues on market-fresh new American fare like pan-roasted chicken with cheddar grits and greens. The back garden is a delight in nice weather. [$] *Average main: $19* ✉ *87 Lafayette Ave., at S. Portland Ave., Fort Greene* ☎ *718/624–9443* 🌐 *www.stonehomewinebar.com* ⏲ *No lunch* [M] *C to Lafayette Ave.* ⊕ *7:C4.*

$$ AMERICAN Fodor's Choice ★ 🍴 **Walter's.** A sister restaurant to Williamsburg's Walter Foods, this buzzy bistro has a seasonal menu, a comely crowd, and rosy-hued lighting that gives the space a glamorous Gallic vibe. Stop in for a cocktail after a day in Fort Greene Park, or come for a heartier repast courtesy of Walter's raw bar, satisfying main dishes (the fried chicken with garlic mashed potatoes is a consistent winner), and market-fresh veggie sides. [$] *Average main: $20* ✉ *166 DeKalb Ave., Fort Greene* ☎ *718/488–7800* 🌐 *www.walterfoods.com/walters* [M] *B, Q, R to DeKalb Ave.; C to Lafayette Ave.; G to Fulton St.* ⊕ *7:C4.*

PARK SLOPE

Park Slope's reputation precedes it: this handsome, gay-friendly family neighborhood also happens to be a great place to fill the tummy. Restaurant-crammed 5th Avenue is not for the indecisive; there's everything from Mexican to Italian to Thai, and it's all quite good.

$$ ITALIAN Fodor's Choice ★ 🍴 **al di là Trattoria.** Roughly translated as "the great beyond," al di là has been consistently packed since it opened in 1998, and it's easy to understand why: perfectly prepared dishes from Northern Italy served at affordable prices, in a relaxed atmosphere. The warm farro salad with seasonal ingredients and goat cheese is perfectly al dente; the hand-pinched ravioli are deliciously homemade; and meatier entrées

like braised rabbit, pork loin scaloppine, and charcoal-grilled young Bo Bo chicken are highlights. The wine bar is a good spot to wait for a table. $ *Average main: $23* ⊠ *248 5th Ave., at Carroll St., Park Slope* ☎ *718/783–4565* ⊕ *www.aldilatrattoria.com* Ⓜ *R to Union St.* ✛ *7:C5.*

$$
MEXICAN

✕ **Fonda.** Authentic and flavorful contemporary Mexican food, perfectly mixed cocktails, and amiable staff define this cozy restaurant—the first of three in New York City overseen by award-winning chef and cookbook author Roberto Santibañez. It's tempting to order by sauce alone: enchiladas with mole, scallops and shrimp with avocado serrano sauce, and poblano peppers with roasted-tomato chipotle sauce. Popular appetizers include the braised duck and the fish salpicon, both served on corn tortillas. The small space is always buzzing and in nice weather there's backyard seating. $ *Average main: $22* ⊠ *434 7th Ave., between 14th and 15th Sts., Park Slope* ☎ *718/369—3144* ⊕ *www.fondarestaurant. com* ☽ *No lunch weekdays* Ⓜ *F, G to 7th Ave. or 15th St.–Prospect Park* ✛ *7:C6.*

$$
ITALIAN

✕ **Franny's.** Local, organic, sustainable, and high-quality are the watchwords at this lively spot known for delicious wood-fired pizzas and inventive Southern Italian dishes. The menu is gently priced but portions run small. Seasonal flourishes might include ramps, roasted fennel, or whipped eggplant, and pizza toppings feature unusual cheeses like nutty grana padano, peppery pecorino, and sharp Ragusano D.O. caciocavallo: all pair well with the extensive list of Italian wines. Watch the crew at work through the open kitchen. $ *Average main: $18* ⊠ *348 Flatbush Ave., between Sterling Pl. and 8th Ave., Park Slope* ☎ *718/230–0221* ⊕ *www.frannysbrooklyn.com* Ⓜ *2, 3 to Grand Army Plaza; B, Q to 7th Ave.* ✛ *7:C5.*

$$
ASIAN FUSION
Fodor'sChoice
★

✕ **Talde.** *Top Chef* alumnus Dale Talde has created a showstopping menu of Asian-American comfort foods at this casual neighborhood restaurant. Taste the bold flavors of staples like the crispy pretzel pork and chive dumplings, tangy Kung Pao chicken wings with cilantro and peanuts, Filipino pork shoulder with pickled papaya, and Korean fried chicken with a kimchee yogurt sauce cooled by sliced grapes. If the Filipino halo-halo dessert is on the menu, you're in for a sugar rush: it's shaved ice with sweetened condensed milk, coconut, tapioca, seasonal fruit, and Cap'n Crunch. Distract yourself with a cocktail at the bar if there's a wait for a table. $ *Average main: $22* ⊠ *369 7th Ave., at 11th St., Park Slope* ☎ *347/916–0031* ⊕ *www.taldebrooklyn.com* ☽ *No lunch weekdays* Ⓜ *F, G to 7th Ave.* ✛ *7:C6.*

PROSPECT HEIGHTS

Once referred to as the "new Park Slope," the neighborhood on the other side of Flatbush has come into its own. Leafy, brownstone-laden streets are increasingly filled with great restaurants.

$$
ITALIAN

✕ **Bar Corvo.** On the Crown Heights–Prospect Heights border (*corvo* means "crow" in Italian, as in Crow Hill, this area's old name) and a stone's throw from the Brooklyn Museum, this handmade-pasta specialist is an offshoot of Park Slope's renowned al di là. Like its sibling, Bar Corvo offers rustic decor alongside refined starches and salads—squid-ink spaghetti with octopus, *malfatti* gnocchi with walnuts, and an impeccable warm farro salad (the fried spicy chickpeas, billed a "snack," are highly addictive). For weekend museumgoers, Bar Corvo's brunch is a refined alternative to Tom's more casual diner fare up the block. [$] *Average main: $18* ✉ *791 Washington Ave., at Lincoln Pl., Prospect Heights* ☎ *718/230—0940* 🌐 *www.barcorvo.com* ⏲ *No lunch weekdays* [M] *2, 3 to Eastern Pkwy.–Brooklyn Museum; 2, 3, 4, 5 to Franklin Ave.; S to Botanic Garden* ⊕ *7:D5.*

$$ JAPANESE Fodor's Choice ★

🍴 **Chuko.** Whether it's because of the miniscule size of the restaurant or the habit-forming flavors of the noodle bowls, there's always a crowd outside this ramen storefront. Since opening in 2011 as an offshoot of Manhattan's Morimoto, Chuko has become a Prospect Heights institution with a small, reliably tasty menu—the signature ramen comes in a simple selection of broths and toppings. The Brooklyn flagship has since spawned **Bar Chuko** (*565 Vanderbilt Ave., at Bergen St.*; *closed Mon.*), a block away, which has a wider selection of *izakaya* small plates—Japanese bar food like yakitori skewers and clams with XO sauce. Wander over there if the mothership is mobbed or to enjoy a shochu cocktail while you wait. [$] *Average main: $13* ✉ *552 Vanderbilt Ave., at Dean St., Prospect Heights* ☎ *718/576—6701* 🌐 *www.barchuko.com* 💳 *No credit cards* [M] *2, 3 to Bergen St.; A, C to Clinton–Washington Aves.; B, Q to 7th Ave.* ⊕ *7:D5.*

$ CARIBBEAN Fodor's Choice ★

🍴 **The Islands.** A Prospect Heights institution since before the neighborhood gentrified, this Caribbean restaurant has a tiny ground-floor kitchen and a steep staircase leading up to an equally small dining room that feels like a crow's nest. The Islands does the area's West Indian heritage proud with signature jerk dishes that are at least two-alarm spicy. Generous portions (a "small" plate is plenty) of chicken, shrimp, goat, and oxtail come with rice and salad—an authentic and delicious low-frills meal. [$] *Average main: $12* ✉ *803 Washington Ave., at Lincoln Pl., Prospect Heights* ☎ *718/398—3575* 💳 *No credit cards* [M] *2, 3 to Eastern Pkwy.–Brooklyn Museum; 2, 3, 4, 5 to Franklin Ave.; S to Botanic Garden* ⊕ *7:D5.*

$ DINER FAMILY

🍴 **Tom's Restaurant.** The legend of Tom's may outstrip the reality (contrary to myth, Suzanne Vega's hit "Tom's Diner" is *not* named for the place), but lines form down the block every weekend around brunchtime for a spot at this snug, old-school lunch-counter joint that serves straight-ahead diner food. Kindly proprietor Jim Kokotas offers the folks in line coffee, orange slices, and sausage bites. When you finally sit, stick to breakfast staples—the lemon ricotta flapjacks are the real standout (ask for the flavored butters). If your party is small enough, counter seats can usually be had more quickly. [$] *Average main: $8* ✉ *782 Washington Ave., at Sterling Pl., Prospect Heights* ☎ *718/636—9738* 🌐 *www.tomsbrooklyn.com* ⏲ *No dinner* 💳 *No credit cards* [M] *2, 3 to Eastern Pkwy.–Brooklyn Museum; 2, 3, 4, 5 to Franklin Ave.; S to Botanic Garden* ⊕ *7:D5.*

$$ MODERN AMERICAN

🍴 **The Vanderbilt.** The mellowest of longtime Brooklyn chef Saul Bolton's several restaurants in the borough, the Vanderbilt offers a broad menu in a large space. Comfort food like meatballs, chicken, and pork chops are joined by creative small plates, a charcuterie menu, a well-chosen craft beer menu, and intriguing cocktails. Weekend brunch is the busier, buzzier meal, with delicious shrimp 'n' grits. For a higher-end,

16

experience, Bolton's eponymous flagship, Saul (closed Monday and Tuesday), moved from Cobble Hill to the Brooklyn Museum several years ago; locals agree the menu became less exceptional after the transfer but the presentation is polished. $ *Average main: $16* ✉ *570 Vanderbilt Ave., Prospect Heights* ☎ *718/623—0570* ⊕ *www. thevanderbiltnyc.com* ☉ *No lunch weekdays* Ⓜ *2, 3 to Bergen St.; C to Clinton–Washington Aves.; B, Q to 7th Ave.* ✛ *7:D5.*

CONEY ISLAND

It's no longer an island, but this amusement park on the sea is salt-of-the-earth paradise. Think pizza and hot dogs and calorie-laden carnival fare. If you're in town during July 4, a Big Apple must-see is the annual Nathan's Famous hot dog eating contest where hundreds of people gather to watch "professional" eaters scarf down tubular meat.

$$

✕ **Totonno's Pizzeria Napolitana.** Thin-crust pies judiciously topped with

PIZZA

fresh mozzarella and tangy, homemade tomato sauce, then baked in

FAMILY

a coal oven—at Totonno's you're not just eating pizza, you're biting

Fodor's Choice

into a slice of New York history. Not much has changed since Anthony

★

(Totonno) Pero first opened the pizzeria, in 1924, right after the subways started running to Coney Island—-the restaurant is at the same location and run by the same family, who use ingredients and techniques that have been handed down through four generations. The casual dining room is old-school, too, with checkerboard linoleum flooring, red-top tables, and wall-to-wall autographed photos, historic news clippings, and awards and accolades (including the James Beard American Classic). $ *Average main: $16* ✉ *1524 Neptune Ave., between 15th and 16th sts., Coney Island* ☎ *718/372–8606* ⊕ *www.totonnosconeyisland. com* ☉ *Closed Mon.–Wed.* ⊟ *No credit cards* Ⓜ *D, F, N, Q to Coney Island–Stillwell Ave.* ✛ *7:G6.*

BRIGHTON BEACH

The subway trains that shuttle people out to this beachside neighborhood could be nicknamed the "time machine" because strolling the wide boardwalk along the sea feels like you've dropped into another time and space. Odessa in the 1980s comes to mind. After all, it was around that time when a mass migration of Russian immigrants settled in Brighton Beach. Today you'll hear more Slavic than English and you'll most certainly be tempted by the vodka and highly entertaining Russian restaurants that line the boardwalk.

$

✕ **Cafe Kashkar.** Uyghur cuisine, from the Chinese region of Xinjiang, is

ASIAN

the focus of the menu at this postage stamp-size café. Standouts include *naryn* (lamb dumplings), *samsa* (empanada-like lamb pies), pickles, vinegary salads, and clay-oven-baked bread. The few Uzbek dishes on the menu are recommended, in particular the pilaf and the lamb and vegetable *dymlama*—-a meat and potato stew that's sometimes made with vegetables and fruit. The portions are definitely shareable. $ *Average main: $6* ✉ *1141 Brighton Beach Ave., at Brighton 15th St., Brighton Beach* ☎ *718/743-3832* ⊕ *www.kashkarcafe.com* Ⓜ *B, Q to Brighton Beach* ✛ *7:H6.*

$$ ╳ **Tatiana Restaurant and Night Club.** There are two prime times at Tatiana's: day and night. Sitting at a boardwalk-side table on a summer afternoon, enjoying the breezes and the views of the Atlantic while eating lunch al fresco, is a quintessential Brighton Beach experience. After dark, a flashier crowd arrives, especially on weekends when Tatiana's hosts an extravagant floor show, with plenty of dancing, costumes, and acrobatics. The menu has a bit of everything: the Ukrainian specialties, like the sweet and savory *varenikis*, a pierogi-like dumpling that's considered the Ukraine's national dish, are especially good, as is the herring, the homemade lox, and the caviar platters. Vodka can be ordered like wine—by the bottle. No sneakers are allowed in the evenings. $ *Average main: $20* ⊠ *3152 Brighton 6th St. (or enter from boardwalk), Brighton Beach* ☎ *718/891–5151* ⊕ *www.tatianarestaurant.com* M *B, Q to Brighton Beach* ✛ *7:H6.*

RUSSIAN
Fodor's Choice
★

QUEENS

ASTORIA

After you're finished with the sights, why head back to Manhattan? End your day with dinner at one of Astoria's legendary Greek restaurants (on or near Broadway), or venture to the Middle Eastern restaurants farther out on Steinway Street.

$$ ╳ **Kabab Café.** Middle-Eastern restaurants are a dime a dozen in NYC, but Egyptian-Mediterranean spots are a rarer find, attracting celebrity chefs and TV personalities like Anthony Bourdain and Andrew Zimmern. This charming yet eccentric 16-seat café, which excels at interesting homestyle dishes, is a true hidden treasure. The menu changes nightly, but think of the fare here as Egyptian-accented comfort food: exceedingly tender lamb stuffed with pomegranate is always great. For the super adventurous eater, try the grilled lamb brain or lamb tongue. When it's available, the roasted goose in a saffron sauce is a must. $ *Average main: $17* ⊠ *25-12 Steinway St., Astoria* ☎ *718/728–9858* ⊘ *Closed Mon.* ⌒ *Reservations not accepted* ═ *No credit cards* M *N, Q to Astoria Blvd.* ✛ *7:F1.*

MIDDLE EASTERN

$$ ╳ **Taverna Kyclades.** The current powerhouse of Hellenic eats in the neighborhood, Taverna Kyclades serves Greek classics at a higher level than you'd expect, given the simple décor and unassuming location. Fried calamari and grilled octopus make appearances at rock-bottom prices, despite their obvious quality, as do more out-of-the-ordinary dishes like "caviar dip" and swordfish kebabs. Lamb chops drip with juice, and grilled sardines are so fresh you'd swear they were just pulled from the sea. Be prepared to wait for a table at peak times, as they don't take reservations. There's also a Manhattan outpost on 1st Avenue and East 13th Street in the East Village. $ *Average main: $16* ⊠ *33-07 Ditmars Blvd., Astoria* ☎ *718/545–8666* ⊕ *www.tavernakyclades.com* ⌒ *Reservations not accepted* M *N, Q to Astoria–Ditmars Blvd.* ✛ *7:F1.*

GREEK

FLUSHING

Manhattan may be known for its fine four-star restaurants, but food lovers know there's one train to take to some of the best eats in the city. The 7 snakes its way through the middle of Queens, and conveniently through some of the best dining neighborhoods in New York. At the end of the line is Flushing, home to the second-largest Chinatown in the United States. (First is San Francisco's.) Wide streets have few tourists and many interesting stores and restaurants, making the long trip worth it. A couple tips: bring cash, because not many of these restaurants accept credit cards, and be prepared to encounter language difficulties, as English speakers are in the minority. In Manhattan, catch the 7 train at Times Square or Grand Central Terminal.

$ CHINESE 🍴 **Spicy and Tasty.** Flushing is crammed with quality salt-of-the-earth Chinese eateries, but Spicy and Tasty is the place to go for stand-out Chinese, particularly if you're a first-timer to the neighborhood. The restaurant lives up to its name with numbing Szechuan peppercorns and slicks of red chili oil. Tea-smoked duck has crispy skin and smoky, salty meat. Eggplant with garlic sauce tastes of ginger, tomatoes, and red chilies. Cool it all down with a Tsingtao beer. The $6.50 lunch special—weekdays only—is quite the deal. [$] *Average main: $10* ✉ *39-07 Prince St., at 39th Ave., Flushing* ☎ *718/359–1601* 🌐 *www.spicyandtasty.com* 💳 *No credit cards* [M] *7 to Flushing–Main St.* ✥ *7:H1.*

LONG ISLAND CITY

Long Island City began attracting more visitors when MoMA PS1 opened in the 1970s.

$ CANADIAN Fodor's Choice ★ 🍴 **M. Wells Dinette.** When the original version of this beloved and experimental restaurant in Long Island City lost its lease and had to shut down, a swath of New York eaters let out a collective groan. But they didn't have to go too long without their foie gras fix because French-Canadian chef Hugue Dufour reopened the restaurant at MoMA PS1. The menu changes depending on the season but diners might find dishes like veal cheek stroganoff, with thick bucatini, or bone marrow and escargot. Finish off with a slice of maple pie and a shot of maple bourbon. Then wander the gallery trying to make sense of the art (and your meal). The restaurant currently closes at 6 pm, leaving time for a leisurely lunch but not dinner. [$] *Average main: $17* ✉ *MoMA PS1, 22–25 Jackson Ave., at 46th Ave., Long Island City* ☎ *718/786–1800* 🌐 *www.momaps1.org/about/mwells* ⏲ *No dinner. Closed Tues. and Wed.* ✍ *Reservations not accepted* [M] *7, G to Court Sq.; E, M to Court Sq.–23rd St.* ✥ *7:F1.*

$$$$ STEAKHOUSE 🍴 **M. Wells Steakhouse.** From the team that made Long Island City a dining destination with the original M. Wells and then the M. Wells Dinette inside MoMA PS1 comes this mecca devoted to meat. Once you find the door—-go through the gate, then walk across the small courtyard—-settle in at a table in the industrial space, order a cocktail (the Canadian sidecar just means there's maple in the classic), and peruse the menu. There are some good but gimmicky options—-a bone-in burger, the short or tall stack of pork chops, foie gras gnocchi—-but we say stick to the steak, particularly the thick, juicy côte de boeuf, and you'll leave a happy diner. [$] *Average main: $40* ✉ *43-15 Crescent St., Long Island City* ☎ *718/786–9060* 🌐 *www.magasinwells.com* ⏲ *Closed Tues. No lunch* [M] *7, N, Q to Queensboro Plaza; E, M, R to Queens Plaza* ✥ *7:F1.*

JACKSON HEIGHTS

One of the most ethnically diverse parts of New York City, Jackson Heights is home to a United Nations of cuisine: from outstanding Indian and Pakistani places to surprisingly excellent taco carts. Most recently, Tibetans and Nepalese have been moving into the neighborhood, setting up small shops selling juicy meat-filled *momos* (dumplings) and other Himalayan treats.

$ ✕ **Phayul.** Step through the doorway with the Himalayan eyebrow
TIBETAN   threading sign above it, head up the twisting and turning stairway, then enter through a beaded curtain and you'll find yourself something of a delicious culinary anomaly: Tibetan-Sichuan cuisine. The traditional *momos* (Tibetan dumplings stuffed with meat) are worth trying, but the most exciting fare here lies in the fusion of the two cultures, like spicy blood sausage or tofu in a fiery chili sauce. The funky beef-studded Tibetan yak cheese soup is for adventurous eaters. [$] *Average main: $9* ✉ *37-65 74th St., Jackson Heights* ☎ *718/424–1869* ▭ *No credit cards* [M] *7 to 74th St.–Broadway; E, F, M, R to Jackson Heights–Roosevelt Ave.* ✛ *7:F1.*

WOODSIDE

It has long been said that to get great Thai food in the Big Apple, you have to go to Queens. While the Thai dining landscape has improved in other parts of the city, Woodside is still its epicenter. But to only associate Woodside with just Thai cuisine is underselling it; you'll find a variety of ethnic eateries here, including Ecuadorian and Italian.

$ ✕ **SriPraPhai.** The main reason foodies flock to Woodside is to go to
THAI   SriPraPhai(pronounced "See-PRA-pie"). It's widely considered the best Thai restaurant in New York. Don't be overwhelmed by the huge menu—it's hard to go wrong. Crispy watercress salad, *larb* (ground pork salad with mint and lime juice), sautéed chicken with cashews and pineapple, *kao-soy* (curried egg noodles), and roasted duck green curry are a few standouts. If you go with a few people, order the delicately flavored whole steamed fish. There's a large separate menu for vegetarians. But prepare your palate: your mouth might feel like a five-alarm fire by the time you're finished. [$] *Average main: $12* ✉ *64-13 39th Ave., Woodside* ☎ *718/899–9599* ⊕ *www.sripraphairestaurant.com* ▭ *No credit cards* ⊙ *Closed Wed.* [M] *7 to 69th St.* ✛ *7:H1.*

16

THE BRONX

People don't really wander into this borough—like they do into Brooklyn and even Queens, hoping to stumble on some gem of an ethnic eatery—but the Bronx actually has a lot going for it, if you know where to look. Dotted throughout the borough are some great Mexican taquerías, African eateries, and old-school Italian joints. Skip Manhattan's Little Italy and head to the Bronx's Arthur Avenue for a real red-sauce treat; it's a much more authentic Italian-American neighborhood and a great place to carb-load.

$$ ✕ **Antonio's Trattoria.** Antonio's bills itself as "an Italian restaurant
ITALIAN   serving simple food," but it's underselling itself. This is fantastic

salt-of-the-earth Italian fare at its best. Start with the mini-meatballs wading in a marinara sauce and move on to baked clams, house-made ravioli, fettuccine carbonara, or excellent pizza, baked in a brick oven in the Neapolitan manner. Only the red-and-white checked tablecloths are missing. It's a bit off the main "Little Italy" strip, but worth the trek. And if you haven't eaten enough, expect a server to come by, prodding you with *"Mangia, mangia!"* $ *Average main: $22* ⊠ *2370 Belmont Ave., Belmont* ☎ *718/733–6630* ⊕ *www.antoniostrattoria.com* Ⓜ *B, D to 182nd–183rd Sts.*

$$
ITALIAN

✕ **Zero Otto Nove.** Though insiders who can get a table swear by Rao's on 114th Street in Manhattan, Zero Otto Nove chugs along as one of the best Italian restaurants north of 96th Street. The draw? A menu that nicely balances authentic Italian fare with good Italian-American classics. Try a woodoven–fired pizza, perfectly chewy and loaded with buffalo mozzarella. The San Matteo, which adds broccoli rabe to the mix, is just as addictive as the plain Jane margherita. Pasta dishes are worthy of your attention, too: the malfade with chickpeas, crispy pancetta, and breadcrumbs might make you want to skip the pizza pie for now. For those who don't feel like a trek to the Bronx, there's an outpost in Chelsea. $ *Average main: $15* ⊠ *2357 Arthur Ave., Belmont* ☎ *718/220–1027* ⊕ *www.roberto089.com* ☾ *Closed Mon.* ⚐ *Reservations not accepted* Ⓜ *B, D to 182nd–183rd Sts.*

STATEN ISLAND

$

ITALIAN
FAMILY

Denino's Pizzeria & Tavern. Arguably the best pizzeria in the borough, Denino's has been run by the same Sicilian family for more than 75 years. Baking thin-crust pizzas in their current location since 1937, this Staten Island institution is worth the trip from from St. George (half an hour by bus; 15-minute drive). For dessert, try Ralph's Famous Italian Ices and Ice Cream, conveniently located across the street. $ *Average main: $17* ⊠ *524 Port Richmond Ave.* ☎ *718/442–9401* ⊕ *www. deninos.com* ▭ *No credit cards* Ⓜ *S44 or S94 bus from Staten Island Ferry Terminal (30 mins).*

NEW YORK CITY DINING AND LODGING ATLAS

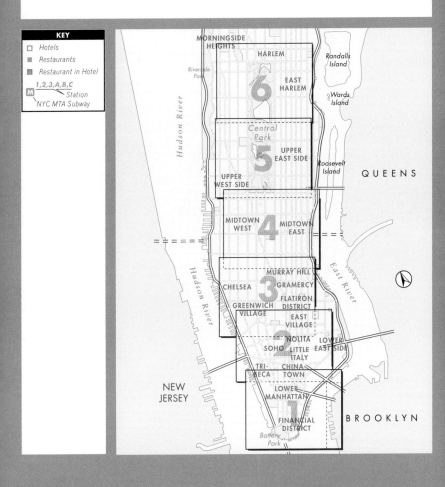

KEY

- ☐ Hotels
- ◼ Restaurants
- ◼ Restaurant in Hotel

1,2,3,A,B,C ──── Station
Ⓜ NYC MTA Subway

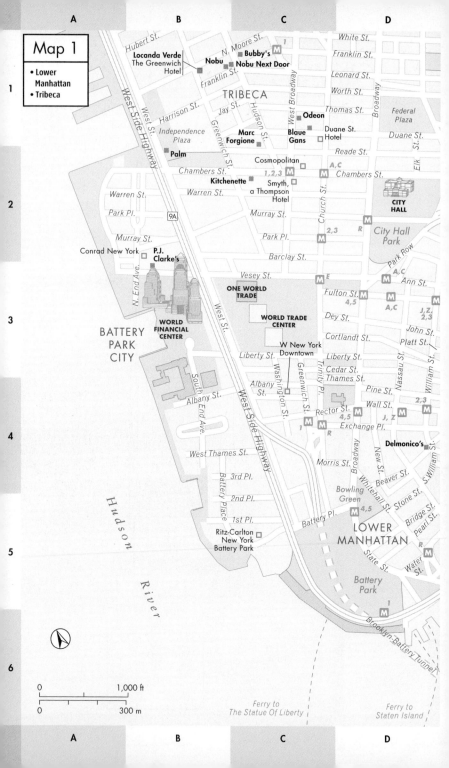

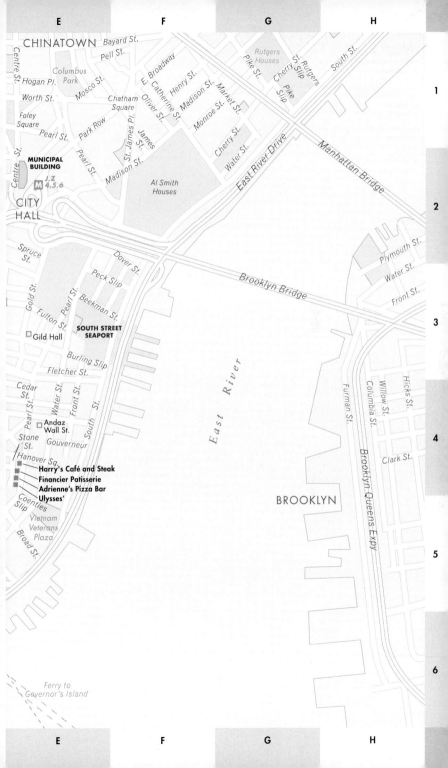

CHINATOWN Bayard St.
Pell St.
E. Broadway
Centre St.
Columbus Park
Hogan Pl.
Mosco St.
Worth St.
Chatham Square
Henry St.
Madison St.
Market St.
Pike St.
Rutgers Houses
Cherry St.
Rutgers Slip
South St.
Foley Square
Park Row
Oliver St.
Monroe St.
Pike Slip
Pearl St.
St. James Pl.
James St.
Cherry St.
Pearl St.
Madison St.
Water St.
East River Drive
Manhattan Bridge
MUNICIPAL BUILDING
J, Z
4, 5, 6
Al Smith Houses
CITY HALL
Spruce St.
Dover St.
Gold St.
Peck Slip
Brooklyn Bridge
Plymouth St.
Water St.
Fulton St.
Pearl St.
Beekman St.
Front St.
Gild Hall
SOUTH STREET SEAPORT
Burling Slip
Fletcher St.
East River
Cedar St.
Pearl St.
Water St.
Front St.
South St.
Furman St.
Columbia St.
Willow St.
Hicks St.
Andaz Wall St.
Stone St.
Gouverneur
Clark St.
Hanover Sq.
Harry's Café and Steak
Financier Patisserie
Adrienne's Pizza Bar
Ulysses'
Coenties Slip
BROOKLYN
Brooklyn Queens Expy
Vietnam Veterans Plaza
Broad St.
Ferry to Governor's Island

E F G H

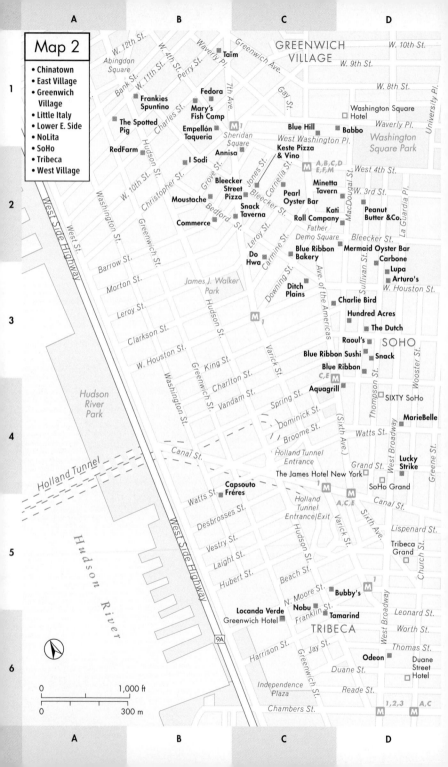

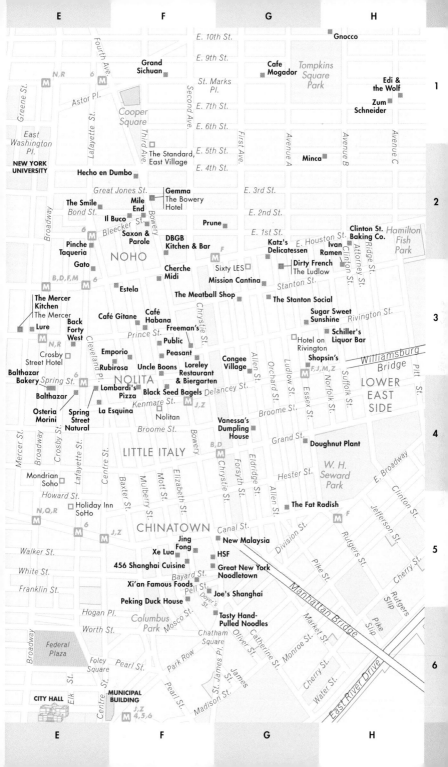

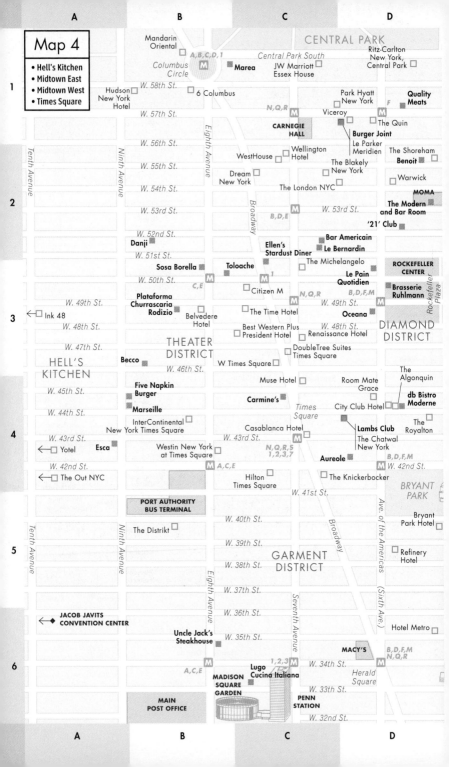

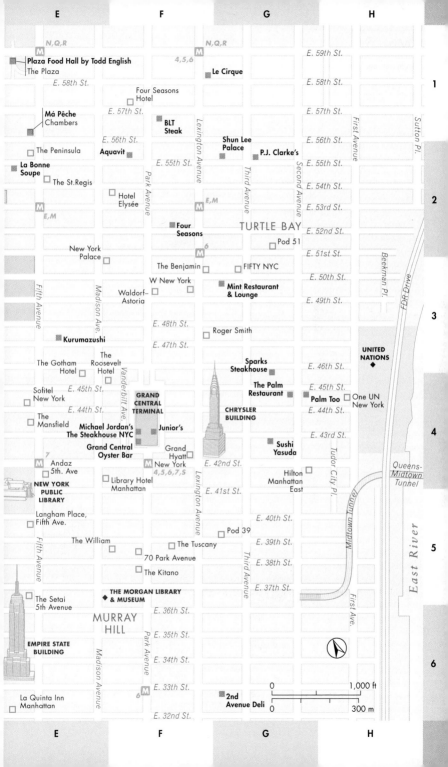

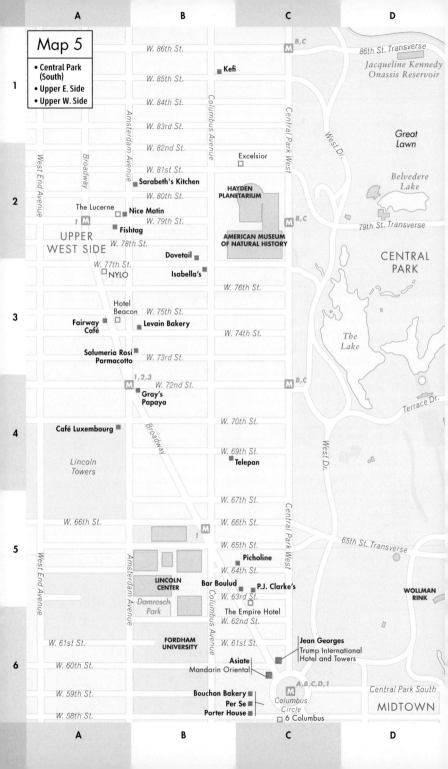

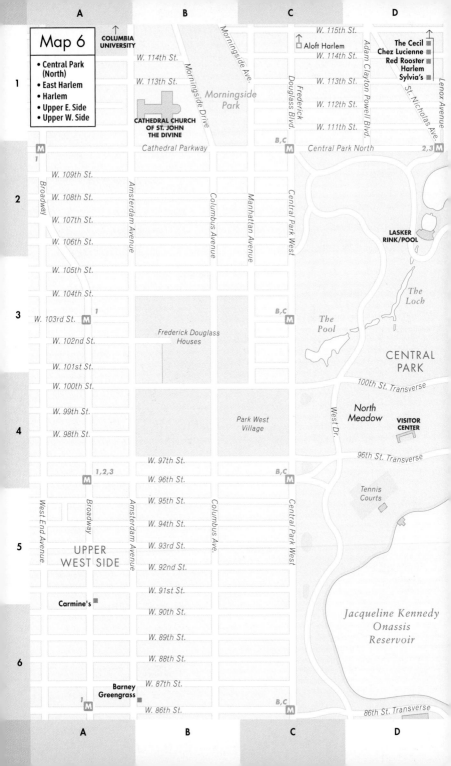

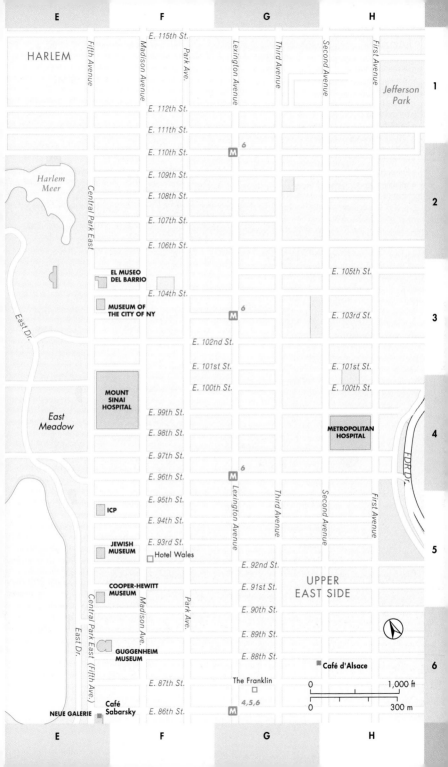

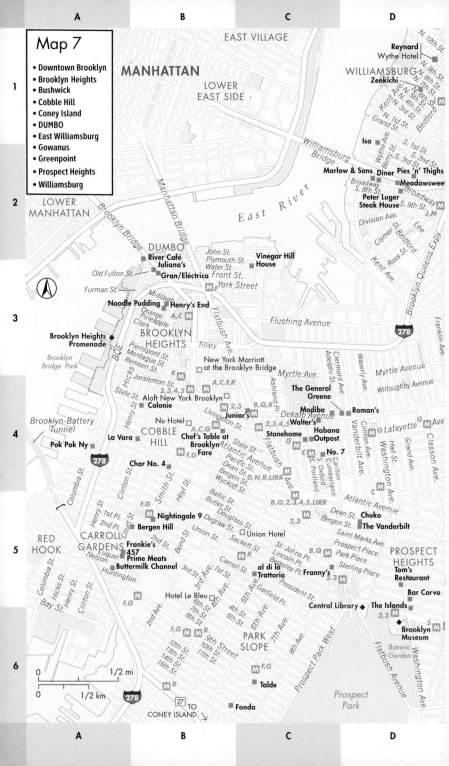

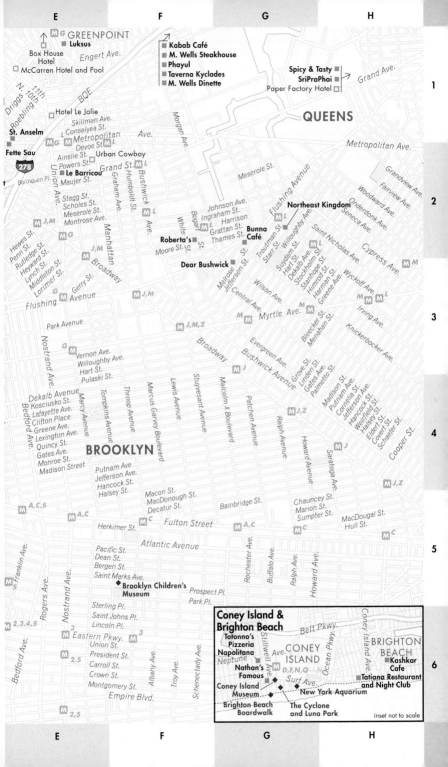

WHERE TO STAY

Updated by
Jessica Colley

There are more hotel rooms than ever in New York City, as exciting new properties continue to open their doors not only in Manhattan proper but in Brooklyn and the outer boroughs as well. But does that mean that New York is cheap? Well, we wouldn't say *cheap,* but you can still find some deals, especially if you're not set on a specific property or neighborhood, and if you don't mind a few extra minutes of commuting time.

Hotels continue to slash rates based on market sensitivity—especially if you and all of those other Internet-savvy room shoppers are willing to wait until the last minute. That said, if you want to stay in a specific place and the rate seems reasonable, book it—it's just as likely to go up, especially during peak seasons (spring and fall).

How to choose? The first thing to consider is location (*Check out our "Where Should I Stay?" chart*). Many New York City visitors insist on staying in the hectic Midtown area—and options are improving there— but other neighborhoods are often just as convenient. Less touristy areas, such as Gramercy, the Lower East Side, the Upper West Side— even Brooklyn—provide a far more realistic sense of New York life.

Also consider timing: the least expensive months to book rooms in the city are January and February. If you're flexible on dates, ask the reservationist if there's a cheaper time to stay during your preferred traveling month—that way you can avoid peak dates, like Fashion Week and the New York City Marathon. Be sure to ask about possible weekend packages that could include a third night free. (The Financial District in particular can be a discount gold mine on weekends.)

Another source of bargains? Chain hotels. Many have moved into the city and charge reasonable room rates. In addition to favorites like the Sheraton, Hilton, and Hyatt brands, there are Best Westerns, Days Inns, and Comfort Inns. These rates aren't as low as you find outside Manhattan, but they're certainly getting closer.

PLANNER

NEED A RESERVATION?

Hotel reservations are a necessity when planning your trip to New York. Competition for clients also means properties must undergo frequent improvements, especially during July and August, so when booking, ask about any renovations, lest you get a room within earshot of noisy construction, or temporarily(and inconveniently) without amenities such as room service or spa access.

SERVICES

Unless otherwise noted, all hotels listed have private baths, central heating, air-conditioning, and private phones. Many now have wireless Internet (Wi-Fi) available, though it's not always free. Most large hotels have video or high-speed checkout capability, and many can arrange babysitting. Pools are a rarity, but most properties have gyms or health clubs, and sometimes full-scale spas; hotels without facilities usually have arrangements for guests at nearby gyms, sometimes for a fee.

FAMILY TRAVEL

New York has gone to great lengths to attract family vacationers, and hotels have followed the family-friendly trend. Some properties provide such diversions as web TV and in-room video games. Most full-service Manhattan hotels provide rollaway beds, babysitting, and stroller rental, but be sure to make these arrangements when booking, not when you arrive.

DOES SIZE MATTER?

If room size is important to you, ask how many square feet a room has, not just if it's big. A hotel room in New York is considered large if it's 500 square feet. Very large rooms are 600 square feet. To stay anywhere larger, book a multiroom suite. Small rooms are a tight 150 to 200 square feet, sometimes less.

PRICES

There's no denying that New York City hotels are expensive, but rates run the full range. For high-end hotels like the Mandarin Oriental at Central Park, prices start at $895 a night for a standard room in high season, which runs from September through December. At the low end of the spending spectrum, a bunk at the Jane starts at $99 for a single. But don't be put off by the prices printed here—many hotels slash their rates significantly for promotions and web-only deals.

Prices in the reviews are the lowest cost of a standard double room in high season.

WHAT IT COSTS			
$	**$$**	**$$$**	**$$$$**
$299 and under	$300–$449	$450–$600	over $600

FOR TWO
PEOPLE

Prices are for a standard double room, excluding 14.75% city and state taxes.

BEST BETS FOR NEW YORK CITY LODGING

Fodor's offers a selective listing of high-quality lodging in every price range. Here we've compiled our top picks by price and experience.

Fodor's Choice ★

Ace Hotel, $$
Andaz Wall Street, $$
The Bowery Hotel, $$$
The Carlyle, $$$$
The Chatwal, $$$$
Crosby Street Hotel, $$$
The Greenwich Hotel, $$$
The High Line Hotel, $$
Hotel on Rivington, $$
Hyatt Union Square, $$
The Inn at Irving Place, $$$
The James Hotel New York, $$$
Library Hotel, $$
The London NYC, $$$
Mandarin Oriental, $$$$
The Mark, $$$
Mondrian Soho, $$$
NoMad, $$
The Out NYC, $$
The Peninsula, $$$$
Refinery Hotel, $$$
Ritz-Carlton New York, Central Park, $$$$
The St. Regis, $$$$
The Standard

Highline, $$$
Wythe Hotel, $$

Best by Price

$

Carlton Arms
The Herald Square Hotel
Holiday Inn SoHo
Hotel Beacon
Hotel Metro
The Jane
La Quinta Inn
The Paper Factory Hotel
Pod 39
Pod 51
Yotel

$$

Ace Hotel
Andaz Wall Street
Casablanca Hotel
Conrad New York
The High Line Hotel
Hotel on Rivington
Library Hotel
The Mansfield
The Maritime Hotel
The Michelangelo
The Out NYC
Room Mate Grace
The Standard Highline

W Hotel New York
Wythe Hotel

$$$

Crosby Street Hotel
The Greenwich Hotel
The Inn at Irving Place
The James Hotel New York
The Mark
Mondrian SoHo
Refinery Hotel
Sixty LES

$$$$

The Carlyle
The Chatwal
Gramercy Park Hotel
Mandarin Oriental
The Mercer
The Peninsula
Ritz-Carlton New York, Central Park
The St. Regis

Best by Experience

BEST BEDS

Four Seasons Hotel
The Greenwich Hotel
Ink48
The Mansfield
The Mark

The Nolitan Hotel
Ritz-Carlton New York, Battery Park

BEST CONCIERGE

Four Seasons Hotel
Le Parker Meridien
The London NYC
Mandarin Oriental
The Quin
Ritz-Carlton New York, Battery Park

BEST GYM

The Grand Hyatt New York
The James Hotel New York
Le Parker Meridien
The London NYC
The Mark
Trump International Hotel and Towers

BEST FOR HISTORY BUFFS

The Algonquin
The Carlyle
The Chatwal
The Inn at Irving Place
The Plaza
The St. Regis

BEST FOR KIDS

Conrad New York
FIFTY NYC
Hotel Beacon
Ink48
Le Parker Meridien
The Plaza
The Tuscany

BEST-KEPT SECRET

Andaz Wall Street
Box House Hotel
The Franklin
The Greenwich Hotel
Gramercy Park Hotel
Hotel on Rivington
The Jane
The Marlton
The Nolitan Hotel
NU Hotel Brooklyn
The Standard
Sixty LES
Wythe Hotel

BEST FOR HISTORY BUFFS

The Algonquin
The Carlyle
The Chatwal
The Inn at Irving Place
The Plaza
The St. Regis

BEST HOTEL BAR

Bemelmans Bar at the Carlyle
The Biergarten at the Standard
Breslin Bar at the Ace Hotel
The Gansevoort Park Avenue NYC
Isola at the Mondrian SoHo
Jimmy at the James Hotel
King Cole Bar at the St. Regis
Lobby Bar at the Bowery Hotel

Oak Bar at the Plaza
Print Lounge at Ink48
Rose Bar at the Gramercy Park Hotel
Winnie's at the Refinery Hotel

BEST FOR KIDS

Conrad New York
FIFTY NYC
Hotel Beacon
Ink48
Le Parker Meridien
The Plaza
The Tuscany

BEST-KEPT SECRET

Andaz Wall Street
Box House Hotel
The Franklin
The Greenwich Hotel
The High Line Hotel
The Inn at Irving Place
The Lowell

BEST LOBBY

Ace Hotel
The Bowery Hotel
Four Seasons
Gramercy Park Hotel
Mandarin Oriental
The Marlton
NYLO
The Peninsula
The St. Regis

BEST NEIGHBORHOOD EXPERIENCE

The Bowery Hotel
The Carlyle
Crosby Street Hotel
The Franklin
The Greenwich Hotel
Hotel on Rivington
The Inn at Irving Place
The Jade
The Mark
The Marlton
The Standard
The Wythe
High Line Hotel
The Marlton
NYLO
The Paper Factory Hotel
Park Hyatt
Refinery Hotel

BEST POOL

Gansevoort Meatpacking NYC
Mandarin Oriental
ONE UN New York
The Peninsula
Trump International Hotel and Towers

BEST SERVICE

The Carlyle
The Chatwal
Four Seasons Hotel
The Greenwich Hotel
The James Hotel New York
The London NYC

The Peninsula
The Mark
The Plaza
Ritz-Carlton New York, Battery Park
SoHo Grand
The St. Regis

BEST VIEWS

The Carlyle
Hotel on Rivington
Mandarin Oriental
Mondrian SoHo
The Nolitan
Ritz Carlton New York, Central Park
The Standard East Village
The Standard
Trump International Hotel and Towers
Wythe Hotel

MOST ROMANTIC

Andaz Wall Street
Gramercy Park Hotel
The Greenwich Hotel
The Inn at Irving Place
Library Hotel
The Lowell
The Marlton
Mondrian SoHo
Ritz-Carlton New York, Battery Park
The Standard
Wythe Hotel

17

WHERE SHOULD I STAY?

	Neighborhood Vibe	Pros	Cons
Lower Manhattan	Mostly skyscraper hotels in an area that buzzes with activity during weekday hours, but can be eerily quiet at night.	Low crime area; easy subway access to uptown sights; great walking paths along the waterfront and in Battery Park.	Construction and congestion near World Trade Center site; limited choice of restaurants and shopping.
SoHo and NoLIta (with Little Italy)	Swanky, high-end hotels with hip restaurants and lounges patronized by New Yorkers and travelers alike.	Scores of upscale clothing boutiques and art galleries nearby; safe area for meandering walks; easy subway access.	Not budget-friendly; streets are crowded on weekends; few major sites nearby.
East Village and the Lower East Side	The epicenter of edgy New York, great for travelers looking to party.	Great low-cost options for young generation. Great restaurants and independent boutiques.	One of the least subway-accessible Manhattan 'hoods; expect late-night noise.
Greenwich Village and the West Village	Hotels in this part of town are few and far between. The ones that are here are small and boutique-y.	Easy subway access to anywhere in town; great shopping, dining, and drinking venues.	Winding streets can be tough to navigate; most hotels are on the pricey side.
Chelsea and the Meatpacking District	More hotels are opening in one of the city's trendiest restaurant and nightlife areas.	"See and be seen";lots of great shopping.	This is a trendy and pricey neighborhood for hotels. Most hotel bars are a real scene.
Union Square, Flatiron District, and Gramercy	A relatively quiet residential area.	Patches of calm respite from the hustleandbustle of downtown and midtown; low crime area.	Limited subway access as you move east; Gramercy may be too quiet for some.
Midtown East and West, and Murray Hill	Mostly big-name hotel chains and luxury business suites around Times Square; lots of tourists.	Near Broadway theaters; budget options are available in chain hotels and indies alike.	Streets are often packed with pedestrians; area around Port Authority is gritty. Murray Hill is pretty quiet.
Upper East Side	Well-heeled residential neighborhood near many museums.	Removed from Midtown hustle; near tourist attractions like Central Park.	Streets are quiet after 9 pm; few budget dining options; limited subway access (just the 6 line).
Upper West Side	Hotels in a residential neighborhood near Central Park, Lincoln Center, and some museums.	Lovely tree-lined streets; laid-back neighborhood eateries.	Weekend trains can be slow; most hotels are on the pricey side.
Brooklyn	Brooklyn has a bit of everything so it depends on where you end up. Williamsburg is all about hipsters, while Downtown Brooklyn and around are quite residential.	You'll find generally smaller boutique-style hotels with personalized service and character, and rates worth traveling for. Plus, a whole new borough to explore.	If you're out late in Manhattan, it'll be a subway or a relatively pricey taxi back to Brooklyn.

HOTEL REVIEWS

Listed alphabetically within neighborhoods. Please visit Fodors.com for expanded reviews. Use the coordinate (1:B2) at the end of each listing to locate a property on the corresponding map preceding this chapter.

LOWER MANHATTAN

FINANCIAL DISTRICT

$$
HOTEL
Fodor's Choice
★

Andaz Wall Street. If space is a priority, head to the southern tip of Manhattan: this sleek hotel has generous rooms with large windows, oak floors, and extra large bathrooms. **Pros:** free Wi-Fi, bikes, snacks, and nonalcoholic beverages; excellent, intuitive lighting controls; good value. **Cons:** limited choice for restaurants and nightlife in the neighborhood; in-house restaurant not open every day. $ *Rooms from: $395* ⊠ *75 Wall St., Financial District* ☎ *212/590–1234* ⊕ *www.newyork. wallstreet.andaz.hyatt.com* ⇨ *213 rooms, 40 suites* ⦿| *No meals* Ⓜ *2, 3 to Wall St.* ✛ *1:E4.*

$$$
HOTEL

Gild Hall. Captains of Industry, here's a boutique hotel for you: operated by the owners of the several Thompson Hotels around the United States and beyond, Gild Hall aggressively courts clientele with a Y chromosome. Beds have padded leather headboards and tartan throw blankets. **Pros:** central Financial District location; eye-popping lobby; stylish room design. **Cons:** small rooms for the price; untraditional location. $ *Rooms from: $499* ⊠ *15 Gold St., at Platt St., Financial District* ☎ *212/232–7700, 800/268–0700* ⊕ *www.thompsonhotels.com* ⇨ *116 rooms, 10 suites* ⦿| *No meals* Ⓜ *2, 3, 4, 5, A, C, J, Z to Fulton St.* ✛ *1:E3.*

$$$
HOTEL

The W New York Downtown. In the heart of the Financial District, this W outpost juxtaposes the gritty feel of the Financial District with sleek surfaces. **Pros:** near popular tourist attractions; restaurant offers some surprisingly affordable fare; modern workout room. **Cons:** scaffolding-dense neighborhood; construction noise of World Trade Center nearby; not family-friendly. $ *Rooms from: $499* ⊠ *123 Washington St., at Albany St., Financial District* ☎ *646/826–8600* ⊕ *www. wnewyorkdowntown.com* ⇨ *214 rooms, 3 suites* ⦿| *No meals* Ⓜ *1, R to Rector St.; 4, 5 to Wall St.* ✛ *1:C4.*

TRIBECA

$$
HOTEL
FAMILY

Conrad New York. A pleasant surprise in a quiet Battery Park City location, this hotel has many coveted amenities: significant square footage, a breezy rooftop bar, and access to green space in nearby Hudson River Park. **Pros:** spacious rooms with separate living space; emphasis on art and design; movie theater and restaurants; near downtown attractions. **Cons:** daily fee for Wi-Fi; removed from Midtown attractions; expensive. $ *Rooms from: $359* ⊠ *102 North End Ave., between Vesey and Murray Sts., TriBeCa* ☎ *212/945–0100* ⊕ *www.conradnewyork.com* ⇨ *463 suites* ⦿| *No meals* Ⓜ *1, 2, 3, A, C to Chambers St.; E to World Trade Center* ✛ *1:B3.*

17

$ ▢ **The Cosmopolitan Hotel.** For a bargain room in a great downtown
HOTEL neighborhood, it's hard to beat this cost-conscious favorite. **Pros:**
friendly staff; great location for power shoppers; recent refresh with
New York-inspired design. **Cons:** sometimes noisy location; small
rooms. Ⓢ *Rooms from: $299 ⊠ 95 West Broadway, at Chambers St.,
TriBeCa* ☎ *212/566–1900* ⊕ *www.cosmohotel.com* ⟿ *130 rooms, 1
suite* ⏣*No meals* Ⓜ *1, 2, 3, A, C to Chambers St.* ✛ *1:C2.*

$$ ▢ **Duane Street Hotel.** Amid TriBeCa's historic warehouses and trendy
HOTEL art galleries sits this boutique hotel, a fashionable addition to the neigh-
borhood. **Pros:** great location; free Wi-Fi; stylish rooms; good pick for
the allergy conscious. **Cons:** off-site gym; no 24-hour room service.
Ⓢ *Rooms from: $399 ⊠ 130 Duane St., TriBeCa* ☎ *212/964–4600*
⊕ *www.duanestreethotel.com* ⟿ *41 rooms, 2 suites* ⏣*No meals* Ⓜ *1,
2, 3, A, C to Chambers St.* ✛ *1:C1; 2:D6.*

$$$ ▢ **The Greenwich Hotel.** This understated, inviting hotel manages to fly
HOTEL under the radar even though Robert De Niro is an owner. **Pros:** fabulous
Fodor's Choice restaurant (Locanda Verde, also available for room service); gorgeous
★ pool; excellent service; luxurious bathrooms. **Cons:** some plumbing
noise; high prices. Ⓢ *Rooms from: $595 ⊠ 377 Greenwich St., TriBeCa*
☎ *212/941–8900* ⊕ *www.thegreenwichhotel.com* ⟿ *75 rooms, 13
suites* ⏣*No meals* Ⓜ *1 to Franklin St.* ✛ *1:B1.*

$$$ ▢ **The Ritz-Carlton New York, Battery Park.** If you're staying this far
HOTEL downtown, the Ritz is your top choice. **Pros:** excellent service; best
FAMILY upscale base for downtown exploring; pet- and kid-friendly; Statue
of Liberty views. **Cons:** removed from Midtown tourist sights; limited
nighttime activities; few neighborhood options for dining and enter-
tainment. Ⓢ *Rooms from: $545 ⊠ 2 West St., at Battery Park, TriBeCa*
☎ *212/344–0800, 800/241–3333* ⊕ *www.ritzcarlton.com/batterypark*
⟿ *259 rooms, 39 suites* ⏣*No meals* Ⓜ *1, R, J to Rector St.; 4, 5 to
Bowling Green* ✛ *1:C5.*

$$ ▢ **Smyth, a Thompson Hotel.** Conveniently located almost on top of a
HOTEL convenient subway stop, this thoroughly modern hotel makes TriBeCa
a welcoming landing spot for visitors. **Pros:** great service; good restaurant; excellent subway access. **Cons:** Wi-Fi not free; only a frosted
glass partition divides bathroom from sleeping area; bathrooms could
have better lighting. Ⓢ *Rooms from: $299 ⊠ 85 West Broadway,
between Chambers and Warren Sts., TriBeCa* ☎ *212/587–7000* ⊕ *www.
thompsonhotels.com/hotels/smyth-tribeca* ⟿ *84 rooms, 16 suites* ⏣*No
meals* Ⓜ *1, 2, 3, A, C to Chambers St.* ✛ *1:C2.*

$$$ ▢ **Tribeca Grand.** Still popular with the glitterati, the scene at the Tribeca
HOTEL Grand centers on the eight-story atrium's Church Lounge bar and café.
Pros: great dining and bar scene; central downtown location; fun social
atrium; pet-friendly. **Cons:** rooms get noise from restaurant below; bath-
rooms have slightly cold design. Ⓢ *Rooms from: $499 ⊠ 2 6th Ave.,
between Walker and White sts., TriBeCa* ☎ *212/519–6600, 800/965–
3000, 212/519–6700* ⊕ *www.tribecagrand.com* ⟿ *187 rooms, 14 suites*
⏣*No meals* Ⓜ *A, C, E to Canal St.* ✛ *2:D5.*

SOHO AND NOLITA

SOHO

> **WORD OF MOUTH**
>
> "[The SoHo Grand] is definitely funky, yet nice. The bar is always packed but a good place to people watch. I have found the rooms small but comfortable and the staff helpful. I find it less pretentious than some 'W' hotels at which I have stayed." —A2

$$$ HOTEL Fodor's Choice ★ **Crosby Street Hotel.** This whimsical boutique hotel, the first branch of a UK chain to open in the U.S., has excellent SoHo views. **Pros:** unique, fun design; big, bright rooms; great bar. **Cons:** small gym. [$] *Rooms from: $555* ✉ *79 Crosby St., between Prince and Spring sts., SoHo* ☎ *212/226–6400* 🌐 *www.firmdalehotels.com* 🛏 *69 rooms, 17 suites* 🍴 *No meals* [M] *6 to Spring St.; N, R to Prince St.; B, D, F, M to Broadway–Lafayette St.* ✣ *2:E3.*

$ HOTEL FAMILY **Holiday Inn SoHo.**"SoHo" and "Holiday Inn" may not sound right together, but here they are. **Pros:** well-priced SoHo solution; well-trained staff. **Cons:** nothing stylish; closer to Chinatown than to SoHo. [$] *Rooms from: $280* ✉ *138 Lafayette St., near Canal St., SoHo* ☎ *212/966–8898, 800/465–4329* 🌐 *www.hidowntown-nyc.com* 🛏 *215 rooms, 12 suites* 🍴 *No meals* [M] *6, J, N, Q, R, Z to Canal St.* ✣ *2:E5.*

$$$ HOTEL FAMILY Fodor's Choice ★ **The James Hotel New York.** This hotel on the edge of SoHo never sacrifices comfort for style, so it's no wonder there's a high percentage of return customers: creative types, businesspeople, fashionistas, and anyone else with deep pockets. **Pros:** stellar service; fabulous views; cool SoHo location. **Cons:** rooftop bar is expensive and sometimes too-cool-for-school. [$] *Rooms from: $549* ✉ *27 Grand St., between Thompson St. and 6th Ave., SoHo* ☎ *212/465–2000* 🌐 *www.jameshotels.com* 🛏 *109 rooms, 5 suites* 🍴 *No meals* [M] *1, A, C, E to Canal St.* ✣ *2:D4.*

$$$$ HOTEL **The Mercer.** Owner André Balazs has a knack for dating Hollywood starlets and channeling a neighborhood sensibility, and here it's SoHo loft all the way. **Pros:** great location; sophisticated design touches; celebrity sightings in lobby. **Cons:** service inconsistent; some tight rooms. [$] *Rooms from: $695* ✉ *147 Mercer St., at Prince St., SoHo* ☎ *212/966–6060, 888/918–6060* 🌐 *www.mercerhotel.com* 🛏 *68 rooms, 7 suites* 🍴 *No meals* [M] *N, R to Prince St.; B, D, F, M to Broadway–Lafayette St.* ✣ *2:E3.*

$$$ HOTEL Fodor's Choice ★ **NoMo SoHo.** Snazzy, fairytale-inspired style and a chic SoHo vibe make the Mondrian a winner for anyone looking for a decadent downtown New York experience. **Pros:** stylish rooms with fairytale-inspired accents; friendly to electronics addicts; fabulous views from floor-to-ceiling windows. **Cons:** elevators can be slow; standard rooms are on the small side; charge for Internet. [$] *Rooms from: $579* ✉ *9 Crosby St., SoHo* ☎ *212/389–1000, 212/389–1001* 🌐 *www.nomosoho.com* 🛏 *263 rooms, 43 suites* 🍴 *No meals* [M] *6, J, N, Q, R, Z to Canal St.* ✣ *2:E4.*

$$$$ HOTEL **SIXTY SoHo.** Formerly SoHo icon 60 Thompson, this hotel received a renovation and rebranding in 2014. **Pros:** central to SoHo nightlife;

good gym; some rooms have balconies. **Cons:** not family-oriented; no pets allowed. [$] *Rooms from: $719* ✉ *60 Thompson St., between Broome and Spring sts., SoHo* ☎ *212/431–0400, 877/431–0400* 🌐 *www.thompsonhotels.com* 🛏 *97 rooms, 10 suites* 🍴 *No meals* [M] *C, E to Spring St.* ✣ *2:D4.*

$$ HOTEL **SoHo Grand.** The SoHo Grand defines what SoHo is today—once pioneering, now expensive, and with a vaguely creative vibe. **Pros:** fashionable, laid-back sophistication; great service; surprisingly discreet setting; diverse eating and drinking options. **Cons:** closer to Canal Street than prime SoHo; rooms on small side. [$] *Rooms from: $329* ✉ *310 West Broadway, at Grand St., SoHo* ☎ *212/965–3000, 800/965–3000* 🌐 *www.sohogrand.com* 🛏 *341 rooms, 12 suites* 🍴 *No meals* [M] *1, A, C, E to Canal St.* ✣ *2:D4.*

NOLITA

$$ HOTEL **The Nolitan Hotel.** A welcome addition to an underserved neighborhood, the Nolitan combines a hip, slightly gritty feel with some luxe touches, but don't expect a lot of space to spread out. **Pros:** cool vibe; fun location convenient to lower Manhattan and Brooklyn; fabulous views from rooftop and some rooms. **Cons:** smallish rooms; gym access five-minute walk away; some street noise. [$] *Rooms from: $409* ✉ *30 Kenmare St., NoLIta* ☎ *212/925–2555* 🌐 *www.nolitanhotel.com* 🛏 *56 rooms, 1 suite* 🍴 *No meals* [M] *J, Z to Bowery; 6 to Spring St.* ✣ *2:F4.*

EAST VILLAGE AND THE LOWER EAST SIDE

EAST VILLAGE

$$$ HOTEL Fodor's Choice ★ **The Bowery Hotel.** The Bowery Hotel is like an English hunting lodge in Manhattan, warmed by rich tapestries, fireplaces, and chandeliers—and there's no shortage of Brits, who flock to the property; the only thing missing is a trusty hound. **Pros:** quirky, fun location; happening bar and lobby-lounge area; celebrity sightings; interesting views. **Cons:** gritty neighbors; rooms lack luxe touches expected at this price. [$] *Rooms from: $535* ✉ *335 Bowery, at 3rd St., East Village* ☎ *212/505–9100* 🌐 *www.theboweryhotel.com* 🛏 *135 rooms, 25 suites* 🍴 *No meals* [M] *6 to Bleecker St.; B, D, F, M to Broadway–Lafayette St.* ✣ *2:F2.*

$$$ HOTEL **The Standard, East Village.** A jarring, 21-story glass-and-steel finger rising up in the low-rise East Village, this hotel was never going to pass under the radar—and that's guaranteed now that André Balazs and company have taken over. **Pros:** stylish, sunny rooms with great views; central location for downtown exploring; free Wi-Fi. **Cons:** out of character with the area; rooms on the small side. [$] *Rooms from: $495* ✉ *25 Cooper Sq., between 5th and 6th sts., East Village* ☎ *212/475–5700* 🌐 *www.standardhotels.com/eastvillage* 🛏 *145 rooms, 8 suites* 🍴 *No meals* [M] *6 to Astor Pl.; N, R to 8th St.–NYU* ✣ *2:F2.*

LOWER EAST SIDE

$$ HOTEL Fodor's Choice ★ **Hotel on Rivington.** A pioneer when it opened back in 2004, this glass-walled hotel on the Lower East Side is still a great choice if you want to be in the thick of the neighborhood's dining and nightlife scene. **Pros:** cool location and vibe; huge windows with wonderful New York views; many rooms have balconies; seriously luxurious bathrooms. **Cons:** feels

clubby on weekends; isolated from some subway lines. $ *Rooms from: $380* ✉ *107 Rivington St., between Ludlow and Essex sts., Lower East Side* ☎ *212/475–2600, 800/915–1537* ⊕ *www.hotelonrivington.com* ↩ *88 rooms, 20 suites* |◎| *No meals* Ⓜ *F to Delancey St.; J, M, Z to Essex St.* ✛ *2:G3.*

$ | 🏨 **The Ludlow.** The latest stylish creation from hotelier Sean MacPher-
HOTEL | son, this new hotel embodies the effortless cool attitude of the Lower East Side, from its cozy lounge with limestone fireplace to the romantic trellis-covered garden. **Pros:** hot restaurant and bar scene; some rooms have terraces and great views; gorgeous bathrooms. **Cons:** lounge and courtyard can get crowded. $ *Rooms from: $295* ✉ *180 Ludlow St., Lower East Side* ☎ *212/432–1818* ⊕ *www.ludlowhotel.com* ↩ *164 rooms, 20 suites* |◎| *No meals* Ⓜ *F to 2nd Ave.; J, M, Z to Essex St.* ✛ *2:G3.*

$$$ | 🏨 **Sixty LES.** This hotel is a great embodiment of the neighborhood
HOTEL | inhabitants: hip, but friendly when you get to know it. **Pros:** in the heart of downtown scene; great views from suites; hip rooftop bar and pool. **Cons:** occasionally snobby staff; rooms stylish but dark. $ *Rooms from: $529* ✉ *190 Allen St., between Houston and Stanton sts., Lower East Side* ☎ *877/460–8888* ⊕ *www.sixtyhotels.com/lowereastside* ↩ *141 rooms, 10 suites* |◎| *No meals* Ⓜ *F to Delancey St.; J, M, Z to Essex St.* ✛ *2:G3.*

GREENWICH VILLAGE AND THE WEST VILLAGE

GREENWICH VILLAGE

$$$ | 🏨 **The Jade.** Among the ghosts of the literary salons and speakeasies
HOTEL | of Greenwich Village is the Jade, a boutique property on a tree-lined street with an Art Deco sensibility. **Pros:** delivers a true Greenwich Village experience; cozy fireplaces; quiet neighborhood location. **Cons:** small rooms; no connecting rooms. $ *Rooms from: $450* ✉ *52 W. 13th St., between 5th and 6th aves., Greenwich Village* ☎ *212/375–1300* ⊕ *www.thejadenyc.com* ↩ *109 rooms, 4 suites* |◎| *No meals* Ⓜ *1, 2, 3, F, M to 14th St.; L to 6th Ave.* ✛ *3:E4.*

$$ | 🏨 **The Marlton.** Built in 1900 and once home to Jack Kerouac, this hotel
HOTEL | has been renovated into a stylish boutique with a residential feel. **Pros:** fresh property with luxurious touches; spacious lobby with coffee bar; great Greenwich Village location. **Cons:** very small rooms; no work desks; no room service. $ *Rooms from: $375* ✉ *5 W. 8th St., Greenwich Village* ☎ *212/321–0100* ⊕ *www.marltonhotel.com* ↩ *105 rooms, 2 suites* |◎| *Breakfast* Ⓜ *A, B, C, D, E, F, M to W. 4th St.* ✛ *3:E5.*

$$ | 🏨 **Washington Square Hotel.** This low-key hotel in Greenwich Village
HOTEL | is popular with visiting New York University parents—the location is also near Washington Square Park and its magnificent arch (and just down the street from Mario Batali's Babbo restaurant). **Pros:** parkside location; deluxe rooms are charming; great hotel bar; free Wi-Fi. **Cons:** NYU students everywhere in the neighborhood; rooms are small. $ *Rooms from: $315* ✉ *103 Waverly Pl., at MacDougal St., Greenwich Village* ☎ *212/777–9515, 800/222–0418* ⊕ *www.*

17

washingtonsquarehotel.com ↻ *152 rooms* |◎| *Breakfast* Ⓜ *A, B, C, D, E, F, M to W. 4th St.* ✛ *2:D1.*

WEST VILLAGE

$

HOTEL

⛱ **The Jane.** To some, the Jane is impossibly chic; to others, the rooms are reminiscent of Sing Sing. **Pros:** extraordinary value for the neighborhood; hot bar scene; gorgeous décor in lounge; great branch of weekend brunch favorite Café Gitane; convenient neighborhood for downtown sightseeing. **Cons:** impossibly tiny standard rooms; some rooms have shared bathrooms; noise from the bar. ⓢ *Rooms from: $125* ✉ *113 Jane St., at West St., West Village* ☎ *212/924–6700* ⊕ *www.thejanenyc.com* ↻ *171 rooms* |◎| *No meals* Ⓜ *A, C, E to 14th St.; L to 8th Ave.* ✛ *3:B5.*

CHELSEA AND THE MEATPACKING DISTRICT

CHELSEA

$

HOTEL

⛱ **Chelsea Lodge.** Popular with Europeans and budget-conscious visitors, the Chelsea Lodge is a great location for guests who don't insist on a lot of amenities. **Pros:** on a gorgeous Chelsea block; residential feel; great bang for the buck. **Cons:** not romantic; shared bathrooms. ⓢ *Rooms from: $169* ✉ *318 W. 20th St., between 8th and 9th aves., Chelsea* ☎ *212/243–4499* ⊕ *www.chelsealodge.com* ↻ *22 rooms, 4 suites* |◎| *No meals* Ⓜ *C, E to 23rd St.; 1 to 18th St.* ✛ *3:C3.*

$$

HOTEL

⛱ **The GEM Hotel Chelsea.** At this stylish, well-priced boutique hotel, the modern rooms are small but designed to make the most of limited space. **Pros:** great Chelsea location; close to several subway lines; in-room coffeemakers. **Cons:** gym and business center, both on the lower level, feel like a work in progress; rooms may be too small for some. ⓢ *Rooms from: $329* ✉ *300 W. 22nd St., Chelsea* ☎ *212/675–1911* ⊕ *www.thegemhotel.com* ↻ *81 rooms* |◎| *No meals* Ⓜ *1, C, E to 23rd St.* ✛ *3:C3.*

$$

HOTEL

Fodor's Choice

★

⛱ **High Line Hotel.** A late 19th-century, red-brick Gothic building on the landscaped grounds of a former seminary was transformed into this lovely hotel, full of original architectural details like stained glass windows and pine floors. **Pros:** historic property with lots of character; gorgeous design from top to bottom; peaceful garden; quality coffee bar in the lobby. **Cons:** doesn't have the best subway access. ⓢ *Rooms from: $300* ✉ *180 10th Ave., at 20th St., Chelsea* ☎ *212/929–3888* ⊕ *www.thehighlinehotel.com* ↻ *60 rooms, 4 suites* |◎| *No meals* Ⓜ *C, E to 23rd St.* ✛ *3:A3.*

$

HOTEL

⛱ **Hilton New York Fashion District.** Fashion is the theme at this Hilton, which is located in the emerging Fashion District neighborhood (previously known as the garment district) on the upper edge of Chelsea. The lobby is done in rich textiles with multicolor spools mounted on a white board behind the front desk. **Pros:** reasonable prices for a good location; rooftop lounge with great skyline views. **Cons:** small closets; trying to be trendy. ⓢ *Rooms from: $249* ✉ *152 W. 26th St., between 6th and 7th aves., Chelsea* ☎ *212/858–5888, 212/858–5889* ⊕ *www3.hilton.com* ↻ *280 rooms* |◎| *No meals* Ⓜ *1 to 28th St.; C, E to 23rd St.* ✛ *3:D2.*

$$ **Hotel Americano.** This boutique property, which overlooks the High
HOTEL Line, captures the artistic and stylish spirit of Chelsea. **Pros:** year-round
rooftop pool and bar; views overlooking the High Line; near the thriv-
ing gallery scene in Chelsea. **Cons:** low beds; bathrooms lack privacy;
some furniture is form over function. $ *Rooms from: $395* ⊠ *518
W. 27th St., between 10th and 11th aves., Chelsea* ☎ *212/216–0000*
⊕ *www.hotel-americano.com* ⌐ *49 rooms, 7 suites* ⦿| *No meals* Ⓜ *C,
E to 23rd St.* ✛ *3:A1.*

$$ **The Maritime Hotel.** The Maritime's white-ceramic tower, the former
HOTEL HQ for the National Maritime Union, was the first luxury hotel to be
built in the Chelsea gallery district, and the property still feels a bit
nautical: the small rooms resemble modern ship cabins, with burnished
teak paneling, sea-blue drapes and bed accents, and 5-foot "portholes"
that face the Hudson River skyline. **Pros:** fun rooms with big porthole
windows; great location near Chelsea Market and the Chelsea galleries.
Cons: street noise; small rooms. $ *Rooms from: $435* ⊠ *363 W. 16th
St., at 9th Ave., Chelsea* ☎ *212/242–4300* ⊕ *www.themaritimehotel.
com* ⌐ *121 rooms, 5 suites* ⦿| *No meals* Ⓜ *A, C, E to 14th St.; L to
8th Ave.* ✛ *3:B4.*

$ **Riff Chelsea.** Formerly the Chelsea Star, this new hotel has a rich music
HOTEL history (Madonna crashed here in the '80s) and a creative spirit, from
the rockstar-inspired rooms to the ground-floor art gallery. **Pros:** central
location near Penn Station; good value option; fresh, bold décor. **Cons:**
some rooms have shared bathrooms. $ *Rooms from: $149* ⊠ *300 W.
30th St., Chelsea* ☎ *212/244–7827* ⊕ *www.riffhotels.com* ⌐ *36 rooms,
7 suites* ⦿| *No meals* Ⓜ *1, 2, 3, A, C, E to 34th St.–Penn Station* ✛ *3:C1.*

MEATPACKING DISTRICT

$$ **Gansevoort Meatpacking NYC.** Though the nearby Standard New York
HOTEL has stolen some of its thunder, there's still plenty to draw guests to
this chic Meatpacking District pioneer, starting with the sleek rooms
that overlook the city or the Hudson River and the rooftop deck with
a 45-foot heated pool. **Pros:** rooftop pool; wonderful art collection;
great location for restaurants and shopping. **Cons:** location can seem
too trendy, especially at night; service can be slipshod. $ *Rooms from:
$445* ⊠ *18 9th Ave., at 13th St., Meatpacking District* ☎ *212/206–6700*
⊕ *www.hotelgansevoort.com* ⌐ *164 rooms, 22 suites* ⦿| *No meals* Ⓜ *A,
C, E to 14th St.; L to 8th Ave.* ✛ *3:B4.*

$$$ **The Standard, High Line.** André Balazs's architectural statement on
HOTEL the West Side is still one of New York's hottest hotels. **Pros:** beautiful
Fodor's Choice building with sweeping views; beautiful people; impressive restaurant
★ space. **Cons:** noisy at night; tight rooms; can be too sceney. $ *Rooms
from: $495* ⊠ *848 Washington St., between 13th and Little W. 12th
Sts., Meatpacking District* ☎ *212/645–4646* ⊕ *www.standardhotels.
com* ⌐ *334 rooms, 4 suites* ⦿| *No meals* Ⓜ *A, C, E to 14th St.; L to
8th Ave.* ✛ *3:B4.*

17

UNION SQUARE, FLATIRON DISTRICT, AND GRAMERCY

UNION SQUARE

$$ **Hyatt Union Square New York.** Experiencing a bit of "real" New York
HOTEL (and getting away from Midtown) got easier when this Hyatt opened
Fodor'sChoice just south of Union Square in a newly built tower with three restaurants,
★ an on-site gym, and bikes and scooters to borrow. **Pros:** convenient and
vibrant location; buzzy dining and drinking outlets. **Cons:** charge for
Internet; some standard rooms are small. $ *Rooms from: $379* ⊠ *134
4th Ave., Union Square* ☎ *212/253–1234* ⊕ *www.unionsquare.hyatt.
com* ⤳ *178 rooms and suites* ⦿ *No meals* Ⓜ *4, 5, 6, L, N, Q, R to
14th St.–Union Sq.* ✛ *3:F4.*

$$$$ **W New York Union Square.** The W chain's iconic New York City prop-
HOTEL erty continues to attract a mix of trendsetters and tourists, thanks to
its downtown location and funky style. **Pros:** fashionable location;
great restaurant. **Cons:** noisy lobby; expensive Wi-Fi. $ *Rooms from:
$650* ⊠ *201 Park Ave. S, at 17th St., Union Square* ☎ *212/253–9119,
877/946–8357* ⊕ *www.wnewyorkunionsquare.com* ⤳ *254 rooms, 16
suites* ⦿ *No meals* Ⓜ *4, 5, 6, L, N, Q, R to 14th St.–Union Sq.* ✛ *3:F3.*

FLATIRON DISTRICT

$$ **Ace Hotel.** The Ace is not your ordinary boutique hotel. **Pros:** in-house
HOTEL destination restaurants; supercool but friendly vibe; unfussy yet stylish.
Fodor'sChoice **Cons:** dark lobby; caters to a young crowd; may be too sceney for some.
★ $ *Rooms from: $399* ⊠ *20 W. 29th St., at Broadway, Flatiron District*
☎ *212/679–2222* ⊕ *www.acehotel.com* ⤳ *274 rooms, 8 suites* ⦿ *No
meals* Ⓜ *N, R to 28th St.* ✛ *3:E1.*

$ **Carlton Arms.** Europeans and students know about the chipper, win-
HOTEL ning attitude of this friendly, no-frills hotel, where the rooms are painted
by artists on a rotating basis. **Pros:** rock-bottom prices; friendly attitude; quieter residential Murray Hill location. **Cons:** no elevator; many
rooms have shared baths. $ *Rooms from: $120* ⊠ *160 E. 25th St., at
3rd Ave., Flatiron District* ☎ *212/684–8337, 212/679–0680 for reservations* ⊕ *www.carltonarms.com* ⤳ *54 rooms (20 with private bath)*
⦿ *No meals* Ⓜ *6 to 23rd St.* ✛ *3:G2.*

$$ **The Eventi.** This hotel adds a touch of style just below Penn Station
HOTEL in an area desperately in need of new lodging options. **Pros:** great loca-
FAMILY tion; relaxing spa; nice gym. **Cons:** crowded lobby. $ *Rooms from:
$350* ⊠ *851 6th Ave., at 30th St., Flatiron District* ☎ *212/564–4567*
⊕ *www.eventihotel.com* ⤳ *239 rooms, 53 suites* ⦿ *No meals* Ⓜ *N, R
to 28th St.* ✛ *3:D1.*

$$ **Gansevoort Park Avenue NYC.** A downtown-hip hotel on the edge of
HOTEL lower Midtown, the Gansevoort Park improves upon its hard-living
Meatpacking District sibling by several degrees. **Pros:** happening bar
and rooftop; location convenient to Union Square; friendly staff. **Cons:**
if you want peace and quiet, this hotel is not for you. $ *Rooms from:
$395* ⊠ *420 Park Ave. S, at 29th St., Flatiron District* ☎ *212/317–2900*
⊕ *www.gansevoortpark.com* ⤳ *213 rooms, 36 suites* ⦿ *No meals* Ⓜ *6
to 28th St.* ✛ *3:F1.*

$$ HOTEL 🏨 **Hotel Giraffe.** A consistent property with friendly service, large rooms, and lots of repeat customers (particularly business travelers) Hotel Giraffe is often noted for its nightly complimentary wine-and-cheese reception. **Pros:** rooftop terrace for guests; quiet hotel; nice extras like free breakfast and coffee all-day. **Cons:** street noise near lower levels; pricey for the quality. [$] *Rooms from: $449* ✉ *365 Park Ave. S, at 26th St., Flatiron District* ☎ *212/685–7700, 877/296–0009* 🌐 *www.hotelgiraffe.com* 🛏 *51 rooms, 21 suites* 🍴 *Breakfast* [M] *6 to 28th St.* ✥ *3:F2.*

$$ HOTEL 🏨 **Martha Washington.** Convenient to the action without being smack in the middle of it is Martha Washington, a sleek new hotel with a hot Danny Meyer restaurant, Marta, on the ground floor (make reservations in advance for this Roman-style pizzeria). **Pros:** trendy but not over-the-top; cozy single rooms are a great option for solo travelers. **Cons:** sceney restaurant can be loud and crowd the lobby; lower floors lack views and can feel a bit basement-y. [$] *Rooms from: $395* ✉ *29 E. 29th St., between Park and Madison aves., Flatiron District* ☎ *212/689–1900* 🌐 *www.chelseahotels.com/us/new-york/martha-washington/about* 🛏 *261 rooms, 6 suites* 🍴 *No meals* [M] *6 to 28th St.* ✥ *3:F1.*

$$ HOTEL Fodor's Choice ★ 🏨 **The NoMad Hotel.** Named for the emerging "North of Madison" (that is, Madison Square Park) neighborhood in which it's located, this upscale-bohemian property was one of the most buzzed-about hotel openings of 2012. **Pros:** 24-hour room service; free Wi-Fi; rooftop terrace; central location. **Cons:** exposed bathtubs lack privacy. [$] *Rooms from: $445* ✉ *1170 Broadway, at 28th St., Flatiron District* ☎ *212/796–1500* 🌐 *www.thenomadhotel.com* 🛏 *154 rooms, 14 suites* 🍴 *No meals* [M] *N, R to 28th St.* ✥ *3:E2.*

$ HOTEL 🏨 **Park South Hotel.** In this beautifully transformed 1906 office building, rooms feel smartly contemporary, though they've retained some period details; request one with a view of the Chrysler Building to avoid overlooking noisy 27th Street and the bar on the ground floor. **Pros:** free breakfast and Internet; turndown service; good value. **Cons:** some noisy rooms; small rooms and bathrooms. [$] *Rooms from: $299* ✉ *124 E. 28th St., between Lexington and Park aves., Flatiron District* ☎ *212/448–0888, 800/315–4642* 🌐 *www.parksouthhotel.com* 🛏 *128 rooms, 3 suites* 🍴 *Breakfast* [M] *6 to 28th St.* ✥ *3:F2.*

$$ HOTEL 🏨 **The Paul.** Another stylish addition to an increasingly trendy neighborhood, this 21-floor hotel has comfortable, modern rooms with big warehouse-style windows and some fun touches like bedside dictionaries (why not learn a new word before calling it a day?) and Rolodexes full of neighborhood tips and staff picks. **Pros:** fun, developing neighborhood; fresh, stylish rooms with big windows; rooftop bar. **Cons:** rooms on small side. [$] *Rooms from: $339* ✉ *32 W. 29th St., between Broadway and 6th Ave., Flatiron District* ☎ *212/204–5750* 🌐 *www.thepaulnyc.com* 🛏 *122 rooms, 2 suites* 🍴 *No meals* [M] *1, N, R to 28th St.* ✥ *3:E1.*

$$ HOTEL 🏨 **The Roger.** A colorful choice in a rather plain neighborhood, the Roger continues to have a following among repeat visitors to New York, especially since its 2012 redesign. **Pros:** colorful room décor; friendly service; good value. **Cons:** no room service; tiny bathrooms. [$] *Rooms from:*

17

$350 ✉ 131 Madison Ave., at 31st St., Flatiron District ☎ 212/448–7000, 877/847–4444 🌐 www.therogernewyork.com 🛏 190 rooms, 2 suites 🍴 No meals [M] 6 to 33rd St. ✥ 3:F1.

GRAMERCY PARK

$$$$ HOTEL 🏨 **Gramercy Park Hotel.** Ian Schrager, boutique hotelier extraordinaire, decorated this property with contemporary art by the likes of Andy Warhol and Jean-Michel Basquiat. **Pros:** trendy bar scene; opulent rooms; great restaurant; parkside location. **Cons:** inconsistent service; expensive bar. [$] *Rooms from: $629 ✉ 2 Lexington Ave., at Gramercy Park, Gramercy Park ☎ 212/920–3300 🌐 www.gramercyparkhotel.com 🛏 139 rooms, 46 suites 🍴 No meals [M] 6 to 23rd St. ✥ 3:G3.*

$$$ HOTEL Fodor's Choice ★ 🏨 **The Inn at Irving Place.** Fantasies of Old New York—Manhattan straight from the pages of Edith Wharton and Henry James, an era of genteel brick townhouses and Tiffany lamps—spring to life at this discreet, romantic inn. **Pros:** romantic and charming; big rooms; excellent breakfast and tea service; Mario Batali's Casa Mono is downstairs. **Cons:** rooms show some wear; some street noise. [$] *Rooms from: $449 ✉ 56 Irving Pl., between 17th and 18th sts., Gramercy Park ☎ 212/533–4600, 800/685–1447 🌐 www.innatirving.com 🛏 5 rooms, 6 suites 🍴 Breakfast [M] 4, 5, 6, L, N, Q, R to 14th St.–Union Sq. ✥ 3:G3.*

$ HOTEL 🏨 **Marcel at Gramercy.** The chic, affordable Marcel gives guests both style and substance in a prime location. **Pros:** outdoor patio has spectacular views of the city; good value. **Cons:** elevators are slow; some rooms are tight on space; décor not to everyone's taste. [$] *Rooms from: $299 ✉ 201 E. 24th St., Gramercy Park ☎ 212/696–3800 🌐 www.themarcelatgramercy.com 🛏 136 rooms 🍴 No meals [M] 6 to 23rd St. ✥ 3:G2.*

MIDTOWN EAST AND MURRAY HILL

MIDTOWN EAST

$ HOTEL 🏨 **70 Park Avenue.** A multimillion-dollar refresh in 2012 brought new life to this Midtown business-traveler favorite, infusing the lobby and rooms with a bright color palette and modern furniture. **Pros:** complimentary evening wine reception; polite service; simple rooms and hotel layout. **Cons:** small rooms; design and art might not suit all tastes. [$] *Rooms from: $299 ✉ 70 Park Ave., at 38th St., Midtown East ☎ 212/973–2400, 800/707–2752 🌐 www.70parkave.com 🛏 202 rooms, 3 suites 🍴 No meals [M] 4, 5, 6, 7, S to Grand Central–42nd St. ✥ 4:F5.*

$$$ HOTEL 🏨 **Andaz 5th Avenue.** The serene and spacious rooms at this chic, modern property evoke that coveted New York loft feel, with floor-to-ceiling windows that look out over 5th Avenue and the New York Public Library. **Pros:** spacious and stylish; big, luxurious bathrooms; good dining and drinking options; suites have outdoor space. **Cons:** pricey; busy location might not suit all guests. [$] *Rooms from: $500 ✉ 485 5th Ave., at 41st St., Midtown East ☎ 212/601–1234 🌐 newyork.5thavenue.andaz.hyatt.com 🛏 142 rooms, 42 suites 🍴 No meals [M] 4, 5, 6, 7, S to Grand Central–42nd St. ✥ 4:E5.*

$$ 🏨 **The Benjamin.** NYC is often called the City that Never Sleeps, but
HOTEL if a good night's rest is essential for your visit, the Benjamin may be
FAMILY your choice accommodation—with a menu of 12 pillows to choose
from (including buckwheat, water, and Swedish memory varieties),
white-noise machines, and 500-thread-count sheets, they've got it cov-
ered. **Pros:** sleep-friendly; great location; gracious staff; kitchenettes
in big rooms; pets stay for free. **Cons:** paid Internet and Wi-Fi; boring
views; dull neighborhood after dark. $ *Rooms from: $429* ✉ *125 E.
50th St., at Lexington Ave., Midtown East* ☎ *212/715–2500* ⊕ *www.
thebenjamin.com* ⮌ *112 rooms, 97 suites* ⫯⊙⫯ *No meals* Ⓜ *6 to 51st St.;
E, M to Lexington Ave./53rd St.* ✛ *4:F3.*

$$ 🏨 **FIFTY NYC.** This popular hotel attracts business travelers but it's also
HOTEL comfortable for families or leisure travelers—especially the studios and
FAMILY spacious suites, which have full kitchens and a clean, playful design that
incorporates oversize chairs and couches. **Pros:** apartment-style living;
large rooms; good value; kid- and pet-friendly. **Cons:** pricey Wi-Fi unless
you get an online deal. $ *Rooms from: $379* ✉ *155 E. 50th St., at 3rd
Ave., Midtown East* ☎ *212/751–5710, 800/637–8483* ⊕ *www.affinia.
com/fifty* ⮌ *233 rooms, 18 suites* ⫯⊙⫯ *No meals* Ⓜ *6 to 51st St.; E, M to
Lexington Ave./53rd St.* ✛ *4:G3.*

$$$$ 🏨 **Four Seasons Hotel.** For better or worse, the Four Seasons remains the
HOTEL blueprint for what a Manhattan luxury hotel should be. **Pros:** spacious
and comfortable rooms; perfect concierge and staff service; afternoon
tea in the lobby lounge. **Cons:** pricey; confusing room controls; some
furniture could use updating. $ *Rooms from: $995* ✉ *57 E. 57th St.,
between Park and Madison aves., Midtown East* ☎ *212/758–5700,
800/487–3769* ⊕ *www.fourseasons.com/newyork* ⮌ *300 rooms, 68
suites* ⫯⊙⫯ *No meals* Ⓜ *4, 5, 6 to 59th St.; N, Q, R to Lexington Ave./59th
St.* ✛ *4:F1.*

$$ 🏨 **The Gotham Hotel.** This sleek hotel has a lot going for it, but a clincher
HOTEL is that every room has outdoor space. **Pros:** welcoming staff; central
location; every room has a balcony. **Cons:** no on-site gym. $ *Rooms
from: $350* ✉ *16 E. 46 St., between 5th and 6th aves., Midtown East*
☎ *212/490–8500* ⊕ *www.thegothamhotelny.com* ⮌ *66 rooms, 10
suites* ⫯⊙⫯ *No meals* Ⓜ *B, D, F, M to 47th–50th Sts./Rockefeller Center;
4, 5, 6, 7, S to Grand Central–42nd St.* ✛ *4:E4.*

$$ 🏨 **Grand Hyatt New York.** This historic hotel has been transformed
HOTEL into a sleek and modern central hub. **Pros:** comfy beds, light-filled
gym on a high floor; refreshing modern design; large, well-planned
rooms. **Cons:** no in-room minibar; Wi-Fi not free. $ *Rooms from:
$359* ✉ *109 E. 42nd St., between Park and Lexington aves., Midtown
East* ☎ *212/883–1234, 800/233–1234* ⊕ *www.grandnewyork.hyatt.
com* ⮌ *1,306 rooms, 43 suites* ⫯⊙⫯ *No meals* Ⓜ *4, 5, 6, 7, S to Grand
Central–42nd St.* ✛ *4:F4.*

$$ 🏨 **Hilton Manhattan East.** This traditional-style, 20-story Tudor City hotel
HOTEL is a stone's throw from the United Nations and Grand Central Termi-
nal, making it fairly convenient but not very glamorous. **Pros:** near
UN; some balconies; convenient location for getting to major sights.
Cons: long walk to subway; unexciting room decor. $ *Rooms from:
$425* ✉ *304 E. 42nd St., between 1st and 2nd aves., Midtown East*

17

☎ *212/986–8800, 800/879–8836* ⊕ *www3.hilton.com* ⇗ *286 rooms, 14 suites* ⦿| *No meals* Ⓜ *4, 5, 6, 7, S to Grand Central–42nd St.* ✛ *4:G4.*

$$$ ⬚ **Hotel Elysée.** This intimate hotel is a favorite for travelers looking
HOTEL   for good value in a desirable Midtown location. **Pros:** complimentary snacks and Wi-Fi; individually decorated rooms; cute library. **Cons:** underwhelming lobby; slightly outdated décor. Ⓢ *Rooms from: $495* ⊠ *60 E. 54th St., between Madison and Park aves., Midtown East* ☎ *212/753–1066, 800/535–9733* ⊕ *www.elyseehotel.com* ⇗ *87 rooms, 16 suites* ⦿| *Breakfast* Ⓜ *E, M to 5th Ave./53rd St.* ✛ *4:F2.*

$$$ ⬚ **The Kitano.** As you might guess from the name, the Kitano imports
HOTEL   much of its sensibility from Japan, with touches that include a bilingual concierge and a high-concept Japanese restaurant—it also makes for a notably service-oriented stay. **Pros:** extra soundproofing in guest rooms; cute mezzanine bar area; good value; excellent live jazz. **Cons:** lower-floor views are limited; expensive restaurant. Ⓢ *Rooms from: $499* ⊠ *66 Park Ave., at 38th St., Midtown East* ☎ *212/885–7000, 800/548–2666* ⊕ *www.kitano.com* ⇗ *149 rooms, 18 suites* ⦿| *No meals* Ⓜ *4, 5, 6, 7, S to Grand Central–42nd St.* ✛ *4:F5.*

$$$$ ⬚ **Langham Place, Fifth Avenue.** Setting new standards for luxury, the
HOTEL   towering, limestone-clad Langham Place, Fifth Avenue (formerly the Setai Fifth Avenue) was conceived as an opulent crash pad for wealthy overseas tourists, captains of industry on long-term stays, and anyone in need of some serious pampering. **Pros:** attentive service; gorgeous spa; great location; quality dining. **Cons:** street noise reported by guests on lower floors. Ⓢ *Rooms from: $745* ⊠ *400 5th Ave., Midtown East* ☎ *212/695–4005* ⊕ *www.langhamhotels.com* ⇗ *157 rooms, 57 suites* ⦿| *No meals* Ⓜ *B, D, F, M, N, Q, R to 34th St.–Herald Sq.* ✛ *4:E5.*

$$ ⬚ **Library Hotel Manhattan.** Bookishly handsome, this stately landmark
HOTEL   brownstone, built in 1900, is inspired by the nearby New York Public
Fodor's Choice Library—each of its 10 floors is dedicated to one of the 10 categories
★   of the Dewey Decimal System and is stocked with art and books relevant to subtopics such as erotica, astronomy, or biography—let your interests guide your room choice. **Pros:** fun rooftop bar; playful book themes; stylish rooms. **Cons:** rooftop sometimes reserved for events; more books in rooms themselves would be nice. Ⓢ *Rooms from: $399* ⊠ *299 Madison Ave., at 41st St., Midtown East* ☎ *212/983–4500, 212/983–4500* ⊕ *www.libraryhotel.com* ⇗ *60 rooms* ⦿| *Breakfast* Ⓜ *4, 5, 6, 7, S to Grand Central–42nd St.* ✛ *4:E4.*

$$$ ⬚ **Loews Regency Hotel.** After a year-long renovation, this snazzy, spa-
HOTEL   cious Park Avenue hotel reopened in early 2014 with state-of-the-art technology, a new 10,000-square-foot spa, and bright, tastefully appointed rooms with notably comfortable beds. **Pros:** friendly and helpful staff; fresh, recently renovated property; huge spa and fitness center; appealing, buzzy bar and restaurant. **Cons:** on the expensive side. Ⓢ *Rooms from: $589* ⊠ *540 Park Ave., at 61st St., Midtown East* ☎ *212/759–4100, 800/233–2356* ⊕ *www.loewshotels.com* ⇗ *321 rooms, 58 suites* ⦿| *No meals* Ⓜ *4, 5, 6 to 59th St.; N, Q, R to Lexington Ave./59th St.* ✛ *5:F6.*

$$$ HOTEL **New York Palace.** From the moment you enter the gilded gates of these connected mansions, originally built in the 1880s by railroad baron Henry Villard, you know you're somewhere special; there's a reason this is called the Palace. **Pros:** fresh property after extensive renovation; great service; unmatched views of St. Patrick's Cathedral. **Cons:** high prices; harried staff. [$] *Rooms from: $599* ✉ *455 Madison Ave., at 50th St., Midtown East* ☎ *212/888–7000, 800/697–2522* 🌐 *www.newyorkpalace.com* 🛏 *822 rooms, 87 suites* 🍴 *No meals* [M] *6 to 51st St.; E, M to Lexington Ave./53rd St.* ✥ *4:E3.*

$ HOTEL **One UN New York.** In a sky-high tower near the landmark United Nations building, the One UN New York starts on the 28th floor and has fabulous views—ask for a room facing west, toward Manhattan's skyline. A multilingual staff caters to a discerning clientele including heads of state. **Pros:** unbeatable East River and city views; good value; great front-door and bell staff. **Cons:** a far walk to the subway; pricey Internet access. [$] *Rooms from: $220* ✉ *1 United Nations Plaza, 44th St. and 1st Ave., Midtown East* ☎ *212/758–1234, 866/866–8086* 🌐 *www.millenniumhotels.com/usa/oneunnewyork* 🛏 *439 rooms, 34 suites* 🍴 *No meals* [M] *4, 5, 6, 7, S to Grand Central–42nd St.* ✥ *4:H4.*

$$$$ HOTEL Fodor's Choice ★ **The Peninsula.** Stepping through the Peninsula's Beaux Arts facade onto the grand staircase overhung with a monumental chandelier, you know you're in for a glitzy treat. **Pros:** brilliant service; fabulous rooms with convenient controls; unforgettable rooftop bar. **Cons:** expensive. [$] *Rooms from: $1045* ✉ *700 5th Ave., at 55th St., Midtown East* ☎ *212/956–2888, 800/262–9467* 🌐 *www.peninsula.com* 🛏 *185 rooms, 54 suites* 🍴 *No meals* [M] *E, M to 5th Ave./53rd St.* ✥ *4:E2.*

$ HOTEL **Pod 51.** If cramped quarters don't bother you, this is one of the best deals in town. **Pros:** great prices; fun design. **Cons:** not for claustrophobes; some shared baths. [$] *Rooms from: $145* ✉ *230 E. 51st St., between 2nd and 3rd aves., Midtown East* ☎ *212/355–0300, 800/742–5945* 🌐 *www.thepodhotel.com* 🛏 *345 rooms (189 with private bath)* 🍴 *No meals* [M] *6 to 51st St.; E, M to Lexington Ave./53rd St.* ✥ *4:G2.*

$$ HOTEL **Roger Smith.** This quirky choice is one of the better affordable stays in the city. The art-filled rooms, matched by the murals in the lobby, are homey and comfortable, with down pillows and quilts on the beds. **Pros:** good location near Grand Central; intimate atmosphere; free Wi-Fi. **Cons:** street noise; small bathrooms. [$] *Rooms from: $379* ✉ *501 Lexington Ave., between 47th and 48th sts., Midtown East* ☎ *212/755–1400, 800/445–0277* 🌐 *www.rogersmith.com* 🛏 *102 rooms, 28 suites* 🍴 *No meals* [M] *6 to 51st St.; E, M to Lexington Ave./53rd St.* ✥ *4:F3.*

$ HOTEL **The Roosevelt Hotel.** Named after Teddy, not Franklin, this Midtown icon just steps from Grand Central has an ornate lobby with cushy couches and an old-school bar detailed in heavy wood that makes the place feel like it's from another time, and it is—the property dates from 1924. **Pros:** great public areas; big bathrooms; comfortable rooftop lounge. **Cons:** dated design; limited in-room amenities. [$] *Rooms from: $299* ✉ *45 E. 45th St., at Madison Ave., Midtown East* ☎ *888/833–3969, 212/661–9600* 🌐 *www.therooseveltfhotel.com*

17

🛏 963 rooms, 52 suites 🍴 No meals [M] 4, 5, 6, 7, S to Grand Central–42nd St. ✣ 4:F4.

$$$$ HOTEL 🏨 **The Sherry-Netherland.** It may come as a surprise to learn that this stately part of the New York landscape is essentially a tall, luxurious apartment building that also has 50 hotel rooms and suites. **Pros:** gorgeous lobby; commanding, impeccable location; Cipriani access. **Cons:** small check-in area; rooms vary in taste and décor; nonsuites are on the small side; interior rooms lack views; guests sometimes feel the cold shoulder from the full-time residents. [$] *Rooms from: $649 ✉ 781 5th Ave., at 59th St., Midtown East ☎ 212/355–2800, 800/247–4377 🌐 www.sherrynetherland.com 🛏 26 rooms, 24 suites 🍴 No meals [M] N, Q, R to 5th Ave./59th St. ✣ 5:E6.*

$$$$ HOTEL Fodor's Choice ★ 🏨 **The St. Regis.** World-class from head to toe, this 5th Avenue Beaux Arts landmark comes as close to flawless as any hotel in New York, with tech-savvy rooms, historic touches, and the iconic King Cole Bar. **Pros:** classic NYC favorite; rooms combine true luxury with helpful technology; easy-access butler service; superb in-house dining; prestigious location. **Cons:** expensive; too serious for families seeking fun. [$] *Rooms from: $1495 ✉ 2 E. 55th St., at 5th Ave., Midtown East ☎ 212/753–4500, 877/787–3447 🌐 www.stregisnewyork.com 🛏 171 rooms, 67 suites 🍴 No meals [M] E, M to 5th Ave./53rd St. ✣ 4:E2.*

$$ HOTEL 🏨 **W Hotel New York.** A hopping bar and sunken lounge in the reception area, funky décor touches like window boxes filled with grass and guest rooms that hew to the classic brand formula—they're small but they look good—make this a quintessential W property. **Pros:** central location; great-looking rooms; Bliss Spa in hotel. **Cons:** thin walls; small rooms; inconsistent service. [$] *Rooms from: $329 ✉ 541 Lexington Ave., between 49th and 50th sts., Midtown East ☎ 212/755–1200, 877/946–8357 🌐 www.wnewyork.com 🛏 696 rooms, 60 suites 🍴 No meals [M] 6 to 51st St.; E, M to Lexington Ave./53rd St. ✣ 4:F3.*

$$ HOTEL 🏨 **Waldorf-Astoria.** The Waldorf is undeniably historic, and presidents usually stay here thanks to the security of the drive-in entrance, but we'd recommend a cocktail at the classic Bull and Bear Bar downstairs rather than a night in one of the small standard rooms, which can feel a bit oppressive with their extensive floral patterns. **Pros:** historic Art Deco building filled with NYC's aristocratic, gangster, and jazz histories; best Waldorf salad in town; knowledgeable doormen. **Cons:** rooms not up-to-date; more about the name than the experience; in-hotel Starbucks costs twice as much as those around the corner. [$] *Rooms from: $379 ✉ 301 Park Ave., between 49th and 50th sts., Midtown East ☎ 212/355–3000, 800/925–3673 🌐 www.waldorfnewyork.com 🛏 1,113 rooms, 300 suites 🍴 No meals [M] 6 to 51st St.; E, M to Lexington Ave./53rd St. ✣ 4:F3.*

$$ HOTEL 🏨 **The William.** What was once two connected brownstones home to a social club for Williams College has now been transformed into a modern, extended-stay hotel. **Pros:** convenient fully equipped kitchens; central location near Grand Central; good eating and drinking options. **Cons:** color and design may be too bright and modern for some guests. [$] *Rooms from: $395 ✉ 24 E. 39th St., between Park and Madison aves., Midtown East ☎ 646/922–8600 🌐 www.thewilliamnyc.*

com ⤸ *26 rooms, 7 suites* ⏀ *No meals* Ⓜ *4, 5, 6, 7, S to Grand Central–42nd St.* ✛ *4:F5.*

MURRAY HILL

$$ 🛏 **The Carlton Hotel.** From the two-story lobby designed by David
HOTEL Rockwell to still-intact, original 1904 Beaux Arts details such as the
stained-glass dome (created by workers from the Tiffany glass factory),
a 40-foot ceiling in the lobby, and a soaring crystal chandelier, the
Carlton is a refurbished gem. **Pros:** spectacular lobby; stylish rooms.
Cons: expensive bar; small rooms; dimly lit bathrooms. Ⓢ *Rooms from:
$449* ✉ *88 Madison Ave., between 28th and 29th sts., Murray Hill*
☎ *212/532–4100, 800/601–8500* ⊕ *www.carltonhotelny.com* ⤸ *294
rooms, 23 suites* ⏀ *No meals* Ⓜ *6 to 28th St.; N, R to 28th St.* ✛ *3:F1.*

$ 🛏 **The Herald Square Hotel.** The sculpted cherubs on the facade and the
HOTEL vintage magazine covers adorning the common areas hint that the great-
value Herald Square Hotel used to be *Life* magazine's headquarters.
Pros: affordable prices; centrally located. **Cons:** unattractive lobby;
readers report inconsistent service. Ⓢ *Rooms from: $199* ✉ *19 W. 31st
St., between 5th Ave. and Broadway, Murray Hill* ☎ *212/279–4017,
800/727–1888* ⊕ *www.heraldnyc.com* ⤸ *100 rooms* ⏀ *No meals* Ⓜ *B,
D, F, M, N, Q, R to 34th St.–Herald Sq.* ✛ *3:E1.*

$ 🛏 **Pod 39.** This cheap and cheerful sibling of the Pod Hotel on 51st
HOTEL Street has tight quarters and trendy amenities. **Pros:** quality taco and
cocktail spot; big rooftop with gorgeous views; lobby lounge with ping-
pong table. **Cons:** tight quarters; buzzy lobby and restaurant might not
suit all guests. Ⓢ *Rooms from: $150* ✉ *145 E. 39th St, between Lexing-
ton and 3rd aves., Murray Hill* ☎ *212/865–5700* ⊕ *www.thepodhotel.
com* ⤸ *366 rooms* ⏀ *No meals* Ⓜ *4, 5, 6, 7, S to Grand Central–42nd
St.* ✛ *4:G5.*

$$$ 🛏 **The Tuscany.** This historic building in Murray Hill was originally
HOTEL apartments—which explains the generous space—and is now a family-
FAMILY friendly hotel in a convenient location near Grand Central. **Pros:** very
large rooms for New York; fresh design and furnishings; art installations featuring local artists. **Cons:** on the expensive side. Ⓢ *Rooms from:
$495* ✉ *120 E. 39th St., between Park and Lexington aves., Murray
Hill* ☎ *212/686–1600* ⊕ *www.stgiles.com* ⤸ *116 rooms, 8 suites* ⏀ *No
meals* Ⓜ *4, 5, 6, 7, S to Grand Central–42nd St.* ✛ *4:F5.*

MIDTOWN WEST

$$ 🛏 **6 Columbus.** This boutique-style hotel in the shadow of the towering
HOTEL Time Warner Center has the vibe and amenities of downtown lodging
with a convenient Midtown location. **Pros:** convenient location; fun in-
hotel restaurant; reasonably priced for neighborhood; family-friendly.
Cons: rooms on lower floors facing 58th Street can be noisy. Ⓢ *Rooms
from: $399* ✉ *6 Columbus Circle, 58th St. between 8th and 9th aves.,
Midtown West* ☎ *877/626–5862* ⊕ *www.sixtyhotels.com/6columbus*
⤸ *88 rooms, 10 suites* ⏀ *No meals* Ⓜ *1, A, B, C, D to 59th St.–Colum-
bus Circle* ✛ *4:B1.*

17

$$$ HOTEL 🏨 **The Algonquin.** One of Manhattan's most historic properties, the Algonquin is a landmark of literary history—think oak paneling and pillars in the lobby—but with modernized rooms and contemporary comforts. **Pros:** free Internet; friendly, knowledgeable staff; central location. **Cons:** some small rooms. [$] *Rooms from: $459* ✉ *59 W. 44th St., between 5th and 6th aves., Midtown West* ☎ *212/840–6800, 800/555–8000* 🌐 *www.algonquinhotel.com* 🛏 *156 rooms, 25 suites* 🍴 *No meals* [M] *7 to 5th Ave.; B, D, F, M to 42nd St.–Bryant Park* ✥ *4:D4.*

$$ HOTEL FAMILY 🏨 **Belvedere Hotel.** Built during the 1920's, the Belvedere's main draw is its Times Square/Theater District location; the rooms tend to be dark and don't stand out designwise, although they are spacious and have kitchenettes with a microwave, minirefrigerator, and coffeemaker. **Pros:** good rates available; renovated rooms are good value. **Cons:** can be loud with street noise; slow elevators; Wi-Fi free in only some room categories. [$] *Rooms from: $329* ✉ *319 W. 48th St., between 8th and 9th aves., Midtown West* ☎ *212/245–7000, 888/468–3558* 🌐 *www.belvederehotelnyc.com* 🛏 *345 rooms* 🍴 *No meals* [M] *C, E to 50th St.* ✥ *4:B3.*

$ HOTEL FAMILY 🏨 **Best Western Plus President Hotel.** The President is the only politically themed hotel in the city, starting with the purple color scheme, a combination of Republican red and Democratic blue. **Pros:** sleek rooms for the price; convenient location; unique theme. **Cons:** cramped lobby; dark bathrooms; poor views. [$] *Rooms from: $249* ✉ *234 W. 48th St., between 8th Ave. and Broadway, Midtown West* ☎ *212/246–8800, 800/828–4667* 🌐 *www.presidenthotelny.com* 🛏 *334 rooms, 45 suites* 🍴 *No meals* [M] *N, Q, R to 49th St.; 1, C, E to 50th St.* ✥ *4:C3.*

$$$ HOTEL FAMILY 🏨 **The Blakely New York.** It may be a tried-and-true design motif, but it's hard to resist the English gentlemen's club when it's done right. **Pros:** all rooms have kitchenettes; central location; good-size rooms; acclaimed restaurant. **Cons:** rooms facing 54th Street can be noisy; some rooms have little natural light; expensive. [$] *Rooms from: $529* ✉ *136 W. 55th St., between 6th and 7th aves., Midtown West* ☎ *212/245–1800, 800/735–0710* 🌐 *www.blakelynewyork.com* 🛏 *60 rooms, 58 suites* 🍴 *Breakfast* [M] *N, Q, R to 57th St.–7th Ave; F to 57th St.* ✥ *4:C2.*

$$ HOTEL 🏨 **Bryant Park Hotel.** A New York landmark that towers over the New York Public Library and Bryant Park, this sleek hotel is still a Midtown hot spot. **Pros:** gorgeous building; fashionable crowd and setting; across from pretty Bryant Park; free Wi-Fi. **Cons:** expensive; Cellar Bar frequently booked for events. [$] *Rooms from: $445* ✉ *40 W. 40th St., between 5th and 6th aves., Midtown West* ☎ *212/869–0100, 877/640–9300* 🌐 *www.bryantparkhotel.com* 🛏 *112 rooms, 16 suites* 🍴 *No meals* [M] *B, D, F, M to 42nd St.–Bryant Park; 7 to 5th Ave.* ✥ *4:D5.*

$$ HOTEL 🏨 **Casablanca Hotel.** A favorite for the comfortable rooms and great location, the Casablanca evokes the sultry Mediterranean. **Pros:** great access to the Theater District; free continental breakfast and evening wine-and-cheese reception; free Wi-Fi. **Cons:** exercise facilities at nearby New York Sports Club, not on premises; heavy tourist foot traffic. [$] *Rooms from: $439* ✉ *147 W. 43rd St., Midtown West* ☎ *212/869–1212*

⊕ *www.casablancahotel.com* 🛏 *42 rooms, 6 suites* ¶◎¶ *Breakfast* Ⓜ *1, 2, 3, 7, N, Q, R, S to Times Sq.–42nd St.* ✛ *4:C4.*

$$$$
HOTEL
Fodor'sChoice
★

The Chatwal New York. A lavishly refurbished reincarnation of a classic Manhattan theater club, the Chatwal delivers a stylish, luxury experience with a matching price tag. **Pros:** gorgeous lobby; state-of-the-art room controls and amenities; excellent service; quality dining, bar, and spa. **Cons:** some visitors may find the price too high for the Times Square location. Ⓢ *Rooms from: $795* ✉ *130 W. 44th St., between 5th and 6th aves., Midtown West* ☎ *212/764–6200* ⊕ *www.thechatwalny. com* 🛏 *50 rooms, 26 suites* ¶◎¶ *No meals* Ⓜ *B, D, F, M to 42nd St.– Bryant Park; 1, 2, 3, N, Q, R, S to Times Sq.–42nd St.; 7 to 5th Ave.* ✛ *4:D4.*

$
HOTEL

Citizen M. A stylish property with a refreshing attitude in Midtown, this hotel is all about giving you everything you need and nothing you don't. **Pros:** all-season rooftop bar; cozy lobby full of books and magazines; 20th floor gym with great views. **Cons:** rooms are tight on space. Ⓢ *Rooms from: $199* ✉ *218 W. 50th St., Midtown West* ☎ *212/461– 3638* ⊕ *www.citizenm.com* 🛏 *230 rooms* ¶◎¶ *No meals* Ⓜ *1, C, E to 50th St.; N, Q, R to 49th St.* ✛ *4:C3.*

$$
HOTEL

City Club Hotel. Oceanliner–inspired rooms at the City Club are brisk, bright, and masculine: they're also about the same size as a room on a cruise ship—that means tight quarters, matey, no matter how much you enjoy sharing space with Jonathan Adler ceramics. **Pros:** free Wi-Fi; great restaurant; personal service. **Cons:** no gym; tiny lobby. Ⓢ *Rooms from: $400* ✉ *55 W. 44th St., between 5th and 6th aves., Midtown West* ☎ *212/921–5500* ⊕ *www.cityclubhotel.com* 🛏 *62 rooms, 3 suites* ¶◎¶ *No meals* Ⓜ *B, D, F, M to 42nd St.–Bryant Park; 7 to 5th Ave.* ✛ *4:D4.*

$$
HOTEL

The Distrikt. Rising high above Port Authority, the Distrikt tries to approximate the boutique hotel experience in an area of town best known for its bus depot, and for the most part, it succeeds. **Pros:** central location; friendly staff; good Midtown views from higher floors. **Cons:** on a gritty block right across from Port Authority; noisy on lower floors. Ⓢ *Rooms from: $429* ✉ *342 W. 40th St., between 8th and 9th aves., Midtown West* ☎ *212/706–6100* ⊕ *www.distrikthotel. com* 🛏 *155 rooms* ¶◎¶ *No meals* Ⓜ *A, C, E to 42nd St.–Port Authority* ✛ *4:B5.*

$$
HOTEL
FAMILY

DoubleTree Suites by Hilton Hotel New York City–Times Square. Space is the draw at this 45-story Times Square top dog; every room is a suite, with a separate bedroom and living room (each with a big flat-screen TV), occupying about 400 square feet overlooking Times Square and Broadway—an especially desirable location during the New Year's Eve ball drop. **Pros:** free 24-hour gym and Wi-Fi in public areas; extremely helpful, informed concierge; convenient to the Theater District; very quiet considering location. **Cons:** paid Wi-Fi in guest rooms; pricey for a DoubleTree. Ⓢ *Rooms from: $349* ✉ *1568 Broadway, at 47th St., Midtown West* ☎ *212/719–1600* ⊕ *doubletree3.hilton.com* 🛏 *460 suites* ¶◎¶ *No meals* Ⓜ *B, D, F, M to 42nd St.–Bryant Park; N, Q, R to 49th St.* ✛ *4:C3.*

17

CLOSE UP

Romantic Retreats

As the English explorer Sir Walter Raleigh once wrote, "Romance is a love affair in other than domestic surroundings." Indeed, many high-end hotels seem custom-built for romance, with plush feather beds, silky linens, and ultrasoft robes. But some properties go above and beyond in catering to couples, offering services like bath butlers and in-room massages. Here's our pick of the city's best spots for an intimate getaway.

At the **Ritz-Carlton New York, Battery Park** (*Lower Manhattan*), your wish is their command. Take advantage of lower-than-normal weekend rates to book a Liberty Suite, with sweeping views of the Statue of Liberty. With a quick call to the concierge you can arrange to have champagne and strawberries waiting in your room when you arrive. A bath butler can then fill your marble tub with a potion of bath oils and flower petals. If you're here in February, don't miss a trip to the penthouse Chocolate Bar, with its aphrodisiac chocolate-and-champagne buffet.

The **Inn at Irving Place** (*Union Square/Gramercy*) does romance the old-fashioned way, with four-poster beds, fireplaces, fur throws, and plenty of privacy in an elegant 1800s brownstone. The complimentary breakfast is served on fine bone china either in the cozy sitting room or in bed.

Few things are as romantic as taking a bath, and at the **Carlyle** (*Upper East Side*) every room has one. Fill the tub with steaming water and some Kiehl's bubble bath, take a soak, then lounge with your lover in a plush terry robe while looking out at some of the city's best views. The 23,000-square-foot Bliss Spa at **W Hotel New York** (*Midtown East*), on Lexington Avenue, is an urban oasis, with men's and women's lounges, a gym, and a full menu of facial and body treatments, massage, waxing, and nail services. Couples can spend a full day being pampered in the spa or unwind in their rooms with an in-room massage, available 24 hours a day.

All the rooms at the **Library Hotel** (*Midtown East*) have an inviting charm that makes them a good choice for a romantic weekend away, but if you're looking for a little mood reading, ask for the Erotic Literature room or the Love Room, curated by Dr. Ruth.

$$ HOTEL 🏨 **Dream New York.** Part hotel, part Kafkaesque dream, this Midtown spot specializes in style over comfort but is still quite livable, despite some over-the-top design features—and noise from the scenesters headed to the rooftop bar. **Pros:** AVA Lounge penthouse bar; large spa; up-to-the-minute electronics. **Cons:** small rooms; spotty service; might be too sceney for some. [$] *Rooms from: $345* ✉ *210 W. 55th St., at Broadway, Midtown West* ☎ *212/247–2000* 🌐 *www.dreamhotels.com/midtown* 🛏 *204 rooms, 12 suites* 🍴 *No meals* [M] *N, Q, R to 57th St.–7th Ave.* ✣ *4:C2.*

$ HOTEL 🏨 **Hilton Times Square.** A glass-and-steel skyscraper atop a 335,000-square-foot retail complex that includes a movie theater and Madame Tussauds Wax Museum, the Hilton Times Square soars 44 stories above Manhattan and overlooks New York City's famous skyline and the Hudson

River. **Pros:** great location for Times Square entertainment; convenient to public transportation; big rooms. **Cons:** impersonal feel; nickel-and-dime charges and overpriced food and drink, especially breakfast. $ *Rooms from: $299* ✉ *234 W. 42nd St., between 7th and 8th aves., Midtown West* ☎ *212/840–8222, 800/445–8667* ⊕ *www.hilton.com* ⤴ *460 rooms, 2 suites* ⦿ *No meals* Ⓜ *1, 2, 3, 7, N, Q, R, S to Times Sq.–42nd St.; A, C, E to 42nd St.–Port Authority* ✛ *4:C4.*

$ 🏨 **Hyatt Herald Square New York.** Business travelers, tourists, and families
HOTEL alike appreciate this fresh property a stone's throw from Penn Station with a scenic rooftop bar featuring Empire State Building views. **Pros:** fresh, stylish rooms with coffeemakers; friendly and efficient service; location in the thick of it. **Cons:** small workout room; location can be noisy. $ *Rooms from: $219* ✉ *30 W. 31st St., between 5th Ave. and Broadway, Midtown West* ☎ *212/330–1234* ⊕ *heraldsquare.hyatt.com/en/hotel/home.html* ⤴ *121 rooms, 1 suite* ⦿ *No meals* Ⓜ *B, D, F, M, N, Q, R to 34th St.–Herald Sq.* ✛ *3:E1.*

$ 🏨 **Hotel Metro.** With mirrored columns and elegant black-and-white
HOTEL photos in the lobby, the Hotel Metro feels distinctively retro. **Pros:** complimentary coffee and tea 24/7; renovated exercise room has flat-screen TVs; free Wi-Fi in rooms. **Cons:** noise seeps in from outside; rooms are tasteful but spartan. $ *Rooms from: $294* ✉ *45 W. 35th St., between 5th and 6th aves., Midtown West* ☎ *212/947–2500* ⊕ *www. hotelmetronyc.com* ⤴ *162 rooms, 20 suites* ⦿ *Breakfast* Ⓜ *B, D, F, M, N, Q, R to 34th St.–Herald Sq.* ✛ *4:D6.*

$$ 🏨 **Hudson New York Hotel.** Budget fashionistas are drawn to the this
HOTEL affordable hotel. **Pros:** fabulous, elegant bar; gorgeous Francesco Clemente fresco in lobby; breathtaking Sky Terrace. **Cons:** staff can be condescending; tiny rooms; overpriced cocktails. $ *Rooms from: $339* ✉ *356 W. 58th St., between 8th and 9th aves., Midtown West* ☎ *212/554–6000* ⊕ *www.hudsonhotel.com* ⤴ *866 rooms, 69 suites* ⦿ *No meals* Ⓜ *1, A, B, C, D to 59th St.–Columbus Circle* ✛ *4:B1.*

$ 🏨 **Ink48.** If you want to be near Midtown but a bit removed from the
HOTEL hustle and bustle, this Kimpton hotel is a great option. **Pros:** friendly
FAMILY staff; great views; large rooms; beautiful rooftop. **Cons:** out-of-the-way location; lobby can feel overly quiet; street noise in lower-floor rooms. $ *Rooms from: $299* ✉ *653 11th Ave., at 48th St., Midtown West* ☎ *212/757–0088* ⊕ *www.ink48.com* ⤴ *196 rooms, 26 suites* ⦿ *No meals* Ⓜ *C, E to 50th St.* ✛ *4:A3.*

$$$ 🏨 **InterContinental New York Times Square.** A central location mere blocks
HOTEL from the heart of Broadway, Times Square, and restaurant-rich Hell's Kitchen makes the InterContinental a conveniently located draw. **Pros:** central for transportation and entertainment; in-house restaurant helmed by celebrity chef; attentive staff. **Cons:** fee for Internet. $ *Rooms from: $459* ✉ *300 W. 44th St., between 8th and 9th aves., Midtown West* ☎ *877/331–5888, 212/315–2535* ⊕ *www.interconny. com* ⤴ *578 rooms, 4 suites, 25 studios* ⦿ *No meals* Ⓜ *A, C, E to 42nd St.–Port Authority* ✛ *4:B4.*

$$ 🏨 **JW Marriott Essex House.** With Central Park views and an Art Deco
HOTEL masterpiece of a lobby, the JW Marriott Essex House is a comfortable Midtown hotel full of character. **Pros:** great service; amazing views;

17

impressive restaurant. **Cons:** overly complex room gadgetry; expensive bar. [$] *Rooms from: $399* ✉ *160 Central Park S, between 6th and 7th aves., Midtown West* ☎ *212/247–0300, 800/937–8461* 🌐 *www.marriott.com* 🛏 *509 rooms, 117 suites* 🍴 *No meals* [M] *N, Q, R to 57th St.–7th Ave.; F to 57th St.* ✥ *4:C1.*

$$$ HOTEL 🏨 **The Knickerbocker.** An oasis of elegant, urban sophistication in the heart of Times Square, the Knickerbocker is a soothing counterpoint to mass of people, lights, and excitement that converge at the crossroads of Broadway and 42nd Street. **Pros:** in Times Square but aesthetically apart from it; spacious gym; fabulous rooftop bar. **Cons:** nearby dining isn't that exciting; small lobby. [$] *Rooms from: $489* ✉ *6 Times Sq., entrance on 42nd St., east of Broadway, Midtown West* ☎ *212/204—4980* 🌐 *www.theknickerbocker.com* 🛏 *299 rooms, 31 suites* 🍴 *No meals* [M] *1, 2, 3, 7, N, Q, R, S to Times Sq.–42nd St.* ✥ *4:C4.*

$ HOTEL 🏨 **La Quinta Inn Manhattan.** Smack in the middle of Koreatown and close to Penn Station, this budget-friendly hotel in a cheerful old Beaux Arts building may be one of the best deals in town. **Pros:** self-check-in machines; gift shop on the premises for necessities; relaxed rooftop bar; complimentary continental breakfast. **Cons:** no room service; no frills. [$] *Rooms from: $180* ✉ *17 W. 32nd St., between 5th Ave. and Broadway, Midtown West* ☎ *212/736–1600* 🌐 *www.laquintamanhattanny.com* 🛏 *182 rooms* 🍴 *Breakfast* [M] *B, D, F, M, N, Q, R to 34th St.–Herald Sq.* ✥ *4:E6.*

$$$ HOTEL FAMILY 🏨 **Le Parker Meridien.** Combining the comforts of a dependable large hotel with whimsical elements, this hotel also keeps visitors coming back with its iconic patty-palace Burger Joint, which serves one of the city's best no-frills burgers from behind a velvet curtain. **Pros:** lively, animated vibe; best hotel gym in the city; fun dining; tech-friendly rooms. **Cons:** lobby is a public space and gets crowded at peak times; small bathrooms. [$] *Rooms from: $450* ✉ *119 W. 56th St., between 6th and 7th aves., Midtown West* ☎ *212/245–5000, 800/543–4300* 🌐 *www.parkermeridien.com* 🛏 *513 rooms, 216 suites* 🍴 *No meals* [M] *N, Q, R to 57th St.–7th Ave.; F to 57th St.* ✥ *4:D1.*

$$$ HOTEL Fodor's Choice ★ 🏨 **The London NYC.** Stylish and sophisticated, the London NYC merges the flair of both its namesake cities in spacious, tech-savvy suites that are some of the largest in New York, starting at 500 square feet. **Pros:** posh atmosphere without prissiness; great fitness club; generous rooms; free Wi-Fi. **Cons:** no bathtubs in most rooms; expensive dining options. [$] *Rooms from: $599* ✉ *151 W. 54th St., between 6th and 7th aves., Midtown West* ☎ *866/690–2029, 212/307–5000* 🌐 *www.thelondonnyc.com* 🛏 *562 suites* 🍴 *No meals* [M] *B, D, E to 7th Ave.; N, Q, R to 57th St.–7th Ave.* ✥ *4:C2.*

$$$$ HOTEL Fodor's Choice ★ 🏨 **Mandarin Oriental.** The Mandarin's commitment to excess is evident in the lobby, on the 35th floor of the Time Warner Center, where dramatic floor-to-ceiling windows look out over Columbus Circle and Central Park. **Pros:** fantastic views from rooms, lounges, and pool; all the resources of the Time Warner Center; expansive suites; gorgeous, upscale restaurant with more amazing views. **Cons:** Trump hotel blocks some park views; expensive; mall-like surroundings. [$] *Rooms from:*

$895 ⊠ 80 Columbus Circle, at 60th St., Midtown West ☏ *212/805–8800* ⊕ *www.mandarinoriental.com/newyork* ☎ *198 rooms, 46 suites* ⫙ *No meals* Ⓜ *1, A, B, C, D to 59th St.–Columbus Circle* ✛ *4:B1; 5:C6.*

$$ 🛏 **The Mansfield.** They sweat the small stuff at the Mansfield: Wi-Fi
HOTEL is free, bathroom products are from Aveda, and even the key cards
are snazzily embossed with scenes of old-timey New York. **Pros:** free
Wi-Fi; business center; 24-hour gym; great bar. **Cons:** small rooms
and bathrooms; air-conditioners are window units. Ⓢ *Rooms from:
$319 ⊠ 12 W. 44th St., between 5th and 6th aves., Midtown West*
☏ *212/277–8700, 800/255–5167* ⊕ *www.mansfieldhotel.com* ☎ *99
rooms, 27 suites* ⫙ *No meals* Ⓜ *B, D, F, M to 42nd St.–Bryant Park;
7 to 5th Ave.* ✛ *4:E4.*

$$ 🛏 **The Michelangelo.** Italophiles feel like they've been transported to the
HOTEL good life in the Mediterranean at this deluxe hotel, where the long,
wide lobby lounge is clad with multi-hue marble and Veronese-style
oil paintings. **Pros:** good location; spacious rooms. **Cons:** noisy air-
conditioning units; some rooms have limited views; small closets; in-
room fixtures need some updating. Ⓢ *Rooms from: $399 ⊠ 152 W.
51st St., at 7th Ave., Midtown West* ☏ *212/765–1900, 800/237–0990*
⊕ *www.michelangelohotel.com* ☎ *123 rooms, 56 suites* ⫙ *Breakfast*
Ⓜ *B, D, E to 7th Ave.; 1 to 50th St.* ✛ *4:C3.*

$$ 🛏 **Muse Hotel.** Surrealist prints and busts of Thalia, the muse of comedy,
HOTEL adorn the lobby of this polished Kimpton property, a good pick for
guests looking for a Midtown boutique-hotel experience. **Pros:** contem-
porary interiors; good Midtown location; pet-friendly; complimentary
morning coffee and tea. **Cons:** street noise; small gym. Ⓢ *Rooms from:
$389 ⊠ 130 W. 46th St., between 6th and 7th aves., Midtown West*
☏ *212/485–2400, 877/692–6873* ⊕ *www.themusehotel.com* ☎ *181
rooms, 19 suites* ⫙ *No meals* Ⓜ *B, D, F, M to 47th–50th Sts./Rock-
efeller Center* ✛ *4:C4.*

$$ 🛏 **The Out NYC.** Billed as a straight-friendly "urban resort" in one of
HOTEL New York's most happening gay neighborhoods, the Out is the incarna-
Fodor'sChoice tion of all things hip and modern. **Pros:** centrally located; affordable;
★ friendly staff. **Cons:** can be noisy at night. Ⓢ *Rooms from: $360 ⊠ 510
W. 42nd St., between 10th and 11th aves., Midtown West* ☏ *212/947–
2999* ⊕ *www.theoutnyc.com* ☎ *87 rooms, 10 suites, 8 quads* ⫙ *No
meals* Ⓜ *A, C, E to 42nd St.–Port Authority* ✛ *4:A4.*

$$$$ 🛏 **Park Hyatt New York.** Occupying the first 25 floors of a towering
HOTEL Midtown skyscraper, this hotly anticipated luxury property is the new
Fodor'sChoice flagship of the global Park Hyatt brand. **Pros:** large guest rooms; luxuri-
★ ous furnishings; stunning décor and art collection. **Cons:** disappointing
views from guest rooms; street noise is audible on lower floors; expensive. Ⓢ *Rooms from: $795 ⊠ 153 W. 57th St., between 6th and 7th
aves., Midtown West* ☏ *646/774—1234* ⊕ *www.newyork.park.hyatt.
com* ☎ *115 rooms, 95 suites* ⫙ *No meals* Ⓜ *N, Q, R to 57th St.–7th
Ave.* ✛ *4:C1.*

17

$$$$ ⊞ **The Plaza.** Eloise's adopted home on the corner of Central Park, the
HOTEL   Plaza is one of New York's most storied hotels, hosting all manner of
Fodor's Choice   dignitaries, moneymakers, and royalty. **Pros:** historic property; lavish
★   rooms. **Cons:** rooms aren't that big for the money. Ⓢ *Rooms from:*
$895 ⊠ *768 5th Ave., at Central Park, Midtown West* ☎ *212/759–3000*
⊕ *www.theplazany.com* ↝ *180 rooms, 102 suites* †⊙† *No meals* Ⓜ *N, Q,*
R to 5th Ave./59th St. ✛ *4:E1.*

$$$ ⊞ **The Quin.** This new luxury hotel just south of Central Park once
HOTEL   housed artists like Marc Chagall and Georgia O'Keeffe. **Pros:** new,
fresh property; spacious rooms; close to neighborhood destinations
like Carnegie Hall. **Cons:** 57th Street location might be too chaotic
for some. Ⓢ *Rooms from: $599* ⊠ *101 W. 57th St., at 6th Ave., Mid-*
town West ☎ *212/245–7846* ⊕ *www.thequinhotel.com* ↝ *208 rooms,*
28 suites †⊙† *No meals* Ⓜ *N, Q, R to 57th St.–7th Ave.; F to 57th St.*
✛ *4:D1.*

$$$ ⊞ **Refinery Hotel.** Set in a former hat factory, this hotel has a gorgeous
HOTEL   year-round rooftop, impressively spacious rooms, and several buzzing
Fodor's Choice   bars and restaurants. **Pros:** lots of character and lovely, detailed design;
★   rooftop lounge with great views; excellent bars and restaurant. **Cons:**
limited dining and nightlife options nearby. Ⓢ *Rooms from: $559* ⊠ *63*
W. 38th St., between 5th and 6th aves., Midtown West ☎ *646/664–0310*
⊕ *www.refineryhotelnewyork.com* ↝ *197 rooms* †⊙† *No meals* Ⓜ *B, D,*
F, M to 42nd St.–Bryant Park; 7 to 5th Ave. ✛ *4:D5.*

$$$ ⊞ **Renaissance Hotel.** After a shift from all-business to a more design-
HOTEL   centric approach, the Renaissance is enjoying a renaissance of its own.
Pros: contemporary design; latest in-room technology. **Cons:** rooms
can be a bit noisy. Ⓢ *Rooms from: $539* ⊠ *714 7th Ave., between 47th*
and 48th sts., Midtown West ☎ *212/765–7676, 800/628–5222* ⊕ *www.*
renaissancehotels.com ↝ *305 rooms, 5 suites* †⊙† *No meals* Ⓜ *N, Q,*
R to 49th St.; 1 to 50th St.; B, D, F, M to 47th–50th Sts./Rockefeller
Center ✛ *4:C3.*

$$$$ ⊞ **The Ritz-Carlton New York, Central Park.** It's all about the park views
HOTEL   here, though the above-and-beyond service, accommodating to a fault,
FAMILY   makes this renowned property popular with celebs and other demand-
Fodor's Choice   ing guests. **Pros:** great concierge; personalized service; stellar location;
★   views. **Cons:** pricey; limited common areas. Ⓢ *Rooms from: $895* ⊠ *50*
Central Park S, at 6th Ave., Midtown West ☎ *212/308–9100, 866/671–*
6008 ⊕ *www.ritzcarlton.com* ↝ *259 rooms, 47 suites* †⊙† *No meals* Ⓜ *F*
to 57th St.; N, Q, R to 5th Ave./59th St. ✛ *4:D1.*

$$ ⊞ **Room Mate Grace.** A favorite of European visitors and business travel-
HOTEL   ers who work in fashion and entertainment, Grace delivers high-design
FAMILY   lodgings on a budget. **Pros:** cool swimming pool lounge; friendly, helpful staff. **Cons:** small rooms; little in-room privacy (no door separating
shower from main room). Ⓢ *Rooms from: $319* ⊠ *125 W. 45th St.,*
Midtown West ☎ *212/354–2323* ⊕ *www.room-matehotels.com* ↝ *139*
rooms †⊙† *No meals* Ⓜ *B, D, F, M to 47th–50th Sts./Rockefeller Center*
✛ *4:D4.*

$$ ⊞ **The Royalton.** Back in the 1990s, the Royalton's lobby bar was one of
HOTEL   the prime meeting spots for local A-listers, and a redesign has attracted a
new generation of movers and shakers—be prepared to run the gauntlet

of the buzzing lounge before reaching your room—but the helpful staff have ensured a smooth transition. **Pros:** hip lobby scene; luxurious beds and bathrooms; helpful service. **Cons:** dark hallways; lighting verges on eye-strainingly dim. [$] *Rooms from: $399* ✉ *44 W. 44th St., between 5th and 6th aves., Midtown West* ☎ *212/869–4400, 800/697–1791* 🌐 *www.royaltonhotel.com* 🛏 *141 rooms, 27 suites* 🍴 *No meals* [M] *B, D, F, M to 42nd St.–Bryant Park; 7 to 5th Ave.* ✣ *4:D4.*

$ HOTEL 🏨 **The Shoreham.** In a neighborhood packed with generic hotels, the Shoreham sports a welcome dose of style, along with proximity to Midtown's attractions. **Pros:** tech-friendly rooms; pet-friendly attitude; stylish décor. **Cons:** not designed for families; limited space. [$] *Rooms from: $259* ✉ *33 W. 55th St., between 5th and 6th aves., Midtown West* ☎ *212/247–6700, 877/847–4444* 🌐 *www.shorehamhotel.com* 🛏 *177 rooms, 42 suites* 🍴 *No meals* [M] *E, M to 5th Ave./53rd St.; F to 57th St.* ✣ *4:D2.*

$$ HOTEL 🏨 **Sofitel New York.** With bilingual signage throughout the hotel, plenty of velvet in the lobby, and European modern design in the rooms—think blond wood and fresh flowers—the Sofitel brings a Gallic flair to Midtown West. **Pros:** central location; great beds; some suites with terraces and views. **Cons:** room views vary. [$] *Rooms from: $350* ✉ *45 W. 44th St., between 5th and 6th aves., Midtown West* ☎ *212/354–8844* 🌐 *www.sofitel.com* 🛏 *346 rooms, 52 suites* 🍴 *No meals* [M] *B, D, F, M to 42nd St.–Bryant Park; 7 to 5th Ave.* ✣ *4:E4.*

$ HOTEL 🏨 **The Time Hotel.** One of the neighborhood's first boutique hotels, this spot half a block from the din of Times Square tempers trendiness with a touch of humor. **Pros:** acclaimed and popular Serafina restaurant downstairs; surprisingly quiet for Times Square location; good turndown service. **Cons:** design makes the rooms a little dated; service is inconsistent; water pressure is lacking. [$] *Rooms from: $275* ✉ *224 W. 49th St., between Broadway and 8th Ave., Midtown West* ☎ *212/246–5252, 877/846–3692* 🌐 *www.thetimeny.com* 🛏 *164 rooms, 29 suites* 🍴 *No meals* [M] *1, C, E to 50th St.; N, Q, R to 49th St.* ✣ *4:C3.*

$$$ HOTEL 🏨 **Viceroy New York.** Handsome and finely tailored, this hotel has functional, tech-focused rooms and lots of amenities. **Pros:** comfortable, quiet library with "cartender" mixing drinks in late afternoon; generous rooftop space with views of Central Park; appealing restaurant. **Cons:** small, crowded lobby; busy 57th Street location might not suit all guests. [$] *Rooms from: $559* ✉ *120 W. 57th, Midtown West* ☎ *212/830–8000* 🌐 *www.viceroyhotelsandresorts.com/newyork* 🛏 *197 rooms, 43 suites* 🍴 *No meals* [M] *N, Q, R to 57th St.—7th Ave.; F to 57th St.* ✣ *4:D1.*

$$ HOTEL 🏨 **W Times Square.** Although it opened back in 2001, the W Times Square still stands out in the craziness of Times Square, thanks to its iconic, 57-story exterior—if you want to be in the thick of the action, this is a fun place to stay. **Pros:** bustling nightlife and happy-hour scene; sleek rooms. **Cons:** if you want quiet, head elsewhere; no bathtubs in the smaller rooms. [$] *Rooms from: $379* ✉ *1567 Broadway, at 47th St., Midtown West* ☎ *212/930–7400, 877/946–8357* 🌐 *www.wnewyorktimessquare.com* 🛏 *466 rooms, 43 suites* 🍴 *No meals* [M] *N, Q, R to 49th St.* ✣ *4:C3.*

$$ ▦ **Warwick.** This grande dame was built by William Randolph Hearst in
HOTEL   1926 for his mistress, Hollywood actress Marion Davies, and it's hosted
many from Tinseltown since then, including Cary Grant in the Presiden-
tial Suite for 12 years. **Pros:** excellent restaurant and bar; historic prop-
erty; spacious suites. **Cons:** some rooms could use a refresh; no a/c in
the hallways. $ *Rooms from: $385* ⊠ *65 W. 54th St., at 6th Ave., Mid-
town West* ☎ *212/247–2700, 800/223–4099* ⊕ *www.warwickhotelny.
com* ⤵ *359 rooms, 67 suites* ⦿ *No meals* Ⓜ *F to 57th St.; B, D, E to
7th Ave.* ✛ *4:D2.*

$ ▦ **Wellington Hotel.** A few blocks south of Central Park and Columbus
HOTEL   Circle, the Wellington is a good base for visitors who want to see the
FAMILY   sights in Midtown and the Upper West Side. **Pros:** central location; chip-
per, helpful staff; good for big families. **Cons:** dark, often small bath-
rooms; limited breakfast options. $ *Rooms from: $275* ⊠ *871 7th Ave.,
at 55th St., Midtown West* ☎ *212/247–3900, 800/652–1212* ⊕ *www.
wellingtonhotel.com* ⤵ *515 rooms, 85 suites* ⦿ *No meals* Ⓜ *N, Q, R
to 57th St.–7th Ave.* ✛ *4:C2.*

$$$ ▦ **WestHouse.** This Art Deco–style hotel is designed to feel like a glam-
HOTEL   orous private residence. **Pros:** many extras included; fresh, luxurious
rooms. **Cons:** guests may have mixed feelings on mandatory daily resident fee; busy Midtown location lacks nearby quality restaurant and
nightlife options. $ *Rooms from: $499* ⊠ *201 W. 55th St., between
7th Ave. and Broadway, Midtown West* ☎ *212/707–4888* ⊕ *www.
westhousehotelnewyork.com* ⤵ *154 rooms, 16 suites* ⦿ *Breakfast* Ⓜ *B,
D, E to 7th Ave.; N, Q, R to 57th St.–7th Ave.* ✛ *4:C2.*

$ ▦ **Westin New York at Times Square.** This giant Midtown hotel has all
HOTEL   the amenities and service you expect from a reliable brand, at fairly
reasonable prices, though without much style. **Pros:** central for Midtown attractions; big rooms; great gym. **Cons:** congested area near Port
Authority; small bathroom sinks; some rooms need to be refreshed.
$ *Rooms from: $299* ⊠ *270 W. 43rd St., at 8th Ave., Midtown West*
☎ *212/201–2700, 866/837–4183* ⊕ *www.westinny.com* ⤵ *873 rooms*
⦿ *No meals* Ⓜ *A, C, E to 42nd St.–Port Authority* ✛ *4:B4.*

$ ▦ **Yotel.** Look beyond the gimmicks (a luggage-storing robot, the futur-
HOTEL   istic white design scheme)and discover one of New York's best-run,
most functional lodgings. **Pros:** great value; large common outdoor
space; access to West Side piers and Javits Center. **Cons:** rooms may be
small for some; limited luggage storage and hanging space; 10th Avenue
is a bit remote. $ *Rooms from: $149* ⊠ *570 10th Ave., at 42nd St., Midtown West* ☎ *646/449–7700* ⊕ *www.yotelnewyork.com* ⤵ *647 rooms,
22 suites* ⦿ *Breakfast* Ⓜ *A, C, E to 42nd St.–Port Authority* ✛ *4:A4.*

UPPER EAST SIDE

$$$$ ▦ **The Carlyle, A Rosewood Hotel.** On the well-heeled corner of Madison
HOTEL   Avenue and 76th Street, the Carlyle's fusion of venerable elegance and
Fodor'sChoice   Manhattan swank calls for the aplomb of entering a Chanel boutique:
★   walk in chin high, wallet out, and ready to impress (and be impressed).
Pros: perhaps NYC's best Central Park views; refined service; delightful
array of dining and bar options; chic shopping in the neighborhood;
great bathtubs. **Cons:** removed from touristy Manhattan; stuffy vibe

may not work for families; every room is different, limiting consistency. [$] *Rooms from: $800* ✉ *35 E. 76th St., between Madison and Park aves., Upper East Side* ☎ *212/744–1600* 🌐 *www.thecarlyle.com* 🛏 *121 rooms, 69 suites* 🍴 *No meals* [M] *6 to 77th St.* ⊕ *5:F3.*

$ HOTEL **The Franklin.** The best luxury boutique hotel north of 57th Street, this nine-story townhouse is a gem in a decidedly residential neighborhood. **Pros:** neighborhood-y location; free Wi-Fi and generous breakfast; pet-friendly. **Cons:** far from many tourist sights except Museum Mile; small rooms. [$] *Rooms from: $279* ✉ *164 E. 87th St., between Lexington and 3rd aves., Upper East Side* ☎ *212/369–1000, 800/607–4009* 🌐 *www.franklinhotel.com* 🛏 *50 rooms* 🍴 *Breakfast* [M] *4, 5, 6 to 86th St.* ⊕ *6:G6.*

$$$$ HOTEL **Hôtel Plaza Athénée.** Positioned unobtrusively by Central Park on the Upper East Side, the Plaza Athénée (now related in name only to its Parisian cousin) makes stellar service a priority, with a personal sit-down check-in off to the side of the lobby, and extravagant in-room dining service with an old-world feel: white tablecloths, candles, and flowers are part of the deal. **Pros:** discerning service; fabulous hotel bar. **Cons:** lobby can feel dark; Wi-Fi costs extra; expensive. [$] *Rooms from: $695* ✉ *37 E. 64th St., at Madison Ave., Upper East Side* ☎ *212/734–9100, 212/606–4600* 🌐 *www.plaza-athenee.com* 🛏 *117 rooms, 25 suites* 🍴 *No meals* [M] *6 to 68th St.–Hunter College; F to Lexington Ave./63rd St.* ⊕ *5:F5.*

$$ HOTEL FAMILY **Hotel Wales.** A favorite for in-the-know travelers, the Wales is a pleasant if unassuming hotel in a sedate neighborhood. **Pros:** on-site fitness facilities; great neighborhood feel; roof garden. **Cons:** standard rooms are tight on space; if seeking nightlife go elsewhere. [$] *Rooms from: $395* ✉ *1295 Madison Ave., between 92nd and 93rd sts., Upper East Side* ☎ *212/876–6000* 🌐 *www.hotelwalesnyc.com* 🛏 *46 rooms, 43 suites* 🍴 *No meals* [M] *6 to 96th St.* ⊕ *6:F5.*

$$$$ HOTEL **The Lowell.** Steps from Madison Avenue shopping and the Museum Mile, this old-money refuge on a leafy residential block was built as an upscale apartment hotel in the 1920s and still delivers genteel sophistication and pampering service in an unbeatable location. **Pros:** great location; service with a personal touch; charming décor; some suites with wood-burning fireplaces. **Cons:** cramped lobby; expensive. [$] *Rooms from: $800* ✉ *28 E. 63rd St., between Madison and Park aves., Upper East Side* ☎ *212/838–1400, 800/221–4444* 🌐 *www.lowellhotel.com* 🛏 *27 rooms, 47 suites* 🍴 *No meals* [M] *N, Q, R to 5th Ave./59th St.; F to Lexington Ave./63rd St.* ⊕ *5:F6.*

$$$ HOTEL Fodor's Choice ★ **The Mark.** The Mark is the perfect combo of uptown panache and downtown chic. **Pros:** hip design; cavernous closet space; great service; scene-making restaurant and bar. **Cons:** expensive; limited budget dining options in neighborhood. [$] *Rooms from: $600* ✉ *25 E. 77th St., at Madison Ave., Upper East Side* ☎ *212/744–4300* 🌐 *www.themarkhotel.com* 🛏 *100 rooms, 50 suites* 🍴 *No meals* [M] *6 to 77th St.* ⊕ *5:F2.*

17

CLOSE UP

Lodging Alternatives

APARTMENT RENTALS VS. SUITE HOTELS

For your trip to New York, you may want a little more space than the city's typically tiny hotel rooms provide. Some travelers consider apartment rentals, but there are many good reasons to stick to hotel suites instead. Why? First, apartment rentals of less than 30 days—with some very limited exceptions—are illegal in New York City. Furthermore, apartment-rental scams are an issue. In some published reports, potential guests have arrived to find that the apartment they rented does not exist, or that they are paying for an illegal sublet. In some cases, travelers have lost their deposit or their prepaid rent (note: never wire money to an account).

There are a few reputable providers of short-term rentals, *noted below,* but many Fodorites have turned to suite hotels and bed-and-breakfasts with apartmentlike accommodations. As Airbnb's attempts to change New York State housing laws continue, consider one of the legal providers below. And if you are going to rent an apartment, be sure to read reviews of individual apartments for first-hand feedback from fellow travelers.

FURNISHED APARTMENTS

Local rental agencies that arrange rentals of furnished apartments include the following.

Abode Limited. ☏ *800/835–8880, 212/472–2000* ⊕ *www.abodenyc.com.*

Manhattan Getaways. ☏ *212/956–2010* ⊕ *www.manhattangetaways. com.*

SUITE HOTELS

Suite hotels like the Conrad New York, the DoubleTree Suites by Hilton Hotel New York City–Times Square, and The London NYC—all in Manhattan—as well as the Box House Hotel, in Brooklyn, are definitely on the spacious side. The Affinia hotel group, which includes the FIFTY NYC, has many suites as well.

BED-AND-BREAKFASTS

B&Bs booked through a service may be either hosted (you're the guest in someone's quarters) or unhosted (you have full use of someone's vacated apartment, including kitchen privileges). Reservation services include the following.

Bed and Breakfast Network of New York. ⊠ *134 W. 32nd St., Suite 602, between 6th and 7th aves.* ☏ *212/645–8134, 888/707–4626* ⊕ *www.bedandbreakfastnetwork.com.*

The City Lights Bed and Breakfast aggregate helps travelers find B&Bs as well as short-term apartments. ☏ *212/737–7049* ⊕ *www. citylightsbedandbreakfast.com.*

UPPER WEST SIDE

$$$ HOTEL **The Empire Hotel.** In a prime Upper West Side spot, the sophisticated Empire Hotel attracts locals for views from the rooftop pool and lounge area underneath the hotel's iconic red neon sign, while guests appreciate the rooms, which are a comfortable and chic escape from the bustle of the city. **Pros:** great location next to Lincoln Center and blocks from Central Park; beautiful rooftop pool and bar; nice turndown service. **Cons:** rooftop bar brings foot traffic through hotel lobby, plus noise to some rooms; some rooms could use a refresh; bathrooms are nicely designed but tiny; pool is quite small. [$] *Rooms from: $519* ✉ *44 W. 63rd St., at Columbus Ave., Upper West Side* ☎ *212/265–7400* 🌐 *www.empirehotelnyc.com* 🛏 *376 rooms, 50 suites* 🍴 *No meals* [M] *1, A, B, C, D to 59th St.–Columbus Circle* ✦ *5:C5.*

$ HOTEL **The Excelsior Hotel.** Directly across the street from the American Museum of Natural History, this well-kept, old-school spot is comfortable but has occasionally inconsistent staff. **Pros:** excellent neighborhood-y Upper West Side location near Central Park; near foodie mecca Zabar's and popular burger joint Shake Shack; tranquil environment. **Cons:** spotty front-desk staff; rooms are inconsistent; Wi-Fi is not free. [$] *Rooms from: $289* ✉ *45 W. 81st St., between Central Park W and Columbus Ave., Upper West Side* ☎ *212/362–9200* 🌐 *www.excelsiorhotelny.com* 🛏 *120 rooms, 80 suites* 🍴 *No meals* [M] *B, C to 81st St.–Museum of Natural History* ✦ *5:C2.*

$ HOTEL FAMILY **Hotel Beacon.** A neighborhood favorite for a reason, this Upper West Side hotel is three blocks from Central Park, ten blocks from Lincoln Center, and steps from great gourmet grocery stores—Zabar's, Fairway, and Citarella. **Pros:** kitchenettes in all rooms; great UWS location; affordable; great service. **Cons:** though comfortable and spacious, rooms aren't winning any design awards. [$] *Rooms from: $299* ✉ *2130 Broadway, at 75th St., Upper West Side* ☎ *212/787–1100, 800/572–4969* 🌐 *www.beaconhotel.com* 🛏 *140 rooms, 136 suites* 🍴 *No meals* [M] *1, 2, 3 to 72nd St.* ✦ *5:A3.*

$$ HOTEL FAMILY **The Lucerne.** Service is the strong suit at this landmark-facade hotel, whose exterior has more pizzazz than the predictable guest rooms decorated with dark-wood reproduction furniture and chintzy bedspreads. **Pros:** free Wi-Fi; clean; great gym; close to Central Park. **Cons:** inconsistent room size; some guests report uncomfortable pillows. [$] *Rooms from: $309* ✉ *201 W. 79th St., at Amsterdam Ave., Upper West Side* ☎ *212/875–1000, 800/492–8122* 🌐 *www.thelucernehotel.com* 🛏 *165 rooms, 37 suites* 🍴 *No meals* [M] *1 to 79th St.* ✦ *5:A2.*

$$ HOTEL **NYLO New York City.** Bringing modern style to the sometimes stodgy Upper West Side, this hotel nods to the jazz era—think raucous bar, decadent living room with a fireplace, and tempting restaurants. **Pros:** short walk from Central Park; quiet, safe location; excellent dining and drinking options; rooms with terraces and dynamite views. **Cons:** lobby might be too hectic for some; Upper West Side location removed from some attractions. [$] *Rooms from: $349* ✉ *2178 Broadway, Upper West Side* ☎ *212/362–1100* 🌐 *www.nylohotels.com* 🛏 *258 rooms, 33 suites* 🍴 *No meals* [M] *1 to 79th St.* ✦ *5:A3.*

$$$$ ⊞ **Trump International Hotel and Towers.** This iconic New York property's
HOTEL incomparable views of Central Park has interior design to match, conceived with the help of the Donald's daughter, Ivanka. **Pros:** fine service;
stellar views; discerning treatment. **Cons:** expensive. $ *Rooms from:*
$800 ⊠ 1 Central Park W, between 59th and 60th sts., Upper West
Side ☏ *212/299–1000, 888/448–7867* ⊕ *www.trumphotelcollection.*
com ⇆ *35 rooms, 141 suites* ⦿ *No meals* Ⓜ *1, A, B, C, D to 59th*
St.–Columbus Circle ✛ *5:C6.*

HARLEM

$ ⊞ **Aloft Harlem.** A reasonably priced option in an increasingly popular
HOTEL area of Harlem (Marcus Samuelsson's hot Red Rooster restaurant is
nearby), this branch of the Aloft chain delivers with cheerful service and
a fun atmosphere, once you get past the confusing front entrance. **Pros:**
good room size for the price; convenient to subways; ever-increasing
local shopping and dining options. **Cons:** rooms have minimal space
for hanging clothes; rooms get some street noise. $ *Rooms from: $289*
⊠ *2296 Frederick Douglass Blvd., between 123th and 124th sts., Har-*
lem ☏ *212/749–4000* ⊕ *www.aloftharlem.com* ⇆ *124 rooms* ⦿ *No*
meals Ⓜ *A, B, C, D to 125th St.* ✛ *6:C1.*

BROOKLYN

DOWNTOWN BROOKLYN

$$ ⊞ **Aloft New York Brooklyn.** A funky boutique operation in the heart
HOTEL of Downtown Brooklyn, Aloft is a lively yet comfortable space.
FAMILY **Pros:** easy subway access; reasonable prices; guests have access to the
adjacent Sheraton's indoor swimming pool and room service. **Cons:**
rumored construction behind the hotel could mean noise in years to
come. $ *Rooms from: $359* ⊠ *216 Duffield St., between Willoughby*
St. and Fulton Mall, Downtown Brooklyn ☏ *718/256–3833* ⊕ *www.*
aloftnewyorkbrooklyn.com ⇆ *170 rooms, 6 suites* ⦿ *No meals* Ⓜ *2, 3*
to Hoyt St.; A, C, F, N, R to Jay St.—Metro Tech ✛ *7:B4.*

$$ ⊞ **New York Marriott at the Brooklyn Bridge.** The rooms at this well-situated
HOTEL hotel are classic Marriott—large and comfortable, if nondescript, and
FAMILY enhanced by high ceilings, massaging showerheads, rolling desks, and
other niceties. **Pros:** near some of Brooklyn's hipper neighborhoods; traditional full-service hotel. **Cons:** on a busy downtown street. $ *Rooms*
from: $369 ⊠ *333 Adams St., between Johnson and Willoughby Sts.,*
Downtown Brooklyn ☏ *718/246–7000* ⊕ *www.marriott.com/nycbk*
⇆ *638 rooms, 28 suites* ⦿ *No meals* Ⓜ *2, 3, 4, 5 to Borough Hall; A,*
C, F, N, R to Jay St.—Metro Tech ✛ *7:B3.*

BOERUM HILL

$ ⊞ **NU Hotel Brooklyn.** The hip-yet-affordable NU, on one of Brooklyn's
HOTEL main nightlife and shopping streets, is perfect for visitors seeking a
perch near the best of the borough. **Pros:** great Brooklyn launching pad;
knowledgeable staff; 24-hour fitness center. **Cons:** subway or cab ride
to anything in Manhattan; bar area can be a little too quiet; limited
in-room amenities. $ *Rooms from: $299* ⊠ *85 Smith St., Boerum Hill*

☎ *718/852–8585* ⊕ *www.nuhotelbrooklyn.com* ↻ *87 rooms, 6 suites* ⬤*❙Breakfast* Ⓜ *F, G to Bergen St.; A, C, G to Hoyt-Schermerhorn Sts.* ✛ *7:B4.*

GOWANUS

$ 🏨 **Hotel Le Bleu.** This hotel, nestled among gorgeous Brooklyn brown-
HOTEL stones, provides comfortable, carpeted rooms, some with terraces fac-
ing the Statue of Liberty or Manhattan. **Pros:** stylish rooms with coffee
makers; some rooms have terraces and Manhattan views; great access to
Brooklyn dining and shopping. **Cons:** far from main NYC attractions.
Ⓢ *Rooms from: $239* ✉ *370 4th Ave., Gowanus* ☎ *718/625–1500*
⊕ *www.hotellebleu.com* ↻ *48 rooms* ⬤*❙Breakfast* Ⓜ *R to 9th St.; F,*
G to 4th Ave. ✛ *7:B5.*

$ 🏨 **The Union Hotel.** When it's not your first time visiting New York, and
HOTEL you want to get away from the crowds, this hotel provides a comfortable Brooklyn retreat from which to explore the borough. **Pros:** location
near the subway; walking distance to great restaurants and shopping;
free Wi-Fi. **Cons:** rooms are tight on space. Ⓢ *Rooms from: $159* ✉ *611*
Degraw St., Gowanus ☎ *718/403–0614* ⊕ *www.unionhotelbrooklyn.*
com ↻ *43 rooms* ⬤*❙Breakfast* Ⓜ *R to Union St.* ✛ *7:C5.*

GREENPOINT

$$ 🏨 **Box House Hotel.** Adventurous travelers are drawn to this all-suites
HOTEL hotel, formerly a door factory, in industrial northern Greenpoint. **Pros:**
FAMILY exciting, developing neighborhood; huge suites with kitchens and living
rooms; free neighborhood transportation. **Cons:** functional bathrooms
not particularly luxurious; no black-out curtains; isolated location in
industrial area isn't for everyone. Ⓢ *Rooms from: $379* ✉ *77 Box St.,*
Greenpoint ☎ *718/383–3800* ⊕ *www.theboxhousehotel.com* ↻ *56*
suites ⬤*❙No meals* Ⓜ *G to Greenpoint Ave.* ✛ *7:E1.*

WILLIAMSBURG

$ 🏨 **Hotel Le Jolie.** This no-frills favorite has excellent service and is con-
HOTEL venient not only to Williamsburg's arts, culture, and dining scenes,
but also to the subway and the Brooklyn-Queens Expressway, the lat-
ter handy should you want to get into Manhattan via car. **Pros:** good
value; free parking on a first-come, first-served basis; convenient part
of Brooklyn. **Cons:** location next to highway can mean noise; can feel
remote even though near to subways. Ⓢ *Rooms from: $199* ✉ *235*
Meeker Ave., between Lorimer St. and Union Ave., Williamsburg
☎ *718/625–2100* ⊕ *www.hotellejolie.com* ↻ *52 rooms* ⬤*❙Breakfast*
Ⓜ *L to Lorimer St.* ✛ *7:E1.*

$$ 🏨 **McCarren Hotel and Pool.** With funky design details like an underfoot,
HOTEL glass-encased river in the lobby (plus a fireplace), and a plum location
overlooking McCarren Park, this hotel sizzles with scenester savvy.
Pros: high hip factor; quality rooftop restaurant-bar; close to main thoroughfare Bedford Avenue. **Cons:** potential for noise from concerts in
McCarren Park; some room details like lighting controls could be more
user-friendly. Ⓢ *Rooms from: $315* ✉ *160 N. 12th St., between Bedford*
and Berry sts., Williamsburg ☎ *718/218–7500* ⊕ *www.chelseahotels.*
com/us/brooklyn/mccarren-hotel-and-pool/about ↻ *60 rooms, 4 suites*
⬤*❙No meals* Ⓜ *L to Bedford Ave.* ✛ *7:E1.*

17

$ B&B/INN Fodor's Choice ★ 🏨 **Urban Cowboy B&B.** Williamsburg's only B&B, which occupies a newly renovated 100-year-old townhouse, combines the neighborhood's renegade spirit with an eye for design. **Pros:** beautiful design with personal touches; backyard jacuzzi; personable staff. **Cons:** most rooms share a bathroom. [$] *Rooms from: $200* ✉ *111 Powers St., North Williamsburg* ☎ *347/840–0525* 🌐 *www.urbancowboybnb.com* 🛏 *4 rooms (3 with shared bath), 1 cabin* 🍴 *Breakfast* [M] *L to Lorimer St., G to Metropolitan Ave.* ✣ *7:E2.*

$$ HOTEL Fodor's Choice ★ 🏨 **Wythe Hotel.** A former cooperage on the Brooklyn waterfront has found new life as the Wythe Hotel, a stunner for its Manhattan-skyline views, locally sourced design touches and amenities, and super-cool restaurant **(Reynard)** and bar **(Ides)**. **Pros:** unique building history; excellent entry into fun neighborhood; Brooklyn-based design and environmentally friendly products; fabulous views from rooms or rooftop bar; destination-worthy restaurant. **Cons:** somewhat removed from the subway; no room service. [$] *Rooms from: $300* ✉ *80 Wythe Ave., at N. 11th St., Williamsburg* ☎ *718/460–8001* 🌐 *www.wythehotel.com* 🛏 *66 rooms, 4 suites* 🍴 *No meals* [M] *L to Bedford Ave.* ✣ *7:D1.*

QUEENS

$ HOTEL FAMILY 🏨 **The Paper Factory Hotel.** Space, style, access to intriguing local neighborhoods, and seriously good value—this paper factory turned chic hotel provides many reasons to stay in Queens. **Pros:** excellent value; one-minute walk to subway; stylish rooms and restaurant; generous space. **Cons:** some street noise reaches rooms. [$] *Rooms from: $199* ✉ *37-06 36th St., Astoria* ☎ *718/392–7200* 🌐 *www.paperfactoryhotel.com* 🛏 *123 rooms, 10 suites* 🍴 *No meals* [M] *M, R to 36th St.* ✣ *7:H1.*

SHOPPING

Updated
by Christina
Valhouli

The Big Apple is one of the best shopping destinations in the world, rivaled perhaps only by London, Paris, and Tokyo. Its compact size, convenient subway system, and plentiful cabs (or Uber or Lyft rides) make it easy to navigate with plenty of bags in tow. But what it really comes down to is the staggering number and variety of stores. If you can't find it in New York, it probably doesn't exist.

If you like elegant flagships and money is no object, head to Midtown, where you find international megabrands like Louis Vuitton, Yves Saint Laurent, and Gucci, as well as famed department stores Bergdorf Goodman and Barneys. Nearby Madison Avenue has couture from Carolina Herrera and Vera Wang, and 5th Avenue is lined with famous jewelry stores like Tiffany, Van Cleef & Arpels, and Harry Winston. This is also the neighborhood to indulge in bespoke goods, such as handmade shoes from John Lobb. If you like designer pieces but can't afford them, don't despair—there are plenty of upscale consignment shops around the city where you can find last season's Chanel suit or a vintage YSL jacket.

The small, independent shops that once lined SoHo have largely been swallowed up by J. Crew and UNIQLO, but if you want to hit the chains, this is a great place to do it, because SoHo also provides high-quality people-watching and superb lunches. If craving some of old SoHo's artistic spirit, don't discount the street vendors' stalls, which sell handmade jewelry and simple cotton dresses. You never know—you might buy something from a soon-to-be-famous designer.

The East Village and Lower East Side are hotbeds of creativity and quirky coolness, with little boutiques selling everything from retro furniture to industrial-inspired jewelry, tucked among bars and tenement apartments. The Meatpacking District is another great shopping destination to find chic stores like Diane Von Furstenberg and Catherine Malandrino along with independently owned boutiques.

Deals and Steals

Everyone loves a bargain—including a temporary New Yorker. Scoring a good deal is a rite of passage, and the city is home to everything from low-cost department stores like Century 21 to hawkers of pseudo-Rolex watches and Kate Spade bags stationed at street corners and Canal Street stalls. Then there are the sample sales.

If a seasonal sale makes New Yorkers' eyes gleam, a sample sale throws them into a frenzy. With so many designer flagships and corporate headquarters in town, merchandise fallout periodically leads to tremendous deals. Although technically the term "sample sale" refers to stock that's a sample design, show model, leftover, or already discounted item, the term is now also used for sales of current-season goods. Location adds a bit of an illicit thrill to the event: sales are held in hotels, warehouses, offices, or loft spaces, where items both incredible and unfortunate jam a motley assortment of racks,

tables, and bins. Generally, there is a makeshift communal dressing room, but mirrors are scarce, so veteran sample-sale shoppers come prepared for wriggling in the aisles; some wear tank tops with tights or leggings for modest quick changes. Two rules of thumb: grab first and inspect later, and call in advance to find out what methods of payment are accepted. One of the ultimate experiences is the Barneys Warehouse Sale, held in February and August in Chelsea. Other luscious sales include the Vera Wang bridal-gown sale (early winter) and Dwell Studio (spring and late fall).

How to find out about these events? The level of publicity and regularity of sales vary. The print and online versions of *New York* magazine are always worth checking for sample sale tip-offs, as are regular bulletins on Racked (⊕ *www.racked.com*). If interested in specific designers, call their shops and inquire—you may get lucky.

18

LOWER MANHATTAN

FINANCIAL DISTRICT

Known primarily as the home of Wall Street, the Financial District isn't the best place for browsing.

BARGAIN SHOPPING

Fodor'sChoice ★ **Century 21.** For many New Yorkers this downtown fixture remains the mother lode of discount shopping. Four floors are crammed with everything from Marc Jacobs shoes and half-price cashmere sweaters to Donna Karan sheets, though you have to sift through racks and fight crowds to find the gems. Best bets for men are shoes and designer briefs; the full floor of designer women's wear can yield some dazzling finds. Don't miss the children's section either, for brands like Ralph Lauren and Ed Hardy. ⊠ *22 Cortlandt St., between Broadway and Church St., Lower Manhattan* ☎ *212/227–9092* ⊕ *www.c21stores.com* Ⓜ *R to Cortlandt St.*

GIFTS AND SOUVENIRS

City Store. The official store of NYC sells anything and everything having to do with the city, from books and pamphlets to fun gifts. Pick up NYPD T-shirts, taxicab medallions, garbage truck toys, and dish towels silkscreened with the skyline. The store shuts at 5 pm weekdays and is closed weekends. ✉ *1 Centre St., at Chambers St., Financial District* ☎ *212/386–0007* ⊕ *http://a856-citystore.nyc.gov/* Ⓜ *4, 5, 6 to Brooklyn Bridge–City Hall.*

TRIBECA

Known for its multimillion-dollar lofts and celebrity residents, TriBeCa is home to some of the most interesting boutiques in the city, most of them seemed geared toward deep pockets, especially the design and clothing stores. Specialty shops such as Korin or J. Crew Men's Shop at the Liquor Store are worth a visit.

CHILDREN'S CLOTHING

FAMILY   **Shoofly.** Stylish children's shoes and accessories imported from all over the world are the name of the game here. Choose from ballet flats, trendy sneakers, and motorcycle boots along with pom-pom hats, brightly patterned socks, eclectic toys, and jewelry. ✉ *42 Hudson St., between Thomas and Duane sts., TriBeCa* ☎ *212/406–3270* ⊕ *www. shooflynyc.com* Ⓜ *1 to Franklin St.*

CLOTHING

Fodor's Choice   **Issey Miyake.** This flagship, designed by Frank Gehry, attracts a non-
★   fashion crowd who come just to gawk at his undulating, 25-foot-high titanium sculpture, *The Tornado.* Miyake's signature style has clothes that are sleek and slim-fitting, and made from polyester or ultrahigh-tech textiles. This flagship carries the entire runway collection, as well as Pleats Please and Issey Miyake Fete. ✉ *119 Hudson St., at N. Moore St., TriBeCa* ☎ *212/226–0100* ⊕ *www.tribecaisseymiyake.com* Ⓜ *1 to Franklin St.*

Nili Lotan. This Israeli-born designer worked for Ralph Lauren and Nautica before launching her own collection for women. Nili Lotan is known for her knitwear, drapey coats, and love of solid colors. Her white-washed retail space also sells rare books. ✉ *188 Duane St., between Greenwich and Hudson sts., TriBeCa* ☎ *212/431–7713* ⊕ *www.nililotan.com* Ⓜ *1, 2, 3 to Chambers St.*

Steven Alan Annex. This TriBeCa flagship sells casual cool sportswear. Steven Alan is the place to come if your preferred uniform is a cashmere beanie, untucked plaid shirt, and skinny jeans. The rustic space stocks clothing for men and women and sells its own line of clothing, as well as beauty products and home accessories. ✉ *103 Franklin St., TriBeCa* ☎ *212/343–0692* ⊕ *www.stevenalan.com* Ⓜ *1 to Franklin St.*

J. Crew Men's Shop at the Liquor Store. It would be easy to walk right past this place and think it's a bar rather than an outpost of J. Crew for men, because it's filled with manly knickknacks like old Jack Kerouac books and vintage photographs. Some of the best finds are the limited-edition suits and cashmere sweaters, as well as non–J. Crew items like Barbour jackets and Ray-Bans. ✉ *235 West Broadway, at White St., TriBeCa* ☎ *212/226–5476* ⊕ *www.jcrew.com* Ⓜ *1 to Franklin St.*

HOME DECOR

Korin. If you're serious about cooking, head to this specialty knife store in TriBeCa. Previously only open to the trade, it is one of the best places to shop for top-quality knives imported from Japan. ✉ *57 Warren St., between West Broadway and Church St., TriBeCa* ☎ *212/587–7021* ⊕ *www.korin.com* Ⓜ *1, 2, 3 to Chambers St.*

SHOES, HANDBAGS, AND LEATHER GOODS

Matt Bernson. Thankfully, the footwear at designer Matt Bernson's new TriBeCa store is both beautiful and blister-proof. Though the native New Yorker's comfy, affordable sandals are staples at Bloomingdale's and Piperlime in SoHo, this shop is his first standalone venture. His shop also stocks accessories such as jewelry and handbags. Don't miss the designer's dog, Abraham, who accompanies him to work every day. ✉ *20 Harrison St., between Greenwich and Staple sts., TriBeCa* ☎ *212/941–7634* ⊕ *www.mattbernson.com* Ⓜ *1 to Franklin St.*

Fodor'sChoice ★ **Shinola.** This World War II–era shoe polish brand, proudly based in Detroit, has been relaunched as a company that builds handcrafted watches, bicycles, leather goods, journals, and pet accessories. Shinola's TriBeCa flagship store also sells American-made products from other brands, such as Filson. ✉ *177 Franklin St., between Greenwich and Hudson sts., TriBeCa* ☎ *917/728–3000* ⊕ *www.shinola.com* Ⓜ *1 to Franklin St.*

SOHO AND NOLITA

SOHO

Head to SoHo for both the cheap and the hyperchic. The narrow sidewalks get very busy, especially on weekends, but this is a fun "see-and-be-seen" neighborhood. There are plenty of familiar high-fashion names like Prada, Chanel, and Louis Vuitton, as well as several less expensive chains, like Banana Republic and Sephora, which have made land-grabs on Broadway. But you can still hit a few clothing and housewares boutiques not found elsewhere in this country. The hottest shopping area runs west from Broadway over to 6th Avenue, between West Houston and Grand streets. Don't overlook a couple of streets east of Broadway, too: Crosby and Lafayette have several intriguing shops.

18

BEAUTY

MiN. If the selection of grooming products at Duane Reade doesn't cut it for you, head to MiN. This wood-paneled shop is decidedly male-friendly, with leather couches and exposed brick walls. Shop for unusual scents from Santa Maria Novella and L'Artisan Parfumeur, shaving products from Old Bond Street, or quirky items like mustache wax. ✉ *117 Crosby St., between Prince and Houston sts., SoHo* ☎ *212/206–6366* ⊕ *minnewyork.com* Ⓜ *N, R to Prince St.*

Fodor'sChoice ★ **Birchbox.** Cult favorite beauty subscription service Birchbox now has a retail space. Visitors to its SoHo store can stock up on best-selling products here, which range from $5–$200 and include everything from lip balm and stylish mugs to curling irons, headphones, and fragrance. There's also a BYOB (Build Your Own Birchbox) section, where users create their own box full of samples. The store also has a separate floor

Street Vendor Shopping

CLOSE UP

If you're looking for original or reproduced artwork, the two areas to visit for street vendors are the stretch of 5th Avenue in front of the Metropolitan Museum of Art (roughly between 81st and 82nd streets) and the SoHo area of West Broadway, between Houston and Broome streets. In both areas are dozens of artists selling original paintings, drawings, and photographs (some lovely, some lurid), as well as photo reproductions of famous New York scenes (the Chrysler Building, South Street Seaport). Prices can start as low as $15, but be sure to haggle.

The east–west streets in SoHo are an excellent place to look for handmade crafts: Spring and Prince streets, especially, are jammed with tables full of beaded jewelry, tooled leather belts, cotton sundresses, and homemade hats and purses. These streets are also great places to find deals on art books; several vendors have titles featuring the work of artists from Diego Rivera to Annie Leibovitz, all for about 20% less than you pay at a chain. It's best to know

which books you want ahead of time, though; street vendors wrap theirs in clear plastic, and can get testy if you unwrap them but don't wind up buying.

Faux-designer handbags, sunglasses, wallets, and watches are some of the most popular street buys in town—but crackdowns on knock-offs have made them harder to find. The hub used to be Canal Street, roughly between Greene and Lafayette streets, but many vendors there have swept their booths clean of fake Vuitton, Prada, Gucci, and Fendi merchandise. You might have better luck finding a "Faux-lex" near Herald Square or Madison Square Garden, and good fake handbags are still sold by isolated vendors around such shopping areas as Rockefeller Center and the lower stretch of 5th Avenue, near Union Square. If looking for bargain luggage, skip Canal Street, as the bags there might not last beyond the flight home, and instead pick up a bargain at Marshalls, TJ Maxx, or Century 21.

---

set aside for makeup, hair, and nail services. ✉ *433 West Broadway, between Spring and Prince sts.* ☎ *646/589–8500* ⊕ *www.birchbox.com* Ⓜ *N, R to Prince St.*

CAMERAS AND ELECTRONICS

Apple Store. Branch location at 103 Prince Street, between Greene and Spring streets. *See Midtown East for full review.*

CHILDREN'S CLOTHING

FAMILY **Giggle.** This high-end baby store is often gridlocked with strollers but stocks nearly everything a stylish parent (and baby) could ever need. The Giggle flagship carries all the gear and accessories to build a chic nursery, including Dwell bedding, plush toys, and bold kids' clothing. Basic gear such as highchairs and strollers are also sold, and the staff makes sure parents know how to fold that complicated stroller before leaving the store. Additional Giggle outlets are located on the Upper West and Upper East sides. ✉ *120 Wooster St., between Spring*

Luxe shops line the streets of SoHo.

and Prince sts., SoHo ☏ *212/334–5817* ⊕ *www.giggle.com* Ⓜ *N, R to Prince St.*

FAMILY **J. Crew.** If want to pick up stylish clothing for yourself as well as your children, head to this location of J.Crew, which stocks women's clothing as well its Crewcuts line. Stocking pint-size versions of the preppy classic clothes the brand is famous for, this shop is replete with cords, cashmere sweaters, and blazers for the junior set as well as moms. ✉ *99 Prince St., between Greene and Mercer sts., SoHo* ☏ *212/966–2739* ⊕ *www.jcrew.com* Ⓜ *C, E to Spring St.*

FAMILY **Les Petits Chapelais.** Designed and made in France, these clothes for kids (from newborn up to age 12) are cute and stylish but also practical. Corduroy outfits have details like embroidered flowers and contrasting cuffs, and soft, fleecy jackets are reversible. There's also a line of sailor-inspired clothes. ✉ *146 Sullivan St., between Houston and Prince sts., SoHo* ☏ *212/625–1023* Ⓜ *C, E to Spring St.*

CLOTHING

& Other Stories. Owned by Swedish megastore H&M, this new space focuses on midrange clothes and bold twists on staples designed in Paris and Stockholm. Come here to browse chunky sweaters, pointy-toed flats, and printed coats. Don't miss the designer collaborations and beauty section. ✉ *575 Broadway, between Houston and Prince sts.* ☏ *646/767–3063* ⊕ *www.stories.com/us* Ⓜ *N, R to Prince St.*

Fodor's Choice ★ **3X1.** In this huge denim shop, which doubles as a factory, customers can watch 3x1 jeans being made. The walls of the pristine white space are lined with an assortment of more than 600 varieties of selvedge denim. Those looking for a bespoke pair start by selecting the perfect denim.

Jeans are hand-cut and sewn by the in-house seamstresses, who work in a glass-enclosed space. Shoppers can also buy off-the-rack jeans, with hems tailored on the spot (starting at $195). ⊠ *15 Mercer St., between Grand and Howard sts., SoHo* 🕾 *212/391–6969* ⊕ *www.3x1.us* Ⓜ *6, J, N, Q, R, Z to Canal St.*

7 for All Mankind. Whether you're hunting for super skinny, high-waisted, or boot-cut jeans in a dark or distressed finish, this temple to denim has it all. The jeans are a firm celebrity favorite (Cameron Diaz is a fan), but be warned: although they are guaranteed to make your derriere look good, they don't come cheap. You also find stylish and sexy dresses here, plus sweaters and jackets for men and women. ⊠ *394 West Broadway, between Broome and Spring sts., SoHo* 🕾 *212/226–8615* ⊕ *www.7forallmankind.com* Ⓜ *C, E to Spring St.*

A Bathing Ape. Known simply as BAPE to devotees, this exclusive label has a cult following in its native Tokyo. At first it may be hard to see what the fuss is about. A small selection of camouflage gear and limited-edition T-shirts is placed throughout the minimalist space; the real scene stealers are the flashy retro-style sneakers in neon colors. ⊠ *91 Greene St., between Prince and Spring sts., SoHo* 🕾 *212/925–0222* ⊕ *www. bape.com* Ⓜ *N, R to Prince St.*

Fodor's Choice ★ **Agent Provocateur.** If Victoria's Secret is too tame for you, try this British lingerie shop, which has a naughty twist. Showpieces include boned corsets, lace sets with contrast-color trim, bottoms tied with satin ribbons, and a few fetish-type leather ensembles. A great selection of stockings is complemented by the garter belts to secure them. ⊠ *133 Mercer St., between Prince and Spring sts., SoHo* 🕾 *212/965–0229* ⊕ *www. agentprovocateur.com* Ⓜ *N, R to Prince St.*

Alexander Wang. *Vogue* darling Alexander Wang's boutique is as unfussy—but cool—as his clothes. In between browsing for perfectly slouchy tank tops, sheath dresses, or edgy ankle boots, shoppers should check out the rotating display of luxe objects tucked inside the store's cage, which has included furry punching bags and marbleized surfboards ⊠ *103 Grand St., between Greene and Mercer sts., SoHo* 🕾 *212/977–9683* ⊕ *www.alexanderwang.com* Ⓜ *6, J, N, Q, R, Z to Canal St.*

Allan & Suzi. The duo behind Allan & Suzi has been selling pristine vintage clothing to celebrities for years—and has also outfitted the cast of *Sex and the City*. Their downtown store sells a mix of new and vintage finds, ranging from the elegant to the wacky. Dig, and you may find a Gaultier gown or a Pauline Trigère dress, along with crazy disco gear. ⊠ *237 Centre St., between Grand and Broome sts., SoHo* 🕾 *212/724–7445* ⊕ *www.allanandsuzi.net* Ⓜ *6, J, N, Q, R, Z to Canal St.*

American Two Shot. This boutique sells a carefully curated mix of contemporary designs for men and women, including clothing from Timo Weiland, Lazy Oaf and Nanushka, as well as rare vintage finds. The displays are fun and witty (you might see a voodoo doll). The space also functions as an art gallery and includes an outpost of Cafe Integral for shoppers in need of a caffeine fix. The shop recently launched its own clothing line, which is made in LA. ⊠ *135 Grand St., between Crosby* *and Lafayette sts., SoHo* ☎ *212/925–3403* ⊕ *www.americantwoshot. com* Ⓜ *6, J, N, Q, R, Z to Canal St.*

Anna Sui. The violet-and-black salon, with its Victorian rock-chick vibe, is the ideal setting for Sui's bohemian and rocker-influenced designs and colorful beauty products. ⊠ *113 Greene St., between Prince and Spring sts., SoHo* ☎ *212/941–8406* ⊕ *www.annasui.com* Ⓜ *N, R to Prince St.*

A.P.C. This hip French boutique sells deceptively simple clothes in an equally understated setting. Choose from sharply cut gabardine and corduroy suits to dark denim jeans and jackets. For women, best bets include striped sweaters and skinny jeans. ⊠ *131 Mercer St., between Prince and Spring sts., SoHo* ☎ *212/966–9685* ⊕ *www.apc.fr* Ⓜ *6 to Spring St.; N, R to Prince St.; B, D, F, M to Broadway–Lafayette St.*

Balenciaga. This glossy new flagship is sheathed in acres of green marble and limestone. The two-story space has a minimalist design, all the better to show off creative director Alexander Wang's structured designs. Don't miss the luxurious handbags and leather shoes. ⊠ *148 Mercer St., between Houston and Prince St., SoHo* ☎ *212/206–0872* ⊕ *www. balenciaga.com* Ⓜ *C, E to 23rd St.*

Bloomingdale's. Branch location at 504 Broadway, between Broome and Spring streets. *See Midtown East for full listing.*

Christopher Fischer. Featherweight cashmere sweaters, wraps, and throws in every hue, from Easter-egg pastels to rich jewel tones, have made Fischer the darling of the preppy set. His shop also carries leather accessories, housewares, and baby clothes. ⊠ *80 Wooster St., between Spring and Broome sts., SoHo* ☎ *212/965–9009* ⊕ *www.christopherfischer. com* Ⓜ *N, R to Prince St.*

Fodor'sChoice
★

Comptoir des Cotonniers. The "cotton counter" angles for multigenerational shopping, lining up stylish, comfortable basics for babies, twentysomethings, ladies of a certain age, and everyone in between. There's a subtle Parisian vibe to the understated tunics, dresses, and separates; colors tend to be muted. The brand's first U.S. branch has a nature-friendly minimalist look, with pale-wood floors and lots of natural light. ⊠ *155 Spring St., at West Broadway, SoHo* ☎ *212/274–0830* ⊕ *www. comptoirdescotonniers.com* Ⓜ *C, E to Spring St.*

Costume National. Everything about this boutique is sexy and minimalist, with a rock'n' roll edge. The clothes—and lighting—are dark. Shoppers find sharply tailored wool pants for men and silky tops for women in muted shades of black, gray, and charcoal, along with motorcycle boots and leather gloves. ⊠ *150 Greene St., between Houston and Prince sts., SoHo* ☎ *212/431–1530* ⊕ *www.costumenational.com* Ⓜ *N, R to Prince St.*

Emporio Armani. At this middle child of the Armani trio, the clothes are elegant without ever being fussy and frequently stocked in cream, muted blues, and ever-cool shades of taupe. ⊠ *410 West Broadway, at Spring St., SoHo* ☎ *646/613–8099* ⊕ *www.armani.com/us/emporioarmani* Ⓜ *C, E to Spring St.*

Etro. This Italian fashion house is known for its trademark paisleys and bold patterns, which cover everything from suits and dresses to

18

lustrous pillows. Etro's downtown location combines the best of Italy with a Soho loft, with high tin ceilings, brightly colored rugs, and industrial lighting. ⊠ *89 Greene St., between Spring and Prince sts., SoHo* ☎ *646/329–6929* ⊕ *www.etro.com* Ⓜ *N, R to Prince St.*

French Connection. This British-owned company stocks an impressive collection of on-trend clothing for men and women at reasonable prices. Some of the best bets are the sharply tailored trench coats and jeans, as well as dresses. For men, try the cashmere sweaters and skinny trousers. ⊠ *435 West Broadway* ☎ *212/219–1197* ⊕ *www.frenchconnection.com* Ⓜ *C, E to Spring St.*

Fodor's Choice ★ **Isabel Marant.** If you're after that casually glamorous Parisian vibe, look no further than Isabel Marant. Long a favorite of globe-trotting fashionistas, this location is the French designer's first U.S. retail store. The tailored jackets, shorts, and flirty dresses are eclectic and sophisticated, with textured, deeply hued fabrics. ⊠ *469 Broome St., at Greene St., SoHo* ☎ *212/219–2284* ⊕ *www.isabelmarant.tm.fr* Ⓜ *N, R to Prince St.*

Kiki de Montparnasse. Named for Man Ray's mistress and muse from the 1940s, this upscale lingerie store serves up decadent styles in a seductive but artistic setting. Shoppers find exquisitely made corsets and bra and underwear sets, but a large portion of the store is used as a rotating art gallery for erotic art. ⊠ *79 Greene St., at Spring St., SoHo* ☎ *212/965–8150* ⊕ *www.kikidm.com* Ⓜ *N, R to Prince St.*

Kirna Zabête. Think of this space as a mini department store for some of the biggest names in fashion, including Alexander Wang, Azzedine Alaïa, Roland Mouret and Valentino Garavani. The multilevel store has a fun, Pop Art–inspired design, complete with neon signs suggesting that shoppers "leave looking lovely" and "life is short, buy the shoes." ⊠ *477 Broome St., between Greene and Wooster sts., SoHo* ☎ *212/941–9656* ⊕ *www.kirnazabete.com* Ⓜ *N, R to Prince St.*

Marc Jacobs. One of Marc Jacobs' various NYC boutiques, this location, housed in a former garage, retails crisply tailored designs for men and women in luxurious fabrics: silk, cashmere, wool bouclé, and tweeds ranging from the demure to the flamboyant. The details, though—oversize buttons, circular patch pockets, and military-style grommet belts—add a sartorial wink. The shoe selection is not to be missed. ⊠ *163 Mercer St., between Houston and Prince sts., SoHo* ☎ *212/343–1490* ⊕ *www.marcjacobs.com* Ⓜ *N, R to Prince St.*

Marni. If you're a fan of the boho-chic look, stock up on Consuelo Castiglioni's brightly colored, happy clothes here. The collection features dresses and jackets in quirky prints and many of the silhouettes are vintage-inspired. Accessories are also eye-popping. ⊠ *161 Mercer St., between W. Houston and Prince sts., SoHo* ☎ *212/343–3912* ⊕ *www.marni.com* Ⓜ *N, R to Prince St.*

Miu Miu. Prada front woman Miuccia Prada established a secondary line (bearing her childhood nickname, Miu Miu) to showcase her more experimental ideas. Look for Prada-esque styles in more daring colors and cuts, such as high-waist skirts with scalloped edges, Peter Pan–collar dresses in bold patterns, and patent-leather pumps. ⊠ *100 Prince*

St., between Mercer and Greene sts., SoHo ☎ *212/334–5156* ⊕ *www. miumiu.com* Ⓜ *N, R to Prince St.*

Moncler. Many New York women swear by Moncler coats to keep them warm but still stylish throughout the winter. This store is the Italian brand's first foray into New York. The knee-length puffer is a firm favorite, but there are stylish ski jackets and accessories, along with pieces created in collaboration with designers like Giambattista Valli. ✉ *90 Prince St., between Mercer St. and Broadway, SoHo* ☎ *646/350– 3620* ⊕ *www.moncler.com* Ⓜ *N, R to Prince St.*

Odin. Gentlemen, if you're tired of the corporate look, head to Odin to spruce up your weekend wardrobe. This boutique, which caters only to men, carries separates from cool brands including Rag & Bone, Thom Browne, and Band Of Outsiders. The cheerful and helpful staff guarantees you will leave looking hip—but not as if you're trying too hard. ✉ *199 Lafayette St., between Broome and Kenmare sts., SoHo* ☎ *212/966–0026* ⊕ *www.odinnewyork.com* Ⓜ *6 to Spring St.*

Fodor's Choice ★ **Opening Ceremony.** Just like Colette in Paris, Opening Ceremony bills itself as a concept store, which means you never know what you'll find. The owners are constantly globetrotting to soak up the work of foreign designers and bring back the best clothing, products, and vintage items to showcase in their store. Hong Kong, Japan, Brazil, and the United Kingdom have all been represented. There's also a gallery space here. ✉ *35 Howard St., between Broadway and Lafayette St., SoHo* ☎ *212/219–2688* ⊕ *www.openingceremony.us* Ⓜ *6, J, N, Q, R, Z to Canal St.*

Paul Smith. Fans love Paul Smith for his classic-with-a-twist clothes, and this 5,000-square-foot flagship is a temple to his design ethos and inspirations. Victorian mahogany cases complement the dandyish British styles they hold. Embroidered vests; brightly striped socks, scarves, and shirts; and tongue-in-cheek cuff links are all signature Paul Smith looks, along with classic suits and outerwear for men and women. Shoppers also find furniture and a selection of photography books and ephemera. ✉ *142 Greene St., between Houston and Prince sts., SoHo* ☎ *646/613–3060* ⊕ *www.paulsmith.co.uk* Ⓜ *N, R to Prince St.*

Fodor's Choice ★ **Piperlime.** This popular e-tailer now has its first brick-and-mortar store. The large loftlike space carries clothing from top designers as well as its own Piperlime Collection. To round out your outfit, browse handbags from Zac Posen and Milly, or shoes from B Brian Atwood and Stuart Weitzman. Visitors can also shop online from in-store kiosks and iPads. ✉ *121 Wooster St., between Prince and Spring sts., SoHo* ☎ *212/343–4284* ⊕ *www.piperlime.com* Ⓜ *N, R to Prince St.*

Prada. This ultramodern space, designed by Rem Koolhaas, incorporates so many technological innovations that it was written up in *Popular Science*. Dressing room glass walls turn opaque at the touch of a button, and instead of mirrors, shoppers can check themselves out in large video panels. ✉ *575 Broadway, at Prince St., SoHo* ☎ *212/334– 8888* ⊕ *www.prada.com* Ⓜ *N, R to Prince St.*

R by 45rpm. This cult favorite Japanese denim brand may be pricey, but fans love the label for its attention to detail, like hand-dyed denim

18

woven on antique looms. The T-shirts are particularly stylish. ✉ *169 Mercer St., between Houston and Prince sts., SoHo* ☎ *917/237–0045* ⊕ *www.rby45rpm.com* Ⓜ *N, R to Prince St.*

Reiss. Think of Reiss as the Banana Republic of Britain—a go-to place for casual-but-tailored clothes at a relatively gentle price. Kate Middleton is a loyal customer. Standouts for women include cowl-neck sweater dresses and A-line skirts. Men's wool combat trousers are complemented by shrunken blazers, military-inspired peacoats, and trim leather jackets. ✉ *387 West Broadway, between Spring and Broome sts., SoHo* ☎ *212/925–5707* ⊕ *www.reissonline.com* Ⓜ *N, R to Prince St.*

Saint Laurent Paris. This fabled French house is now under the direction of Hedi Slimane, who is revitalizing the brand and opened a new downtown flagship, with high ceilings and a monochromatic palette. The new Saint Laurent nods to the past, with a refined, polished elegance. Don't miss the sleek shoes and structured handbags. ✉ *80 Greene St., between Spring and Broome sts., SoHo* ☎ *212/431–3240* ⊕ *www.ysl. com* Ⓜ *N, R to Prince St.; 6 to Spring St.*

Sean. This French-pedigreed shop carries classic, understated menswear imported from Europe at reasonable prices. Linen and corduroy painter's coats are best sellers, along with V-neck sweaters and a respectable collection of slim-cut suits. ✉ *181 Prince St., between Sullivan and MacDougal Sts., SoHo* ☎ *212/598–5980* ⊕ *www.seanstore.com* Ⓜ *N, R to Prince St.*

Seize sur Vingt. Head to this boutique if you're ready to splurge on an exquisitely tailored shirt or suit. Men and women can pick out an off-the-rack item and have it tailored in-house for a perfect fit, or create a fully bespoke shirt from a mind-boggling array of fabrics (linen, broadcloth oxford, flannel). To complete the look, sweaters, shoes, and accessories are also available. ✉ *78 Greene St., between Spring and Broome sts., SoHo* ☎ *212/625–1620* ⊕ *www.16sur20.com* Ⓜ *N, R to Prince St.*

Stella McCartney. McCartney's flagship store has a luxe look, thanks to parquet flooring and touches of gold found in the Art Deco sculptures and clothing racks. Her main collection, done mostly in gauzy, muted colors, is on the top floor, while children's, Adidas by Stella McCartney, and lingerie are on the lower level. In keeping with McCartney's vegetarianism, fur and leather are verboten. ✉ *112 Greene St., between Spring and Prince sts., SoHo* ☎ *212/255–1556* ⊕ *www.stellamccartney. com* Ⓜ *N, R to Prince St.*

Tess Giberson. This Rhode Island School of Design graduate is making waves for her eponymous women's collection. The boutique has an airy, minimalist feel, with whitewash walls and rotating art exhibits that perfectly match the clothing's pared-down aesthetic. Your best bets are floaty silk dresses and striking knitwear. ✉ *97 Crosby St., between Prince and Spring sts., SoHo* ☎ *212/226–1932* ⊕ *www.tessgiberson. com* Ⓜ *N, R to Prince St.*

Topshop. British cult favorite Topshop, which has only a handful of U.S. stores, is a master at pumping out of-the-minute-fashion at reasonable prices. It can be a madhouse, and items sell quickly, but it's worth fighting the crowds. Slinky dresses are around $130, and jeans and jumpsuits are about $90. Coats and shoes are also standouts. Male stylistas can browse through the ground-level Topman. ⊠ *478 Broadway, between Broome and Grand sts., SoHo* ☎ *212/966–9555* ⊕ *www.topshop.com* Ⓜ *6 to Spring St.; N, R to Prince St.*

Trademark. Retail is in the blood of Trademark founders Pookie and Louisa Burch, the daughters of C. Wonder founder Chris Burch. Both their boutique and clothing line reflect a restrained American design aesthetic. Their collection ranges from boxy jackets to totes and turtleneck sweaters. ⊠ *95 Grand St., between Greene and Mercer sts.* ☎ *212/206–8206* ⊕ *www.trade-mark.com* Ⓜ *6, J, N, Q, R, Z to Canal St.*

Woolrich. In a nod to this brand's almost 200-year history, Woolrich's first retail space is decorated with vintage shearing tools and catalogs from the original Pennsylvania mill. The space is cozy, thanks to throw rugs and industrial-style lighting, and the full Woolrich product line is sold here, from sweaters to blankets and thick winter coats. ⊠ *125 Wooster St., between Prince and Spring sts.* ☎ *646/371–9968* ⊕ *www. woolrich.com* Ⓜ *N, R to Prince St.*

Vera Wang. Not content designing just wedding dresses, Wang is also a star at evening wear and casual-but-chic daywear. Her entire ready-to-wear collection is showcased here in this gleaming, all-white store. Choose from clothes ranging from sexy one-shouldered satin gowns to cashmere sweaters and wool pencil skirts. Don't miss the shoe collection. ⊠ *158 Mercer St., between Houston and Prince sts., SoHo* ☎ *212/382–2184* ⊕ *www.verawang.com* Ⓜ *N, R to Prince St.*

Vivienne Tam. Known for her East-meets-West designs, Tam makes dresses, blouses, and trousers with clean lines and bold prints in luxurious fabrics like silk. ⊠ *40 Mercer St., at Grand St., SoHo* ☎ *212/966–2398* ⊕ *www.viviennetam.com* Ⓜ *N, R to Prince St.*

Fodor's Choice ★ **Warm.** If you want to feel the love, come to this little boutique owned by lifelong surfers Winnie Beattie and her husband Rob Magnotta. Everything has a sunny, beachy vibe, from leather sandals, bikinis, and bleached sweaters to hand-blown glass vases. There's also a collection of children's books, housewares, and menswear. ⊠ *181 Mott St., between Kenmare and Broome sts., SoHo* ☎ *212/925–1200* ⊕ *www.warmny. com* Ⓜ *6 to Spring St.*

Fodor's Choice ★ **What Goes Around Comes Around.** Professional stylists and celebrities flock here to dig up pristine vintage items like Levi's and Azzedine Alaïa dresses, as well as Hermès scarves and Chanel jewelry. The vintage rock tees (think Black Sabbath, Mötley Crüe) are great finds but can set you back an eye-watering $300–$600. ⊠ *351 West Broadway, between Broome and Grand sts., SoHo* ☎ *212/343–1225* ⊕ *www. whatgoesaroundnyc.com* Ⓜ *6, J, N, Q, R, Z to Canal St.*

CRAFTS

Fodor's Choice ★ **Purl.** Anyone with a crafty bent will fall in love with this colorful paradise of top-quality knitting and sewing supplies, gorgeous craft books, and much, much more. Prices aren't cheap but the sales people are extra friendly. It's worth a browse even if you're not planning to buy anything. ⊠ *459 Broome St., between Mercer and Green sts., SoHo* ☎ *212/420—8796* ⊕ *www.purlsoho.com* Ⓜ *6 to Spring St.*

18

FOOD AND TREATS

Fodor's Choice **Harney & Sons.** Fancy a cuppa? Harney & Sons produce more than 250
★ varieties of loose tea, which can be sampled at their store and tea salon
in SoHo. The design is sleek and dramatic, with a 24-foot-long tasting
bar and floor-to-ceiling shelves stocked with tea. Shoppers find classic
brews like English Breakfast and Oolong, along with interesting herb-
als (ginger and liquorice, or mint verbena). Enjoy a cup with a scone or
other light fare, available at the tea salon. ⊠ *433 Broome St., between
Broadway and Crosby St., SoHo* ☏ *212/933–4853* ⊕ *www.harney.com*
Ⓜ *6 to Spring St.*

Fodor's Choice **Jacques Torres Chocolates.** Visit the café and shop here and be literally
★ surrounded by chocolate. The glass-walled downtown space also houses
Torres's chocolate factory, so you can watch the goodies being made
while sipping a richly spiced cocoa or nibbling on a Java Junkie bar.
Signature taste: the "wicked" chocolate, laced with cinnamon and chili
pepper. ⊠ *350 Hudson St., at King St., SoHo* ☏ *212/414–2462* ⊕ *www.
mrchocolate.com* Ⓜ *1 to Houston St.*

Kee's Chocolates. Owner Kee Ling Tong whips up delicious truffles and
macaroons with unusual, Asian-inspired flavors. Try the ginger peach
and rosewater lychee macaroons, or truffles flavored with lemongrass
mint and tamarind. ⊠ *80 Thompson St., between Spring and Broome
sts., SoHo* ☏ *212/334–3284* ⊕ *www.keeschocolates.com* Ⓜ *C, E to
Spring St.*

MarieBelle. The handmade chocolates here are nothing less than works of
art. Square truffles and bonbons—in flavors like Earl Grey, cappuccino,
passion fruit, and saffron—are painted with edible dyes (cocoa butter
dyed with natural coloring) so each resembles a miniature painting.
Relax in the Cacao Bar and Tea Salon while sipping an Aztec hot chocolate, made from rich cacao, rather than cocoa powder. ⊠ *484 Broome
St., between West Broadway and Wooster St., SoHo* ☏ *212/925–6999*
⊕ *www.mariebelle.com* Ⓜ *N, R to Prince St.; 6, C, E to Spring St.*

Fodor's Choice **Vosges Haut Chocolat.** This chandeliered salon lined with apothecary
★ shelves takes a global approach to chocolate. Many of the creations
are travel-inspired: the Budapest bonbons combine dark chocolate and
Hungarian paprika, and the Black Pearls contain wasabi. Don't miss the
best-selling chocolate bacon bars. ⊠ *132 Spring St., SoHo* ☏ *212/625–
2929* ⊕ *www.vosgeschocolate.com* Ⓜ *N, R to Prince St.*

HOME DECOR

de Vera. Owner Federico de Vera crisscrosses the globe searching for
unique decorative products, so shoppers never know what they might
find here. Venetian glass vases, Thai Buddhas, and antique rose-cut
diamond rings are typical finds. ⊠ *1 Crosby St., at Howard St., SoHo*
☏ *212/625–0838* ⊕ *www.deveraobjects.com* Ⓜ *6, J, N, Q, R, Z to
Canal St.*

Fodor's Choice **Jonathan Adler.** Everything at this flagship store, housed in a former
★ plumbing factory, is fun and happy. Adler boldly funks up midcen-
tury modern design, with striped, striated, or curvy handmade pottery
(ranging from a $30 vase to a chunky $400 lamp) and hand-loomed
wool pillow covers, rugs, and throws. Pull up to the Gift Bar if you

need inspiration for a present. ⊠ *53 Greene St., between Broome and Grand sts., SoHo* ☎ *212/941–8950* ⊕ *www.jonathanadler.com* Ⓜ *6, J, N, Q, R, Z to Canal St.*

Fodor's Choice ★ **Matter.** This beautifully curated store appeals to fans of sleek, modern furniture—if money is no object. How about the iconic Tank armchair by Alvar Aalto for a cool $5,000? Or a smoked-glass coffee table by Established & Sons for $1,400? Even if your budget is limited, Matter is worth a visit for inspiration. ⊠ *405 Broome St., between Centre and Lafayette sts., SoHo* ☎ *212/343–2600* ⊕ *www.mattermatters.com* Ⓜ *6 to Spring St.; J, Z to Bowery.*

Room & Board. Fans of streamlined, midcentury modern furniture ascend to heaven here. This location is stocked with sleek sofas, beds, and children's furniture as well as accessories like rugs and lamps—-90% of it made in America. Design aficionados can choose from iconic pieces like seating cubes from Frank Gehry and Eames molded plywood chairs, or items from up-and-coming designers. ⊠ *105 Wooster St., between Spring and Prince sts., SoHo* ☎ *212/334–4343* ⊕ *www.roomandboard. com* Ⓜ *N, R to Prince St.*

JEWELRY AND ACCESSORIES

Fodor's Choice ★ **Alexis Bittar.** This Brooklyn-born designer began selling his first jewelry line, made from Depression-era glass, on a corner in SoHo. Now, Bittar counts A-list celebs and fashion editors among his fans. He makes clean-line, big-statement jewelry from vermeil, colored Lucite, pearls, and vintage glass. The store mirrors this aesthetic with a mix of old and new, like antique-white Victorian-era lion's-claw tables and Plexiglas walls. ⊠ *465 Broome St., between Mercer and Greene sts., SoHo* ☎ *212/625–8340* ⊕ *www.alexisbittar.com* Ⓜ *N, R to Prince St.*

Fodor's Choice ★ **Aurélie Bidermann.** This French jeweler's New York boutique is all white with pops of color, and includes a mural commissioned from a street artist. Bidermann's signature look is bold and inspired by her travels and nature. Look out for lace filigree gold cuffs, large turquoise necklaces, and drop earrings in the shape of gingko leaves. ⊠ *265 Lafayette St., between Prince and Springs sts.* ☎ *212/335–0604* ⊕ *www. aureliebidermann.com* Ⓜ *N, R Prince St.*

Fodor's Choice ★ **Broken English.** This L.A. favorite has now made its way to New York. Owner Laura Freedman sells a well-curated selection of jewelry from designers including Anita Ko and Carla Amorim. Expect delicate and whimsical pieces, from diamond-encrusted ear cuffs to geometric rings. ⊠ *56 Crosby St., between Spring and Broome sts.* ☎ *212/219–1264* ⊕ *www.brokenenglishjewelry.com* Ⓜ *6 to Spring St.*

Ivanka Trump. The Donald's daughter would like to see you dripping in her diamonds. Her SoHo location has an Art Deco look, with black-and-white furniture and plenty of glittering chandeliers. But the real bling is the jewelry—drop earrings, tassel lariats, and bold cocktail rings. Don't miss the elegant Bridal Bar for wedding jewelry. ⊠ *109 Mercer St., between Prince and Spring sts., SoHo* ☎ *212/756–9912* ⊕ *www.ivankatrumpcollection.com* Ⓜ *N, R to Prince St.*

Robert Lee Morris. If you buy into the mantra that bigger is better, make a stop here. Morris designs big, chunky jewelry that is anything but

18

understated. Gold and silver cuffs have serious weight, and necklaces and earrings dangle with hammered disks for a "wind chime" effect. Some pieces incorporate diamonds; others have semiprecious stones like turquoise or citrine. ⊠ *400 West Broadway, between Broome and Spring sts., SoHo* ☎ *212/431–9405* ⊕ *www.robertleemorris.com* Ⓜ *C, E to Spring St.*

Stuart Moore. Everything about this boutique is minimalist, from the architecture to the jewelry. Most of the designs (from Henrich & Denzel to Beatrice Mueller) have a streamlined, almost industrial look: diamonds are set in brushed platinum, and gold bangles are impossibly delicate. ⊠ *411 West Broadway, at Spring St., SoHo* ☎ *212/941–1023* ⊕ *www.stuartmoore.com* Ⓜ *C, E to Spring St.; N, R to Prince St.*

Versani. Shoppers find innovative combinations of silver, gold, and platinum teamed with wood, leather, semiprecious stones, and diamonds at this bold jewelry store. There is also a wide selection of wedding bands, cufflinks, earrings, and pendants. ⊠ *152 Mercer St., between Houston and Prince sts., SoHo* ☎ *212/941–7770* ⊕ *www.versani.com* Ⓜ *N, R to Prince St.*

SHOES, HANDBAGS, AND LEATHER GOODS

Camper. Urbanites love this Spanish footwear company for its funky but comfortable shoes. Their flagship store has an unusual pagoda-style roof made from tubes. Inside the store, there's a vertical garden. All the slip-ons and lace-ups here have generously rounded toes and a springy feel. ⊠ *110 Prince St., between Wooster and Greene sts., SoHo* ☎ *212/343–4220* ⊕ *www.camper.com* Ⓜ *N, R to Prince St.*

Fodor's Choice
★
The Frye Company. This 6,000-square-foot mecca to boots has an old western feel, thanks to the exposed brick walls and reclaimed barn doors. Boots can be tattooed—or hot stamped—with your initials while you wait in the lounge. In addition to Frye's famed boots, shoppers can also pick from flats, oxfords, clogs, and mules. ⊠ *113 Spring St., between Mercer and Greene sts., SoHo* ☎ *212/226–3793* ⊕ *www. thefryecompany.com* Ⓜ *N, R to Prince St.*

Longchamp. Their Le Pliage foldable nylon bags may have become a preppy staple but don't think this label is stuffy—or all about nylon. There's a wide selection of leather handbags as well as wallets, belts, and shoes. Kate Moss also designs a line for Longchamp. ⊠ *132 Spring St., at Elizabeth St., SoHo* ☎ *212/343–7444* ⊕ *www.longchamp.com* Ⓜ *N, R to Prince St.*

NOLITA

NoLIta("North of Little Italy") is a shopping mecca, thanks to the abundance of boutiques that range from quirky to elegant. Like SoHo, NoLIta has changed from an understated, locals-only area to a crowded weekend magnet, as much about people-watching as shopping. Still, unlike those of its SoHo neighbor, these stores remain largely independent. Running along the parallel north–south spines of Elizabeth, Mott, and Mulberry streets, between Houston and Kenmare streets, NoLIta's boutiques tend to be small and, as real estate costs dictate, somewhat pricey.

BEAUTY

Lafco New York. A heavy, iron-barred door leads to a hushed, scented inner sanctum of beauty products. This location is the official retailer of the 600-year-old Santa Maria Novella products from Italy, which include intriguingly archaic colognes, creams, and soaps such as Dental Elixir and rose rice powder. Everything is packaged in bottles and jars with antique-style apothecary labels. There's also a wide selection of fragrances. ⊠ *285 Lafayette St., between Houston and Prince sts., NoLIta* ☎ *212/925–0001* ⊕ *www.lafcony.com* Ⓜ *N, R to Prince St.*

Fodor's Choice ★ **Le Labo.** If you're bored with the perfume stock at department stores, come to this tiny boutique with a rustic industrial vibe and resident mixologist who helps create your ideal perfume. After choosing your favorite scents, the perfume is mixed and a personalized label created for your bottle. ⊠ *233 Elizabeth St., between Prince and Houston sts., NoLIta* ☎ *212/219–2230* ⊕ *www.lelabofragrances.com* Ⓜ *B, D, F, M to Broadway–Lafayette St.*

BOOKS AND STATIONERY

Fodor's Choice ★ **McNally Jackson.** This cozy, independent bookstore is a bibliophile's dream. The bright two-story space has hardwood floors, a café, and plenty of chairs for lounging and curling up with a book. More than 50,000 books are stocked and the literary section is organized geographically. Budding authors can self-print their tomes on a device called the Espresso Book Machine. ⊠ *52 Prince St., between Lafayette and Mulberry sts., NoLIta* ☎ *212/274–1160* ⊕ *www.mcnallyjackson. com* Ⓜ *N, R to Prince St.; 6 to Spring St.*

CLOTHING

Creatures of Comfort. Owner Jade Lai has brought her popular L.A. outpost to New York. The open, airy boutique racks cool clothes from emerging designers alongside products from around the world. Most of the colors are muted, and brands carried include Acne, Band of Outsiders and the house label, Creatures of Comfort. There's a small selection of shoes, as well as under the radar beauty products, such as Rodin hand cream. ⊠ *205 Mulberry St., between Spring and Kenmare sts., NoLIta* ☎ *212/925–1005* ⊕ *www.creaturesofcomfort.us* Ⓜ *6 to Spring St.*

Fodor's Choice ★ **Duncan Quinn.** Described as "Savile Row meets Rock 'n' Roll" by GQ, this designer provides full bespoke and ready-to-wear services for everything from chalk-stripe suits to cuff links and croquet shirts, all in a shop not much bigger than its silk pocket squares. Off-the-rack shirts are handmade in Italy, but if you want to splurge, get fitted for a shirt with mother-of-pearl buttons. ⊠ *70–80 Kenmare St., between Mott and Mulberry sts., NoLIta* ☎ *212/226–7030* ⊕ *www.duncanquinn.com* Ⓜ *6 to Spring St.*

INA. The clothing at this couture consignment store harks back only one or two seasons, and in some cases, the items have never been worn. Browse through the racks to spot gems from Lanvin, Chanel, and Alexander McQueen. There are multiple locations around the city; this outpost also carries menswear. ⊠ *15 Bleecker St., at Elizabeth St., NoLIta* ☎ *212/228–8511* ⊕ *www.inanyc.com* Ⓜ *6 to Bleecker St.*

18

Jay Kos. There aren't too many boutiques where the owner sometimes whips up a snack for customers in the boutique's custom kitchen, but this designer—famous for dressing Diddy and Johnny Depp—wanted his boutique to have a homey feel. The clothes veer toward the fabulous: suede shoes, linen suits, and cashmere sweaters, which are displayed in armoires. ✉ *293 Mott St., at Houston St., NoLIta* ☏ *212/319–2770* ⊕ *www.jaykos.tumblr.com* Ⓜ *B, D, F, M to Broadway–Lafayette St.*

Fodor'sChoice
★
Malia Mills. Fit fanatics have met their match here—especially those gals who are different sizes on top and bottom (bikini tops go up to size E). Flattering bikini tops and bottoms are sold separately: halters, bandeaus, and triangle tops, plus boy-cut, side-tie, and low-ride bottoms. There's a collection of one-pieces as well. ✉ *199 Mulberry St., between Spring and Kenmare sts., NoLIta* ☏ *212/625–2311* ⊕ *www.maliamills. com* Ⓜ *6 to Spring St.*

Margaret O'Leary. Born in Ireland but settled in California, O'Leary is known for her knitwear. Her NoLIta boutique stocks everything from cashmere to cable knit in sweaters, tunics, and capes. Come here when the temperature starts to drop and you want to feel cozy. ✉ *279 Mott St., between Prince and Houston sts., NoLIta* ☏ *646/274–9498* ⊕ *www. margaretoleary.com* Ⓜ *N, R to Prince St.*

Nanette Lepore. Feminine and flirty are the best way to describe the line at this cheerful shop; skirts are pleated, shift dresses have lace appliqués, and fur shrugs have tiny sleeves. ✉ *423 Broome St., between Lafayette and Crosby sts., NoLIta* ☏ *212/219–8265* ⊕ *www.nanettelepore.com* Ⓜ *6 to Spring St.*

Oak. Most of the clothing here comes in black or leather, and the store carries high-end designers in addition to its own line. Come here for skinny jeans, capes, and draped jersey dresses. ✉ *28 Bond St., between Lafayette St. and Bowery, NoLIta* ☏ *212/677–1293* ⊕ *www.oaknyc. com* Ⓜ *6 to Bleecker St.*

Resurrection. If you're serious about vintage—and have deep pockets—Resurrection stocks a treasure trove of pristine pieces from Chanel, Gucci, Halston, Alaia, and YSL among others. Kate Moss is a fan, and designers like Marc Jacobs and Anna Sui have sought inspiration among the racks. ✉ *217 Mott St., between Prince and Spring sts., NoLIta* ☏ *212/625–1374* ⊕ *www.resurrectionvintage.com* Ⓜ *6 to Spring St.*

JEWELRY AND ACCESSORIES

Dinosaur Designs. This Antipodean-owned brand designs jewelry and housewares inspired by nature and organic shapes. Resin is used to craft jewelry and vases in bold colors like hot pink and orange. Don't miss the striking tableware. ✉ *211 Elizabeth St., between Houston and Prince sts., NoLIta* ☏ *212/680–3523* ⊕ *www.dinosaurdesigns.com.au* Ⓜ *N, R to Prince St.*

Erica Weiner. This eponymous designer specializes in vintage-inspired jewelry and antiques: delicate Art Deco earrings, vintage lockets, and necklaces fashioned from antique charms. The Erica Weiner collection includes pieces under $200. ✉ *173 Elizabeth St., between Kenmare and Spring sts., NoLIta* ☏ *212/334–6383* ⊕ *www.ericaweiner.com* Ⓜ *6 to Spring St.; J, Z to Bowery.*

Me&Ro. Minimalist, Eastern styling has gained these designers a cult following. The Indian-inspired, hand-finished gold bangles, earrings, and necklaces are covered in delicate jewels. Although the fine jewelry is expensive, small sterling silver pendants start at around $170. ⊠ *241 Elizabeth St., between Houston and Prince sts., NoLIta* ☎ *917/237–9215* ⊕ *www.meandrojewelry.com* Ⓜ *N, R to Prince St.*

SHOES, HANDBAGS, AND LEATHER GOODS

Clare V. L.A.-based designer Clare Vivier's first New York store displays her signature simple-but-elegant leather fold-over clutches in every size and color, as well as understated totes and duffels. There is a line of men's accessories, plus iPad cases, sunglasses, and other sundries. ⊠ *239 Elizabeth St., between Houston and Prince sts., NoLIta* ☎ *646/484–5757* ⊕ *www.clairevivier.com* Ⓜ *N, R to Prince St.*

High Way. The bags here marry form and function. Totes and messenger bags come in durable leather and nylon, and some handbags have a wealth of inner pockets. ⊠ *238 Mott St., between Prince and Spring sts., NoLIta* ☎ *212/966–4388* ⊕ *www.highwaybuzz.com* Ⓜ *6 to Bleecker St.*

John Fluevog Shoes. The inventor of the "Angel" sole (protects against water, acid, and "Satan"), Fluevog designs chunky, funky shoes and boots for men and women that are popular with rock stars and those that want to look like one. ⊠ *250 Mulberry St., at Prince St., NoLIta* ☎ *212/431–4484* ⊕ *www.fluevog.com* Ⓜ *N, R to Prince St.*

Kathryn Amberleigh. This designer, a graduate of the Fashion Institute of Technology, has perfected the sexy-but-edgy look in her handcrafted shoes. There are simple flats and wedges along with peep-toe ankle boots and sky-high heels. Most designs hover around the $250 mark. ⊠ *219 Mott St., between Prince and Spring sts., NoLIta* ☎ *212/842–2134* ⊕ *www.kathrynamberleigh.com* Ⓜ *6 to Spring St.*

Sigerson Morrison. The details—just-right T-straps, small buckles, a perfectly pointy toe—make these women's shoes irresistible. Prices start around $300, so the sales are big events. ⊠ *28 Prince St., between Mott and Elizabeth sts., NoLIta* ☎ *212/219–3893* ⊕ *www.sigersonmorrison.com* Ⓜ *6 to Spring St.; N, R to Prince St.*

Manhattan Portage/Token. Although messenger bags are now ubiquitous, pay homage to the store that started it all. Super durable, they come in waxed canvas as well as nylon, and the line has expanded to include totes, duffels, and travel bags, all in unadorned, simple styles. ⊠ *258 Elizabeth St., between Houston and Prince sts., NoLIta* ☎ *212/226–9655* ⊕ *www.manhattanportage.com* Ⓜ *N, R to Prince St.*

EAST VILLAGE AND LOWER EAST SIDE

EAST VILLAGE

The East Village is a fabulous hunting ground for independent boutiques.

ANTIQUES AND COLLECTIBLES

Lost City Arts. This sprawling shop is one of the best places to shop for 20th-century–design furniture, lighting, and accessories. Lost City can help you relive the Machine Age with an in-house, retro-modern line of furniture. ⊠ *18 Cooper Sq., at 5th St., East Village* ☎ *212/375–0500* ⊕ *www.lostcityarts.com* Ⓜ *6 to Astor Pl.*

BEAUTY

Fodor'sChoice
★

Bond No. 9. Created by the same fragrance team as Creed, this line of scents is intended to evoke the New York City experience, with a scent for every neighborhood: Central Park, a men's fragrance, is woodsy and "green," and Park Avenue is discreet but not too sweet. This flagship also carries candles and body creams. ⊠ *9 Bond St., between Lafayette St. and Broadway, East Village* ☎ *212/228–1732* ⊕ *www.bondno9.com* Ⓜ *6 to Bleecker St.*

Fodor'sChoice
★

Kiehl's Since 1851. At this favored haunt of top models and stylists, white-smocked assistants help you choose between the lotions and potions, all of which are packaged in simple-looking bottles and jars. Some of the products, such as the Ultra Facial Cream, Creme with Silk Groom hairstyling aid, and super-rich Creme de Corps, have attained near-cult status among fans. ⊠ *109 E. 3rd Ave., at 13th St., East Village* ☎ *212/677–3171* ⊕ *www.kiehls.com* Ⓜ *L to 3rd Ave.*

BOOKS AND STATIONERY

St. Mark's Bookshop. This legendary indie bookstore finally has a new home. The new space is smaller than the original, but has a sleeker, more functional design thanks to gleaming white bookshelves and display tables that can be reconfigured to chairs during readings. The store's specialties include poetry and graphic design, and it stays open until 11 pm. ⊠ *136 E. 3rd St., between 1st Ave. and Ave. A, East Village* ☎ *212/260–7853* ⊕ *www.stmarksbookshop.com* Ⓜ *F to 2nd Ave.*

CLOTHING

Cloak & Dagger. Come here if you like refined but on-trend looks. The racks are lined with tulip skirts, belted dresses, and trenches handpicked by owner and designer Brookelynn Starnes. ⊠ *334 E. 9th St., between 1st and 2nd aves., East Village* ☎ *212/673–0500* ⊕ *www.cloakanddaggernyc.com* Ⓜ *6 to Astor Pl.*

Fodor'sChoice
★

John Varvatos. This menswear designer has long been inspired by rock 'n' roll. His ad campaigns have starred Franz Ferdinand and Green Day, so it is fitting that he transformed the former CBGB club into his New York flagship. The space is dotted with vintage pianos, guitars, and vinyl records. And the clothes? The jeans, leather pants, and suede shoes give you rockstar cred, but there are also classic, understated styles for the corporate set. ⊠ *315 Bowery, between 1st and 2nd sts., East Village* ☎ *212/358–0315* ⊕ *www.johnvarvatos.com* Ⓜ *6 to Bleecker St.*

Pas de Deux. Fashion editors love this little boutique—which looks like it was imported straight from Paris—thanks to the marble checkerboard floor, chandeliers, and fine woodwork. The well-curated selection includes dresses, trench coats, and denim from Isabel Marant, Thakoon Panichgul, and Alexander Wang. There are also lots of lovely little accessories, like eyeglasses, cardholders, and delicate necklaces. ⊠ *328 E. 11th St., between 1st and 2nd aves., East Village* ☎ *212/475–0075* ⊕ *www.pasdedeuxny.com* Ⓜ *6 to Astor Pl.; L to 1st Ave.*

Patricia Field. If you loved Carrie Bradshaw's wild outfits on *Sex and the City*, this is the place for you. As well as designing costumes for the show, Field has been a longtime purveyor of flamboyant and campy club-kid gear. Her 4,000-square-foot East Village emporium is chockablock with teeny kilts, lamé, marabou, pleather, and vinyl, plus wigs in every color and stiletto heels in some very large sizes. ⊠ *306 Bowery, between Bleecker and Houston sts., East Village* ☎ *212/966–4066* ⊕ *www.patriciafield.com* Ⓜ *6 to Bleecker St.*

Screaming Mimi's. Browse through racks bulging with vintage finds from the 1920s through '90s. Retro wear includes everything from dresses to soccer shirts and prom dresses. Although most of the non-designer finds are affordable, Screaming Mimi's also carries vintage designer duds from Valentino, Chloe, and Gaultier. ⊠ *382 Lafayette St., between 4th and Great Jones sts., East Village* ☎ *212/677–6464* ⊕ *www.screamingmimis.com* Ⓜ *6 to Bleecker St.*

Tokio 7. Even fashion designers like Alexander Wang have been known to pop into this high-end consignment store to browse. Racks are loaded with goodies from A-list designers such as Gucci, Stella McCartney, Diane von Furstenberg, and Phillip Lim, and the inventory changes almost daily. ⊠ *83 E. 7th St., between 1st and 2nd aves., East Village* ☎ *212/353–8443* ⊕ *www.tokio7.net* Ⓜ *6 to Astor Pl.*

Trash and Vaudeville. This punk mecca is famous for dressing stars like Debbie Harry and the Ramones back in the '70s, and its rock 'n' roll vibe lives on. Goths, punks, and pro wrestlers shop here for bondage-inspired pants and skirts, as well as vinyl corsets and mini-kilts. ⊠ *4 St. Marks Pl., between 2nd and 3rd aves., East Village* ☎ *212/982–3590* ⊕ *www.trashandvaudeville.com* Ⓜ *6 to Astor Pl.*

HOME DECOR

White Trash. Looking for a midcentury modern Danish desk? This is your place. Owner Stuart Zamsky crams his store with surprisingly affordable pieces that are mostly from the '40s through '70s, including tables, lamps, and chairs. Quirkier pieces include paper mobiles from the '70s, old fondue sets, and antique medical-office cabinets. ⊠ *304 E. 5th St., between 1st and 2nd aves., East Village* ☎ *212/598–5956* ⊕ *www.whitetrashnyc.com* Ⓜ *6 to Astor Pl.*

JEWELRY AND ACCESSORIES

Verameat. All the jewelry here is handmade in New York City, and none of it is typical. Design motifs include wrenches, Big Macs, and grenades. Tilda Swinton is a fan. ⊠ *315 East 9th St., between 1st and 2nd aves., East Village* ☎ *212/388–9045* ⊕ *www.verameat.com* Ⓜ *6 to Astor Pl.*

MUSIC STORES

Other Music. DJs and musicians flock here for hard-to-find genres on CD and LPs, ranging from Japanese electronica and Krautrock to acid folk and Americana. You can buy concert tickets at the in-house box office. There's also a great selection of used CDs, including seminal punk classics from the Clash and Stooges. ⊠ *15 E. 4th St., between Lafayette St. and Broadway, East Village* ☎ *212/477–8150* ⊕ *www.othermusic. com* Ⓜ *6 to Astor Pl.*

18

The Lower East Side is a great area to shop for funky home furnishings.

TOYS

Dinosaur Hill. Forget about Elmo and Barbie. This little shop is crammed with quirky gifts for kids like hand puppets and marionettes from Asia, telescopes and wooden rattles. Don't miss the unusual instruments, such as a cedar kalimba. ⊠ *306 E. 9th St., between 1st and 2nd aves., East Village* ☎ *212/473–5850* ⊕ *www.dinosaurhill.com* Ⓜ *6 to Astor Pl.*

WINE

Astor Wines & Spirits. Stock up on wine, spirits, and sake at this beautiful shop. To unwind and learn more about food and wine, there's a wine library and a kitchen for cooking classes. ⊠ *399 Lafayette St., at 4th St., East Village* ☎ *212/674–7500* ⊕ *www.astorwines.com* Ⓜ *6 to Astor Pl.*

LOWER EAST SIDE

Head to the Lower East Side for excellent vintage finds and edgy looks. Once home to multitudes of Jewish immigrants and crumbling tenement buildings, the Lower East Side has transformed from New York's bargain hunting ground into a hotbed for indie design that includes everything from clothing to furniture. Ludlow Street, one block east of Orchard, is the main drag for boutiques, bars, and low-key restaurants. Head here if you want to revamp your look with a trendier style. For the full scope of this area, prowl from Allen to Essex streets, and south of Houston Street down to Broome.

ANTIQUES AND COLLECTIBLES

Las Venus. Fans of midcentury modern design and sleek lines need to make a beeline here. Las Venus stocks upscale vintage furniture and accessories in excellent condition. While most of the items are sleek, this is also the place to indulge in Lucite and zebra-print fantasies.

✉ *113 Stanton St., between Ludlow and Essex sts., Lower East Side* ☎ *212/982–0608* ⊕ *www.lasvenus.com* Ⓜ *F to 2nd Ave.*

SHOES, HANDBAGS, AND LEATHER GOODS

Altman Luggage. Having trouble fitting all your purchases into your bag? Altman sells top-of-the-line luggage from Rimowa, Samsonite, and Tumi at discount prices. A selection of watches and cosmetic bags are also for sale. ✉ *135 Orchard St., between Delancey and Rivington sts., Lower East Side* ☎ *212/254–7275* ⊕ *www.altmanluggage.com* Ⓜ *J, M, Z to Essex St.; F to Delancey St.*

GREENWICH VILLAGE AND WEST VILLAGE

GREENWICH VILLAGE

The Beats were born and raised in the Village, but today, the poets and have artists have long been replaced by New York University buildings and apartments with sky-high rent. There are still charmingly off-beat stores worth exploring here that retain the flavor of the glory days.

BEAUTY

C. O. Bigelow. Founded in 1838, this is the oldest apothecary-pharmacy in the United States; Mark Twain used to fill prescriptions here. They still fill prescriptions, but the real reason to come is for the hard-to-find brands like Klorane shampoo and Elgydium toothpaste. Bigelow also has its own line of products, including green-tea lip balm and quince hand lotion. ✉ *414 6th Ave., between 9th and 10th sts., Greenwich Village* ☎ *212/533–2700* ⊕ *www.bigelowchemists.com* Ⓜ *A, B, C, D, E, F, M to W. 4th St.*

CLOTHING

Denim & Supply. Owned by Ralph Lauren, this boutique has a rustic, utilitarian look, with distressed wood floors and plenty of Americana. Jeans, denim shirts and jackets are available in every hue along with T-shirts, dresses, and cargo pants. ✉ *99 University Pl., between 11th and 12th sts., Greenwich Village* ☎ *212/677–1895* ⊕ *www.denimandsupply. com* Ⓜ *4, 5, 6, L, N, Q, R to 14th St.–Union Sq.*

Fodor's Choice ★ **La Petite Coquette.** Everything at this lingerie store is unabashedly sexy, and the helpful staff can find the perfect fit. The store's own line of corsets, camisoles, and other underpinnings comes in a range of colors. ✉ *51 University Pl., between 9th and 10th sts., Greenwich Village* ☎ *212/473–2478* ⊕ *www.thelittleflirt.com* Ⓜ *N, R to 8th St.–NYU.*

Personnel of New York. "Lifestyle boutique" is an overused term, but it is the best way to describe this indie favorite, which specializes in men's and women's clothing from New York and L.A. designers. The boutique also stocks unusual home goods, such as bottle openers by Japanese designer Tadanori Baba and soap from Juniper Ridge. ✉ *9 Greenwich Ave., between Christopher and 10th sts., Greenwich Village* ☎ *212/924–0604* ⊕ *www.personnelofnewyork.com* Ⓜ *1 to Christopher St.–Sheridan Sq.; A, B, C, D, E, F, M to W. 4th St.*

18

WEST VILLAGE

One of the most beautiful spots in New York, the West Village is filled with charming boutiques, restaurants, and bars—many of which have retained their vintage charm thanks to exposed brick walls and pressed tin ceilings. Stroll around, get lost on a cobblestone street, and finish a day of shopping with a drink at a cozy bar.

Bleecker Street is a particularly good place to indulge all sorts of shopping appetites. Foodies love the blocks between 6th and 7th avenues for the specialty purveyors like Murray's Cheese *(254 Bleecker St.)*. Fashion fans forage the stretch between West 10th Street and 8th Avenue. Hudson Street and Greenwich Avenue are also prime boutique-browsing territory. Christopher Street, true to its connection with the lesbian and gay community, has a handful of shops sporting rainbow flags.

ANTIQUES AND COLLECTIBLES

Kaas Glassworks. From the outside, this shop is beyond cute, thanks to its old-fashioned sign and sandwich board. The specialty here is decoupage that has been turned into quirky trays and paperweights. Owner Carol Kaas uses antique prints, vintage postcards, historical maps, and ephemera in her works and customizes decoupage trays from wedding invitations, photos, baby announcements, or other paper keepsakes. ⊠ *117 Perry St., between Greenwich and Hudson sts., West Village* ☎ *212/366–0322* ⊕ *www.kaas.com* Ⓜ *1 to Christopher St.–Sheridan Sq.*

BEAUTY

Fodor'sChoice
★

Aedes De Venustas. Arguably the best place to buy fragrance in town, this boutique's super-knowledgeable staff helps shoppers find the perfect scent. High-end brands like L'Artisan Parfumeur and Annick Goutal are stocked, along with luxurious skincare products, pricey candles, and room diffusers. The shop's signature gift wrap is as beautiful as what's inside the box. ⊠ *9 Christopher St., between 6th and 7th aves., West Village* ☎ *212/206–8674* ⊕ *www.aedes.com* Ⓜ *1 to Christopher St.–Sheridan Sq.*

Jo Malone. This crisp black and white boutique sets a serene backdrop to sample tangy scents like lime blossom and mandarin, or Earl Grey and cucumber. Fragrances can be worn alone or layered. The flagship gives complimentary hand massages (by appointment) and has a sampling bar to create a bespoke scent. ⊠ *330 Bleecker St., between 10th and Christopher sts., West Village* ☎ *212/242–1454* ⊕ *www.jomalone.com* Ⓜ *1 to Christopher St.–Sheridan Sq.*

BOOKS AND STATIONERY

bookbook. This small, independent bookstore is crammed with the latest new releases as well as a thoughtful assortment of general nonfiction, guidebooks, and children's books. But when the weather cooperates, the real focus here is the carefully selected sale tables that spill out onto the sidewalk, with deals on everything from Graham Greene to Chuck Palahniuk. ⊠ *266 Bleecker St., between 6th and 7th aves., West Village* ☎ *212/807–8655* ⊕ *www.bookbooknyc.com* Ⓜ *1 to Christopher St.–Sheridan Sq.; A, B, C, D, E, F, M to W. 4th St.*

Three Lives & Company. One of the city's best book selections is displayed on the tables and counters of this bookshop, which highlights the latest literary fiction and serious nonfiction, classics, quirky gift books, and gorgeously illustrated tomes. The staff members' literary knowledge is formidable, so don't be afraid to ask for their own picks. ⊠ *154 W. 10th St., at Waverly Pl., West Village* ☎ *212/741–2069* ⊕ *www.threelives. com* Ⓜ *1 to Christopher St.–Sheridan Sq.*

CLOTHING

CAP Beauty. The new CAP Beauty is a one stop shop for natural skin care, which means that 100% of the products are free from synthetic ingredients. Brands carried include Elizabeth Dehn, Tata Harper and Ko Denmark. CAP also does spa treatments, facials, and acupuncture. ⊠ *238 W. 10th St., at Hudson St., West Village* ☎ *212/645–6572* ⊕ *www.capbeauty.com* Ⓜ *1 to Christopher St.–Sheridan Sq.*

Cynthia Rowley. This boutique delivers flirty, whimsical dresses that are perfect for cocktail parties. To complete the look, throw on some of her colorful pumps and sharply tailored coats. ⊠ *376 Bleecker St., between Charles and Perry sts., West Village* ☎ *212/242–3803* ⊕ *www. cynthiarowley.com* Ⓜ *1 to Christopher St.–Sheridan Sq.*

Fisch for the Hip. This high-end consignment store sells carefully curated men's and women's clothing and accessories, from top designers including Tom Ford, Balenciaga, and Lanvin. Hermès bags are a specialty. ⊠ *90 7th Ave., between 15th and 16th sts., West Village* ☎ *212/633–6965* ⊕ *www.fischforthehip.com* Ⓜ *A, C, E to 14th St.; L to 8th Ave.; 1 to 18th St.*

Hotoveli. This unprepossessing nook stocks some of the most elegant (and expensive) designers in the world, ranging from Alexander McQueen to Vivienne Westwood. If you have to ask how much an item costs, don't try it on. ⊠ *378 Bleecker St., between Charles and Perry sts., West Village* ☎ *212/206–7475* ⊕ *www.hotoveli.com* Ⓜ *1 to Christopher St.–Sheridan Sq.*

Khirma Eliazov. This former magazine editor now designs an elegant line of handbags, clutches, and accessories that are favorites among stars like Blake Lively and J. Lo. She uses luxury materials, including python, alligator, crocodile, and stingray skins. ⊠ *102 Charles St., between Hudson and Bleecker sts., West Village* ☎ *646/998–5240* ⊕ *www.khirmaeliazov.com* Ⓜ *1 to Christopher St.–Sheridan Square.*

FOOD AND TREATS

Chocolate Bar. What sets this chocolate emporium apart is minimalist design, which also turns up in the groovy packaging. Scoop up chocolate bars, whose flavors include salted caramel and milk Cheerios, or try a coffee cardamom truffle washed down with a steaming cup of spicy hot chocolate. ⊠ *19 8th Ave., between Jane and 12th sts., West Village* ☎ *917/388–3761* ⊕ *www.chocolatebarnyc.com* Ⓜ *A, C, E, to 14th St.; L to 8th Ave.*

Li-Lac Chocolates. Feeding the Village's sweet tooth since 1923, Li-Lac indulges with almond bark and coconut clusters as well as such specialty items as chocolate-molded Statues of Liberty. The coconut rolls and chocolate-covered graham crackers tempt even the most stubborn dieter. To see how the small batch chocolates are made, visit Li-Lac's

Brooklyn factory. ⊠ *40 8th Ave., at Jane St., West Village* ☎ *212/924–2280* ⊕ *www.li-lacchocolates.com* Ⓜ *A, C, E to 14th St.; L to 8th Ave.*

Sockerbit. Who knew Scandinavians were obsessed with candy? There's much more than Swedish fish at this gleaming white candy emporium that stocks hard candies, gummies, licorice, and chocolate. Have fun pronouncing the names of treats like Bumlingar Jordgubb and Zoo Klubba. ⊠ *89 Christopher St., between Bleecker and 4th sts., West Village* ☎ *212/206–8170* ⊕ *www.sockerbit.com* Ⓜ *1 to Christopher St.–Sheridan Sq.*

SHOES, HANDBAGS, AND LEATHER GOODS

Fodor's Choice
★
Flight 001. Frequent flyers can one-stopshop at this travel-themed store that puts a creative spin on everyday accessories. Shop for bright luggage tags, passport holders, satin sleep masks, and innovative storage for everything from shoes to toiletries. ⊠ *96 Greenwich Ave., between 12th and Jane sts., West Village* ☎ *212/989–0001* ⊕ *www.flight001.com* Ⓜ *1, 2, 3 to 14th St.*

Fodor's Choice
★
Leffot. This simple, understated store focuses on one thing: selling top-quality men's shoes. Owner Steven Taffel, who previously worked at Prada, has stocked his shop with selections from John Lobb, Church's and Edward Green. These shoes are meant to last a lifetime, and many have a price tag to match. Bespoke footwear is also available. ⊠ *10 Christopher St., at Gay St., West Village* ☎ *212/989–4577* ⊕ *www.leffot.com* Ⓜ *1 to Christopher St.–Sheridan Sq.; A, B, C, D, E, F, M to W. 4th St.*

Lulu Guinness. Hit this black-and-white-boutique for cheerfully eccentric accessories such as handbags printed with images of lips, dolls, and cameos. Other accessories, including umbrellas and luggage, are equally fun. ⊠ *394 Bleecker St., between 11th and Perry sts., West Village* ☎ *212/367–2120* ⊕ *www.luluguinness.com* Ⓜ *1 to Christopher St.–Sheridan Sq.*

CHELSEA AND THE MEATPACKING DISTRICT

CHELSEA

Chelsea offers one-stop shopping for some of the biggest retail brands.

BOOKS AND STATIONERY

FAMILY **Books of Wonder.** Readers young and old delight in Manhattan's oldest and largest independent children's bookstore. The friendly, knowledgeable staff can help select gifts for all reading levels. Don't miss the extensive Oz section, plus the collection of old, rare, and collectible children's books and original children's book art. ⊠ *18 W. 18th St., between 5th and 6th aves., Chelsea* ☎ *212/989–3270* ⊕ *www.booksofwonder.com* Ⓜ *F, M to 14th St.; L to 6th Ave.*

Posman Books. Posman Books has an outstanding selection of contemporary and classic books across genres. Don't miss the cheeky and serious high-quality greeting cards. ⊠ *Chelsea Market, 75 9th Ave., between 15th and 16th sts., Chelsea* ☎ *212/627–0304* ⊕ *www.posmanbooks.com* Ⓜ *A, C, E to 14th St.; L to 8th Ave.*

CLOTHING

Comme des Garçons. The designs in this swoopy, gold-adorned space consistently push the fashion envelope with brash patterns, unlikely juxtapositions (tulle and neoprene), and cuts that are meant to be thought-provoking, not flattering. Architecture students come just for the interior design. ⊠ *520 W. 22nd St., between 10th and 11th aves., Chelsea* ☎ *212/604–9200* ⊕ *www.comme-des-garcons.com* Ⓜ *C, E to 23rd St.*

New York Vintage. Stylists to the stars, TV costumers, and the deep-pocketed descend upon this boutique to browse racks of prime vintage clothing. Everything is high-end, so don't expect any bargains. Take your pick from Yves Saint Laurent, Madame Grès, and Thierry Mugler items. There's a good selection of handbags and stilettos, too. ⊠ *117 W. 25th St., between 6th and 7th aves., Chelsea* ☎ *212/647–1107* ⊕ *www.newyorkvintage.com* Ⓜ *1 to 28th St.*

Fodor's Choice ★ **Story.** Launched by former consultant Rachel Shechtman, Story is a concept store with a twist. Every few weeks, it partners with a new sponsor to develop a retail "story," like a magazine spread, which ranges from wearable tech to "home for the holidays." Pop by often to admire the artful displays, and you never know what will be for sale, from chocolates to clothing and books. Story also hosts events such as talks with TED speakers. ⊠ *144 10th Ave., at 19th St., Chelsea* ☎ *212/242–4853* ⊕ *www.thisisstory.com* Ⓜ *A, C, E to 14th St.; L to 8th Ave.*

GIFTS AND SOUVENIRS

Eleni's. Take a bite out of the Big Apple—in cookie form—with these perfectly decorated treats, shaped like yellow cabs, the New York skyline, and police cars. It's not just New York depicted here; the iced cookies come in every design imaginable, from iPhones to bottles of nail polish. Photos of loved ones can be transferred onto cupcakes—if you don't mind taking a bite. ⊠ *Chelsea Market, 75 9th Ave., between 15th and 16th sts., Chelsea* ☎ *212/255–6804* ⊕ *www.elenis.com* Ⓜ *A, C, E to 14th St.; L to 8th Ave.*

MUSIC STORES AND MEDIA

Jazz Record Center. If you're seeking rare or out-of-print jazz recordings, this is your one-stop shop. Long-lost Ellingtons and other rare pressings come to light here; the jazz-record specialist also stocks books, collectibles, DVDs, posters, CDs, and LPs. ⊠ *236 W. 26th St., 8th fl., between 7th and 8th aves., Chelsea* ☎ *212/675–4480* ⊕ *www.jazzrecordcenter. com* Ⓜ *1 to 28th St.*

WINE

Bottlerocket Wine & Spirit. Fun and approachable, this shop puts a new spin on wine shopping. Vintages are organized by quirky factors like their compatibility with Chinese takeout and whom they'd best suit as gifts (ranging from "Third Date" to "The Boss"). A kids' play nook and doggie area make the space extra-welcoming. ⊠ *5 W. 19th St., between 5th and 6th aves., Chelsea* ☎ *212/929–2323* ⊕ *www.bottlerocketwine. com* Ⓜ *4, 5, 6, L, N, Q, R to 14th St.–Union Sq.*

18

MEATPACKING DISTRICT

For nearly a century, the industrial western edge of downtown Manhattan was defined by slaughterhouses and meatpacking plants, blood-splattered cobblestone streets, and men lugging carcasses into warehouses before dawn.

But in the late 1990s the area bounded by 14th Street, Gansevoort Street, Hudson Street, and 11th Avenue speedily transformed into another kind of meat market. Many of the old warehouses now house ultra-chic shops, nightclubs, and restaurants packed with angular fashionistas. Jeffrey, a pint-size department store, was an early arrival, followed by bigger brands such as Diane von Furstenberg and a few lofty furniture stores. Despite the influx of a few chains—albeit stylish ones like Scoop—eclectic boutiques keep popping up. The one thing that's hard to find here is a bargain.

CAMERAS AND ELECTRONICS

Apple Store. Branch location at 401 West 14th Street. *See Midtown East for full review.*

CLOTHING

Catherine Malandrino. Celebs like Halle Berry love this French-born designer for her sexy-without-trying-too-hard looks. Shop for silk V-neck gowns or one-shouldered ruched wool dresses. ⊠ *652 Hudson St., at 13th St., Meatpacking District* ☎ *212/929–8710* ⊕ *www. catherinemalandrino.com* Ⓜ *A, C, E to 14th St.; L to 8th Ave.*

Fodor's Choice ★   **Diane von Furstenberg.** At this light-filled New York flagship, try on the iconic DVF wrap dress in myriad patterns. The blouses, shorts, and skirts are equally feminine. ⊠ *874 Washington St., at 14th St., Meatpacking District* ☎ *646/486–4800* ⊕ *www.dvf.com* Ⓜ *A, C, E to 14th St.; L to 8th Ave.*

Jeffrey. The Meatpacking District really arrived when this Atlanta-based mini-Barneys opened its doors. You can find an incredible array of designer shoes—Valentino and red-soled Christian Louboutin are some of the best sellers—plus top labels such as Yves Saint Laurent and Lanvin. ⊠ *449 W. 14th St., between 9th and 10th aves., Meatpacking District* ☎ *212/206–1272* ⊕ *www.jeffreynewyork.com* Ⓜ *A, C, E to 14th St.; L to 8th Ave.*

Owen. Fashion Institute of Technology grad Phillip Salem transformed this space into a whimsical place to shop, thanks to the 25,000 paper bags that line the arched ceiling. This upscale boutique sells men's and women's wear from 70 established and independent designers. Come here for skinny jeans, luxurious sweaters, and dresses from J. Brand, Garter+Derringer, and Roksanda Ilincic. ⊠ *809 Washington St., between Gansevoort and Horatio sts., Meatpacking District* ☎ *212/524–9770* ⊕ *www.owennyc.com* Ⓜ *A, C, E to 14th St.; L to 8th Ave.*

Rebecca Taylor. This designer is known for her soft, feminine work, which runs the gamut from sexy to understated, all with a slightly vintage flair. Taylor's downtown location is a serene, spacious environment for browsing racks of silky shirtdresses, embroidered tunics, and ruffled overcoats. Her shoes, handbags, and jewelry are equally romantic. ⊠ *34 Gansevoort St., between Greenwich and Hudson sts., Meatpacking*

District ☎ *212/243–2600* ⊕ *www.rebeccataylor.com* Ⓜ *A, C, E to 14th St.; L to 8th Ave.*

Trina Turk. Make a bee-line to this boutique if you like bright, happy colors and 1970's-influenced clothing. The shop, designed by Jonathan Adler, showcases Turk's ready-to-wear clothing in a bright, airy setting. Swimwear is a standout, and menswear is also sold here. ✉ *67 Gansevoort St., between Washington and Greenwich sts., Meatpacking District* ☎ *212/206–7383* ⊕ *www.trinaturk.com* Ⓜ *A, C, E to 14th St.; L to 8th Ave.*

JEWELRY AND ACCESSORIES

Ten Thousand Things. You might find yourself wishing for 10,000 things from the showcases in this elegant boutique. Designs run from delicate gold and silver chains to long Peruvian opal earrings. Many shapes are abstract reflections of natural forms, like twigs or seedpods. Prices start around $180 but quickly rise. ✉ *423 W. 14th St., between 9th and 10th aves., Meatpacking District* ☎ *212/352–1333* ⊕ *www.tenthousandthingsnyc.com* Ⓜ *A, C, E to 14th St.; L to 8th Ave.*

UNION SQUARE AND THE FLATIRON DISTRICT

UNION SQUARE

The several blocks around Union Square—which itself is home to the city's best greenmarket, and a holiday market leading up to Christmas—is a bit south of the Flatiron District and has large retail chains such as LuLu Lemon, J.Crew, Banana Republic, and Anthropologie

BEAUTY

Fresh. Long a beauty favorite, with ingredients that are good enough to eat (think brown sugar, soy, and black tea), the Fresh flagship has an apothecary-inspired look, with beautifully packaged soaps displayed like pastries in a glass case. Pull up a seat at the communal Kitchen Table to try out a new product. ✉ *872 Broadway, between 18th and 19th sts., Union Square* ☎ *212/477–1100* ⊕ *www.fresh.com* Ⓜ *4, 5, 6, L, N, Q, R to 14th St.–Union Sq.*

BOOKS AND STATIONERY

Fodor's Choice
★

The Strand. Opened in 1927, and still run by the same family, this monstrous book emporium—home to 2 million volumes, or "18 Miles of Books"—is a symbol of a bygone era, a mecca for serious bibliophiles, and a local institution. The store has survived the Great Depression, World War II, competition from Barnes & Noble, and the Kindle. The stock includes new and secondhand books, plus thousands of collector's items and merchandise. A separate rare-book room is on the third floor (it closes at 6:15 daily). The basement has discounted, barely touched review copies of new books, organized by author. If you're looking for souvenirs, visit the New York section of the bookstore for New York–centric literature, poetry, and cookbooks, as well as T-shirts and totes. Visitors should also check the Strand's events calendar and try to attend an author or artist event. Headliners have ranged from Anne Rice to James Franco. ✉ *828 Broadway, at 12th St., Union Square*

18

☎ *212/473–1452* ⊕ *www.strandbooks.com* Ⓜ *4, 5, 6, L, N, Q, R to 14th St.–Union Sq.*

CLOTHING

Beacon's Closet. Brooklyn favorite Beacon's Closet now has a Big Apple outpost. This simple space, which is lit by multiple chandeliers, has a wide selection of gently used modern and vintage clothes. Comb through the racks and you might find pieces from Christian Dior, Marc Jacobs, or AllSaints as well as stylish items from under-the-radar labels. ✉ *10 W. 13th St., between 5th and 6th aves., Union Square* ☎ *917/261–4863* ⊕ *www.beaconscloset.com* Ⓜ *4, 5, 6, L, N, Q, R to 14th St.–Union Sq.*

Forever 21. Branch location at 40 East 14th Street. *See Midtown West for full review.*

J.Crew. This preppy-chic staple in so many people's closets continues to push the envelope under superstar Jenna Lyons. Yes, you can still get cardigans, cords, and tees in every pastel color of the rainbow, but the clothes today are sometimes downright sexy. The leather jackets and sequined skirts are also perfect for that casual, thrown-together look. This flagship carries women's, men's, and Crewcuts for children as well as a wedding gown collection. ✉ *91 5th Ave., between 15th and 16th sts., Union Square* ☎ *212/255–4848* ⊕ *www.jcrew.com* Ⓜ *4, 5, 6, L, N, Q, R to 14th St.–Union Sq.*

FOOD AND WINE

Fodor's Choice ★ **Max Brenner: Chocolate by the Bald Man.** This shop and restaurant is all about a Wonka-ish sense of entertainment. The café encourages the messy enjoyment of gooey creations like chocolate pizzas for kids, but there are also savory options to soak up all that sugar. Take-away treats include caramelized pralines and tins of hot-chocolate mix. ✉ *841 Broadway, between 13th and 14th sts., Union Square* ☎ *646/467–8803* ⊕ *www.maxbrenner.com* Ⓜ *4, 5, 6, L, N, Q, R to 14th St.–Union Sq.*

Fodor's Choice ★ **Union Square Wine & Spirits.** Tastings are easy at this well-stocked store, thanks to Enomatic machines. These card-operated contraptions let you sample dozens of wines. If machines don't do it for you, generous tastings are held most Fridays and Saturdays. ✉ *140 4th Ave., at 13th St., East Village* ☎ *212/675–8100* ⊕ *www.unionsquarewines.com* Ⓜ *4, 5, 6, L, N, Q, R to 14th St.–Union Sq.*

HOME DECOR

Fodor's Choice ★ **ABC Carpet & Home.** If you love eclectic goods from around the world, this is your place. Spread over 10 floors is a superb selection of rugs, antiques, textiles, furniture, and bedding, including sleek sofas and Balinese daybeds. The ground floor is a wonderland of silk pillows and jewelry. To refuel, there's an in-house restaurant from Jean-Georges Vongerichten. More rugs and carpets are unrolled across the street at 881 Broadway. ✉ *888 Broadway, at 19th St., Union Square* ☎ *212/473–3000* ⊕ *www.abchome.com* Ⓜ *4, 5, 6, L, N, Q, R to 14th St.–Union Sq.*

JEWELRY AND ACCESSORIES

Beads of Paradise. Not your ordinary bead store, the baubles here are sourced from around the world. Shoppers can choose silver from Bali and Mexico and ancient glass beads from China, along with semiprecious stones. Sign up for a class to learn how to put it all together. ⊠ *16 E. 17th St., between 5th Ave. and Broadway, Union Square* ☎ *212/620–0642* ⊕ *www.beadsofparadisenyc.com* Ⓜ *4, 5, 6, L, N, Q, R to 14th St.–Union Sq.*

FLATIRON DISTRICT

The Flatiron District, north of Union Square, stretches from about 17th Street up to 29th Street, and us between 6th Avenue and Lexington, This is one of the buzziest areas in New York, brimming with both large and small stores. Come here if you want to shop the big chains minus the Midtown tourist crowds.

BOOKS AND STATIONERY

Idlewild Books. Named for the pre-1960's JFK Airport, this travel-inspired bookstore is one of the last of its kind in America. They stock guidebooks, novels, and children's books grouped by destination, and also run foreign-language classes, ranging from Arabic to German. If those chairs look familiar, it may be because you huddled in one during a layover at the American Airlines terminal. ⊠ *12 W. 19th St., 2nd fl., at 5th Ave., Flatiron District* ☎ *212/414–8888* ⊕ *www.idlewildbooks. com* Ⓜ *4, 5, 6, L, N, Q, R to 14th St.–Union Sq.*

CHILDREN'S CLOTHING

FAMILY **Space Kiddets.** The funky (Elvis-print rompers, CBGB onesies) mixes with the old-school (retro cowboy-print pants, brightly colored clogs, Bruce Lee T-shirts) and the high-end (Lili Gaufrette, Kenzo, Boo Foo Woo from Japan) at this casual, trendsetting store. ⊠ *26 E. 22nd St., between Broadway and Park Ave., Flatiron District* ☎ *212/420–9878* ⊕ *www.spacekiddets.com* Ⓜ *6 to 23rd St.*

CLOTHING

Anthropologie. Bohemian-chic is the aesthetic of this popular women's clothing and home accessories chain. ⊠ *85 5th Ave., Flatiron District* ☎ *212/627–5885* ⊕ *www.anthropologie.com* Ⓜ *4, 5, 6, L, N, Q, R to 14th St.–Union Sq.*

Club Monaco. In addition to the brand's signature clothing (think of a hipper Banana Republic), this flagship includes an outpost of Williamsburg favorite Toby's Estate Coffee, as well as a bookstore operated by the Strand. ⊠ *160 5th Ave., between 20th and 21st sts., Flatiron District* ☎ *212/352–0936* ⊕ *www.clubmonaco.com* Ⓜ *N, R to 23rd St.*

Madewell. This J.Crew spinoff is ideal for casual women's staples like jeans, t-shirts, and sweaters with a vintage look. The two-story Manhattan flagship has a quirky, homespun design; merchandise is displayed on everything from old mill tables to meat hooks. Don't miss the shoe shop and home goods collection. ⊠ *115 5th Ave., between 18th and 19th sts., Flatiron District* ☎ *212/228–5172* ⊕ *www.madewell.com* Ⓜ *4, 5, 6, L, N, Q, R to 14th St.–Union Sq.*

Fodor'sChoice **Maison Kitsuné.** This decades-old French fashion and music label made
★ its stateside debut in this airy, sunwashed boutique for men's and womenswear classics with a stylish Gallic twist, ranging from cardigans and loafers to blazers and dresses. ⊠ *NoMad Hotel, 1170 Broadway, at 28th St., Flatiron District* ☎ *212/481–6010* ⊕ *www.kitsune.fr* Ⓜ *N, R to 28th St.*

18

Holiday Markets

Between Thanksgiving and Christmas, holiday markets—rows of wooden stalls, many with red-and-white-stripe awnings—spring up around town. The gifts and goods vary from year to year, but there are some perennial offerings: colorful handmade knitwear and jewelry; sweet-smelling soaps, candles, and lotions with hand-lettered labels; glittery Christmas ornaments of every stripe; and New York–theme gift items (a group called Gritty City sell T-shirts, coin purses, and undies printed with pictures of taxicabs and manhole covers).

While the holiday market in Grand Central Terminal's Vanderbilt Hall is indoors, most vendors set up outside. There's one every year at Columbus Circle, near the southwest entrance to Central Park, and another at Bryant Park, behind the New York City Public Library. The largest and most popular, however, is at the south end of Union Square, where you can go from the greenmarket to the stalls, just like the downtowners who meet in the afternoon or after work to look for unique or last-minute gifts.

HOME DECOR

Fodor's Choice
★
Fishs Eddy. The dishes, china, and glassware for resale come from all walks of crockery life, including corporate dining rooms and failed restaurants, so you never know what you might find. Fishs Eddy also sell their own line of dishes, which has a classic look. The shop is a great place to pick up New York–themed gifts, such as mugs and trays. ⊠ *889 Broadway, at 19th St., Flatiron District* ☎ *212/420–9020* ⊕ *www.fishseddy.com* Ⓜ *4, 5, 6, L, N, Q, R to 14th St.–Union Sq.*

Marimekko. If you love bright, cheerful patterns, make a beeline to the Marimekko flagship. This 4,000-square-foot store is primarily white, so the colorful merchandise pops. Everything from pot holders and shower curtains to coats and dresses is available here in the bold signtaure Marimekko prints. If feeling crafty, pick up a few yards of fabric to create something of your own. ⊠ *200 5th Ave., between 23rd and 24th sts., Flatiron District* ☎ *212/843–9121* ⊕ *www.marimekko.com* Ⓜ *N, R to 23rd St.*

TOYS

Kidding Around. This independent shop is piled high with old-fashioned wooden toys, sturdy musical instruments, and plenty of arts-and-crafts materials. The costume racks are rich with dress-up potential. ⊠ *60 W. 15th St., between 5th and 6th aves., Flatiron District* ☎ *212/645–6337* ⊕ *www.kiddingaroundtoys.com* Ⓜ *F, M to 14th St.; 4, 5, 6, L, N, Q, R to 14th St.–Union Sq.*

MIDTOWN EAST

If money is no object, put on your best shopping shoes and most glamorous sunglasses and head to Midtown East. Some of the world's most luxurious brands—from Gucci to Christian Dior—have their flagship stores along 5th Avenue. All the stores *on* 5th Avenue are included in

Midtown East, although some might be on the west side of the street and have West in their address.

ANTIQUES AND COLLECTIBLES

A La Vieille Russie. Antiques dealers since 1851, this shop specializes in European and Russian decorative arts, jewelry, and paintings. Behold bibelots by Fabergé and others, enameled or encrusted with jewels. If money is no object, there are also antique diamond necklaces and pieces of china once owned by Russian nobility. ⊠ *781 5th Ave., at 59th St., Midtown East* ☎ *212/752–1727* ⊕ *www.alvr.com* Ⓜ *N, Q, R to 5th Ave./59th St.*

The Chinese Porcelain Company. Though the name of this prestigious shop indicates one of its specialties, its stock covers more ground, ranging from lacquerware to Khmer sculpture as well as work by contemporary Chinese artists. ⊠ *475 Park Ave., at 58th St., Midtown East* ☎ *212/838–7744* ⊕ *www.chineseporcelainco.com* Ⓜ *4, 5, 6 to 59th St.; N, Q, R to Lexington Ave./59th St.*

Flying Cranes Antiques. At this world leader in Japanese antiques, shoppers find rare, museum-quality pieces from the Meiji period, Japan's Golden Age. Items include ceramics, cloisonné, metalwork, baskets, and samurai swords and fittings. ⊠ *Manhattan Art and Antiques Center, 1050 2nd Ave., between 55th and 56th sts., Midtown East* ☎ *212/223–4600* ⊕ *www.flyingcranesantiques.com* Ⓜ *E, M to Lexington Ave./53rd St.*

Leo Kaplan Ltd. The impeccable items here include Art Nouveau glass and pottery, porcelain from 18th-century England, antique and modern paperweights, and Russian art. ⊠ *114 E. 57th St., between Park and Lexington aves., Midtown East* ☎ *212/355–7212* ⊕ *www.leokaplan. com* Ⓜ *4, 5, 6 to 59th St.; N, Q, R to Lexington Ave./59th St.*

Newel Art Galleries. Housed in a renovated six-story building, this huge collection spans the Renaissance through the 20th century. The nonfurniture finds, from figureheads to bell jars, make for prime conversation pieces. Newel is a major supplier of antiques for Broadway showsand luxury department store windows. ⊠ *425 E. 53rd St., between 1st Ave. and Sutton Pl., Midtown East* ☎ *212/758–1970* ⊕ *www.newel.com* Ⓜ *E, M to Lexington Ave./53rd St.*

BOOKS AND STATIONERY

Fodor's Choice
★ **Argosy Bookstore.** Family owned since 1925, Argosy is a charmingly old-fashioned place to browse for both bargain and priceless books. The shop keeps a scholarly stock of rare books and autographs. It's also a great place find low-price maps and prints for gifts. ⊠ *116 E. 59th St., between Park and Lexington aves., Midtown East* ☎ *212/753–4455* ⊕ *www.argosybooks.com* Ⓜ *4, 5, 6 to 59th St.; N, Q, R to Lexington Ave./59th St.*

CAMERAS AND ELECTRONICS

Fodor's Choice
★ **Apple Store.** New York's flagship Apple Store features a 32-foot-high glass cube that appears to float over its subterranean entrance. The Apple-obsessed will be happy to know this location is open 24/7, holidays included. Make an appointment at the Genius Bar if you need

18

tech help. ⊠ *767 5th Ave., between 58th and 59th sts., Midtown East* ☎ *212/336–1440* ⊕ *www.apple.com* Ⓜ *N, Q, R to 5th Ave./59th St.*

SONY Style. Located on the ground floor of the Sony Building, this sunny space is a wonderland of electronics, with all the latest home-theater equipment, cameras, tablets, and smartphones. ⊠ *550 Madison Ave., at 55th St., Midtown East* ☎ *212/833–8800* ⊕ *www.store.sony.com* Ⓜ *E, M to 5th Ave./53rd St.*

CLOTHING

Abercrombie & Fitch. This brand is known for its casual preppy clothes for men, women, and kids—but brace yourself for the thumping club music and dim lighting. ⊠ *720 5th Ave., Midtown East* ☎ *212/306—0936* ⊕ *www.abercrombie.com* Ⓜ *F to 57th St.; N, Q, R to 5th Ave./59th St.*

Banana Republic. Although there are nearly a dozen Banana Republic stores around the city, come to the flagship for the biggest selection of clothing. Don't miss the Heritage collection or the big clearance racks. ⊠ *Rockefeller Center, 626 5th Ave., at 51st St., Midtown East* ☎ *212/974–2350* ⊕ *www.bananarepublic.gap.com* Ⓜ *B, D, F, M to 47th–50th Sts./Rockefeller Center; E, M to 5th Ave./53rd St.*

Brooks Brothers. The clothes at this classic American haberdasher are, as ever, traditional, comfortable, and fairly priced. Summer seersucker, navy-blue blazers, and the peerless oxford shirts have been staples for generations; the women's and boys' selections have variations thereon. Get scanned by a digital tailor for precisely measured custom shirts or suits; an appointment is recommended. ⊠ *346 Madison Ave., at 44th St., Midtown East* ☎ *212/682–8800* ⊕ *www.brooksbrothers.com* Ⓜ *4, 5, 6, 7, S to Grand Central–42nd. St.*

Burberry. This six-story glass-and-stone flagship is a temple to all things plaid, British, and Cara Delevingne. The iconic trench coat can be made-to-measure here, and the signature plaid can be found on bikinis, scarves, and wallets. For children, there are mini versions of quilted jackets and cozy sweaters. ⊠ *9 E. 57th St., between 5th and Madison aves., Midtown East* ☎ *212/407–7100* ⊕ *www.us.burberry.com* Ⓜ *N, Q, R to 5th Ave./59th St.*

Chanel. The Midtown flagship has often been compared to a Chanel suit—slim, elegant, timeless, and decorated in the signature black-and-white colors. Come here for the iconic suits and quilted handbags, along with other pillars of Chanel style: chic little black dresses, evening gowns, and yards of pearls. There's also a cosmetics area where you can stock up on the famed scents and nail polish. ⊠ *15 E. 57th St., between 5th and Madison aves., Midtown East* ☎ *212/355–5050* ⊕ *www.chanel.com* Ⓜ *N, Q, R to 5th Ave./59th St.*

Christian Dior. This very white, very glossy space sets a serene background to showcase the luxe ready-to-wear collection along with handbags and accessories. If you're not in the market for an investment gown or fine jewelry, peruse the latest status bag. The Dior menswear boutique is next door; the cigarette-thin suits are often snapped up by women. ⊠ *21 57th St., at Madison Ave., Midtown East* ☎ *212/931–2950* ⊕ *www.dior.com* Ⓜ *N, Q, R to 5th Ave./59th St.*

Fodor's Choice ★ **Dover Street Market.** The New York location is the only U.S. outpost of Rei Kawakubo's Dover Street Market (the others are in London, Tokyo and Beijing). It's basically a multilevel fashion-store emporium: each floor has miniboutiques from brands including Prada, Alaïa, and Alexander Wang alongside lesser-known designers. The seven-story building is worth a look just for people-watching. The in-house Rose Bakery is the perfect spot to refuel with an espresso or iced pound cake. ✉ *160 Lexington Ave., at 30th St., Midtown East* ☎ *646/837–7750* ⊕ *newyork.doverstreetmarket.com* Ⓜ *6 to 33rd St.*

Fodor's Choice ★ **Dunhill.** If you're stumped on what to buy the man in your life, head to Dunhill. The menswear is exquisitely tailored, and the accessories, like wallets and cufflinks, are somewhat affordable. The walk-in humidor stores top-quality tobacco and cigars. ✉ *545 Madison Ave., at 55th St., Midtown East* ☎ *212/753–9292* ⊕ *www.dunhill.com* Ⓜ *E, M to 5th Ave./53rd St.*

Gianni Versace. The architecture here, with its marble floor and glittering chandeliers, provides the perfect backdrop for the outrageous designs and colors of Versace clothes. The brand's housewares and bedding collection are also available here. ✉ *647 5th Ave., near 51st St., Midtown East* ☎ *212/317–0224* ⊕ *www.versace.com* Ⓜ *E, M to 5th Ave./53rd St.*

Gucci. Located in the Trump Building, this 46,000-square-foot flagship with floor-to-ceiling glass windows is the largest Gucci store in the world. Here, shoppers find a special "heritage" department, plus goods exclusive to the store. The clothing is edgy and sexy. Skintight pants might be paired with a luxe leather jacket; silk tops leave a little more to the imagination. Many of the accessories, like wraparound shades or snakeskin shoes, have Gucci's signature horse bit detailing. ✉ *725 5th Ave., at 56th St., Midtown East* ☎ *212/826–2600* ⊕ *www.gucci. com* Ⓜ *N, Q, R to 5th Ave./59th St.*

18

H&M. Of-the-moment trends are packaged for the mass market at this affordable Swedish clothing chain, which has numerous stores in the city. H&M has collaborated with many designers, including Karl Lagerfeld and Isabel Marant. ✉ *640 5th Ave., between 51st and 52nd sts., Midtown East* ☎ *212/489–0390* ⊕ *www.hm.com* Ⓜ *E, M to 5th Ave./53rd St.*

Joe Fresh. Think of this brand as the Canadian version of H&M crossed with the Gap, selling stylish but classic clothes for men and women at affordable prices. The New York flagship stocks everything from sweaters and denim to button-down shirts and shoes in a rainbow of colors. Just about all items are under $100. ✉ *510 5th Ave., between 42nd and 43rd sts., Midtown East* ☎ *212/764–1730* ⊕ *www.joefresh. com* Ⓜ *7 to 5th Ave.*

Massimo Dutti. Owned by Zara, think of this brand as its older, more sophisticated sibling. The three-story space specializes in sleek basics that are perfect for work or the weekends, such as blazers, trench coats, and silky sweaters. ✉ *689 5th Ave., between 54th and 55th sts., Midtown East* ☎ *212/371–2555* ⊕ *www.massimodutti.com* Ⓜ *E, M to 5th Ave./53rd St.*

Tommy Hilfiger. The global flagship oozes old-school Americana, with its dark-wood paneling, shirts displayed on bookshelves, and scattering of antiques. It's filled with tailored suits for men, smart sweater sets and pencil skirts for women, and evening wear along with sportswear, plus a whole floor devoted to denim. ⊠ *681 5th Ave., at 54th St., Midtown East* ☎ *212/223-1824* ⊕ *usa.tommy.com* Ⓜ *E, M to 5th Ave./53rd St.*

UNIQLO. At 89,000 square feet, this location is the biggest UNIQLO in the world (there are also branches in SoHo and near Herald Square). Shoppers can scoop up staples such as sweaters, skinny jeans, and button-down shirts in a rainbow of colors. Don't miss the limited edition collaborations with big-name designers and stylists. The Heattech clothing range is always a big hit. Weekday mornings are the best time to avoid long lines for the dressing rooms. ⊠ *666 5th Ave., between 52nd and 53rd sts., Midtown East* ☎ *877/486-4756* ⊕ *www.uniqlo.com* Ⓜ *E, M to 5th Ave./53rd St.*

Zara. This massive store is one of Zara's biggest in the U.S. and the place to come for affordable, stylish fashion. New merchandise arrives twice a week and ranges from classics like blazers to edgier skinny trousers. There are also two lounge areas, in case you need a shopping break. ⊠ *666 5th Ave., between 52nd and 53rd sts., Midtown East* ☎ *212/765-0477* ⊕ *www.zara.com* Ⓜ *E, M to 5th Ave./53rd St.*

DEPARTMENT STORES

Bergdorf Goodman. This luxury department store is the ultimate shopping destination, offering ladies (and men) who lunch designer clothes, a stellar shoe department, and top-notch service. The fifth floor is where to go for contemporary lines. The range of products in the beauty department is unparalleled, and shoppers can complete their look with highlights at the in-house John Barrett salon. If you need to refuel, grab a bite at the seventh-floor BG Restaurant, with Central Park views, or a quick bite at the beauty-level Good Dish. ⊠ *754 5th Ave., between 57th and 58th sts., Midtown East* ☎ *212/753-7300* ⊕ *www. bergdorfgoodman.com* Ⓜ *N, Q, R to 5th Ave./59th. St.*

Fodor's Choice
★
Bloomingdale's. Only a few stores in New York occupy an entire city block; the uptown branch of this New York institution is one of them. The main floor is a crazy, glittery maze of mirrored cosmetic counters and perfume-spraying salespeople. Once you get past this dizzying scene, you can find good buys on designer clothes, bedding, and housewares. ⊠ *1000 3rd Ave., main entrance at 59th St. and Lexington Ave., Midtown East* ☎ *212/705-2000* ⊕ *bloomingdales.com* Ⓜ *4, 5, 6 to 59th St.; N, Q, R to Lexington Ave./59th St.*

Henri Bendel. Behind the graceful Lalique windows, discover a world of luxe accessories, all from Henri Bendel's own collection. Work your way through two floors of jewelry, scarves, handbags, and sunglasses. If you really want to pamper yourself, visit Frédéric Fekkai's hair salon on the fourth floor. ⊠ *712 5th Ave., between 55th and 56th sts., Midtown East* ☎ *212/247-1100* ⊕ *www.henribendel.com* Ⓜ *E, M to 5th Ave./53rd St.*

Lord & Taylor. This is not your mother's Lord & Taylor. The department store has been working hard to attract a younger, hipper crowd. Shoppers find classic brands like Coach and Ralph Lauren along with skinny jeans from Seven for All Mankind and Trina Turk tops. Don't miss the lovely ground-floor beauty department. Best of all, it isn't nearly as crowded as competitor Macy's. ✉ *424 5th Ave., between 38th and 39th sts., Midtown East* ☎ *212/391–3344* ⊕ *www.lordandtaylor.com* Ⓜ *B, D, F, M, N, Q, R to 34th St.–Herald Sq.*

Saks Fifth Avenue. This iconic store has been upping its fashion stakes and revamping its résumé, by adding more contemporary lines such as Proenza Schouler and Victoria Beckham. The department store now has a designer sneaker shop, as well as an enormous Christian Louboutin shop-within-a-shop. The ground-floor beauty department stocks everything from the classics to the edgy. ✉ *611 5th Ave., between 49th and 50th sts., Midtown East* ☎ *212/753–4000* ⊕ *www.saksfifthavenue.com* Ⓜ *E, M to 5th Ave./53rd St.*

GIFTS AND SOUVENIRS

New York City Transit Museum Gift Shop. Located in the symbolic heart of New York City's transit system, the store features an eclectic array of merchandise all linked to the MTA (Metropolitan Transportation Authority), from straphanger ties to earrings made from old subway tokens. ✉ *Grand Central Terminal, Vanderbilt Pl. and 42nd St., Midtown East* ☎ *212/878–0106* ⊕ *www.transitmuseumstore.com* Ⓜ *4, 5, 6, 7, S to Grand Central–42nd St.*

HOME DECOR

Armani Casa. In keeping with the Armani aesthetic, the minimalist furniture and housewares here have a subdued color scheme (gold, gray, cream, and black). Big-ticket items include luxuriously upholstered sofas and sleek coffee tables. The desk accessories and throw pillows are equally understated. ✉ *Decoration & Design Building, 979 3rd Ave., Suite 1424, between 58th and 59th sts., Midtown East* ☎ *212/334–1271* ⊕ *www.armanicasa.com* Ⓜ *4, 5, 6 to 59th St.; N, Q, R to Lexington Ave./59th St.*

JEWELRY AND ACCESSORIES

Bulgari. This Italian company is certainly not shy about its name, which encircles gems, watch faces, and an ever-growing accessories line. There are beautiful, weighty rings and other pieces mixing gold with stainless steel, porcelain, and the brand's signature cabochon multicolored sapphires. Wedding and engagement rings are slightly more subdued. ✉ *730 5th Ave., at 57th St., Midtown East* ☎ *212/315–9000* ⊕ *www. bulgari.com* Ⓜ *N, Q, R to 5th Ave./59th St.*

Cartier. Established in 1914, this legendary French jeweler, and firm favorite among royals and celebrities, is the place to come for exquisite engagement rings, luxury watches, or cufflinks. Cartier's iconic designs include the panther motif, the Trinity ring, and Tank watches. ✉ *767 5th Ave., between 58th and 59th sts., Midtown East* ☎ *212/457–3202* ⊕ *www.cartier.com* Ⓜ *N, Q, R to 5th Ave./59th St..*

H. Stern. Sleek designs pose in an equally modern 5th Avenue setting; smooth cabochon-cut stones, most from South America, glow in pale wooden display cases. The designers make notable use of semiprecious stones such as citrine, tourmaline, and topaz. ✉ *645 5th Ave., between*

18

51st and 52nd sts., Midtown East ☎ *212/655–3910* ⊕ *www.hstern.net* Ⓜ *E, M to 5th Ave./53rd St.*

Harry Winston. These jewels regularly adorn celebs at the Oscars, and you need an A-list bank account to shop here. The ice-clear diamonds are of impeccable quality and set in everything from emerald-cut solitaire rings to wreath necklaces resembling strings of flowers. No wonder the jeweler was immortalized in the song "Diamonds Are a Girl's Best Friend." ⊠ *718 5th Ave., at 56th St., Midtown East* ☎ *212/399–1000* ⊕ *www.harrywinston.com* Ⓜ *F to 57th St.; N, Q, R to 5th Ave./59th St.*

Mikimoto. The Japanese originator of the cultured pearl, Mikimoto presents a glowing display of high-luster pearls. Besides the creamy strands from their own pearl farms, check out diamond-and-pearl earrings, bracelets, and rings. ⊠ *730 5th Ave., between 56th and 57th sts., Midtown East* ☎ *212/457–4600* ⊕ *www.mikimotoamerica.com* Ⓜ *F to 57th St.; N, Q, R to 5th Ave./59th St.*

Fodor'sChoice
★
Tiffany & Co. It's hard to think of a more iconic New York jewelry store than Tiffany, along with its unmistakable blue box. Daydream among the displays of platinum-and-diamond bracelets and massive engagement rings, but head to the sterling-silver floor for more affordable baubles. The new Tiffany T line is streamlined and modern. ⊠ *727 5th Ave., at 57th St., Midtown East* ☎ *212/755–8000* ⊕ *www.tiffany.com* Ⓜ *N, Q, R to 5th Ave./59th St.*

Van Cleef & Arpels. This French jewelry company is considerably more low-key than many of its blingy neighbors, in both design and marketing ethos (you won't see them opening a store in your average mall). Their best-known design is the cloverleaf Alhambra, which can be found on rings, necklaces, and earrings. ⊠ *744 5th Ave., between 57th and 58th sts., Midtown East* ☎ *212/644–9500* ⊕ *www.vancleef-arpels. com* Ⓜ *N, Q, R to 5th Ave./59th St.*

SHOES, HANDBAGS, AND LEATHER GOODS

Bally. If you want to channel your inner princess, you can't go wrong with the ladylike pumps and high-heeled boots here. The accessories and clothing are equally tasteful. ⊠ *628 Madison Ave., at 59th St., Midtown East* ☎ *212/751–9082* ⊕ *www.bally.com* Ⓜ *N, Q, R to 5th Ave./59th St.*

Bottega Veneta. The signature crosshatch weave graces leather handbags, slouchy satchels, and shoes; the especially satisfying brown shades extend from fawn to deep chocolate. The stylish men's and women's ready-to-wear collection is also sold here. ⊠ *699 5th Ave., between 54th and 55th sts., Midtown East* ☎ *212/371–5511* ⊕ *www.bottegaveneta. com* Ⓜ *4, 5, 6 to 59th St.; N, Q, R to Lexington Ave./59th St.; E, M to 5th Ave./53rd St.*

Cole Haan. This brand is known for its comfortable but stylish footwear—many shoes have Nike Air cushioning in the heel. Everything from sandals to boots and pumps is available. ⊠ *620 5th Ave., between 49th and 50th sts., Midtown East* ☎ *212/765–9747* ⊕ *www.colehaan. com* Ⓜ *E, M to 5th Ave./53rd St.*

Department Store Discounts

If you don't have one of these stores in the state where you live, take advantage of special discounts available by showing a state ID card.

Bloomingdale's: Go to the visitor center on the balcony level between the ground and second floors for a 10% discount on all purchases bought that day.

Lord & Taylor: Hit the ground-floor information desk to pick up a coupon for 15% off that day's purchases.

Macy's: Stop by the visitor center on the balcony level between the ground and second floors for a 10% discount voucher. The coupon is valid for five days for U.S. visitors and one month for international visitors.

Fendi. Once known for its furs, Fendi is now synonymous with decadent handbags. The purses are beaded, embroidered, and fantastically embellished within an inch of their lives. Buttery soft leathers, ladylike evening dresses, structured handbags, and other accessories are also available. ⊠ *677 5th Ave., between 53rd and 54th sts., Midtown East* ☎ *212/759–4646* ⊕ *www.fendi.com* Ⓜ *E, M to 5th Ave./53rd St.*

Fratelli Rossetti. Don't come here expecting sexy, skyscraper stilettos. This Italian leather goods company excels at classic shoes. Riding boots are among the most popular items, but there are also pumps, loafers, and slouchy ankle boots. Men can choose from oxfords and boots. There's also a line of leather handbags. ⊠ *625 Madison Ave., between E. 58th and E. 59th Sts., Midtown East* ☎ *212/888–5107* ⊕ *www. fratellirossetti.com* Ⓜ *N, R, Q, 5th Ave./59th St.; 4, 5, 6 to 59th St.*

Fodor's Choice **Louis Vuitton.** In the mammoth 57th Street flagship, shoppers get their
★ fill of LV-emblazoned handbags and accessories, as well as the more subtle Damier check pattern and colorful striated leathers. The clothes and shoes here are devastatingly chic. ⊠ *1 E. 57th St., at 5th Ave., Midtown East* ☎ *212/758–8877* ⊕ *www.louisvuitton.com* Ⓜ *N, Q, R to 5th Ave./59th St.*

Salvatore Ferragamo. Elegance and restraint typify these designs, from patent leather ballet flats to weekender ankle boots. The company rework some of their women's styles from previous decades, like the girlish Audrey (as in Hepburn) ballet flat, released seasonally for limited runs. Don't miss the silk ties for men. ⊠ *655 5th Ave., at 52nd St., Midtown East* ☎ *212/759–3822* ⊕ *www.ferragamo.com* Ⓜ *E, M to 5th Ave./53rd St.*

Stuart Weitzman. The broad range of styles, from wingtips to strappy sandals, is enhanced by an even wider range of sizes and widths. Bridal shoes are hugely popular, if pricey. ⊠ *625 Madison Ave., between 58th and 59th sts., Midtown East* ☎ *212/750–2555* ⊕ *www.stuartweitzman. com* Ⓜ *N, Q, R to 5th Ave./59th St.; 4, 5, 6 to 59th St.*

18

TOYS

American Girl Place. Grade school kids are crazy for American Girl dolls, whose line ranges from historically accurate characters to contemporary girls with all the accompanying clothes and accessories. Bring your doll here for a doll hairdressing station, café, and Dress Like Your Doll shop. ✉ *609 5th Ave., at 49th St., Midtown East* ☎ *212/371–2220* ⊕ *www. americangirl.com* Ⓜ *B, D, F, M to 47th–50th Sts./Rockefeller Center.*

MIDTOWN WEST

Whether you're window-shopping or have money to burn, Midtown West includes some of the best (and priciest) department stores, including Bergdorf Goodman and Henri Bendel.

CAMERAS AND ELECTRONICS

B&H Photo & Video. Low prices, good customer service, and a liberal returns policy make this a favorite with pros and amateurs alike looking for audio and video equipment, new cameras, or a laptop. Be sure to leave a few extra minutes for the checkout procedure; also, keep in mind that the store is closed Saturday. B&H is also known for its ceiling-height conveyor belt system to move packages. ✉ *420 9th Ave., between 33rd and 34th sts., Midtown West* ☎ *212/444–6615* ⊕ *www. bhphotovideo.com* Ⓜ *1, 2, 3, A, C, E to 34th St.–Penn Station.*

CLOTHING

Forever 21. The pounding music, plethora of jeggings, and graffiti-covered NYC taxicabs parked inside appeal to tween shoppers. But even if you are older than 21, there's still reason to shop here. This location, clocking in at a whopping 90,000 square feet, is crammed with supertrendy clothes that won't break the bank, such as slouchy sweaters, shirtdresses, and pouffy skirts. Menswear and children's clothes are also sold here, and the jewelry is surprisingly well done. There are several other locations in Manhattan, including Union Square. ✉ *1540 Broadway, between 45th and 46th sts., Midtown West* ☎ *212/302–0594* ⊕ *www.forever21.com* Ⓜ *N, Q, R to 49th St.*

Gap. Gap may be as ubiquitous as Starbucks, but it is still a go-to place for classic denim, khakis, and sweaters in a rainbow of colors as well as on-trend capsule collections from top designers. This flagship also carries GapBody, GapMaternity, GapKids, and babyGap. ✉ *60 W. 34th St., at Broadway, Midtown West* ☎ *212/760–1268* ⊕ *www.gap.com* Ⓜ *B, D, F, M, N, Q, R to 34th St.–Herald Sq.*

Norma Kamali. A fashion fixture from the 1980s has a thoroughly modern, though still '80s-influenced, line. Her luminously white store carries graphic bathing suits, Grecian-style draped dresses, and her signature poofy "sleeping-bag coats." The in-house Wellness Café sells olive oil–based beauty products. ✉ *11 W. 56th St., between 5th and 6th aves., Midtown West* ☎ *212/957–9797* ⊕ *shop.normakamali.com* Ⓜ *N, Q, R 5th Ave./59th St.*

DEPARTMENT STORES

Macy's. Macy's headquarters are in the midst of a multiyear renovation, and visitors can expect a glossier, grander look with acres of marble and new video screens. On both the cosmetics and clothing floors, the focus has been shifted to prestige brands such as Gucci jewelry and Kate Spade. There is over one million square feet of retail space, so it would be easy to spend an entire day shopping here. ✉ *Herald Sq., 151 W. 34th St., between 6th and 7th aves., Midtown West* ☎ *212/695–4400* ⊕ *www.macys.com* Ⓜ *B, D, F, M, N, Q, R to 34th St.–Herald Sq.*

FOOD AND TREATS

Morrell & Company. This high-end, sprawling wine shop also includes a wine bar and auction division. Come by for a free tasting or if money is no object, head to the rare wine vault. More than 100 fine wines are available by the glass at the store's café. ✉ *1 Rockefeller Plaza, at 49th St., Midtown West* ☎ *212/688–9370* ⊕ *morrellwine.com* Ⓜ *B, D, F, M to 47th–50th Sts./Rockefeller Center.*

HOME DECOR

Muji. If you're into simple, chic, cheap style, Muji will be your trifecta. The name of this Japanese import translates to "no brand," and indeed, you don't find logos plastered on the housewares or clothes. Instead, their hallmark is a streamlined, minimalist design. The whole range of goods, from milky porcelain teapots to wooden toys, is invariably user-friendly. ✉ *620 8th Ave., at 40th St., Midtown West* ☎ *212/382–2300* ⊕ *www.muji.us* Ⓜ *A, C, E to 42nd St.–Port Authority.*

JEWELRY AND ACCESSORIES

Skagen. Brave the crowds in Times Square to head to Skagen's flagship, which sells watches, handbags, and leather accessories inspired by Danish design. Many of the time pieces and satchels have a unisex design and are logo-free. ✉ *1585 Broadway, between 47th and 48th sts., Midtown West* ☎ *845/384–1221* ⊕ *www.skagen.com* Ⓜ *N, Q, R to 49th St.*

18

MUSEUM STORES

Museum of Arts and Design. This well-curated gift shop stocks crafts like beautiful handmade tableware, unusual jewelry, and rugs, often tied into ongoing exhibits. It's a great place to stock up on gifts. ✉ *2 Columbus Circle, at 8th Ave., Midtown West* ☎ *212/299–7700* ⊕ *thestore. madmuseum.org* Ⓜ *1, A, B, C, D to 59th St.–Columbus Circle.*

Museum of Modern Art Design and Book Store. The MoMA's in-house shop stocks a huge selection of art reproductions and gorgeous coffee-table books about painting, sculpture, film, and photography. Across the street is the MoMA Design Store, where you can find Charles and Ray Eames furniture reproductions, vases designed by Alvar Aalto, and lots of clever toys. ✉ *11 W. 53rd St., between 5th and 6th aves., Midtown West* ☎ *212/708–9700* ⊕ *www.moma.org/visit/plan/stores* Ⓜ *E, M to 5th Ave./53rd St.*

PERFORMING ARTS MEMORABILIA

Drama Book Shop. If you're looking for a script, be it a lesser-known Russian translation or Broadway hit, chances are you can find it here. The range of books spans film, music, dance, TV, and biographies. The shop also hosts Q&As with leading playwrights. ✉ *250 W. 40th St., between 7th and 8th aves., Midtown West* ☎ *212/944–0595* ⊕ *www. dramabookshop.com* Ⓜ *A, C, E to 42nd St.–Port Authority; 1, 2, 3, 7, N, Q, R, S to Times Sq.–42nd St.*

One Shubert Alley. This was the first store to sell Broadway merchandise outside of a theater. Today souvenir posters, tees, and other knickknacks memorializing past and present Broadway hits still reign at this Theater District shop. ⊠ *1 Shubert Alley, between 44th and 45th sts., Midtown West* ☎ *212/944–4133* Ⓜ *1, 2, 3, 7, N, Q, R, S to Times Sq.–42nd St.*

Triton Gallery. Theatrical posters both large and small are available, and the selection is democratic, with everything from Marlene Dietrich's *Blue Angel* to recent Broadway shows represented. ⊠ *The Film Center, 630 9th Ave., Suite 808, between 44th and 45th sts., Midtown West* ☎ *212/765–2472* ⊕ *www.tritongallery.com* Ⓜ *A, C, E to 42nd St.–Port Authority.*

SHOES, HANDBAGS, AND LEATHER GOODS

Manolo Blahnik. These sexy status shoes are some of the most expensive on the market. The signature look is a pointy toe with a high, delicate heel, but there are also ballet flats, gladiator sandals, and over-the-knee dominatrix boots that cost nearly $2,000. Pray for a sale. ⊠ *31 W. 54th St., between 5th and 6th aves., Midtown West* ☎ *212/582–3007* ⊕ *www.manoloblahnik.com* Ⓜ *E, M to 5th Ave./53rd St.*

Fodor's Choice ★   **Smythson of Bond Street.** Although Smythson still sells stationery fit for a queen—check out the royal warrant from England's HRH—it is also a place to scoop up on-trend handbags, iPad cases, and wallets. The hues range from sedate brown and black to eye-popping tangerine. The softbound leather diaries, address books, and travel accessories make ideal gifts. ⊠ *4 W. 57th St., between 5th and 6th aves., Midtown West* ☎ *212/265–4573* ⊕ *www.smythson.com* Ⓜ *F to 57th St.; N, Q, R to 5th Ave./59th St.*

TOYS

Toys "R" Us. The first thing that shoppers see when they walk into the Times Square megastore is a revolving 60-foot-high Ferris wheel. There's also a life-size T. Rex that roars and a 4,000-square-foot Barbie dollhouse. With all the movie tie-in merchandise, video games, yo-yos, stuffed animals, and what seems to be the entire Mattel oeuvre, good luck extracting your kids from here. ⊠ *1514 Broadway, at 44th St., Midtown West* ☎ *646/366–8800* ⊕ *www.toysrus.com* Ⓜ *1, 2, 3, 7, N, Q, R, S to Times Sq.–42nd St.*

THE UPPER EAST SIDE

This neighborhood is known for its antiques shops and high-end designers, such as Carolina Herrera, Oscar de la Renta, and Tom Ford. They are primarily sprinkled along Madison Avenue.

ANTIQUES AND COLLECTIBLES

Florian Papp. Established in 1900, this store has an unassailable reputation among knowledgeable collectors. Expect to find American and European antiques and paintings from the 18th to 20th century. Gilt mirrors, chandeliers, and mahogany tables abound. ⊠ *962 Madison Ave., between 75th and 76th sts., Upper East Side* ☎ *212/288–6770* ⊕ *www.florianpapp.com* Ⓜ *6 to 77th St.*

Cool Local Chains

New Yorkers in the know hit these fabulous local chains for unique frocks and the best of the city's one-stop shopping.

Ricky's. Loud and fun, these drugstores sprinkled around the city attract a young, eclectic crowd who come just as often for the crazy-color wigs as they do for Dove body wash and toothpaste. If you're feeling spendy, high-end haircare and makeup is also sold here. Every fall the stores turn into Halloween Central, with a huge assortment of costumes referencing everything from Avatar to Jersey Shore. ⊠ 375 Broadway, between White and Franklin sts., TriBeCa ☎ 212/925-5490 ⊕ www.rickysnyc.com Ⓜ 6, J, N, Q, R, Z to Canal St.

Scoop. If you want to look stylish without trying too hard, come here to stock up on jeans (Rag & Bone, Citizens of Humanity), slinky tops, vintage-looking tees, and cozy knits from designers like Stella McCartney, Theory, and Veronica Beard. Other locations in the city sell menswear. ⊠ 473–475 Broadway, between Broome and Grand sts., SoHo ☎ 212/925-3539 ⊕ www.scoopnyc.com Ⓜ 6 to Spring St.

Keno Auctions. Leigh Keno of *Antique Roadshow* fame presides over this auction house, which specializes in Americana. As expected, he has a good eye and an interesting inventory; he's sold silver sauceboats from Paul Revere, masterpiece paintings, and Chippendale furniture. ⊠ *127 E. 69th St., between Park and Lexington aves., Upper East Side* ☎ *212/734–2381* ⊕ *www.kenoauctions.com* Ⓜ *6 to 68th St.–Hunter College.*

BEAUTY

NARS. Women adore NARS for their iconic products such as Jungle Red Lipstick and multiuse sticks. The NARS flagship has glossy white walls and a red counter, and stocks the full NARS makeup range as well as a collection of "François' Favorite Things," which includes books, films, and photographs that have served as inspiration. ⊠ *971 Madison Ave., between 75th and 76th sts., Upper East Side* ☎ *212/861-2945* ⊕ *www.narscosmetics.com* Ⓜ *6 to 77th St.*

BOOKS AND STATIONERY

Crawford Doyle Booksellers. You're as likely to see an old edition of Wodehouse as a bestseller in the window of this shop. Bibliophiles find a high-quality selection of fiction, nonfiction, and biographies, plus some rare books on the balcony. Salespeople offer their opinions *and* ask for yours. ⊠ *1082 Madison Ave., between 81st and 82nd sts., Upper East Side* ☎ *212/288–6300* ⊕ *www.crawforddoyle.com* Ⓜ *4, 5, 6 to 86th St.*

CHILDREN'S CLOTHING

FAMILY **Bonpoint.** Celebrities love this French children's boutique for the beautiful designs and impeccable workmanship—think pony-hair baby booties and hand-embroidered jumpers and cashmere onesies. The flagship has a loftlike design with whimsical touches, such as a large indoor tree and a cloud sculpture. ⊠ *805 Madison Ave., between 67th and 68th*

18

sts., Upper East Side ☎ *212/879–0900* ⊕ *www.bonpoint.com* Ⓜ *6 to 68th St.–Hunter College.*

FAMILY **Infinity.** Prep-school girls and their mothers giggle and gossip over the tween clothes (with more than a few moms picking up T-shirts and jeans for themselves) with Les Tout Petits dresses, Juicy Couture jeans, and tees emblazoned with Justin Bieber. ✉ *1116 Madison Ave., at 83rd St., Upper East Side* ☎ *212/734–0077* Ⓜ *4, 5, 6 to 86th St.*

CLOTHING

Fodor's Choice ★ **Alexander McQueen.** The New York flagship of this iconic fashion designer is full of rich details like intricately patterned floors, and tiny architectural details meant to draw the eye, such as feathers in the molding. Now under the helm of Sarah Burton, this location sells menswear and womenswear, which lean towards edgy gothic. ✉ *747 Madison Ave., between 64th and 65th sts., Upper East Side* ☎ *212/645–1797* ⊕ *www.alexandermcqueen.com* Ⓜ *6 to 68th St.–Hunter College.*

Barbour. The signature look here is the company's waxed cotton and quilted jackets, available for men and women. The quilted jackets, tweeds, moleskin pants, lamb's-wool sweaters, and tattersall shirts invariably call up images of country rambles. ✉ *1047 Madison Ave., at 80th St., Upper East Side* ☎ *212/570–2600* ⊕ *www.barbour.com* Ⓜ *6 to 77th St.*

BCBG Max Azria. This brand's initials are short for "bon chic, bon genre,"which means stylish sportswear and embellished, embroidered evening dresses here. The collection ranges from leather pants to maxi dresses. ✉ *770 Madison Ave., at 66th St., Upper East Side* ☎ *212/717–4225* ⊕ *www.bcbg.com* Ⓜ *6 to 68th St.–Hunter College.*

Belstaff. Nearly a century old, this British brand specializes in motorcycle gear that has quite the pedigree—both Che Guevara and Steve McQueen have worn Belstaff. The relaunched company have expanded their collection to include luxury basics for men and women, including peacoats, waxed jackets, and body-hugging dresses with luxury touches like python and crocodile. ✉ *814 Madison Ave., between 68th and 69th sts., Upper East Side* ☎ *212/897–1880* ⊕ *www.belstaff.com* Ⓜ *6 to 68th St.–Hunter College.*

Bra Smyth. Chic and sexy underthings in soft cottons and silks line the shelves of this uptown staple. In addition to the selection of bridal-ready white bustiers and custom-fit swimsuits (made, cleverly, in bra-cup sizes), the store is best known for its knowledgeable staff, many of whom can give tips on proper fit and size you up on sight. Cup sizes run from AA to J. ✉ *905 Madison Ave., at 73rd St., Upper East Side* ☎ *212/772–9400* ⊕ *www.brasmyth.com* Ⓜ *6 to 68th St.–Hunter College.*

Calvin Klein. Though the namesake designer has bowed out, the label keeps channeling his particular style. This stark flagship store emphasizes the luxe end of the clothing line. Men's suits tend to be soft around the edges; women's evening gowns are often a fluid pouring of silk. There are also shoes, accessories, housewares, and makeup. ✉ *654 Madison Ave., at 60th St., Upper East Side* ☎ *212/292–9000* ⊕ *www.*

calvinklein.com Ⓜ *4, 5, 6 to 59th St.; N, Q, R to Lexington Ave./59th St.*

Calypso St. Barth. Catch an instant island-vacation vibe from Calypso's colorful women's wear, which includes caftans, tunics, and dangly jewelry. To complete the look, there are also boho housewares at the brand's New York flagship, which has a suitably beachy vibe (check out the shell chandeliers). There are multiple branches throughout the city with different themes, including an outlet on Broome Street. ✉ *900 Madison Ave., between 72nd and 73rd sts., Upper East Side* ☎ *212/535–4100* Ⓜ *6 to 77th St.*

Carolina Herrera. A favorite of the high-society set (and A-list celebs), Herrera's designs are ladylike and elegant. Her suits, gowns, and cocktail dresses in luxurious fabrics make for timeless silhouettes. ✉ *954 Madison Ave., at 75th St., Upper East Side* ☎ *212/249–6552* ⊕ *www.carolinaherrera.com* Ⓜ *6 to 77th St.*

Dolce & Gabbana. It's easy to feel like an Italian movie star amid these exuberant (in every sense) clothes. Corseted dresses are a favorite; the fabric could be sheer, furred, or leopard-print. Men's suits are slim and sharp. ✉ *825 Madison Ave., between 68th and 69th sts., Upper East Side* ☎ *212/249–4100* ⊕ *www.dolcegabbana.com* Ⓜ *6 to 68th St.–Hunter College.*

Judith & Charles. This Canadian import is an ideal place to shop for work clothes that have an edge (think shift dresses in bold stripes). The clothing here is separated by color and style, so it's easy to rifle through racks of blazers, office-appropriate dresses, and well-cut tees. ✉ *1355 3rd Ave., between 77th and 78th sts., Upper East Side* ☎ *212/988–4411* ⊕ *www.judithandcharles.com* Ⓜ *6 to 77th St.*

Juliette Longuet. This French-born designer's boutique is housed inside an elegant townhouse. Her designs combine the best of New York and Parisian chic; think leather leggings, chiffon blouses, and little black dresses. ✉ *153 E. 70th St., at Lexington Ave., Upper East Side* ☎ *646/360–3300* ⊕ *www.juliettelonguet.com* Ⓜ *6 to 68th St.–Hunter College.*

Fodor's Choice ★ **Kate Spade.** The new Kate Spade flagship is located in a townhouse, so it feels like shopping in a well-appointed home—albeit one with oversize chandeliers and glamorous custom rugs. The nearly 8,000-square-foot space contains every Kate Spade product, from clothing to shoes and beauty. ✉ *789 Madison Ave., between 65th and 66th sts., Upper East Side* ☎ *212/988–0259* ⊕ *www.katespade.com* Ⓜ *6 to 68th St.–Hunter College.*

Fodor's Choice ★ **Lanvin.** This French label has been around since 1889 and is the oldest French fashion house still in existence. With Alber Elbaz at the helm, Lanvin's signature look is fluid and sexy; think one-shouldered cocktail dresses, cigarette pants, and ruffled blouses. This elegant town house is the first U.S. outpost. The interior design itself is a showstopper; the three-story space oozes old money and glamour with its Art Deco chandeliers and soothing gray walls. And the clothes? Just as slinky. ✉ *815 Madison Ave., between 68th and 69th sts., Upper East Side* ☎ *646/439–0381* ⊕ *www.lanvin.com* Ⓜ *6 to 68th St.–Hunter College.*

18

La Perla. If money is no object, shop here for some of the sexiest underthings around. The collection includes lace sets, corsets, and exquisite bridal lingerie. ⊠ *803 Madison Ave., between 67th and 68th sts., Upper East Side* ☎ *212/570–0050* ⊕ *www.laperla.com* Ⓜ *6 to 68th St.–Hunter College.*

Lisa Perry. This designer takes an artist's approach in her gleaming white space. She has created dresses printed with famous Andy Warhol photographs, such as the image of him drowning in a Campbell's Soup can. Pop Art aside, her store is filled with a mix of '60s and '70s vintage clothes, as well as her own designs. ⊠ *988 Madison Ave., between 76th and 77th sts., Upper East Side* ☎ *212/431–7467* ⊕ *www.lisaperrystyle. com* Ⓜ *6 to 77th St.*

Fodor's Choice
★
Ludivine. Make a beeline for this store if you love French designers. Owner Ludivine Grégoire showcases of-the-moment Gallic (and a few Italian) designers like Vanessa Bruno, Jerome Dreyfuss, and Carvin. ⊠ *1216 Lexington Ave., between 82nd and 83rd sts., Upper East Side* ☎ *212/249–4053* ⊕ *www.boutiqueludivine.com* Ⓜ *4, 5, 6 to 86th St.*

Marina Rinaldi. If you are a curvy gal and want to celebrate your figure rather than hide it, shop here. Marina Rinaldi sells form-flattering knit dresses, wool trousers, and coats that are tasteful and luxurious. ⊠ *13 E. 69th St., between Madison and 5th aves., Upper East Side* ☎ *212/734–4333* ⊕ *www.marinarinaldi.com* Ⓜ *6 to 68th St.–Hunter College.*

Max Mara. Think subtle colors and classics in plush fabrics—pencil skirts in heathered wool, tuxedo-style evening jackets, and several choices of wool and cashmere camel overcoats. The suits are exquisitely tailored. ⊠ *813 Madison Ave., at 68th St., Upper East Side* ☎ *212/879–6100* ⊕ *www.maxmara.com* Ⓜ *6 to 68th St.–Hunter College.*

Michael Kors. This designer keeps rolling out boutiques in the city. This location, spread over two levels, showcases his clean-cut, American classic clothing and accessories. If you need fashion inspiration, images from his runway shows are screened on an 18-foot high television. ⊠ *667 Madison Ave., between E. 60th and E. 61st Sts., Midtown West* ☎ *212/980–1550* ⊕ *www.michaelkors.com* Ⓜ *N, Q, R to 5th Ave./59th St.*

Milly. These bright, cheerfully patterned clothes look as at home on the Upper East Side as they would in Palm Beach or Marrakech. At designer Michelle Smith's U.S. flagship, find flirty cocktail dresses, beach-ready maxis, and boldly patterned bathing suits. ⊠ *900 Madison Ave., between 72nd and 73rd sts., Upper East Side* ☎ *212/395–9100* ⊕ *www.millyny.com* Ⓜ *6 to 77th St.*

Morgane Le Fay. The clothes here have a dreamy, ethereal quality that is decidedly feminine. Silk gowns are fluid and soft, while blazers and coats are more tailored. Her dresses are also popular with brides who want a minimalist look. ⊠ *980 Madison Ave., between 76th and 77th sts., Upper East Side* ☎ *212/879–9700* ⊕ *www.morganelefay.com* Ⓜ *6 to 77th St.*

Oscar de la Renta. Come here for the ladylike but bold runway designs of this upper-crust favorite. Skirts swing, ruffles billow, embroidery brightens up tweed, and even a tennis dress looks like something you could go dancing in. ⊠ *772 Madison Ave., at 66th St., Upper East Side* ☎ *212/288–5810* ⊕ *www.oscardelarenta.com* Ⓜ *6 to 68th St.–Hunter College.*

Otte. This stylish mini-chain has outposts around the city, but the Upper East Side location has the biggest selection of clothing from on-trend designers such as Helmut Lang and Band of Outsiders, as well as its own line of clothing. If you want that nonchalant chic look, like a tailored cape thrown over skinny jeans, this is your place. ⊠ *1232 3rd Ave., between 71 and 72nd sts., Upper East Side* ☎ *212/744–4002* ⊕ *otteny. com* Ⓜ *6 to 68th St.–Hunter College.*

Fodor's Choice
★
Polo Ralph Lauren. Even if you can't afford the clothes, come just to soak up the luxe lifestyle. This women's flagship is housed in a 22,000-square-foot building built to look like a historic Beaux Arts mansion (or a small palace), complete with a curving marble staircase and stone floors. In addition to the complete women's collection, the brand's lingerie, homewares, and fine-jewelry and watch salon are here. ⊠ *888 Madison Ave., at 72nd St., Upper East Side* ☎ *212/434–8000* ⊕ *www.ralphlauren.com* Ⓜ *6 to 68th St.–Hunter College.*

Reed Krakoff. This former Coach creative director has branched out to launch his own luxury lifestyle store. The clothing has an edgy look, with little black dresses in heavy wool and massive cuff bracelets. The handbags and shoes, however, are more feminine. ⊠ *831 Madison Ave., between 69th and 70th sts., Upper East Side* ☎ *212/988–0560* ⊕ *www. reedkrakoff.com* Ⓜ *6 to 68th St.–Hunter College.*

Roberto Cavalli. Rockstar style (at rockstar prices) means clothing decked out with fur, feathers, and lots of sparkle. Animal prints are big in this temple to the over-the-top. ⊠ *711 Madison Ave., at 63rd St., Upper East Side* ☎ *212/755–7722* ⊕ *www.robertocavalli.com* Ⓜ *N, Q, R to 5th Ave./59th St.*

Tom Ford. Famous for revamping Gucci, Ford does not disappoint with his eponymous line. Women's stilettos and clutches are unabashedly sexy, while men's selections veer towards the traditional and are impeccably tailored. Shirts come in more than 300 hues, and off-the-rack suits start around $3,000. His Black Orchid unisex fragrance is a cult favorite. ⊠ *845 Madison Ave., at 70th St., Upper East Side* ☎ *212/359–0300* ⊕ *www.tomford.com* Ⓜ *6 to 68th St.–Hunter College.*

Tomas Maier. The creative director of luxury Italian company Bottega Veneta now has an eponymous store in Manhattan. The elegant, wood-floored space showcases Tomas Maier's understated clothing for men and women as well as jewelry and home goods, such as candles. Best bets include classic black dresses and structured handbags. ⊠ *956 Madison Ave., between 75th and 76th sts., Upper East Side* ☎ *212/988–8686* ⊕ *www.tomasmaier.com* Ⓜ *6 to 77th St.*

Tory Burch. The global flagship of this preppy boho label is housed in an elegantly restored townhouse. The five-story space features Tory Burch's signature orange lacquer walls, purple curtains, and gold hardware. If

18

you already own her iconic ballet flats, browse through the ready-to-wear collection, handbags, shoes, and jewelry. ✉ *797 Madison Ave., between 67th and 68th sts., Upper East Side* ☎ *212/510–8371* ⊕ *www.toryburch.com* Ⓜ *6 to 68th St.–Hunter College.*

Valentino. No one does a better red than Valentino, and the mix here at this four-story townhouse is at once audacious and beautifully cut; the fur or feather trimmings, low necklines, and opulent fabrics are about as close as you can get to celluloid glamour. Big spenders can request the VIP suite. ✉ *821 Madison Ave., between 68th and 69th sts., Upper East Side* ☎ *212/772–6969* ⊕ *www.valentino.com* Ⓜ *6 to 68th St.–Hunter College.*

Vera Wang Bride. This star wedding-dress designer churns out dreamy dresses that are sophisticated without being over-the-top. Choose from A-line and princess styles, and slinky sheaths. If money is no object, bespoke wedding dresses are available. An appointments is essential. ✉ *991 Madison Ave., at 77th St., Upper East Side* ☎ *212/628–3400* ⊕ *www.verawang.com* Ⓜ *6 to 77th St.*

Vilebrequin. Allow St-Tropez to influence your swimsuit; these striped, floral, and solid-color French-made trunks come in sunny hues as well as matching boys' styles. Waterproof pocket inserts keep your essentials safe from beachcombers. The company now has a women's line as well. ✉ *1007 Madison Ave., between 77th and 78th sts., Upper East Side* ☎ *212/650–0353* ⊕ *us.vilebrequin.com* Ⓜ *6 to 77th St.*

DEPARTMENT STORES

Barneys New York. This luxury boutique continues to provide fashion-conscious and big-budget shoppers with irresistible, must-have items at its uptown flagship store. The extensive menswear selection has a handful of edgier designers, though made-to-measure is always an option. The women's department showcases posh designers of all stripes, from the subdued lines of Armani and Nina Ricci to the irrepressible Alaïa and Zac Posen. The shoe selection trots out Prada boots and strappy Blahniks; the cosmetics department keeps you in Kiehl's, Sue Devitt, and Chantecaille; jewelry runs from the whimsical (Jennifer Meyer) to the classic (Ileana Makri). ✉ *660 Madison Ave., between 60th and 61st sts., Upper East Side* ☎ *212/826–8900* ⊕ *www.barneys.com* Ⓜ *4, 5, 6 to 59th St.; N, Q, R to Lexington Ave./59th St.*

Fodor'sChoice
★

Fivestory. This luxurious mini department store, located inside a townhouse, carries clothing, accessories, shoes, and home décor for men, women, and children in an elegant setting (think marble floors and lots of velvet and silk). It specializes in independent designers but also showcases designs from heavy-hitters such as Jason Wu and Lanvin. ✉ *18 E. 69th St., between 5th and Madison aves., Upper East Side* ☎ *212/288–1338* ⊕ *www.fivestoryny.com* Ⓜ *6 to 68th St.–Hunter College.*

FOOD AND TREATS

FP Patisserie. Famed French patissier François Payard has multiple boutiques around the city but this location is the flagship. Chocolates, pastries, and macarons are displayed like jewels in glass cases. If you need to calm the sugar rush, there's a small dining area serving dishes like croque-monsieur. ⊠ *1293 3rd Ave., between 74th and 75th sts., Upper East* ☎ *212/717–5252* ⊕ *www.payard.com* Ⓜ *6 to 77th St.*

Fodor's Choice
★ **La Maison du Chocolat.** Stop in at this chocolatier's small tea salon to dive into a cup of thick, heavenly hot chocolate. The Paris-based outfit sells handmade truffles, chocolates, and pastries that could lull you into a chocolate stupor. ⊠ *1018 Madison Ave., between 78th and 79th sts., Upper East Side* ☎ *212/744–7117* ⊕ *www.lamaisonduchocolat. com* Ⓜ *6 to 77th St.*

HOME DECOR

Fodor's Choice
★ **Ankasa.** Owners Sachin and Babi Ahluwalia used to source textiles for luxury designers like Oscar de la Renta. Now they are using that same design sensibility to produce a gorgeous line of housewares, womenswear and accessories, which are globally inspired. The embroidery is exquisite. ⊠ *1200 Madison Ave., between 87th and 88th sts., Upper East Side* ☎ *212/996–5200* ⊕ *www.ankasa.com* Ⓜ *4, 5, 6 to 86th St.*

JEWELRY AND ACCESSORIES

Asprey. This luxury retailer's claim to fame is jewelry; its own eponymous diamond cut has A-shape facets but this British brand caters to all tastes. Everything from leather goods and rare books to polo equipment and scarves is available. ⊠ *853 Madison Ave., between 70th and 71st sts., Upper East Side* ☎ *212/688–1811* ⊕ *www.asprey.com* Ⓜ *6 to 68th St.–Hunter College.*

Fred Leighton. If you're in the market for vintage diamonds, this is the place, whether your taste is for tiaras, Art Deco settings, or sparklers once worn by a Vanderbilt. The skinny, stackable diamond eternity bands are hugely popular. ⊠ *773 Madison Ave., at 66th St., Upper East Side* ☎ *212/288–1872* ⊕ *www.fredleighton.com* Ⓜ *6 to 68th St.– Hunter College.*

18

MUSEUM STORES

Fodor's Choice
★ **Cooper Hewitt, Smithsonian Design Museum.** Prowl the shelves here for intriguing urban oddments and ornaments, like sculptural tableware, Alexander Girard dolls, housewares by Alessi and Japanese notebooks by Postalco. ⊠ *2 E. 91st St., at 5th Ave., Upper East Side* ☎ *212/849– 8400* ⊕ *www.cooperhewitt.org* Ⓜ *4, 5, 6 to 86th St.*

Metropolitan Museum of Art Shop. This sprawling shop has a phenomenal book selection, as well as posters, Japanese print note cards and decorative pillows covered in William Morris prints. Reproductions of statuettes and other objets d'art fill the gleaming cases in every branch. Don't miss the jewelry selection, with its Byzantine- and Egyptian-inspired baubles. ⊠ *1000 5th Ave., at 82nd St., Upper East Side* ☎ *212/570– 3894* ⊕ *store.metmuseum.org* Ⓜ *4, 5, 6 to 86th St.*

Museum of the City of New York. Satisfy your curiosity about New York City's past, present, or future with the terrific selection of books, cards, toys, and photography posters. ⊠ *1220 5th Ave., at 103rd St., Upper East Side* ☎ *212/534–1672* ⊕ *www.mcny.org* Ⓜ *6 to 103rd St.*

Neue Galerie. Like the museum, the in-house bookshop and design store focuses on German, Austrian, and Central European art. Everything from children's toys to accessories and home décor is available here. ✉ *1048 5th Ave., between 85th and 86th sts., Upper East Side* ☎ *212/628–6200* ⊕ *www.neuegalerie.org* Ⓜ *4, 5, 6 to 86th St.*

SHOES, HANDBAGS, AND LEATHER GOODS

Anya Hindmarch. Although arguably most famous for her "I'm Not a Plastic Bag" tote, Hindmarch's real standouts are buttery leather shoulder bags and hobos, which are decidely understated. Her designs run the gamut from cheeky to ladylike. Leather goods can be embossed with monograms, entire sentences, or a sketch. ✉ *795 Madison Ave., between 67th and 68th sts., Upper East Side* ☎ *646/852–6233* ⊕ *www. anyahindmarch.com* Ⓜ *6 to 68th St.–Hunter College.*

Fodor's Choice ★   **Charlotte Olympia.** The Art Deco–inspired space at this British shoe store showcases very sexy and expensive stilettos, pumps, and flats. Accessories such as shoulder bags and clutches are also available. ✉ *22 E. 65th St., at Madison Ave., Upper East Side* ☎ *212/744–1842* ⊕ *www. charlotteolympia.com* Ⓜ *6 to 68th St.–Hunter College.*

Christian Louboutin. Lipstick-red soles are the signature of Louboutin's delicately sexy couture slippers and stilettos, and his pointy-toe creations come trimmed with beads, buttons, or "tattoos." ✉ *965 Madison Ave., between 75th and 76th sts., Upper East Side* ☎ *212/396–1884* ⊕ *www.christianlouboutin.com* Ⓜ *6 to 77th St.*

Church's English Shoes. Beloved by bankers and lawyers, these shoes are of indisputable quality. You could choose something highly polished for an embassy dinner, a classic penny loafer, or a suede ankle boot for a country weekend. ✉ *689 Madison Ave., at 62nd St., Upper East Side* ☎ *212/758–5200* ⊕ *www.church-footwear.com* Ⓜ *N, Q, R to 5th Ave./59th St.; F to Lexington Ave./63rd St.*

Devi Kroell. You may have spotted her snakeskin hobo on celebs such as Halle Berry and Ashley Olsen. This serene space is a perfect backdrop for the designer's luxury handbags and shoes, which are crafted from premium leather. Roomy shoulder bags come in python and calf leather, and evening bags have a touch of sparkle. There's also a selection of jewelry and scarves. ✉ *717 Madison Ave., between 63rd and 64th sts., Upper East Side* ☎ *212/644–4499* ⊕ *www.devikroell.com* Ⓜ *N, Q, R to 5th Ave./59th St.*

Hermès. This legendary French retailer is best known for its iconic handbags, the Kelly and the Birkin, named for Grace Kelly and Jane Birkin, as well as its silk scarves and neckties. True to its roots, Hermès still stocks saddles and other equestrian items in addition to a line of beautifully simple separates. ✉ *691 Madison Ave., at 62nd St., Upper East Side* ☎ *212/751–3181* ⊕ *www.hermes.com* Ⓜ *N, Q, R to 5th Ave./59th St.; F to Lexington Ave./63rd St.*

Jimmy Choo. Pointy toes, low vamps, narrow heels, ankle-wrapping straps—these British-made shoes are sometimes more comfortable than they look. ✉ *716 Madison Ave., between 63rd and 64th sts., Upper East Side* ☎ *212/759–7078* ⊕ *www.jimmychoo.com* Ⓜ *F to Lexington Ave./63rd St.*

Fodor's Choice ★   **Jack Rogers.** This brand, beloved by prepsters everywhere, is most famous for its Navajo sandal, worn by Jackie Onassis. You can still buy the

Navajo at the Jack Rogers flagship store, as well as other footwear like ballet pumps, boots, and wedges. ⊠ *1198 Madison Ave., between 87th and 88th sts., Upper East Side* ☎ *212/259–0588* ⊕ *www.jackrogersusa. com* Ⓜ *4, 5, 6 to 86th St.*

John Lobb. If you truly want to be well-heeled, pick up a pair of these luxury shoes, whose prices start at around $1,200. Owned by Hermès, John Lobb offers classic styles such as oxfords, loafers, boots, and slippers. ⊠ *800 Madison Ave., between 67th and 68th sts., Upper East Side* ☎ *212/888–9797* ⊕ *www.johnlobb.com* Ⓜ *6 to 68th St.–Hunter College.*

Robert Clergerie. Although best known for its chunky, comfy wedges, this French brand is not without its sense of fun. The sandal selection includes beaded starfish shapes, and for winter, the ankle boots have killer heels but the soles are padded. ⊠ *19 E. 62nd St., between 5th and Madison aves., Upper East Side* ☎ *212/207–8600* ⊕ *www. robertclergerie.com* Ⓜ *N, Q, R to 5th Ave./59th St.; F to Lexington Ave./63rd St.*

Tod's. These coveted driving moccasins, loafers, and boots are the top choice for jet-setters who prefer low-key, logo-free, luxury goods. Though most of the women's selection is made up of low-heel or flat styles, an increasing number of high heels are bent on driving sales, rather than cars. The handbags feature the same fine craftsmanship. ⊠ *650 Madison Ave., near 60th St., Upper East Side* ☎ *212/644–5945* ⊕ *www.tods.com* Ⓜ *N, Q, R to 5th Ave./59th St.*

THE UPPER WEST SIDE

18

Although largely a residential neighborhood, the Upper West Side has some excellent food (Zabar's) as well as smaller boutiques.

BOOKS AND STATIONERY

Westsider Books & Westsider Records. This wonderfully crammed space is a lifesaver on the Upper West Side. Squeeze in among the stacks of art books and fiction, or pop outside for the $1 bargains. Don't miss the rare book collection. ⊠ *2246 Broadway, between 80th and 81st sts., Upper West Side* ☎ *212/362–0706* ⊕ *www.westsiderbooks.com* Ⓜ *1 to 79th St.*

CAMERAS AND ELECTRONICS

Apple Store. Branch location at 1981 Broadway. *See Midtown East for full review.*

CHILDREN'S CLOTHING

FAMILY **A Time for Children.** When you shop at this funky boutique, you'll also be doing some good, as 100% of the profits go to the Children's Aid Society. Choose from toys, books, and clothing, which include classic brands such as Petit Bateau as well as graphic-print footed PJs. ⊠ *506 Amsterdam Ave., between 84th and 85th sts., Upper West Side* ☎ *212/580–8202* ⊕ *www.atimeforchildren.org* Ⓜ *1 to 86th St.*

CLOTHING

BOC. Who needs to go downtown for cutting-edge designers? This store stocks sleek designs from Ulla Johnson, Destin, and A.L.C. The selection of bags, shoes, and jewelry is just as stylish. ✉ *410 Columbus Ave., between 79th and 80th sts., Upper West Side* ☎ *212/799–1567* ⊕ *www.bocnyc.com* Ⓜ *1 to 79th St.; B, C, to 81st St.–Museum of Natural History.*

Fodor'sChoice ★ **Intermix.** Whether you're looking for the perfect daytime dress, a pair of J Brand jeans, or a puffer coat that doesn't make you look like the Michelin man, Intermix sells a well-curated assortment of emerging and established designers. Expect to see designs from DVF, Rag & Bone, and Missoni. There are a number of locations in the city. ✉ *210 Columbus Ave., between 69th and 70th sts., Upper West Side* ☎ *212/769–9116* ⊕ *www.intermixonline.com* Ⓜ *1, 2, 3, B, C to 72nd St.*

Mint. Trendy pieces that don't break the bank are what Mint is all about. The collection includes Alice & Olivia, Susana Monaco, and Joe's Jeans. The walls are painted, of course, in mint. ✉ *448 Columbus Ave., between 81st and 82nd sts., Upper West Side* ☎ *212/362–6250* ⊕ *www.shopmint.com* Ⓜ *1 to 79th St.; B, C to 81st St.–Museum of Natural History.*

Pachute. This cozy boutique, which means "simple" in Hebrew, specializes in stylish casual wear. If your weekend uniform consists of button-down shirts, understated jewelry, and espadrilles, then make a beeline here. ✉ *57 W. 84th St. , between Columbus Ave. and Central Park W, Upper West Side* ☎ *212/501–9400* ⊕ *www.pachute.com* Ⓜ *B, C to 86th St.*

FOOD AND TREATS

Le Palais des Thés. If you prefer a mellower caffeine kick, come to this French-owned tea boutique. All varieties of black and green teas are available as well as rarer leaves and globally inspired blends, such as a Turkish hammam flavor that includes roses and dates. The box sets and canisters make excellent gifts. ✉ *194 Columbus Ave., at 69th St., Upper West Side* ☎ *646/664–1902* ⊕ *www.palaisdesthes.com* Ⓜ *1 to 66th St.–Lincoln Center; B, C to 72nd St.*

Zabar's. When it comes to authentic New York food, it's hard to beat rugelach, bagels, or lox from this favorite specialty food emporium. ✉ *2245 Broadway, at 80th St., Upper West Side* ☎ *212/787–2000* ⊕ *www.zabars.com* Ⓜ *1 to 79th St.*

SHOES, HANDBAGS, AND LEATHER GOODS

Fodor'sChoice ★ **Tani.** Fashionable Upper West Side ladies love this shoe store for its huge selection and patient staff. Tani's selection is mostly classic-with-a-twist, and shoppers find brands that are more cool than sexy, such as Doc Martens and Camper. ✉ *2020 Broadway, between 69th and 70th sts., Upper West Side* ☎ *212/873–4361* Ⓜ *1, 2, 3 to 72nd St.*

NIGHTLIFE

Updated by
Jessica Colley

New Yorkers are fond of the "work hard, play hard" maxim, but the truth is, Gothamites don't need much of an excuse to hit the town. Monday is the new Thursday, which replaced Friday and Saturday, but it doesn't matter: the bottom line is that there's always plenty to do in this 24-hour city. Whether it's raising a glass in a divey 1930's saloon, a gay sports bar, the latest dimly lit cocktail den, or a swanky rooftop lounge; checking out the latest band, or laughing it up at a comedy show, it isn't hard for visitors to get a piece of the action.

The nightlife scene still resides largely downtown—in the dives of the East Village and Lower East Side, the classic jazz joints of the West Village, and the Meatpacking District's and Chelsea's "see-and-be-seen" clubs. Midtown, especially around Hell's Kitchen, has developed a vibrant scene, too, and plenty of preppy hangouts dot the Upper East and Upper West sides. Brooklyn, especially Williamsburg, is the destination for hipsters.

Keep in mind that *when* you go is just as important as *where* you go. A club that is packed at 11 pm might empty out by midnight, and a bar that raged last night may be completely empty tonight. *Paper* magazine has a good list of roving parties. You can check their online nightlife guide, *PM*, via their website (⊕ *www.papermag.com*). Another streetwise mag, the *L Magazine* (⊕ *www.thelmagazine.com*), lists what's happening at many of the city's lounges and clubs, as well as dance and comedy performances. Scour industry-centric websites, too, like *Eater* and *Grub Street,* which catalog the comings and goings of many a nightlife impresario. The *New York Times* has listings of cabaret and jazz shows, most comprehensively in their Friday and Sunday Arts sections. Bear in mind that a venue's life span is often measured in months, not years. Phone ahead or check online to make sure your target hasn't closed or turned into a polka hall (although, you never know—that could be fun, too).

LOWER MANHATTAN

FINANCIAL DISTRICT

BARS

Fodor's Choice ★ **The Dead Rabbit.** For exquisite cocktails without the dress code or pretentious door policy typical of some New York cocktail dens, venture to the tip of Manhattan for a night of Irish hospitality in a 19th-century-inspired saloon. The ground-floor taproom serves craft beers and whiskeys of the world, while the upstairs parlor shakes and stirs craft cocktails, many utilizing Irish whiskey—accompanied by ragtime music played live on the piano. ⊠ *30 Water St., Financial District* ☎ *646/422–7906* ⊕ *www.deadrabbitnyc.com* Ⓜ *1 to South Ferry; R to Whitehall St.*

TRIBECA

BARS

B-flat. The design is red-on-red here, and the Asian-style cocktails are particularly groovy (literally—one, with citrusy Japanese yuzu juice and vodka, has been dubbed the Groovy) at this Japan-meets-'50s-America lounge. Listen to live jazz while nibbling on American and Japanese-inflected treats. ⊠ *277 Church St., between Franklin and White sts., TriBeCa* ☎ *212/219–2970* ⊕ *www.bflat.info* Ⓜ *1 to Franklin St.; 6, A, C, E, J, N, Q, R, Z to Canal St.*

Brandy Library. Alas, the only book in this exquisite, wood-paneled room is the leather-bound menu listing hundreds of brandies and single-malt scotches. The bottles are on gorgeous backlighted "bookshelves," though, and you can learn what makes each of them special by chatting with the spirit sommelier—or by attending the twice-weekly Spirit School tasting classes. ⊠ *25 N. Moore St., between Varick and Hudson sts., TriBeCa* ☎ *212/226–5545* ⊕ *www.brandylibrary.com* Ⓜ *1 to Franklin St.; A, C, E to Canal St.*

M1-5. For the more bohemian of TriBeCa pubgoers, this lipstick-red, high-ceiling spot is a vast playground (as in, billiards and darts). There is a reggae jukebox, huge screens for sports, live shows, and DJ nights on the weekends—all without a pesky cover charge. Extra points, too, for the bar's name, which cites TriBeCa's warehouse zoning law. ⊠ *52 Walker St., between Broadway and Church St., TriBeCa* ☎ *212/965–1701* ⊕ *www.m1-5.com* Ⓜ *6, A, C, E J, N, Q, R, Z to Canal St.*

Smith and Mills. Attractive scenesters frolic at this tiny gem of a gin mill, where mixologists who resemble Daniel Day-Lewis dispense elixirs (and caviar) from a bar hung with pots and pans. There are cozy table-nooks for couples, and while the food is worth a visit, many locals come here late when a cocktail craving hits. ⊠ *71 N. Moore St., between Hudson and Greenwich sts., TriBeCa* ☎ *212/226–2515* ⊕ *www.smithandmills. com* Ⓜ *1 to Franklin St.*

Terroir Wine Bar. If the tag line—the Elitist Wine Bar for Everyone—isn't enough to get you in the door, the extensive wine list, including options by the glass, bottle, or adorable 3-ounce "taste" should do the

19

trick. This low-lit neighborhood wine bar is easy to walk right by on charming Harrison Street, but once inside you find seats at the bar for wine-centric conversations with the sharp staff, or more private nooks for a romantic evening of wine and cheese. ⊠ *24 Harrison St., TriBeCa* ☎ *212/625–9463* ⊕ *wineisterroir.com/tribeca* Ⓜ *1 to Franklin St.*

Ward III. You can get a solid Negroni or Manhattan at this exposed-brick watering hole, but where the bar really shines is in its bespoke cocktails. Fight for a seat at the bar if possible to watch the sharply clad mixologists whip up house specialties, or simply give them a few descriptive words ("spirit-forward," "something with bourbon," "light and refreshing") and let them create a cocktail on the spot to match your thirst. ⊠ *111 Reade St., between West Broadway and Church St., TriBeCa* ☎ *212/240–9194* ⊕ *www.ward3.com* Ⓜ *1, 2, 3 to Chambers St.*

Warren 77. Exposed brick walls, Dr. John on the jukebox, framed sports portraits on the wall, a dark setting that seems to glow, and the biggest, chunkiest banquettes in the whole wide world (or at least south of Canal Street) distinguish this TriBeCa beatnik boîte, co-owned by ice hockey god Sean Avery. ⊠ *77 Warren St., between West Broadway and Greenwich St., TriBeCa* ☎ *212/227–8994* ⊕ *www.warren77nyc.com* Ⓜ *1, 2, 3 to Chambers St.*

DANCE CLUBS AND DJ VENUES

Santos Party House. "Now *this* is what I call a dance club," says Arthur Baker, the legendary DJ (and legendary record producer), about this glorious downtown dance club, where the velvet ropes part for everyone. Co-owned by rocker Andrew W. K., the bilevel Santos ain't fancy, but that's the point, and the customers are as eclectic (everybody from punks to Upper East Siders) as the DJs, including Mr. Baker, who flies in regularly from London. Hence the musical vibe—underground dance, mostly—is simply kaleidoscopic. ⊠ *96 Lafayette St., between White and Walker sts., TriBeCa* ☎ *212/584–5492* ⊕ *www.santospartyhouse.com* Ⓜ *6, J, N, Q, R, Z to Canal St.*

CHINATOWN, NOHO, NOLITA, AND SOHO

CHINATOWN

BARS

Apotheke. Tucked away down a winding lane deep in Chinatown, this cocktail apothecary is a surprising find in a neighborhood known more for soup dumplings than creative tipples. Influenced by the 19th-century absinthe parlors of Paris, this historically inflected spot is all about drama and presentation. Think more chemistry lab than traditional bar—the results are not only delicious, but a feast for the eyes. ⊠ *9 Doyers St.* ☎ *212/406–0400* ⊕ *www.apothekenyc.com* Ⓜ *6, J, N, Q, R, Z to Canal St.; 4, 5, 6 to Brooklyn Bridge–City Hall.*

NOHO

BARS

Madam Geneva. Adjacent to the stylish and packed restaurant Saxon + Parole, this gin den is named after the 18th-century English term for the clear spirit. The brick-lined, dimly lit bar and lounge is a natural spillover space after dinner next door; you can also nibble on Asian-inspired snacks here (from the same kitchen). The crowd is thirsty, polished, and often on the prowl. There's a DJ on weekends. ⊠ *4 Bleecker St.* ☎ *212/254–0350* ⊕ *www.madamgeneva-nyc.com* Ⓜ *6 to Bleecker St.; F to 2nd Ave.; B, D, F, M to Broadway–Lafayette St.*

NOLITA

BARS

Sweet and Vicious. The name of this unpretentious butterfly-logo lounge doesn't signify the looks (sweet) and attitude (vicious) of certain downtown pretty things that frequent the bars on this stretch. So what makes this bar in particular so sweet? A lovely back garden that's more private than the sceney bars they might otherwise hit in SoHo and NoLIta. ⊠ *5 Spring St., between the Bowery and Elizabeth St., NoLIta* ☎ *212/334–7915* ⊕ *www.sweetandviciousnyc.com* Ⓜ *6 to Spring St.; J, Z to Bowery.*

SOHO

BARS

City Winery. Is it the city's most creative wine bar? Or its most impressive concert space? Both, actually. Pairing killer music (Nick Lowe, Shawn Colvin, War, Los Lobos) with unique events (Klezmer Breakfast, Cheese Brunch, tours of its in-house winery, special "Vinofile" memberships, and a Twitter wine-tasting party called Spit and Twit), the City Winery has ample room for customers with "good taste" in every sense of the term. ⊠ *155 Varick St., at Vandam St., SoHo* ☎ *212/608–0555* ⊕ *www.citywinery.com* Ⓜ *1 to Houston St.*

Ear Inn. Since the early 1800s this sturdy old New York classic (at one time also a bordello) has been packing in, and amiably spooking, customers. According to legend, the place is haunted by a randy ghost, so beware—that hand you feel in your lap might not be your lover's. This hardly scares away patrons—in fact, it may be a selling point (the staff encourage you to report all sightings). ⊠ *326 Spring St., between Greenwich and Washington sts., SoHo* ☎ *212/226–9060* ⊕ *www.earinn.com* Ⓜ *1 to Houston St.; C, E to Spring St.*

Fanelli's. Linger over the *New York Times* at this terrific neighborhood bar and restaurant, which is pretty down-to-earth for a SoHo landmark that's been serving drinks (and solid cuisine—dig those burgers!) since 1847. Check out the hilarious old-timey photos on the walls, too. ⊠ *94 Prince St., at Mercer St., SoHo* ☎ *212/226–9412* Ⓜ *N, R to Prince St.; B, D, F, M to Broadway–Lafayette St.*

Jimmy. Located on the 18th floor of the trendy James Hotel, Jimmy is a rooftop bar with stellar views. Sit in a corner nook for Empire State Building vistas, or head toward the outdoor pool area to survey the bridges over the East River. Cocktails are a highlight, featuring seasonal ingredients and novelties like ice cubes made from cinnamon water.

19

✉ *15 Thompson St., at Grand St., SoHo* ☎ *212/201–9118* ⊕ *www. jimmysoho.com* Ⓜ *C, E to Spring St.; 1 to Canal St.*

La Compagnie des Vins Surnaturels. Cheese, charcuterie, and chocolate are all temptations at this cozy wine bar, lined with exposed-brick walls and shelves stocked with wine (the complete list is over 600 bottles). This is the dimly lit sister property of a bar of the same name in Paris; the wine list leans heavily toward French options. ✉ *249 Centre St.* ☎ *212/343–3660* ⊕ *www.compagnienyc.com* Ⓜ *6 to Spring St.*

Pegu Club. Modeled after an officers' club in Myanmar, the Pegu manages to feel expansive and calm even when packed. The well-dressed and flirtatious come here partly for the exotically lovely surroundings, but primarily for the cocktails, which are innovative, prepared with superlative ingredients, and predictably pricey. ✉ *77 W. Houston St., 2nd fl., between West Broadway and Wooster St., SoHo* ☎ *212/473–7348* ⊕ *www.peguclub.com* Ⓜ *B, D, F, M to Broadway–Lafayette St.; 6 to Bleecker St.*

Fodor'sChoice ★ **Pravda.** This Russian retreat has more than 70 different vodkas, including 10 house-infused flavors, which means the choices of martini is nearly endless. The speakeasy feel of this underground spot is comfortable enough to spend the entire night, and Russian-inspired nibbles including caviar with blini provide longevity to try yet another vodka variation, from cucumber-dill to ginger-infused flavors. ✉ *281 Lafayette St., between Houston and Prince sts., SoHo* ☎ *212/226–4944* ⊕ *www.pravdany.com* Ⓜ *N, R to Prince St.; B, D, F, M to Broadway–Lafayette St.*

EAST VILLAGE AND LOWER EAST SIDE

EAST VILLAGE
BARS

Beauty Bar. Grab a seat in a barber chair or under a dryer at this made-over hair salon where, during happy hour, the manicurist will do your nails for a fee that includes a drink. (How's that for multitasking?) The DJ spins everything from Britpop to rock—a great soundtrack for primping. ✉ *231 E. 14th St., between 2nd and 3rd aves., East Village* ☎ *212/539–1389* ⊕ *www.thebeautybar.com/New_York* Ⓜ *4, 5, 6, L, N, Q, R to 14th St.–Union Sq.*

Death + Company. Theater behind the bar, inventive cocktails, and decadent bar bites bring thirsty New Yorkers to the sister lounge of the equally imaginative and classy nearby bar Mayahuel. Check out the hilarious wall mural toward the rear, setting the tone for the tongue-and-cheek satanic vibe of this watering hole. ✉ *433 E. 6th St., between 1st Ave. and Ave. A, East Village* ☎ *212/388–0882* ⊕ *www. deathandcompany.com* Ⓜ *F to 2nd Ave., 6 to Astor Pl.*

Fodor'sChoice ★ **Mayahuel.** The Agave goddess is behind the name of this cocktail den, where all manner of Aztec spirits (raspberry tea–infused tequila, pineapple-infused mescal) make for the fiendishly rococo concoctions, courtesy of master mixologist Philip Ward. Equally good are snacks such as popcorn with lime, cheese, and chili. The bilevel setting conjures a

Kickin' Karaoke

If you're looking for a venue other than your shower to bust out a rendition of Queen's "Somebody to Love," you're in good company. Otherwise-jaded New Yorkers have become hooked on the goofy, addictive pleasure of karaoke. The K-word means "empty orchestra" in Japanese, and seems to tickle both downtown hipsters (who dig the irony of kitsch) and uptown financiers (who need a good rebel yell at the end of a workday), and everybody in between who loves to flex the golden pipes after a few drinks.

There are three ways of getting your lead-vocalist groove on: doing it in public at a barwide Karaoke Night; reserving a private space at a bar ("karaoke boxes," they're called), where only your friends can hear you scream—er, sing; and bounding up onstage in front of a live band.

The hardcore karaoke places tend to be either grungy or glitzy, with as many as 15 available boxes for rent by the hour or night (each box includes a music machine, microphones, and bar service), as well as up to 80,000 songs on tap for you to warble. (Don't worry, that figure includes stuff by Journey, REO Speedwagon, Britney Spears, and other grotesquely catchy Top 40 music.) There are two locations of **Sing-Sing Karaoke** (*9 St. Marks Pl., 212/387–7800 and 81 Ave. A, 212/674–0700*), the triple serving of cheesiness at Midtown's **Pulse** (*135 W. 41st St., between Broadway and 6th Ave.; 646/461–7717*), and just about anywhere else in the unofficial Koreatown that sprawls around Herald Square are a blast—try **Karaoke Duet 35** (*53 W. 35th St., 2nd fl., between 5th and 6th Aves.; 646/233–2685*).

For live-band karaoke, head to the Lower East Side's hottest song-fest: Monday-night rock 'n' roll karaoke at **Arlene's Grocery** (*95 Stanton St.; 212/995–1652*).

19

south-of-the-border bordello feel. ✉ *304 E. 6th St., between 1st and 2nd aves., East Village* ☎ *212/253–5888* ⊕ *www.mayahuelny.com* Ⓜ F to 2nd Ave.; 6 to Astor Pl.; N, R to 8th St.–NYU.

McSorley's Old Ale House. One of New York's oldest saloons (it claims to have opened in 1854) and immortalized by *New Yorker* writer Joseph Mitchell, McSorley's is a must-visit for beer lovers, even if only two kinds of brew are served: McSorley's Light and McSorley's Dark. It's also essential for blarney lovers, and much friendlier to women than it was before the '80s. (The motto here once was "Good ale, raw onions, and no ladies.") Go early to avoid the down-the-block lines on Friday and Saturday nights. ✉ *15 E. 7th St., between 2nd and 3rd aves., East Village* ☎ *212/473–9148* Ⓜ 6 to Astor Pl.

Otto's Shrunken Head Tiki Bar & Lounge. Who says NYC doesn't appeal to all tastes? Should you get a sudden urge to visit a tiki bar while in the East Village—and who doesn't sometimes?—the ultrapopular Otto's is your ticket. You'll find more than just a bamboo bar here, namely fish lamps, a tattooed, punk-rock crowd, cute little banquettes, drinks served in shrunken-head mugs, beef jerky for sale, and DJs prone to spinning anything from '50s rock to "Soul Gidget" surf music. ✉ *538 E.*

14th St., between Aves. A and B, East Village ☎ *212/228–2240* ⊕ *www.ottosshrunkenhead.com* Ⓜ *L to 1st Ave.*

PDT. Those who crave their cocktails with a little cloak-and-dagger really flip over PDT (which stands for "Please Don't Tell"). Housed beside the unassuming hot-dog joint, Crif Dogs, this pseudo-speakeasy can be reached only through a phone booth. Patrons with phoned-in reservations are escorted through the phone booth's false back into the cocktail bar, which is decorated with warm wooden beams and tongue-in-cheek taxidermy. ✉ *113 St. Marks Pl., between 1st Ave. and Ave. A, East Village* ☎ *212/614–0386* ⊕ *www.pdtnyc.com* Ⓜ *6 to Astor Pl.*

Fodor's Choice ★ **Pouring Ribbons.** This polished second-floor cocktail bar is named after the way a drink forms iridescent liquid ribbons when it is expertly poured. Coiffed bartenders shake or stir your concoction of choice from a grid-based menu that allows you to visualize just how "spirit-forward" or "refreshing" you want your drink to be. Elaborate cocktail garnishes on the bar look tempting enough to eat, but order some cheese and charcuterie to accompany your drinks instead. ✉ *225 Ave. B, , 2nd fl., between 13th and 14th sts.* ☎ *917/656–6788* ⊕ *www.pouringribbons.com* Ⓜ *L to 1st Ave.*

Summit Bar. Manhattan's easternmost cocktail bar, Summit Bar serves up high-end sips in a low-key environment. Still, much thought and care is put into the drinks, right down to the herbs that come from the Summit's rooftop garden. The menu aims to please, and splits between "classic" and more ambitious "alchemist" sections, the latter boasting drinks with caraway-infused agave and shiso leaf. There's a snug outdoor patio as well, ideal for sampling the Summit's surprising take on a margarita come summer. ✉ *133 Ave. C, between 8th and 9th sts., East Village* ☎ *917/261–7708* ⊕ *www.thesummitbar.net* Ⓜ *L to 1st Ave.*

Temple Bar. Unmarked and famous for its classic cocktails and romantic atmosphere, the Temple is prime first-date territory, especially once you drift past the sleekly wonderful bar to the back, where, swathed in almost complete darkness, you can lounge on a comfy banquette, order an old-fashioned, and do what people on first dates do. ✉ *332 Lafayette St., East Village* ☎ *212/925–4242* ⊕ *www.templebarnyc.com* Ⓜ *B, D, F, M to Broadway–Lafayette St.; 6 to Bleecker St.*

CABARET AND PIANO BARS
Joe's Pub. Wood paneling, red-velvet walls, and comfy sofas make a lush setting for top-notch performers and the A-list celebrities who love them(or pretend to). Named for the Public Theater's near-mythic impresario Joe Papp, and located inside the Public, Joe's doesn't have a bad seat—but if you want to occupy one, buy tickets beforehand and/or arrive at least half an hour early for the Italian-inspired dinner menu. ✉ *425 Lafayette St., between 4th St. and Astor Pl., East Village* ☎ *212/539–8778* ⊕ *www.joespub.com* Ⓜ *6 to Astor Pl.*

ROCK CLUB
Fodor's Choice ★ **Lit Lounge.** With a rock roster that's included musical forces as diverse as Devendra Banhart and the Hold Steady, Lit is a wonderfully grungy East Village classic. The raucous arty crowd hits not only shows but its charming art gallery Fuse and theme parties, which cater to fans

of specific bands (the White Stripes, Devo, and the Buzzcocks, to name just three). ⊠ *93 2nd Ave., between 5th and 6th sts., East Village* ☎ *212/777–7987* ⊕ *www.litloungenyc.com* Ⓜ *F to 2nd Ave., 6 to Astor Pl.*

LOWER EAST SIDE

BARS

Fodor'sChoice
★
Back Room. The Prohibition-era atmospheric touches here include tin ceilings, chandeliers, velvet wallpaper, mirrored bars, an amply sized fireplace, and a "hidden" outdoor entrance (which you can find easily enough, though the backalley). The music consists of rock CDs rather than a live spinmeister, and the drinks come in old-fashioned teacups or wrapped in paper bags. These, and other prize quirks, attract a slightly older clientele than many of its rowdier neighbors. ⊠ *102 Norfolk St., between Delancey and Rivington sts., Lower East Side* ☎ *212/228–5098* ⊕ *www.backroomnyc.com* Ⓜ *F to Delancey St.; J, M, Z to Essex St.*

Spitzer's Corner. No, you won't rub shoulders with ex-governor Eliot Spitzer here, but you can find 40 types of beer on tap plus a selection of the bottled variety, good food, floor-to-ceiling windows that pop open in fine weather, and wooden walls supposedly taken from pickle barrels (fortunately, the air is free of any scent from their former contents). ⊠ *101 Rivington St., at Ludlow St., Lower East Side* ☎ *212/228–0027* ⊕ *www.spitzerscorner.com* Ⓜ *F to Delancey St.; J, M, Z to Essex St.*

LIVE MUSIC VENUES

Arlene's Grocery. On Monday nights, crowds pack into this former Puerto Rican bodega for Rock 'n' Roll Karaoke, where they live out their rock-star dreams by singing favorite punk anthems on stage with a live band. The other six nights of the week are for local bands, and accordingly hit-or-miss. ⊠ *95 Stanton St., between Ludlow and Orchard sts., Lower East Side* ☎ *212/358–1633* ⊕ *www.arlenesgrocery.net* Ⓜ *F to 2nd Ave.*

Fodor'sChoice
★
Bowery Ballroom. This theater with Art Deco accents is probably the city's top midsize concert venue. Packing in the crowds here is a rite of passage for musicians on the cusp of stardom, including the Gossip, Manic Street Preachers, and the exuberant Go! Team. Grab one of the tables on the balcony (if you can), stand (and get sandwiched) on the main floor, or retreat to the comfortable bar in the basement, which really fills up after each show. ⊠ *6 Delancey St., between the Bowery and Chrystie St., Lower East Side* ☎ *212/533–2111* ⊕ *www.boweryballroom.com* Ⓜ *J, Z to Bowery.*

The Delancey. From the palm-studded rooftop deck (heated in winter, hosting barbecues in summer) down to the basement, where noisy rock and punk bands hold court, the multifaceted Delancey, at the foot of the Williamsburg Bridge, strikes an invigorating balance between classy and trashy. ⊠ *168 Delancey St., between Clinton and Attorney sts., Lower East Side* ☎ *212/254–9920* ⊕ *www.thedelancey.com* Ⓜ *F to Delancey St.; J, M, Z to Essex St.*

Mercury Lounge. You have to squeeze past all the sardine-packed hipsters in the front bar to reach the stage, but it's worth it. Not only does this top-quality venue, a "little sister to the Bowery Bar," specialize in cool

19

bands on the indie scene (Holly Golightly, Echo and the Bunnymen, and the Apostle of Hustle, anyone?), but it was where the late, great Jeff Buckley used to stop by to do spontaneous solo shows. ✉ *217 E. Houston St., at Ave. A, Lower East Side* ☎ *212/260–4700* ⊕ *www. mercuryloungenyc.com* Ⓜ *F to 2nd Ave.*

Pianos. With two venues for live music and DJs—the Showroom downstairs and Lounge upstairs—as well as a full bar that serves food downstairs, there's something for everyone at this Lower East Side staple. It's a blast late nights. ✉ *158 Ludlow St., just south of Stanton St., Lower East Side* ☎ *212/505–3733* ⊕ *www.pianosnyc.com* Ⓜ *F to Delancey St.; J, M, Z to Essex St.*

Rockwood Music Hall. Musicians and DJs rev up the crowd seven days a week at this intimate, multi-stage venue. Performances start as early as 3 pm on the weekends and 6 pm during the week—meaning you can get your live music fix and catch up on your sleep, too. Many shows are free. ✉ *196 Allen St., Lower East Side* ☎ *212/477–4155* ⊕ *www. rockwoodmusichall.com* Ⓜ *F to 2nd Ave.; J, Z to Bowery.*

GREENWICH VILLAGE AND WEST VILLAGE

GREENWICH VILLAGE
BARS
The Dove Parlour. On a colorful block that evokes the Greenwich Village of yore—a cigar store, vegetarian cafés, a bootleg music shop, a store specializing in chess—is this wonderful bar, whose elegant atmosphere (red-velvet wallpaper, white-wood paneling) is belied by the revelry of the sexy young customers sipping cocktails. ✉ *228 Thompson St., between 3rd and Bleecker sts., Greenwich Village* ☎ *212/254–1435* ⊕ *www.thedoveparlour.com* Ⓜ *N, R to 8th St.–NYU; A, B, C, D, E, F, M to W. 4th St.*

Vol de Nuit. Tucked away from the street, the "Belgian Beer Bar" (as everybody calls it) features a European-style, enclosed outdoor courtyard and a cozy interior, all red light and shadows. NYU grad-student types come for the mammoth selection of beers on tap as well as the fries, which are served with Belgian flair, in a paper cone with an array of sauces on the side. ✉ *148 W. 4th St., at 6th Ave., Greenwich Village* ☎ *212/982–3388* ⊕ *www.voldenuitbar.com* Ⓜ *A, B, C, D, E, F, M to W. 4th St.*

JAZZ VENUES
Fodor's Choice ★ **Blue Note.** Considered by many (not least its current owners) to be "the jazz capital of the world," the Blue Note was once the stomping ground for such legends as Dizzy Gillespie, and still hosts a variety of acts, from Chris Botti to the Count Basie Orchestra to Boz Scaggs. Expect a steep cover charge except for late shows on weekends, when the music goes from less jazzy to more funky. ✉ *131 W. 3rd St., near 6th Ave., Greenwich Village* ☎ *212/475–8592* ⊕ *www.bluenote.net* Ⓜ *A, B, C, D, E, F, M to W. 4th St.*

Knickerbocker Bar and Grill. Jazz is on the menu Friday and Saturday nights at this old-fashioned steakhouse, a longtime staple of the city's more intimate music scene. ⊠ *33 University Pl., at 9th St., Greenwich Village* ☎ *212/228–8490* ⊕ *www.knickerbockerbarandgrill.com* Ⓜ *N, R to 8th St.–NYU; 6 to Astor Pl.*

LIVE MUSIC VENUES

(Le) Poisson Rouge. Underneath the site of the late, lamented Village Gate jazz emporium is this cutting-edge jewel of a place, whose name means "the Red Fish" (and whose parentheses around "Le" remain a mystery). Blending just the right mix of posh notes (lush décor, fine dining) and brave music programming (jazz, classical, electronic, cabaret, rock, folk—even, with the splendiferous Ralph's World, children's music), the Poisson is quite simply an essential NYC fixture. ⊠ *158 Bleecker St., at Thompson St., Greenwich Village* ☎ *212/505–3474* ⊕ *www. lepoissonrouge.com* Ⓜ *A, B, C, D, E, F, M to W. 4th St.*

WEST VILLAGE

BARS

Corner Bistro. Opened in 1961, this charming neighborhood saloon serves what many think are the best (and most affordable) burgers in town. Once you actually get a seat, the space feels nice and cozy, but until then, be prepared to drink a beer amid lively and hungry patrons. ⊠ *331 W. 4th St., at 8th Ave., West Village* ☎ *212/242–9502* ⊕ *www. cornerbistrony.com* Ⓜ *1, 2, 3, A, C, E to 14th St.; L to 8th Ave.*

Fodor's Choice
★

Employees Only. The dapper, white-coated bartenders (many of them impressively mustachio'd) at this speakeasy-style bar mix delicious, well-thought-out cocktails with debonair aplomb and freshly squeezed mixers. Sip one in the dimly lit bar area and you might feel like you've stepped back in time—if it weren't for the crush of trendy West Village locals and visitors in-the-know at your back. Look for the green awning that says EO and the neon Psychic sign out front. Dinner is served in the restaurant at the back: it's quality, but pricey. ⊠ *510 Hudson St., between Christopher and 10th sts., West Village* ☎ *212/242–3021* ⊕ *www.employeesonlynyc.com* Ⓜ *1 to Christopher St.–Sheridan Sq.; A, B, C, D, E, F, M to W. 4th St.*

Hudson Bar and Books. Along with its sister branches—Beekman Bar and Books on Beekman Place and Lexington Bar and Books on, yep, Lexington—the Hudson reflects a literary bent in its cocktails, with names like the Dewey Decimal, the Cervantes Spritzer, and Alphabet Absinthe (topped off with floating letter-shape sugar cubes). Despite that, it's hardly a hushed library where well-read butlers serve you; the atmosphere here is more about book decor than serious literature. It's seriously clubby, with wood paneling and leather banquettes. And it's one of the few places where you can still smoke. ⊠ *636 Hudson St., at Horatio St., West Village* ☎ *212/229–2642* ⊕ *www.barandbooks.cz* Ⓜ *A, C, E to 14th St.; L to 8th Ave.*

Fodor's Choice
★

Little Branch. Top-quality cocktails, dim lighting and snug booths make this the ideal spot for a conversation with friends (that you can actually hear) or an intimate date. ⊠ *20 7th Ave., at Leroy St., West Village* ☎ *212/929–4360* Ⓜ *1 to Houston St.*

Otheroom. Ever wish that the bar you're drinking in had something more interesting on its walls than Budweiser signs? Head to the far

19

west Otheroom, art gallery by day, upscale drinking spot by night. The menu is pretty creative, too, with dozens of microbrews and American wines available by the glass. ⊠ *143 Perry St., between Greenwich and Washington sts., West Village* ☎ *212/645–9758* Ⓜ *1 to Christopher St.–Sheridan Sq.*

White Horse Tavern. According to New York legend, writer Dylan Thomas drank himself to death in this historic West Village tavern founded in 1880. The Horse remains perpetually popular with literary types, but thankfully it's lacking more death-by-alcohol-poisoning cases of late. When the weather's nice, try to snag a seat at one of the sidewalk tables for prime—and, given the neighborhood, we do mean prime—people-watching. ⊠ *567 Hudson St., at 11th St., West Village* ☎ *212/989–3956* Ⓜ *1 to Christopher St.–Sheridan Sq.*

Wilfie & Nell. Combine the beloved cozy atmosphere and frothy pints standard at Irish pubs with a well-heeled West Village crowd and you get Wilfie & Nell, a candlelit bar full of communal tables for making new friends. This perpetually crowded neighborhood favorite, with its low ceilings and locally sourced food, is a popular singles spot as well as a good match for night owls: food and brews are served into the wee hours. ⊠ *228 W. 4th St., between 10th St. and 7th Ave. S, West Village* ☎ *212/242–2990* ⊕ *www.wilfieandnell.com* Ⓜ *1 to Christopher St.–Sheridan Sq.; A, B, C, D, E, F, M to W. 4th St.*

CABARET AND PIANO BARS

The Duplex. No matter who's performing, the largely gay audience hoots and hollers in support of the often kitschy performers at this music-scene staple on busy Sheridan Square since 1951. Singers and comedians hold court in the cabaret theater, while those itching to take a shot at open mic head downstairs to the lively piano bar. ⊠ *61 Christopher St., at 7th Ave. S, West Village* ☎ *212/255–5438* ⊕ *www.theduplex.com* Ⓜ *1 to Christopher St.–Sheridan Sq.*

GAY NIGHTLIFE

Cubbyhole. Early in the evening the crowd is mixed at this neighborhood institution, where the DJs, unpretentious décor, and inexpensive margaritas are popular. Later on, the women take charge. ⊠ *281 W. 12th St., at 4th St., West Village* ☎ *212/243–9041* ⊕ *www.cubbyholebar.com* Ⓜ *1, 2, 3, A, C, E to 14th St.; L to 8th Ave.*

Fodor's Choice
★

Henrietta Hudson. The nightly parties at this laid-back West Village HQ for the Sapphic set attract young professional women, out-of-towners, and longtime regulars. Because the DJ and pool table quickly create a crowd, though, stake your claim to a spot early, especially on weekends. ⊠ *438 Hudson St., at Morton St., West Village* ☎ *212/924–3347* ⊕ *www.henriettahudson.com* Ⓜ *1 to Christopher St.–Sheridan Sq.*

JAZZ VENUES

Garage Restaurant & Café. Good news for you budget-minded jazzers: there's no cover *and* no minimum at this West Village hot spot, where two jazz groups jam seven nights a week and a fireplace sets the mood upstairs. ⊠ *99 7th Ave. S, between Bleecker and Christopher sts., West Village* ☎ *212/645–0600* ⊕ *www.garagerest.com* Ⓜ *1 to Christopher St.–Sheridan Sq.*

Fodor's Choice **Village Vanguard.** This prototypical jazz club, tucked into a cellar in
★ Greenwich Village since the 1940s, has been the haunt of legends like
Thelonious Monk and Barbara Streisand. Today you can hear jams
from the likes of Bill Charlap and Ravi Coltrane, and on Monday
night the sizable resident Vanguard Jazz Orchestra blowtheir collective
heart out. ⊠ *178 7th Ave. S, between 11th and Perry sts., West Village*
☎ *212/255–4037* ⊕ *www.villagevanguard.com* Ⓜ *1, 2, 3 to 14th St.*

LIVE MUSIC VENUES

SOB's. The initials stand for "Sounds of Brazil" (no, not what you—and
everybody else—might think), and this is *the* place for reggae, African,
and Latin music, with some jazz gigs sprinkled in. The late, great Cuban
sensation Cachao used to hold court here, as does calypso's Mighty
Sparrow when he's up north. Don't miss the Haitian dance parties, the
afterwork Latin groove happy hour, or the bossa nova brunches. Dinner is served as well. ⊠ *204 Varick St., West Village* ☎ *212/243–4940*
⊕ *www.sobs.com* Ⓜ *1 to Houston St.*

CHELSEA AND THE MEATPACKING DISTRICT

CHELSEA

BARS

Half King. Writer Sebastian Junger (*The Perfect Storm*) is one of the owners of this would-be literary mecca. We say "would-be," because the
ambience can be more publike than writerly—and that's fine, since the
King draws such a friendly crowd (media types, mostly). We like it best
for its frequent readings, gallery exhibits, and Irish-American menu.
⊠ *505 W. 23rd St., between 10th and 11th aves., Chelsea* ☎ *212/462–
4300* ⊕ *www.thehalfking.com* Ⓜ *C, E to 23rd St.*

COMEDY CLUBS

Fodor's Choice **Upright Citizens Brigade Theatre.** Raucous sketch comedy, audience-
★ initiated improv, and classic stand-up take turns onstage here at the
city's absolute capital for alternative comedy. There are even classes
available;. ⊠ *307 W. 26th St., between 8th and 9th aves., Chelsea*
☎ *212/366–9176* ⊕ *www.ucbtheatre.com* Ⓜ *C, E to 23rd St.*

GAY NIGHTLIFE

Gym Sports Bar. At New York's first gay sports bar, the plentiful flat-
screen TVs and cheap Budweisers draw athletic enthusiasts of every
stripe, from athlete to armchair. Nobly, the bar sponsors—and frequently hosts parties for—a number of local gay sports teams. ⊠ *167
8th Ave., at 18th St., Chelsea* ☎ *212/337–2439* ⊕ *www.gymsportsbar.
com* Ⓜ *A, C, E to 14th St.; L to 8th Ave.; 1 to 18th St.*

THE MEATPACKING DISTRICT

BARS

Hogs & Heifers. This raucous place is all about the saucy barkeeps using
megaphones to berate male customers and bait the females to get up
on the bar and dance (and add their bras to the collection on the wall).
⊠ *859 Washington St., at 13th St., Meatpacking District* ☎ *212/929–
0655* ⊕ *www.hogsandheifers.com* Ⓜ *A, C, E to 14th St.; L to 8th Ave.*

19

Plunge. The Gansevoort Hotel's slick rooftop bar would be worth visiting even without its mouthwatering views. The adjectives sleek and glossy could easily be illustrated by Plunge, where the lighting is soft, the furnishings are cool and comfy (at least to a degree), the music isn't too loud, servers of both sexes are sexy, and there is ample space—indoors as well as out. ⊠ *18 9th Ave., at 13th St., Meatpacking District* ☎ *212/660–6736* ⊕ *www.hotelgansevoort.com* Ⓜ *A, C, E to 14th St.; L to 8th Ave.*

The Standard Hotel Biergarten, Grill, and Living Room. Practically the official bar of the High Line park, the Standard Biergarten is a sprawling, riotous space complete with ping pong tables and big steins of beer. There's also a grill bar and indoor Living Room lounge. As for the chic hot spot on the top floor, unofficially called the Boom Boom Room, it's currently the hardest door in town ("hardest," that is, to get through), but given the quality of the accessible fun down below, we forgive the snobbery. ⊠ *848 Washington St., at 13th St., Meatpacking District* ☎ *212/645–4646* ⊕ *www.standardhotels.com* Ⓜ *A, C, E to 14th St.; L to 8th Ave.*

DANCE CLUBS AND DJ VENUES

Cielo. Relatively mature dance clubgoers (if the word "mature" can ever be applied to such a crowd) gravitate to this small but sturdy Meatpacking District music-head mecca to toss back cocktails, dig the high-quality sound system, groove to top-flight DJs spinning soulful Latin beats and techno, boogie on the sunken dance floor, and smoke in the no-frills garden outside. Monday nightis home to the award-winning Deep Space parties, where resident DJs (as well as guest spinmeisters like Dimitri from Paris) rev up the faithful with everything from dubstep to Stravinsky. ⊠ *18 Little W. 12th St., between 9th Ave. and Washington St., Meatpacking District* ☎ *212/645–5700* ⊕ *www.cieloclub.com* Ⓜ *A, C, E to 14th St.; L to 8th Ave.*

UNION SQUARE, GRAMERCY, AND THE FLATIRON DISTRICT

UNION SQUARE

BARS

Rye House. A welcoming bar with slick cocktails and a clever take on comfort food, the Rye House beckons just steps from the chain store overload of Union Square. From boiled peanuts and fried pickles to their own take on a Sazerac, the space is a welcome respite from the hustle and bustle outside. ⊠ *11 W. 17th St., between Broadway and 5th Ave., Union Square* ☎ *212/255–7260* ⊕ *www.ryehousenyc.com* Ⓜ *4, 5, 6, L, N, Q, R to 14th St.–Union Sq.*

GRAMERCY

BARS

Dear Irving. This cocktail parlor invites Gramercy locals inside with its name, the beginning of a letter to the lovely Irving Place on which the bar resides. Interiors are chic and refined, and just like at sister property Raines Law Room, there are private sections of tables and couches for intimate conversations. Reservations are recommended, especially during prime weekend hours. ⊠ *55 Irving Pl., between 17th and 18th sts.* ⊕ *www.dearirving.com* Ⓜ *4, 5, 6, L, N, Q, R to 14th St.–Union Sq.*

Old Town Bar. The proudly unpretentious bilevel Old Town is redolent of old New York, and why not? It's been around since 1892. Tavern-style grub, mahogany everywhere, and atmosphere, atmosphere, atmosphere make this a fun stop on any pub crawl. Men: don't miss the giant, person-size urinals. ⊠ *45 E. 18th St., between Broadway and Park Ave. S, Gramercy* ☎ *212/529–6732* ⊕ *www.oldtownbar.com* Ⓜ *4, 5, 6, L, N, Q, R to 14th St.–Union Sq.*

Pete's Tavern. This historic landmark (where O. Henry was a loyal customer) is one of the bars that claims to be the oldest continuously operating watering hole in the city. Pete's has charm to spare, with its long wooden bar and cozy booths, where locals crowd in for a beer or a fantastic burger. When weather warms up, sidewalk tables with red-and-white-checker tablecloths on scenic Irving Place are a neighborhood favorite. ⊠ *129 E. 18th St., at Irving Pl., Gramercy* ☎ *212/473–7676* ⊕ *www.petestavern.com* Ⓜ *4, 5, 6, L, N, Q, R to 14th St.–Union Sq.*

JAZZ VENUES

FAMILY

Fodor's Choice

★

Jazz Standard. The Standard's sizable underground room draws top names in the business. As a part of Danny Meyer's southern-food restaurant Blue Smoke, it's one of the few spots where you can get dry-rubbed ribs to go with your bebop. Bring the kids for the Jazz Standard Youth Orchestra concerts every Sunday afternoon. ⊠ *116 E. 27th St., between Park and Lexington aves., Gramercy* ☎ *212/576–2232* ⊕ *www.jazzstandard.com* Ⓜ *6 to 28th St.*

LIVE MUSIC VENUES

Fodor's Choice

★

Irving Plaza. This two-story venue is known for its solid rock performances, both indie (DJ Shadow and Sleater-Kinney) and more mainstream (Lenny Kravitz)—even if they can get a little pricey. Red walls and chandeliers add a Gothic touch. If the main floor gets too cramped, seek sanctuary in the chill bar upstairs. ⊠ *17 Irving Pl., at 15th St., Gramercy* ☎ *212/777–6800* ⊕ *www.irvingplaza.com* Ⓜ *4, 5, 6, L, N, Q, R to 14th St.–Union Sq.*

FLATIRON DISTRICT

BARS

The Ace Hotel. A hot spot for the digital set, this hotel's lobby and adjoining restaurant spaces—the Breslin and the John Dory—have been packed since they opened at this Pacific Northwest import. If your bearded hipster friend came into some cash, his place would look like the lobby here, with reclaimed-wood tables, beer signs, and beautiful folks in oversize eyeglasses drinking coffee by day or a craft brew by night (while a DJ spins in the background). ⊠ *20 W. 29th St., between Broadway and 5th Ave., Flatiron District* ☎ *212/679–2222* ⊕ *www. acehotel.com* Ⓜ *R to 28th St.*

Flatiron Lounge. Here, resident mixologists rely on the freshest (and sometimes most exotic) ingredients available. The cocktail menu changes often, but if you're stumped, tell the bartenders what you like and they'll happily invent a bespoke concoction on the spot. ⊠ *37 W. 19th St., between 5th and 6th aves., Flatiron* ☎ *212/727–7741* ⊕ *www. flatironlounge.com* Ⓜ *1 to 18th St.; F, M to 14th St.; L to 6th Ave.; 6 to 23rd St.*

19

Fodor's Choice
★

The NoMad Bar. A sultry space from the team behind the NoMad Hotel (with a separate entrance on 28th Street) this bilevel bar impresses with its inviting leather banquettes, extensive golden-lit bar, and tempting list of craft cocktails. The food leans towards comfort classics, such as chicken pot pie and bacon-wrapped hot dogs, but the design is pure sophistication. ⊠ *10 W. 28th St., at Broadway, Flatiron District* ☎ *347/472–5660* ⊕ *www.thenomadhotel.com* Ⓜ *N, R to 28th St.; 6 to 28th St.*

Raines Law Room. There's no phone number or big sign for this cocktail bar; just ring the bell to enter. Wood-burning fireplaces, deep banquettes, and curtains for privacy all contribute to the comfortable, living room–like vibe—perfect for a date or intimate group gathering. An outdoor garden lighted by candle is functional, too: herbs grown here are used in the carefully crafted cocktails. ⊠ *48 W. 17th St., Flatiron District* ⊕ *www.raineslawroom.com* Ⓜ *F, M to 14th St.; 4, 5, 6, L, N, Q, R to 14th St.–Union Sq.*

MIDTOWN EAST AND MURRAY HILL

MIDTOWN EAST
BARS

The Bar Downstairs. The bar without a name in the basement of the Andaz 5th Avenue may lack a moniker, but it certainly has pedigree. Alchemy Consulting, a joint venture from Chicago's Violet Hour and New York's Death and Co., designed the cocktails here; look for spins on the Negroni and Manhattan in the sleek subterranean space. The food menu is similarly up-market, with a variety of nebulously Spanish small plates. ⊠ *485 5th Ave., at 41st St., Midtown East* ☎ *212/601–1234* ⊕ *newyork.5thavenue.andaz.hyatt.com/en/hotel/dining/thebardownstairs.html* Ⓜ *B, D, F, M to 42nd St.–Bryant Park; 7 to 5th Ave.; 4, 5, 6, S to Grand Central–42nd St.*

Fodor's Choice
★

Campbell Apartment. Commuting professionals pack into this Grand Central Terminal bar on their way to catch trains home during the evening rush, but don't let the crush of humanity scare you away—you can have a romantic time here in one of Manhattan's more beautiful rooms. The restored space dates to the 1920s, when it was the private office of an executive named John W. Campbell, and as the exquisite décor suggests, old JWC knew how to live. Sample the good life as you knock back a well-built cocktail from an overstuffed chair. Just try to avoid that weekday evening rush. ⊠ *Grand Central Terminal, 15 Vanderbilt Ave. entrance, Midtown East* ☎ *212/953–0409* ⊕ *www.grandcentralterminal.com* Ⓜ *4, 5, 6, 7, S to Grand Central–42nd St.*

King Cole Bar. A justly beloved Maxfield Parrish mural of "Old King Cole" himself, as well as his psychedelic court, adds to the already considerable elegance at this romantic and essential Midtown meeting place. Try a Bloody Mary—this is where the drink was introduced to Americans. Be warned: prices for a single cocktail are steep. ⊠ *St. Regis Hotel, 2 E. 55th St., between 5th and Madison aves., Midtown East* ☎ *212/339–6857* ⊕ *www.kingcolebar.com* Ⓜ *E, M to 5th Ave./53rd St.*

P. J. Clarke's. Mirrors and polished wood and other old-time flair adorn New York's most famous Irish bar, a red-brick brawler of a joint. Steeped in Hollywood lore—Steve McQueen was once a regular, and scenes from the 1945 movie *Lost Weekend* were shot here—Clarke's draws in the after-work crowd that appreciates drinking beer and eating exceptionally juicy burgers immersed in history. ⌧ *915 3rd Ave., at 55th St., Midtown East* ☎ *212/317–1616* ⊕ *www.pjclarkes.com* Ⓜ *6 to 51st St.; E, M to Lexington Ave./53rd St.; 4, 5, 6 59th St.; N, Q, R to Lexington Ave./59th St.*

GAY NIGHTLIFE

Evolve Bar and Lounge. Rising from the ashes of a popular gay club on the same site, this glossy, raucous Chelsea-style bar–club gets Midtown East rocking, with its sexy-yet-genial staff and theme nights like Pop-off Thursday, Bulge Friday, and Disco Balls Sunday. ⌧ *221 E. 58th St., between 2nd and 3rd aves., Midtown East* ☎ *212/355–3395* Ⓜ *4, 5, 6 to 59th St.; N, Q, R to Lexington Ave./59th St.*

Townhouse Bar. It's the elegant yin to the rowdy yang of Evolve, which is just across the block at East 58th Street. Distinguished mature men from the Upper East Side meet younger would-be versions of themselves at this "gentlemen's club," which looks like the home of a blueblood with superb taste. The attire is "uptown casual" if not fancier. ⌧ *236 E. 58th St., between 2nd and 3rd aves., Midtown East* ☎ *212/754–4649* ⊕ *www.townhouseny.com* Ⓜ *4, 5, 6 to 59th St.; N, Q, R to Lexington Ave./59th St.*

MURRAY HILL

BARS

Galway Pub. This welcoming spot is sought out as one of Midtown's best Irish pubs. Even on a block with a high number of fine drinking establishments, Galway Pub stands out thanks to its gorgeous circular bar, intriguing orange lighting, spirited after-work crowd, and bartenders, some of whom may actually hail from the Emerald Isle. Snag one of their business cards, too—on the back are words of wisdom from the best Irish writers. ⌧ *7 E. 36th St., between 5th and Madison aves., Murray Hill* ☎ *212/725–2353* ⊕ *www.galwaypubnyc.com* Ⓜ *6 to 33rd St.*

Middle Branch. Sasha Petraske's speakeasy-style cocktail bars have expanded into Murray Hill with Middle Branch, a two-story space and former antiques store with no sign outside to announce its presence. Cocktail lovers find the brick townhouse anyway, and inside, linger over small plates, live jazz, and a long list of sophisticated drinks. ⌧ *154 E. 33rd St., Murray Hill* ☎ *212/213–1350* Ⓜ *6 to 33rd St.*

MIDTOWN WEST

BARS

Cellar Bar. Underneath the Bryant Park Hotel—and a tiled, arched ceiling—is one of the more spectacular spaces in Midtown. As a DJ with a taste for classic R&B spins the night away, a fashion-industry crowd gets up to dance—and spill their collective drink. ⌧ *40 W. 40th St., between 5th and 6th aves., Midtown West* ☎ *212/642–2211* ⊕ *www.*

19

cellarbarbryantparkhotel.com Ⓜ *B, D, F, M to 42nd St.–Bryant Park; 7 to 5th Ave.*

Joe Allen. Everybody's en route either to or from a show at this "old reliable" on the boisterous Restaurant Row, celebrated in the musical version of *All About Eve.* Chances are you'll even spot a Broadway star at the bar or in the dining room. Still, our favorite thing about Joe's is not the show crowd but the hilarious "flop wall," adorned with posters from musicals that bombed, sometimes spectacularly. (Check out the ones for *Paradox Lust, Got Tu Go Disco,* and *Dude,* the unfortunate sequel to *Hair.*) ✉ *326 W. 46th St., between 8th and 9th aves., Midtown West* ☎ *212/581–6464* ⊕ *www.joeallenrestaurant.com* Ⓜ *A, C, E to 42nd St.–Port Authority; N, Q, R to 49th St.*

Lantern's Keep. The elegance of cocktail culture from another era is alive and well at Lantern's Keep, an intimate lounge tucked behind the lobby of the Iroquois Hotel. Reservations are recommended for this watering hole, where plush seats are huddled around a fireplace. There is no standing room here, resulting in a luxurious, leisurely vibe. Cocktails are works of art and bartenders are helpful at identifying your perfect poison. ✉ *Iroquois Hotel, 49 W. 44th St., between 5th and 6th aves., Midtown West* ☎ *212/453–4287* ⊕ *www.iroquoisny.com/lanternskeep* Ⓜ *B, D, F, M to 42nd St.–Bryant Park.*

The Rum House. A bar beloved by locals in Midtown may be an urban legend, but consider the Rum House the exception to the rule. Among the glittering lights of Broadway theaters, this is a destination bar for their attention to the craft of mixing cocktails. The sister property to downtown favorite Ward III, this bar has nightly live piano music and creative libations in addition to all the classic cocktails. ✉ *228 W. 47th St., between 7th and 8th aves., Midtown West* ☎ *646/490–6924* ⊕ *www.edisonrumhouse.com* Ⓜ *N, Q, R to 49th St.; A, C, E to 42nd St.–Port Authority.*

Russian Vodka Room. Forget Russian Samovar across the block—here's where the serious vodka drinking goes down, along with (almost) everything that goes along with serious vodka drinking. The Vodka Room features a glowing, sophisticated front room with nightly piano player (and the superlative Dmitri Kolesnik on Monday, free of charge), a more sumptuous back room, a generous Attitude Adjustment Hour (that's Russki for "Happy Hour"), and more exotically infused vodkas (horseradish! ginger! pepper!) than you can shake a babushka at. For those who crave variety, a vodka tasting menu is available, as are culinary standards like borscht. ✉ *265 W. 52nd St., between Broadway and 8th Ave., Midtown West* ☎ *212/307–5835* ⊕ *www.russianvodkaroom. com* Ⓜ *1, C, E to 50th St.*

Salon de Ning. Take a break from 5th Avenue shopping at this glass-lined penthouse bar on the 23rd floor of the ritzy Peninsula Hotel. Drinks are pricey, of course, but what isn't in this neighborhood? The views are worth it, especially from the rooftop terraces. ✉ *Peninsula Hotel, 700 5th Ave., at 55th St., Midtown West* ☎ *212/956–2888* ⊕ *www. salondening.com* Ⓜ *E, M to 5th Ave./53rd St.*

COMEDY CLUBS

Caroline's on Broadway. This high-gloss club presents established names as well as comedians on the edge of stardom. Janeane Garofalo, David Alan Grier, Colin Quinn, and Gilbert Gottfried have all headlined. ⊠ *1626 Broadway, between 49th and 50th sts., Midtown West* ☎ *212/757–4100* ⊕ *www.carolines.com* Ⓜ *N, Q, R to 49th St.; 1 to 50th St.*

Chicago City Limits. This crew tout themselves as performing in the longest-running improv show in the city. Heavy on audience participation, the improv shows take place Friday and Saturday (with stand-up comics taking the stage the rest of the week) and seldom fail to whip visitors into what the comics might call a "phun phrenzy."⊠ *318 W. 53rd St., between 8th and 9th aves., Midtown West* ☎ *212/888–5233* ⊕ *www.chicagocitylimits.com* Ⓜ *C, E to 50th St.*

DANCE CLUBS AND DJ VENUES

Pacha. Maybe you've been to the exclusive Pacha clubs in Buenos Aires, Ibiza, and London. But the jewel in the crown of the Pacha empire may well be here. Assuming you pass muster to enter, you find four stories' worth of high-tech fittings (blinding lights, go-go girls, humungous sound), plus celeb DJs and celeb customers. ⊠ *618 W. 46th St., between 11th and 12th aves., Midtown West* ☎ *212/209–7500* ⊕ *www. pachanyc.com* Ⓜ *C, E to 50th St.*

GAY NIGHTLIFE

Posh. Lest you think that Hell's Kitchen has no fine gay lounges, Posh has walls covered in fine canvases by local artists, trophies over the bar, ample room for kibitzing and dancing, plenty of neon décor, and hours that are "4 pm to 4 am GUARANTEED." Who says nothing is certain anymore in these confusing times? ⊠ *405 W. 51st St., at 9th Ave., Midtown West* ☎ *212/957–2222* ⊕ *www.poshbarnyc.com* Ⓜ *C, E to 50th St.*

JAZZ VENUES

Birdland. This place gets its name from saxophone great Charlie "Yardbird" (or just "Bird") Parker, so expect serious musicians such as John Pizzarelli, the Dave Holland Sextet, and Arturo O'Farrill's Afro-Cuban Jazz Orchestra (on Sunday night). The dining room serves moderately priced American fare with a Cajun accent. ⊠ *315 W. 44th St., between 8th and 9th aves., Midtown West* ☎ *212/581–3080* ⊕ *www. birdlandjazz.com* Ⓜ *A, C, E to 42nd St.–Port Authority.*

Dizzy's Club Coca Cola. For a night of jazz without the pretension, turn to Dizzy's, an intimate club with Manhattan skyline views and Southern-inflected cuisine (okra, fried chicken, catfish) and cocktails. Late night sessions are ideal for an after dinner night cap; some of the drinks, such as the Dizzy Gillespie, are named after jazz legends. ⊠ *10 Columbus Circle, Midtown West* ☎ *212/258–9595* ⊕ *www.jazz.org/dizzys* Ⓜ *1, A, B, C, D to 59th St.–Columbus Circle.*

Iridium. This cozy, top-drawer club is a sure bet for big-name talent like the David Murray Black Saint Quartet and Michael Wolff. The sight lines are good, and the sound system was designed with the help of Les Paul, the inventor of the solid-body electric guitar, who used to play

19

here every Monday night. The rest of the week sees a mix of artists like Chuck Mangione and the Eddie Daniels Band. ✉ *1650 Broadway, at 51st St., Midtown West* ☎ *212/582–2121* ⊕ *www.theiridium.com* Ⓜ *1 to 50th St.; N, Q, R to 49th St.*

LIVE MUSIC VENUES

B. B. King Blues Club & Grill. This lavish Times Square club is vast, shiny, and hosts a range of musicians, from the Harlem Gospel Choir to George Clinton and the P-Funk All-Stars. It's also where surviving rock legends like Little Richard and Chuck Berry play as well. ✉ *237 W. 42nd St., between 7th and 8th aves., Midtown West* ☎ *212/997–4144* ⊕ *www.bbkingblues.com* Ⓜ *A, C, E to 42nd St.–Port Authority; 1, 2, 3, 7, N, Q, R, S to Times Sq.–42nd St.*

UPPER EAST SIDE

BARS

American Trash. You might tell from the name that this isn't exactly your granddad's UES drinking establishment. Bicycle tires, golf clubs, and other castoffs cover the walls and ceiling, ensuring that the 20-year-old Trash, a sanctum of sleaze, merits its descriptive name. Eight plasma TVs, three video games, a defiantly rock 'n' roll jukebox, and a pool table keep the neighborhood crowd (as well as stray bikers who hate them) busy. Some nights local bands play classic rock. ✉ *1471 1st Ave., between 76th and 77th sts., Upper East Side* ☎ *212/988–9008* ⊕ *www. americantrashnyc.com* Ⓜ *6 to 77th St.*

Fodor's Choice ★ **Auction House.** This Victorian-style lounge brings a touch of downtown chic to the sometimes suburban-feeling Upper East Side with candlelit tables, high tin ceilings, and velvet couches. Rap and hip-hop fans should look elsewhere (the only tunes coming out of this joint are alternative and rock), and baseball caps and sneakers are strictly forbidden, as are—at the other end of the spectrum—fur coats. ✉ *300 E. 89th St., between 1st and 2nd aves., Upper East Side* ☎ *212/427–4458* Ⓜ *4, 5, 6 to 86th St.*

Bar Pleiades. The cocktail bar companion to Café Boulud, also in the Surrey Hotel, Bar Pleiades is a livelier alternative to the more staid atmosphere at the Carlyle's Bemelmans Bar. The design is classic to a fault, employing a black-and-white theme that's positively Audrey Hepburn–esque. Drinks rotate seasonally, and there are tasty nibbles from the café kitchen. Though it doesn't have the same drink menu, the rooftop bar is a cozy aerie good for people- and skyscraper-watching. ✉ *Surrey Hotel, 20 E. 76th St., between 5th and Madison aves., Upper East Side* ☎ *212/772–2600* ⊕ *www.barpleiades.com* Ⓜ *6 to 77th St.*

Opia. The motto for this upscale-yet-unpretentious bar-restaurant—"If you like us, tell your friends, and if you don't, tell your enemies!"—isn't necessary, given its manifold charms: a drop-dead-gorgeous design, plenty of space for canoodling and cavorting, a romantic balcony (though 57th Street isn't exactly a scenic beach), plus live jazz on Tuesday and Saturday nights. Opia is ideal for couples in full-on infatuation or spouses hoping to remember the wine-and-roses days before kids. ✉ *130 E. 57th St., between Lexington and 3rd aves., Upper East Side*

☎ *212/688–3939* ⊕ *www.opiarestaurant.com* Ⓜ *4, 5, 6 to 59th St.; N, Q, R to Lexington Ave./59th St.*

CABARET AND PIANO BARS

Fodor's Choice **The Carlyle.** The hotel's discreetly sophisticated Café Carlyle hosts such
★ top cabaret and jazz performers as Christine Ebersole, John Pizzarelli, and Steve Tyrell. Stop by on a Monday night and take in Woody Allen, who swings on the clarinet with the Eddy Davis New Orleans Jazz Band. The less fancy-schmancy (though still pricey) Bemelmans Bar, with a mural by the author of the *Madeline* books, features a rotating cast of pianist-singers. ✉ *35 E. 76th St., between Madison and Park aves., Upper East Side* ☎ *212/744–1600* ⊕ *www.thecarlyle.com* Ⓜ *6 to 77th St.*

GAY NIGHTLIFE

Fodor's Choice **Brandy's Piano Bar.** A singing waitstaff warm up the mixed crowd at this
★ delightful and intimate Upper East Side lounge, getting everyone in the mood to belt out their favorite tunes. In fact, the Brandy's scene is so cheerful that some patrons call it musical Prozac, keeping depression at bay. ✉ *235 E. 84th St., between 2nd and 3rd aves., Upper East Side* ☎ *212/744–4949* ⊕ *www.brandyspianobar.com* Ⓜ *4, 5, 6 to 86th St.*

UPPER WEST SIDE

BARS

The Empire Hotel Rooftop Bar. The only thing better than hanging out in Lincoln Center on a lovely night is hanging out a dozen stories above Lincoln Center. Thanks to the radically refurbished Empire Hotel's sprawling rooftop bar, you can enjoy that pleasure even on nights that are less than lovely. We're talking thousands of square feet here, most of it outdoors, and heated in winter. ✉ *44 W. 63rd St., between Broadway and Columbus Ave., Upper West Side* ☎ *212/265–7400* ⊕ *www. empirehotelnyc.com* Ⓜ *1 to 66th St.–Lincoln Center.*

JAZZ VENUES

Smoke. If you can't wait until sunset to get your riffs on, head uptown to this lounge near Columbia University, where the music starts as early as 6 pm. Performers include some of the top names in the business, including turban-wearing organist Dr. Lonnie Smith and the drummer Jimmy Cobb (who kept time on Miles Davis's seminal album *Kind of Blue*). ✉ *2751 Broadway, between 105th and 106th sts., Upper West Side* ☎ *212/864–6662* ⊕ *www.smokejazz.com* Ⓜ *1 to 103rd St.*

19

HARLEM

BARS

Corner Social. With nearly 20 beers on tap, sports on big screens, and bar food that's anything but boring, it's no surprise that this neighborhood favorite is packed on weekends. In warm weather an outdoor patio gives you a front-row seat to the scene on Lenox Avenue. ✉ *321 Lenox Ave., at 126th St., Harlem* ☎ *212/510–8552* ⊕ *www.cornersocialnyc. com* Ⓜ *2, 3 to 125th St.*

Fodor'sChoice	**Ginny's Supperclub.** Head downstairs from Marcus Samuelsson's re-
★	nowned Red Rooster restaurant and find yourself in a glamorous lounge
that seems right out of the 1920s. The cocktails are classic with a modern flair and there is live music and/or DJs most Saturday evenings
and some weeknights, as well as a gospel brunch. ⊠ *310 Lenox Ave.,
at 125th St., Harlem* ☎ *212/421–3821* ⊕ *www.ginnyssupperclub.com*
Ⓜ *2, 3 to 125th St.*

Harlem Public. A juicy burger, live music, and more than a dozen craft
beers on tap makes this the type of neighborhood watering hole every
New Yorker wants on their corner. Plenty of stools fill the exposed brick
space, along with a scattering of tables on the sidewalk during warm
weather. It's an unfussy spot to raise a glass after a day of exploring
vibrant Harlem. ⊠ *3612 Broadway, at 149th St., Harlem* ☎ *212/939–
9404* ⊕ *www.harlempublic.com* Ⓜ *1, A, B, C, D to 145th St.*

Shrine. It doesn't look like much from the outside, but this small performance venue with a global slant hosts multiple events each night,
including live music, DJs, spoken word, and dance. ⊠ *2271 Adam Clayton Powell Jr. Blvd. , between 133rd and 134th sts.* ☎ *212/690–7807*
⊕ *www.shrinenyc.com* Ⓜ *2, 3 to 135th St.*

JAZZ VENUES

Minton's. Welcome back. The jazz institution that once featured big-name
performers such as Dizzy Gillespie and Duke Ellington has reopened
as a sophisticated supper club with a roster of house-band jazz performers and featured musicians. The southern revival food is garnering
acclaim (the kitchen is shared with the Cecil restaurant next door). It's
not a cheap night out but worth the splurge. Jackets are required for
men. ⊠ *206 W. 118 St., near Adam Clayton Powell Jr. Blvd., Harlem*
☎ *212/243–2222* ⊕ *www.mintonsharlem.com* Ⓜ *2, 3, B, C to 116th St.*

BROOKLYN

CARROLL GARDENS
BARS

Fodor'sChoice	**Clover Club.** Long recognized for excellent drinks—both classic and
★	inspired by the classics—and a cozy vibe, this is one of the best cock-
tail bars in Brooklyn. The whole operation is thanks to Julie Reiner, a
passionate mixologist and businesswoman who has long been a leader
in the industry. Each quarter, she and her barstaff write a seasonal
cocktail list, inspired perhaps by a spirit (Chartreuse, for example) or
a classic drink style (like the flip). Weekends get busy; we recommend
weekdays in the early evening when you can sit at the bar and call
bartender's choice. Weekend brunch is very good, too, and not just for
the bloody mary: the lamb buger is excellent and there's a nice selection of baked eggs. ⊠ *210 Smith St., Carroll Gardens* ☎ *718/855–7939*
⊕ *www.cloverclubny.com* Ⓜ *F, G to Bergen St.*

DUMBO
BARS

Superfine. The narrow bar and bilevel floor plan might seem a little odd, but friendly service and a convivial crowd transform this renovated warehouse into a welcoming neighborhood spot. The kitchen's organic menu changes seasonally, but the real action is at the bar, where stiff libations are poured near the popular, orange-felt pool table. ✉ *126 Front St., between Jay and Pearl Sts., DUMBO* ☎ *718/243–9005* ⊗ *Closed Mon.* Ⓜ *A, C to High St.; F to York St.*

WILLIAMSBURG
BARS

Barcade. Stop reminiscing about your arcade-loving youth and start playing the more than 30 vintage video games (most cost a mere quarter) lining the walls of this high-spirited bar-arcade. Challenge yourself with favorites like Ms. Pacman or rarities like Rampage. Barcade isn't just about the games, though: there's a good selection of microbrews, as well as snacks. ✉ *388 Union Ave., between Ainslie and Powers Sts., North Williamsburg* ☎ *718/302–6464* ⊕ *www.barcadebrooklyn.com* Ⓜ *G to Metropolitan Ave., L to Lorimer St.*

Fodor's Choice ★ **Ides Bar.** Without a doubt the buzziest bar in Williamsburg, the Ides benefits from its privileged position on the Wythe Hotel's rooftop. Well-heeled patrons from all over the world line up for entry and the jaw-dropping views of the Manhattan skyline. It's a hot spot on weekends, and crowded—-its more than worth it to go early and have that memorable view all to yourself. ✉ *Wythe Hotel, 80 Wythe Ave., 6th fl., North Williamsburg* ☎ *718/460-8006* ⊕ *www.wythehotel.com/the-ides* Ⓜ *L to Bedford Ave.*

Fodor's Choice ★ **Maison Premiere.** Step inside this buzzy bar and restaurant, marked only by a small "Bar, Oysters" sign, and you'll instantly feel whisked away to New Orleans. Sip expertly made cocktails at the horseshoe-shape bar, or dine on platters of oysters at one of the café tables (there are full dinner and brunch menus as well). In spring and summer, the back garden is a lush oasis with cast-iron tables amid wisteria and palms. ✉ *298 Bedford Ave., at S. 1st St., South Williamsburg* ☎ *347/335–0446* ⊕ *www.maisonpremiere.com* Ⓜ *L to Bedford Ave.*

Radegast Hall & Biergarten. The vibe is boisterous at this sprawling beer garden, with plenty of communal tables that foster a convivial atmosphere. The Central European beers on tap and in bottles pair well with hearty foods like schnitzel, goulash, and delicious hot pretzels. There's live music most nights. ✉ *113 N. 3rd St., North Williamsburg* ☎ *718/963-3973* ⊕ *www.radegasthall.com* Ⓜ *L to Bedford Ave.*

Spuyten Duyvil. You might need to be a beer geek to recognize the obscure names of the more than 100 imported microbrews available here, but the connoisseurs behind the bar are more than happy to offer detailed descriptions and make recommendations. They'll also help you choose cheese and charcuterie platters to match your beverages. The space is narrow, with limited seating: all the more reason to take advantage of the huge backyard in summer. ✉ *359 Metropolitan Ave.,*

19

near Havemeyer St., North Williamsburg ☎ *718/963–4140* ⊕ *www. spuytenduyvilnyc.com* Ⓜ *L to Lorimer St., G to Metropolitan Ave.*

LIVE MUSIC VENUES

Bembe. This steamy, bilevel lounge is Williamsburg's answer to Miami clubbing, though decorated with salvaged items including an old redwood front door from a New York State winery. The crowd is as eclectic as the DJ-spun beats, from reggae to Brazilian—often accompanied by live drumming. The tropical bar menu gives the place its Latin cred. ✉ *81 S. 6th St., at Berry St., South Williamsburg* ☎ *718/387–5389* ⊕ *www.bembe.us* Ⓜ *J, M, Z to Marcy Ave.*

Music Hall of Williamsburg. This intimate, trilevel music venue in a former mayonnaise factory has excellent acoustics, so it's no surprise that it draws die-hard fans of rock and indie music. There's balcony seating and an additional bar upstairs. If you love Manhattan's Bowery Ballroom, you'll feel the same way about this venue; in fact, it's run by the bookers at Bowery Presents, so expect the same quality lineups. ✉ *66 N. 6th St., near Wythe Ave., North Williamsburg* ☎ *718/486–5400* ⊕ *www.musichallofwilliamsburg.com* Ⓜ *L to Bedford Ave.*

Union Pool. This former pool-supply store is a funky multipurpose venue, complete with a corrugated tin–backed bar, a photo booth, a small stage for live music, and cheap PBR. It's a popular spot on the Friday-night circuit, especially for late-night dancing. The back patio has a taco truck and a fire pit. ✉ *484 Union Ave., near Meeker Ave., North Williamsburg* ☎ *718/609–0484* ⊕ *www.union-pool.com* Ⓜ *G to Metropolitan Ave., L to Lorimer St.*

BUSHWICK AND EAST WILLIAMSBURG

BARS

Fodor's Choice
★

Featherweight. The cocktail list at this small spot is full of the hits you'd expect at a bar run by the experts behind the two Weather Up spaces in Manhattan and Prospect Heights. Part of the allure, though, is that bartenders will mix a cocktail to your precise specifications. Prime time here is late night. Finding the entrance is part of the fun: look for the painted feather and the three-story-tall mural of a boxer. ✉ *135 Graham Ave., at Johnson Ave., East Williamsburg* ⊕ *www.featherweightbk.com* Ⓜ *J, M to Lorimer St.; L to Montrose Ave.*

PARK SLOPE

BARS

Union Hall. This neighborhood standby has something going on just about every night. On the main floor, two bocce courts and a library nook with couches and fireplace are popular hangouts; downstairs, there are smart comedy shows featuring *Daily Show* and *Saturday Night Live* regulars, eclectic talks, or DJs spinning. The outdoor patio is open in good weather. The menu of perfectly tasty burgers, sandwiches, and bar snacks (the beer cheese is a highlight) means the patrons tend to settle in for the evening. Events are either free or have a modest cover ($5 to $20). ✉ *702 Union St., at 5th Ave., Park Slope* ☎ *718/638–4400* ⊕ *www.unionhallny.com* Ⓜ *R to Union St.*

LIVE MUSIC VENUES

Fodor's Choice ★ **Barbès.** Outstanding regulars like the Django Reinhardt mantle-bearer Stephane Wrembel, western-swingers Brain Cloud, and Slavic Soul Party spin threads of folk and "ethnic" into 21st century music, while the Erik Satie Quartet keep Satie, Britten, and other classical composers relevant. Performances take place in the back room, where a pitcher is passed to collect the $10 suggested cover. Up front, the somewhat musty bar has a laid-back vibe and a full cocktail menu. ⊠ *376 9th St., at 6th Ave., Park Slope* ☎ *347/422–0248* ⊕ *www.barbesbrooklyn.com* Ⓜ *F, G to 7th Ave.*

QUEENS

ASTORIA

BARS

Bohemian Hall & Beer Garden. Warm summer nights and cold beers have been savored by locals for over 100 years at the Bohemian Hall & Beer Garden. With pitchers of beer, picnic tables, live music, and Czech dishes from the kitchen, this sunny garden is an ideal spot for getting together with old friends—or making new ones over big mugs of Staropramen and Pilsner Urquell. ⊠ *29-19 24th Ave., Astoria* ☎ *718/274–4925* ⊕ *www.bohemianhall.com* Ⓜ *N, Q to Astoria–Ditmars Blvd.*

LONG ISLAND CITY

BARS

Dutch Kills. The dark bar and cozy wooden booths at Dutch Kills—a cocktail den with a nod to the neighborhood's historic roots—serves up finely crafted drinks at a few dollars cheaper than similar Manhattan watering holes. Expect precisely chiseled chunks of ice and skilled bartenders that, with a few queries into your preferences and curiosities, can create a concoction just to your taste. ⊠ *27-24 Jackson Ave., Long Island City* ☎ *718/383–2724* ⊕ *www.dutchkillsbar.com* Ⓜ *E, M, R to Queens Plaza; G to Court Sq.; 7, N, Q to Queensboro Plaza.*

19

PERFORMING ARTS

Updated by
John Rambow

"Where do you wait tables?" is the not-so-ironic question New York performers get when they say they're in the arts. Even more telling is that most of these toughened artists don't miss a beat when they respond with the restaurant's name. Fact is, if you're an aspiring performer here, you'd better be tough and competitive. There is a constant influx of artists from around the globe, and all these actors, singers, dancers, and musicians striving for their big break infuse the city with a crackling creative energy.

Just as tough are the audiences. Although rising ticket prices have made attending a Broadway show a less common outing for even the most devout theater-loving New Yorkers, that's not true of many other kinds of performances. Whether the audiences are primarily local or not, it's their discernment that helps drive the arts scene, whether they are flocking to a concert hall to hear a world-class soprano deliver a flawless performance, or crowding into a cramped café to support fledgling writers reading from their own work.

New York has somewhere between 200 and 250 "legitimate" theaters (meaning those with theatrical performances, not movies), and many more ad hoc venues—parks, churches, lofts, galleries, rooftops, even parking lots. The city is also a revolving door of special events: summer jazz, one-act-play marathons, film festivals, and music and dance celebrations from the classical to the avant-garde, to name just a few. It's this unrivaled wealth of culture and art that many New Yorkers cite as the reason they're here, and the reason why millions more make the migration.

PLANNING

DANCE, OPERA, MUSIC, AND MORE

In addition to theater, New York is one of the premier cities in the world for ballet and contemporary dance, opera, and classical music. Start your search with a visit to the websites of the three biggest performing-arts centers: Lincoln Center (⊕ *www.lincolncenter.org*), Carnegie Hall (⊕ *www.carnegiehall.org*), and the Brooklyn Academy of Music (⊕ *www.bam.org*). They all have detailed events calendars, and their listings demonstrate the sheer depth of great performances available in New York. It's also helpful to consider the time you're visiting. Many arts groups schedule their local performances from September through May, with special holiday events planned in November and December. Although the number of performances in many venues taper off in the dog days of summer, the period also brings lots of festivals and outdoor performances, many of them inexpensive or free. Finally, it's smart to also check out the websites of any museums you think you might want to visit while in town. The Frick, for instance, has been hosting world-class classical-music concerts in its 175-seat Music Room since 1939, the Metropolitan Museum of Art periodically stages concerts on its rooftop, or near the Egyptian Temple of Dendur, or in its enviable gallery of musical instruments.

WHAT'S ON?

The *New York Times* (⊕ *www.nytimes.com/events*) listings are probably the single best place to find out what's happening in the city. The *New Yorker* (⊕ *www.newyorker.com*) is more selective; its "Goings On" app lets you filter performances and other events by location. *New York* magazine (⊕ *www.nymag.com*) gives a slightly more opinionated spin on the performing arts. All three publish preview issues listing the major events coming in the season ahead. The theater sites ⊕ *www.playbill.com*, ⊕ *www.theatermania.com*, and ⊕ *www.offoffonline.com* (for Off-Off-Broadway) provide synopses, accessibility info, run times, seating charts, and links to buy tickets.

BROADWAY AND OFF-BROADWAY— WHAT'S THE DIFFERENCE?

There are roughly 40 Broadway theaters in New York, and although you might expect their shows to be the best ones in town, the definition depends on theater capacity, not quality. Per the Actors' Equity union, which determines such matters, a Broadway theater must have at least 500 seats, though most have at least 1,000. Nearly all are within a few blocks of Times Square. A show must be performed in a Broadway theater to be eligible for a Tony Award. Off-Broadway theaters, which are scattered throughout Manhattan, have 100 to 499 seats; Off-Off-Broadway venues seat fewer than 100.

BUYING TICKETS AT FULL PRICE

How much do tickets sell for, anyway? The average price paid for a Broadway show hovers around $100; not counting the limited "premium seat" category (or discount deals), the low end for musicals is in the $50–$75 range. Nonmusical comedies and dramas start at about

20

$60 and top out at about $120. Off-Broadway show tickets average $60–$90, and Off-Off-Broadway shows can run as low as $15–$25, or even less if you find a deal. Tickets to an opera start at about $25 for nosebleed seats and can soar to more than $400 for prime locations. Classical music concerts go for $25 to $100 or more, depending on the venue and the performers. Dance performances are usually in the $15 to $60 range, but expect choice seats for the ballet to cost more, especially around the holidays.

Scoring tickets is fairly easy, especially if you have some flexibility. Always start with the website of the venue or theater company to see what deals and prices are available. If timing or cost is critical, the only way to ensure the seats you want is to make your purchase in advance—and that might be months ahead for a hit show. In general, tickets for Saturday evening and for weekend matinees are the toughest to secure, and the priciest.

For smaller performing-arts companies, and especially for Off-Broadway shows, try **Ticket Central,** on Theater Row; service charges are nominal here. **SmartTix** is a reliable resource for (usually) smaller performing-arts companies, including dance and music; their service charges are nominal as well.

Sure bets for Broadway (and some other big-hall events) are the box office or either **Telecharge** or **Ticketmaster.** Virtually all larger shows are listed with one service or the other, but never both; specifying "premium" helps get elusive—and expensive (sometimes topping $500)—seats. A broker or your hotel concierge should be able to procure last-minute tickets, but prices may even exceed "premium" rates. Be prepared to pay steep add-on fees (per ticket *and* per order) for all ticketing services.

■TIP➡ Although online ticket services provide seating maps to help you choose, the advantage of going to the box office is twofold: there are no add-on service fees, and a ticket seller can personally advise you about sight lines—and knee room—for the seat location you are considering. Broadway box offices do not usually have direct phone lines; their walk-in hours are generally 10 am until curtain.

BUYING DISCOUNT TICKETS

The cheapest—though chanciest—ticket opportunities are found at participating theater box offices on the day of the performance. These rush tickets, usually about $25–$40, may be distributed by lottery and are usually for front-row (possibly neck-craning) seats, though it can vary by theater. Check the comprehensive planner on ⊕ *www.nytix.com* or go to the box office of the show you are interested in to discover whether they make such an offer and how to pursue it. Obstructed-view seats or those in the very rear balcony are sometimes available for advance purchase; the price point on these is usually in the $35–$40 range.

For advanced discount purchases, the best seating is likely available by using a discount code. Procure these codes, good for 20% to 50% off, online. (You need to register on each website.) The excellent no-subscription-required ⊕ *www.broadwaybox.com* posts all discount

Best Tips for Broadway

Whether forking over hundreds of dollars for a top seat or shoestringing it with a standing-room ticket, you'll have better Broadway experiences to brag about if you take our advice.

Do your homework. Remember—your friend's must-see may not be yours. Subscribe to online newsletters ahead of your trip for access to show synopses, special ticket offers, and more. If it's a classic play or opera, you may enjoy it more if you've read a synopsis before you go.

Reserve ahead. The TKTS booth is great if you're up for what the fates make available, but for must-sees, book early. While you're at it, ask whether the regular cast is expected. (An in-person stop at the box office is the most reliable way to score this information, but don't hold them to it unless it's the day of the performance. If there is a change then—and the replacement cast is not acceptable to you—you may get a refund.) For musicals, live music often adds a special zing; confirm when ticketing to avoid surprises on the rare occasion when recorded music is used.

Check theater seating charts. Front mezzanine is a great option; with seats that overhang the orchestra section, they can be better (though not always less expensive) than many orchestra seats. Book with a seating chart at hand (available online and at the box office). Check accessibility, especially at older theaters with multiple flights of stairs and few elevators.

Know when to go. Typically, Broadway shows give eight performances a week. There are nightly performances from Tuesday through Saturday night, and matinees at 2 pm on Wednesday and Saturday and at 3 pm on Sunday (on Monday most theaters are closed, or "dark"). Saturday night and Wednesday matinee are the most difficult. Weeknights are popular with locals. Tuesday is especially promising, and typically an earlier curtain—7 or 7:30 instead of the usual 8 pm—helps ensure a good night's sleep for your next day of touring.

Dress right. You can throw on jeans to go to the theater these days, but personally we feel shorts and sneakers have no place on Broadway (at least in the audience). Bring binoculars if your seats are up high, leave behind the bulky coat (coat checks are *not* the norm), and drop bags and packages off at your hotel room in advance—theater seats tend to be narrow, with little leg room.

Travel smart. Trying to get to the show on time? Unless you don't mind watching the meter run up while you're stuck in traffic, avoid cabs into or out of Times Square. Walk, especially if you're within 10 blocks of the theater. Otherwise, take the subway; many train lines converge in the area.

Dine off Broadway. Dining well on a budget and doing Broadway right are not mutually exclusive. The key is to avoid eating in Times Square itself—even the national chains are overpriced. Consider eating earlier instead, in whatever neighborhood you're visiting that day. If you're already in Midtown, head west to 9th or 10th Avenue, where prix-fixe deals and ethnic eateries are plentiful and many actors and theater folk live. You never know whom you'll see on the street or at the next table.

20

codes currently available for Broadway shows. As with all discount codes provided through online subscriber services—**TheaterMania, Playbill,** and **Best of Off Broadway** among them—to avoid service charges, you must bring the printout to the box office, and make your purchase there.

For seats at 25% to 50% off the usual price, go to one of the **TKTS booths** (⊕ *www.tdf.org*): there's one in Times Square, another at South Street Seaport, and a third in downtown Brooklyn. Although they do tack on a $4-per-ticket service charge, and not all shows are predictably available, the broad choices and ease of selection—and, of course, the solid discount—make TKTS the go-to source for the flexible theatergoer. You can browse available shows for that day online or via a TKTS app, or check the electronic listings board near the ticket windows to mull over your options while you're in line. At the Times Square location (look for the red glass staircase), there is a separate "Play Express" window (for nonmusical events) to further simplify (and expedite) things. Times Square hours are: Monday and Wednesday–Saturday 3–8, and Tuesday 2–8 for evening performances; for Wednesday and Saturday matinees 10–2; for Sunday matinees 11–3; and for Sunday evening shows, from 3 until 7. The South Street Seaport location, at the corner of Front and John streets, is open Monday–Saturday 11–6, and Sunday 11–4, except in winter. Brooklyn hours are Tuesday–Saturday 11–3 and 3:30–6. All ticket sales are for shows on that same day (one exception: the Brooklyn location's matinee tickets are for next-day performances only). Credit cards, cash, or traveler's checks are accepted at all locations. ■TIP→ **Ticket-booth hours may vary over holiday periods.**

Contacts Best of Off Broadway. ☎ 212/874–5348 ⊕ *www.bestofoffbroadway. com.* **Playbill.** ⊕ *www.playbill.com.* **SmartTix.** ☎ 212/868–4444 ⊕ *www. smarttix.com.* **Telecharge.** ☎ 212/239–6200, 800/447–7400 outside NYC ⊕ *www.telecharge.com.* **TheaterMania.** ☎ 212/947–8844 ⊕ *www.theatermania. com.* **Ticket Central.** ☎ 212/279–4200 ⊕ *www.ticketcentral.com* Ⓜ 1, 2, 3, 7, N, Q, R, S to Times Sq.–42nd St.; A, C, E to 42nd St.–Port Authority. **Ticketmaster.** ☎ 866/448–7849 for automated service, 800/745–3000 ⊕ *www.ticketmaster. com.* **TKTS.** ☎ 212/912–9770 ⊕ *www.tdf.org* Ⓜ 1, 2, 3, 7, N, Q, R, S to Times Sq.–42nd St. **TKTS.** ☎ 212/912–9770 ⊕ *www.tdf.org* Ⓜ A, C, F, R to Jay St.–MetroTech; 2, 3, 4, 5 to Borough Hall. **TKTS.** ☎ 212/912–9770 ⊕ *www.tdf.org* Ⓜ 2, 3, 4, 5, A, C, J, Z to Fulton St.

PERFORMING ARTS IN NEW YORK CITY

Listings are alphabetical by neighborhood.

LOWER MANHATTAN

FINANCIAL DISTRICT
MUSIC
FAMILY **Brookfield Place Winter Garden.** This office complex across the street from the World Trade Center hosts occasional musical performances, which have included jazz, gospel, avant-garde, and site-specific sound installations, as well as a little theater, dance, and film. Events are presented within Brookfield Place's spectacular 10-story glass-covered Winter

Garden atrium, or on its outdoor plaza, overlooking the Hudson, and are almost always free. ⊠ *World Financial Center, West St., between Vesey and Liberty sts., Financial District* ⊕ *www.brookfieldplaceny. com/EventsCalendar* Ⓜ *E to World Trade Center; 1 to Rector St.*

TRIBECA
MUSIC

FAMILY **Tribeca Performing Arts Center.** This center celebrates theater (with a clever children's series) and dance but is primarily known for jazz. Highlights in Jazz and Lost Jazz Shrines are two of its special series. ⊠ *199 Chambers St., at Greenwich St., TriBeCa* ☎ *212/220–1459* ⊕ *www. tribecapac.org* Ⓜ *1, 2, 3 to Chambers St.*

READINGS AND LECTURES

Poets House. Situated in a bright and airy building in the residential area of Battery Park City and near the Hudson River, this reading room is an open resource for all ages, with a 50,000-volume library, readings, and other poetry-centric events. ⊠ *Battery Park City, 10 River Terr., at Murray St., TriBeCa* ☎ *212/431–7920* ⊕ *www.poetshouse.org* ⊙ *Reading room Tues.–Fri. 11–7, Sat. 11–6* Ⓜ *E to World Trade Center; 1, 2, 3, A, C, E to Chambers St.*

SOHO
READINGS AND LECTURES

Fodor's Choice **The Greene Space** (*Jerome L. Greene Performance Space*). The local
★ public radio stations WNYC and WQXR invite the public into their intimate (125 seats) studio for live shows featuring classical, rock, jazz, and new music; audio theater; conversation; and interviews. It's a great place to get up-close with writers and newsmakers, as well as musicians and actors who might be playing Carnegie Hall, Broadway, or the Met Opera a few days later. ⊠ *44 Charlton St., at Varick St., SoHo* ☎ *646/829–4000* ⊕ *www.thegreenespace.org* Ⓜ *C, E to Spring St.; 1 to Houston St.*

Housing Works Bookstore Cafe. Amid roughly 25,000 books and CDs for sale, Housing Works hosts a wide range of literary and cultural events, including quirky readings, sometimes with unannounced surprise guests; journal and book launches; and storytelling or music nights. This cozy store is staffed largely by volunteers, and all profits go toward fighting homelessness and HIV/AIDS. ⊠ *126 Crosby St., between Houston and Prince sts., SoHo* ☎ *212/334–3324* ⊕ *www.housingworks.org/ bookstore* ⊙ *Weekdays 9–9, weekends 9–5* Ⓜ *N, R to Prince St.; B, D, F, M to Broadway–Lafayette St.; 6 to Bleecker St.*

THEATER

HERE. Celebrating all manner of contemporary, genre-bending productions, the original home of Eve Ensler's *The Vagina Monologues* and Basil Twist's *Symphonie Fantastique* also houses art exhibitions and a café. ⊠ *145 6th Ave., between Spring and Broome sts., SoHo* ☎ *212/352–3101 for tickets* ⊕ *www.here.org* Ⓜ *C, E to Spring St.*

20

EAST VILLAGE AND LOWER EAST SIDE

EAST VILLAGE

DANCE

Danspace Project. Founded to foster the work of independent choreographers such as Lucinda Childs and David Gordon, Danspace Project sponsors performances that are as fresh—and idiosyncratic—as the historic church space they occupy. Performance series curated by guest artists are also a regular part of the calendar. ⊠ *St. Mark's Church in-the-Bowery, 131 E. 10th St., at 2nd Ave., East Village* ☎ *212/674–8112, 866/811–4111 for tickets* ⊕ *www.danspaceproject.org* Ⓜ *6 to Astor Pl.; N, R to 8th St.–NYU.*

FILM

Fodor's Choice

★

Anthology Film Archives. Dedicated to preserving and exhibiting independent and avant-garde film, Anthology Film Archives is made up of two screening rooms that seat 187 and 75 as well as a film repository, all inside a renovated red-brick courthouse. Cofounded in the 1960s by the downtown legend and filmmaker Jonas Mekas, Anthology remains a major destination for adventurous and unusual movies, new as well as old. The Essential Cinema series delves into the works of canonized, groundbreaking directors; the frequent festivals are more eclectic and may cover under-recognized auteurs, such as a series devoted to the director Edgar G. Ulmer, as well as hard-to-see films of all types. This is an experience for film lovers, not casual moviegoers, so don't expect the amenities you'd find at a multiplex. ⊠ *32 2nd Ave., at 2nd St., East Village* ☎ *212/505–5181* ⊕ *www.anthologyfilmarchives.org* Ⓜ *F to 2nd Ave.*

MUSIC

SubCulture. With its exposed brick, structural pillars, theater-style seating, and industrial-chic bar, this intimate subterranean concert hall could just as easily be a cool lounge as a venue for classical (especially chamber), jazz, and new music. Series here have included performances of all of Beethoven's string quartets, as well as an annual PianoFest, which brings in some of the most exciting pianists from across many genres. The calendar also finds room for singer-songwriters, comedians, and performers of world music. ⊠ *Downstairs, 45 Bleecker St., between the Bowery and Lafayette St., East Village* ☎ *212/533–5470* ⊕ *www. subculturenewyork.com* Ⓜ *6 to Bleecker St.; B, D, F, M to Broadway–Lafayette St.; N, R to Prince St.*

READINGS AND LECTURES

KGB Bar. A nexus of the downtown literary scene, KGB keeps a busy calendar of readings and discussions: start with Sunday Night Fiction or KGB Poetry on Monday night. The name and the Soviet kitsch are a nod to the bar's history as a speakeasy for leftist Ukrainians. ⊠ *85 E. 4th St., between the Bowery and 2nd Ave., East Village* ☎ *212/505–3360* ⊕ *www.kgbbar.com* Ⓜ *F to 2nd Ave.*

Fodor's Choice

★

The Moth. Founded in 1997 and dedicated to first-person storytelling, this roving series has spread far beyond just New York, where it was founded in 1997 by the writer George Dawes Green. But it's still going strong here: the Mainstage shows bring together luminaries to tell their stories and maybe dish a little too. At the much looser open-mic Story-SLAMs, competitors are randomly selected and given just five minutes to tell their story, which must tie in with the night's theme. These tales get told at Housing Works and other venues downtown and in Brooklyn. ⊠ *Housing Works Bookstore Cafe, 126 Crosby St.* ☎ *212/742–0551* Ⓜ *B, D, F, M to Broadway–Lafayette St.: N, R to Prince St.*

Nuyorican Poets Cafe. The reigning arbiter of poetry slams, the Nuyorican Poets Cafe hosts open-mic events and the influential granddaddy (b. 1989) of the spoken-word scene, the Friday Night Poetry Slam. Other performances, including hip-hop open mics, jazz acts, and theatrical performances, round out the schedule. Though there are a small number of reserved tickets for popular shows like the Friday Night Poetry Slam and the Monday night open mics, it's still a good idea to line up early; the small venue gets packed quickly. ⊠ *236 E. 3rd St., between Aves. B and C, East Village* ☎ *212/780–9386* ⊕ *www.nuyorican.org* Ⓜ *F to 2nd Ave.; J, M, Z to Essex St.*

The Poetry Project. Launched in 1966, the Poetry Project has been a source of sustenance for poets (and their audiences) ever since. This place has seen performances by Allen Ginsberg, Amiri Baraka, Sam Shepard, Patti Smith, Anne Waldman, and many others. At current readings you might find artists of the same caliber. Prime times are Monday, Wednesday, and Friday. ⊠ *St. Mark's Church in-the-Bowery, 131 E. 10th St., at 2nd Ave., East Village* ☎ *212/674–0910* ⊕ *www. poetryproject.org* Ⓜ *6 to Astor Pl.; L to 3rd Ave.*

THEATER

Classic Stage Company. At the CSC's cozy 199-seat theater you can see excellent revivals—such as Chekhov's *Three Sisters,* Shakespeare's *Romeo and Juliet,* or several plays of Euripides—often with a modern spin, reigning theatrical stars, and new scores. ⊠ *136 E. 13th St., between 3rd and 4th aves., East Village* ☎ *212/677–4210* ⊕ *www. classicstage.org* Ⓜ *4, 5, 6, L, N, Q, R to 14th St.–Union Sq.*

La MaMa E.T.C. Ellen Stewart (1919–2011) founded La MaMa E.T.C. in 1961 in a small Manhattan basement. Since that time, the Experimental Theatre Club has grown continuously, all the while taking risks on unknown works that cross cultures and performance disciplines. ⊠ *66 E. 4th St., between the Bowery and 2nd Ave., East Village* ☎ *646/430–5374 for tickets* ⊕ *www.lamama.org* Ⓜ *F to 2nd Ave.; B, D, F, M to Broadway–Lafayette St.; 6 to Bleecker St.*

20

New York Theatre Workshop. Works by new and established playwrights anchor this theater's repertoire. Jonathan Larson's *Rent* got its start here before going to Broadway, as did the hit musical *Once.* Works by Tony Kushner (*Homebody/Kabul*), Caryl Churchill, Amy Herzog, and Paul Rudnick have also been staged here. Hit the box office for Sunday night CheapTix; those seats are $20—in cash—as available (advance purchase is recommended). ⊠ *79 E. 4th St., between the Bowery and 2nd Ave., East Village* ☎ *212/279–4200 for tickets* ⊕ *www.nytw.org* Ⓜ *F to 2nd Ave.; B, D, F, M to Broadway–Lafayette St.; 6 to Astor Pl.*

Performance Space 122 (PS122). Founded in 1979 inside a 19th-century public school building, Performance Space 122 has helped launch the careers of many a downtown musician and artist, both super-fringey and otherwise. After an extensive overhaul that's scheduled to be finished in 2016, it will reopen with two new theaters and a much modernized interior. Until then you can catch performances in other venues around town, particularly during the two-week COIL festival, held in January. ⊠ *150 1st Ave., at 9th St., East Village* ☎ *212/477–5829 for tickets* ⊕ *www.ps122.org* Ⓜ *6 to Astor Pl.; L to 1st Ave.*

The Public Theater. Fresh theater, such as *Here Lies Love,* David Byrne' and Fatboy Slim's "poperetta" about Imelda Marcos, keep people talking about the Public Theater. Many noted productions that began here (*Hair, A Chorus Line*) went on to Broadway and beyond. Some shows release limited-availability $20 or $40 rush standby tickets at the box office (two tickets max; cash only). Check online for available performances. ⊠ *425 Lafayette St., south of Astor Pl., East Village* ☎ *212/539–8500, 212/967–7555 for tickets* ⊕ *www.publictheater.org* Ⓜ *6 to Astor Pl.; N, R to 8th St.–NYU.*

Theater for the New City. This four-theater cultural complex stages three- or four-week-long runs of new shows by emerging and mid-career American playwrights. The socially conscious group also runs a free summer program of street theater, performed in all five boroughs. ⊠ *155 1st Ave., between 9th and 10th sts., East Village* ☎ *212/254–1109* ⊕ *www.theaterforthenewcity.net* Ⓜ *6 to Astor Pl.; L to 1st Ave.*

LOWER EAST SIDE

FILM

Sunshine Cinema. Talk about busy: according to a *Village Voice* article, this storied building, which supposedly dates back to 1844, has served as "a church, an immigrant meeting hall, a boxing venue, a nickelodeon, a Yiddish vaudeville house, a hardware warehouse, a graffiti showcase, and an indie-rock playroom." Since 2001, it's been a great neighborhood theater showing a mix of art-house and smaller-release mainstream-independent films on five decent-size screens. Great midnight movies play, too. ⊠ *143 E. Houston St., between 1st and 2nd aves., Lower East Side* ☎ *212/260–7289* ⊕ *www.landmarktheatres.com* Ⓜ *F to 2nd Ave.*

THEATER

Dixon Place. Founded back in the rough-and-ready 1980s, this small theater continues to host worthy, and frequently whacked-out and hilarious, performances. Its popular HOT! Festival of Queer Performance, held in July, is the longest-running LGBTQ festival in the world. Whatever you're seeing, the Lounge, Dixon Place's cheerful bar, is a great place to meet up before the show and connect with artists after. ⊠ *161A Chrystie St., between Rivington and Delancey sts., Lower East Side* ☎ *212/219–0736* ⊕ *www.dixonplace.org* Ⓜ *J, Z to Bowery; B, D to Grand St.; F to 2nd Ave.*

GREENWICH VILLAGE AND WEST VILLAGE

GREENWICH VILLAGE

FILM

Angelika Film Center. Foreign, independent, and some mainstream films are screened here. Despite its (six) tunnel-like theaters, small screens, and the occasionally audible subway rumble below, it's usually packed; get a snack at the café while you wait for your movie to be called. ✉ *18 W. Houston St., at Mercer St., Greenwich Village* 🕾 *212/995–2570* ⊕ *www.angelikafilmcenter.com/nyc* Ⓜ *B, D, F, M to Broadway–Lafayette St.; 6 to Bleecker St.; N, R to Prince St.*

IFC Center. Sharing the same owner as the IFC cable channel, the IFC Center shows a mix of repertory and first-run independent, art-house, shorts (including cartoons), and foreign movies. Despite the modern wire-mesh facade, there are still clues that this was once the much-beloved Waverly Theater. ✉ *323 6th Ave., at 3rd St., Greenwich Village* 🕾 *212/924–7771* ⊕ *www.ifccenter.com* Ⓜ *A, B, C, D, E, F, M to W. 4th St.*

READINGS AND LECTURES

Center for Architecture. This contemporary glass-faced gallery near Washington Square hosts lively discussions (which may be accompanied by films or other visuals) on topics like radical architecture in Mexico City or what to expect when you renovate an apartment. ✉ *536 LaGuardia Pl., between 3rd and Bleecker sts., Greenwich Village* 🕾 *212/683–0023* ⊕ *www.aiany.org* ☉ *Exhibits weekdays 9–8, Sat. 11–5* Ⓜ *A, B, C, D, E, F, M to W. 4th St.*

New York Studio School. The venerable New York Studio School hosts two—always free, almost always on Tuesday and Wednesday—evening lecture series on contemporary issues in art. Hear from both emerging and established artists and curators, as well as some of the biggest names in art history and criticism. The school building served as the original location of the Whitney Museum. ✉ *8 W. 8th St., between 5th and 6th aves., Greenwich Village* 🕾 *212/673–6466* ⊕ *www.nyss.org* Ⓜ *A, B, C, D, E, F, M to W. 4th St.*

THEATER

FAMILY
Fodor'sChoice
★

Monday Night Magic. Since 1997, Michael Chaut and four other magician producers have been running these weekly performances in and around Greenwich Village. The acts, usually four per night, come from all over the world and often include performers you'd see in much bigger theaters and clubs on other nights. The mind-reading and sleight-of-hand with birds, cards, balls, and handkerchiefs come at a fast pace and don't let up during intermission, when a couple additional magicians appear in the lobby and back of the theater for card tricks and other "close-up magic." Although the acts are tailored for an adult audience, they're also suitable for younger prestidigitators. ✉ *The Players Theatre, 115 MacDougal St., between 3rd and Bleecker sts.* 🕾 *212/615–6432* ⊕ *www.mondaynightmagic.com* Ⓜ *A, B, C, D, E, F, M to W. 4th St.*

20

FAMILY   **Skirball Center for the Performing Arts.** This pristine, wood-lined theater on the NYU campus supports emerging artists, with interesting dance, music, and theater events, often in collaboration with international companies. Conferences and even a circus or two round out the calendar, which also includes many family-friendly events. ⊠ *566 LaGuardia Pl., at Washington Sq. S, Greenwich Village* ☎ *212/998–4941 for tickets, 888/611–8183 for tickets* ⊕ *www.nyuskirball.org* Ⓜ *A, B, C, D, E, F, M to W. 4th St.; N, R to 8th St.–NYU.*

WEST VILLAGE

FILM

Fodor's Choice   **Film Forum.** In addition to premiering new international features and
★   documentaries that are otherwise hard to catch on the big screen, this nonprofit theater with three small screening rooms hosts movies by canonized directors such as Hitchcock, Godard, and Bertolucci; in-depth film series devoted to particular actors or genres; and newly restored prints of classic works. The small café in the lobby serves tasty cakes and freshly popped popcorn. This is no megaplex; be prepared for small seats and screens and a cash-only box office (credit cards can be used to buy tickets online in advance). ⊠ *209 W. Houston St., between 6th Ave. and Varick St., West Village* ☎ *212/727–8110* ⊕ *www.filmforum. org* Ⓜ *1 to Houston St.*

CHELSEA

DANCE

Fodor's Choice   **Joyce Theater.** In a former Art Deco movie house in Chelsea, the 472-seat
★   Joyce Theater has superb sightlines and presents a full spectrum of contemporary dance. Pilobolus, Ballet Hispanico, and the taut and athletic Parsons Dance are regulars in the Joyce's always rewarding lineup, as are the ridiculous (and ridiculously talented) Les Ballets Trockadero de Monte Carlo, a male troupe who perform travesties of classic works in tutus and pointe shoes—the whole nine yards. ⊠ *175 8th Ave., at 19th St., Chelsea* ☎ *212/691–9740, 212/242–0800 for tickets* ⊕ *www.joyce. org* Ⓜ *A, C, E to 14th St.; L to 8th Ave.*

New York Live Arts. This Chelsea space serves as the home stage for the innovative Bill T. Jones/Arnie Zane Dance Company. It's also a laboratory for new choreographers and artists in residence, and hosts nonchoreographed events such as panel discussions. ⊠ *219 W. 19th St., between 7th and 8th aves., Chelsea* ☎ *212/691–6500, 212/924–0077 for tickets* ⊕ *www.newyorklivearts.org* Ⓜ *1 to 18th St.; A, C, E, to 14th St.; L to 8th Ave.*

THEATER

FAMILY   **TADA!** Vibrant musical theater pieces for kids are performed by all-kid casts. Most shows are on weekends, and children's tickets start at $10. ⊠ *15 W. 28th St., between Broadway and 5th Ave., Chelsea* ☎ *212/252–1619* ⊕ *www.tadatheater.com* Ⓜ *N, R to 28th St.*

MIDTOWN WEST

DANCE

Baryshnikov Arts Center. Famed dancer and actor Mikhail Baryshnikov's longtime vision came to fruition in this modern venue for contemporary dance and other performance. The center hosts a range of resident artists, including dancers and musical groups, as well as productions by boundary-breaking international choreographers. The vibrant programming is presented in the center's 238-seat Jerome Robbins Theater and the 136-seat Howard Gilman Performance Space. ⊠ *450 W. 37 St., between 9th and 10th aves., Midtown West* ☎ *646/731–3200* ⊕ *www. bacnyc.org* Ⓜ *A, C, E to 34th St.–Penn Station.*

FILM

Fodor'sChoice ★ **Museum of Modern Art (MoMA) films.** You'll find some of the most engaging international film repertory around at Roy and Niuta Titus Theaters 1 and 2, in MoMA's basement. Sometimes the films tie in with current art exhibitions; the Contenders series, which starts each fall, is a chance to catch up on the past year's releases that are likely to win awards, or at least stand the test of time. Movie tickets are available at the museum for same-day screenings (a limited number are released up to one week in advance for an extra fee). They're free if you have purchased museum admission ($25); otherwise they cost $12. ⊠ *11 W. 53rd St., between 5th and 6th aves., Midtown West* ☎ *212/708–9400* ⊕ *www.moma.org/ visit/films* Ⓜ *E, M to 5th Ave./53rd St.; B, D, F, M to 47th–50th Sts./ Rockefeller Center.*

The Paris Theatre. Across from the Plaza Hotel stands the Paris—a rare, stately remnant of the single-screen era. Opened in 1948, it retains its wide screen (and balcony) and is a fine showcase for new movies, often foreign and with a limited release. ⊠ *4 W. 58th St., between 5th and 6th aves., Midtown West* ☎ *212/688–3800* ⊕ *www.theparistheatre.com* Ⓜ *N, Q, R to 5th Ave./59th St.; F to 57th St.*

FAMILY **Ziegfeld Theatre.** Its vintage is late-1960s, but the Ziegfeld Theatre is as close as you come to a classic movie-palace experience in New York today. Its chandeliers and crimson décor, raised balcony, wide screen, some 1,100 seats, good sightlines, and solid sound system make the Ziegfeld a special place to view anything it shows. Grand-opening red-carpet galas often take place here as well. ⊠ *141 W. 54th St., between 6th and 7th aves., Midtown West* ☎ *212/765–7600 for showtimes* ⊕ *www.bowtiecinemas.com/locations/ziegfeld* Ⓜ *F to 57th St.; N, Q, R to 57th St.–7th Ave.; B, D, E to 7th Ave.*

MUSIC

FAMILY
Fodor'sChoice ★ **Carnegie Hall.** Carnegie Hall is, of course, one of the world's most famous concert halls. Its incomparable acoustics make it one of the best venues in the world to hear classical music, but it's also strong in jazz, pop, cabaret, and folk music. Since the opening-night concert on May 5, 1891, which Tchaikovsky conducted, virtually every important musician the world has known has performed in this Italian Renaissance–style building. Leonard Bernstein had his debut here; Vladimir Horowitz made his historic return to the concert stage here. The world's top orchestras perform in the grand and fabulously steep 2,804-seat

20

Isaac Stern Auditorium, the 268-seat Weill Recital Hall often features young talents making their New York debuts, and the subterranean 599-seat Judy and Arthur Zankel Hall attracts big-name artists such as the Kronos Quartet and Milton Nascimento to its modern and stylish space. A noted roster of family concerts is also part of Carnegie's programming. The Carnegie box office releases $10 rush tickets for some shows on the day of performance, or you may buy partial-view seating in advance at 50% off the full ticket price. ⊠ *881 7th Ave., at 57th St., Midtown West* ☎ *212/247–7800* ⊕ *www.carnegiehall.org* Ⓜ *N, Q, R to 57th St.–7th Ave.; B, D, E to 7th Ave.*

The Town Hall. Garrison Keillor's *A Prairie Home Companion* radio show sometimes broadcasts from this historic venue, which was founded by suffragists and built in 1921 by McKim, Mead& White. Richard Strauss, Winston Churchill, Theodore Roosevelt, and Bob Dylan have all appeared on stage here; these days it hosts programs that include pop and rock, jazz, gospel, blues, folk, show tunes, political humor, theater, dance, and world music. ⊠ *123 W. 43rd St., between 6th and 7th aves., Midtown West* ☎ *212/840–2824, 800/982–2787 (Ticketmaster)* ⊕ *www.thetownhall.org* Ⓜ *1, 2, 3, 7, N, Q, R, S to Times Sq.–42nd St.*

OPERA

Gotham Chamber Opera. This opera company presents lesser-known chamber works as well as new ones in inspired productions, many of them mounted in surprising New York locations, such as St. Paul's Chapel, the Metropolitan Museum, and among the cherry trees at the Brooklyn Botanic Garden. Recent standout works have included a production of Nico Muhly's 2011 work *Dark Sisters,* as well as Marc-Antoine Charpentier's Baroque opera *La descente d'Orphée aux enfers,* written in 1686 and never before performed in New York. ⊠ *410 W. 42nd St., between 9th and 10th aves., Midtown West* ☎ *212/868–4460* ⊕ *www.gothamchamberopera.org* Ⓜ *A, C, E to 42nd St.–Port Authority.*

PERFORMANCE CENTERS

Fodor's Choice ★ **New York City Center.** Pause as you enter this neo-Moorish building, built in 1923 for the Shriners (cousins of the Freemasons), and admire the beautifully ornate tile work that plasters the lobby. City Center's 2,200-seat main stage is perfectly suited for dance and special theatrical events. The very popular Encores! series, generally in spring, revisits musicals of the past in a concert format—an event that has led to shows returning to Broadway, with the long-running *Chicago* among them. Tickets for City Center's annual Fall for Dance festival sell out quickly. ⊠ *131 W. 55th St., between 6th and 7th aves., Midtown West* ☎ *212/581–1212 (CityTix)* ⊕ *www.nycitycenter.org* Ⓜ *N, Q, R to 57th St.–7th Ave.; F to 57th St.*

Radio City Music Hall. This landmark was built shortly after the stock market crash of 1929; John D. Rockefeller wanted to create a symbol of hope in what was a sad, broke city. He partnered with the Radio Corporation of America to build a grand theater. When it opened, some said Radio City Music Hall was so grand that there was no need for performances, because people would get more than their money's

20

worth simply by sitting there and enjoying the space. Despite being the largest indoor theater in the world with its cityblock–long marquee, it feels warm and intimate. Hour-long "Stage Door" walking tours run year-round, but access is limited during show times. Day-of-tour tickets are sold at the Radio City Avenue Store; advance tickets are available by phone or through the website.

Although there are concerts and other events here year-round, the biggest draw is the Radio City Christmas Spectacular: more than a million visitors every year come to see the iconic Rockettes. Make reservations as early as possible, especially if you want to attend near Christmas or on a weekend. Certain dates and times tend to sell out, but you can usually find tickets for all shows until mid-October. Tickets cost a hefty $45–$299 per person for the 90-minute show, although there are often promotions and deals available, especially for nonpeak times. In 2015, Radio City premiered its New York Spring Spectacular, creating another opportunity to see a Rockettes kickline. ⊠ *1260 6th Ave., between 50th and 51st sts., Midtown West* ☎ *212/247–4777, 866/858–0007 for tickets* ⊕ *www.radiocity.com* Ⓜ *B, D, F, M to 47th–50th Sts./Rockefeller Center; N, Q, R to 49th St.*

READINGS AND LECTURES

LIVE from the NYPL. The New York Public Library's discussion series includes a rich program of lectures and reading events from the biggest names in books and culture in general. Most programs are held at the famous main library. ⊠ *Stephen A. Schwarzman Building, 42nd St. at 5th Ave., Midtown West* ☎ *212/930–0855, 888/718–4253 for tickets* ⊕ *www.nypl.org/events/live-nypl* Ⓜ *B, D, F, M to 42nd St.–Bryant Park; 7 to 5th Ave.*

THEATER

Roundabout Theatre Company. This nonprofit theatrical company is known for its revivals of classic musicals and plays, including *Anything Goes* and *The Importance of Being Earnest*. Its main stage, the American Airlines Theatre, is the former Selwyn—the venerable home to the works of Coward, Kaufman, and Porter in their heyday. The Roundabout's other Broadway venues are Studio 54, the longtime home of its successful *Cabaret* revival, and the Stephen Sondheim Theatre. The two Off-Broadway stages at the Harold and Miriam Steinberg Center for Theatre show a mix of classics and works from up-and-coming playwrights. ⊠ *American Airlines Theatre, 227 W. 42nd St., between 7th and 8th aves., Midtown West* ☎ *212/719–1300 for tickets* ⊕ *www. roundabouttheatre.org* Ⓜ *1, 2, 3, 7, N, Q, R, S to Times Sq.–42nd St.; A, C, E to 42nd St.–Port Authority.*

New Amsterdam Theater. In 1997 Disney refurbished the elaborate 1903 Art Nouveau New Amsterdam Theater, where Bob Hope, Jack Benny, Fred Astaire, and the *Ziegfeld Follies* once drew crowds. *The Lion King* ruled here for the first nine years of its run, followed by *Mary Poppins* and then *Aladdin* starting in 2014. ⊠ *214 W. 42nd St., between 7th and 8th aves., Midtown West* ☎ ⊕ *www.disneyonbroadway.com* Ⓜ *1, 2, 3, 7, N, Q, R, S to Times Sq.–42nd St.; A, C, E to 42nd St.–Port Authority.*

FAMILY

Fodor's Choice

★

The New Victory Theater. In a magnificently restored space from 1900, the New Victory Theater presents an international roster of supremely kid-pleasing plays, music, dance, opera, and circus performances. Through the organization's workshops and exhibits, children and their parents can also learn more about other parts of theater (writing, for instance) and kinds of performance, such as break dancing. Count on reasonable ticket prices, high-energy and high-class productions, and the opportunity for kids to chat with the artists after many performances. ⊠ *209 W. 42nd St., between 7th and 8th aves., Midtown West* ☎ *646/223–3010* ⊕ *www.newvictory.org* Ⓜ *1, 2, 3, 7, N, Q, R, S to Times Sq.–42nd St.; A, C, E to 42nd St.–Port Authority.*

Playwrights Horizons. Known for its support of new work by American playwrights, this Off-Broadway theater was the first home for eventual Broadway hits such as *Grey Gardens* and Wendy Wasserstein's *Heidi Chronicles.* ⊠ *416 W. 42nd St., between 9th and 10th aves., Midtown West* ☎ *212/564–1235, 212/279–4200 for tickets* ⊕ *www.phnyc.org* Ⓜ *A, C, E to 42nd St.–Port Authority.*

Signature Theatre Company. Designed by the architect Frank Gehry, the company's Pershing Square Signature Center houses three theater spaces. All tickets are $25 for a show's initially announced run. A central space with a café and bookstore connects the theaters, so come early, or stay late; the café is open until midnight Tuesday through Sunday. ⊠ *Pershing Square Signature Center, 480 W. 42nd St., between 9th and 10th aves., Midtown West* ☎ *212/244–7529* ⊕ *www.signaturetheatre. org* Ⓜ *A, C, E to 42nd St.–Port Authority.*

UPPER EAST SIDE

PERFORMANCE CENTERS

FAMILY

92nd Street Y. Well-known soloists, jazz musicians, show-tune stylists, and chamber music groups perform in the 92Y's 905-seat Kaufmann Concert Hall. But the programming is hardly limited to music—its online calendar bristles with popular lectures-and-readings series featuring big-name authors, poets, playwrights, political pundits, and media bigwigs (many events are live-streamed or archived online). Also worth the Upper East Side trek are the Harkness Dance Festival, film programs, and many family-friendly events. ⊠ *1395 Lexington Ave., at 92nd St., Upper East Side* ☎ *212/415–5500 for tickets* ⊕ *www.92y. org* Ⓜ *6 to 96th St.*

Fodor's Choice

★

Park Avenue Armory. Built in 1879 and occupying an entire city block, this handsome Gothic brick building was used as the headquarters, drill hall, and social club for the Seventh Regiment, a National Guard unit called the "Silk Stocking" regiment because its members were mainly drawn from wealthy Gilded Age WASPs. The sumptuous interiors (like the building itself, done at members' expense) were decorated by Louis Comfort Tiffany, Stanford White, and other fashionable designers of the time. After World War I, the armory began to decay, and its opulent rooms were in danger of ruin. Help came in the form of a major restoration that began in 2010 and is ongoing. The armory was put back into service, but this time in the service of art. The huge installations,

20

plays, and immersive concerts here take advantage of the massive space its 55,000-square-foot (5,100-square-meter) drill hall provides. A couple standouts: the Royal Shakespeare Company summer-long series of plays, performed inside a replica of its theater in Stratford-upon-Avon, and an installation by the artist Douglas Gordon that turned the hall into a massive reflecting pool. ⊠ *643 Park Ave., between 66th and 67th sts., Upper East Side* ☎ *212/616–3930* Ⓜ *6 to 68th St.–Hunter College, F to Lexington Ave./63rd St.*

READINGS AND LECTURES

Works & Process. Insight into the creative process is what the Works & Process program is all about. Often drawing on dance and theater works-in-progress, the live performances are complemented by illuminating discussions with their choreographers, playwrights, and directors. There are very popular holiday concerts, too. ⊠ *Guggenheim Museum, 1071 5th Ave., at 89th St., Upper East Side* ☎ *212/423–3587* ⊕ *www.worksandprocess.org* Ⓜ *4, 5, 6 to 86th St.*

UPPER WEST SIDE

MUSIC

Great Music in a Great Space. This organ and choral concert series is aptly named, set in St. John the Divine's massive, atmospheric Gothic space. Any music you come to hear at St. John the Divine will likely be an unforgettable experience, but the Christmastime programming of the Early Music New York (*www.earlymusicny.org*) ensemble is especially moving in this space. ⊠ *The Cathedral Church of St. John the Divine, 1047 Amsterdam Ave., at 112th St., Upper West Side* ☎ *212/316–7540* ⊕ *www.stjohndivine.org* Ⓜ *1, B, C to Cathedral Pkwy.–110th St.*

FAMILY **Jazz at Lincoln Center.** A few blocks south of Lincoln Center itself, this Columbus Circle venue is almost completely devoted to jazz, with a sprinkling of other genres mixed in. Stages in Rafael Viñoly's crisply modern Frederick P. Rose Hall include the 1,200-seat Rose Theater, where a worthy Jazz for Young People series joins buoyant adult programming a few times each year. Also here is the Allen Room, an elegant theater with a glass wall overlooking Columbus Circle, and the smaller Dizzy's Club Coca-Cola, where there are two sets nightly, and often more that go late into the night. All are accompanied by a full bar and restaurant here. ⊠ *Time Warner Center, 10 Columbus Circle, Broadway at 60th St., Upper West Side* ☎ *212/258–9800* ⊕ *www.jazz.org* Ⓜ *1, A, B, C, D to 59th St.–Columbus Circle.*

Merkin Concert Hall at Kaufman Music Center. A destination for both old-school and cutting-edge musical performances, this concert hall around the corner from Lincoln Center is a lovely, acoustically advanced 450-seater that presents chamber pieces. It's also known for jazz, world, new music, and especially its Ecstatic Music Festival in January, when an eclectic group of indie-classical artists more than lives up to its billing. ⊠ *129 W. 67th St., between Broadway and Amsterdam Ave., Upper West Side* ☎ *212/501–3300* ⊕ *www.kaufmanmusiccenter.org/mch* Ⓜ *1 to 66th St.–Lincoln Center.*

Jazz at Lincoln Center

Miller Theatre. Adventurous programming of jazz, classical, early and modern music, and dance makes up the calendar at this university theater, founded in 1988. A well-designed 688-seater, this is a hall that rewards serious listeners. ⊠ *Columbia University, 2960 Broadway, at 116th St., Upper West Side* ☎ *212/854–1633, 212/854–7799 for box office* ⊕ *www.millertheatre.com* Ⓜ *1 to 116th St.–Columbia University.*

PERFORMANCE CENTERS

FAMILY

Fodor's Choice

★

Lincoln Center for the Performing Arts. This massive and somewhat fortress-like, white travertine-clad complex contains 23 theaters, as well as the Juilliard School, the New York City Ballet, the Film Center of Lincoln Center, and a branch of the New York Public Library, making it one of the most concentrated places for the performing arts in the nation. Its 16-acre campus, planned by the master architect Philip Johnson and built as part of an urban-renewal effort, arose over the course of several years from 1962 to 1969; some 40 years later, it was given a thorough remodeling to better integrate into the neighborhood.

To get oriented, start across the street, on Broadway between 62nd and 63rd streets, at the David Rubenstein Atrium. There you'll find free Wi-Fi, tables, a café, free concerts (Thursday at 7:30 pm) and that rarest of NYC commodities, a public restroom. In addition, discounted day-of-show tickets for many Lincoln Center venues may be purchased in person here; there is a limit of four tickets per customer, and the amount of discount depends on the performance. Because the box office is closed on Monday, any available tickets for Monday performances are sold on Sunday.

The acoustics in Alice Tully Hall are top-notch; the hall's primary resident is the Chamber Music Society of Lincoln Center (*www.chambermusicsociety.org*). Avery Fisher Hall is home to the New York Philharmonic (*www.nyphil.org*); the season is late September to late June. Orchestra rehearsals are open to the public on selected weekday mornings ($20, usually Wednesday or Thursday). A popular Young People's Concert series takes place Saturday afternoon, four times throughout the season.

The largest hall, the Metropolitan Opera House is notable for its dramatic arched entrance as well as its lobby's immense Swarovski crystal chandeliers and Marc Chagall paintings, both of which can be seen from outside later in the day. The titan of American opera companies and an institution since its founding in 1883, the Metropolitan Opera (*www.metopera.org*) brings the world's leading singers to the vast stage here from September to May. All performances, including those sung in English, are subtitled on small screens on the back of the seat in front of you. Also resident at the Met is the American Ballet Theatre (*www. abt.org*), renowned for its gorgeous full-program renditions of the 19th-century classics (*Swan Lake, Giselle, The Sleeping Beauty*) with choreography reenvisioned by 20th-century or contemporary masters. A limited number of same-day $20 rush orchestra seats are available at the Met's website. These tickets go on sale for Sunday through Friday evening performances at noon, for matinees four hours before curtain, and for Saturday evenings at 2 pm.

The David H. Koch Theater is the home of the formidable New York City Ballet (*www.nycballet.com*), and has an unmatched repertoire of 20th-century works, predominantly by George Balanchine, Jerome Robbins, and Peter Martins. The company particularly excel at short-form programs. Their fall season starts in September and early October, then returns in late November through December for their beloved annual production of Balanchine's *The Nutcracker*. Their winter repertory program runs in January and February, and a spring season runs from April into May. Sharing the theater is a mix of other internationally famous dance troupes.

The Lincoln Center Theater complex houses the Vivian Beaumont Theater, the smaller Mitzi E. Newhouse Theater, and the rooftop Claire Tow Theater, which has 131 seats and a small outdoor terrace.

The auditorium of the Walter Reade Theater (*www.filmlinc.com*) shows film series devoted to "the best in world cinema," including silents, documentaries, retrospectives and recent releases, often on the same theme or from the same country. The Elinor Bunin Munroe Film Center has two small screening rooms, a café, and an amphitheater that hosts lectures and panel discussions.

In addition to extensive musical and theatrical holding, the New York Public Library for the Performing Arts mounts periodic exhibitions related to major artists and composers. At the library's free Silent Clowns series (*www.silentclowns.com*), held Sunday afternoon in its auditorium from September to May, rarely seen prints of the silent era's comedy masters are paired with live piano music.

Tours of Lincoln Center, including the Met, take place daily and leave from the atrium; reservations are recommended and can be made from the website or in person. They do not include backstage areas but sometimes do include parts of the auditoriums. Backstage tours of the Met ($22) are held during the performance season. ⊠ *From 62nd to 66th St., between Broadway/Columbus and Amsterdam aves., Upper West Side* ☎ *212/875–5000 for main switchboard, 212/721–6500 (CenterCharge)* ⊕ *www.lincolncenter.org* ☉ *David Rubinstein Atrium: weekdays 8 am– 10 pm, weekends 9 am–10 pm* Ⓜ *1 to 66th St.–Lincoln Center.*

FAMILY **Symphony Space.** Although Symphony Space runs an energetic roster of classical, jazz, international, and other kinds of music, it also excels with many other kinds of art programming. On the literary front, its two halls—the Peter Jay Sharp Theatre and the Leonard Nimoy Thalia— host a celebrated roster of literary events, including Bloomsday on Broadway, the Thalia Book Club, and the famed Selected Shorts series: stories read by prominent actors and broadcast live on National Public Radio. Plays, films, and "Thalia Docs" on Sunday (usually true-to-their-roots art-house screenings) round out the adult programming. For the family, turn to their hugely popular Just Kidding lineup for a nonstop parade of zany plays, sing-alongs, midday Saturday (and sometimes Sunday) movies, and animation. ⊠ *2537 Broadway, at 95th St., Upper West Side* ☎ *212/864–5400* ⊕ *www.symphonyspace.org* Ⓜ *1, 2, 3 to 96th St.*

THEATER

Shakespeare in the Park. Some of the best things in New York are, indeed, free—including this summer festival presented by the Public Theater and performed at an open-air stage in Central Park. Many notable performers have appeared here, including Meryl Streep, Michelle Pfeiffer, Christopher Walken, Helen Hunt, Morgan Freeman, Al Pacino, Anne Hathaway, and Kevin Kline. The tickets are given out (limit two per person) starting at noon on the day of each show, and always sell out. What you save in money, you make up for in time and tedium—lines are usually *long*. Plan to line up by midmorning or earlier if there have been good reviews. The easiest way to score these scarce tickets is to register via an online lottery between midnight and noon on the day you'd like to attend; an email response after noon confirms (or denies) success. Making a donation to the Public Theater is one way to avoid the lines and be sure you get a ticket. ⊠ *Delacorte Theater, Central Park, midpark near 81st St., Upper West Side* ☎ *212/539–8500* ⊕ *www.shakespeareinthepark.org* ☑ *Free* Ⓜ *B, C to 81st St.–Museum of Natural History.*

20

HARLEM

Apollo Theater. Michael Jackson, Ella Fitzgerald, and James Brown are just a few of the world-class performers who have appeared on this equally famed stage, which first opened back in 1934 and is Harlem's oldest surviving stage. If the Apollo's Amateur Night doesn't get you up to 125th Street, consider its more intimate Apollo Music Café events on Friday and Saturday nights, featuring a variety of underground jazz,

FILM SERIES AND REVIVALS

Although many of the screens listed here show first-run releases, old favorites and rarities are the heart of their programing. These gems—which include just about every kind of film, from silent and noir to the most au courant experimental work—are frequently screened at museums, cultural societies, and other institutions, such as the French Institute (*212/355–6100* ⊕ *www.fiaf. org*), Scandinavia House (*212/779–3587* ⊕ *www.scandinaviahouse. org*), and major branches of the New York Public Library (⊕ *www. nypl.org*). A reliably creative range of repertory screenings can always be found at Anthology Film Archives (*212/505–5181* ⊕ *www. anthologyfilmarchives.org*), Film Forum (*212/727–8110* ⊕ *www. filmforum.org*), the Museum of Modern Art (MoMA) (*212/708–9400* ⊕ *www.moma.org*), the Museum of the Moving Image (*718/784–0077* ⊕ *www.movingimage.us*), the Brooklyn Academy of Music (*718/636–4100* ⊕ *www.bam.org*), and Lincoln Center's Walter Reade Theater (*212/875–5600* ⊕ *www.filmlinc.com*).

pop, hip-hop, and rock performers. ✉ *253 W. 125th St., at Frederick Douglass Blvd., Harlem* ☎ *212/531–5300, 800/745–3000 for tickets (Ticketmaster)* ⊕ *www.apollotheater.org* Ⓜ *2, 3, A, B, C, D to 125th St.*

Harlem Stage. Set in a perfectly restored 1890 Croton Aqueduct facility, Harlem Stage is a cozy 192-seat uptown venue for jazz, world music, and dance. ✉ *The Gatehouse, 150 Convent Ave., at 135th St., Harlem* ☎ *212/281–9240* ⊕ *www.harlemstage.org* Ⓜ *B, C to 135th St.; 1 to 137th St.–City College.*

BROOKLYN

FORT GREENE
PERFORMANCE CENTERS

Fodor's Choice
★
Brooklyn Academy of Music (BAM). Founded in 1861, BAM is a multi-use performing arts center spanning three Instagram-worthy edifices, including the seven-story, Beaux Arts Peter Jay Sharp building. Facilities include an unadorned "black box" theater, dance venues, a four-screen movie theater, an opera house, a ballroom, and a café. Cyclists park in style at the David Byrne–designed bike rack on Lafayette Avenue between St. Felix Street and Ashland Place. ✉ *30 Lafayette Ave., Fort Greene* ☎ *718/636–4100* ⊕ *www.bam.org* Ⓜ *2, 3, 4, 5, B, D, N, Q, R at Atlantic Ave.–Barclays Center.*

PARK SLOPE
THEATER

FAMILY
Puppetworks. Finely detailed wooden marionettes and hand puppets are on the bill at Puppetworks. Kid-friendly performances like *The Prince and the Magic Flute* come to life on weekends in this 75-seat neighborhood theater. Reservations are required; credit cards are not accepted. ✉ *338 6th Ave., at 4th St., Park Slope* ☎ *718/965–3391* ⊕ *www. puppetworks.org* Ⓜ *F, G to 7th Ave.*

CLOSE UP

New York's Film Festivals

New York's extreme diversity is what makes it a cinephile's heaven: you find dozens of festivals for niche interests and those just wanting to be at the front end of what's out there. New releases and premieres dominate the festival scene, but the city has its share of retrospective events, especially in summer.

The city's preeminent film event is the annual New York Film Festival (⊕ *www.filmlinc.com*), sponsored by the Film Society of Lincoln Center, from late September into October. Screenings are announced more than a month in advance and often sell out quickly. Film venues are usually Lincoln Center's Alice Tully Hall and Walter Reade Theater. In January, the Film Society join forces with the Jewish Museum to produce the New York Jewish Film Festival (⊕ *www. nyjff.org*); in March they join MoMA to present New Directors/New Films (⊕ *www.newdirectors.org*), and June brings their collaboration on the Human Rights Watch Film Festival (⊕ *ff.hrw.org*).

The Tribeca Film Festival (⊕ *www. tribecafilm.com/festival*) takes place in mostly downtown venues for about two weeks starting mid-April and shows mainstream premieres along with indie flicks, as well as a Family Festival, which attracts big crowds to its street fair and movies for all ages.

Fans also flock to other noteworthy annuals like the Asian American International Film Festival (⊕ *www. asiancinevision.org*) from late July to early August; and the Margaret Mead Film Festival (⊕ *www.amnh.org/ explore/margaret-mead-film-festival*) and DOC NYC (⊕ *www.docnyc.net*),

two November festivals that both focus on documentaries from all over.

For kids, the year-round programs of the New York International Children's Film Festival (NYICFF) (⊕ *www.gkids. com*) peak in March with an extravaganza of about 100 new films and videos for ages 3–18.

Summer in New York sees a bonanza of alfresco film; screenings are usually free (but arrive early to secure a space; screenings begin at dusk). The HBO Bryant Park Summer Film Festival (*212/512–5700* ⊕ *www.bryantpark. org*) shows classic films at sundown on Mondays, June–August. The Hudson River Park RiverFlicks (⊕ *www. riverflicks.org*) series in July and August has movies for grown-ups on Wednesday evening on Pier 63; River-Flicks for kids are at Pier 46 on Friday. The Upper West Side has Summer on the Hudson (⊕ *www.nycgovparks.org*) with Wednesday night screenings on Pier 1, near West 70th Street. Rooftop Films' (⊕ *www.rooftopfilms.com*) Underground Movies Outdoors is more eclectic than most other film series, with shows outdoors in summer on rooftops in all five boroughs. Check their schedule for off-season screenings as well. On Thursday nights in summer, check out Movies with a View in Brooklyn Bridge Park (⊕ *www. brooklynbridgepark.org*).

20

DUMBO

THEATER

Fodor's Choice
★

St. Ann's Warehouse. Everyone from Marianne Faithfull to August Wilson has played St. Ann's, a veritable arts arena that has commissioned cutting-edge theater, music, and a surprising amount of high-art puppeteering since 1980. The venue is set to relocate to a stunningly refurbished,1860 tobacco warehouse in Brooklyn Bridge Park in time for the 2015 fall season. ⊠ *Tobacco Warehouse, 45 Water St., DUMBO* 🕾 *718/254–8779* ⊕ *www.stannswarehouse.org* Ⓜ *A, C to High St.; F to York St.*

BROOKLYN HEIGHTS

MUSIC

Bargemusic. This "cozy floating concert hall moored just south of the Brooklyn Bridge," as the *New York Times* once described it, keeps chamber music groups busy year-round on a renovated harbor barge that has a fabulous view of the Manhattan skyline. Since you really are on the water, you probably want to skip this if susceptible to seasickness. ⊠ *Fulton Ferry Landing, Old Fulton and Furman sts., Brooklyn Heights* 🕾 *718/624–4924* ⊕ *www.bargemusic.org* Ⓜ *A, C to High St.; F to York St.; 2, 3 to Clark St.*

QUEENS

FILM

FAMILY **Museum of the Moving Image Films.** Video art, digital screenings, live musical collaborations, and in-person appearances by moviemaker luminaries join retrospectives and themed repertory such as Chuck Jones cartoons, Recovered Treasures (from world archives), or Avant-Garde Masters. Daily short films are screened in Tut's Fever Movie Palace, a fab Red Grooms and Lysiane Luong–designed installation. Weekend Family Film matinees make this museum a great choice for kids. ⊠ *3601 35th Ave., at 37th St., Astoria* 🕾 *718/784–0077* ⊕ *www.movingimage. us* Ⓜ *M, R to Steinway St.; N, Q to 36th Ave.*

TRAVEL SMART
NEW YORK CITY

GETTING HERE AND AROUND

New York City packs a staggering range of sights and activities into the 301 square miles (780 square km) of its five boroughs. You probably want to focus most of your visit in Manhattan, but with more time, taking a trip to Brooklyn or one of the other "outer" boroughs (Queens, the Bronx, or Staten Island) is worthwhile.

If flying into one of the three major airports that service New York—John F. Kennedy (JFK), LaGuardia (LGA), or New Jersey's Newark (EWR)—pick your mode of transportation for getting to Manhattan before your plane lands. Tourists typically either take a car service or head to the taxi line, but those aren't necessarily the best choices, especially during rush hour. Public transportation is inexpensive and should be considered, especially if traveling light and without young children. Keep in mind that it's particularly expensive to take a cab from Newark, making the AirTrain or another form of public transportation a better deal.

Once you're in Manhattan, getting around can be a breeze when you get the hang of the subway system. When not in a rush and the weather's cooperating, just walk—it's the best way to discover the true New York. Not quite sure where you are or how to get where you're headed? Ask a local. You may be surprised at how friendly the city's inhabitants are, debunking their reputation for rudeness. In the same getting-there-is-half-the-fun spirit, there are water, land, and air journeys that let you see the city from a whole new perspective.

∎ AIR TRAVEL

Generally, international flights go in and out of John F. Kennedy or Newark airport, while domestic flights go in and out of both of these, as well as LaGuardia Airport.

AIRLINES AND AIRPORTS
Airline and Airport Links.com. For direct links to many of the world's airlines and airports, check this website. ⊕ *www.airlineandairportlinks.com.*

AIRLINE SECURITY ISSUES
Transportation Security Administration (*TSA*). The TSA has answers for almost every question that might come up. ⊕ *www.tsa.gov.*

AIRPORTS
The major air gateways to New York City are LaGuardia Airport (LGA) and JFK International Airport (JFK) in the borough of Queens, and Newark Liberty International Airport (EWR) in New Jersey.

Airport Information JFK International Airport (*JFK*). ☎ 718/244–4444 ⊕ *www.jfkairport.com.* **LaGuardia Airport** (*LGA*). ☎ 718/533–3400 ⊕ *www.laguardiaairport.com.* **Newark Liberty International Airport** (*EWR*). ☎ 973/961–6000, 888/397–4636 ⊕ *www.newarkairport.com.*

TRANSFERS—CAR SERVICES
Car services can be a great convenience, because the driver often meets you in the baggage-claim area and helps with your luggage. The flat rates are often comparable to taxi fares, but some car services charge for parking and wait time at the airport. To eliminate these expenses, other car services require you to telephone their dispatcher when you land so they can send the next available car to pick you up. The New York City Taxi and Limousine Commission rules require all car services be licensed and pick up riders only by prior arrangement; if possible, call 24 hours in advance for reservations or at least a half day before your flight's departure. Drivers of non-licensed vehicles ("gypsy cabs") often solicit fares outside the terminal in baggage-claim areas. Don't take them: you run the risk of an unsafe ride and will definitely pay more

than the going rate. Getting a car via the Uber ride-sharing service or one of its competitors is another option.

For phone numbers, see Taxi Travel.

TRANSFERS—TAXIS AND SHUTTLES

Outside the baggage-claim area at each of New York's major airports are taxi stands where a uniformed dispatcher helps passengers find taxis (*see Taxi Travel*). Cabs are not permitted to pick up fares anywhere else in the arrivals area, so if you want a taxi, take your place in line. Shuttle services generally pick up passengers from a designated spot along the curb.

New York Airport Service, NYC Airporter, and SuperShuttle run vans and some buses from JFK, Newark, and LaGuardia airports to Grand Central Terminal, the Port Authority Bus Terminal, Penn Station, and hotels in Manhattan. Fares cost about $15–$18 one-way and $33–$38 round-trip, per person. Those rates are significantly cheaper than taking a taxi if you're on your own, but probably not if there's two or more of you traveling together. If you choose to use such services, keep in mind that customers' satisfaction with them is very mixed; online reviews often complain of rude employees and significant waits for vans to both arrive and reach their destinations. In any case, allow lots of time for the shuttle's other pick-ups and drop-offs along the way.

Shuttle Service GO Airlink NYC.
☎ 877/599–8200, 212/812–9000 ⊕ www. nyairportservice.com. **NYC Airporter.** ☎ 855/269–2247 ⊕ www.nycairporter.com. **SuperShuttle.** ☎ 800/258–3826 ⊕ www. supershuttle.com.

TRANSFERS FROM JFK INTERNATIONAL AIRPORT

The rate for traveling between JFK and Manhattan by yellow cab in either direction is a flat fee of $52.50 plus tolls (which may be as much as $6.50). The trip takes 35–60 minutes. Prices are roughly $25–$55 for trips to most other locations in New York City. You should also tip the driver.

JFK's AirTrain ($5) connects JFK Airport to the New York City Subway (A, E, J, and Z trains) and the Long Island Railroad (LIRR)—both of which take you to Manhattan or Brooklyn. The monorail system runs 24 hours. ■TIP➔ Not sure which train to take? Check ⊕ www. hopstop.com and ⊕ www.citymapper.com (or their corresponding apps) for the best route to your destination. Subway travel between JFK and Manhattan takes less than an hour and costs $3.50 in subway fare (including $1 to buy a MetroCard) plus $5 for the AirTrain. The LIRR travels between JFK's AirTrain stop (Jamaica Station) and Penn Station in around 30 minutes, for about $17, including the AirTrain fee. When traveling *from* Manhattan to the Howard Beach station, be sure to take the A train marked "Far Rockaway" or "Rockaway Park," not "Lefferts Boulevard."

JFK Transfer Information AirTrain JFK.
☎ 718/244–4444 ⊕ www.airtrainjfk.com. **Long Island Railroad.** ☎ 718/217–5477 ⊕ www. mta.info/lirr.

TRANSFERS FROM LAGUARDIA AIRPORT

Taxis cost $30–$50 plus tip and tolls (which may be as high as $6.50) to most destinations in New York City, and take at least 20–40 minutes.

For $2.75 (pay with a MetroCard or exact change in coins, no pennies) you can ride the Q70 bus to the Jackson Heights–Roosevelt Avenue subway station, where you can transfer to the E, F, M, R, and 7 trains and reach many points in Manhattan and Brooklyn. Another option is to take the M60 bus to 106th Street and Broadway on Manhattan's Upper West Side, with connections en route to several New York City Subway lines (2, 3, 4, 5, 6, A, B, C, D, N, and Q trains). Allow at least 90 minutes for the entire trip to Midtown, and perhaps a bit more during heavy traffic or rain.

TRANSFERS FROM NEWARK AIRPORT

Taxis to Manhattan cost $50–$70 plus tolls and tip and take 20–45 minutes. "Share and Save" group rates are available for up to four passengers between 8 am and midnight—make arrangements with the airport's taxi dispatcher. If you're heading to the airport from Manhattan, there's a $17.50 surcharge on top of the normal taxi rate.

AirTrain Newark, an elevated light-rail system, can take you from the airline terminal to the Newark Liberty International Airport Station. From here you can take New Jersey Transit (or, for a much higher price, Amtrak) trains heading to New York Penn Station. It's an efficient and low-cost way to get to New York City, particularly if you don't have many in your group and aren't carrying massive amounts of luggage. Total travel time to New York Penn Station via New Jersey Transit is approximately 30 minutes and costs $12.50. By contrast, a similar, slightly faster trip via Amtrak costs roughly $35. The AirTrain runs every 3 minutes from 5 am to midnight and every 15 minutes from midnight to 5 am. Note that New Jersey Transit trains first make a stop at the confusingly named Newark Penn Station before they reach New York Penn Station, their final stop. If you're not sure when to get off the train, ask a conductor or fellow passenger.

Coach USA with Olympia Trails buses leave for Manhattan stops at Port Authority, Bryant Park (at 42nd Street and 5th Avenue), and Grand Central Terminal about every 15 to 30 minutes until midnight. The trip takes roughly 45 minutes, and the fare is $16. Buses headed to Newark Airport depart from near Grand Central, Bryant Park, and Port Authority every 20 to 30 minutes. The trip takes 55 to 65 minutes.

Newark Airport Information AirTrain Newark. ☎ 888/397–4636 ⊕ www. airtrainnewark.com. **Coach USA.** ☎ 877/863–9275 ⊕ www.coachusa.com.

TRANSFERS BETWEEN AIRPORTS

There are several transportation options for connecting to and from area airports, including shuttles, AirTrain and mass transit, and car service or taxi. New York Airport Service and NYC Airporter run vans and buses between Newark, JFK, and LaGuardia airports. AirTrain provides detailed, up-to-the-minute recorded information on how to reach your destination from any of New York's airports. Note that if you arrive after midnight at any airport, you may wait a long time for a taxi. Consider calling a car service, as there is no shuttle service at that time.

Contacts AirTrain. ☎ 800/247–7433 ⊕ www. panynj.gov/airtrain.

▌ BOAT TRAVEL

The Staten Island Ferry runs across New York Harbor between Whitehall Street next to Battery Park in Lower Manhattan and St. George terminal in Staten Island. The free 25-minute ride gives you a view of the Financial District skyscrapers, the Statue of Liberty, and Ellis Island.

New York Water Taxi, in addition to serving commuters, shuttles tourists to the city's many waterfront attractions between the West and East sides and Lower Manhattan (including the 9/11 Memorial), the South Street Seaport, and Brooklyn's waterfront parks.

An all-day pass on the water taxi is $30; a similar pass that also allows passengers to visit the 9/11 Memorial as part of their sightseeing package is $32. Another package includes an eight-hour bike rental for $54.

Information New York Water Taxi (*NYWT*). ☎ 212/742–1969 ⊕ www.nywatertaxi.com. **Staten Island Ferry.** ⊕ www.siferry.com.

▌ BUS TRAVEL

Most city buses in Manhattan follow easy-to-understand routes along the island's street grid. Routes go north and south on the avenues and east and west on the major two-way crosstown streets: 96th, 86th, 79th, 72nd, 66th, 57th, 42nd, 34th, 23rd, and 14th. Bus routes usually operate 24 hours a day, but service is infrequent late at night. Traffic jams can make rides maddeningly slow, especially along 5th Avenue in Midtown and on the Upper East Side. Certain bus routes provide "limited-stop service" during weekday rush hours, which saves travel time by stopping only at major cross streets and transfer points. A sign posted at the front of the bus indicates limited service; ask the driver whether the bus stops near where you want to go before boarding.

To find a bus stop, look for a light-blue sign (green for a "limited" bus, which skips more stops) on a green pole; bus numbers and routes are listed, with the stop's name underneath.

Bus fare is the same as subway fare: $2.75. Pay when you board with exact change in coins (no pennies, and no change is given) or with a MetroCard.

MetroCards (*see Public Transportation*) allow you one free transfer between buses or from bus to subway; when using coins on the bus, you can ask the driver for a free transfer coupon, good for one change to an intersecting route. Legal transfer points are listed on the back of the slip. Transfers generally have time limits of two hours.

Several routes in the city now have so-called Select Bus Service (SBS) rather than limited-stop service. These routes include those along 1st and 2nd avenues and 34th Street in Manhattan, as well as the M60, which travels between LaGuardia Airport and 125th Street in Harlem. The buses, which are distinguished from normal city buses by flashing blue lights on the front, make fewer stops. In addition, riders must pay for their rides before boarding with either a MetroCard or coins at a machine mounted on the street. The machine prints out a receipt. This receipt is the only proof of payment, so be sure to hold onto it for your entire SBS trip or risk a fine for fare evasion.

Bus route maps and schedules are posted at many bus stops in Manhattan, major stops throughout the other boroughs, and ⊕ *MTA.info*. Each of the five boroughs of New York has a separate bus map; they're available from some station booths, but rarely on buses. The best places to obtain them are the information kiosks in Grand Central Terminal and Penn Station, and the MTA's website.

Most buses that travel outside the city depart from the Port Authority Bus Terminal, on 8th Avenue between 40th and 42nd streets. You must purchase your ticket at a ticket counter, not from the bus driver, so give yourself enough time to wait in line. Several bus lines serving northern New Jersey and Rockland County, New York, make daily stops at the George Washington Bridge Bus Station from 5 am to 1 am. The station is connected to the 175th Street station on the A line of the subway, which travels down the West Side of Manhattan.

A variety of discount bus services, including BoltBus and Megabus, run direct routes to and from cities such as Philadelphia, Boston, and Washington, D.C., with the majority of destinations along the East Coast. These budget options, priced from about $20 one-way, depart from locations throughout the city and can be more convenient than traditional bus services, although not always as comfortable.

Buses in New York Metropolitan Transit Authority (MTA) Travel Information Line. ☎ *511* ⊕ *www.mta.info.*

Buses to New York Academy Bus Lines. ☎ *201/420–7000, 800/442–7272* ⊕ *www.academybus.com.* **BoltBus.** ☎ *877/265–8287* ⊕ *www.boltbus.com.* **Coach.** ☎ *800/631–8405* ⊕ *www.coachusa.com.* **Greyhound Lines Inc.** ☎ *800/231–2222* ⊕ *www.greyhound.com.* **Megabus.** ☎ *877/462–6342* ⊕ *us.megabus.com.* **New Jersey Transit.** ☎ *973/275–5555* ⊕ *www.njtransit.com.* **Trailways.** ☎ *800/225–6815* ⊕ *www.trailways.com.* **Vamoose Bus.** ☎ *212/695–6766* ⊕ *www.vamoosebus.com.*

Bus Stations George Washington Bridge Bus Station. ☎ 800/221-9903 ⊕ www. panynj.gov. **Port Authority Bus Terminal.** ☎ 212/564-8484 ⊕ www.panynj.gov.

▌ CAR TRAVEL

If you plan to drive into Manhattan, try to avoid the morning and evening rush hours and lunch hour. Tune in to traffic reports online or on the radio (e.g., WCBS 880 or 1010 WINS on the AM radio dial) before you set off, and don't be surprised if a bridge is partially closed or entirely blocked with traffic.

Driving within Manhattan can be a nightmare of gridlocked streets, obnoxious drivers, and seemingly suicidal jaywalkers and bicyclists. Narrow and one-way streets are common, particularly downtown, and can make driving even more difficult. The most congested streets of the city lie between 14th and 59th streets and 3rd and 8th avenues. In addition, portions of Broadway near Times Square (from 42nd to 47th Street) and Herald Square (33rd to 35th) are closed to motorized traffic. This can create gridlock and confusion in nearby streets.

GASOLINE

Gas stations are few and far between in Manhattan. If you can, fill up at stations outside the city, where prices are 10¢ to 50¢ cheaper per gallon. In Manhattan, you can refuel at stations along the West Side Highway and 11th Avenue south of West 57th Street and along East Houston Street. Some gas stations in New York require you to pump your own gas; others provide attendants. Across the river in New Jersey, all gas stations are required to offer full service only; turn off the engine and wait for the attendant to help you.

PARKING

Free parking is difficult to find in Midtown, and on weekday evenings and weekends in other neighborhoods. If you find a spot on the street, check parking signs carefully, and scour the curb for a faded yellow line, the bane of every driver's existence. Violators may be towed away or ticketed literally within minutes. If you do drive, use your car sparingly in Manhattan. Instead, park it in a guarded parking garage for at least several hours; hourly rates (which can be $40 or more for just two hours) decrease somewhat if a car is left for a significant amount of time. ▌TIP➔ Best Parking (⊕ nyc.bestparking. com) helps you find the cheapest parking-lot options for your visit; search by neighborhood, address, or attraction.

RULES OF THE ROAD

On city streets the speed limit is 25 mph, unless otherwise posted. No right turns on red are allowed within city limits, unless otherwise posted. Be alert for one-way streets and "no left turn" intersections.

The law requires that front-seat passengers wear seat belts at all times. Children under 16 must wear seat belts in both the front and back seats. Always strap children under age four into approved child-safety seats. It is illegal to use a handheld cell phone while driving in New York State. Police will immediately seize the car of anyone arrested for DWI (driving while intoxicated) in New York City.

CAR RENTALS

When you reserve a car, ask about cancellation penalties, taxes, drop-off charges (if you're planning to pick up the car in one city and leave it in another), and surcharges (for being under or over a certain age, additional drivers, or driving across state or country borders or beyond a specific distance from your point of rental). All these things can add substantially to your costs. Request car seats and extras such as GPS when you book.

Rates are sometimes—but not always—better if you book in advance or reserve through a rental agency's website. There are other reasons to book ahead, though: for popular destinations, during busy times of the year, or to ensure that you get certain types of cars (vans, SUVs, exotic sports cars).

■TIP➜ Make sure that a confirmed res-ervation guarantees you a car. Agencies sometimes overbook, particularly for busy weekends and holiday periods.

Rates in New York City are around $50–$110 a day and $350–$500 a week for an economy car with air-conditioning, automatic transmission, and unlimited mileage. This includes the state tax on car rentals, which is 19.87%. Rental costs are lower outside New York City, specifically in such places like Hoboken, New Jersey, and Yonkers, New York. If you already have a membership with Zipcar or a simi-lar short-term car-rental service, consider using them for your car needs in the city.

CAR-RENTAL INSURANCE

If you own a car and carry comprehensive car insurance for both collision and liabil-ity, your personal auto insurance probably covers a rental, but read your policy's fine print to be sure. If you don't have auto insurance, you should probably buy the collision- or loss-damage waiver (CDW or LDW) from the rental company. This eliminates your liability for damage to the car. Some credit cards offer CDW cover-age, but it's usually supplemental to your own insurance and rarely covers SUVs, minivans, luxury models, and the like. If your coverage is secondary, you may still be liable for loss-of-use costs from the car-rental company (again, read the fine print). But no credit-card insurance is valid unless you use that card for *all* transactions, from reserving to paying the final bill.

■TIP➜ Diners Club offers primary CDW coverage on all rentals reserved and paid for with the card. This means that Din-ers Club's company—not your own car insurance—pays in case of an accident. It doesn't mean that your car-insurance company won't raise your rates once it discovers you had an accident.

You may also be offered supplemental lia-bility coverage. The car-rental company is required to carry a minimal level of liability coverage insuring all renters, but it's rarely enough to cover claims in a really serious accident if you're at fault. Your own auto-insurance policy protects you if you own a car; if you don't, you have to decide whether you are willing to take the risk.

U.S. rental companies sell CDWs and LDWs for about $20–$40 a day; supple-mental liability is usually more than $10 a day. The car-rental company may offer you all sorts of other policies, but they're rarely worth the cost. Personal accident insurance, which is basic hospitalization coverage, is an especially egregious rip-off if you already have health insurance.

■TIP➜ You can decline insurance from the rental company and purchase it through a third-party provider such as Travel Guard (⊕ *www.travelguard.com*)—$9 per day for $35,000 of coverage. That's sometimes just under half the price of the CDW offered by some car-rental companies.

▮ PUBLIC TRANSPORTATION

When it comes to getting around New York, you have your pick of transporta-tion in almost any neighborhood you're likely to visit. The subway and bus net-works are extensive, especially in Man-hattan, although getting across town can take some extra maneuvering. If you're not pressed for time, consider taking a public bus (*see Bus Travel*); they generally are slower than subways, but you can also see the city as you travel. Yellow cabs (*see Taxi Travel*) are abundant, except during the evening rush hour, when many driv-ers' shifts change, and in bad weather, when they get snapped up quickly. If it's late at night or you're outside Manhat-tan, using a ride-sharing service such as Lyft or Uber may be a good idea. Like a taxi ride, the subway (*see Subway Travel*) is a true New York City experience; it's also often the quickest way to get around. However, New York (especially Manhat-tan) is really a walking town, and depend-ing on the time of day, the weather, and your destination, hoofing it could be the easiest and most enjoyable option.

During weekday rush hours (from 7:30 am to 9:30 am and 5 pm to 7 pm) avoid Midtown if you can—subways and streets are jammed, and travel time on buses and taxis can easily double.

Subway and bus fares are $2.75 per ride. Reduced fares are available for senior citizens and people with disabilities during non–rush hours.

You pay for mass transit with a MetroCard, a plastic card with a magnetic strip. There is a $1 fee for any new MetroCard purchase but there is an 11% bonus added to the card if you put $5.50 or more on the card. (There is a $5.50 minimum card purchase at station booths; this minimum does not apply at vending machines.) A Single Ride Ticket (sold only at Metro-Card vending machines) is $3. To help calculate the exact number of rides you need without having a balance left over, note that putting $9.91 on an existing MetroCard will get you $11 value, equal to 4 rides (add $1 for any new MetroCard purchase). As you swipe the card through a subway turnstile or insert it in a bus's card reader, the cost of the fare is automatically deducted. With the MetroCard, you can transfer free from bus to subway, subway to bus, or bus to bus, within a two-hour period.

MetroCards are sold at all subway stations and some stores—look for an "Authorized Sales Agent" sign. The MTA sells two kinds of MetroCards: unlimited-ride and pay-per-ride. Seven-day unlimited-ride MetroCards ($31) allow bus and subway travel for a week. If you expect to ride more than 11 in one week, this is the card to get.

Unlike unlimited-ride cards, pay-per-ride MetroCards can be shared between riders. (Unlimited-ride MetroCards can be used only once at the same station or bus route in an 18-minute period.)

You can buy or add money to an existing MetroCard at a MetroCard vending machine, available at most subway station entrances (usually near the station booth). The machines accept major credit cards and ATM or debit cards. Many also accept cash, but note that the maximum amount of change they return is $6, which is doled out in dollar coins.

SUBWAY TRAVEL

The subway system operates on more than 840 miles of track 24 hours a day and serves nearly all the places you're likely to visit. It's cheaper than a cab, and during the workweek it's often faster than either taxis or buses. The trains are well-lighted and air-conditioned. Still, the New York subway is hardly problem-free. Many trains are crowded, the older ones are noisy, the air-conditioning can break, and platforms can be dingy and damp. Homeless people sometimes take refuge from the elements by riding the trains, and panhandlers and buskers head there for a captive audience. Although trains usually run frequently, especially during rush hours, you never know when some incident somewhere on the line may stall traffic. In addition, subway construction sometimes causes delays or limitation of service, especially on weekends and after 10 pm on weekdays.

You can transfer between subway lines an unlimited number of times at any of the numerous stations where lines intersect. If you use a MetroCard (*see Public Transportation*) to pay your fare, you can also transfer to intersecting MTA bus routes for free. Such transfers generally have a time limit of two hours.

Most subway entrances are at street corners and marked by lampposts with an illuminated Metropolitan Transportation Authority (MTA) logo or globe-shape green or red lights—green means the station is open 24 hours and red means the station closes at night (though the colors don't always correspond to reality). Subway lines are designated by numbers and letters, such as the 3 line or the A line. Some lines run "express" and skip stops, and others are "local" and make all stops. Each station entrance has a sign indicating the lines that run through the station. Some entrances are also marked "uptown only" or "downtown only." Before entering subway stations, read the signs carefully. One of the most frequent mistakes visitors make is taking the train in the wrong direction. Maps of the full subway system are posted in every train car and usually on the subway platform (though these are sometimes out of date). You can usually pick up free maps at station booths.

For the most up-to-date information on subway lines, call the MTA's Travel Information Center or visit its website. The Hopstop and Citymapper apps and websites are a good source for figuring out the best line to take to reach your destination, as are Google Maps. Alternatively, ask a station agent.

Pay your subway fare at the turnstile, using a MetroCard bought from a vending machine.

Schedule and Route Information Metropolitan Transit Authority (MTA) Travel Information Line. ☎ 511 ⊕ www.mta.info.

Subway Information Citymapper. ⊕ www.citymapper.com. HopStop. ⊕ www.hopstop.com. Metropolitan Transportation Authority (MTA) Travel Information Line. ☎ 511 ⊕ www.mta.info.

▌ TAXI TRAVEL

Yellow cabs are almost everywhere in Manhattan, cruising the streets looking for fares. They are usually easy to hail on the street or from a cabstand in front of major hotels, though finding one at rush hour or in the rain can take some time (and assertiveness). Even if you're stuck in a downpour or at the airport, do not accept a ride from a "gypsy cab." If a cab is not yellow and does not have a numbered aqua-color plastic medallion riveted to the hood, you could be putting yourself (or at least your wallet) in danger by getting into the car.

You can see whether a taxi is available by checking its rooftop light. If the center panel is lit and the side panels are dark, the driver is ready to take passengers—he is required to take passengers to any location in New York City as well as Newark Airport and two adjoining counties, although only NYC and Newark locations are metered. Once the meter is engaged (and if it isn't, alert your driver; you seldom benefit from negotiating an off-the-record ride), the fare is $2.50 just for entering the vehicle and 50¢ for each unit thereafter. A unit is defined as either ⅕ mile when the cab's cruising at 6 mph or faster or as 60 seconds when the cab is either not moving or moving at less than 6 mph. New York State adds 50¢ to each cab ride. There's also a 50¢ night surcharge added between 8 pm and 6 am, and a much-maligned $1 weekday surcharge is tacked on between 4 pm and 8 pm. All taxi drivers are required to accept credit cards as payment. Occasionally, some who prefer cash claim their machines are broken when that isn't actually the case. If a driver waits until the end of the ride to mention a broken machine and you want to pay by credit card, you may wish to ask the driver to turn off the meter and drive you to an ATM to see if this extra hassle is worth it.

One taxi can hold a maximum of four passengers (an additional passenger under the age of seven is allowed if the child sits on someone's lap). You must pay any bridge or tunnel tolls incurred during your trip (a driver usually pays the toll himself to keep moving quickly, but the amount is added to the final fare). Taxi drivers expect a 15% to 20% tip.

To avoid unhappy taxi experiences, try to know where you want to go and how to get there before you hail a cab. ▌TIP→ **Know the cross streets of your destination (for instance, "5th Avenue and 42nd Street") before you enter a cab; a quick call to your destination will give you cross-street information, as will a glance at a map. Also, speak simply and** clearly to make sure the driver has heard you correctly—few are native English-speakers, so it never hurts to make sure you've been understood. If headed for a far-flung location in Brooklyn or Queens, it can be helpful to pull up the location using Google Maps or a similar app, especially if the driver doesn't have GPS of his own. When you leave the cab, remember to take your receipt. It includes the cab's medallion number, which can help you track the cabbie down in the event that you've left your possessions in the cab or if you want to report an unpleasant ride. Any charges, such as those for bridges, are itemized on the receipt; you can double-check to make sure you were charged correctly.

Yellow taxis can be difficult to find in parts of Brooklyn, Queens, the Bronx, and Staten Island. To help with this issue, in 2013 the city of New York allowed car-service companies to convert their vehicles to apple-green Boro Taxis, which act like yellow taxis: they charge the same metered rates, accept credit cards, and must take you to any location within the city of New York. The difference is that green taxis are only allowed to pick up fares in non-Manhattan boroughs and in Manhattan locations above 96th Street.

If you're outside Manhattan and can't find a yellow or green taxi, you may have no choice but to call a car service. Locals and staff at restaurants and other public places can often recommend a reliable company. Always confirm the fee beforehand; a 10%–15% tip is customary.

Another increasingly popular option is booking a car through one of the car service apps like Uber, Lyft, Gett, or SheRides, which match passengers with potential car-service drivers. After booking a car through one of their respective apps, you can trace its journey to you via GPS, and you get a text message once it has arrived. These services are sometimes cheaper than a taxi but sometimes more, especially if "surge pricing" is in effect (when it's raining or at other high-demand

times). The apps do let you get an estimate on rates before you book, so check to see if the convenience is worth the cost. Payment (which includes a tip) is also done via the apps.

Car-Service Companies Boro Taxi information. ⊕ www.borotaxis.org. **Carey.** ☏ 800/336–4646 ⊕ www.carey.com. **Carmel Car Service.** ☏ 212/666–6666, 866/666–6666 ⊕ www.carmelcarservice.com. **Dial 7 Car Service.** ☏ 212/777–7777 ⊕ www.dial7. com. **London Towncars.** ☏ 212/988–9700, 800/221–4009 ⊕ www.londontowncars.com. **Gett.** ⊕ www.gett.com. **Lyft.** ⊕ www.lyft.com. **She Rides.** ⊕ www.sheridesnyc.com. **Uber.** ⊕ www.uber.com.

▮ TRAIN TRAVEL

For information about the subway, see Subway Travel.

Metro-North Railroad trains take passengers from Grand Central Terminal to points north of New York City, both in New York State and Connecticut. Amtrak trains arrive at Penn Station. For trains from New York City to Long Island and New Jersey, take the Long Island Rail Road and New Jersey Transit, respectively; both operate from Penn Station. The PATH trains offer service to Newark, Jersey City, and Hoboken.

Information Amtrak. ☏ 800/872–7245 ⊕ www.amtrak.com. **Long Island Rail Road.** ☏ 511 ⊕ www.mta.info/lirr. **Metro-North Railroad.** ☏ 212/532–4900, 511 ⊕ www.mta. info/mnr. **New Jersey Transit.** ☏ 973/275–5555 ⊕ www.njtransit.com. **PATH.** ☏ 800/234–7284 ⊕ www.pathrail.com.

Train Stations Grand Central Terminal. ⊠ 87 E. 42nd St., at Park Ave., Midtown East, New York ⊕ www.grandcentralterminal. com. **Penn Station.** ⊠ From 31st to 33rd St., between 7th and 8th aves., Midtown West, New York.

ESSENTIALS

■ COMMUNICATIONS

INTERNET

You can check your email or surf the Internet at all public libraries, many cafés and public parks, and most hotels. In addition, all of New York's subway stations are on target to have both Wi-Fi and mobile service; about 80 stations in Manhattan and Queens currently have it. The organization NYCwireless keeps track of free Wi-Fi hot spots in the New York area; the apps WiFi Finder (for Android devices) and Free Wi-Fi Finder (for iOS) can also help you track down hot spots.

Contacts NYCwireless. ⊕ *www.nycwireless. net.*

■ DISABILITIES AND ACCESSIBILITY

New York has come a long way in making life easier for people with disabilities. At most street corners, curb cuts allow wheelchairs to roll along unimpeded. Many restaurants, shops, and movie theaters with step-up entrances have wheelchair ramps. Though some New Yorkers may rush past those in need of assistance, you'll find plenty of people who are more than happy to help you get around.

NYC & Company's website has information on the accessibility of many landmarks and attractions, as well as a downloadable guide. If you need to rent a wheelchair or scooter while in New York, Scootaround will deliver it to your hotel or another location, and reservations can be made up to a year in advance.

Local Resources NYC & Company. ⊕ *www. nycgo.com/accessibility.* **Scootaround.** ☎ *888/441–7575* ⊕ *www.scootaround.com/ rentals/n/newyork.*

LODGING

Despite the Americans with Disabilities Act (ADA), the definition of accessibility seems to differ from hotel to hotel. Some properties may be accessible by ADA standards for people with mobility problems but not for people with hearing or vision impairments, for example.

If you have mobility problems, ask for the lowest floor on which accessible services are available. If you have a hearing impairment, check whether the hotel has devices to alert you visually to the ring of the telephone, a knock at the door, and a fire/emergency alarm. Some hotels provide these devices without charge. Discuss your needs with hotel personnel if this equipment isn't available, so that a staff member can personally alert you in the event of an emergency.

If you're bringing a guide dog, get authorization ahead of time and write down the name of the person with whom you spoke.

SIGHTS AND ATTRACTIONS

Most public facilities in New York City, whether museums, parks, or theaters, are wheelchair-accessible. Some attractions have tours or programs for people with mobility, sight, or hearing impairments.

TRANSPORTATION

Although the city is working to retrofit stations to comply with the ADA, not all stations, including many major ones, are accessible and unlikely to be so in the near future. Accessible stations are clearly marked on subway and rail maps. Visitors in wheelchairs have better success with public buses, all of which have wheelchair lifts and "kneelers" at the front to facilitate getting on and off. Bus drivers provide assistance.

Reduced fares are available to disabled passengers; if paying with cash, you need to present a Medicare card or Paratransit card. You may also apply for a Temporary Reduced-Fare MetroCard in advance of your visit. Visitors to the city are also eligible for the same Access-a-Ride program benefits as New York City residents.

Drivers with disabilities may use windshield cards from their own state or Canadian province to park in designated handicapped spaces.

The U.S. Department of Transportation Aviation Consumer Protection Division's online publication, *New Horizons: Information for the Air Traveler with a Disability,* has advice for travelers with a disability, and outlines basic rights. Visit ⊕ *www.disability.gov* for general information.

Information and Complaints Reduced-Fare Metrocard. ☏ *511* ⊕ *www.mta.info/ accessibility/transit.htm.* **U.S. Department of Transportation Aviation Consumer and Protection.** ⊕ *airconsumer.dot.gov/ publications/horizons.htm.*

▌ GAY AND LESBIAN TRAVEL

Attitudes toward same-sex couples are very tolerant in Manhattan and most other parts of the city. Hell's Kitchen, Chelsea, and (to a lesser degree) Greenwich Village are the most prominently gay neighborhoods, but gay men and lesbians feel at home almost everywhere. The world's oldest gay-pride parade takes place on 5th Avenue the last Sunday in June.

PUBLICATIONS

For listings of gay events and places, check out *Next,* which is online and also distributed in many gay bars throughout Manhattan. Local publications like The *New York* and *Time Out New York* magazines have a gay-friendly take on what's happening in the city.

Gay Publications Gay City News. ⊕ *www. gaycitynews.com.* **Next.** ⊕ *www.nextmagazine. com.*

Local Information The Center (*Lesbian, Gay, Bisexual & Transgender Community Center*). ☏ *212/620–7310* ⊕ *www.gaycenter.org.*

▌ KIDS IN NEW YORK

For listings of children's events, consult *New York* magazine and other local media. The Friday *New York Times* arts section also includes children's activities. Other good sources on happenings for youngsters are the websites NYMetroParents and New York Family (and their respective magazines). If you have access to cable television, check the local all-news channel New York 1, where you'll find a spot aired several times daily that covers current and noteworthy children's events. *Fodor's Around New York City with Kids* (available in bookstores everywhere) can help you plan your days together.

LODGING

Before you consider using a cot or fold-out couch for your child, ask how large your hotel room is—New York City rooms are usually small. Most hotels in New York allow children under a certain age to stay in their parents' room at no extra charge, but others charge for them as extra adults; be sure to find out the cutoff age for children's discounts.

PUBLIC TRANSPORTATION

Children shorter than 44 inches (about 1.1 meters) ride for free on MTA buses and subways. If pushing a stroller, don't struggle through a subway turnstile; ask the station agent to buzz you through the gate (the attendant will ask you to swipe your MetroCard through the turnstile nearest the gate). Keep a sharp eye on your kids while in the subway; at some stations there is a gap between the train doors and the platform.

▌ MEDIA

NEWSPAPERS AND MAGAZINES

The major daily newspapers in New York are the *New York Times* and *Wall Street Journal,* both broadsheets, and the *Daily News* and *New York Post,* which are tabloids. The *Village Voice* is a free alternative weekly. Local magazines and websites include the *New Yorker* and *New York*. All of these are widely available online and at newsstands and shops around town.

MONEY

In New York, it's easy to get swept up in a debt-inducing cyclone of $60-per-person dinners, $120 theater tickets, $20 nightclub covers, and $300 hotel rooms. But one of the good things about the city is that you can spend in some areas and save in others. Within Manhattan, a cup of coffee can cost from $1 to $4, a pint of beer from $5 to $8, and a sandwich from $7 to $10. Generally, prices in the outer boroughs are lower than those in Manhattan.

The most generously bequeathed treasure of the city is the arts. The stated admission fee at the Metropolitan Museum of Art is a suggestion; you can donate a lesser amount and not be snubbed. Many other museums in town have special times during which admission is free. The Museum of Modern Art, for instance, is free on Friday from 4 to 8. In summer a handful of free music, theater, and dance performances, as well as films (usually screened outdoors), fill the calendar each day.

Prices here are given for adults. Substantially reduced fees are typically available for children, students, and senior citizens.

CREDIT CARDS

Record all your credit card numbers—as well as the phone numbers to call if your cards are lost or stolen—in a safe place, so you're prepared should something go wrong. Both MasterCard and Visa have general numbers you can call if your card is lost, but you're better off calling the number of your issuing bank, since MasterCard and Visa usually just transfer you anyway. Your bank's number is typically printed on your card.

Reporting Lost Cards American Express. ☎ *800/528–4800 in U.S.* ⊕ *www. americanexpress.com.* **Diners Club.** ☎ *800/234–6377* ⊕ *www.dinersclub.com.*

Discover. ☎ *800/347–2683 in U.S.* ⊕ *www. discovercard.com.* **MasterCard.** ☎ *800/627–8372* ⊕ *www.mastercard.com.* **Visa.** ☎ *800/847–2911* ⊕ *www.visa.com.*

RESTROOMS

Public restrooms in New York are few and far between. If you find yourself in need of a restroom, head for Midtown department stores, museums, or the lobbies of large hotels to find the cleanest bathrooms. Public atriums, such as those at the Citicorp Center and Trump Tower, also provide good public facilities, as do Bryant Park and the many Starbucks coffee shops in the city.

Restaurants usually allow only patrons to use their restrooms, but if you're dressed well and look as if you belong, you can often just sail right in. If too self-conscious for this brand of nonchalance, just ask the host or hostess nicely. Be aware that cinemas, Broadway theaters, and concert halls have limited amenities, and there are often long lines before performances and during intermissions.

SAFETY

New York City is one of the safest large cities in the country. However, do not let yourself be lulled into a false sense of security. As in any large city, travelers in New York remain particularly easy marks for pickpockets and hustlers.

After the September 11, 2001, terrorist attacks security was heightened throughout the city. Never leave any bags unattended, and expect to have yourself and your possessions inspected thoroughly in such places as airports, sports stadiums, museums, city buildings, and sometimes even subway stations.

Ignore the panhandlers on the streets and subways, people who offer to hail you a cab (they often appear at Penn Station, the Port Authority, and Grand Central), and limousine and gypsy-cab drivers who (illegally) offer you a ride.

Keep jewelry out of sight on the street; better yet, leave valuables at home. Don't carry wallets, smartphones, or other gadgets in your back pockets, and make sure bags and purses stay closed.

Avoid deserted blocks in unfamiliar neighborhoods. A brisk, purposeful pace helps deter trouble wherever you go.

The subway runs around the clock and is generally well trafficked until midnight (and until at least 2 am on Friday and Saturday nights), and overall it is very safe. If you do take the subway late at night, ride in the center car, with the conductor. Watch out for unsavory characters lurking around the inside or outside of stations.

When waiting for a train, head to the center of the platform, and stand far away from its edge, especially when trains are entering or leaving the station. Once the train pulls into the station, avoid empty cars. While on the train, don't engage in verbal exchanges with aggressive riders. If a fellow passenger makes you nervous while on the train, trust your instincts and change cars. When disembarking, stick with the crowd until you reach the street.

Travelers Aid International helps crime victims, stranded travelers, and wayward children, and works closely with the police.

■TIP➔ Distribute your cash, credit cards, IDs, and other valuables between a deep front pocket, an inside jacket or vest pocket, and a hidden money pouch. Don't reach for the money pouch once you're in public.

Information Travelers Aid International. ☎ 718/656–4870 ⊕ www.travelersaid.org/ta/jfk.html. **Travelers Aid International.** ☎ 973/623–5052 ⊕ www.travelersaid.org.

■ SENIOR-CITIZEN TRAVEL

The Metropolitan Transportation Authority (MTA) charges lower fares for passengers 65 and over.

To qualify for age-related discounts, mention your senior-citizen status up front when booking hotel reservations (not when checking out). Be sure to have identification on hand. When renting a car, ask about promotional car-rental discounts, which can be cheaper than senior-citizen rates.

■ SPORTS AND THE OUTDOORS

The City of New York's Parks & Recreation division lists all of the recreational facilities and activities available through New York's Parks Department. The *New York Times*'s sports section lists upcoming events, times, dates, and ticket information.

Contact Information Department of Parks & Recreation. ☎ 311 in New York City, 212/639–9675 ⊕ www.nycgovparks.org.

BASEBALL

The subway gets you directly to the stadiums of both New York–area major-league teams: the New York Mets play at Citi Field, at the next-to-last stop on the 7 train in Queens, while the Yankees defend their turf at Yankee Stadium in the Bronx, accessible via the B, D, and 4 trains. The Mets-affiliated, minor-league Brooklyn Cyclones are named for Coney Island's famous wooden roller coaster. They play 38 home games at MCU Park, next to the boardwalk, with views of the Atlantic over the right-field wall and historic Astroland over the left-field wall. Most people make a day of it, with time at the beach and amusement rides before an evening game. Take the D, F, or Q subway to the end of the line, and walk one block to the right of the original Nathan's Famous hot dog stand.

For another fun, family-oriented experience, check out the Staten Island Yankees, one of New York's minor-league teams, which warms up many future New York Yankees players. The stadium, a five-minute walk from the Staten Island Ferry terminal, has magnificent views of Lower Manhattan and the Statue of Liberty.

Contact Information Brooklyn Cyclones.
☎ 718/372-5596, 718/507-8499 for tickets ⊕ www.brooklyncyclones.com Ⓜ D, F, N, Q to Coney Island–Stillwell Ave. **New York Mets.** ☎ 718/507-8499 ⊕ www.mets.com Ⓜ 7 to Mets–Willets Point. **New York Yankees.** ☎ 718/293-6000 ⊕ www.yankees.com Ⓜ 4, B, D to 161st St.–Yankee Stadium. Metro-North (Hudson line) to Yankees–E. 153rd St. **Staten Island Yankees.** ☎ 718/720-9265 ⊕ www. siyanks.com.

BASKETBALL

The New York Knicks arouse intense hometown passions, which means tickets for home games at Madison Square Garden are hard to come by. Try StubHub to score tickets. The Brooklyn Nets are across the river, in the swanky Barclays Center. The stadium is easily reachable by nine different subway lines. The men's basketball season runs from late October through April. The New York Liberty, a member of the Women's NBA, had its first season in 1997. The season runs from mid-May through August, with home games played at Madison Square Garden.

Contact Information Brooklyn Nets.
☎ 917/618-6700 for box office ⊕ www.nba. com/nets Ⓜ 2, 3, 4, 5, B, D, N, Q, R to Atlantic Ave.–Barclays Center. **Madison Square Garden.** ☎ 212/465-6741 ⊕ www.msg.com Ⓜ 1, 2, 3 to 34th St.–Penn Station. **New York Knicks.** ☎ 212/465-5867 ⊕ www.nba.com/ knicks. **New York Liberty.** ☎ 212/465-6766 for tickets, 212/564-9622 for fan hotline ⊕ www.wnba.com/liberty.

BICYCLING

In the past couple years, bicycling the streets of Manhattan and many parts of Brooklyn has become more mainstream and much less the sole province of bike messengers and zealots. The city government and biking organizations have both helped make it safer than it had been for decades, and drivers and pedestrians are more aware that bikes are likely to be on the road, too. Check the Department of

THE FODORS.COM CONNECTION

Before your trip, be sure to check out what fellow travelers are saying in Talk on ⊕ www.fodors.com.

Transportation's website for a cycling map that shows the best routes and roads with designated bike lanes, as well as local road rules, including for taking a bike on public transit.

For biking under more controlled conditions, head to New York's major parks. Central Park has a six-mile circular drive with a couple of decent climbs. It's closed to car traffic from 10 am to 3 pm (except the southeast portion between 6th Avenue and East 72nd Street), from 7 pm to 7 am on weekdays, and from 7 pm Friday to 7 am Monday. On holidays it's closed to car traffic from 7 pm the night before until 7 am the day after.

Beware of renting a bike from the vendors that hang out on the streets near Central Park, especially by Columbus Circle. These bikes tend to be old and mismatched and are also often stolen. It's better to rent from someone with an actual storefront. Most bike-rental stores have copies of the very handy official Bike Map, which is published annually and shows traffic flow and bike lanes for all of New York City.

The bike lane along the Hudson River Park's esplanade parallels the waterfront from West 59th Street south to the esplanade of Battery Park City. The lane also heads north, connecting with the bike path in Riverside Park and the promenade between West 72nd and West 110th streets, continuing all the way to the George Washington Bridge. A two-way bike lane runs along the park's Terrace Drive, a popular route across the park at 72nd Street. From Battery Park it's a quick ride to the Wall Street area, which is deserted on weekends, and over to South Street and a bike lane along the East River.

The 3.3-mile circular drive in Brooklyn's Prospect Park is closed to cars year-round except from 7 am to 9 am (on the northbound East Drive) and 5 pm to 7 pm (on the southbound West Drive) on weekdays. It has a long, gradual hill that tops off near the Grand Army Plaza entrance.

Bike Rentals & Information New York City Department of Transportation. ⊕ www.nyc.gov/bikes. **Bicycle Rentals at Loeb Boathouse.** ☎ 212/517–2233 for Boathouse, 212/260–0400 for Tavern on the Green ⊕ www.centralparknyc.org Ⓜ 6 to 68th St.–Hunter College.**Pedal Pusher Bike Shop.** ☎ 212/288–5592 ⊕ www.pedalpusherbikeshop.com Ⓜ 6 to 68th St.–Hunter College. **Toga Bike Shop.** ☎ 212/799–9625 ⊕ www.togabikes.com Ⓜ 1 to 66th St.–Lincoln Center. **Waterfront Bicycle Shop.** ☎ 212/414–2453 ⊕ www.bikeshopny.com Ⓜ 1 to Christopher St.–Sheridan Sq.

CITI BIKE BICYCLING SHARE

New York's bike-sharing program debuted in 2013 with hundreds of stations, the majority in Manhattan south of Central Park and northern Brooklyn. The three-speed, 40-pound, bright-blue bikes, which are either charming or clunky depending on your perspective, are outfitted with lights and bungee cords to secure small bags and other items. They don't come with helmets, though: wearing one is recommended but not mandatory.

After buying a Citi Bike pass, you are able to borrow an unlimited number of the bikes for either 24 hours ($9.95) or 7 days ($25). What is limited is your time with a particular bike: the time between unlocking a bike at one station at returning it to another must be 30 minutes or under, or you face additional charges, and these overtime charges add up quickly (all the way to $1,200 for never returning a bike at all). As soon as you return one bike, you're free to get another—even one from the same location.

Before you pull a bike from one of the bays and start the 30-minute clock running, spend a little time planning your route. Citi Bike's apps are helpful with this, because they show which of the computerized outdoor stations have bikes available, and—just as important—which have empty bays available for when it's time to return your bike.

Contact Information Citi Bike. ☎ 855/245–3311 for customer service ⊕ www.citibikenyc.com.

GROUP BIKE RIDES

Bike New York runs a 40-mile, five-borough bike ride the first Sunday in May. The Five Borough Bicycle Club organizes day and weekend rides. The New York Cycle Club sponsors weekend rides for every level of ability. Time's Up!, a non-profit advocacy group, leads free recreational rides at least twice a month for cyclists as well as skaters; the Central Park Moonlight Ride, departing from Columbus Circle at 10 pm the first Friday of every month, is a favorite.

Contact Information Bike New York. ☎ 212/870–2080 ⊕ www.bikenewyork.org. **Five Borough Bike Club.** ☎ 347/688–2925 ⊕ www.5bbc.org. **New York Cycle Club.** ☎⊕ www.nycc.org. **Time's Up!** ☎ 212/802–8222 ⊕ www.times-up.org.

BOATING, KAYAKING & SUP

Central Park has rowboats (plus one Venetian gondola for glides in the moonlight) on the 22-acre Central Park Lake. Rent your rowboat, which holds up to four people, at Loeb Boathouse, near East 74th Street, from April through November ($15 an hour).Gondola rides (complete with gondolier) are available only in summer and can be reserved ($30 per half hour); the gondolas hold up to six people.

In summer at the Pier 96 Boathouse in Midtown West, you can take a sturdy kayak out for a paddle for free on weekends and weekday evenings from mid-May through mid-October. Pier 40, in the West Village, and the pier at West 72nd Street have similar schedules. Beginners learn to paddle close to shore until they feel ready to venture farther out into open water. More experienced kayakers can partake in the three-hour trips conducted every weekend and on holiday mornings. Because of high demand, there is a lottery to determine who gets to go out each morning; to be entered, you must be at the pier to sign up before 8 am. No reservations are taken in advance. Manhattan Kayak Company gives kayak and stand-up paddleboard (SUP) lessons for all levels and runs trips on the Hudson River between May and late September, including a fun New York After Dark tour for $80.

Contact Information Loeb Boathouse. ☎ 212/517–2233 ⊕ *www.thecentralparkboathouse.com/boats.php* Ⓜ *6 to 68th St.–Hunter College.* **Manhattan Kayak Company.** ☎ 212/924–1788 ⊕ *www.manhattankayak.com* Ⓜ *A, C, E to 42nd St.–Port Authority.* **Pier 96 Boathouse.** ⊕ *www.downtownboathouse.org* Ⓜ *1, A, B, C, D to 59th St.–Columbus Circle.*

FOOTBALL

The football season runs from September through December. The enormously popular New York Giants play at MetLife Stadium in East Rutherford, New Jersey. Most seats for Giants games are sold on a season-ticket basis—and there's a long waiting list for those. However, single tickets are occasionally available at the stadium box office or on ticket resale sites like StubHub. The New York Jets also play at MetLife Stadium. Although Jets tickets are not as scarce as those for the Giants, most are snapped up by fans before the season opener.

Contact Information New York Giants. ☎ 201/935–8222 for tickets ⊕ *www.giants.com.* **New York Jets.** ☎ 800/469–5387 for tickets ⊕ *www.newyorkjets.com.*

HOCKEY

The New York Islanders hockey team is moving from their suburban Long Island stadium to the Barclays Center in Brooklyn for the 2015/16 season.

Contact Information New York Islanders. ⊕ *www.islanders.nhl.com* Ⓜ *2, 3, 4, 5, B, D, N, Q, R to Atlantic Ave.–Barclays Center.*

ICE-SKATING

The outdoor rink in Rockefeller Center, open from October through early April, is much smaller in real life than it appears on TV and in movies—though it *is* as beautiful, especially when Rock Center's enormous Christmas tree towers above it. Tickets are first-come, first-served, so be prepared to wait—especially around the holidays. Be prepared to pay, too: skating rates are $27–$30 for adults, which doesn't include skate rental ($12), and that only pays for admission during a single 90-minute skating session. The city's outdoor rinks, open from roughly November through March, all have their own character. Central Park's beautifully situated Wollman Rink has skating until long after dark beneath the lights of the city. Be prepared for daytime crowds on weekends. The Lasker Rink, at the north end of Central Park, is smaller and usually less crowded than Wollman. Chelsea Piers' Sky Rink has two year-round indoor rinks overlooking the Hudson. Skate rentals are available at all rinks. The skating rink at the Winter Village at Bryant Park has "free" skating, although this doesn't include skate rental ($15–$19) or the likely fee to either buy a lock for a locker or have bags checked ($8–$10). Winter Village's rink is open from November through early March, daily from 8 am to 10 pm. A FastPass (available online, includes skate rental and bag check) allows you to skip the line; it costs $22–$28. ■TIP➜ Every winter the trendy Standard Hotel, in the Meatpacking District near the High Line, makes its own tiny ice rink. Skate tickets are $12 and skate rental is $3; the rink, at 848 Washington Street at West 13th Street, is open from 9 am until at least midnight on weekends and from noon on weekdays. When you're done, hot chocolate, toddies, waffles, and doughnuts are ready to take the edge off any chill.

Contact Information Lasker Rink. ⊕ www. laskerrink.com Ⓜ B, C to Cathedral Pkwy.–110th St.; 2, 3 to Central Park North–110th St. **Rockefeller Center.** ☎ 212/332–7654 ⊕ www.therinkatrockcenter.com Ⓜ B, D, F, M to 47th–50th Sts./Rockefeller Center; E, M to 5th Ave./53rd St. **Sky Rink.** ☎ 212/336–6100 ⊕ www.chelseapiers.com/sr Ⓜ C, E to 23rd St. **Trump Wollman Skating Rink.** ⊕ www. wollmanskatingrink.com Ⓜ 1, A, B, C, D to 59th St.–Columbus Circle.

Winter Village at Bryant Park. ✉ 1065 6th Ave., between 40th and 42nd sts., Midtown West, New York ☎ 212/661–6640 ⊕ wintervillage.org Ⓜ B, D, F, M to 42nd St.–Bryant Park.

JOGGING

All kinds of New Yorkers jog, some with dogs or babies in tow, so you always have company on the regular jogging routes. What's not recommended is setting out on a lonely park path at dusk. Go running when and where everybody else does. On Manhattan streets, roughly 20 north-south blocks make a mile.

In Manhattan, Central Park is the busiest spot, specifically along the 1.6-mile path circling the Jacqueline Kennedy Onassis Reservoir, where you jog in a counterclockwise direction. A runners' lane has been designated along park roads; the entire loop road is a hilly 6 miles. A good 1.75-mile route starts at the Tavern on the Green along the West Drive, heads south around the bottom of the park to the East Drive, and circles back west on the 72nd Street park road to your starting point. Riverside Park, along the Hudson River bank in Manhattan, is glorious at sunset. You can cover 4.5 miles by running from West 72nd to 116th Street and back, and the Greenbelt trail extends 4 more miles north to the George Washington Bridge at 181st Street. Other favorite Manhattan circuits are the Battery Park City esplanade (about 2 miles), which connects to the Hudson River Park (about 1½ miles), and the East River Esplanade (just over 3 miles from East 63rd to East 125th streets).

■ STUDENTS IN NEW YORK

New York is home to Columbia University, New York University, Fordham University, and the City College of New York. With other colleges scattered throughout the five boroughs, and a huge population of public and private high-schoolers, it's no wonder the city is rife with student discounts. Wherever you go, especially museums, sightseeing attractions, and performances, identify yourself as a student and ask if a discount is available, but be prepared to show your ID.

High 5 for the Arts is a great program for teens 13 and 18 (or anyone in middle or high school). Tickets to a wide variety of performances (though only rarely Broadway shows) are sold for $5 online or by phone. Check the website to find out about upcoming events.

Contact Informatoin High 5 for the Arts. ☎ 212/302–7433 ⊕ teens.artsconnection. org/faq-high5.**STA Travel.** ☎ 212/473–6100, 800/781–4040 for 24-hr service center ⊕ www.sta.com.

■ TAXES

A sales tax of 8.875% applies to almost everything you can buy retail, including restaurant meals. However, prescription drugs and non-prepared food bought in grocery stores are exempt. Clothing and footwear costing less than $110 are also exempt.

■ TIPPING

The customary tipping rate for taxi drivers is 15%–20%, with a minimum of $2; bellhops are usually given $2 per bag in luxury hotels, $1 per bag elsewhere. Hotel maids should be tipped $2 per day of your stay. A doorman who hails or helps you into a cab can be tipped $1–$2. You should also tip your hotel concierge for services rendered; the size of the tip depends on the difficulty of your request, as well as the quality of the concierge's work. Waiters should be tipped 15%–20%, though at higher-end restaurants, a solid 20% is more the norm. Tip $1 or $2 per drink you order at the bar, or possibly more if you're ordering something especially time-consuming to make.

▌ VISITOR INFORMATION

The Grand Central Partnership (a business-improvement district) has installed a number of information booths in and around Grand Central Terminal (there's one near Vanderbilt Avenue and East 43rd Street). They're loaded with maps and helpful brochures on attractions throughout the city and staffed by friendly, knowledgeable, multilingual New Yorkers.

NYC & Company runs Official NYC Information Centers at Macy's as well as in Lower Manhattan at City Hall Park, South Street Seaport, and in Chinatown, at the triangle where Canal, Walker, and Baxter streets meet. Its official visitor guide and map, both downloadable from NYC & Company's website as well as in hard copies available around town, are both very useful.

The Downtown Alliance has information on the area encompassing City Hall south to Battery Park, and from the East River to West Street. For a free booklet listing New York City attractions and tour packages, contact the New York State Division of Tourism.

CONTACTS

City Information Downtown Alliance.
☎ *212/566–6700* ⊕ *www.downtownny.com.*
Grand Central Partnership. ☎ *212/883–2420*
⊕ *www.grandcentralpartnership.org.* **NYC &**
Company Information Center at Macy's.
☎ *212/484–1222* ⊕ *www.nycgo.com* Ⓜ *B,*
D, F, M, N, Q, R to 34th St.–Herald Sq. **Times**
Square Alliance. ⊕ *www.timessquarenyc.org.*

Statewide Information New York State
Division of Tourism. ☎ *800/225–5697*
(weekdays 8–5) ⊕ *www.iloveny.com.*

INDEX

PHOTO CREDITS

Front cover: Stockelements/Shutterstock and Rockefellercenter.com. [Description: Atlas at Rocke-feller Center]. 1, Songquan Deng/Shutterstock. 2, Kord.com/age fotostock. 5, Liberty Helicopters, Inc. Chapter 1: Experience New York City: 8-9, Sean Pavone / Shutterstock.11, Oote Boe Photography/ Alamy. 14, Ace Stock Limited/Alamy. 16, Alija/iStockphoto. 18A, Xuan Che/Flickr, [CC BY 2.0]. 18B, Andreykr I Dreamstime.com. 18C, Sylvian Granadam/age fotostock. 18 D, Dmitro2009 / Shutterstock. 19 (top left), Revoc9 I Dreamstime.com. 19 (bottom left), Craig Chesek/AMNH. 19 (right), Picture-Quest. 24, Brooklyn Bridge Park Etienne Frossard/www.brooklynbridgeparknyc.org. 25, adactio/ Flickr, [CC BY 2.0]. 29, emilydickinsonridesabmx/Flickr. 31, Jeff Greenberg/Alamy. 37, Corbis. 39, Photodisc. 41 (top), Liberty Helicopters, Inc. 41 (bottom), Joshua Haviv/shutterstock. 43 (top), Library of Congress Prints and Photographs Division. 43 (bottom), Library of Congress Prints and Photo-graphs Division. Chapter 2: Lower Manhattan: 45, Sepavo I Dreamstime.com. 47, Heeb Christian/age fotostock. 48, Chuck Pefley/Alamy. 52, Silverstein Properties. 53 (top), White House Photo/Alamy. 53 (bottom), Sondra Paulson/iStockphoto. 54 (top left), Robert/Flickr, [CC BY-SA 2.0]. 54 (top right), Jim Watson/CHINFO, Navy Visual News Service (Public Domain), via Wikimedia Commons. 54 (bottom), RodneyRamsey/Flickr. 55 (left), Jim Watson/CHINFO, Navy Visual News Service (Public Domain), via Wikimedia Commons. 55 (center), Peter Comitini/Flickr. 55 (right), Denise Gould (Public Domain), via Wikimedia Commons. 56-57 (top), Silverstein Properties. 56 (bottom), Silverstein Properties. 57 (bottom left), meunierd/Shutterstock. 57 (bottom right), Joe Woolhead/Silverstein Properties. 58 (top left), Luca Cepparo/iStockphoto. 58 (top right), FaceMePLS/Flickr. 58 (bottom left), p_c_w/Flickr. 58 (bottom right), cytech/Flickr. 62, kropic1/Shutterstock. 65, Estormiz/Wikimedia Commons. Chapter 3: SoHo, NoLIta, Little Italy, and Chinatown: 67, Art Kowalsky/Alamy. 69, Ambient Images Inc./Alamy. 70, Adeliepenguin I Dreamstime.com. 72-73, Renault Philippe/age fotostock. 75, OK Harris Works of Art. 77, Philip Lange/Shutterstock. Chapter 4: The East Village and the Lower East Side: 79, Jeff Greenberg/Alamy. 81, Bruce Monroe/Flickr, [CC BY-SA 2.0]. 82, Tomás Fano/Flickr, [CC BY-SA 2.0]. Chapter 5: Greenwich Village and the West Village: 89, wdstock/iStockphoto. 91, Evelyn Proimos/ Flickr, [CC BY 2.0]. 92, wdstock/iStockphoto. 93, Ambient Images Inc./Alamy. 96, Jennifer Arnow. Chapter 6: Chelsea and the Meatpacking District: 99, Kobby_dagan I Dreamstime.com. 101 and 102, Jennifer Arnow. 104, Timothy Schenck. 106, Marco Rubino / Shutterstock. 107, Kokyat Choong/ Alamy. Chapter 7: Union Square, the Flatiron District, and Gramercy Park: 111, David Shankbone/ Wikipedia.org. 113, Kord.com/age fotostock. 114, Yadid Levy/Alamy. 115, Russell Kord/Alamy. 117, naphtalina/iStockphoto. Chapter 8: Midtown East: 121, Kord.com. 123, Jaap Hart/iStockphoto. 124, svlumagraphica/iStockphoto. 126, Rudy Sulgan/age fotostock. 131, Stuart Monk/iStockphoto/Think-stock. 132, Sylvain Grandadam/age fotostock. Chapter 9: Midtown West: 137, Dibrova I Dreamstime. com. 139, Bruno Perousse/age fotostock. 140, Mirceanil Dreamstime.com. 143, Tomás Fano/Flickr, [CC BY-SA 2.0]. 144, oversnap/iStockphoto. 148, Tomás Fano/Flickr, [CC BY-SA 2.0]. Chapter 10: The Upper East Side: 151, Nicholas Pitt/Alamy. 153, Mary Robnett. 154, Janine Wiedel Photolibrary/ Alamy. 158, Doug Scott/age fotostock. 160, Sampete I Dreamstime. 161, Renaud Visage/age fotostock. 162 (top), Renaud Visage/age fotostock. 162 (center), Metropolitan Museum of Art. 162 (bottom), An East Greek Late Archaic Alabastron in the Form of a Kore by http://www.flickr.com/photos/antiquities project/5515795335/Attribution License. 164 (top), Kristen Bonardi Rapp/Flickr, [CC BY-SA 2.0]. 164 (bottom), Metropolitan Museum of Art. 165, Wild Bill Studio/Metropolitan Museum of Art. 166 (top and bottom), Metropolitan Museum of Art. Chapter 11: Central Park: 169 and 170 (top), Piero Ribelli. 170 (center), Rudy Sulgan/age fotostock. 170 (bottom), Library of Congress Prints & Photographs Division.171 (left), Chase Guttman. 171 (right), Sandra Baker/Alamy. 172, Worldscapes/age foto-stock. 173 (left), Chris Lee. 173 (right), Michal Daniel. 174, Peter Arnold, Inc./Alamy. 175 (left), Craig Hale/iStockphoto. 175 (right), Agency Jon Arnold Images/age fotostock. 176 (top left), Sean Pavone/ Shutterstock. 176 (top right), Terraxplorer/iStockphoto. 176 (bottom), Sandra Baker/Alamy. 177 (bot-tom), Darren Green Photography/Alamy. 177 (top left), Chuck Pefley/Alamy. 177 (right), Chase Gutt-man. 178, Piero Ribelli. 179 (left), Sandra Baker/Alamy. 179 (right), Piero Ribelli. 180-181 (bottom), gary718/Shutterstock. 180 (top left), Peter Arnold, Inc./Alamy. 180 (top right), TNT Magazine/Alamy. 181 (top left), johnandersonphoto/iStockphoto. 181 (top right), LMR Group/Alamy. 182 (left), Piero Ribelli. 182 (right), Jon Arnold/Agency Jon Arnold Images. 183, Christian/Flickr, [CC BY-NC-SA 2.0]. 184, Mario Savoia/iStockphoto. Chapter 12: The Upper West Side: 185, Kord.com/age fotostock. 187, Momos/Wikimedia Commons. 188, Kord.com/age fotostock. 190 and 191, Jennifer Arnow. 192 (top left), Sepavo I Dreamstime.com. 192 (top right), Craig Chesek/AMNH. 192 (bottom), Dennis Fin-nin/AMNH. 194, American Museum of Natural History. 195 and 196, Denis Finnin/AMNH. 197 (top), C. Chesek/AMNH. 197 (bottom), D. Finnin/C. Chesek/AMNH. Chapter 13: Harlem: 201, Cris-tian Baitg/iStockphoto. 203, Joe Malone/Agency Jon Arnold Images/age fotostock. 204, SuperStock/

NOTES

NOTES

NOTES

NOTES

NOTES

NOTES

NOTES

NOTES

NOTES

ABOUT OUR WRITERS

Jessica Colley is a travel and food writer based in Harlem. She adores New York for its bubbling pizza pies, storied cobbled streets, and picnics on the bank of the Hudson River. Jessica shares her travels and New York tips on Twitter at @jessicacolley.

David Farley is the author of the award-winning travel memoir *An Irreverent Curiosity* and writes about food and travel for *AFAR* magazine, the *New York Times,* and *National Geographic Traveler.* He teaches writing at Columbia University and New York University.

Laura Itzkowitz writes for *Travel + Leisure, Refinery29,* and *Saveur,* among others. She is the co-author of a forthcoming guide to New York City's hidden bars and restaurants. She lives in Greenpoint.

Kristin Iversen is a writer and editor who has lived in Brooklyn for 15 years. She is the managing editor for *Brooklyn* and *The L* magazines, and her work has appeared in the New York *Observer* and *The Nervous Breakdown,* among others.

Christina Knight has lived in Park Slope since 1995 and is a senior multimedia producer at WNET/Thirteen where she works with *American Masters, Great Performances,* and NYC-ARTS.org.

From sailing the Nile in a *felucca* to eating street-cart tacos in Mexico City, **Anuja Madar**'s best memories are from her travels. She was a travel editor for nearly six years and has spent nearly 11 years calling NYC home.

Megan Eileen McDonough splits her time between Brooklyn, San Francisco, and Hong Kong. She runs Bohemian Trails, a blog for the savvy traveler and she also contributes to the *Huffington Post, WIRED,* and *Budget Travel.*

Marisa Meltzer is a writer based in Brooklyn. She currently resides in Red Hook but has also lived in Brooklyn Heights and Prospect Heights. Her work has appeared in the *New York Times, Elle, AFAR,* and others.

Chris Molanphy is a pop-chart analyst, feature writer, music critic, and Brooklyn native. His work has appeared in *Slate, Pitchfork,* the *Village Voice,* NPR Music's The Record, RollingStone.com, *Billboard,* and CMJ. He is a frequent guest on National Public Radio (All Things Considered, Soundcheck, On the Media). He lives in Brooklyn.

Irish-born writer **Jacinta O'Halloran** has been calling New York City home for more than two decades. She can walk the part (i.e., fast) and talk the part (i.e., when she's mad at cabdrivers, ordering bagels, or giving directions) of a local, but she still sees and feels the city like a visitor (i.e., she still looks up!).

John Rambow has written for *Travel + Leisure, Fast Company,* and *New York* magazines, as well as Medium and several other blogs and guidebooks. From a base in Queens, he aims to stay on top of all the amazing things happening in this New York City. He tweets at @johnrambow.

Matt Rodbard lives in Carroll Gardens and writes about restaurants, chefs, drinks, music, and New York City as a place to enjoy all of it. He is the executive editor at Food Republic and is writing a book about Korean food in America.

Josh Rogol, a native of Stamford, Connecticut, now makes his home in Brooklyn. He is a licensed New York City tour guide, freelance travel writer, and a video producer for *USA Today Sports.* His quest to sample the best of New York's culinary world is a passion that spans all five boroughs.

Emily Saladino lives in Brooklyn's Clinton Hill neighborhood. She contributes food, culture, and travel stories to *BBC, Conde Nast Traveler, USA Today, Travel + Leisure,* and others.

Sarah Spagnolo is editor-at-large at Foursquare; before that spent a decade at *Travel + Leisure.* She's been based in Bed-Stuy since 2013.

Christina Valhouli writes about travel, lifestyle, and beauty for a variety of publications including the *New York Times* and the *New York Post*. She is the former staff travel writer at *Forbes.com* and has contributed to several Fodor's guidebooks in addition to *Fodor's New York City*. Her travels have taken her to more than 30 countries but she now calls the New York City area home.

Manhattan Subway Lines